Langua

1749
Walter de Gruyter
250
Berlin · New York
1999

Language, Power and Social Process 2

Editors

Monica Heller
Richard J. Watts

Mouton de Gruyter
Berlin · New York

Language Ideological Debates

Edited by

Jan Blommaert

W DE G Mouton de Gruyter
Berlin · New York 1999

Mouton de Gruyter (formerly Mouton, The Hague)
is a Division of Walter de Gruyter GmbH & Co. KG, Berlin.

⊗ Printed on acid-free paper which falls within the guidelines
of the ANSI to ensure permanence and durability.

Library of Congress Cataloging-in-Publication Data

Language ideological debates / edited by Jan Blommaert.
p. cm. – (Language, power, and social process : 2)
Includes bibliographical references (p.) and index.
ISBN 3-11-016350-0. – ISBN 3-11-016349-7 (pbk.)
1. Sociolinguistics. 2. Language and languages – Political aspects. I. Blommaert, Jan. II. Series.
P40.I2965 1999
306.44–dc21 99-32848
CIP

Die Deutsche Bibliothek – Cataloging-in-Publication Data

Language ideological debates / ed. by Jan Blommaert. – Berlin ; New York : Mouton de Gruyter, 1999
(Language, power and social process ; 2)
ISBN 3-11-016349-7 brosch.
ISBN 3-11-016350-0 gb.

Disk conversion: Amir Moghaddass Esfehani, Berlin.
Printing: WB-Druck GmbH & Co., Rieden/Allgäu.
Binding: Lüderitz & Bauer GmbH, Berlin.
Cover design: Christopher Schneider, Berlin.
Printed in Germany.

... and language, after all, is a purely historical phenomenon

V. N. Voloshinov

Preface

This book is very much the product of a collaborative effort of all the authors. The hardship of the editorial work (a kind of work I rarely enjoy) was greatly relieved by their enthusiasm and by the amount of work each of the authors was prepared to invest in his/her chapter. Chapters were revised over and over again, by authors drawing inspiration from each other's work and suggestions, in an attempt to improve the overall coherence and clarity of the volume. In the very true sense of the word, this book is a debate in its own right, one which I had the privilege to chair. I thank all the authors for the spirit and the commitment with which they contributed to this effort. I owe a special debt to Monica Heller and Dick Watts, the series editors. They were initially bigger fans of this project than I was myself, and they certainly had a clearer idea of what the book should become than I did. They coached me all along in a most vigorous, yet compassionate way. As for compassion, both of them wrote an excellent chapter themselves. Their contribution to the style, shape and content of this volume is enormous. Thanks also to Anke Beck and her Mouton de Gruyter team for great editorial guidance and assistance, and for the generosity in which she handled my problems with editorial deadlines. Three people closer to home actively assisted me in the tedious work of final editing. Pika took care of my least favorite job: getting lists of references right; Katrijn Maryns checked the language, orthography and style of the chapters; Chris Bulcaen took care of the index. And Pika, Frederik and Alexander tolerated me at home while I was finishing the book. To all of them: *merci*.

Gent, January 1999 *Jan Blommaert*

Contents

Preface vii

Notes on contributors xi

The debate is open
Jan Blommaert 1

Locating power: Corsican translators and their critics
Alexandra Jaffe 39

The ideology of dialect in Switzerland
Richard J. Watts 67

Language ideological debates in an Olympic city:
Barcelona 1992–1996
Susan M. DiGiacomo 105

Heated language in a cold climate
Monica Heller 143

The debate on bilingual education in the U.S.:
Language ideology as reflected in the practice of bilingual teachers
Sheila M. Shannon 171

The Ebonics controversy in context:
Literacies, subjectivities, and language ideologies in the United States
James Collins 201

Singapore's *Speak Mandarin Campaign*:
Language ideological debates in the imagining of the nation
Wendy Bokhorst-Heng 235

Linguistic and political attitudes towards Israeli Hebrew: Ongoing revival versus normalcy
Ron Kuzar 267

Politics, ideology and poetic form: The literary debate in Tanzania
Joshua Madumulla, Elena Bertoncini and Jan Blommaert 307

Portuguese as ideology and politics in Mozambique: Semiotic (re)constructions of a postcolony
Christopher Stroud 343

Flemish nationalism in the Belgian Congo versus Zairian anti-imperialism: Continuity and discontinuity in language ideological debates
Michael Meeuwis 381

The debate is closed
Jan Blommaert 425

Name index 439

Subject index 441

Notes on contributors

Elena Bertoncini Zúbková is Professor of Swahili language and literature at the Istituto Universitario Orientale in Naples (Italy) and she teaches Swahili literature at the INALCO in Paris (France). Her publications include *Outline of Swahili Literature* (Brill, 1989), a Swahili grammar called *Kiswahili kwa Furaha* (IUO, 1987), essays on Swahili language and style as well as translations of Swahili poetry, short stories and plays into Italian and Slovak.

Jan Blommaert is Professor of African linguistics and sociolinguistics at the University of Gent (Belgium). He was a research director at the IPrA Research Center (University of Antwerp) from 1991 untill 1997. He is a co-editor of the *Handbook of Pragmatics* (Benjamins, since 1995). Other publications include *Debating Diversity* (with Jef Verschueren, Routledge, 1998), *Political Linguistics* (co-edited with Chris Bulcaen, Benjamins, 1997) and articles on language ideologies, language policy and language planning in Belgium, Europe and Africa.

Wendy D. Bokhorst-Heng (PhD) is a part-time lecturer at the University of Singapore. Her main research interests are in issues relating to discourse, language planning (with a focus on education), language ideology, and nationalism. Her publications include reviews on international comparative education and nationalism in education. She also published various articles relating to issues of language planning and language ideology in Singapore that have appeared as chapters in books.

James Collins is Professor in the Departments of Anthropology and Reading at the State University of New York at Albany. He has researched and written on social theory and linguistics, critical studies of language and education, and Native American languages and cultures. Major publications include *Understanding Tolowa Histories: Western Hegemonies and Native American Responses* (Routledge, 1998), "Literacy and literacies" (*Annual Review of Anthropology*, 1995) and "Structure and contradiction" in Calhoun, LiPuma & Postone (eds.), *Bourdieu, A critical reader* (Polity Press, 1993)

Susan M. DiGiacomo, an adjunct Professor in the Department of Anthropology, University of Massachusetts at Amherst, started research on Catalan nationalism in 1977. Her interests in ideology, discourse, and power in complex societies also include cancer treatment and epidemiology, and the changing nature of work in the academy. A contributor to collected volumes of essays on both nationalism and medical anthropology, and a translator of Catalan authors, she has also published articles in *Anthropological Quarterly* (1987), *Medical Anthropology* (1992), *Medical Anthropology Quarterly* (forthcoming), and *Critique of Anthropology* (1997).

Monica Heller is Professor in the Department of Sociology and Equity Studies in Education and the Centre de recherches en éducation franco-ontarienne at the Ontario Institute for Studies in Education of the University of Toronto. Her most recent publications include *Linguistic Minorities and Modernity: A Sociolinguistic Ethnography* (Longman, 1999) and *Voices of Authority: Education and Linguistic Diversity* (co-edited with Marilyn Martin-Jones, Ablex, to appear in 2000).

Alexandra Jaffe received her PhD from Indiana University (1990) and taught at SUNY-Cortland before coming to the University of Southern Mississippi. In her research on Corsica, she has been particularly interested in how dominant language ideologies are reproduced and challenged, and explores these issues in her forthcoming book in this series. She is currently analysing data on Corsican bilingual radio practice and its popular reception, and continues fieldwork in Corsica. Other research interests include the social uses of greeting cards, and the connection between non-standard orthography and stigmatized images of Southern varieties of American English.

Ron Kuzar teaches in the Department of English Language and Literature at the University of Haifa and in the Department of Hebrew and Semitics at Tel-Aviv University. His academic interests are syntax, English and Hebrew linguistics, and cultural studies of language and linguistics.

Joshua S. Madumulla is a senior lecturer in Swahili literature at the Department of Kiswahili of the University of Dar es Salaam. He also worked with the Institute of Kiswahili Research of the same university for over a decade. He is a literary scholar specialized in modern literature in Swahili. His publications include several articles and a book, *Proverbs and sayings: theory and practice* (IKR, 1995).

Michael Meeuwis studied African Languages and History at the University of Gent and Linguistics at the University of Antwerp, where he graduated with a PhD dissertation on the Congolese community in Belgium. He is a postdoctoral fellow of the Fund for Scientific Research-Flanders, currently affiliated to the University of Antwerp. His domains of interest include the grammar and history of Lingala, the linguistic and sociolinguistic history of Central Africa (western Congo in particular), language ideologies and intercultural communication.

Sheila M. Shannon is Associate Professor and Chair of Language, Literacy and Culture at the School of Education, University of Colorado at Denver. Her work focuses on the politics of language status and its impact on educational practice. She has conducted fieldwork in the U.S. on Spanish and in Ireland on Irish. She is co-author of *Pushing Boundaries: Language and Culture in a Mexicano Community* (with Olga A. Vásquez and Lucinda Pease Alvarez, Cambridge, 1994). Other publications include "Mexican immigrants in U.S. schools: Targets of symbolic violence" (with Kathy Escamilla, *Educational Policy*, forthcoming), and "The hegemony of English: A case study of one bilingual classroom as a site of resistance" (*Linguistics and Education*, 1995).

Christopher Stroud is an Associate Professor in bilingualism research, currently employed at the Centre for Research on Bilingualism, Stockholm University. His field of speciality is in sociolinguistics where he has worked with issues in language, literacy, interethnic communication and education in multilingual developing contexts. The focus of his work is on the relationship of language to social change and transformation and on how issues of language tie into and are affected by local strivings for identity and empowerment in situations of global change. He has worked extensively in Mozambique and in Papua New Guinea.

Richard J. Watts is Professor of English Linguistics at the University of Berne (Switzerland). He is the editor of the international journal *Multilingua: Journal of Cross-Cultural and Interlanguage Communication* and co-editor (with Monica Heller) of the present book series for Mouton de Gruyter. Among his publications are *Power in Family Discourse, Politeness in Discourse* (with Sachiko Ide and Konrad Ehlich), *Cultural Democracy and Ethnic Pluralism* (with Jerzy Smolicz) and *Standard English: The Widening Debate* (with Tony Bex). He is currently editing a volume of papers on alternative histories of English.

The debate is open

Jan Blommaert

1. The purpose

How do language ideologies come about? What makes the difference between a successful language ideology —one that becomes dominant— and other, less successful ones? What is the connection between language ideologies and broader political and ideological developments in a society? How did we arrive at our contemporary views and perspectives on language and our assessments of current linguistic situations? These are among the central questions that will be discussed in this volume.

The starting point of this interrogation is the observation that, until now, these questions have rarely been explored by scholars studying language ideologies. As a consequence, the *historiography of language ideologies* is something that remains to be constructed. The socioculturally motivated ideas, perceptions and expectations of language, manifested in all sorts of language use and in themselves objects of discursive elaboration in meta-pragmatic discourse, seem to have no history. There is now a widespread recognition of language ideologies as a crucial topic of debate in the study of language and society, especially when it comes to assessing the relationships between language and power/social structure, and when it comes to assessing the motives and causes for certain types of language change. (For general discussions of language ideologies, see Joseph and Taylor (eds.) 1990; Kroskrity, Schieffelin and Woolard (eds.) 1992; Schieffelin, Woolard and Kroskrity (eds.) 1998; Woolard and Schieffelin 1994; Woolard 1992, 1998). But one area of study, the historical production and reproduction of language ideologies, needs to be filled in.[1]

In their attempt to scratch the surface of this type of sociolinguistic historiography, the authors in this volume have chosen *debates* as their main objects of analysis. Debates, that is, in which language is central as a topic, a motif, a target, and in which language ideologies are being articulated, formed, amended, enforced. The debates that will be discussed in the various contributions to this volume all deal with debates that had some impact on (or at least a very close connection with) the "language situation" in the society in which it takes place. They are organized around issues of purity and impurity of languages, the social "value" of some language(s) as opposed to (an)other(s), the sociopolitical desirability of the use of one language or language variety over another, the symbolic "quality" of languages and varieties as emblems of nationhood, cultural authenticity, progress, modernity, democracy, self-respect, freedom, socialism, equality, and many more "values" (in fact, sociopolitical ideals) that remain to be discovered when reading the chapters. The debates are usually developed with considerable *sérieux* and with continuous signalling of importance, relevance and salience. They develop against a wider sociopolitical and historical horizon of relationships of power, forms of discrimination, social engineering, nation-building and so forth. Their outcome always has connections with these issues as well: the outcome of a debate directly or indirectly involves forms of conflict and inequality among groups of speakers: restrictions on the use of certain languages/varieties, the loss of social opportunities when these restrictions are not observed by speakers, the negative stigmatization of certain languages/varieties, associative labels attached to languages/varieties. Language ideological debates are part of more general sociopolitical processes, and one of the contributions of the studies collected here may consist of a clearer understanding of the precise role played by language ideologies in more general sociopolitical developments, conflicts and struggles. Thus our effort can be inserted in an emerging tradition of work in which the relationships between discourse on the one hand and social conflict, struggle and inequality on the other hand are central concerns (see e.g. Briggs (ed.) 1996, 1997; Hymes 1996; Heller 1994).

Before giving the floor to the different authors of the chapters in this collection, I will specify some of the central issues, concepts and concerns that have motivated and inspired the authors, and that have ran through the different discussions that took place during the construction of this book. The dialogue was not always easy and clear, and the collection will bear traces of a gradual and incomplete convergence in terminology, perception of the issues, theoretical preferences, historical scope and intertextual connections to other traditions and disciplines —traces reflecting the (debate-internal) genesis of a small tradition, a way of speaking about language, history, social forces and actors, ideologies, co-constructed and shared by the authors in the volume.

The genesis of this book starts with a concept paper which I wrote and sent to the invited authors in late 1996, and in which I formulated some general questions and suggested some concepts that could be useful in answering them. One of the starting observations I made was that history is still a difficult concept in the study of language. I will therefore start with a set of comments on history, historical time and linguistics. I will, after that, formulate a proposal for a historical perspective on language data. Next I will turn to the central object of the studies in this volume: debates. Finally, I will provide a brief survey of the chapters in the book, and conclude by identifying a number of target domains for which the study of language ideological debates may be particularly useful.

2. Problems of history

> The other social sciences are rather badly informed about the crisis that our discipline [historiography, JB] has undergone during the last twenty or thirty years. Their tendency is to ignore together with the works of historians an aspect of social reality of which historiography has always been a faithful servant, if not a skilful vendor: that social *durée*, these multiple and contradictory temporalities in the life of human beings that are not only the substance of the past but also the fabric of the present social life. The more relevant it is in the unfolding debate between the social sciences to emphasize the importance and the usefulness of history, or rather of the dialectic of the *durée* .... For nothing is in our view more important and central to social reality than this vivid, intimate and infinitely repeated opposition between the single moment and the slow unfolding time. In relation to the past as well as to the present, a clear awareness of this plurality of temporalities is indispensable to any common methodology for the social sciences.
>
> (Braudel 1958 [1969]: 43, my translation)

This is one of the classic formulations of *durée* given by Fernand Braudel. Braudel argues with considerable force for the acceptance of a layered and multiple concept of time —a concept of time that recognizes both different "objective", chronological speeds and different ways of perceiving time by subjects. "Traditional" historical time, called "*courte durée*" by Braudel (and "*événement*" by most other authors) is qualified as "the short time, measured on individuals, everyday life, our illusions, our understandings and awareness" (45–46). It is the time people can see, feel and control. But apart from that time, there are other times or temporalities: slow processes that are beyond the reach of individuals, the time of social, political and economic systems; and even slower: the ultra-slow time documented in climate and geology. History, according to Braudel, is the study of overlapping, intertwining and conflicting temporalities in the lives of people. And this insight, according to Braudel, could be historiography's main contribution to the other social sciences.

I start with this longish commentary on one of the classic historiographical concepts for a variety of reasons. First, it is undoubtedly an attractive and useful concept, of which numerous empirical correlates can be explored and found. As said above, the various temporalities are not only objective chronometrical phenomena; they also refer to perceptions and experiences of time by humans, in other words (and this is an essential ingredient of the Braudelian conception of historical time) to the social nature of time. To this contemporary students of language would add: time is social, hence also interactional, shared, collaboratively accomplished, managed, enacted, inhabited (made part of the *habitus*) by social beings. It is an object of power and control, of discipline and regimentation (for the origins of the latter, see E.P. Thompson 1991, chapter 6). All these things, the irregular and fragmented flow of time(s) as seen and perceived by social beings, can be fruitfully researched in relation to language and communicative phenomena.

And so we arrive at the second reason why this (type of) concept is attractive. Mainstream linguistics has so far not been able to incorporate a full and rich historical concept of time into its analytical toolkit. Foucault (1966, chapter 4) observed that in traditional grammar, external time was motivated by language-internal features, so that time collapsed *in* language. Edwin Ardener's review of classical historical linguistics led to the conclusion that

> [t]he grandeur of the Neogrammarian model for historical linguistics literally left nothing more to be said. This grandeur lay in its perfect generativeness. It did not, however, generate history.
>
> (Ardener 1971: 227)

Meeuwis and Brisard, discussing a wide range of approaches from historical linguistics as well as from sociolinguistics and anthropological linguistics, and covering a variety of linguistic paradigms, note "how an essentially 'adynamic' and 'achronic' approach to time prevails throughout these paradigms" (1993: 7). Time and temporal dynamics are often reduced to degrees of linguistic complexity (the most elaborate structures being the most stable ones, the simpler lexemes being the oldest), to a tentative timescale which is projected onto sound change and degrees of lexical similarity between languages (as in glottochronology), to a generative principle based on a schema of systemic development. Too often, the historicity of linguistic data is taken for granted. The question as to why certain data are *historical* (and would hence be objects of historical-linguistic analysis) is supposed to be answered by history itself: this text is dated 1689; therefore it is historical, therefore any analysis of this text is historical analysis.[2]

There is an admirable record of dissenting views in the study of language, in which more elaborate, richer and more valuable connections between language and history are being advocated (e.g. Thomason and Kaufman 1988; Nurse and Spear 1985; Burke 1993). The influence of deeply dynamic perspectives on language and communication, articulated in the works of e.g. Bakhtin and Voloshinov, or in the works of Roman Jakobson and his Prague School colleagues cannot be overlooked (e.g. Jakobson 1985). To some of these perspectives I shall return below. But the fact remains that language history as something that pertains to speakers, to societies, to social and cultural systems, is only rarely the history used in linguistics or adjacent sciences. References to the past are still, by and large, impressionistic or prima facie, and quite a bit of idealization goes on when it comes to understanding the historical forces that made us speak, write, listen, read the way we do now. It is our ambition to add to the history of language and languages a dimension of human agency, political intervention, power and authority, and so make that history a bit more *political* (a road previously explored by e.g. Grillo 1989 and Fabian 1986). Simple and linear concepts of historical time do not offer much hope in that respect.

Let us briefly dwell on the dissenting views hinted at above, for they constitute a third reason why a Braudelian concept of historical time may be interesting. In fields as diverse as ethnography, literary analysis, poetics and folklore, deeply dynamic views of language and language behavior have been articulated. Now-classic concepts such as intertextuality, contextualization, performance and entextualization all point towards the intrinsically historical, action-related and socioculturally anchored nature of all phenomena of language (for a survey see Bauman and Briggs 1990). Every text incorporates, reformulates, reinterprets or re-reads previous texts, every act of communication is grounded in semantic and pragmatic histories which are not simple and linear, but complex, multilayered and fragmented. Texts generate their publics, publics generate their texts, and the analysis of "meanings" now has to take into account a historiography of the context of production, the mechanisms and instruments of reproduction and reception, ways of storage and remembering (Gal and Woolard (eds.) 1995; Gal 1989). The fact is that discourses, texts, talk all have their "natural history" —a chronological and sociocultural anchoring which produces meaning and social effects in ways that cannot be reduced to text-characteristics alone (see the essays in Silverstein and Urban (eds.) 1996). Context, in this approach, is historical and the dynamics of textualization is not restricted to the event in which discourse is produced and exchanged. Every event —dynamic and processual in itself— is situated as part of a tradition of events, and this tradition contributes heavily to what happens in each concrete event.[3] Hence, texts are not stable over time: each reproduction of a text shapes a new text. One of the problems with attempts such as that of historical linguistics and historical pragmatics (cf. above) is that the stability of texts over time is taken for granted, and that inferences about genre, tradition, meaning and effect are based on a nuanced linguistic analysis of the text itself. The texts are *historical*, but the analysis simply treats them as *old*.

3. Intrinsic historicity

In the concept paper circulated among the authors of the chapters in this volume, I advocated the incorporation of a historical dimension *intrinsic to language data*. This historical dimension could be organized along two lines: (i) Braudelian *durée* as a perspective on language —viz. a perspective which captures both the intrinsic historicity as well as the social nature of language and language use; (ii) materialism as a methodological point of departure —viz. a heuristic in which language processes are seen as real, socioculturally and historically anchored phenomena, not epiphenomenal to reality but co-constructive of reality (a consequence, I believe, of the intrinsic historicity of language data). What we need to look for, in my opinion, is a formulation of the historicity of language data *as part of the definition of our object*. In other words, the historical dimension should be intrinsic to every synchronic or diachronic observation made in and about language. Every language fact is intrinsically historical.

I have given some space to *durée* in the previous section. Now, some clarification is in order with regard to the materialist orientation I advocated. It is a common move in the linguistic tradition (including sociolinguistics), to adopt idealist approaches to language-related ideational phenomena such as attitudes or ideologies (see Williams 1992). They are often seen as ideas which people just happen to have. One effect of this is an abstraction of the historical process in which the genesis of such ideational phenomena is contained, sometimes amounting, in fact, to a dehistorization of the phenomena. The preferred locus of analysis is the synchronic plane, where questions about the origin and the causes of distribution and impact of ideologies can be avoided.

This idealization leads to a number of problems. Power can hardly be seen as a purely local/synchronic concept. Insights into the development of power relations are of the utmost importance for an accurate understanding of the synchronic use of power, especially when we are dealing with societally established forms of power and forms of power which come about through a long and intricate process of social and political manoeuvring and engineering (e.g. Gramsci's hegemony with all its social and political mechanisms, Foucault's normalized, "capillary" power, or Althusser's ideological state apparatuses). The same comment can in fact be made for all group-related concepts in sociolinguistic analysis. One cannot define a speech community in purely synchronic terms. And if one does define it in historical terms, this historical dimension should make itself felt at the analytical level. The problem is, indeed, analytical and descriptive. The social formations involved in the production and reproduction of power in societies need to be identified in more detail than is customary in various branches of sociolinguistics and discourse analysis, where seemingly unambiguous labels (the authorities, the ruling classes, the masses, the laymen, institutions...) are taken to tell the whole story. The social formations need to be identified ethnographically, specifying the practices they use, when they use them, where they come from and so on. If language is used by real people and not by abstract social categories, then these real people must have names, faces, ages, occupations, and so on.

I am advocating a type of materialism which should replace the current idealism characterizing the use of ideational concepts, but which should not lapse into too rigid interpretations of Marxism as economism. What I mean by materialism is an ethnographic eye for the real historical actors, their interests, their alliances, their practices, and where they come from, in relation to the discourses they produce —where discourse is in itself seen as a crucial symbolic resource onto which people project their interests, around which they can construct alliances, on and through which they exercise power. Power (including the (re)production of ideology) must be identified as a form of practice, historically contingent and socially embedded.[4] I find admirable examples of this approach in Monica Heller's (1994) work, which is in turn inspired by Bourdieu (e.g. 1982). It is, in Bourdieu's terms, an investigation into praxis, be it with a stronger focus on the precise developments and activities captured under "praxis" and more in particular on the interactional and discursive dimensions of these developments and activities. The precise discursive mechanisms by means of which linguistic symbolic resources are being produced, distributed or circulated, and the value attached to these resources, are the foci of our attention.

What counts for power also counts for its results: conflict, inequality, injustice, oppression, or delicate and fragile status-quo. There, too, a perspective which puts emphasis on the historical conditions and the genesis of patterns of conflict, inequality and so forth can prove very fruitful. If some group or individual does not succeed in having their voices heard (or if, in fact, they don't even seem to *have* a voice), then the reason for this is rarely purely synchronic. It usually has to do with slowly or dramatically *emerged* forms of inequality sedimented in the differential allocation of speaking rights, attributions of status and value to speech styles, uneven distribution of speech repertoires and other historical developments. Such forms of inequality are transcontextual, translocal, certainly not one-time (see Briggs 1997: 534–538). Bourdieu meets Hymes at this point: there is a difference between potential and actual fact, says Hymes, and whereas *potentially* anything can happen in language, and *potentially* all languages and their speakers are equal, "[t]o a great extent, languages ... are what has been made of them". And the fact is that "languages are not found unmolested, as it were, one to a community, each working out its destiny autonomously" (Hymes 1996: 57). Behind every instance of violence, conflict, oppression or injustice, there is a history of violence, conflict, oppression or injustice. A study of language which aims at dealing adequately with power has to rely on the precise identification of conditions, actors, structures and patterns, over time and resulting in intertextualities for power and power effects. It is to loci of such intertextualities that I shall now turn.

4. Debates: A tentative model

In the field of politics, discursive struggle and contestation are generically captured under the label of debate. The political process develops through a series of exchanges involving a variety of social actors: politicians and policy-makers themselves, academic and non-academic experts, interested members of the public, the media. Debates are, political-ideologically, the points of entrance for civil society into policy making: they are (seen as) the historical moments during which the polity gets involved in shaping policies. And for our purpose here, it is crucial to note that this shaping process is mainly a process of shaping textual tools captured under terms such as public opinion: interpretations of policies, illustrative applications of policy statements to various areas of social life and social experience (see also Blommaert 1997a).

Though there may be a prototypical perception of political debates, it is hard to provide conclusive criteria for identifying them, both in terms of discourse event-type (identities of participants, genres, time span, setting, etc.) and in terms of their relation to the outcome of decision-making procedures. They are patterns of interrelated discourse activities (Stroud, this volume, calls them "discourse projects") often with a fuzzy beginning and end, of which we usually only remember the highlights, the most intense and polarized episodes. In the light of the textual nature of the process, it would be accurate to characterize debates as historical episodes of textualization, as histories of texts in which a struggle is waged between various texts and metatexts. Debates are more or less historically locatable periods in which a "struggle for authoritative entextualization" takes place (Silverstein and Urban 1996: 11): "[p]olitics can be seen ... as the struggle to entextualize authoritatively, and hence, in one relevant move, to fix certain metadiscursive perspectives on texts and discourse practices". Metadiscursive entextualization —inserting texts into a chosen metadiscursive context and hence indicating the preferred way(s) of "reading" these texts— is then a strategic practice often aimed at the "acceptance of a metadiscourse by a community", a process that may be "at the very center of a community's organizing social categories and their relationship, including political hierarchies" (1996: 12).

The struggle for authoritative entextualization involves ideology brokers: categories of actors who, for reasons we set out to investigate, can claim authority in the field of debate (politicians and policy-makers, interest groups, academicians, policy implementers, the organized polity, individual citizens). The struggle develops usually over *definitions* of social realities: various representations of reality which are pitted against each other —discursively— with the aim of gaining authority for one particular representation. Mehan (1996) calls this "the politics of representation":

> Proponents of various positions in conflicts waged in and through discourse attempt to capture or dominate modes of representation .... This competition over the meaning of ambiguous events, people, and objects in the world has been called the "politics of representation". ... Indeed, the process of lexical labeling is itself an entextualization process. Complex, contextually nuanced discussions get summed up in (and, hence, are entextualized through) a single word.
>
> (Mehan 1996: 253)

Debates are excellent linguistic-ethnographic targets. They are textual/ discursive, they produce discourses and metadiscourses, and they result in a battery of texts that can be borrowed, quoted, echoed, vulgarized etc. In sum, they are moments of textual formation and transformation, in which minority views can be transformed into majority views and vice versa, in which group-specific discourses can be incorporated into a master text, in which a variety of discursive means are mobilized and deployed (styles, genres, arguments, claims to authority), and in which sociopolitical alliances are shaped or altered in discourse.

Debates about language ideologies define or redefine the language ideologies (often through conflicting representations) in the same way as debates about languages define or redefine these languages. They shape or reshape them, and so become the locus of *ideology (re)production*. A particular (set of) text(s), the outcome of the conclusion of the debate, may become the canon on which echoes, borrowings etc. are based, and from which other discourses or political practices can be derived, or on the basis of which they can be motivated and legitimized. In turn, the origin of debates often presupposes the existence of language ideologies, and debates often graft new priorities and directions (e.g. radicalization, the highlighting of particular aspects) onto existing language ideologies.

It is essential to identify the participants in such debates, as well as to question the hows and whys of the particular moment of occurrence of debates and their outcomes. Some debates are highly formative. They not only provide a lexicon and a set of stock arguments which underly the construction of authoritative (folk as well as expert) rhetoric about the issue, but they may also instigate implementation practices and hegemonize the field. Some debates, however, remain inconsequential. In terms of power effects, they failed. Still they may be highly illustrative of political and ideological traditions in the field of language in a particular society at a particular moment. The difference between formative and inconsequential ideologies often does not lie in the nature and structure of the ideologies themselves, but rather in what kind of *reproduction* they are subject to.

For this is the second part of the model: ideologies do not win the day just like that, they are not simply picked up by popular wisdom and public opinion. They are being reproduced by means of a variety of institutional, semi-institutional and everyday practices: campaigns, regimentation in social reproduction systems such as schools, administration, army, advertisement, publications (the media, literature, art, music) and so on (J.B. Thompson 1990). These reproduction practices may result —willingly or not— in *normalization*, i.e. a hegemonic pattern in which the ideological claims are perceived as "normal" ways of thinking and acting (thus, Bourdieu qualified standard language as *un produit normalisé*: Bourdieu 1982: 28). There is no public opinion, no social consensus which can be detached from real processes of hegemonization. For this reason, analyses of debates have to make reference to the forms of *stasis* preceding or following them. The more or less stable situations which generate debates or are the effect of debates may be understood more fully when looking at the structure, the causes and the development of the debates. Also, the connection between normalization and institutionalization can be explored in more detail: are normalized practices/ideas *eo ipso* "institutional", either in the broad sense of conventional practices/ideas that are ratified through structures of power, or in a more narrow sense as mediated and channeled through formal systems of authority and control?

These processes of hegemonization may account for the success versus failure of some debates. What means were mobilized, what kind of institutional muscle was deployed, and why and when? This way, we could also question some of the preconditions for the reproduction of language ideologies: for instance, what means can one deploy in a largely illiterate environment, given the fact that some of the traditional instruments (based on literacy) would be ineffective? What kind of preconditions do ideology brokers take for granted? And what can be revealed about their target audiences through this?

Note that I want to remain far removed from Big Brother fantasies, and that I do not want to project a fixed set of ideology brokers onto each case of (re)production. It is not always the State that is the main actor, and neither are all attempts at hegemony aimed at maximizing (malevolent) control over the polity. In a similar vein, the hegemony of one ideology does not necessarily imply total consensus or total homogeneity. On the contrary, ambiguity and contradiction may be key features of every ideology, and subjects' adherence to one ideology or another is often inconsistent or ambivalent. The point is precisely to reach a more refined understanding of the processes of power, by identifying the actors, the practices and the contextual factors involved in specific historical processes.

One final comment is terminological. I have described debates in this section as slowly unfolding processes of discursive exchange. There is, of course, a well-established usage of the term debate, one which takes debates to be clearly delineated and demarcated speech events, one-time "*événements*" that proceed almost ritually and that mark important phases of decision-making. "Parliamentary debates on voting rights for immigrants" as well as "the Clinton-Dole presidential debate" would fit this description. Such debates will occur in the volume, but they will be treated as parts of and moments in another type of debate: the larger, slower type of debate that is central to the discussions in the chapters of this volume.

5. The book

Les us now try to give a more structured survey of the various contributions in the book. The chapters have been put in a loosely geographical order, starting with three papers on debates in European states (Jaffe, Watts, DiGiacomo) and one on Canada (Heller), where a situation occurs which is germane to some of the European cases. The second bloc consists of two papers on the United States (Shannon and Collins). Next, two papers will discuss debates in post-World War II states in which nation-building had to start from scratch, but in a socio-economic and sociopolitical environment which is "first world", i.e. highly literate, economically prosperous and technologically advanced, as well as geopolitically influential: Singapore (Bokhorst-Heng) and Israel (Kuzar). Finally, three chapters discuss cases from African states: Tanzania (Madumulla, Bertoncini and Blommaert), Mozambique (Stroud) and Congo-Zaire (Meeuwis). The African cases also have to be situated in a context of emerging state structures, but in contrast to Singapore and Israel, socio-economic and sociopolitical conditions are marked by extreme poverty, marginalization and underdevelopment.

Europe and Canada

Alexandra Jaffe's paper "Locating power: Corsican translators and their critics" opens the volume and foreshadows a number of recurrent themes. The case she discusses is a debate between Corsican translators and their critics during the late 1980s about the translation of a well-known French novel, *Knock*, into Corsican. The debate has to be situated in a long history of regionalism and cultural nationalism in Corsica, in which French —the hegemonic language of the oppressor— came to be seen as an enemy in its own right, and Corsican came to stand metonymically for the totality of the struggle for nationhood (and indeed, peoplehood) of the Corsicans. Language and nation do all but coincide in Corsica as well as in some other contemporary European regional nationalisms. The deeper meanings of the debate therefore revolve around how translations of French (hegemonic) literature into Corsican correspond to political and language-ideological claims related to the promotion of Corsican language-and-nation building. The central issue in the debate, identified by Jaffe, is an opposition between two language ideologies. The first one is an instrumentalist ideology, in which language is seen as a tool for transforming ideas into new linguistic patterns. The second one is a romantic ideology, in which language is an abstract idea inextricably linked with a people's "soul". The first ideology would allow translations of French works into Corsican to be seen as acts of "promotion" of Corsican (or even "improvement" —Jaffe quotes a translator who uses the expression "putting the language to the test"). The translators argue that they are "expanding" the language, "proving" its expressive qualities, and so penetrating into domains of power hitherto exclusively reserved to French. Corsican is used *as if* it were a language of power —*as if*, indeed, it were French. On the other hand, the second ideology would see translations as acts of perversion, since only creative literature in Corsican would realize the ideal mapping of language and soul, whereas translations would bring a foreign "essence" into the language. Translations of French novels perpetuate the role of French as an input language, a source language without which Corsican would not exist as a literate language. Thus translations reinforce the "colonial" (a term often used by Jaffe) linguistic power relations that hold between French and Corsican. Empowerment and alienation are played off against each other in a debate of which the outcome is hard to foretell.

The actors in this debate are all elite figures. One the one hand, there are the translators: highly articulate, multilingual and sophisticated intellectuals often with an impressive cultural erudition. Their critics too are amongst the most vociferous and influential intellectuals on the island. The particular form of nationalism in Corsica, regional and cultural in bias, has pushed intellectuals into the battle zone. In particular, Jaffe identifies literacy, or rather, writing, as a crucial theme in Corsican nationalism. Jaffe writes: "All Corsican texts could be seen as game pieces in a war for symbolic territory." The writing of grammars and dictionaries of Corsican provided legitimacy for the Corsicans' claim to peoplehood, since what they spoke was a language, not a "*dialecte*" or "*idiome*". The production of literature would demonstrate that this language was, moreover, beautiful, flexible, creative, artistic, in short: cultural. Given the history of powerlessness of the Corsicans in the face of the metropolitan French language and culture, and given the role of the written word in the struggle for empowerment, representational strategies in writing can become topics of heated debate.

Jaffe focuses strongly on the case at hand. But of course, the particular debate cannot be understood without taking into account the long history of mobilization of symbolic resources such as writing in Corsican, against the power, the institutions and the language of the "colonizer", France. French is perceived as monolithic, massive, suffocating, even dehumanizing. The roots of such language perceptions may be local; but their intertextuality with other times and places is impressive. The pattern described by Jaffe, of a Corsican anti-(French)-language which is used in a struggle for a "decolonization of the mind" (the term is Ngugi wa Thiong'o's), is indeed colonial and reminiscent of similar struggles both in the Third World and elsewhere. It is a classic case of Herderian logic that comes to the rescue of people who feel oppressed. Similar cases will appear further in the volume.

Richard Watts discusses "The ideology of dialect in German-speaking Switzerland". We are still in the First World, in a country that boasts a long history of democratically-channeled multilingualism without big conflicts, and —at least to the outsider— without much in the way of a language of its own. The three main languages of Switzerland (French, German and Italian) are the national languages of the neighboring countries. Rhaeto-Romantsch, the only "true" Swiss language, was later added to the list of national languages. But Watts describes the way in which, since World War II, an ideology of dialect has emerged in German-speaking Switzerland (demographically the largest part of the country), to the extent that the standard variety of German now enjoys an overall lower prestige than its dialect varieties. The various Swiss dialects of German —*Schwyzertüütsch*— are ideologically qualified as "open", "direct", "spontaneous" and so forth, *and* as "typically Swiss". At the same time, however, only standard German is used in official communication and in education to non-German speaking Swiss. Consequently, intercommunity communication between members of the German-speaking community and members of other communities risks to be impeded by the use of a dialect which only the German-speaking Swiss can understand. In other words: the official language policy is subverted by the "indigenization" of one of the official languages by its speakers.

Watts sketches a complex network of Swiss myths, ranging from William Tell over Swiss materialism and the idea of Switzerland as a mountain fortress which maintains strict neutrality in international conflicts. These myths, Watts argues, have crystallized into language and into an ideology of dialect among German-speaking Swiss because of three historical factors: (i) the economic depression of the 1920s-1930s, (ii) the rise of fascism in Germany and Italy, and (iii) the second World War. In particular, the ideology of dialect served to build and reinforce a Swiss self-image of anti-fascism through a symbolic —linguistic— closure of Switzerland against Italy (Rhaeto-Romantsch) and Germany (Schwyzertüütsch). In the meantime, dialect has been profusely used in education as well as in the media, and language behavior in everyday life shows the default nature of dialect use as opposed to standard German (which, significantly, is called *Schriftdeutsch* 'German for writing'). Watts sees distinct dangers in this situation: the closure generated by the ideology of dialect has now turned inwardly, and German dialects create a barrier between the German-speaking community and the non-German-speaking communities and so create conditions for a regionalism based on an identity of ethnolinguistic uniqueness. Especially the Swiss Francophones, says Watts, "feel that the insistence on dialect ... is a betrayal of Swiss identity" which to them appears to reside in the quadrilingual character of the nation and the multilingualism of its citizens.

In the case of Switzerland (as in the Canadian case discussed by Heller, see below), the debate is slowly unfolding. It is a gradual emergence of ideas and practices, stimulated by historical turning points such as the War, but with an important role (as in Canada) for institutions as centers in which ideologies can be anchored and made societally relevant and productive. In Switzerland —and this is Watts' main concern— education and the media have tuned into the ideology of dialect and now account for and contribute to an acceleration and a deepening of the process of ideological reproduction.

In line with the conclusions of the previous chapter, Susan DiGiacomo's paper on "Language ideological debates in an Olympic city: Barcelona 1992–1996" focuses on the press as a channel and a medium of ideological production and reproduction. According to DiGiacomo, journalistic texts are "themselves elements in and of ideological practice that must be taken seriously". Hence, in contrast to the slow processes described by Watts, DiGiacomo puts emphasis on contemporary history and recent events, as they are articulated in and by the media. Her case is Catalonia, and more in particular the way in which Catalan linguistic capital was bartered during that high point in Catalonia's post-Franco history: the Barcelona Olympics of 1992. DiGiacomo follows the way in which the organization of the Olympics in a city which, apart from being the Olympic city is also the capital of an outspokenly autonomist region in Spain, becomes a historical moment (an "*événement*") in which symbols of Catalan nationhood, of power and of cultural greatness are articulated and played out against competing Spanish symbols. The momentary perspective is of course only apparent.

Catalonia's bid for linguistic and cultural power in 1992 cannot be dissociated from the long period of anti-Catalan and anti-regionalist oppression under Franco, nor from the attempts towards maintaining a centralist and uniformly Castilian image of Spain by both the post-Franco Spanish governments and the contemporary conservative and centrist forces in Spain. There is a long tradition in Catalonia of cherishing the language in the context of the political goal of autonomy (documented in the works of Kathryn Woolard, e.g. 1989), and the "*événement*" of 1992 derives its salience, its violence and explicitness, from the slower history of Spanish-Catalan political relations.

The tropes articulated in the debate, in which journalists, columnists and editorialists play important parts alongside international figures such as Vargas Llosa, are familiar. The nation Catalonia has gradually acquired "state" symbols: a flag, an anthem, a standardized language; and the organization of a great international event such as the Olympics offers a chance to play these symbols out against those of the Spanish state. As a consequence, the play of hierarchies starts: which symbol should come first, which anthem should be sung first, which language should dominate the press briefs... The undercurrent to these practical issues is a more theoretical issue, in which international figures such as Vargas Llosa try to intervene: that of the *value* of a nation-(sub)state such as Catalonia, set against the context of the Spanish nation-State as well as against that of more abstract units such as the Hispanic "world". It is a competition between abstractions, of course, but a heated one and at times a bitter one.

Symbols and history are the two main components of DiGiacomo's account: it is on the basis of battles over interpretations of symbols and history (e.g. the Franco period) that contemporary politics is being looked at. Contemporary politics itself is a highly complex pattern of actors and events, in which local, regional and national politicians, experts, intellectuals and journalists, socialists and conservatives, Catalans, centralist Spaniards, international intellectuals, the leading members of the International Olympic Committee, international journalists, all produce competing interpretations and representations. And the main vehicle for these battles, argues DiGiacomo, is the looking-glass of the press. In newspapers, "things happen": people choose sides, quote and comment, represent, criticize, and they do all this through influential channels that articulate a "massive" voice —the presumed voice of the masses.

Monica Heller's paper "Heated language in a cold climate", also discusses language-ideological debates in the context of a modern, First World society, Canada. Like in the European cases discussed by Jaffe,

Watts and DiGiacomo, a strong regionalist movement using an ethno-linguistic image of uniqueness as the backbone of its claims to identity and nationhood is central in the debate. Heller describes the developments of Anglophone-Francophone relations in Canada since the second World War. Her approach generates one very long debate spanning the last half century (but evidently building further on conditions from a more remote past). In a case such as Canada (as in Watts' discussion of Switzerland), the *durée* appears to be the most appropriate frame to describe chronic language conflicts. Heller notes how, prior to World War II, an imperialist policy of separateness had shaped a situation in which the French-speaking Canadians had been socio-economically and politically minorized, but had at the same time developed institutions of their own (mainly through the Catholic church), a small elite made up of intellectuals and Catholic clergy, and an ideology based on the idea of a separate nation (or "race") characterized by French and Catholicism. This idea of separateness left the existing power relations intact. While some space was left for "Canadianisms" in French, the overall attitude towards the language was purist, thus maintaining a sharply marked boundary with the Anglophone world. After World War II, a new elite generation and an emerging middle class rose to power, and religion lost ground in Francophone nationalism. The new elite challenged both the supremacy of the Anglophones in Canada and the conservatism of the Church in their own community. Ideologically, Heller writes, "French Canadian spiritual nationalism was re-invented as Québécois state nationalism", in which separateness as a nation was seen as the key argument for obtaining a "state", i.e. an autonomous region. From the 1960s onwards, institutional dynamics assumes an important role in shaping a Québécois nation-state through decision-making processes in the field of education, language policy and so forth. Gradually and by means of legal and institutional instruments, the Québécois elite redefined the value of linguistic capital in the country.

From then onwards, Heller identifies an opposition between two ideologies of the nation-state. Quebec bases its legitimacy and identity on the shaping of a monolingual territorial unit, causing uncertainty among other Francophone communities outside Quebec as well as doubts about the democratic caliber of the nation-state. The Federal authorities, on the other hand, elaborate an ideology of bilingualism as the key to a "uniquely Canadian" identity, in turn generating suspicion among Francophones who resent being treated as a minority on a par with others, and whose ideal lies in "monolingual zones" (seen as the best way to promote bilingualism, for, as Heller notes, Québécois and minority Francophones "[b]oth hold ... that as members of a minority, in order to be bilingual, one has to maintain one's first language.")

The debate is perpetual here. It develops on the rhythm of political decision-making processes, demographic and economic evolutions, election results, institutional changes, and so on. The picture we are offered by Heller is one of slowness: the two opposing ideologies come about slowly, gradually, not at all explosively or as a result of conflicts which made the situation unbearable. On the ground, quite a few conflicts must have occurred, of course, but the most important changes —those within the Francophone Québécois community after World War II— do not seem to come about as the result of such individual conflicts but rather as the product of a long history of minorization, ideological build-up, and economic dynamics both locally and on a nation-wide scale.

The opposition between a Québécois monolingual ideal and a Federal Canadian bilingual ideal can also be traced in expert traditions in Canada, Heller argues, and

> [s]ociology, anthropology and political science have tended to become engaged in the theorizing of social visions or of relations of power in Canadian society, in which language is not understood as social process, but rather as an essential characteristic, or label. Thus much of the work on language in Canada, motivated by political interests, takes language as a unified given.

The similarity with Jaffe's description of the language ideology of the translators' critics is striking and unavoidable: essentialist and homogeneistic ideologies of language appear better suited for nationalistic purposes, and better fit nationalist rhetorical frames, than others. Also important to note is the way in which scientific endeavors get shaped by political agendas. Québécois linguistics focuses on the characteristics and adequacy of Canadian French and contributes to the construction of a normative variety; linguistics inspired by the Federal agenda focuses on the nature and features of bilingualism. Work on both topics clearly sustains crucial political arguments, and scientific work is an indirect form of political discourse. Interestingly, Heller notes the political suitability of a particular sociolinguistic school, variationism:

> [h]ere the sociolinguistic stance that language is inherently variable, which does not mean it is not rule-governed, served well the interests of a political movement attempting to construct its own linguistic variety as both authentic ... and authoritative ....

Restricted and specific language ideologies such as variationism, mediated through expert voices speaking on "local" cases, data and issues (or at least: cases, data, and issues that can be "repatriated" to fit the local situation), provide the building stones for a muscled societal and political ideology of language which is articulated through the words and actions of politicians, institutions, councils and so on, in the slow and big debate sketched by Heller for post-World War II Canada.

The United States

Few states look as homogeneous and integrated as the United States, despite the presence and salience of obvious social, ethnic and cultural cleavages. Billig (1995: 143–153) identifies the U.S. as a society in which "banal nationalism" is very strong: the "normal" and almost unnoticed "flagging" of the nation by means of multiple everyday signals that refer to the normal unit of political and social thinking, the United States. In turn, Silverstein (1996) describes the American preoccupation with the nation as based on an ideology of homogeneous, monolingual standard English and finds that "we might say that we live in a society with a culture of monoglot standardization underlying the constitution of our linguistic community and affecting the structure of our various overlapping speech communities" (1996: 284). The two authors of the chapters on the U.S. both delve into the structure of this image of homogeneity. Following the Bilingual Education Act of 1968, there have been numerous debates on the role of languages other than standard (American) English in the American education system. Shannon's and Collins' chapters each document particular cases, the former focused on the debate on Spanish in American schools, the latter on the "Ebonics" debate (African-American varieties of English).

Sheila Shannon argues that by absence of a codified language policy in the U.S., English monolingualism (Silverstein's "culture of monoglot standardization") is the *de facto* norm, the default order of sociolinguistic life. The monoglot ideology is the backbone of language practices, linguistic debates, perceptions of ethnolinguistic stratification and so on, it is the neutral point used to measure and evaluate events and phenomena that are congruent or deviant. In the case Shannon documents, debates and measures related to bilingual education thus display a considerable paradox. Bilingual education in the U.S. seems to be aimed at increased competence in English. In other words, an assimilationist ideal underlies pluralist interventions in social life, and diversity is something which can be tolerated to a certain extent only. In light of what we have already witnessed in the previous chapters, it comes as no surprise that particular arguments are being used in defense of a monoglot ideal: English is the mark of Americanness, of good citizenship, of a will to integrate into U.S. society, and so on. A lack of proficiency in English displayed by Hispanics is quickly interpreted as an unwillingness to adapt to the dominant values and norms, and hence, as a rejection of the American way of life, an act of subversion.

Significantly, in the debate about Spanish in U.S. schools, just like in most other debates documented here, the conflict is not one of equals. One language is hegemonic and symbolically constructed as "in everyone's best interest". It is the high status language, the prestige language, the language of the socio-economic elite and middle class. The other language is a low-prestige and low status language, spoken by people in the periphery, both on a world scale (Mexicans and Cubans *vis-à-vis* Americans) as well as within one and the same society (low-skilled workers, high unemployment and low-education communities). Pluralism is rarely about reaching a patchwork of differences, it usually revolves around inequality and hierarchies.

Shannon describes the debate on bilingualism in U.S. education against the background of American nationalism. In particular, she contextualizes the case in the Reagan years, an era marked by high-flying national symbols, new dreams of world leadership and national greatness. Protagonists in the debate, such as Sam Hayakawa and William Bennett, emphasized the need for a unifying ideal of American identity, an ideal built on tradition and an essentialized notion of ownership of the nation. One could comment that strangely enough, tradition and ownership of the nation were associated during the Reagan years with white Anglo-Saxon immigration and not with either native Americans or non-white and non-Anglo-Saxon immigration. The case of the Reagan years is interesting, and further research would undoubtedly draw interesting parallels between the language ideological debate and debates in other spheres of society, such as international relations, welfare, economics and trade, and ethics.

James Collins' chapter on the contextualization of the Ebonics debate also stresses the intertextuality of the particular debate with other debates, and also situates the particular debate as a sub-debate of something larger: the historically phased unfolding of different American conceptions of the nation. Ebonics kept American linguists, educators and members of the general public busy for the best part of 1997. The issue was whether the varieties of English spoken by African-Americans —Ebonics— should be recognized as a legitimate language in education. The proposition itself, the very idea of the institutional fragmentation of English into a number of "ethnic" varieties, sparked an intense and heated debate in which all kinds of historical, sociological, linguistic-anthropological and political arguments were mobilized. Just like in the case discussed by Shannon, issues of linguistic diversity in institutions quickly turned into issues of the coherence and even the survival of the nation. Language was essentialized as "political otherness", then transformed into a political statement indicating the refusal to accept American "normalcy", and then confronted to the monolithical ideology of monoglot standard. Collins identifies the multiple sites of the debate, noting how the conflict over Ebonics quickly turned into a struggle over symbolic domination conceptualized as linguistic capital.

But Collins takes his analysis further than that. He sketches a historical evolution in which ideas about the nation are accompanied by ideas of the kind of (language-and-) literacy required for that particular idea of a nation. Thus, he identifies a "moral" complex of language-literacy, a "technical" complex and a "cultural" complex. The first two complexes, characteristic of earlier phases of nation-building, are centripetal: they stress the importance of monoglot standard English in the construction of an (ideal) American society. The third complex is centrifugal and stresses variability, difference, and alternative routes to prosperity, happiness, and nationhood. The claims to institutional equality for Ebonics (as well as for Spanish in Shannon's chapter) belong to this centrifugal complex. But they meet a reinforced centripetal ideology of standard, and the confrontation of both ideological currents can clearly be seen in the Ebonics debate.

Not surprisingly, central ingredients in the Ebonics debate are linguistic status definitions. Is Ebonics a "language"? a "dialect"? or just "gibberish"? Linguistic-definitional hierarchies reflect the ideological positions outlined by Collins, and labeling a linguistic phenomenon as a "language" involves far more than the expert-induced neutralization that often accompanies it (cf. Blommaert 1997b: 85–92 for a discussion of labeling in colonial linguistics; see also Calvet 1974). Such battles over linguistic status, symbolic ranking and claims to *langue*-hood are at the heart of many language ideological debates (remember Jaffe's "*mais où sont vos Rimbaud?*"), and they demonstrate precisely how deeply entrenched language ideological key concepts are in larger political-ideological schemes and models. Collins provides yet another clear case of the inextricable intertwining of different fields related to the conception of sociocultural and sociopolitical units such as nation, culture, ethnic group, minority, but also class, state and society.

Singapore and Israel

The next "bloc" in the book consists of two papers on countries in which a relatively short national history competes with relatively long and complex histories of identity. The countries are Singapore and Israel —both post-World War II states and both historically affiliated with Britain. Singapore and Israel are new nations, but they are not postcolonial in the way that e.g. African countries are. For one thing, both geopolitically as well as socio-economically, they belong to the "first world": they are relatively prosperous countries (e.g. compared to some of their neighbors) of some regional (or wider) importance in terms of political and economic weight. In both cases, young statehood has to be neutralized by old nationhood, so to speak. The quest for nation-building in the new state makes use of discourses emphasizing oldness, tradition, pedigree.

Wendy Bokhorst-Heng discusses the Singaporean "Speak Mandarin Campaign" and places the attempt by the Singaporean government to gain control over language use and language practices in the Chinese community of Singapore squarely in the realm of the "imagining of the nation". In the case of Singapore —an affluent, pocket-size but highly diversified South-East Asian community— this imagined nation is explicitly mixed. Prime Minister Lee Kuan Yew (himself a major player in the language ideological debate and an influential broker in ethnolinguistic theories) sets as target for his nation-building efforts the construction of a multilingual, multi-ethnic and multicultural nation, quite unlike the strongly homogeneistic concepts of the nation we have seen in the discussions of the European and Canadian cases.

Or is it? Bokhorst-Heng describes how the Speak Mandarin Campaign precisely aims at reducing (or indeed eliminating) the internal diversity within the community of Singaporean Chinese. Instead of the eleven dialects currently spoken by Chinese in Singapore, the Campaign intends to introduce the generalized use of Mandarin Chinese. The arguments used in favor of this homogenization are already well known. The Singaporean campaigners differentiate between good and bad language. "Good" is standard Mandarin; "bad" are the dialects. Standard Mandarin is associated with a long, rich and noble cultural tradition (that of *the* Chinese), which is supposed to provide a sense of orientation and belonging in the fast-changing world which Singapore intends to spearhead. Inferiority is engraved onto the everyday language use of the people, and progress can only be attained by bringing one's language use under stricter control from the authorities: the campaign is strongly hegemonic, massive and hardly nuanced. And apart from the active "imagining of a language" that goes on in the discourse on Mandarin, a number of ideological contrastive schemata arise. Thus, standard is not only opposed to dialect, but Chinese and the other community languages ("ethnic languages") are also opposed to English. Whereas the ethnic languages are associated with culture and tradition and hence with the past, with history, with stability, English is not "cultural" (in the sense of "traditional"). It refers to the future, to new ideas and values, with change. This way, Lee Kuan Yew and his followers construct an intricate symbolic pattern in which the whole Singaporean national project can be captured. Singapore is an Asian nation, firmly embedded in the traditions of the region and cherishing local values and cultural traditions. At the same time, Singapore is a modern society, strongly internationally oriented and preoccupied with economic progress. This, apparently, requires a different kind of symbolic alignment, not with Asian traditions but with the language of international commerce and communication: English. This layered linguistic-symbolic pattern is projected onto Singaporean society, and has given rise to the peculiar notion of "English-knowing bilingualism" often attributed to Singapore.

In Singapore, the debate is state-controlled and makes use of a variety of channels and media. Political speeches are one of the most visible vehicles by means of which language-ideological tropes and themes are being transmitted. Apart from that, the newspapers and the TV-channels appear to be important carriers of messages, often articulated by politicians themselves. The debate is relatively recent —Singapore evidently has no long tradition to build upon, either as a state or as a nation endowed with a rich treasure of national historical narratives— and the technology of ideological production and reproduction is undoubtedly state-of-the-art. But the ideas are old, deeply entrenched in European ways of imagining nations and their attributes, but slightly adapted so as to fit the imagining of a multicultural nation of the type outlined above.

Ron Kuzar's chapter on "Linguistic and political attitudes towards Israeli Hebrew: Ongoing revival versus normalcy" deals with a debate —or a series of debates— between prominent scholars of Hebrew in Israel during the 1950s. The historical period is highly significant. After its foundation in 1947, the State of Israel under David Ben-Gurion was faced with a number of extremely demanding challenges, summarized by Kuzar as "the building of a Jewish-Israeli nation-state, which would maximally match all parameters of a prototypical nation-state." First, the state itself had to be consolidated and fortified against attacks from without and within. An economy had to be developed, capable of feeding and supporting Israel's population, which doubled within a few years after the cease-fire of 1949 due to massive Jewish immigration. And on top of that, the state should also be made into a cohesive and united nation as part of what Kuzar calls the "untying of the Zionist package". National characteristics had to be assembled in such a way that the newness as well as the extreme "mixedness" of the young state could be compensated by symbols of unity and tradition. Three ideological currents are identified by Kuzar as "shades of Zionist ideology": socialist Zionism, capitalist statehood, and avant-garde individualistic modernism. The field of tension between these three currents (big enough to create political conflicts, but not big enough to become a threat to national cohesion) serves as the background for the debates about Hebrew.

Kuzar offers a detailed account of the way in which prominent Hebrew scholars (Rosén, Blanc, Ben-Hayyim, Tsemakh ...) produce discourses on language that can be aligned with larger political-ideological developments of the time. Thus, and not surprisingly, the debate starts with a controversy over the *language name*. Rosén had used the term "*Israeli* Hebrew", suggesting that the existence of the State of Israel could be a relevant (socio)linguistic condition giving rise to a "new" language. This terminology was challenged by others, who claimed that Hebrew was Israeli by definition and suggested that the term "*New* Hebrew" be used to identify the new massified forms of Hebrew language use. Both positions drew not only on political-ideological discourses about the nation, but also on linguistic traditions. Proponents of "Israeli" Hebrew could be aligned with structuralism, and therefore regarded Hebrew to be a fully developed language. Opponents of this view took a more philological stance, in which the "quality" of Hebrew was associated to the old written texts, and in which all speakers of Hebrew were defined as "newcomers" to the language. Both positions generate very different discourses on language purity, language ownership, and authority in knowledge of the language. Buried in these discourses are images of the nation, of Jewishness, and ultimately of different conceptions of nation-building and of Jewish national destiny.

Kuzar's chapter confirms insights already gathered from preceding chapters in the book, and anticipates a number of insights in later chapters. First, expert voices can hardly be expected to be heard as neutral and political-ideologically inconsequential when produced in a context in which their topic is politically sensitive. Talking about language in the context of an emerging nation, the object of energetic nation-building practices, is a form of political action and always involves (regardless of the expert's intention) taking political sides. Second, and in line with the foregoing remark, the creation of a scholarly tradition is often seen as a major nation-building activity, especially when national symbols (or symbols eligible to that status) are at stake. Third, theories are not necessarily harmless; some theories of language prove to fit better into certain political projects and vice versa. In the case documented by Kuzar, theories of language which allow for atemporal views of language fit better into an a-social and essentializing image of the "people" and the "nation" than theories which allow for flexibility, adaptability, diversity, change and so on. The use of a particular theory of language may provoke reflections and discourses on time, tradition, continuity, as well as on (im)purity, ownership and authority —usually all elements that are at the heart of nation-building projects.

Africa

The final part of the volume comprises three papers on cases in African countries: Tanzania, Mozambique and Congo (formerly Zaire). In this part, we enter a world in which communicative sociologies and economies are quite different from the ones we encountered in the case studies on Europe, North America, and new states such as Singapore and Israel. Apart from the highly unequal distribution of literacy, the near-absence of genuine mass-media (in the literal sense of the term), postcolonial African states are all characterized by considerable degrees of multilingualism, and by a historically inherited belief in the *problematic nature* of multilingualism. The degrees of multilingualism can be shocking to some observers —countries in Sub-Saharan Africa average more than 40 languages per country— but need to be put in perspective. Depending on how one looks at the case, apparently monolingual countries can be highly multilingual too. Herriman (1996) lists 29 non-aboriginal languages and 50 aboriginal languages in Australia, a figure that would place Australia far higher than e.g. South Africa in terms of languages spoken on its territory. What is different is the degree to which this multilingualism is perceived as an obstacle and as something that needs to be dealt with by means of planning, policy and expert interventions. The three chapters in this part will all be concerned with issues related to language planning and language policy, and the background to each case will be a field of tension between multilingualism-as-a-threat and the demands of postcolonial nation-building, or as in part of Meeuwis' paper, those of colonial state-organization.

Joshua Madumulla, Elena Bertoncini and Jan Blommaert discuss "Politics, ideology and poetic form: The literary debate in Tanzania". The context of the case is that of a socialist revolution (admittedly a quiet one), that took place in Tanzania in 1967. The transition to socialism intensified the nation-building projects that had been set in motion after independence in the early 1960s (and in which a local language, Swahili, had been promoted to the status of national language), and streamlined these projects. From now on, a clear sociocultural target for the new nation would be set, and Tanzania would become a united socialist and Swahili-speaking country. The socialist revolution generated enthusiasm among the population, and also appealed to the emerging class of intellectuals and artists concentrated at the University of Dar es Salaam.

It was there that a group of young and committed poets started experimenting with new forms of poetry in Swahili, forms that did away with the centuries-old tradition of Swahili verse writing which was (and still is) widely practiced in East Africa. By introducing blank and free verse, they intended to liberate traditional Swahili poetry from the bonds of tradition, sectarianism and elitism that had hitherto characterized it, and thus they wanted to contribute to the establishment of a *socialist* Swahili poetry, which was the expression of the newly unified socialist national culture. The new poets never failed to identify the political-ideological links between poetic form and a particular sociocultural and political project. But by doing this, they ran into an establishment of "traditional" poets, who had in the meantime also been mobilized for nation-building purposes.

It is at this point that the poetry debate, which revolved around aesthetics and poetic expression, became an almost unambiguous political debate, for both parties in the literary controversy appeared to defend different *theories*, of society, of socialism, of culture, and of language and history. Thus, what started as a debate on free verse versus rhyme and meter quickly became a debate between moderate interpretations of socialism and more radical, Marxist interpretations of socialism. The young poets shared a view in which the socialist revolution marked a radical break between past and present, which called for the abolishment of all pre-revolutionary social and cultural traditions and the construction of a new, unified mass culture. The traditionalist poets defended the value of pre-revolutionary local cultures and regarded them as a reservoir for "Africanizing" the post-colonial nation.

The debate shows how deeply nation-building practices (including the politization of symbols) can penetrate into a society mobilized for a particular nationalist goal. Intellectuals and artists joined the revolutionary party in its endeavor to establish a socialist society, and they did so by elaborating on and theorizing symbols of nationhood. At the same time, the logic of their theories pushed them to the margins of the political process and turned them into dissidents, who became disappointed with the development of socialism in their society. But in the process, intellectuals formed themselves into a vociferous and influential social class and political actor, and they produced an impressive amount of theorizing on language, culture, tradition, history and so on.

Christopher Stroud's paper on "Portuguese as ideology and politics in Mozambique: Semiotic (re)constructions of a postcolony" treats the way in which the former colonial language Portuguese was appropriated, remodeled and re-historicized by the postcolonial Mozambican nation-builders. Similar to Tanzania, the political-ideological profile of the country is also that of socialism; but in contrast to Tanzania, the Mozambican socialist leaders used a European language —that of the former Portuguese oppressor— as their national linguistic symbol. But this could not be done without an accompanying discourse which aligned Portuguese with the revolutionary socialist goals of the independent state. Stroud writes that

> [Portuguese] ownership was challenged, its alliances reconceived, and its boundaries redrawn —the language was, to all intents and purposes, symbolically taken ... and subsequently transformed into a weapon of the revolution.

The semiotic processes by means of which this appropriation proceeds are complex. They involve irony, recontextualization and revoicing, as well as pragmatic and afterwards metapragmatically theorized practices such as using Portuguese to learn, and become conscious of, what the oppressor wrote about "us". It also involves a re-invention of Mozambican history, in which Portuguese could feature as the cultural link connecting dozens of groups whose only historical relation lies in their joint colonization by a Portuguese-speaking power.

The language becomes different because it is re-invented. One could speak of the linguistic as well as symbolic "indigenization" of Portuguese. Stroud describes how Mozambican Portuguese is presented as "better" than metropolitan Portuguese, because it has been "enriched" by the socialist-revolutionary experiences of the Mozambicans. Hence, Mozambique sought the construction of a *particular* variety of Portuguese, one that would mark the country off against other Portuguese-speaking countries, and one that would embody the spirit of the state ideology. In Stroud's terms, Portuguese came to delineate the space in which the nation-building socialist government could exercise power and control. Not surprisingly, the opposition movement that challenged the state through a protracted guerilla war placed the rejection of Portuguese on its agenda. Instead of Portuguese (now symbolizing FRELIMO power), RENAMO advocated the use of local languages in its "liberated territories". In an interestingly ironical twist, FRELIMO then reinforced a homogeneous and normative (almost purist) image of Portuguese while simultaneously derogating the local Bantu languages, thus recreating the rhetorical opposition between "good" European languages and "bad" African ones which characterized colonial language ideologies. With the shifting political and economic conditions of the 1980s, in which FRELIMO gradually lost its hegemonic grip on society, Portuguese more and more became the identifying feature of FRELIMO as a party, rather than of the nation.

Stroud demonstrates how crucial discourses on language can be in the construction of political-ideological hegemony in contexts such as those of emerging states aspiring to nation-status. Similar patterns could be witnessed in many other chapters of the book, but the Mozambican case is particularly outspoken. Here, more than elsewhere, the postcolonial nation-state seems to be modeled on a European concept of the *cultural* nation, unified and controlled through processes of normalization in fields as diverse as language, law, economy and politics. *Pace* Foucault, Stroud's chapter demonstrates the way in which linguistic regimentation can become a powerful surveillance system (or at least, how people can attempt this), capable of distinguishing the good citizens from the bad ones and of imposing order and clarity on a society marked by deep conflicts and inequalities.

The final chapter in the book, by Michael Meeuwis, treats "Flemish nationalism in the Belgian Congo versus Zairian anti-imperialism: Continuity and discontinuity in language ideological debates". Meeuwis presents two historical vignettes, taken from two different periods in the history of the Congo (Zaire). I shall discuss them in the reverse order.

The second vignette presented by Meeuwis takes us back in time to the first half of the century and to the heyday of colonization. Certain Flemish missionaries in the Congo brought with them a background of Flemish nationalism, and they started to elaborate the premises of this nationalism on local languages and cultures in the Belgian Congo. Flemish nationalism strongly revolved around an association between religion and language-and-culture. The Catholic faith provided a "theory of the natural": human kind was divided into "natural" linguistic-cultural groups, and hence each group had to be able to keep its original language-and-culture, as part of

God's will. As soon as the missionaries arrived in Africa, this ideological frame was projected onto (as well as further developed on the basis of) the ethnolinguistic situation in the colony. More in particular, some missionaries started advocating the use of local, "ethnic" languages —people's "mother tongues"— in various domains, and fought against the use of lingua francas such as Lingala and Swahili. Despite the fact that such lingua francas were by all standards "African" languages, they were not people's *original* languages, and thus distorted the "natural" order of things.

Meeuwis' first vignette treats the postcolonial (Zairian) period, and more precisely the period in which Mobutu's power was at its zenith. In the early 1970s, after the introduction of the state ideology of "*authenticité*", intellectuals started debating language issues. *Authenticité* was aimed at a complete re-Africanization of social, political and cultural life in Zaire. Yet, curiously, this large-scale transformation (involving e.g. the obligatory Africanization of personal names) did not contain a language policy in which African languages would gain prominence. French remained the language of the state. Intellectuals claimed that full Africanization would require the eradication of "foreign" languages such as French, and the vigorous promotion of "national" (i.e. African) languages. This form of "ideological hypercorrection", as Meeuwis calls it, reminds us of the Tanzanian intellectuals' radical interpretation of socialism described in Madumulla et al.'s paper. The Zairian intellectuals effectively ended up in opposition against the state ideology, but not because of disloyalty to the authorities. It was the logic of their theoretical approach which compelled them to state what they believed to be the obvious.

Both debates discussed by Meeuwis were inconsequential debates — they were "losers". Mobutu obviously was not impressed by the anti-French argument constructed by fervently pro-*authenticité* intellectuals. And in the Belgian Congo, four lingua francas eventually became the "African languages" that found their way into the language pyramid of the colony (and of the postcolonial state). No investment was made in the local languages so vigorously defended by the likes of Van Hencxthoven and Hulstaert. But the interesting point is the discontinuity that emerges from pasting both vignettes. The Zairian intellectuals oppose *European* languages versus *African* languages, and develop a theoretical framework for discussing the value or disadvantages of both. The colonial missionaries opposed *different African languages*: lingua francas versus mother tongues. The missionaries' preoccupation with this opposition, as well as their theoretical elaboration of this opposition, has been completely lost over time.

So to the extent that colonial legacies can be identified in postcolonial language situations, things that never became part of that legacy deserve some attention as well (if for nothing else, because they might yield a more fragmented and complex picture of "colonial ideology").

Now that the main patterns and themes of the book have been identified, I can move on to point out some potential areas of application. The research contained in the chapters has, I believe, much to offer to a variety of sociolinguistic, pragmatic and discourse-analytical domains, and I shall briefly suggest some potential contributions to such domains in the next section.

6. Target domains

There is a variety of target domains for the analysis of language ideological debates, all to be situated at the crossroads of discursive practices and sociopolitical processes. The first domain that offers itself is of course the domain of *language policy and language planning*, in which authoritative metadiscourses on the preferred language situation in a society are the central instrument. The study of language planning (and policy) has been plagued by a number of theoretical defects (discussed by Williams 1992; see also Blommaert 1996), and one of them is certainly an idealization of the effectiveness of political decisions on social change. A linear model is often used, in which societal changes appear to be triggered by expert-backed (and expert institution-mediated) government decisions. Too little space is left for cultural and social resistance against such decisions, and the change-inducing effect of language is strongly overrated. Similarly, in the literature, developments in one country are rarely connected to larger-scale developments: issues of global capitalism and imperialism and the way in which language ideologies in peripheral countries get aligned with or subversive to dominant ideologies from central countries are rare in the literature (but see Parakrama 1995). It would be interesting to look into the ways in which language policy options are motivated, projected onto specific domains (education, literature...), so as to get a grasp of what went on behind the scenes of language planning. Also, we might come up with tentative answers to (acutely relevant) questions such as why certain cases of language planning failed despite the best of efforts from language planners and policy-makers. A number of papers in this volume will explicitly comment on diverse forms of explicit and implicit language planning.

On a wider scale, the role of *language in nation-building processes* is an obvious target domain. Most of the papers in this volume look into the ways in which language is ideologized and "promoted" as a crucial ingredient of national identity (and hence a central ingredient in national mobilization and nation-building) through, for instance, standardization and codification practices, language purism, language engineering and so on (as in most cases), or through de-hegemonization and the particularization of local varieties of widespread languages (as in Switzerland). The nation-building processes can be broadly interpreted here, involving "typical" cases of new states searching for a nation (Mozambique, Tanzania, Zaire) but also including forms of ethnic mobilization against a multi-ethnic state perceived as an oppressive regime (as e.g. in Catalonia, Corsica or Canada), as well as practices aimed at consolidating the power of the state (as e.g. in Singapore, Israel and the U.S.). Also included under this rubric would be practices aimed at modeling a colonial "civilization" by imposing a language regime on the colonial subjects (as in the former Belgian Congo).

Third, the theoretical issue of *language and symbolic power* will emerge as one of the issues to be commented upon in most papers. If for no other purpose, our approach might serve to concretize phenomena such as the linguistic marketplace, the unequal distribution of linguistic symbolic capital, a linguistic economy and so on, as well as to locate the role and function of linguistic-symbolic power in relation to "harder" social power relations. Debates on ethnolinguistic pluralism in powerful institutional channels such as education are often cases in point, and even well-established nations such as the United States do not escape occasional heated debates on the unquestioned (and unquestionable) hegemonic status of a monolingual ideal of society, as will be shown in the papers by Shannon and Collins in the volume.

A fourth field of application would be *language change* (language decay, language shift and so on). In the literature, the importance of attitudes is sometimes stressed as a factor in determining processes of language change. By stressing attitudes, ideologies are involved and we enter our field of study. We might be able to adjust some of the existing models of language change on the basis of a set of thorough historical case-analyses. In Tanzania, the age-old opposition between English and Swahili has consumed most of the energy of language planners, linguists and other experts. Very little was left for the study of local ("ethnic") languages, and clear patterns of language shift and the reordering of the language repertoire of speakers of local languages can be observed (Mekacha 1993; Msanjila 1998).

Fifth, a spin-off of this type of work could be a reflection on the nature of *politics as a discursive/textual process*. Especially the role of discursive "hot points" such as debates in the process of political decision-making could introduce important amendments to views of political processes strongly focused on interests, fixed ideological camps and so on, by stressing the importance of a more general architecture of discursive praxis in political developments. Not much innovation can be expected in this field, but for the formulation and exploration of a potentially relevant unit of political-discursive analysis, the debate. One outcome of this exploration will be that intertextualities in the discursive work we observe could be better grounded in a social, political and even cultural-historical perspective. The analyses of some authors in this volume will show how some language ideological debates can only be described and explained as long-term phenomena —not *événement* but *durée*— while others are dealt with on the basis of an almost journalistic time frame. Examples of the former are the papers on Canada (Heller) and Mozambique (Stroud). The most explicit example of the latter is the Catalan case documented by DiGiacomo. In between are various forms of relationships between longitudinal developments and explosive or remarkable discontinuities (as in Tanzania, Congo-Zaire, the U.S., Switzerland). Also the issue of actors can be salient in reformulating current conceptions of the "political" in political discourse. Kuzar's paper on Israel is interesting in showing how prominent linguists can become strongly political communicators on language, and how their scientific ideologies can be turned into political ideologies. Jaffe turns to Corsican writers and translators as ideology brokers with considerable influence; a similar focus on literature as a source and an instrument for political communication can be detected in Madumulla et al.'s Tanzanian case. The Ebonics debate discussed by Collins also involved academics whose pronouncements clashed with the hegemonic consensus in ways that are politically and academically significant.

Sixth, we might arrive at a better understanding of *ideology and ideological processes*, by specifying the historical processes in which they are formed and articulated. In particular, we might be able to highlight the connection between existing traditions of perceiving and conceptualizing reality, points of formulation and mediation of these traditions, and new forms of perceiving and conceptualizing in ideological processes. In other words, we might be able to identify ideologies as discontinuous but not necessarily revolutionary cultural phenomena. Collins places the Ebonics debate squarely in an American history of ideologies of the nation and concomitant ideologies of literacy. Meeuwis identifies an important undercurrent of Flemish nationalism in the ways in which Flemish missionaries in the Belgian Congo debated linguistic issues (involving an interesting example of what would now be called the "transnational flow" of ideologies —Appadurai's "ideoscapes" have a respectable historical pedigree).

In all these target domains, powerful debates as well as inconsequential debates can be equally relevant. Cases of defeat, of marginality and of dissidence are very salient when it comes to getting insights into the structure of power and hegemony.

7. Concluding remarks

The project we foresee in this book is programmatic, in the sense that it explicitly attempts to reformulate and re-document key processes in the domain of language in society. Although the main thrust of our endeavor is to look for a more fruitful integration of linguistics, social theory and historical "*métier*", our focus will be on a refined approach to discourse data in such a way as to do full justice to the ongoing, practical dimension of ideology and to avoid, in the same move, the reification of concepts such as ideology, hegemony, consensus and so on. No doubt, an ethnography (here seen in close connection with historiography) of discourse data provides us with an adequate tool to expose the ongoing, contingent and practical processes of ideological (re)production. At the same time, the meta-dimension of this approach should not be overlooked. Depending on one's point of view, the ideologies of language we investigate can be seen as "theories" of language, and our option to view these theories as discourses aligns us with the postmodernist conceptualization of theories as reductive mechanisms highlighting some aspects of reality while backgrounding others. We may now be in a position to grasp the hows and whys of such theorizing, and thus to lay bare some of the mechanisms by means of which power is being distributed and exercised.

All these are promises, of course, and perhaps some of these promises will not be kept. I will return to some of these issues at the end of the book. In the meantime, I can give the floor to the authors. The debate is open.

Acknowledgments

Most of the authors of this book commented extensively on the various versions of this introductory chapter, and the final version has benefitted enormously from their comments and suggestions. I am particularly grateful to Monica Heller, Dick Watts, Michael Meeuwis, Susan DiGiacomo, Roni Kuzar, Jim Collins and Ben Rampton.

Notes

1. I hasten to add that I am familiar with work on aspects of the history of linguistics, and I want to acknowledge the fact that a good number of these works contain very useful insights in what we would now call language-ideological aspects of linguistics. A good example is Land (1974), and some of the papers in Joseph and Taylor (eds.) (1990) are cases in point. A historical account of a debate within linguistics with considerable theoretical and metatheoretical implications is given in Huck and Goldsmith (1995). At the same time, language-ideological debates should not be narrowed down to debates in linguistics, as the papers in this volume will demonstrate.
2. See e.g. Jacobs and Jucker's (1995: 5) attempt at formulating a historical pragmatics: "the task of historical pragmatics is to describe pragmatically how language was used in former times as transmitted in historical texts."
3. I dwell on this point at some length to avoid misunderstandings with regard to what I call "dynamic views of language and language behavior". There is a body of conversation-analytical literature that qualifies its approach as "dynamic" because of its focus on sequentiality and the "doing" and "becoming" of meaning and sense in conversations. In contrast to the views I outline in this paragraph, the perspective adopted by such conversation-analytical work is strictly "local", and textual dynamics is located solely within the conversation (see Schegloff 1988 for an example and for a motivation for this approach).
4. It is at this point that some critical discourse analysis (including conversation analysis) seems to fall into the trap of situating power *inside* textual structures or discourse patterns, assuming a too self-evident stance with regard to the producers, the audience, the setting —in short, the context of the discourse. For a discussion at length, see Blommaert (1997c).

References

Ardener, Edwin
1971 Social anthropology and the historicity of historical linguistics. In: Ardener, Edwin (ed.), *Social Anthropology and Language*. London: Tavistock, 209–242.

Bauman, Richard and Charles Briggs
1990 Poetics and performance as critical perspectives on language and social life. *Annual Review of Anthropology* 19: 59–88.

Billig, Michael
1995 *Banal Nationalism*. London: Sage.

Blommaert, Jan

1996 Language planning as a discourse on language and society: The linguistic ideology of a scholarly tradition. *Language Problems and Language Planning* 20(3): 199–222.

1997a The slow shift in orthodoxy: (Re)formulations of "integration" in Belgium. In: Briggs, Charles (ed.), *Conflict and Violence in Pragmatic Research*. Special issue, *Pragmatics* 7: 499–518.

1997b *State Ideology and Language: The Politics of Swahili in Tanzania*. Duisburg: Gerhard-Mercator University (LICCAP 3).

1997c *Workshopping: Notes on Professional Vision in Discourse Analysis*. Wilrijk: UIA-GER (Antwerp Papers in Linguistics 91).

Bourdieu, Pierre

1982 *Ce Que Parler Veut Dire: L'Économie des Échanges linguistiques*. Paris: Fayard.

Braudel, Fernand [1969]

1958 Histoire et sciences sociales: La longue durée. In: *Écrits sur l'Histoire*. Paris: Flammarion, 41–83.

Briggs, Charles

1997 Notes on a "confession": On the construction of gender, sexuality, and violence in an infanticide case. In: Briggs, Charles (ed.), *Conflict and Violence in Pragmatic Research*. Special issue, *Pragmatics* 7: 519–546.

Briggs, Charles (ed.)

1996 *Disorderly Discourse: Narrative, Conflict, and Inequality*. New York: Oxford University Press.

1997 *Conflict and Violence in Pragmatic Research*. Special issue, *Pragmatics* 7: 451–633.

Burke, Peter

1993 *The Art of Conversation*. Cambridge: Polity Press.

Calvet, Louis-Jean

1974 *Linguistique et Colonialisme: Petit Traité de Glottophagie*. Paris: Payot.

Fabian, Johannes

1986 *Language and Colonial Power. The Appropriation of Swahili in the Former Belgian Congo, 1885–1938*. Cambridge: Cambridge University Press.

Foucault, Michel

1966 *Les Mots et les Choses*. Paris: Gallimard.

Gal, Susan
1989 Language and political economy. *Annual Review of Anthropology* 18: 345–367.

Gal, Susan and Kathryn Woolard (eds.)
1995 *Constructing Languages and Publics*. Special issue, *Pragmatics* 5: 129–282.

Grillo, Ralph
1989 *Dominant Languages: Language and Hierarchy in Britain and France*. Cambridge: Cambridge University Press.

Heller, Monica
1994 *Crosswords: Language, Ethnicity and Education in French Ontario*. Berlin: Mouton de Gruyter.

Herriman, Michael
1996 Language policy in Australia. In: Herriman, Michael and Barbara Burnaby (eds.), *Language Policies in English-Dominant Countries*. Avon: Multilingual Matters, 35–61.

Huck, Geoffrey J. and John A. Goldsmith
1995 *Ideology and Linguistic Theory: Noam Chomsky and the Deep Structure Debates*. London: Routledge.

Hymes, Dell
1996 *Ethnography, Linguistics, Narrative Inequality: Toward an Understanding of Voice*. London: Taylor and Francis.

Jacobs, Andreas and Andreas Jucker
1995 The historical perspective in pragmatics. In: Jucker, Andreas (ed.), *Historical Pragmatics*. Amsterdam: John Benjamins, 3–33.

Jakobson, Roman
1985 *Verbal Art, Verbal Sign, Verbal Time*. Minneapolis: University of Minnesota Press.

Joseph, John E. and Talbot J. Taylor (eds.)
1990 *Ideologies of Language*. London: Routledge.

Kroskrity, Paul, Bambi Schieffelin and Kathryn Woolard (eds.)
1992 *Language Ideologies*. Special issue, *Pragmatics* 2: 235–453.

Land, Stephen K.
1974 *From Signs to Propositions: The Concept of Form in Eighteenth-Century Semantic Theory*. London: Longman.

Meeuwis, Michael and Frank Brisard
1993 *Time and the Diagnosis of Language Change*. Antwerp: UIA-GER (Antwerp Papers in Linguistics 72).

Mehan, Hugh
1996 The construction of an LD student: A case study in the politics of representation. In: Silverstein, Michael and Greg Urban (eds.), *Natural Histories of Discourse* Chicago: University of Chicago Press, 253–276.

Mekacha, Rugatiri
1993 *The Sociolinguistic Impact of Kiswahili on Ethnic Community Languages in Tanzania: A Case Study of Ekinata.* Bayreuth: Bayreuth African Studies.

Msanjila, Yohani
1998 *The Use of Kiswahili in Rural Areas and its Implications for the Future of Ethnic Languages in Tanzania.* PhD. dissertation, University of Dar es Salaam.

Nurse, Derek and Thomas Spear
1985 *The Swahili: Reconstructing the History and Language of an African Society, 800–1500.* Philadelphia: University of Pennsylvania Press.

Parakrama, Arjuna
1995 *De-hegemonizing Language Standards: Learning from (Post)colonial Englishes about "English".* London: Macmillan.

Schegloff, Emanuel A.
1988 Description in the social sciences I: Talk-in-interaction. *IPrA Papers in Pragmatics* 2: 1–24.

Schieffelin, Bambi B., Kathryn A. Woolard and Paul V. Kroskrity (eds.)
1998 *Language Ideologies: Practice and Theory.* New York: Oxford University Press.

Silverstein, Michael
1996 Monoglot "standard" in America: Standardization and metaphors of linguistic hegemony. In: Brenneis, Donald and Ronald Macaulay (eds.), *The Matrix of Language: Contemporary Linguistic Anthropology.* Boulder: Westview, 284–306.

Silverstein, Michael and Greg Urban
1996 The natural history of discourse. In: Silverstein, Michael and Greg Urban (eds.), *Natural Histories of Discourse.* Chicago: University of Chicago Press, 1–17.

Silverstein, Michael and Greg Urban (eds.)
1996 *Natural Histories of Discourse.* Chicago: University of Chicago Press.

Thomason, Sarah and Terrence Kaufman
1988 *Language Contact, Creolization and Genetic Linguistics*. Berkeley: University of California Press.

Thompson, Edward P.
1991 *Customs in Common*. London: Merlin.

Thompson, John B.
1990 *Ideology and Modern Culture*. Cambridge: Polity Press.

Williams, Glyn
1992 *Sociolinguistics: A Sociological Critique*. London: Routledge.

Woolard, Kathryn
1989 *Double Talk: Bilingualism and the Politics of Ethnicity in Catalonia*. Stanford: Stanford University Press.

1992 Language ideology: Issues and approaches. In: Kroskrity, Paul, Bambi Schieffelin and Kathryn Woolard (eds.), *Language Ideologies*. Special issue, *Pragmatics* 2: 235–249.

1998 Introduction: Language ideology as a field of inquiry. In: Schieffelin, Bambi, Kathryn Woolard and Paul. Kroskrity (eds.); *Language Ideologies: Practice and Theory*. New York: Oxford University Press, 3–47.

Woolard, Kathryn and Bambi Schieffelin
1994 Language ideology. *Annual Review of Anthropology* 23: 55–82.

Locating power: Corsican translators and their critics

Alexandra Jaffe

1. Introduction

In 1989, a translation of a French novel, *Knock*, into Corsican by the Corsican writer and translator Jean-Joseph Franchi ignited a small but intense debate in Corsican cultural and literary circles. The debate was on the nature of translations from French into Corsican, or rather, about the various ways in which such translations could be politicized and made to symbolize power relations on a wider historical and societal level. This debate spilled over into the public domain, and received considerable media coverage. Translators and their critics shared fundamental assumptions about language, identity and power but disagreed about the function/outcomes of translation in the project of resistance to French language domination. This disagreement rested in part on their contrasting focuses on language-as-system versus language as practice/experience. Yet the analysis I will provide in this paper also shows that in some respects, translators challenged the insistence on a monolingual-monocultural norm and its essentialist view of relationship between linguistic, political and cultural identity. Translators also resisted the hobbling of personal artistic freedom imposed by the politics of language in contexts of minority language revitalization. Personal freedom became a metaphor for collective liberation, and suggested a model of resistance that located power in the prerogative to set and choose criteria of value.

In this paper, I use this debate over the politics of representation on Corsica to explore how enactments of linguistic and social identity are shaped by ambient ideological structures, and how "dominant" ideologies of language and identity can be resisted or transformed. Analysis of this debate over the value of translations illustrates John B.Thompson's general point that the minority experience and acceptance of dominance is not uniform; that we should not assume that the social reproduction of relations of inequality involves or requires perfect consensus (1984: Chapter 2). In the translation debate in Corsica we can see the ample space for dissent and contestation created by local interpretations of dominant ideas about the connection between language, identity and power.

Corsica is one of the many places in Western Europe where there has been language shift away from a "regional", predominantly oral language (Corsican) towards the official, written language of the state (French).[1] In the early seventies, the Corsican ethnonationalist movement was the catalyst for efforts at language revitalization. The philosophies and strategies of the past thirty years of Corsican language activism have been shaped by a number of ideological and political forces. These include macro-level language politics: the influence of dominant European ideas about the link between language, cultural identity and nationhood/autonomy. They also include how these broad themes have been translated into specific French language policies. Corsican language activists have also been influenced by academic explanations about the causal connections between French language policies and popular language attitudes and linguistic practices.

A central element of what I am labeling as "dominant language ideology" is the conflation of language, culture and national identity. This is the foundation of Western European "cultural nationalism", in which having a unique language is proof of a unique culture, which in turn legitimates claims to political sovereignty (Hobsbawm 1990; Anderson 1983; Balibar 1991; Grillo 1989). The influence of this dominant language ideology is evident in numerous postcolonial contexts and in many places in the developing world. It is also one of the most widespread scientific ideologies of language: as Blommaert (1996) points out, many linguists and sociolinguists involved in language planning in multilingual contexts subscribe to an "organic" model of language and culture, and to the assumption that linguistic/cultural homogeneity is "normal".

In Western Europe, France has one of the longest histories of using the dominant language as a symbol of political/social incorporation and exercising State control through what Cameron (1995) calls "verbal hygiene". Not surprisingly, therefore, political resistance to French domination in Corsica has been played out on linguistic and cultural terrain. Corsican nationalists made the Corsican language a centerpiece of their claims on peoplehood and political autonomy. As Handler (1988), Gal (1989) and others have pointed out, when language plays this key role in the legitimation of political boundaries, it is not language as communicative practice that is invoked, but rather language as a bounded, pure, autonomous code. In other words, in the European politics of language, there is a monolingual norm and an essentialist philosophical bias (cf. Lüdi 1992; Blommaert and Verschueren 1992).

All of the actors involved in the translation debate were self-labeled *culturels* ('culturals'): teachers, linguists and writers who had been actively involved in the promotion of Corsican language and culture for years. In these circles, the sociolinguistic concept of diglossia had been widely circulated, and constituted the baseline for both their understanding of the processes involved in language shift and their strategies for the revitalization of Corsican. Diglossia described the hierarchical, oppositional relationship between Corsican and French. It indexed language practices (specifically, the exclusion of Corsican from the powerful public sphere) as well as language attitudes. These were intimately connected, for the dominance of French in education and public life and the restriction of the use of Corsican to informal and family domains led many Corsicans to view the languages as *intrinsically* intimate/solidary (Corsican) or distant/powerful (French). When Corsican intellectuals wrote and talked about a "diglossic mentality" they were referring to the way that this compartmentalization of values effectively reproduced and legitimated Corsican's low status. Diglossia was seen as the outcome of both the practical and the symbolic domination of French, which not only had enormous pragmatic value but was also the center of French ideologies of moral and civic virtue (Lüdi 1992; Weinstein 1990). Reversing language shift thus involved tipping the balance of power between Corsican and French in order to simultaneously influence attitudes and practices.

How does one tip that balance of power? One major trend in Corsican language activism was to claim/build for the minority language the attributes and domains of power from which it had been excluded. This is why *writing* assumed such an important role in the process. Writing in Corsican was central to a number of strategies. First of all, the writing of grammars, orthographies and dictionaries played a key role in the construction of Corsican linguistic identity and legitimacy. These texts "proved" that Corsican met conventional and dominant criteria of "languageness": that it had internal unity and structure, and was clearly differentiated from other linguistic codes. Secondly, because the power of French was reflected in its command of public domains, writing in Corsican also played the critical symbolic role of displacing the sole dominion of French in literary, public and official contexts. All Corsican texts could be seen as game pieces in a war for symbolic territory. In the context of French language ideology, the production of written literary texts had particular value as a legitimation of Corsican's claim to be a real language. As late as 1991, during a debate over a proposed law on Corsican language education, a non-Corsican senator who was critical of the measure said: "*Mais où sont vos Rimbaud?*" ('Where are your Rimbauds?') in a reference to the lack of a literary tradition in Corsican that was clearly made to disparage Corsican's language status. It is here that we begin to see the crux of the disagreement over the status of translation. Translation contributed to the corpus of written documents in Corsican, but it did not contribute to the goal of establishing an independent Corsican literary tradition.

2. The political nature of translation

There is an underlying political dimension to all translations, for each act of translation posits a relationship of power (whether equal or unequal) between languages and cultures. In contexts which are by definition hierarchical, the political significance of translation is heightened. Well before the postmodern critique of ethnographic practice, Crick (1976) underscored the issue of power in his definition of anthropology as "translation-for". By this he meant that translation is never neutral: it is an ideologically-grounded interpretation which is intimately linked to issues of power and legitimacy of the translator/anthropologist and his/her discipline (1976: 166). Gupta (1990) also points out the ways in which the process of cultural translation serves to ratify the authenticity of the anthropological construction of "self" and "other". Writing about translation in another context in which power relations are imbalanced (colonialism), Rafael points to "the fact that translation lends itself to either affirmation or evasion of the social order" (1988: 211). Translation is by definition a commentary on power relations, a point also made by Klor de Alva (1989: 143).[2]

Thus translation is metalinguistic and metacultural activity which makes explicit contrasts and conflicts between modes of discourse and models of linguistic value and power which are able to remain buried or implicit in much of everyday life and in some other forms of writing. The interpretation of the "meta" message of translations in contexts of ethnic and/or linguistic militancy takes place against two backdrops: (1) knowledge of the role and meaning of translation in conventional contexts and (2) knowledge of cultural and linguistic hierarchies.

As for (1), most translations are done in order to make a document accessible to people who cannot read it in the original. A translation that openly violates this pragmatic, communicative function acquires a certain metalinguistic force: it insures that the translation will be "read" as a political statement. Given the fact that not all Corsicans speak or read Corsican but all Corsicans speak and read French, translations from French to Corsican actually narrow, rather than broaden the reading audience and thus constitute one of these open violations. In the preface to his bilingual French-Corsican book *Cavalleria Paisana*, Rochiccioli (1982: 9) writes:

"To write in French and hope to be read is a form of optimism. To write in Corsican and cling to the same hope is to dream in vain." In the case of the translation of *Knock*, the metalinguistic dimension is not just part of the message; it *is* the message.

As for (2), there is a precedent for the successful political use of symbolic translations by other Western European ethnic minorities. Typically, ethnic militants have made an issue of translation of official and legal documents into the minority language as a way of asserting their right to cultural and linguistic difference and the government's responsibility to legitimize their language and culture. These translations of the key forms and legal texts of government bureaucracies are counter-symbols which draw on the dense and powerful associations of power, rationality and value of the dominant state. The Welsh nationalist movement, for example, has successfully imposed a parallel Welsh-language structure of forms and documents (Khleif 1980). This is also true of the Basques (Urla 1987), the Catalans (Woolard 1989), and the Québecois (Handler 1988).

However, this particular brand of militant translation has been very little used in Corsica, probably because nationalist or autonomist parties have never had political control. There was a brief (and I suspect, not entirely serious) production of Corsican identification cards, but no other official forms have been translated. In sum, attempts to create official documents in Corsican have been sporadic and have usually met with apathy or disapproval from the political class.

Thus the symbolic literary translation that sparked the debate was not building on a base of existing militant practice. No one had any experience of the social effects of such translations. Translators and their critics brought a variety of theoretical perspectives to their assessment of what translating from the dominant to the minority language did to the existing imbalance of linguistic power. The critics of translation looked at translation from a macropolitical perspective: they interpreted its symbolic value from within the diglossic model. The translators argued from the "bottom up"; they used the micropolitics of their own experiences as a metaphor for sociolinguistic relations of power in translation.

3. The critics

In a magazine article devoted to translation, Santarelli wrote (here and elsewhere in the paper, translations from French and Corsican are my own):

> [for many people, translation is] a dangerous symptom of a serious psychological complex that keeps Corsican literature in a state of infantile dependence on its French "big sister"... a destructive force which prevents it from finding its unique voice ... with Corsican creation in crisis, translation is an evasion of the facts: the language is moribund. It is premature to waste time and energy on translating foreign works while Corsican literature is only in its first stammerings...
>
> (Santarelli 1989: 21)

An angry reader wrote in to amplify on this theme, stating that the "soul of the nation" was best served by documents created in its own language, and called translation "imported foreign philosophy, the reproduction of outside identity". "If Corsican culture is sterile", he concluded, "then better not to deceive ourselves with translations, and to wait with patience for future literary harvests of genuine identity" (Anonymous 1989).

It is obvious that these criticisms have nothing to do with the author's creativity, the artistic validity or the cultural fidelity of the text of the translation. They stem from the knowledge of a political context in which

> translation has been largely a one-way street: the small nations hasten to translate all that is worthwhile of the great nations' literature into their own language but not vice versa ... Small nations cannot afford to be parochial and ignorant, while the great, it seems, can. And do.
>
> (Boldizsar 1979: xi)

The interpretation of translation primarily as a symbol of defeat in a cultural power struggle was expressed in less extreme terms by the literary editor of the Corsican page in the island's weekly magazine. He argued that in the current sociological context, only page-by-page bilingual editions of translations had pedagogical value and that only translations of works that had not been translated into French had philosophical merit. Translation in any other form was simply a "trap" into which minority languages in "diglossic" situations were often lured. Like the other critics, he assumed that the primary motive for translation was to prove the value, or raise the stature of the language in the idiom of power. "*Scrivi tu è scrivi toiu, O Ghjuanghjasè*" ('Write of yourself and of your own, O Jean-Joseph') he wrote, advising Franchi not to waste his considerable creative talents on more translations (Fusina 1989b: 61).

It was true that Franchi had translated Montesquieu and other French classics, and could be suspected of being motivated by the hope that some of the status and legitimacy of the original text would rub off on the minority language. But he had made no particular claims for the greatness of *Knock*; one of his primary motivations for choosing it, he wrote, was that it was widely read in schools (Franchi 1989b). In Franchi's view, translating a familiar text was pedagogically useful. But the ordinariness of the original text was a much more subtle and specific issue than the ones the critics were engaging. They were using Franchi's work as emblem of all translation from the French, and they interpreted his motives against the backdrop of the history of Corsican language planning. That is, as language activists themselves, the critics had often heard arguments such as: "Corsican has no grammar —it has no literature— it is incapable of expressing abstract ideas" from both Corsicans and French as a way of rationalizing French language dominance. They also knew that there was already a long (and I would argue inevitable) tradition in Corsican language activism of countering such arguments by attempting to show that Corsican met French criteria of linguistic value. They recognized that this form of resistance to French left the French-Corsican hierarchy undisturbed, since France and French were still the sources of authority.

While all the translators vociferously denied that they were using the French texts as entrance exams for Corsican legitimacy, some of their comments suggested otherwise. For example, D. Geronimi was challenged during a literary gathering to explain why he had translated *Waiting for Godot*. One of his responses was that the translation served to "put the language to the test". In his written rebuttal to criticism of his translation of *Knock*, Franchi phrased the value of translation in these terms:

> You say that Corsican is concrete? Certainly, and this is its opportunity to bring to European consciousness this mass of images and sensations which until this day have remained *literally virgin*.
>
> (Franchi 1989b: 59, italics added)

Here, "literally" can be translated as "literarily"; for the virginity of Corsican has to do with the written, not the oral tradition. Franchi's statement is based on the cultural norm that attributes superior status and value to written genres, and suggests that the value of the Corsican language is virtual until it is put into writing, which allows it to be measured and assessed in some wider social context. I do not want to make too much of these comments, because they are only part of a complex set of linguistic and social motivations that I will expand on below. But I do believe that they reflect an underlying tension of experience. That is, all Corsican writers, in their natural desire to legitimate their activity, have only French literary precedents to turn to. As Niranyana puts it, people in postcolonial contexts live lives that are already always "in translation" (1994: 38). One could argue that for any educated Corsican, French literature was an inevitable point of reference for all acts of reading and writing (including in Corsican); that even when they wrote original works and did not translate, the implicit comparison between the hegemonic French literary tradition and Corsican literary production was unavoidable. We can see this in the remarks made by Jacques Thiers in a newspaper interview regarding the publication of his book *A Funtana d'Altea*, in Corsican. He refused the label of "novel", because

> being able to write a novel in Corsican is seen as one of the ultimate proofs of the dignity of our language. But do we really need to have novels to believe that Corsican is a distinct language? This is why I prefer to say that my book is a story. Corsican writers do not write in order to show that Corsican is a language.
>
> (Cerani 1991)

The critics of translation viewed any use of French as the source language as an implicit acknowledgment of the superiority of French. They wanted to exercise power by policing the boundaries of the Corsican literary corpus. Given the power imbalance between French and Corsican, it was important to withhold from French any ownership of the "source" text. Translators challenged this reading of the authority of the source text, offering a reverse reading of the relations of authority between source and target language. Rafael provides the groundwork for this sort of reading in his discussion of the relationship of translation to social process. Translation, he writes, "arises from the need to relate one's interest to that of others and so to encode it appropriately ... it thus coincides with the need to submit to the conventions of a given social order" (1988: 210). The translators took the position that translation into the minority language encoded a *reformulated* social order in which habitual relations of power were reversed and the "minority" language was established as the set of conventions to which the majority language had to submit. They claimed that this symbolic empowerment of Corsican was heightened in translations for which there was no practical need, since historically, the "need" for translations in either direction had been defined and imposed on the minority by dominant linguistic and social groups. That is, they were arguing that in their translations, the power balance was on their side since French was being used for Corsican purposes.

4. Translation as practice: The translatable and the untranslatable

The translators' reformulation of the power structure was based in part on their experience of the constant tension, in the act of translation, between what can and what cannot be translated; between the power of the translator to breach chasms of linguistic equivalence and the power of language to resist this forced journey from one culture and frame of reference to another. This tension is central to much of the abundant literature on translation, in which the proof of the translators' skill lies in their ability to recognize its limits: to identify what cannot be completely successfully communicated across languages and cultures. In a volume entitled *Small countries, great literatures*, the editor remarks in the introduction that "*Latva, lasnak* is untranslatable. *Seen, seeing* appears incomplete in English, while the Hungarian has disarming force" (Boldiszar 1979: ix).

Writers on translation always return to the topic of the untranslatable. Rabassa (1984: 24) comments on the untranslatability of local experience of words. He gives the example of the problem the name of a tree posed in a translation he made from Spanish to English. The tree, which has no English counterpart, was identified by its Mayan name in the Spanish text. None of the available choices of translation seemed satisfactory. The local flavor and exoticism connoted by the linguistic contrast of the Mayan name in the Spanish text could not be faithfully reproduced by using either the Mayan or the Spanish name for the tree in the English text. The experiential equivalent (a tree called by an exotic, indigenous name in English) would be geographically inauthentic. In a similar vein, Tedlock (1989: 167) writes about the untranslatability of names in his one act play dramatizing the translation of *Popol Vuh*. The characters debate whether or not a proper name in a Mayan text that means "crocodile" in Nahua should be left in Mayan or written "crocodile" in English. And Eva Hoffman (1989) reflects on her sister's adult decision to use her Polish name in her English life jars her ear:

> Its syllables don't fall as easily on an English speaker's tongue. In order to transpose a single word without distortion, one would have to transport the entire language around it.
>
> (Hoffman 1989: 272)

It is the knowledge of the "entire language" and culture that translators are reminded of by failures in translation. In one respect, their mastery of two codes and movement between them emphasizes linguistic and cultural boundaries. This is the "going across" in the experience of translation. When translators talk about the untranslatable, they often reinforce the notion that each language has its own "genius", an essence that "naturally" sets it apart from all other languages and reflects something of the "soul" of its culture or people. Three comments by Franchi illustrate this point. In a magazine article in which he discussed translation, Franchi used, and then reflected on his use of a Corsican idiom. He wrote: "Quant'au reste, inutile de *'piattassi daretu un ditu'*... tiens! Comment dit-on cela en Français?" ('As for the rest, it's useless to "*hide behind a finger*"... tell me, how do you say that in French?') (1989b: 58). In a fieldwork interview, Franchi also told me an anecdote which emphasized the role of translation in maintaining the integrity and boundaries of both languages in question. He recounted that he had "faithfully" translated Yves Morel's song *'Tu ne me quittes pas'* into Corsican for a Corsican singer. The singer, he said, had then "ruined" the translation by "Corsicanizing" the original music and singing so that the words, so clearly articulated in the original version, were unintelligible. Here, Franchi emphasized the translator's obligation to render the *essence* of the original —the relation of words to music, the tone, the style— in a manner that was also faithful to the structures and style of the target language. In another part of the interview, he took up the topic of language boundaries once again, asserting that the very nature of Corsican guaranteed a distance between source text and translation. He explained that because Corsican is less standardized and more archaic than other latinate languages, a Corsican version of a text would never be "a simple copy of the original" that he claimed one would find, for example, in a translation from French to Spanish.

But the "untranslatable" is also a momentary failure, for translators often do arrive at felicitous translations. These successes are made possible by translators' knowledge of the social, contextual and experiential grounds of meaning in the two languages and cultures that they broker. The process of translating heightens and hones the translator's experience of cultural and linguistic mastery. Translation requires what the Corsican poet Biancarelli described to me as "*un œuil intermédiaire*" ('an intermediate eye'). For him, translating was a rich source of self-knowledge and creative stimulus; it was a metalinguistic experience, an orchestration of the tension between two sets of metaphors. Translators also talked about the exercise of the imagination that translation provoked in the search for a phrase, a tone or a style that they might never have considered in the absence of the requirement to shuttle between two worlds of discourse.

There is another sense in which translation was particularly empowering for Corsican writers. They were able to experience what Roland Barthes calls the "*jouissance*" ('pure pleasure') of the text which comes from playing with or violating norms of style, grammar, register and so on *in Corsican*. I emphasize this because this "*jouissance*" can usually only be experienced in languages with a written tradition. A writer who creates an original text in Corsican cannot violate a norm because there are hardly any (except for the hegemonic French norms); today, even Corsican spelling norms are contested. Translation gave these authors a chance to activate the sociolinguistic elements of oral style that, because of the small corpus of Corsican literature, were largely unexploited. In the translation of *Knock*, the characters were given identities and Corsican dialects from distinct microregions. As a stylistic strategy, the author was playing off the reader's understanding of the social connotations of accent and dialect and regional identity in *both* French and Corsican. This was one of the reasons why it was important for the text to be familiar: it allowed a wide public to appreciate his stylistic strategies. Reviews in the paper printed bits of the dialogue, asking "what do you think of character x speaking as if he came from Sartène?" The point is that the meaning of the author's use of Corsican dialects was sharpened and focused by its relationship with the French work; a similar strategy in an original Corsican work might not have had the same resonances.

Furthermore, as another translator, Jean-Marie Arrighi, pointed out to me, translation provided a unique opportunity to experience that "*jouissance*" without risk for Corsican. This was because translation provided the writer with an outside language of norms which could be violated, thus sparing the fragile oral code from a form of play it might not withstand. That is, there were norms in Corsican, but they were uncodified norms of usage; in Arrighi's words, "one does not feel free to break with those norms which it is still a question of trying to save."

In the arguments so far for and against translation, we can see that translation does not just reflect static relations of social power; it is a forum in which linguistic and social authority is discursively constituted. And, as Balibar writes (joining to some extent the translators' position), "it is in translations that the weaker partner appropriates the language of the stronger" (Balibar 1987: 19). This point is illustrated in Rafael's (1988: xi) elegant analysis of the meaning of translation for Tagalogs and Christian missionaries. Seen from a Tagalog perspective, translation of Spanish texts and discourse was a way of domesticating the forces of Spain and Christianity, it was "a process of demarcation and appropriation" which subverted the notion of linguistic consensus.[3] Similarly, Crowley (1996: 118) notes that for Irish Protestants, the translation of the Bible into Irish was a way of taking popular control of the word of God; it was a form of liberation from English social control.

We can readily draw the analogy with the Corsican case, where translators saw themselves as appropriating linguistic space and the critics of translations took the latter perspective, substituting the authority of French for God's will. In the Corsican case, we can also note the tension (in the translators' discourse) between adherence to an essentialist model of language which emphasizes the naturalness of linguistic and cultural boundaries and the expression of a sense of personal pleasure and identity in which Corsican and French are not separated but integrated.

Another important theme in Corsican translators' defense of their craft was that producing or reading translations involved an intense and simultaneous experience of both the universal and the particular in a way that emphasized cultural interactions rather than cultural boundaries. Several translators emphasized that the positive experience of the particular was generated by a *dialogue* with another culture in the act of translation. For example, in the literary forum mentioned above, Geronimi declared: "I translated *Waiting for Godot* because I am not Becket. I wanted to write it as if Becket were Corsican, as if he had never known another language than Corsican." Franchi justified his translations in similar terms: "so that the [Corsican] language has the chance to know, to experience the works in question" (1989b: 59). Santu Casta, who translated *The Little Prince*, said in an interview in *Kyrn*, "All cultures are intertwined. It always does good to go and see and try to understand the ways others see life, the world" (1990: 35). Often, translators selected their source texts because their relevance to Corsican society. Biancarelli, for example, chose to translate *Waiting for Godot* for its theme of the absurd, for the confrontation between tradition and modernity and the conflict and confusion of identity that he felt characterized Corsican society. A similar theme (as well as the book's familiarity) had motivated Franchi's choice of *Knock*. On another occasion, Biancarelli had translated Gabriel de Lorca in order to explore cultural rather than thematic resonances.

Very explicitly, the translators rejected the exclusionary logic of minority self defense —the wholesale rejection of all that is "foreign", especially if it comes from the dominant culture. They insisted on the "link with the outside" (Geronimi), "the impossibility of living in autarchy," and the necessity of "rubbing up against other writers and cultures" (Biancarelli). In the introduction of his translation of some short pieces by Woody Allen and John Steinbeck (from the French) for the radio, Petru Mari (1986) wrote to an imaginary skeptical audience:

> Yes, of course our literature is able to produce the same pearls as any other ... what do you say? That we don't need anyone? Yes, but if we want to do without them, they will certainly do without us ... what do you think of that?
>
> (Mari 1986: 1)

All of the translators insisted that this relationship with the other was not a dependent one.

5. Walking the line between alienation and empowerment

Crowley writes that

> The monoglossic language, at once familiar and foreign, necessary but felt to be alien ... presents the colonial subject with a problem: how to engage in that language without, in using the oppressor's language, reinforcing one's own dispossession.
>
> (Crowley 1996: 51)

This dilemma is a fundamental one which is not perfectly resolved for those who defend the practice of translation. One response to this dilemma is to emphasize non-equivalence in the form of the text. James Joyce, Crowley adds, did so by using the dominant language in such a novel way as to make it new and make it his. What we find in the Corsican context is a move by several Corsican authors to avoid labeling what they did as "translation". Petru Mari (cited above), Jacques Fusina (who had translated an opera and several song lyrics), and Santu Casta (who had translated *The Little Prince*) all insisted that they only "adapted" or "interpreted". While it was not necessarily the case that "adaptations" were more different from the original texts than "translations", using the term "adaptation" stressed the significance and the authenticity of the final text in Corsican terms, rather than its fidelity to the original. Mari made it clear that for him, the question was less what translators could do for the original than what the original could do for them. The foreign voices in the text might be "imported" (as one of the attacks on translations had claimed), but they were firmly in the representational control of their importers. Mari commented that he had not invested a great deal of time in the mechanics of translation: “I did it quickly,” he told me, “with an ear for how these pieces would work on the radio for a Corsican audience.”

The preface to Grimaldi’s (1989) bilingual collection of stories (*U stringagliulu di sigolu*) is a strong expression of non-equivalent adaptation philosophy. Although this is not a completely parallel example (the author wrote the original in Corsican and had someone else do a French version), the description of that version is illustrative here:

> [it] is neither a direct translation, nor even an adaptation ... the French text is born out of the Corsican one, without being dependent on it; there is no hierarchy in this musical piece, where the two versions are like point and counterpoint.
>
> (Fusina 1989a: 5)

Here, we can note that the rhetorical force of the emphasis on equality and independence in “adaptations” depends on the contrast with “translations”, and thus reinforces the association of translation with linguistic hierarchy.

Some of the authors mentioned so far —Franchi, Fusina, Biancarelli, Geronimi— had superlative command both of written French and written Corsican. They belonged to the very top echelon of the Corsican bilingual intelligentsia. Their exceptional linguistic facility was a vital ingredient in the experiences of personal linguistic empowerment which served as the basis for their judgments about the sociolinguistic meaning of translations.

The experience, and the meaning of translation was rather more ambiguous for those who could not alternate between the two written codes with the same agility. Perhaps the most reflective and self-conscious of these was Jean-Marie Arrighi. He had translated some official reports of the Regional Assembly’s Cultural Council, of which he was a member. He did this because he was committed to the principal of using translations as a way of legitimizing Corsican in the political domain. His experience of translating, however, was ambiguous. To be sure, the process highlighted the difference between the two languages. But it also underscored his very different levels of mastery and experience of Corsican versus French. As he tried to translate, he realized that his abstract thoughts were in French; he could only voice them in Corsican with great and painful effort. Translation made him struggle with his French intellectual heritage; although he rejected its powerful, authoritative and authoritarian linguistic ideology, his entire academic identity and practical consciousness was a function of his experience in this system. For Arrighi, creating an abstract, intellectual document in Corsican was a difficult exercise in which he inevitably reworked French models of expository prose in his head. If Arrighi used his experience of translation as a metaphor for its political significance (as the previous translators did), it was the dominance of French and the weakness of Corsican in public, literary domains that prevailed.

Another question raised for Arrighi by his experience of translation had to do with the nature of the linguistic and cultural divide between Corsican and French. From a political perspective, using Corsican in official domains (and thus, creating new registers in the minority language) was a step forward in a process of linguistic development and legitimation. But from another more emotional and experiential vantage point, this "new" Corsican had no cultural resonances. As he translated, Arrighi sometimes had the impression that he was forcing Corsican into a mold which had no intrinsic value in the Corsican universe. Was a bureaucratic Corsican a "deformation" of Corsican? Was it recognizable *as Corsican* to the average reader? In these questions we can see a reflection of the workings of the diglossic model: the compartmentalization of domains of practice and experience is translated into judgments about linguistic essence. That is, the things that Corsican and French are habitually used to do are read in the popular imagination as part of their inherent capacities.

Arrighi translated the documents because of his conviction that occupying public space with Corsican was important. But his own experience told him that he could not completely control or predict the effect of these symbolic translations on popular attitudes. On the one hand, it was possible that texts such as the ones he produced could be the catalyst for new understandings and acceptance of different registers of Corsican. That is, they might chip away at the logic of diglossia, with its polarized and essentialized identities. On the other hand, the texts might be dismissed out of hand as irrelevant and/or "not Corsican". At the time that Arrighi wrote, it was very difficult to gauge the results of any piece of writing in Corsican, since the reading and writing public was so very small.

One of Arrighi's responses to the dilemma posed by the imbalance in his mastery of written Corsican and French was to write the Corsican version first. He did this to insure a radical difference between the two texts; in particular, to prevent himself from producing a text with Corsican words and French linguistic and conceptual structures. Writing the Corsican text first forced him to ask himself, "how would one *think* this in Corsican?" and finding an authentic Corsican voice to express those thoughts. This voice was partly his, partly his ancestors'; Arrighi himself had not thought these abstractions in Corsican before. Ultimately, he said that his experience of writing these documents was linguistically integrative. He noted that expressing the abstract in a language he had only known as concrete was a way of rediscovering the inherent metaphorical nature of all signs for abstractions, rediscovering the "*pensée sauvage*" in the language of reason and owning them both, in their simultaneous sameness and difference.

But Arrighi did acknowledge that for the inexpert translator, it was indeed the source document and language that dominated. This, I believe, is the nature of most bilingual Corsicans' experiences of translation in their everyday lives. When older speakers of Corsican heard people make errors in French or in Corsican, they often attributed them to failures in translation. These failures of translation were interpreted within the framework of their experience of French language domination and the stigma attached to speaking Corsican. Thus "not being able to find the right words" in Corsican was a form of linguistic alienation that also symbolically highlighted the power of French to erode minority language competence. But the converse, "not being able to find the right words" in French, was seldom seen as proof of the uniqueness and authority of Corsican; it was experienced as a failure to command French that was personally embarrassing and disempowering.[4]

The potential for translation to highlight linguistic alienation is illustrated quite dramatically in a class of "surrogate" translations. One author and illustrator of children's books, Francette Orsoni, does not write in Corsican, but said that she "felt in it"; her stories emanated from childhood images of the village and the world of the fantastic; both of which she associated with Corsican. She created a rudimentary text in Corsican, gave it to a "specialist" friend and collaborated with him over the Corsican turns of phrase, which came "naturally" to him. Even though they did not "come naturally" to her, she represented them as her latent Corsican voice: she knew when the Corsican text was "right".

Another writer (Mattei 1971) had a book of poems he wrote in French translated by a friend in much the same fashion and for the same reason, although his edition was bilingual, with Corsican and French versions printed on facing pages. Mattei, however, made no claims for his own Corsican competence. In a poem thanking his translator, he wrote:

Je remercie Nicole	I thank Nicole
Qui sait avec adresse	Who has the skill
Et avec délicatesse	And delicacy
Utiliser ses connaissances	To use her knowledge
N'importe qui	Not anyone
Ne peut traduire de la poésie	Can translate poetry

Je dis que la langue maternelle	I say, the mother tongue
Est à celle adoptée	Is to the one I use
Qu'une flamme moderne	Like a modern light
Est au feu de cheminée	Is to the fireplace's fire
Elle est froide et fade	It is cold and pale
Et sort de moi toujours	And always comes out of me
toujours forcée	forced
De toutes ses articulations	In all its articulations
Cette langue sans chaleur	This language without warmth
Me fait peu envie	Hardly attracts me
Comme un fruit hybride	Like a hybrid fruit
Issu des pires conjonctures	Born of the worst circumstances
On m'a toujours reproché	I have always been reproached
Le français de mon écriture	For writing in French

Both Orsoni's and Mattei's works are a curious blend of alienation and intense connection with the language and its cultural resonances. The alienation is particularly striking in Mattei's poem, where he characterizes the language that he commands in writing (French) as "forced", "cold" and culturally inauthenticating. There is also Mattei's use of the metaphor of the "hybrid fruit" to describe his own mixed identity. Far from exploiting the association of horticultural hybrids as a positive source of genetic resilience, Mattei represents hybridization as a disastrous genetic aberration. This metaphor shows the strength of the monocultural-monolingual norm, with its images of linguistic and cultural purity: hybridization equals bastardization. These two authors' very desires for surrogate translation invoke an ideology in which the value of the final product is called into doubt: is not the "translated" text a hybrid one?

Surrogate translators were also sometimes used in the nationalist press, and the end results were no less ambiguous than the texts described above. An editor of an autonomist newspaper told me that he felt a political obligation to print serious articles in Corsican. But he and most of the members of his staff did not feel they were competent to write such Corsican texts. The editor tended to draw on a pool of specialists, sending them a French text to turn into a Corsican piece. These same people were called upon to produce Corsican pamphlets and program announcements for political events. The meaning of these translations can be interpreted in a number of different ways. On one hand, the fact of translation was very thinly disguised. The common knowledge that there was a handful of language specialists producing in Corsican emphasized the marginality of writing in Corsican even amongst people who were politically committed to Corsican language and culture. In this sense, these translations drew attention to the lack of fit between political will and linguistic practice, as well as to the power imbalances between French and Corsican that were the causes of the belated development of Corsican literacy. On the other hand, the translation created Corsican linguistic space whose meaning was not entirely bound to the context of its production.

6. Representation and representativity: Politics versus creative license

As we have seen, translators' discussions of the meanings of translation often revolved around their personal experience of translating. In many cases, translation was experienced as a rich arena of creative practice, a source of self-discovery and heightened metaphorical awareness. The nature of the criticisms of translation show, however, that cultural production in Corsica is often cast and always interpreted as political. Writing in Corsican entails social responsibility to represent and promote Corsican culture and language; personal, creative, artistic fidelity takes a distant second place.[5] For a Corsican writer, all creative choices in the process of writing –the use of French versus Corsican, genre, register, topic, spelling– are also political and ideological positions about the nature of Corsicanness.

The political facet of minority expressive culture often coincides with Corsican writers' and artists' personal and political agendas; an overwhelming percentage of Corsican expression is both politically-oriented and focused on Corsicanness. To take a popular example, there is the following commentary from a record jacket of the group *A Filetta*, whose very name (the fern) is "a symbol of tenacity and rootedness".

> the themes taken up are meant to be representative of the joys, the sorrows, the suffering and also the hopes of our people. In them, we denounce repression, the abandonment of the terrain, the loss of our language ...

The moment writers or singers strayed from this path, however, they risked being seen as traitors by other cultural militants. On a personal level, this pressure was fatiguing and frustrating, and ran counter to individual expectations of artistic liberty and the pleasures of self-expression. This was brought home to me one day in a conversation with Fusina, one of the key figures from the "seventies generation" of linguistic militants. As we parted, he said that frankly, he was "just tired"; tired of having to represent something, tired of being a symbol. He just wanted to write, for himself. We can find echoes of this sentiment in comments made by Geronimi (the translator of Becket) and Thiers (the author of numerous works in Corsican and French). Challenged to explain why he had translated from French in the literary meeting alluded to above, Geronomi enumerated all the social justifications for translation. Repeated questioning from the audience then drew a slightly defensive response: "I did it for me, for my pleasure", he said, looking around the room in a way that dared anyone to challenge his right to textual "*jouissance*" and self-representation. Similarly, in the newspaper interview cited above, Thiers' response to the journalist's query about why he wrote a book in Corsican was:

> Pleasure! pleasure! When we speak about Corsican ... we speak about its ruined state, its protection, and of sacrifice. Certainly, there is little to rejoice in, but should we refuse our enjoyment and never speak about the satisfaction and liberation we get from expressing ourselves in Corsican?
>
> (Cerani 1991)

In addition to being an assertion of individual rights, the translators' claim that they translated for their own pleasure had a political and ideological foundation. In fact, I would argue that it was through staking a claim to artistic freedom that Corsican translators proposed their most radical reworking of concepts of linguistic power.

Specifically, the translators appeared to be aware that the social ideology of art reflects relations of power; that the relentless insistence on cultural representativity and fidelity to the exclusion of any other form of expression was in itself evidence of a "colonized" mentality. Translating was a way of demonstrating a new confidence in Corsican language and identity by acting *as if* it were a language of power. Powerful languages are threatened neither by other languages nor by individual activity. Waiting, as the one critic recommended, for Corsica to produce a body of literature that could stand up to French was a denial of the value of both Corsican linguistic history —an oral tradition— and of present-day literary activity, with the normal range of talent and genres it represented.

It is in this sense that the personal experience of power in translation from French into Corsican had a unique political weight. It has to be remembered that most of these writers had not come by their mastery of two languages painlessly. For those who learned French for the first time in school, the first translations they experienced were violations of categories of identity and knowledge embedded in their knowledge of their mother tongue. The shock caused by these translation experiences is well documented, as it occurs in most immigrant contexts. Thus, as Eva Hoffman writes (1989), these were translations in which

> the signifier [is] severed from the signified ... "river" in Polish was a vital sound, energized with the essence of riverhood, of my rivers, of my being immersed in rivers. "River" in English is cold —a word without an aura.
>
> (Hoffman 1989: 106)

Even personal names, the most intimate link of language and self, are strangely altered in this first translation of cultures in school. Richard Rodriguez remembers his first day in an American school, his first extended contact with English:

> The nun said in a friendly but oddly impersonal voice, Boys and Girls, this is Richard Rodriguez. (I heard her sound out: *Rich-heard Road-ree-guess*). It was the first time I had heard anyone name me in English...
>
> (Rodriguez 1982: 11)

And Eva Hoffman recounts the day she and her sister are given English versions of their Polish names:

> My sister and I hang our heads wordlessly under this careless baptism ... the twist of our name takes them a tiny distance from us —but it's a gap into which the infinite hobgoblin of abstraction enters. Our Polish names didn't refer to us, they were us as surely as our eyes and hands. These new appellations ... are not us. They are ... disembodied signs pointing to objects that just happen to be my sister and myself.
>
> (Hoffman 1989: 105)

This symbolic violation, for Hoffman, for Rodriguez and, I suspect, for Corsican writers, heralded their entry into a world they had to obsessively translate —a world of words that they had to possess, precisely *because* they had been cut off from the resonances of those words as children. It was a quest, as Rodriguez says, for an a sense of identity and individuality in the public language, a desire to belong in order to escape undifferentiated otherness. For Hoffman, liberation from the need, and then the desire to translate, signaled the end of her personal sense of alienation. For Rodriguez, this liberation took the form of being able to use the public language to address an anonymous reader, to write about intimate subjects —in short, to dissolve his diglossic experience of Spanish and English. In a sense, Corsican writers can be seen as taking up translation from French as a way of asserting this sort of liberation. Rather than working within dominant structures of value by reversing the habitual identities of source and target language, they took hold of the power to define the meanings of linguistic acts, and declared their translation into Corsican a demonstration of their freedom from the *requirement* to translate (possess) French and a manifestation of their desire to possess Corsican. That is, they defined power as the prerogative not to censor those acts that could be interpreted as powerless.

7. Conclusion: The perils of asserting virtual power in written genres

What is the difference between asserting this sort of power through literacy and literature and asserting it in oral practice? By way of answering this question, let me contrast Petru Mari's translation of Steinbeck's and Woody Allen's plays for radio with some of the other kinds of documents we have considered.

First of all, Mari's published text was a by-product of a translation that had been intended for purely oral consumption. Mari told me that he had only published the translation at the urging of one of his academic friends. In the original broadcast, the textual and foreign origins were clearly subordinated to the entertainment value of the spoken piece. Moreover, since the original texts were in English, they were not accessible to most Corsicans in the original. They were not, therefore as purely symbolic — and hence, as political— as Franchi's translation of *Knock*. They required no prior knowledge of the originals; their meaning and value was not dependent on a bilingual consciousness or a literary background. They were accessible, therefore, to a majority of radio listeners. The political was also de-emphasized by the programming patterns at the radio station. Broadcasts alternated between French and Corsican throughout the day, in all varieties of programming. This meant that the choice of language in any one broadcast did not carry particular ideological weight. Because of this language policy, listeners could enjoy the programming throughout the day without having to have perfect competence in Corsican. And the fact was, there were many Corsicans who could enjoy a radio program in Corsican who were not capable of or interested in reading a Corsican text. The radio, in other words, played to the sociolinguistic reality of the island.

In contrast, the literary translations were premised on the existence of a fairly sophisticated, or at least, a strongly motivated audience. The sophisticated reader, like the translator, would experience the translated text as the expression of universal themes as well as a celebration of Corsican linguistic and cultural particularities. Since the meaning of the translated text would be located in both French and Corsican worlds, as well as in the dynamic space of movement between them, the sophisticated reader would be able to savor, alternately, a divided and an integrated cultural and linguistic heritage. The experience of reading would constitute a new experience of linguistic hierarchy, for the relations between French and Corsican would either be leveled or reversed.

The problem was that there were so very few of these sophisticated readers to write for. The translations in question were thus written for a virtual audience. This meant that these translations were simultaneously writing *as if* Corsican were a language of power (that had nothing to lose from translation) and *as if* Corsican were a language of widespread, everyday literacy in Corsican society.

The latter fiction, it seems to me, is what made the social and symbolic status of translation on Corsica so volatile, so precarious. Part of this has to do with the way that the emphasis on the written rather than the oral risks what Bourdieu and Boltanski (1975) call "the fetishism of language". As Bonn puts it, one of the fundamental paradoxes of writing in a minority language is that:

> a project which makes out to be looking for a place in which to express being as identity ends up looking for this place in the quest itself: in writing ....a "place" which is impossible to seize and hold ... identity becomes confused with the desire for identity ... is the existence of discourse *of* place whose function is to refer to itself possible?
>
> (Bonn 1985: 193)

We can easily recognize the way that French-Corsican translations magnify the self-referential quality of minority literature. Bonn suggests that such a discourse can never truly be about *place* —shared, embodied, situated experiences of identity. Writing about cultural "places" can be complex, ambiguous, unresolved; the boundaries and borders can be fuzzy and loose.

Expert translators found such a place in the dynamic of translation, but for most Corsicans, the location of translation was a detached and abstract domain.

Here it bears reiterating that it was the experience and the intellectual consciousness of diglossia that made literacy and literature so important in Corsican militant circles. Diglossia was a result of symbolic and practical dominance; writing was therefore inevitably interpreted from within this framework.

In the translation debate, we can see some of the consequences of this implicit framework of experience and interpretation. First, there is the powerful hold of "essential" linguistic and cultural identities; as we have seen, concepts of linguistic "essence" and boundaries permeate the arguments of both translators and their critics. Embedded in this linguistic and cultural essentialism is a logic of oppositional identity. At least at some level, translators like Franchi were attempting to transcend this logic. But they did so on terrain that was almost exclusively defined in terms of that logic: writing was defined as a place for displacing French control.

Here, the self-referential quality of purely symbolic translations was a handicap, since it drew attention to power relations of literary production and consumption. As we have seen in the examples of (mild to extreme) linguistic and cultural alienation, translation from the dominant language automatically invokes the experience of linguistic hierarchy. Arrighi's example also illustrates that when writing is detached from vital social practices and exists purely as a symbol, it is the macropolitics of diglossic relations that often prevails. Because of the depth and intensity of Corsicans' shared experiences of powerlessness, subtle representational strategies of expert translators are swept aside by simple, oppositional meanings. In recognition of this, we find Arrighi turning to translation tactics (doing the Corsican version first) that ensure radical difference.

The translation debate underscores an old idea: how critical it is for ideological and political control to be instantiated in everyday practices. As Corsican activists certainly know, French language dominance has been embedded in multiple ways in Corsican social life. This has been difficult for Corsican language activists to replicate for Corsican, for unlike the French state, they have had no access to economic, institutional or political coercion to further the cause of the minority language. Translators tried to locate power in the prerogative to deny and transcend linguistic hierarchy, but did not have a strong enough base of consumers to instill this new vision of power in lived experience. The mere presence of French in the ghost of the original overshadowed the political implications of the translators' craft, and as a result, the non-apologetic, non-dependent aspects of literary translation were only perceived by a very few. In the absence of a healthy spoken language and a sophisticated reading public which is literate in two languages, translation in Corsica was left with contested, virtual value —a pale "as if" in the face of a problematic reality.

Notes

1. See for example Khleif (1980) on Welsh, Woolard (1989) and DiGiacomo (this volume) on Catalan, Boyer (1991) and Garavini (1988) on Occitan, McDonald (1989) on Breton, Urla (1988) on Basque.
2. Klor de Alva also observes that the politics of translation "are more likely to be configured by the unspoken and usually unperceived assumptions making up the reigning ideas and exegetical rules that guide the translator" (1989: 143).
3. Although, from the point of view of Spanish missionaries, translation was an act of linguistic appropriation and an exercise of power for different reasons. They saw translation as the illustration of the "natural" relationship of the world and God's will: "the promise of a fully transparent language ruling over linguistic diversity" (Rafael 1988: 7).
4. Gobard views the inability to translate as one of the foundations of diglossia and linguistic alienation. He writes: "To know two languages apart from one another, without being able to translate one into the other, is precisely the diglossic situation that risks to end in the different specialization of each of the languages" (1976: 179). See also Bourdieu (1982: 64).
5. This is revealed in the nature of three out of six questions asked of Santu Casta, the translator of *The Little Prince*, in a magazine interview: (1) *Traduttore, traditore?* ('translator, traitor?'), (2) Why translate from a language everyone understands to one that only few do?, (3) How does the text you chose relate to Corsican culture? (Anonymous 1990)

References

Anderson, Benedict
1983 *Imagined Communities: Reflections on the Origin and Spread of Nationalism*. London: Verso.

Anonymous
1989 Letter to the Editor. *Kyrn* 193: 4.

Anonymous
1990 Traddutore, traditore? *Kyrn* 336: 35.

Balibar, Etienne
1987 La langue de France exercée au pluriel. In: Vermès, G. and J. Boutet (eds.), *France, Pays Multilingue*, Vol. 2. Paris: L'Harmattan, 9–21.
1991 The nation form: history and ideology. In: Wallerstein, Immanuel and Etienne Balibar (eds.), *Race, Nation, Class: Ambiguous Identities*. New York: Routledge, Chapman and Hall, 86–106.

Blommaert, Jan
1996 Language planning as a discourse on language and society: The linguistic ideology of a scholarly tradition. *Language Problems and Language Planning* 20: 199–222.

Blommaert, Jan and Jef Verschueren
1992 The role of language in European nationalist ideologies. In: Kroskrity, Paul, Bambi Schieffelin and Kathryn Woolard (eds.), *Language Ideologies*. Special issue, *Pragmatics* 2(3): 355–375.

Bonn, Charles
1985 Entre ville et lieu, centre et periphérie: La difficile localisation du roman algérien de langue française. *Peuples Méditerranéens* 30: 185–195.

Bourdieu, Pierre
1982 *Ce Que Parler Veut Dire: L'Économie des Échanges linguistiques*. Paris: Fayard.

Bourdieu, Pierre and Luc Boltanski
1975 Le fétichisme de la langue. *Actes de la Recherche en Sciences Sociales* 1: 2–32.

Boldiszar, Ivan
1979 *Small Countries, Great Literatures?* Budapest: Publishers and Booksellers Association.

Boyer, Henri
1991 *Langues en Conflit: Études sociolinguistiques*. Paris: L'Harmattan.

Cameron, Deborah
1995 *Verbal Hygiene*. London: Routledge.

Casta, Santu
1990 *Principellu*. Ajaccio: Akenaton è Squadra di u Finusellu.

Cerani, Daniel
1991 A Funtana d'Altea: Un récit de Ghjacumu Thiers. Interview in *Le Corse*, 27 July.

Crick, Malcolm
1976 *Towards a Semantic Anthropology: Explorations in Language and Meaning*. London: Malaby.

Crowley, Tony
1996 *Language and History: Theories and Texts*. New York: Routledge.

Franchi, Jean Joseph
1989a *Knock*. Ajaccio: Editions La Marge.
1989b Editorial: Lingua Corsa. *Kyrn* 210: 45.
1992 Interview. *Études Corses*, 29–36.

Fusina, Jacques
1989a Preface to *U Stringagliulu di Sigolu*, by Lisandrina Grimaldi. Bastia: Scola Corsa.
1989b Editorial: Lingua Corsa. *Kyrn* 203.

Gal, Susan
1989 Language and political economy. *Annual Review of Anthropology* 18: 345–367.

Garavini, Fausta
1988 Quelle langue pour la prose d'oc contemporaine? *Lengas* 24: 33–88.

Gobard, Henri
1976 *L'Aliénation linguistique*. Paris: Flammarion.

Grillo, Ralph D.
1989 *Dominant Languages: Language and Hierarchy in Britain and France*. Cambridge: Cambridge University Press.

Grimaldi, Lisandrina
1989 *U Stringagliulu di Sigolu*. Bastia: Scola Corsa.

Gupta, Akhil
1990 Translation and the politics of writing. Paper, American Anthropological Association Annual Meeting, New Orleans.

Handler, Richard
1988 *Nationalism and the Politics of Culture in Quebec*. Madison: University of Wisconsin Press.

Hobsbawm, Eric J.
1990 *Nations and Nationalism since 1780: Programme, Myth, Reality*. New York: Cambridge University Press.

Hoffman, Eva
1989 *Lost in Translation*. New York: Penguin.

Khleif, Bud
1980 *Language, Ethnicity and Education in Wales*. New York: Mouton.

Klor de Alva, J. Jorge
1989 Language, politics and translation: Colonial discourse and classic Nahuatl in New Spain. In: Warren, Rosanna (ed.), *The Art of Translation*. Boston: Northeastern University Press, 140–158.

Lüdi, Georges
1992 French as a pluricentric language. In: Clyne, Michael (ed.), *Pluricentric Languages*. Berlin: Mouton de Gruyter, 149–177.

Mari, Petru
1986 *Scritti d'Altrò*. Bastia: Stamperia Sammarcelli.

Mattei, Francescu
1971 *Febre Maligne*. Ajaccio: Cyrnos et Méditerranée.

McDonald, Maryon
1989 *We Are Not French*. London: Routledge.

Niranyana, Tejaswini
1994 Colonialism and the politics of translation. In: Arteaga, Alfred (ed.), *An Other Tongue: Nation and Ethnicity in the Linguistic Borderlands*. Durham, NC: Duke University Press, 35–52.

Rabassa, Gregory
1984 If this be treason: Translation and its possibilities. In: Frawley, William (ed.), *Translation: Literary, Linguistic and Philosophical Perspectives*. Newark: University of Delaware Press, 21–29.

Rafael, Vicente
1988 *Contracting Colonialism: Translation and Christian Conversion Under Early Spanish Rule*. Ithaca: Cornell University Press.

Rochiccioli, Natale
1982 *Cavalleria Paesana*. Paris: ERTI-LECERF.

Rodriguez, Richard
1982 *Hunger of Memory*. Boston: David R. Godine.

Roseman, Sharon
1995 "Falamos como falamos": Linguistic revitalization and the maintenance of local vernaculars in Galicia. *Journal of Linguistic Anthropology* 5: 3–32.

Santarelli, Paule
1989 Traddutore, traditore? *Kyrn* 200: 21–22.

Tedlock, Dennis
1989 The translator: Or, why the crocodile was not disillusioned. In: Warren, Rosanna (ed.), *The Art of Translation*. Boston: Northeastern University Press, 159–174.

Thompson, John B.
1984 *Studies in the Theory of Ideology*. Berkeley: University of California Press.

Urla, Jacqueline
1987 *Being Basque, Speaking Basque: The Politics of Language and Identity in the Basque Country*. Ph.D. dissertation, University of California, Berkeley.
1988 Ethnic protest and social planning: A look at Basque language revival. *Cultural Anthropology* 3: 379–394.

Weinstein, Brian
1990 Language policy and political development: An overview. In: Weinstein, Brian (ed.), *Language Policy and Political Development*. Norwood, Ablex, 1–22.

Woolard, Kathryn
1989 *Double Talk: Bilingualism and the Politics of Ethnicity in Catalonia*. Stanford: Stanford University Press.

The ideology of dialect in Switzerland

Richard J. Watts

1. Introduction

The purpose of the present chapter is not to identify and analyze a specific language ideological debate, but rather to sketch out the genesis of a language ideology which, in the European context, appears to be unique to Switzerland and which I shall call the "ideology of dialect".[1] Although all the elements which I discuss as being germane to this language ideology have been around in one form or another for several centuries, it is not until the time of World War I that we begin to recognize those features which tend to be associated in general with a language ideology, and it is not until after World War II that we can justifiably categorize them as constituting an ideology. Among those features we can list the following: the symbolic representation of "national" identity in the pre-modern and modern nation-state by a highly codified standard language variety, the degree to which a language variety is "prescribed" as legitimate within the educational system and the non-print media, the ways in which a language variety can be infused with the values of cultural and political resistance toward potential invasion, etc.

Hence my principal argument will be that a language ideology can only be recognized as such when the time is ripe for it to appear, although the major features of that ideology must already be in place as a coherent system of communal myths. In section 3, I therefore deal with the historicity of ideologies in order to discuss the reasons for the emergence of a language ideology, the length of time during which that ideology holds sway over the minds of community members, and the degree of resistance to change and adaptation that the ideology displays.

Obviously, the ideology of dialect in Switzerland has given rise to a wide range of debates both within the dialect communities, and between them and other ethnolinguistic groups in Switzerland, and as I unravel the threads of the ideology, these debates will be touched upon. It is not my purpose to focus on any single debate in detail. However, in the final section I will briefly indicate how three of these debates (one revolving around the resistance of French native speakers in Switzerland to the functional spread of the dialects in the non-print media, another focusing on the status of standard German and the Swiss German dialects in the school system and the third revolving around the maintenance of Romansch) reveal alternative ideologies, although at the present point in time the ideology of dialect is proving to be remarkably resistant to change.

My main focus will be on the relationship between standard German in Switzerland and the Swiss German dialects, and the bulk of the chapter will therefore focus on that relationship. However, there is a tangential problem concerning the status of Romansch which may also be looked at from the perspective of the ideology of dialect, and for this reason I shall also refer to that problem in the following section of the chapter and return to it briefly in the final section. My review of the complex language situation in Switzerland in section 2 thus begins with a lengthy reference to Romansch. In section 3 I shall link the concepts of ideology and myth. Section 4 will develop the term "ideology of dialect" in more detail as it is revealed in the Swiss situation, but since it is essential to locate the mythical elements which contribute towards the genesis of the ideology, I will discuss these first in section 5 before showing explicitly how they relate to the ideology itself in section 6. In section 7, I shall offer narrative examples of mythical accounts of language use and language structure which I have collected over the years, all of which bear on the ideology of dialect in one way or another. Section 8 will be devoted to showing how the ideology of dialect is reproduced in the educational system and the non-print media, and in the final section I shall focus briefly on the three debates indicated above and indicate how they give evidence of alternative ideologies. Before I proceed to section 2, however, I shall define what I understand by the terms "language ideology" and "the ideology of dialect".

I define a language ideology as a set of beliefs about the structure of language and/or the functional uses to which language is put which are shared by the members of a community (cf. also Milroy and Milroy 1985). The beliefs have formed part of that community's overall set of beliefs and the life-styles that have evolved on the basis of those beliefs for so long that their origins seem to have been obscured or forgotten. They are thus socioculturally reproduced as constituting a set of "true" precepts in what appears to the community members to be a logically coherent system. In other words, for the members of the community the precepts of the ideology are superior to other beliefs in possible alternative ideologies. A language ideology is political inasmuch as it forms part of the total set of social principles by which the community organizes itself institutionally. Like any other set of sociopolitical principles, a language ideology may be challenged and the points at which those challenges appear discursively can be termed "ideological debates" (cf. Blommaert's introductory chapter to this volume).

The term "ideology of dialect" is used to refer to any set of beliefs about language in which, in a scenario in which a standardized written language coexists with a number of non-standard oral dialect varieties, the symbolic value of the dialects in the majority of linguistic marketplaces in which they are in competition with the standard is not only believed to be much higher than that of the standard but is also deliberately promoted as having a higher value. In the German-speaking part of Switzerland this is effectively the dominant scenario, whereas in the Romansch-speaking area there is, as we shall see, no standard to compete with the Romansch dialects. Instead competition is with the local Swiss German dialects.

Hence, the fundamental belief which underpins what I take to be the ideology of dialect in German-speaking Switzerland is that the local dialect is that language variety in which all social interactions except for those in the written medium are carried out.[2] The local dialect thus serves as one of the most powerful markers if not *the* most powerful marker, of local, rather than national identity. As we shall see later, local identity is the foundation upon which any form of cantonal or Swiss identity is constructed from the bottom up. In the Romansch-speaking areas of Switzerland the range of social interactions in which the dialect is used is restricted to fewer social domains than in the German-speaking part of the country. Nevertheless, it is highly significant that Romansch speakers will switch to the local German dialect in those residual domains rather than to standard German. As we will see, a standardized oral variety of Romansch is in any case not available to them.

2. Quadrilingual Switzerland?

In 1996 a referendum was held to decide on whether Romansch should or should not be given a measure of officiality in comparison with the other three official languages of Switzerland, German, French and Italian. The vote was overwhelmingly in favor of granting Romansch limited official status and thereby raising it from its previous status of "national" language to one in which it enjoys some of the constitutional powers of German, French and Italian.

This all sounds very democratic and eminently sensible to an outsider, but there are a number of unsolved problems involved in such a political decision. First and foremost is the vexing question of which variety of

Romansch should be chosen as the official "language" (cf. Arquint 1982). Romansch is spoken in five dialect areas, and until the 1980s no attempt to standardize the language had been successful. The present "standardized" version, developed by the Romanist Heinrich Schmid in Zurich in the 1980s and called "Romansch Grischun" (Schmid 1982, 1989), is a bone of contention for many native speakers of Romansch, since it has been put together from the two demographically largest dialect areas with admixtures from the others and is consequently perceived to be no-one's mother tongue.

The dispute over Romansch Grischun is not simply about how the artificial written standard has been put together, although of course this is often how it is presented in the media, but rather about whether it is even desirable to "raise" any standardized version of the language to a more authoritative position than that of the local dialects.[3] In this respect the dispute has rapidly become ideologized and thus politicized, since the symbolic value of dialects as an outward sign of local patriotism in the non-French-speaking parts of the country is the cornerstone of a language ideology which I choose to call "the ideology of dialect".[4] Before I elaborate in more detail in section 4 on the term "ideology of dialect", I would like to dwell a little on the situation of Romansch within the overall linguistic landscape of Switzerland and then move on to the more familiar relationship between standard German and the Swiss German dialects. (For general surveys of Swiss sociolinguistics, see Schläpfer (ed.) 1982 and Werlen (ed.) 1993; see also Watts 1991, 1996.)

The first point that needs clarification is one of terminology, since the Swiss Federal Constitution makes use of two terms, "national language" and "official language". "Official" in this case refers to two major functions that a language should fulfil in Switzerland; it must be able to be used in public debate, either in the federal or the cantonal parliament, or in the media, and it must be able to be used as a written medium. Romansch Grischun can certainly fulfil the second function, but it is a hotly debated point as to whether it will ever be able to fulfil the former. The ideology of language standardization (Milroy and Milroy 1985) rests fundamentally on the social functions a standardized variety fulfils at the level of the written medium (cf. Joseph 1987). However, if we accept Joseph's dictum that the standard languages of Europe are "synecdochic dialects", i.e. that one dialect has been raised to the status of standard so that that "part" of the language stands for the "whole", it must be possible at any time to extend the ideology into the oral medium simply by "decreeing" that certain forms of pronunciation are also perceived to be part and parcel of the synecdochic dialect and by developing political strategies to enforce its oral use. In the case of Romansch Grischun and, as we shall see, in the case of standard German within Switzerland that has never been and will never be an option.

With respect to Romansch the problem lies not only in the fact that the area of Switzerland in which it is spoken is geographically fragmented, i.e. it does not form a homogeneous, unified language territory (Schmid 1989; Billigmeier 1979), but also in the lack of a hinterland beyond the borders of Switzerland. In the case of the other three official languages, French, German and Italian, not only is that hinterland there, but it is also, in each case, demographically strong. The standard variety of each of these languages is in use as the official variety —at least in the written medium— but that is where our problems begin.

There are two further difficulties facing Romansch. Firstly, in the 1990 census a number of non-indigenous languages in daily use in Switzerland were found to have a significantly larger number of native speakers living and working in Switzerland than Romansch. Whereas the number of native speakers of Romansch in terms of the overall population of Switzerland turned out to be only 0.6%, the total number of Turkish and Spanish speakers was found to be closer to 1%, and the total number of native English speakers was around 0.5%. Secondly, beyond the first two to four grades of primary school it is almost impossible for any native speaker of Romansch to be monolingual, since the local German dialects and standard German are omnipresent in both the print and the non-print media.

The relationship between the standard varieties of French, Italian and German in Switzerland is reasonably well-known both inside and outside the country. However, the complex relationship between the Swiss German dialects and standard German is still either not well understood or simply played down and trivialized outside Switzerland. In this chapter I shall argue that at least since World War I, but certainly since World War II an ideology of dialect has developed within German-speaking Switzerland (cf. Sieber and Sitta 1986), which not only bears similarities with the present-day situation with respect to Romansch, but may also have had a fundamental influence on the sociocultural reproduction of that situation.

Officially, German is spoken by around 65% of the total population. Unofficially, of course, the "mother tongue" of the majority of German speakers is one of over 30, mostly Alemannic dialects, which are, generally speaking, mutually intelligible (Haas 1982a, 1982b). On the other hand, the linguistic "distance" between standard German and the Swiss German dialects is great enough to cause considerable difficulty in mutual comprehension between a German-speaking Swiss national and a German speaker from beyond the Alemannic dialect area.

In addition, the Alemannic dialects in Switzerland are in far greater use than Ferguson (1959) would have us believe. The neat distinction between a high and a low variety which Ferguson thought he saw in German-speaking Switzerland simply does not hold water. Dialects are in use in church services, in a number of cantonal parliaments, in the courts, on radio and television. Although there is, to my knowledge, no published research on the proportion of dialect to standard German currently in use on German-speaking television, my own very rough unofficial estimate is that it has reached the level of almost 50%. The version of standard German generally used in Switzerland displays a number of significant lexical and phonological differences from standard German elsewhere. It even contains morphosyntactic differences with respect to strong verb forms, the gender marking of certain nouns and case marking after certain prepositions. At school, however, these forms often suffer from the tendency on the part of the teacher to hypercorrect and are stigmatized as "*nicht richtiges Deutsch*" ('not correct German').

However, just as Romansch speakers perceive themselves to be native speakers of their local variety of the language, i.e. *Ladin* (or even *Vallader* or *Puter*, the two varieties of *Ladin*), *Surmiran*, *Sutsilvan* or *Sursilvan*, rather than of Romansch, most adult German speakers will also state that their "mother tongue" is either "*Schwyzertüütsch*" or a local dialect, e.g. "*Bärntüütsch*", "*Züritüütsch*", "*Wallisertüütsch*", etc. They will also classify standard German as *Schriftdeutsch* (i.e. 'written German' or 'German for writing') and maintain that it is their first "foreign language". Interestingly, however, primary school children in the German-speaking part of the country, on entry into first grade, almost invariably state that their mother tongue is "*Tüütsch*" ('German'), apart, that is, from the children of migrant workers in Switzerland or of internal migrants within the country.

In the following section I shall discuss the notion of historicity of an ideology. My understanding of the term "historicity" rests crucially on the notion of "myth", and I will therefore need to explain how I understand "myth" before outlining some of the mythical elements which go to make up the ideology of dialect in Switzerland.

3. The historicity of an ideology

Stories shared by the members of a community, traditions that belong to that community, its social institutions, prejudices that may or may not be shared by members of the community, sets of communal beliefs and superstitions —all these come into being, or are produced and reproduced through the course of time. They only make sense if we can make sense of their historicity. The same goes for a language ideology, which is a set of communally shared beliefs about language. In other words, if we want to make sense of the ideology, we have to establish its historicity.

I shall posit in this section that there is a right time and a wrong time for a language ideology to take a hold in the thinking of a community and to exert a dominant influence over language attitudes and the conceptualization of the structure of a language and the role it plays in the community. There are bound to be possible competing ideologies against which it must assert itself and that other nonlinguistic sociohistorical, sociopolitical factors will exert a crucial role in the emergence of a dominant ideology. The length of time through which a dominant ideology of language may exert its hegemony depends on the complex interplay between the linguistic and the nonlinguistic factors through which it originally emerged as dominant. In order to unravel the complex threads that lead through time to the moment or period at which a dominant language ideology emerges, we need to locate and trace out the myths that have been and still are fundamental in the construction of a communal ethnic identity. Many of those myths may have little to do with language; others will bear directly on the role language plays in identity construction. But, assuming that we can locate the "right time" for an ideology of language to emerge, we also need to explain what confluence of sociopolitical factors made it the "right time".

My hypothesis is that the historicity of any ideology, how it emerges, why it emerges when it does, and how long it remains dominant, resides in the complex of myths that go to make it up and the relative strength of those myths in relation to the social factors impinging on the community through the course of time. The term "myth", however, should not be understood negatively as a false, unfounded or wrong-headed belief in the origin of a phenomenon. Myths are, of course, essentially fictive, but they always contain elements of reality within them since they are derived from the past experiences of members of the community. There is no point in looking at myths from the present point in time and from a purely rational or common-sense point of view. If we do, we will simply have to dismiss them as fantasy.

Myths are essentially narrative, i.e. they tell part of the "story" of a sociocultural group. They are shared stories; they are not the property of any one individual, and the telling of the stories helps to reconstruct and validate the cultural group. This endows them with explanatory force such that they can be used to justify present patterns of behavior simply by invoking their past validity. They can also be changed, altered, lost, abandoned, inverted, etc., i.e. they are continually reproduced and reconstructed socially. Myths may have either a long or a relatively recent history in the minds of the members of the cultural group.

In section 4 I shall attempt to unravel what I have termed the ideology of dialect in German-speaking Switzerland, most of the features of which are also applicable to the Romansch-speaking part of the country. I shall then identify some of the myths that have contributed toward its emergence. However, identifying those myths is one thing and explaining why and how the ideology came about is another. The explanation will take me outside the realm of language *per se*. Sociopolitical events inside and outside Switzerland during this century will have to be invoked and linked to attitudes toward language. In addition, the ideology of dialect, in my estimation at least, is still very much in evidence and shows absolutely no signs of abating.

4. Features of the ideology of dialect

As we saw in section 1, the set of beliefs that constitute the ideology of dialect in German-speaking Switzerland includes the conviction that "*Schwyzertüütsch*", or some more localized dialect such as "*Bärntüütsch*", "*Züritüütsch*", "*Baseltüütsch*", etc. is the "mother tongue" of the speaker and that standard German is the "first foreign language". The first part of this conviction is universally held, the second, on the other hand, is not always expressed. As a corollary to this belief it is generally felt that standard German, which first-grade schoolchildren learn for the purposes of reading and writing, will be difficult and that it is best to use the dialect in the majority of school internal situations to avoid misunderstandings (Sieber and Sitta 1986).

Standard German is reserved for the written functions of linguistic communication and thus takes on the aura of a school-internal language. Unless the child reads a great deal outside school, standard German will be seen as the language of bureaucracy, the language of formality, the language of institutions, etc. This set of attitudes is constructed largely through the education system. For example, let us consider statements made in an open-ended interview by a first-grade teacher who participated in a project carried out at the University of Berne to assess the relationship between dialect and standard German in the first two grades of primary school. In contrast to the other teachers who participated, this teacher does her best to stick to standard German during her teaching. In the course of the interview she continually returns to the apparent difficulties first-graders have with standard German, e.g. "For example, *Schriftdeutsch* is an enormous problem for most of them," "to see whether they've understood or not, and *Schriftdeutsch*, they really fight against it," "then I say, 'Now we'll try a little *Schriftdeutsch* again,' even if it sometimes goes wrong, so that they learn the use of the language, quite automatically, so that they know whenever they're writing, 'Aha, this is the other language'," etc. I shall comment on the belief that *Schriftdeutsch* is another language and what may give rise to that belief in a later section.

In the German-speaking part of Switzerland command of a Swiss German dialect takes precedence over the command of standard German in evaluating whether a person is or is not a "good Swiss". Naturalization proceedings in some cantons still include a language test in which candidates are required to display their ability to speak and understand a Swiss German dialect, whether or not they are already speakers of standard German. My observation of German-speaking television in Switzerland leads me to estimate that almost 50% of all current television programs in the German-speaking part of the country are conducted in Swiss German, standard German being reserved for the official news bulletins, imported German-language films and those films that have been dubbed from some other language.

Part of the ideology of dialect is a conviction that Swiss German is more down-to-earth, more honest, more communicative, more direct and, in general, more Swiss than standard German, and this part is also shared by speakers of the Romansch dialects. For the German-speaking Swiss, the dialect functions, in other words, as a badge of Swissness, an emblem of "belonging" to Switzerland, which is more powerful than any other emblem. The reason is quite simple: Swiss German is markedly different from other varieties of German (with the possible exception of other related Alemannic dialects in Alsace, Vorarlberg and Baden-Württemberg) and at the same time it does not really exist except in the form of over 30 more or less mutually intelligible dialects. It therefore allows the Swiss to be Swiss and at the same time to be Bernese, Zurichois, Basler, Walliser, etc. Standard German, on the other hand, is necessary for written communication and for oral communication with French- and Italian-speaking compatriots and with those who only speak a form of standard German. In fact, my impression is often that the German-speaking Swiss would far rather communicate in English to a foreigner than in standard German.

But what justifies my evaluation of this set of attitudes toward the dialects and standard German as constituting a language ideology? Firstly, if the beliefs provide a basis for political decision-making processes and social practices, i.e. if the beliefs have become institutionalized as part of an officially sanctioned set of social procedures, it is justified to label them as an ideology. Secondly, if the beliefs link up with other, nonlinguistic beliefs which are crucially significant in the definition of a communal identity (i.e. with other nonlinguistic myths) —and I shall show in the next section that they do— and if they underwrite nonlinguistic aspects of social institutions and social practices, they may also be evaluated as ideological. Thirdly, if those working in influential social institutions such as public education and the media make statements which are not questioned but simply accepted as facts, the set of beliefs even determines *individual* social practices and we are justified in using the term ideology to refer to them.

All three conditions listed above hold for the set of beliefs connected with standard German and the Swiss German dialects and also, partly at least, for the rejection of Romansch Grischun in the Romansch-speaking area. Although I suggested in section 2 that one of the criteria for a language to be given official status in Switzerland is its ability to be used in the media, it would appear that standard German is used in not much more than 50% of all television programs and appears to be losing ground to the dialects. I shall sketch out the relationship between dialect and standard in the medium of radio in a subsequent section.

Statements like those quoted above from one of the primary school teachers we have observed over a two-year period indicate the extent to which those working in primary school classrooms actually believe that what they say about pupils' difficulty with standard German is true despite empirical evidence to the contrary from research carried out in the Canton of Zurich by Häcki Buhofer et al. (Häcki Buhofer et al. 1994; Häcki Buhofer and Studer 1993) and by E. Werlen and Ernst in the Canton of Aargau (E. Werlen and Ernst 1993, 1994). From our own research in the Canton of Berne we reach the following partial conclusion:

> In relation to the constructive process of teaching and learning the language as a subject in the school curriculum we have observed in the first two grades of primary school that any oral knowledge of standard German that might have been acquired through "TV-language" is substituted by Swiss standard German which is oriented toward the teacher and the practice of reading.
> (Werlen et al. 1997: 248)

Aside from the family, the education system and the media are probably the most influential social institutions in molding attitudes toward language and in socializing the individual. They help to shape gate-keeping practices, and they rely on language beliefs having a high value as symbolic resources in the social marketplace (Bourdieu 1991). I therefore conclude that we are indeed dealing with a language ideology here, which I have chosen to call the ideology of dialect. In the following section I will discuss some of the most potent myths that are embedded within the ideology of dialect and sketch out some of the sociopolitical events which have made the period after World War I and especially after World War II the "right" point in time for the emergence of that ideology.

5. Swiss myths

The federal Vice-Chancellor, Achille Casanova from the Italian-speaking part of Switzerland, gave a talk in 1989 at a symposium on the relationship between the official languages of Switzerland in the federal administration in which he referred to Switzerland as a "*coalition de résistances*" ('a coalition of resistances'). He explained this concept by referring to one of the most fundamental Swiss myths, viz. that in times of crisis, i.e. if the country is under threat from outside, or if the freedom to act according to one's own laws is in danger, or if there is any movement towards the centralization of political power, the Swiss feel themselves to be "Swiss" rather than "Romands", "Deutschschweizer" or "Ticinesi".

In the case of any threat to Swiss independence from outside Switzerland the German term "*fremder Vogt*" ('foreign overlord') stands symbolically for this type of "resistance" (Andres 1990), and the archetypical narrative here is that of William Tell.[5] The last point in time at which the myth was invoked for the whole country was during World War II, which helps to explain why the recent need to reassess Switzerland's role during the war is currently being experienced as such a painful process, at least by the older generation who were in their teens or twenties during the war years. The rejection of the referendum on entry into the European Economic Area on December 6, 1992 is explicable as a reaction against the "*fremder Vogt*" of the E.U. on the part of the German- and Italian-speaking Swiss. The fact that the French-speaking Swiss did not invoke this fundamental Swiss myth almost split the country apart.

The second type of "resistance" is expressed in the term "*fremder Richter*" ('foreign judge'). At the time of the occupation of Switzerland by Napoleon I this part of the myth became particularly acute, and once again, in the E.E.A. referendum it was only valid for the German- and Italian-speaking parts of the country. The third type of "resistance", that against centralized state control, is continually used against decisions of the federal parliament and against the federal administration, regardless of what ethnolinguistic group invokes the myth.

Closely connected to the "*coalition de résistances*" are stories that glorify the independence of the commune, the canton, the valley, the region, etc. In other words, Switzerland is not only a "*coalition de résistances*" but also a "*coalition de localités*" ('coalition of localities') (cf. Pichard 1975, 1978). The key feature of this typically Swiss local patriotism is that the myth can be, and frequently is, directed against other "localities" and ethnolinguistic groups simply by linking it with aspects of the "*coalition de résistances*".

Steinberg (1976) refers to the Swiss political system as a "bottom-heavy democracy", by which he means not only that a direct democracy expressed through referenda renders change cumbersome, if not sometimes downright impossible, but also that it is based on a bottom-up political structure resting crucially on a form of concensus democracy that is founded on local patriotism. This can sometimes be interpreted as the betrayal of the idea of a Swiss "nation" if it leads, as it all too often does, to the minorization of one part of the population.

The myth of the materialistic Swiss is well-known both in- and outside Switzerland and is encapsulated in jokes like the following (which is said to have originated in France): "If you see a Swiss jump out of a fifth floor window, jump with him. There's sure to be money at the bottom." In local terms, this Swiss myth leads to a preference of the physical and financial well-being of even the smallest communes to cultural and spiritual well-being, an argument which is supported by the large numbers of Swiss who have sought their academic, artistic or intellectual fortunes abroad. To be fair, however, there are just as many if not more Swiss artists and academics who have been successful within their own country.

Associated with this myth is the continually reiterated story of larger communes and cantons who have helped out financially smaller and weaker ones. In effect the myth of materialism here links up with the myth of the stronger who feels morally obliged to come to the aid of the weaker. It is a story which goes back at least to the warlike events of the 14th and 15th centuries in central Europe, to which the Swiss provided an almost endless number of mercenary soldiers. Its more benevolent aspect is reflected in the myth of Henri Dunant and the Red Cross, to which I shall shortly turn.

The physical topography of Switzerland has given rise to what is probably the most potent myth of all, that of the Gotthard or the mountain "*réduit*". The fundamental idea is that Switzerland is protected geographically by the Alps from outside interference and that the Alps also provide an ideal defensive "fortress" in the eventuality of attack. Its potency is derived from the fact that it can be linked to all the other myths in an endless number of ways, leading to its continual reconstruction and adaptation. For example, the “creation myth” of William Tell is intimately linked with the Gotthard myth along the lines I have just outlined. However, Peyer (1972) argues quite convincingly that the real reason for the rebellion against Habsburg hegemony in the 13th century was that the people of Uri, Schwyz and Unterwalden (now Nidwalden and Obwalden) wanted economic control over the Gotthard pass into northern Italy and the other passes leading over the mountain barrier to the Gotthard. Hence the Gotthard myth is closely connected with the myth of materialism.

The most important aspect of this myth is that of the fortress, the “*réduit*”. It is this which has united the different ethnolinguistic groups within Switzerland more than any other in this century, and it is also this aspect which is being rapidly eroded by recent revelations concerning the financial and economic collaboration of Swiss banks, Swiss industrialists and, partially at least, Swiss politicians with the Nazis during World War II. The extensive military installations, and reserves of ammunition and supplies built into the mountains are the physical expression of the myth.

Closely connected with this myth is the myth of armed neutrality, which goes back to the Congress of Vienna and was written into the first Swiss Federal Constitution of 1848. Continual recourse to this myth has allowed Switzerland not only to avoid being drawn into the armed conflicts that have dogged Europe in the 19th and 20th centuries —or at least this is the way the Swiss would like to interpret events. In effect it is also used constantly and so far quite effectively in referenda to argue against Switzerland becoming a member of either the U.N. or the E.U. At the same time, however, neutrality was also the driving force behind Henri Dunant’s creation of the Red Cross in the 19th century. Part of the Henri Dunant myth is that Switzerland willingly offers herself in times of crisis as a haven for refugees, and the majority of Swiss citizens still believe this despite clear evidence to the contrary from World War II.

6. Relating the myths to language and the emergence of the ideology

How does language play a part in acting out the myriad reconstructions of these myths and the complex interrelationships between them? In particular, how does language play a role in the demographically strongest ethnolinguistic group, that of the German speakers, and the demographically weakest, that of the Romansch speakers?

Before I focus in more detail on this second question, a few general remarks are in order with respect to the historical development of the relationships between the four languages of Switzerland. The present-day language borders can be seen as a reflection of the migration of Alemannic tribes from Southern Germany into the Swiss Alpine areas between the 6th and the 9th centuries (cf. *Zustand und Zukunft der viersprachigen Schweiz* 1989: 14–15). The report on the language situation in Switzerland commissioned by the Department of the Interior with a view to revising the language article in the constitution to include Romantsch (*Zustand und Zukunft der viersprachigen Schweiz*, 'Present and Future State of Quadrilingual Switzerland') summarizes the language situation in the old Confederation up to the Napoleonic invasion of Switzerland as follows:

> The old confederation with its 13 member states since 1513 ... was from 1291 on essentially German-speaking, although Fribourg was always bilingual. The associated areas can be described as follows: the Valais was German-speaking (with French-speaking bailywicks in the lower Valais), the Grisons was German-, Romantsch- and Italian-speaking, whereas parts of the vassal areas remained French-speaking (the Vaud) and Italian-speaking (the Ticino). However, an important factor was the early alliance of certain members of the old confederation with the Republic of Geneva from 1526 on, so that for the old confederation there was already a certain expansion deeper into French-speaking territory. (1989: 16)

It is important to note here that until the beginning of the 19th century French was under the domination of German in both the Valais and Fribourg, even though French speakers represented and still represent a large majority in Fribourg, and that the Vaud was a vassal area under the control of the Canton of Berne. Only in the Republic of Geneva was French the language of administration, education, religion, etc. and Geneva did not become a Swiss canton till after the Treaty of Vienna in 1815. The feeling of minorization thus runs very deep in the French-speaking part of Switzerland, and the resistance to German is greatest in the Canton of Geneva.

Let us now turn to the second question concerning the role that German plays in the construction of the myths. Firstly, the rebellion against Austrian domination at the end of the 13th century —the myth of William Tell— was the rebellion of local groups of Alemannic dialect speakers, who had found strength in their opposition to Habsburg rule by entering into an alliance with one another but were also fiercely opposed to giving up their own local autonomy. Local dialects were thereby associated with difference and independence within alliance. They became constructed as one of the strongest features of local patriotism and at the same time of membership in the confederation through which the Swiss could guarantee their liberty, their freedom to organize their own affairs locally, and protection in alliance.

For as long as the German-speaking states to the north of the Rhine remained a disparate, heterogeneous set of small kingdoms, duchies, principalities, etc. loosely organized within the framework of the Holy Roman Empire, they did not represent much of a threat to the confederation. In addition, movements towards codifying the written language in the 15th and 16th centuries came largely from the chancelleries of the south of Germany, in particular from the Alemannic areas. The notion of a "standard" language in which a synecdochic dialect gains in hegemony over other dialects and is used symbolically to represent the "territory" of a unified state could only develop along with the centralized expansion of state power. The Swiss myths that I outlined in the previous section, however, would lead us to presuppose the rejection of any such centralization, hence the rejection of any process of linguistic standardization.[6] In fact it was not until the rise of the Kingdom of Prussia in the 18th century and its consequent rivalry with the Austro-Hungarian Empire that a North German standard linking unity of territory with unity of language began to develop, and even then there was no imminent danger to the Swiss Confederation.

After German unification in 1871, however, the problem of distinguishing between a north German standard language, the oral model for which was the language of the serious theater in the late 19th century (so-called *Bühnendeutsch*, 'stage German'), and the Swiss-German dialects began to pose itself. It was not that standard German was rejected by the German-speaking middle-class Swiss. There was, after all, not much reason for any such rejection. Switzerland had produced several well-known authors who have since become part of the canon of German literature, and several members of the intelligentsia and the wealthy middle classes insisted on using only standard German at home and in their more close-knit social networks (e.g. the writer Gottfried Keller and the "general" at the time of the first World War, General Wille).[7] The problem lay with the everyday mode of communication amongst members of virtually all the social classes, which had always been, as it is now, dialect. During World War I, the bulk of the German-speaking population, whether or not they regularly spoke standard German, sympathized with the German Empire, whereas the bulk of the Italian- and French-speaking population sympathized with the allies. The risk of Switzerland falling apart along ethnolinguistic lines was greater during the time of World War I than it has been at any other time throughout this century.

The catalyst which created an ideology of dialect out of the connections between language and the myths outlined in the previous section consisted, I maintain, of three historical events: the economic depression at the end of the 1920s and the beginning of the 1930s, the rise of Nazi Germany (and, more obliquely, the rise of Italian fascism which prefigured it) and World War II. I shall exemplify each of these factors in turn.

In November 1918, the Swiss socialist movement and the trade unions called a national strike to implement a wide range of reforms ranging from the 48-hour week to votes for women on the local and federal levels. The army were called out in most large towns in Switzerland to put a stop to the demonstrations held between November 12 and 14. Fortunately, no one was killed, but the use of the army to end a general strike was totally unprecedented in Switzerland. The army is a militia army in which all able-bodied male Swiss citizens are legally required to serve for an initial training period of 17 weeks (recently reduced to 15 weeks) and for three (later two) weeks every year for a number of years. Hence calling on the army to disperse a demonstration is equivalent to asking those who might otherwise be demonstrating to use force to prevent others from demonstrating. During the twenties the army were called out a few more times to disperse workers' demonstrations, resulting in a small number of deaths. The preferred language of the Swiss commander-in-chief during World War I, standard German, which was also the preferred language of a number of industrialist and financier families, may thus have been seen as the language of federal domination, i.e. the language of a federal administration attempting to use force to impose centralization. In addition the force that was used was the very guarantor of armed neutrality, and thereby indirectly of the independence of the dialects, the militia army itself.

In 1932 a right-wing political organization bordering on fascism, the Union Nationale, held a convention in Geneva. A large demonstration was called by parties on the left and in the centre of the political spectrum. The federal government decided once again to use the army to break up the demonstration, but the nearest available units to Geneva were companies of recruits in Lausanne. The demonstration turned into a riot in which several demonstrators were killed by the army. What had been a link between dialect and the working classes, dialect and opposition to political centralizing tendencies, dialect against the internal use of an army that was only ostensively there to protect Swiss citizens from invasion from outside the country, i.e. to defend Swiss neutrality, now became a link between dialect and anti-fascism.

It was also during the 1930s that two related, sociolinguistically significant events took place. On the one hand, Romansch was elected by referendum to the status of national language in 1938, i.e. it became recognized as one of the four national (rather than "official") languages of Switzerland. The referendum itself can be interpreted as a gesture of defiance towards Mussolini's irredentism, his claim that all territories speaking Italian (in which he mistakenly included Romantsch) should eventually become part of Italy (cf. Viletta 1984). On the other hand, Professor Eugen Dieth at the University of Zurich was given the task of preparing an orthography in which Swiss dialects could be written, thus giving a measure of "official" academic recognition to the status of the dialects.

During and immediately after World War II Swiss German dialects regained the symbolic value they had always potentially possessed since the rebellion against the Habsburgs in 1291. They became symbolic guarantors of opposition against invasion from outside Switzerland, particularly against invasion from Germany; they became overt symbols of "non-Germanness", i.e. they openly displayed that the speaker was Swiss, not German or Austrian; they now became recognized explicitly as what they had always been, viz. the vehicles for the expression of local patriotism and local traditions; they became vehicles for resistance against any tendency towards over-centralization; but they also became vehicles of exclusion, i.e. the symbolic opposition towards the large-scale migration of workers from countries such as Italy, Spain, Portugal, Yugoslavia, Turkey, etc. to Switzerland.

Evidence that the ideological nature of this process is recognized by all ethnolinguistic groups in Switzerland is provided by the folklinguistic term "dialect wave" which is used to refer to it. The first "dialect wave" occurred around the turn of the century and can be interpreted as a neo-Romantic "folkloric" desire to preserve the dialects from "extinction". The very fact that amateur dialectologists, folklore collectors and others felt the need to protect the dialects is an indication of the degree to which the shift towards standard German was perceived. The second dialect wave, in the 1930s, was in effect a precursor to the dialect wave of the war years and the immediate post-war era. The third dialect wave began around the year 1968, after a period of unprecedented material and financial prosperity during the 1950s and 1960s. Unfortunately, it coincided with the growth of ultra rightwing nationalist parties and the first referenda to restrict the migration of foreign workers to Switzerland. Since then, however, the ideology of dialect has become so entrenched in the institutional structures of German-speaking Switzerland, particularly, as we shall see, in the education system and in the media that it can be easily invoked and pressed into service for a variety of political goals, e.g. to argue against the integration of Switzerland into Europe or the United Nations, against the granting of automatic naturalization to second generation children of non-Swiss migrant families and, since 1996, to justify Swiss politics during World War II and to protest at alleged unfairness in foreign attitudes toward Switzerland as a result of those events. In the following section I shall deal with a number of apparently isolated, but nevertheless significant everyday events in the coherent practices of the ideology of dialect, after which I shall turn in the penultimate section to a discussion of the ideology in the media and in education.

7. "That's written in standard German. You won't be able to understand it." Everyday anecdotes relating to dialect and standard

Since any language ideology is constructed from mythical accounts of language use and language structure, it is important to locate examples of those accounts when observing the social practices of everyday life. This essentially entails collecting narratives. I therefore offer no apologies for presenting a set of small cameo narratives in this section, some of them derived from my own personal experience and others from the experiences of others, which, if augmented and enriched by interpretive comment, will add to the "essential texture" of the ideology. After almost thirty years of living and working in Switzerland, I have had to try to piece together the ideology of dialect that has somehow become part of a Swiss identity for the German-speaking Swiss, i.e. for 68% of the Swiss population. In the concluding section of this chapter I shall argue that the ideology is fragile because it reconstructs boundaries between German-speaking Switzerland and the other ethnolinguistic areas of the country.

The title of this section is taken from my first anecdote. From 1993 to 1999 I lived very close to the small town of Thun at the head of the Lake of Thun on the very edge of the Bernese Oberland. Rather grandiosely the tourist office has labeled Thun "the City of the Alps". In many ways Thun and its surrounding countryside epitomize much that is traditionally thought of as typically Swiss. The Alpine valleys of the Bernese Oberland with their large Bernese farmhouses, barns and chalets, meadows with cows grazing in the summer and with the skilifts up to the skiing areas operating in the winter provide a picture postcard landscape. For the Swiss themselves the area epitomizes solid local patriotism, hard-headed stubborn realism and one of the traditional heartlands of the rightwing Swiss People's Party, supported by farmers and small business people. One Saturday morning I was browsing through the selection of literature in Bernese German in a bookshop in Thun, consisting of poetry, collections of short stories and even detective novels. Alongside this section was a section devoted to children's books in standard German, and leafing through the pages of one of these books with obvious interest was a girl of about 7 years of age. The girl suddenly turned to her mother and asked in the Bernese Oberland form of the Bernese dialect whether she could buy her the book. "No, don't be silly dear," said her mother. "That's written in standard German. You won't be able to understand it." The situation at first appeared rather absurd to me —an Englishman looking at books written in Bernese German, and a mother telling her child in Bernese German that she would not be able to understand a book written in standard German. That same mother probably let her child watch films for children on television which have either been dubbed into standard German or produced in standard German. If she were then asked whether the girl was able to understand the language, she might have looked at the addressee quizzically. Of course her daughter could understand what was spoken, but standard German written down was a different matter. It had to be difficult and beyond the capabilities of the child.

The second anecdote has an unsavory racist element to it. Not being Swiss (particularly if one does not have the right skin color) and not being able to use a Swiss German dialect can lead one into various forms of racial discrimination. My wife once witnessed a scene at a butcher's shop in which a Tamil refugee wanted to order one thousand five hundred grams of chopped chicken. He made his request in impeccable standard German. The shop was full, the butcher perhaps overworked, but this does not excuse the his reaction. He simply said "What?", whereupon the Tamil repeated his order for one thousand five hundred grams of chopped chicken. In Bernese German the butcher then said loudly and aggressively, "You mean one and a half kilos, don't you?" The Tamil became flustered and then muttered, again in standard German, that yes, he supposed he did. "Then why the hell couldn't you say so?" shouted the butcher, again in Bernese German. "If you mean one and a half kilos, you should say one and a half kilos." What was it that the butcher felt to be wrong here, the fact that the Tamil was speaking standard German, rather than dialect, the fact that he was a Tamil refugee, the fact that the Tamil had made the very insignificant mistake of ordering in grams rather than kilos? Whatever interpretation we choose to give here, the important aspect of the event was the butcher's loud use of Bernese German to assert to the other customers in the shop that the addressee was an outsider, not just a non-Swiss-German-speaker, not just a non-Swiss, but also a colored refugee.

The third anecdote is less aggressive but just as unsettling. I had gone into a shoe-shop in Berne to buy a new pair of shoes and was sitting down to try a few pairs on. Outside the shop window I noticed two tall middle-aged ladies, who looked as if they came from the north of Germany. They entered the shop and asked the young shop-assistant very politely in the standard German of the Hamburg area whether one of them could try on a pair of shoes they had seen in the window. The young shop-assistant became flustered and asked them in Bernese German to repeat their request, which they did. The shop-assistant asked them, again in Bernese German, to wait a moment and came to the back of the shop, where she asked an older assistant if she could serve the two ladies. As she explained in Bernese German, she could not deal with the customers in standard German. After years of schooling in standard German she was simply unable to deal with a standard salesperson-customer interaction. Standard German for her was indeed that language variety which was restricted to the social institution of the school, and was in any case always associated with artificiality and the written medium of communication. In the next section I shall return in more detail to how the ideology of dialect is actually used in the German-speaking school system to reconstruct standard German as a dispreferred language variety restricted to very few formal, mainly written discourse genres.

The fourth anecdote is taken from the school milieu once again, but this time from the grammar school. My son once had to give an oral presentation in the German class. At the time he had a standard German-speaking girlfriend whom he had met in the south of France. He chose a topic from history, which was his favorite subject at school, and spent days gathering all his facts, putting the text together and then practising his oral delivery. At the time he was rather proud of his fluency in standard German and was determined to put up a good show. He delivered his presentation well and the class reacted very favorably. At the end, his German teacher praised the contents but had a number of critical comments to make about his delivery. "Christian," he said, "why do you have to sound like a German? You're Swiss, not German, and there's no point in trying to pretend you're not." This anecdote derives from the same process of the institutional construction of standard German and is clearly predicated on the ideology of dialect.

The fifth story is one of my own and is taken from the first few months of my life in Switzerland. As it happens, it effected me very deeply and very decisively with respect to the way in which I constructed my future life in this country. As a student of German in Britain I was obliged during my time as an undergraduate to spend a year in a German-speaking country, and I was fortunate enough to spend my year in the city of Freiburg im Breisgau in the Alemannic dialect area of Baden in Baden-Württemberg. While I was there, I learnt a great deal of the local dialect and was rather proud of the fact. After leaving university I worked in an English language school on the south coast of England at which there were a majority of Swiss students, which meant that my passive understanding of the Swiss dialects increased considerably. In 1969 I was working at a school in Zurich and had decided to go into town by tram. From my experience of trams in Freiburg I simply assumed that there would be a conductor or conductress in both cars of the tram and got into the second car without reading the notices at the tram-stop telling passengers to buy their tickets from the ticket machines at the tram-stop. Five minutes into the journey an official came by and asked me to show him my ticket, whereupon I told him, in the dialect I had acquired in Freiburg, that I wanted to buy a ticket to the town center. He asked me where I came from and I said from Britain. He then demanded to see proof of this statement, for example whether I could show him my passport. Of course I could not and I remember getting very annoyed at what I considered to be offensive and arrogant behavior when all I wanted to do was buy a ticket. The truth of the matter was that he took me to be German, would not believe that I had not read the instructions at the tram-stop, and had become very unfriendly and unpleasant indeed. The 50 Swiss Franc fine he gave me was soon recovered from the tram company after I had registered a vehement protest, but I resolved from that moment on to use no more standard German with Swiss interlocutors but to try to activate my passive knowledge of Swiss German dialects. The inspector was simply reconstructing the enmity of the German-speaking Swiss toward the Germans, in particular to those from Baden-Württemberg. Unwittingly, however, he became my first "instructor" in the ideology of dialect.

The sixth cameo narrative concerns a Swiss film made in the 1950s and entitled *Der zehnte Mai* ('The 10th of May'). The film was shown on German-speaking Swiss television in 1997 as a response to the rather undifferentiated and somewhat insensitive criticism of Swiss foreign policy during World War II by certain contemporary American and British politicians. One of the demands made of Switzerland is that the Swiss need to reassess and re-evaluate their own recent history particularly in the light of claims by the survivors of Jewish families who were victims of the holocaust that the Swiss banks have withheld any information on accounts opened with them before and during World War II. The aim of the television programmers was to show that even as early as the 1950s Swiss film producers had already embarked on that historical reassessment and had produced a number of extremely sensitive, well-made films in Swiss German, *Der zehnte Mai* being one of them.

For my present purposes, however, the film is interesting because it also illuminates significant elements of the ideology of dialect. On May 10, 1940 German armies marched into the Netherlands, Belgium and Luxemburg, and the Swiss population (although perhaps not the Swiss government) were expecting the imminent invasion of Switzerland by German troops massed along the border. The film does not glorify the Swiss will to resist; it does not present an idealized picture of the Swiss army. On the contrary, it implies rather strongly that despite the will to resist the chances of success were virtually non-existent. The audience is thus presented with a version of the "resistance" myth without the film suggesting that resistance will be either glorious or successful.

On the morning of May 10 a young German dissident flees across the Rhine into Switzerland. His aim is to get to Zurich where he hopes to contact a family who had shown him hospitality and given him temporary refuge as an orphan child immediately after World War I and to locate a Swiss woman from Zurich who was his childhood companion during that time. Here we have a version of the Henri Dunant myth. He makes his way to a railway station in a border town to buy a ticket to Zurich, but realizes that he has no Swiss money with him and witnesses the treatment of an elderly Jewish man who is handed over to the authorities after trying to pay for his ticket with German marks. He catches a lift from a lorry driver with an Eastern Swiss dialect (probably St. Gallen) who is going as far as Zurich. The lorry driver has also witnessed the incident with the Jewish man and expresses his disgust and anger at the collaboration between the border guards and the Nazi authorities. They stop on the way at a roadside restaurant for breakfast when the news comes through on the radio of the German invasion of the Low Countries. The people in the restaurant are horrified and convinced that Switzerland will be invaded that very night, and they express their anger at and contempt of "the Germans". The lorry driver, who has paid for his and the young German's breakfast, tells him that he refuses to drive "a German" any further and that he should find his own way to Zurich. All communication between the Swiss participants takes place in dialect, but the young German only speaks standard German.

From that point on in the story, he is mortally afraid that his language will give him away, as indeed it does at the end of the film. There are of course several other important events in the film, but the significant point here is the way in which standard German becomes a stigma despite the fact that the young German is fleeing for his life to Switzerland. The dialect, on the other hand, is elevated to a position in which it becomes the symbol of resistance and liberty, but resistance against and liberty from Germany and standard German. That, I maintain, is the quintessence of the ideology of dialect as it emerged after World War II.

These and many other narratives contain various aspects of the same story; they reveal significant points in the same language ideology. The point that I wish to make in the next section is that the reconstruction of the ideology starts early, at the latest in the first-grade of primary school, and is supported by the differential treatment of standard German and the dialect in the media.

8. The reproduction of the ideology of dialect in the educational system and the media

One of the major professional functions of primary school teachers in the German-speaking part of Switzerland, although most of the time they are unaware of the fact, is to help to reconstruct for each new generation of schoolchildren the ideology of dialect. Some of the results are revealed in the anecdotes narrated in the previous section; others can be observed in other spheres of Swiss professional life, e.g. in banking, in diplomacy, in the chemical industry, in the hotel and restaurant industry, etc. In this section it is not possible to present and analyze lengthy extracts from the extensive data corpus we have gathered during the course of a research project on how standard German is taught at the level of primary school in the German-speaking part of Switzerland and how the perceptions of first-grade primary school children are socially constructed to create different sets of values between "*Schwyzertüütsch*" and "*Schriftdeutsch*". I will simply restrict myself to some of our most important findings.

The historicity of the institution "school" implies that certain social frames will be re-enacted in every generation of children with a minimum number of changes and adaptations. Primary school teachers can thus be looked at, from this point of view, as professionals, one of the major aspects of whose job is to re-create the evaluative frameworks in which language varieties are to be seen by the learners.

Language is presented, at the latest in the first-grade of primary school, as a significant "*etiquette*" for another culture, considering the lexeme "another" as meaning literally "an other", i.e. a different, alien, out-group culture. The significance of language and forms of verbal interaction is central to the set of mental propositions an individual will develop concerning her/his perceptions of the world, and this includes mental propositions about language itself. The interaction at school is almost always unidirectional, from teacher to pupil, in which the teacher, while simulating communicative interaction, in fact talks for 80 to 90% of the lesson time. Thus the construction of a set of beliefs about language varieties is institutionalized through the social processes of schooling, which involves a wide range of partially overlapping, partially distinct communicative frames.

In the Canton of Berne the majority of primary school teachers openly defy the instructions from the Department of Education that standard German is the official language of public education, preferring to use Bernese German even in literacy classes. When it is used as the language of instruction, it is presented in an artificial way which is noticeably different from the standard German children hear on television programs. For example, teachers make great efforts to stress lexeme boundaries when normal fluent standard German, like Bernese German, would make great use of prosodic structures involving elision, the non-release of stop consonants, the destressing of vocalic segments, etc. They introduce dialect lexemes into their standard German and stick to grammatical patterns that are not only unusual, but often even impossible in standard German.

Lessons usually contain a range of different communicative frames such as the "surrogate parent" frame in which the teacher takes parental responsibility for the well-being and also for the disciplining of the children, the "organization" frame in which everything pertaining to the setting up and organization of the teaching activity is carried out (usually covering a warm-up phase before the lesson begins in earnest), the "content" frame, in which the teacher focuses on the central content of the lesson, the "pupil-pupil interaction" frame in which pupils interact with one another outside the "content" or "organization" frame.

The most informal of these frames is clearly the "pupil-pupil interaction" frame, and in that frame interaction is carried out in Bernese German. The most formal frame is the "content" frame, and even there the majority of teachers will still use Bernese German, switching from time to time for short sequences into standard German. The language variety used in the "surrogate parent" frame is uniquely Bernese German, regardless of whether the teacher uses standard German for the "content" frame or not. The "organization" frame is generally carried out in Bernese German. Hence, whether or not a teacher uses standard German during the "content" frame, the children always know that her/his "mother tongue" is Bernese German. Thus standard German is framed as the language variety in use for the purposes of writing/reading and for highly formal occasions, whereas Bernese German is framed as everyone's "mother tongue" (even though some of the children may have a non-indigenous language). Bernese German is the language of proximity, everyday organization, emotional affect (either positive or negative) and is even framed as the "normal" language in which standard German is presented as an out-group variety, something to learn about, as a metalanguage used for official writing and reading purposes. Codeswitching from one variety into the other generally corresponds to switching from one communicative frame into another and thereby helps to construct the two language varieties as having distinctly different social functions.

Frequent references are made to standard German as a language for writing or as a language in the written medium, e.g. through exercises involving written lexemes in standard German, through reading short text extracts, by orthographizing oral mistakes (i.e. getting the children to spell and write out words they have used wrongly in oral standard German), by getting pupils to write in standard German and then to comment orally on what they have written in Bernese German. When children respond to a standard German question in Bernese German, they are frequently asked to say it in "*Schriftdeutsch*", e.g. "*Kannst du das auf Schriftdeutsch sagen?*" ('Can you say that in German for writing?') or "*Sag's auf Schriftdeutsch*" ('Say it in German for writing').

In addition, Bernese German speaking teachers (and this can be generalized across the whole country to refer to teachers with Swiss German as their mother tongue) have a tendency to over-correct their pupils, aiming at hypercorrect forms just as foreign language teachers often do if they do not have the target language as their mother tongue. There are also practice materials aimed at raising pupils' awareness of the differences between dialect and the standard language, and exercises are often framed to highlight these differences.

Standard German is presented as if it were a foreign language, particularly by those teachers who use Bernese German almost exclusively. Teachers thus set up learning situations which are remarkably similar to those which are in use in foreign language classes. They will structure games in Bernese German which aim at the recognition and manipulation of lexemes, phrases and sentences of standard German. Children are invited to simulate situations in standard German with which they are already familiar in Bernese German. Songs are sung in standard German and commented on in Bernese German. Teachers even resort at times to a form of translation, specifically asking the whole class or individual pupils what a word in standard German means in Bernese German, or vice versa.

At the beginning of first-grade we carried out matched guise tests, which revealed insignificant differences between pupils' attitudes towards and perception of Bernese German, the Swiss form of standard German and a north German variety of the standard. Children did of course favor Bernese German, but the differences were not particularly great. At the beginning of second-grade, however, there were wide divergences in pupils' reactions to these three varieties. Bernese German had apparently increased in acceptance whereas the two varieties of standard German had decreased markedly. These tests and the results of interviews with both pupils and teachers provide very strong evidence that standard German, or "*Schriftdeutsch*" as it is so often called in Bernese classrooms, is constructed as "different", "foreign", "used for the purposes of writing", "un-Swiss", etc. Our initial hypothesis would thus seem to be confirmed.

What I have sketchily described so far in this section is the professional practices of first-grade primary school teachers in the German-speaking part of Switzerland. By examining those practices closely through ethnographic research on the institution of the school, it becomes clear how the ideology of dialect is constructed as part of their professional calling. Discussing educational ethnography, Hymes (1980: 88–103) concludes that anyone who carries out an ethnography of individual classes by merely recording individual lessons is not doing good ethnography. I agree with him, but sometimes, as in the case of our own research, limited funding prevents the setting up of a more comprehensive ethnography. To counteract this criticism and to support my interpretation of the reconstruction of the ideology of dialect through the school system I would therefore like to discuss briefly the use of standard German and the dialect in the media.

The medium of radio in the German-speaking part of Switzerland is dominated by the three channels of the public service of Schweizer Radio DRS, in which standard German still has a significant role to play. The plethora of private local radio stations, on the other hand, overwhelmingly use the local dialect. Even so, however, in a pamphlet published and distributed by Schweizer Radio DRS and intended for use by its employees, a pamphlet which argues very forcefully for the use of a Swiss version of the standard when the standard is required for the relevant programs, we read the following statements in a foreword by Andreas Blum, the director of Schweizer Radio DRS:

> Language culture and the culture of speaking are an essential element of the public image of SR DRS ... We are a Swiss German, not a German radio station, even in areas in which we make use of the "written" language [i.e. "*Schriftdeutsch*"]. The language culture north of the Rhine can therefore not be a model for us —and certainly not the culture of the German theater, with the possible exception of radio plays. Doing radio for German-speaking Switzerland means cultivating a language which has its roots in our language history. Anything other than that is a contribution to the falsification and alienation of our identity, quite apart from whether or not an orientation toward false models based on a lack of preconditions is in most cases doomed to failure.
>
> (Burri et al. 1993: 4)

The "public image" of SR DRS, on which its selling power in competition with local radio stations depends, is interpreted as residing in the form of oral language used by its moderators, newsreaders, interviewers, etc. rather than in the content of the programs themselves. Blum does not of course mean when he writes "we are a Swiss German radio" that the official language of SR DRS is dialect, but rather than it should be standard German with a decidedly Swiss pronunciation and with those lexical and morphosyntactic forms peculiar to Switzerland.

What is interesting in the quotation given above is that Blum explicitly denies the validity of the "language culture" north of the Rhine, i.e. in Germany, as a model for SR DRS. But he also states that the Swiss variety of standard German "has its roots in our language history" and that it is a fundamental element in the construction of a Swiss identity. Note, however, that he is not prepared to admit that it is really the dialects which have this function, not a Swiss form of standard German, even though he might want to say this. We have seen from our discussion of how standard German is reconstructed in the educational system that it is in fact systematically denied that function. The rationale behind the ideology of dialect is to admit standard German in those social arenas in which it is unavoidable, but to reject the notion that it has "its roots in our language history."

SR DRS thus finds itself in a very difficult, and somewhat compromising position. On the one hand, it has to present the Swiss variety of standard German as a medium of oral communication within Switzerland, particularly in programs of an official nature such as news bulletins, political and cultural commentary and discussion, in interviews with non-dialect speakers, etc. On the other hand, it has to present and promote the image of being a Swiss German radio, which means explicitly using dialect in other types of programms. With the majority of the population, however, Swiss standard German is not a medium of oral communication at all, since it is continually reproduced in the education system as a "foreign language", or at least an alien variety that will cause the learners difficulty, as a means of written communication, with correctness rather than fluency projected as the ultimate goals of learning, etc. In this sense Blum is wrong in assuming that it has its roots in Swiss language history, or perhaps I should rather say that he is a victim of the ideology of dialect.

The ideology of dialect is even more in evidence in *Schweizer Fernsehen DRS*, the German-speaking Swiss television network, in which strange mixtures of dialect and standard German occur as a result of the greater commitment toward dialect in television than in radio. Live reports of sports events, e.g. football, ice-hockey, tennis, athletics, etc. are given in standard German, a policy which is based on the very flimsy argument that foreign workers in Switzerland would not be able to understand the commentary if this were not the case. The argument is absurd from at least two points of view. Firstly, most migrant workers in Switzerland are far more likely to have a working knowledge of dialect than they are of standard German. Secondly, the audience of a live sports report does not really need a commentary at all if they understand the rules of the sport. The flimsiness of the argument is compounded by the tendency to hold interviews with experts and players, wherever possible, in dialect. In some instances, long studio discussions often precede and follow the game itself in dialect, if the reporter's interlocutors are dialect speakers.

There are two major news broadcasts every evening on SF DRS, the normal news program at 19.30, in which not only the moderators but also all interviewees and reporters are expected to use standard German, and a news magazine at 21.50 called "*Zehn vor Zehn*" ('Ten to Ten'), in which all interviews are conducted in dialect but all the moderating is carried out in standard German. Interviews are frequently given by the same person in standard German for the 19.30 news broadcast and in dialect for 'Ten to Ten'. It is in situations such as these that any support of and sympathy for standard German in the medium of television is immediately subverted by the ideology of dialect.

9. Competition from alternative ideologies: Locating the ideological debates

The ideology of dialect in German-speaking Switzerland does not show signs of abating. If anything, it has become stronger over the years and has influenced ever wider circles of language usage. One reason for this might be that it has become institutionalized in the educational system and is at present becoming institutionalized in the non-print media. This is of course a hypothesis which would need a great deal of very careful research to confirm or reject. In addition nothing depends on whether it is simply classified as a trend or a dialect wave rather than an ideology. After all, at least the term "ideology" evokes concepts of power, domination, political struggle, etc., which is what we are really dealing with here. It is important, however, to take a wider view of the issue and to try and assess whether or not there are any alternative language ideologies competing with the ideology of dialect.

In section 2, I gave a brief summary of the situation for Romansch, and I argued that the ideology of dialect might also be seen as helping to construct the present opposition to Romansch Grischun. The reason for this is quite simple. All native speakers of Romansch quickly become bilingual, not in Romansch (and certainly not in Romansch Grischun) and standard German but in their dialect of Romansch and the Grisons dialect of German. Their acquisition of literacy in Romansch is deeply effected by their acquisition of literacy in standard German. They are, in other words, exposed to the institutional reproduction of standard German as an alien variety used for written purposes. The introduction of Romansch Grischun for the purposes of literacy will simply underwrite the rejection of a standard form of the language.

Since Romansch Grischun is in any case a synthetic form of Romansch which no one speaks as her/his mother tongue, the consequences of rejection could be far more serious than the rejection of standard German. There is absolutely no danger of the Swiss dialects dying out since they are a fundamental cornerstone in the continued mythical reproduction of what Switzerland is and what it means to be Swiss. There is, however, a very real danger of Romansch dying out. The demise of the language has been high on the agenda of language politics at least since the referendum of 1938. The rationale behind creating Romansch Grischun was that it is only through the creation of a written standard form of the language that it will have any chance of survival. But that rationale simply flies in the face of the ideology of dialect. In German-speaking Switzerland —and we should not forget that the Romansch-speaking area is situated geographically within the German-speaking area— it is the oral forms of language which guarantee survival, not the written forms. In fact, Switzerland might even give the lie to the hypothesis that only a written standard can guarantee the survival of a language.

The alternative ideology here lies precisely in the arguments presented in favor of creating a written medium through which some sense of unity might be recreated in the geographically fragmented heartlands of Romansch speakers. The ideology rests on the belief in the function of a written standardized language variety as an "official" language within Switzerland. This is not the same as pressing for a "one-state-one-language" policy, since Switzerland is, almost by definition, a multilingual, multiethnic state. What the alternative ideology aims at doing is to create a measure of ethnic unity amongst Romansch speakers as a first step towards ensuring that effective policies are developed for the maintenance of the language. The suggestion has also been made that Romansch Grischun should take over the role of a teaching medium in the planned extension of Romansch-medium education through the whole school curriculum.

What the ideology does not seem to take account of, however, is that it is a relatively small step between imposing a teaching medium and creating standards of correctness for it and its imagined speakers and writers. Given the fact that there are only speakers of dialect in the Romansch-speaking area and that virtually all these speakers are bilingual with the Grisons dialect of German, the alternative ideology, borrowed as it is from the ideology of standardization, has little chance of success when pitted against the ideology of dialect. After all, given the Swiss myths dealt with in section 5, there seems little to motivate a Romansch speaker to accept an artificial standard simply to be able to participate in the affairs of the federal government in Berne. Local patriotism is just as strong in the Grisons as it is elsewhere in Switzerland. However, unless these competing language ideologies are fully understood and evaluated, not much progress can be made toward developing effective strategies of language maintenance and language revival.

In the course of this chapter I have referred briefly to two situations when the unity of Switzerland was at stake, the divided loyalties of the ethnolinguistic groups in Switzerland during World War I and the failure of the francophone Swiss (and also of the Cantons of Basel-City and Basel-Land, I need to add) to counterbalance the German- and Italian-speaking Swiss in the EEA referendum in 1992. In the latter situation the ideology of dialect played an indirect role in that the protests of the French-speaking Swiss against what they perceived to be increasing minorization had become more vociferous during the 1980s than ever before. Minorization can of course be realized in a wide range of sociopolitical situations, but in Switzerland the first level at which it is articulated is always that of language and the relationships between the ethnolinguistic groups. The major argument in the expression of protest concerned the increasing use of dialect rather than standard German (cf. Lüdi 1992; Watts 1988). The French-speaking Swiss feel that the insistence on dialect, which I have interpreted here as a language ideology, is a betrayal of Swiss identity. As we have seen, however, one of the major expressions of Swiss identity for the German-speakers is precisely the use of dialect rather than standard German.

Needless to say, the spread of the dialects in the German-speaking part of the country has raised, and continues to raise, a storm of protest in the French-speaking part of Switzerland. The French-speaking Swiss, who make up around 19% of the total population of the country, protest, rightly or wrongly, that they are forced to learn "*le bon allemand*" at school, which they cannot use in German-speaking Switzerland, since they are usually addressed in Swiss German. The truth of the matter is often that they simply expect the German-speaking Swiss to speak French and make little or no effort to speak German of any kind, but this does not invalidate the fact that the use of Swiss German dialects has become a salient feature in inter-ethnic relationships within Switzerland.

The ideological debate over the use of the dialect that is carried on across the French-German language border within Switzerland thus concerns the conflicting claims to "being Swiss" made by French speakers and German speakers. Although the reasons for French speakers' grievances are ultimately to be found in a complex interrelationship of historical, political and socio-economic factors, they are regularly reinterpreted as problems of ethnicity and, in particular, problems of language. French speaking commentators have expressed the conviction that Swiss German as it is used in the non-print media is in the process of what they refer to as "Hollandization", i.e. that there is a move towards separating Swiss German from standard German and creating a "new" standard language out of it. The evidence for this is, needless to say, very flimsy, but it nevertheless expresses the French speakers' fear of Swiss isolationism within Europe (cf. Watts 1997).

The debate reveals an alternative language ideology in the French-speaking part of the country in which the standard language is interpreted as reflecting a higher degree of education, learning and culture than any dialect. Knowing and using standard French implies participating in a world-wide culture, "*la francophonie*", and sharing in a "glorious" past. It also means involving oneself in the global struggle against domination by English. In the French-speaking part of Switzerland there is thus a widely held belief that all French speakers speak standard French and that the Savoyan dialects of French have disappeared. However, one only has to visit some of the more remote valleys of the Fribourg Alps and most of the side valleys of the Canton of Valais leading into the Rhone valley, to discover that the local "*patois*" have not died out at all (cf. Andres 1997). In effect the French-speaking Swiss have simply taken over the French language-ideological contempt for dialects. In that alternative ideology, a dialect is perceived to be a sign of rusticity, lack of education, backwardness, poverty, etc., whereas speaking standard French is associated with culture, sophistication, an openness toward Europe and the world, and, above all, the centralizing tendency of political organization within France.

However, in Switzerland there are grave inconsistencies with this ideology. First and foremost, the French-speaking Swiss do not consider themselves as French, but as Swiss. Secondly, they are just as locally patriotic as the German-speaking Swiss (cf. Pichard 1975, 1978), except that dialect does not serve the purpose of stressing that local patriotism. Thirdly, the French-speaking Swiss are in the forefront of criticism directed at the federal government and espouse the essentially German-speaking myth of the "*fremder Vogt*" as assiduously as the German speakers —without admitting it of course. The common notion of "*le bon français*" is just as much an illusion as their projection of "*le bon allemand*" onto the German speakers. No one can define adequately what either concept refers to, and it remains an elitist vision of a standard language which denies variability, change and development. It blinds the average French-speaking Swiss citizen to understanding the underlying reasons for the ideology of dialect and only helps to exacerbate the problem.

Although the ideology of the standard (which is different from the ideology of standardization evident in the debate over Romansch) is not espoused to nearly the same extent in the German-speaking as in the French-speaking part of Switzerland, it exists there nevertheless. It reveals itself in notions of correctness in language teaching which derive from a hypercorrect notion of what constitutes standard German. Apart from classes in standard German at high school level in preparation for the so-called "*Maturität/maturité*" which enable students to enter university, the overemphasis on language correctness in the secondary school system is felt most acutely in French as a "*langue nationale 2*", but it frequently makes itself felt in the teaching of English as well. As with the "ideology of the standard" with the French speakers, the problem with this alternative ideological mind-set is its lack of flexibility and its uniformity. In English teaching it has often led to a rejection of any other variant of English than British RP in the school system, thus excluding variants from North America, Australasia, or even Scotland and Ireland. The greatest problem with the "ideology of the standard" as it is realized in the German-speaking part of the country, however, is that it effectively plays into the hands of the ideology of dialect. It leads dialect speakers into believing that standard German really *is* a foreign language and that they will never be able to gain similar communicative skills in standard German as a native speaker of the standard. It also helps to restrict the range of standard German usage in Switzerland to written forms of communication.

The ideology of dialect has thus created a potentially divisive situation which could cause a dangerous rift between German speakers and non-German speakers. It is not always a wise idea to exaggerate the political potential of a language ideology, but it might help if educationalists, media experts and politicians in Switzerland were to consider their language practices more seriously as stemming from competing language ideologies and not to remain deaf to protests of the French speakers or the rejection of Romansch Grischun by the Romansch speakers. Political decisions are, after all, frequently made on the basis of language ideologies. The moment may not yet have come for the break-up of the Swiss Confederation, but to prevent it from happening alternative language ideologies other than the ideology of dialect are badly needed. This is not an argument against the dialects, but it *is* an argument for a re-evaluation of the relationship between standard German and the Swiss German dialects and for a re-assessment and reform of how that relationship is socially reproduced in education and the media.

Notes

1. Peter Trudgill (personal communication) has pointed out to me that the situation in Norway may be compared to that in Switzerland with respect to the relationship between the dialects and the standard. Whether or not the notion of ideology of dialect can also be extended to cover the linguistic situation in Norway, however, must remain an open question for the moment.
2. There are of course notable exceptions. Bernese German can boast of a very active and creative written literary tradition which encompasses works of prose fiction (novels, short stories) as well as poetry. There is also a tradition amongst young people throughout Switzerland writing their personal letters in the dialect, and several advertising slogans contain written dialect.
3. For example, there already exists a written literary tradition in a number of Romansch dialects, thus appearing to make Romansch Grischun superfluous as a written standard.
4. The Italian dialects in the Ticino are still very much alive, although a form of standard Italian is generally found to be in use in the major urban areas of the canton, Lugano, Locarno, Bellinzona. The relationship between the dialects and standard Italian, however, is not comparable to that between Swiss

German dialects and standard German or between the dialects of Romansch and Romansch Grischun. For this reason I have excluded Italian from my discussion of the ideology of dialect. See Lurati (1976) and Lurati and Pinana (1983) for details.

5. Tell was said to have been one of the leading rebels against Habsburg tyranny in the Canton of Uri in the late 13th century, who secured his own personal freedom and that of his people from the Austrian overlord Gessler by shooting an apple off his son's head with his crossbow. The story has been immortalized in one of Friedrich Schiller's dramas with the title *Wilhelm Tell* written at the turn of the nineteenth century.
6. In point of fact, however, Swiss printers opted at an early stage to adopt versions of the "standard". This does not, of course, invalidate the general argument with respect to oral forms of standard German, but it does indicate that a great deal more research into standardization in Switzerland is called for.
7. The term "general" is only in use in wartime to refer to the Commander-in-Chief of the army.

References

Andres, Franz
1990 Language relations in multilingual Switzerland. *Multilingua* 9: 11–45.
1997 *Language Choice in Bilingual Education: Sociolinguistic, Social and Political Issues in the Case of Switzerland.* PhD. dissertation, University of Bern.

Arquint, J. C.
1982 Die rätoromanische Schweiz. Stationen der Standardisierung. In: Schläpfer, Rudolf (ed.), *Die viersprachige Schweiz.* Zürich: Benziger, 273–300.

Billigmeier, R.
1979 *A Crisis in Swiss Pluralism.* The Hague: Mouton.

Bourdieu, Pierre
1991 *Language and Symbolic Power.* Cambridge: Polity Press.

Burri, Ruth Maria, Werner Geiger, Roswita Schilling and Edith Slembek
1993 *Deutsch sprechen am Radio.* Brig-Glis: SrZ Print AG.

Casanova, Achille
1989 Gestire il mandato costituzionale delle lingue ufficiali. Bern: Bundeskanzlerei. Mimeograph.

Department of the Interior
1989 *Zustand und Zukunft der viersprachigen Schweiz.* Bern.

Ferguson, Charles
1959 Diglossia. *Word* 15: 325–340.

Haas, Walter
1982b Sprachgeschichtliche Grundlagen. In: Schläpfer, Rudolf (ed.), *Die Viersprachige Schweiz.* Zürich: Benziger, 21–70.
1982b Die deutschsprachige Schweiz. In: Schläpfer, Rudolf (ed.), *Die Viersprachige Schweiz.* Zürich: Benziger, 73–160.

Häcki Buhofer, Annelies, Harald Burger, Hansjakob Schneider and Thomas Studer
1994 Hochspracherwerb in der deutschen Schweiz: Der weitgehend ungesteuerte Erwerb durch sechs- bis achtjährige Deutschschweizer Kinder. In: Burger, Harald and Annelies Häcki Buhofer (eds.), *Sprachwerwerb im Spannungsfeld von Dialekt und Hochsprache.* Bern: Lang, 147–198.

Häcki Buhofer, Annelies and Thomas Studer
1993 Sprachdifferenzbewusstsein und Einstellung zu den Varianten des Deutschen in der deutschen Schweiz. In: Werlen, Iwar (ed.), *Schweizer Soziolinguistik — Sozoilinguistik der Schweiz.* Special issue of *Bulletin CILA* 58: 169–199.

Hymes, Dell
1980 *Language in Education: Ethnolinguistic Essays* Washington, DC: Center for Applied Linguistics.

Joseph, John
1987 *Eloquence and Power.* London: Francis Pinter.

Lüdi, Georges
1992 Internal migrants in a multilingual country. *Multilingua* 11(1): 45–74.

Lurati, O.
1976 *Dialetto e Italiano nella Svizzera Italiana.* Lugano: Solari e Blum.

Lurati, O. and I. Pinana
1983 *Le Parole di una Valle. Dialetto, Gergo e Toponimia della Val Verzasca.* Lugano: Fondazione Arturo e Margherita Lang.

Milroy, James and Lesley Milroy
1985 *Authority in Language.* London: Routledge.

Peyer, Hans-Conrad
1972 Frühes und hohes Mittelalter. Die Entstehung der Eidgenossenschaft. In: *Handbuch der Schweizer Geschichte* Vol. 1. Zürich.

Pichard, A.
1975 *Vingt Suisse à découvrir*. Lausanne. Editions 24 heures.

1978 *La Romandie n'existe pas*. Lausanne: Editions 24 heures.

Sieber, Peter and Horst Sitta
1986 Schweizerdeutsch zwischen Dialekt und Sprache. *Der Deutschunterricht* 6(92): 8–42.

Schläpfer, Rudolf (ed.)
1982 *Die Viersprachige Schweiz*. Zürich: Benziger.

Schmid, Heinrich
1982 *Richtlinien für die Gestaltung einer gesamtbünderromanischen Schriftsprache, Rumantsch Grischun*. Zürich: Langenscheidt.

1989 *Eine einheitliche Schriftsprache: Luxus oder Notwendigkeit? Zum Problem der überregionalen Normierung bei Kleinsprachen. Erfahrungen in Graubünden*. San Martin de Tor: Istitut Ladin "Micurà de Rü".

Steinberg, Jonathan
1976 *Why Switzerland?* London: Cambridge University Press.

Viletta, R.
1984 Die Rätoromanen. Geduldetes Relikt oder gleichberechtigter Teil der Eidgenossenschaft? In: Cattani, A. and A. A. Hälser (eds.), *Minderheiten in der Schweiz. Toleranz auf dem Prüfstand.* Zürich: Verlag "Neue Zürcher Zeitung".

Watts, Richard J.
1988 Language, dialect and national identity in Switzerland. *Multilingua* 7: 313–334.

1991 Linguistic minorities and language conflict in Switzerland: Learning from the Swiss experience. In: Coulmas, Florian (ed.), *Language Policy for the European Community*. Berlin: Mouton, 75–101.

1996 Schweizerische Identität und der schweizerische Beitrag an Europa: Aus der Sicht eines Ausländers. In: Linder, Wolf, Prisca Lanfranchi and Ewald Weibel (eds.), *Schweizer Eigenart — eigenartige Schweiz. Der Kleinstaat im Kräftefeld der europäischen Integration.* Bern: Haupt, 129–142.

1997 Language policies and education in Switzerland. In: Watts, Richard J. and Jerzy J. Smolicz (eds.), *Cultural Democracy and Ethnic Pluralism: Multicultural and Multilingual Policies in Education.* Frankfurt: Lang, 271–302.

Werlen, Erika and Karl Ernst
1993 Zwischen Muttersprache und Fremdsprache: Hochdeutscherwerb in der deutschsprachigen Schweiz. Empirische Zugänge zum schulischen Aspekt. In: Werlen, Iwar (ed.), *Schweizer Soziolinguistik — Soziolinguistik der Schweiz*. Special issue of *Bulletin CILA* 58: 202–212.
1994 Dialektale und hochsprachliche Kommunikationskultur von Schulkindern. Hypothesen und Zugänge. In: Burger, Harald and Annelies Häcki Buhofer (eds.), *Sprachwerwerb im Spannungsfeld von Dialekt und Hochsprache*. Bern: Lang, 215–241.

Werlen, Iwar (ed.)
1993 *Schweizer Soziolinguistik — Soziolinguistik der Schweiz*. Special issue of *Bulletin CILA* 58.

Werlen, Iwar, Jürgen Oelkers, Martina Späni, Richard J. Watts, Jakob Wüest, Johanna Ziberi and Hansmartin Zimmermann
1997 "*Zweitsprachunterricht im obligatorischen Schulsystem*". *Schlussbericht.* Bern (mimeo).

Language ideological debates in an Olympic city: Barcelona 1992–1996

Susan M. DiGiacomo

1. Introduction

This chapter follows the debate over language set off by the 1992 Olympic Games in Barcelona and its sequels up to 1996, examining a series of relative setbacks and victories through extensive use of journalistic coverage of and commentary on that debate. In this, I want to stress the point that the press is one of the principal sites where the struggle for "authoritative entextualization" takes place (Silverstein and Urban 1996: 11), and that this happens on more than one level simultaneously. Newspapers are self-conscious loci of ideology production. In taking editorial positions on social and political issues, they become actors in ideological debates, quoting and debating each other. The print media also play an important double role in the reproduction of linguistic ideology in at least two ways. First, they are places where public figures (not only political leaders, but such representatives of civil society as educators, intellectuals, activists and others) argue the merits of their positions and the faults of their opponents' positions to the general public directly in interviews and articles in the op-ed pages, and indirectly in news reports. Second, as literal texts they embody a particular ideology of orthography, syntax, and usage (see, for example, the style manual developed by the *Diari de Barcelona*, "Un model de llengua pels mitjans de comunicació", published in 1987, and the recent linguistic guidelines for translation and dubbing published by Televisió de Catalunya). The process of journalistic reproduction itself can occasionally become an object of debate and contention, as it did in the tense negotiations between the Spanish and Catalan electronic media over television broadcast rights to the Games. Newspapers, then, are primary sources of data, and I have always treated them as such in my research on nationalist politics generally, and specifically on language planning and ideology.[1]

As the Catalan literary critic Enric Bou noted in a public lecture (1996), the English-speaking world formed its impressions of Catalonia prior to the

Olympic Games of 1992 in Barcelona through only four of its five senses —taste and smell, sight and touch— aided by the publication of Colman Andrews' excellent book *Catalan Cuisine: Europe's Last Great Culinary Secret* (1988), followed by the art historian Robert Hughes' (1992) social history of urban form, *Barcelona*. Cuisine and architecture, however attractive, are the easily exportable parts of Catalan culture, those that bypass the fifth sense —hearing— required for access to language.

Language, however, was at the heart of a public debate in which all parties had very substantial stakes. Whose Olympic Games were these? Would they belong to the Spanish state, whose calendar of major events in 1992 also included Seville's Expo 92, and Madrid's turn as cultural capital of Europe? Would they belong to the city of Barcelona, whose charismatic socialist mayor Pascual Maragall was having difficulty negotiating some of the other symbols —principally the Barcelona city crest and the Catalan national flag— that were central in defining the identity of the Games (Pi-Sunyer 1995; see Cardona i Martí 1995: 169–188 for a compilation of newspaper articles concerning this highly polemical issue)? And where did the Catalan autonomous government, the Generalitat, and its president, Jordi Pujol, fit into this complex equation of political forces?

Language is the key symbol of what Catalans call *el fet diferencial*, 'the fact of difference' that, whether implicitly or explicitly, underlies all variations of contemporary Catalan nationalism across the political spectrum from the center-right to the left. As Catalans sought to claim the Olympics for Catalonia by making sure that the symbols of Catalan identity (not only the visible ones, such as the Catalan national flag and the heraldic crest of the city of Barcelona, but the ones dependent on that fifth sense: the Catalan national anthem and the Catalan language) were officially and prominently present, countervailing forces both within and outside Spain attempted to minimize the impact of the language on foreign ears. The buildup to the Olympics coincided in time with the resurgence of the Spanish right, which was gaining in respectability as the major political alternative to a socialist government deeply mired in scandal and corruption after a decade in power. As the opening ceremonies drew closer, both ends of the Spanish political spectrum, as if in an effort to outdo each other, became increasingly vocal about Catalan threats to the seamlessly perfect surface of Spanish unity they wished the inaugural celebration to reflect. Literary figures of international distinction, Robert Hughes among them, visited Barcelona and added their own disparaging voices to the chorus of disapproval. Even Catalan political leaders —Mayor Pascual Maragall and President Jordi Pujol— did not see eye to eye on the matter.

All parties had formidably high stakes in the outcome and wanted desperately —as much as the athletes arriving to compete in the Games— to win.

Two sections on antecedent linguistic ideological debates establish the intrinsic historicity of Catalan, and contextualize the present case in the struggle for cultural sovereignty that draws its moral force from resistance to the Franco regime and Catalonia's role in the transition to democracy following the dictator's death in 1975. It is not possible to understand either social patterns of language use, or the ideological uses of language, without sensitivity to time, place, and political circumstances as characteristics of language, not as independent variables affecting language. The emphasis on contemporary history and recent events in an ongoing process stresses the social and political dynamics of language ideological debates, rather than focusing on language as a static and formally defined object.

2. Antecedents: Normalizing social use

Public debate about the relationship between language, nationhood, and political power has been continuous since the transition to democracy following the death of General Franco and his regime in 1975, though its history reaches back to the first stirrings of Catalan cultural nationalism in the early decades of the 19th century. The new Spanish Constitution of 1978 recognized that the transition to democracy required restoration of the political autonomy enjoyed by the three "historical autonomies" —Catalonia, the Basque Country, and Galicia— before the outbreak of the Civil War in 1936. The preamble reads in part,

> The Spanish nation, wishing to establish justice, liberty, and security and promote the good of all those who form it, ... proclaims its desire to ... protect all Spaniards and peoples of Spain in the exercise of human rights, their cultures and traditions, languages and institutions.

Article 3 of the Catalan Statute of Autonomy, approved by referendum in 1979 and ratified by the Spanish Cortes, establishes Catalan, "the language proper to Catalonia", as "the official language of Catalonia, as is Castilian, the official language of the whole of the Spanish State", and charges the Generalitat with guaranteeing

> normal and official use of both languages, adopting all measures necessary to ensure they are known, and creating those conditions which shall make possible their full equality with regard to the duties and rights of the citizens of Catalonia.

During the late 1970s and early 1980s, language ideological debates in Catalonia centered primarily on how to reclaim the social space for Catalan that was lost during the four decades of the Franco dictatorship. Not content with erasing Catalan from the schools, the press, radio and film, public acts of worship, street and shop signs, product labels, restaurant menus, contracts and deeds, and communication by telephone or telegraph, the regime reached even into the intimacy of family life in an effort to eradicate the language (see Benet 1978; Ainaud de Lasarte 1995: 68–69, 75–76; Ferrer i Gironès 1985: 179). Following the Civil War of 1936–39, parents were forbidden to enter the names of their children in the Civil Register in Catalan, and the use of Catalan in inscriptions on tombstones was prohibited.

The language survived underground at first, in conversations among families and friends behind closed doors and in clandestine literary discussion groups, poetry readings, and language classes. As early as the mid-1940s, however, it began slowly, and at great risk to those willing to test the limits of the regime's anti-Catalan policies, to reclaim a public presence through Catalan cultural organizations funded by private contributions; voluntary associations such as choral societies and sports clubs; Catholic groups and institutions, most notably the Abbey of Montserrat; and the growing *nova cançó* (new song) movement (DiGiacomo 1985: 208–217). The music of singer-songwriters such as Raimon and Lluís Llach accompanied forms of resistance that became less testimonial and more pragmatic. By the early 1970s, the identification of cultural resistance with political opposition to the Franco regime was complete and embodied in the *Assemblea de Catalunya*, a large umbrella association uniting political parties, trade unions, intellectuals, artists, and citizen groups. In 1973 the Assemblea created a special commission to develop and launch a campaign in favor of restoring the official status of Catalan. The commission's final report, submitted in January 1974, described this campaign as a "fundamental component of the democratic struggle" (cited in Guardiola 1980: 262–263), a position echoed later in the final document on language prepared by the *Congrés de Cultura Catalana*, founded in 1975. The claim to cultural sovereignty is unmistakable: "Each people has the inalienable right to develop its own personality, and thus its own language and culture" (Congrés de Cultura Catalana 1978: 73).

However, this was more easily said than done. As both the Spanish state and Catalonia recovered their institutions of democratic government in a series of referenda and elections between 1977 and 1980, linguistic normalization debates turned on the question of whether Catalan was already too far down the path to extinction (Argente et al. 1979). During a 20-year period —roughly from 1950 to 1970— large numbers of Castilian-speaking people from the impoverished agricultural regions of Andalusia and Murcia (southern Spain) arrived in Barcelona and its industrial environs in search of jobs (see Recolons i Arquer 1979a and 1979b). The rapid and anarchic development of "immigrant ghettoes" on Barcelona's periphery created social conditions in which it was practically impossible for the "immigrants" to come into normal contact with native Catalan speakers (Strubell i Trueta 1978, 1981). This phenomenon had serious consequences for any program of linguistic normalization in a political context in which the language of the schools, mass media, and officialdom was exclusively Castilian from 1939 until the mid-1970s.

From this time until the early 1980s, i.e. the period roughly corresponding to the Spanish transition to democracy, education was highly contested political ground. Left-wing Catalan parties with ties to state-level parties supported a bilingual policy, arguing that a democratic respect for the rights of individual citizens required that parents should be free to choose education in the child's mother tongue. This was the position of the Catalan Socialist Party, linked to the Spanish Socialist Workers' Party (PSOE), then the main opposition party in the Spanish government; and of PSUC, the Catalan communists with links to the Spanish Communist Party. Their political constituency lay in Spain as well as in Catalonia, and if they were to realize their ambition of sharing power in the central government when PSOE became the ruling party in the next elections, they would have to take care not to seem too partisan about Catalan language rights (DiGiacomo 1985, 1986: 78–80). Catalan nationalist parties from the center leftwards argued that a bilingual education policy, based on the erroneous assumption that Catalan and Castilian occupied separate but equal positions in law and society, was the surest way to finish the work the Franco regime had begun. They proposed instead that Catalan be a required subject of study in all schools as the first step in a process leading to the eventual use of Catalan as the vehicle of instruction (DiGiacomo 1985, 1986). In fact, the complex sociolinguistic realities of Catalan society made both strategies problematic, but in different ways. Despite decades of political persecution, Catalan had retained a strong association with social prestige. However, the etiquette of language choice that developed during the Franco period ensured that Catalan was spoken between native Catalan speakers, but not between native Catalan and native Castilian speakers (Woolard 1984, 1985a and 1985b, 1986, 1989; Woolard and Tae-Joong Gahng 1990).

This phase of the debate reached the height of tension in the spring of 1981. Almost a year earlier, in May 1980, Dr. Aina Moll had been appointed by the president of the Generalitat to the position of director general of language policy, and immediately began to develop an agenda for guaranteeing the "normal and official use" of both Catalan and Castilian through a kind of linguistic affirmative action strategy for Catalan. The reaction came on March 12, 1981 in the form of a "Linguistic Manifesto" (subtitled "For Equal Language Rights in Catalonia") published in a Madrid newspaper, *Diario 16*, and endorsed by a group of 2,300 "professionals and intellectuals", all of whom were Castilian speakers resident in Catalonia. Among the 20 names that appeared in the newspaper (an editorial note pleaded "lack of space" to include all the signatures although, despite the efforts of Dr. Moll to learn their identities as a first step in opening a dialogue, the remaining 2,280 names were never revealed) as signatories to the Manifesto, two were identified as Socialist Party militants, two as militants in the socialist labor union, UGT, and others, like Amando de Miguel and Benjamín Oltra, two sociologists prominent in the intellectual resistance to the Franco regime, were publicly known as Socialist Party adherents. Voices once raised in Catalonia's defense during the Franco years were now raised against what they characterized as the Generalitat's "antidemocratic" and even "totalitarian" plan for linguistic normalization, responsible for an act of "cultural genocide" against "the language of Cervantes" and its speakers in Catalonia, the "immigrants", especially schoolchildren who would be "traumatized" by the use of Catalan as the language of instruction in the schools. The structure of this argument would repeat itself in future episodes of the language debate.

The Manifesto came on the heels of an attempted military coup in February, the last gasp of Spanish fascism: an assault on the Congress of Deputies in Madrid led by Lieutenant-Colonel Antonio Tejero and some 200 Civil Guards, and General Milans del Bosch in Valencia (for an account of events, see Gilmour 1985: 240–246). Four days after the publication of the Manifesto, *Diario 16* (March 16, 1981) ran an article entitled "Recuperemos España" ('Let us regain Spain') explicitly linking the attempted coup not only to "the criminality of some military officers", but also to "our collective weakness in allowing the symbols of our [Spanish] identity to drift aimlessly", and adding that public statements made in response to the Manifesto by Heribert Barrera, then president of the Catalan Parliament, "prove that [anti-Spanish] discrimination exists and is impregnated with aggressive and even racist components". The argument, in the simplest terms, was that the causes of the coup should be sought in Catalan home rule.

The response in Catalonia was swift: an eight-point counter-manifesto headed "Crida a la solidaritat en defensa de la llengua, la cultura, i la nació catalana" ('Call to solidarity in defense of the Catalan language, culture, and nation'), read aloud to to some two to three thousand people who filled the University's main lecture hall, adjacent corridors and central courtyard (the organizers had anticipated a turnout of only two or three hundred people). The original document was signed by 160 representatives of the Catalan world of arts and letters, but the signatures began to multiply rapidly: 6,000 more by March 19, a total of 10,000 bẏ March 26, and, by the end of May, 250,000 individual signatures and 1,300 organizations (Monné and Selga 1991: 34–36). On June 24, Midsummer Eve, traditionally a Catalan celebration, some 90,000 people responded to the same "call to solidarity", filling the Barcelona Football Club's Camp Nou stadium to overflowing in order to affirm beyond any doubt that *Som una nació* ('We are a nation') (Monné and Selga 1991: 48). By that time the Crida had coalesced into a civic movement. A Valencian artist, Joan Genovès, designed a striking logo for it in red and gold: the Catalan flag held aloft by a running human figure. Featured on posters announcing demonstrations, campaigns, and other public activities, the symbol quickly became a familiar sight.

3. Antecedents: Normalizing a linguistic standard

In this atmosphere of broad consensus, the Law of Linguistic Normalization was passed by the Catalan Parliament in 1983, establishing the rights of Catalans to use their language for all official purposes, in education, and in the media. In the same year, TV3, the Catalan-language television channel licensed to the Catalan government, began broadcasting. By the mid-1980s, the terrain of the debate had shifted to questions of linguistic standardization, of what kind of Catalan people should be learning and speaking, reading in the press and hearing on radio and television (DiGiacomo, in press). Correct speech is not a new concern, or even one limited to modern life; the earliest known treatise on what Catalans call "barbarisms" dates to 1487 (Solà 1977: 11). The meaning of incorrect speech has, however, changed from "uncultivated" to inauthentic, from "coarse words and rustic usages" to the substitution of Castilian for Catalan lexical items, and, less obvious to those without the philologist's expert knowledge, the substitution of Castilian for Catalan syntax.

The origins of the modern debate on linguistic correctness lie in the 19th-century beginnings of cultural nationalism. Starting in 1859, the Barcelona city government sponsored a yearly poetry competition, the "Jocs

Florals" ('Floral Games'), a kind of living monument to the greatness of medieval Catalan literature. Controversy broke out almost immediately, and two currents of opinion formed: a linguistic aesthetic that reached self-consciously toward archaisms as the source of authenticity; and the partisans of *el català que ara es parla* ('the Catalan we speak now'): that is to say, a standard for the written and formal registers of the language that located authenticity in everyday spoken usage. When, in the early years of the 20th century, the the philologist Pompeu Fabra undertook the task of developing a modern unified orthographic and grammatical standard for Catalan, he made a consistent and explicit choice to keep the written standard close to the spoken language, *el català tal com se parla* (Fabra 1891, cited in Solà 1980: 53).

In the early 1980s, the 19th-century polemic was brought back to life (Tubau 1990), but animated by a different range of meanings. There was rising concern that the 40-year absence of Catalan from school curricula and the mass media was producing two trends that would be very difficult to reverse: the substitution of Catalan lexical items and syntactic structures by Castilian; and the fragmentation of the language into its four main dialectal variants (Eastern, Western, Valencian, and Balearic; see Fuster 1978: 117). Again, the worst-case scenario was that Catalans themselves would unwittingly bring to completion the program of linguistic genocide the Franco regime began, and that it would be the death of Catalonia as a nation.

In 1986, a maverick socialist politician from Girona, Francesc Ferrer i Gironès, found in the experience of consumer society a particularly apt metaphor for the consequences of his own party's temporizing on Spanish government policies adversely affecting Catalan autonomy. "If 'light' tobacco is without nicotine," he wrote, "if 'light' coffee is without caffeine; if 'light' cola is without sugar, etc., then it is absolutely clear that 'light' nationalism is nationalism without the nation" (1986: 14). The metaphor was almost instantly transferred to public discourse on language planning and linguistic authenticity.

However, considerable pressure had built in favor of the acceptance of spoken Catalan —Castilianisms and all— as the only valid standard against which to measure the authenticity of the written and formal spoken registers of the language. Some of the print and electronic media dismissed the Fabrian standard (the early 20th century equivalent of "light" Catalan, now cast as the "heavy" model) as a straitjacket that imprisons the language in stilted formalisms that constitute a barrier to access, not only for "immigrants" but for native speakers as well (see, for example, *Diari de Barcelona* 1987).

In this debate between the defenders of "heavy" and "light" Catalan, there is a most ingenious paradox at work. Those in favor of "light" Catalan are generally located on the left wing of the political spectrum, many of them Catalan socialists who have made an uneasy peace with a party that governed Spain very much from Madrid for more than a decade, continues to wield substancial influence as the main opposition party. In their eagerness to cast aside "artificial" rules for correct usage, they have returned, in a way, to turn-of-the-century romantic ideas of language as a "natural" expression of nationhood (see Prat de la Riba 1978 [1906]: 76). They would, of course, be surprised to find themselves allied with an ideology that, for them, represents the most politically and socially conservative tradition of Catalan nationalism.

4. Whose games? Symbols of Catalan identity in the 1992 Olympics

Until 1986, then, the outer limits of the frame of reference within which language ideological debates were contained were the boundaries of the Spanish state. The 1992 Olympic Games changed this.

The outpouring of general support for Barcelona's Olympic candidacy by ordinary citizens cannot be accounted for in strictly economic terms, although given the potential profits to be made, it is not hard to understand why the business community enthusiastically supported Barcelona's Olympic candidacy.[3] By the time of the International Olympic Committee's announcement, a group of 96 Catalan entrepreneurs had raised $10 million between them, and banks eagerly offered investments and loans to finance construction and restoration projects (*The New York Times*, October 17, 1986: A4).

The 1992 Olympics gave Catalans a chance to stand on the world stage as themselves rather than as counterfeit Spaniards, an opportunity that simultaneously presented itself through the integration of the Spanish state into the European Community. European unity would, Catalans hoped, reduce the importance of states and make it possible for stateless nations to enjoy a greater degree of cultural and political sovereignty (Concepció Ferrer, "Donar veu a les regions", AVUI, 9 March 1992: 14). Indeed, many Catalans argued that the European Union would surely fail unless it gave nations such as Catalonia, Lombardy, Flanders, the Basque Country, and Scotland the freedom to develop new forms of technological, economic, and cultural cooperation (Albert Alay, "Coherència europea i sobirania", AVUI, 22 April 1992: 13).

Spain elected its first representatives to the European Parliament in the spring of 1987, an election that coincided with the municipal elections in which Pascual Maragall was returned to office as Barcelona's mayor and embarked immediately on a massive six-year program of new construction, urban renewal and restoration for the Olympic Games. Maragall's vision of the European Union is one in which cities and regions assume center stage (AVUI, 9 May 1992: 7), and the theme of his 1987 reelection campaign — *Barcelona més que mai* ('Barcelona, now more than ever')— condensed his hopes and intentions for transforming the city from a point on Europe's southern periphery to a place much nearer the conceptual center as one of the principal stars in the constellation of economically and culturally dynamic cities Maragall calls the *eix mediterrani* ('the Mediterranean axis') (see 'A Survey of Spain: After the Fiesta', in *The Economist*, April 25, 1992: 9), an arc joining Valencia, Barcelona, Marseilles, and the industrial cities of northern Italy: Turin, Milan, and Genoa (cf. Newhouse 1997: 78). In 1992, Maragall's intention to use the Olympics as a springboard to attaining the designation of cultural capital of Europe for the year 2000 was clearly articulated by his lieutenant mayor, Lluís Armet, in an interview published in AVUI (19 August 1992: 7).

The 1992 Olympics quickly became a test for Catalans, perhaps even the greatest test to date, of their cultural sovereignty. The question in everyone's mind, as preparations for the Games accelerated in early 1992, was how Catalan the Spanish central government, the Spanish Olympic Committee (COE), the International Olympic Committee (IOC), and the Barcelona Olympic Organizing Committee (COOB) would allow the Olympics to be. Astonishingly, as late as April, there was still no public information on exactly how, where, and with what frequency the Catalan symbols —flag, anthem, and language— would be deployed (see Josep Espinàs, "Símbols en joc", in AVUI, 1 April 1992: 48). No one seemed to want responsibility for ensuring their presence in the opening and closing ceremonies, where they would have the greatest impact, or in the course of the Games. Joan Antoni Samaranch, the president of the IOC, while agreeing publicly with the president of the Generalitat, Jordi Pujol, that "the reality of Catalonia should be recognized and respected in the Games", said that responsibility for ensuring this belonged properly to the Spanish Olympic Committee and COOB. Carles Ferrer Salat, the president of the COE, speaking both for the COE and COOB, denied any such responsibility (AVUI, 27 March 1992: 44). On April 10, the mayor of Barcelona and president of COOB, Pascual Maragall, met with Samaranch, and announced at a joint press conference that the Catalan flag and national anthem would form part of the opening ceremonies "as planned in the script" (which remained secret). The anthem, "Els segadors", would not, however, be played in the event that a Catalan athlete won a gold medal (AVUI, 11 April 1992: 15). President Pujol expressed his satisfaction with this outcome, but, as a news report the following day (AVUI, 12 April 1992: 17) noted, Maragall and Samaranch would not specify the precise role the Catalan symbols would play in the Games.

This mystery, and the tension surrounding it, remained unresolved until the opening ceremony itself. In September 1988, during the ceremony formally inaugurating the finished Olympic stadium, peaceful demonstrators had had their Catalan flags snatched from them by police and thrown into dumpsters, and the arrival of King Juan Carlos was met with a chorus of angry and derisive whistles. The COOB and COE feared that similar protests would mar the opening ceremonies. Despite official assurances that the flag and the Catalan national anthem would be treated with all due respect, many Catalans feared, as Pilar Rahola wrote in her April 12 column in AVUI (p. 14), that

> The *senyera* [the Catalan national flag] will be flown only as part of a spectacle and the Catalan presence will be reduced to the folkloric. Anthem, flag, symbols, *castellers* [human towers], *sardanes* [the national dance of Catalonia], all in the same package, in a sort of Olympic version of *La comarca nos visita* [a regional folklore program on Spanish television].

As a matter of fact, something very close to this *did* happen during the opening ceremonies, although the composition of the audience in the stadium was not such that the incident provoked a demonstration of protest. "Els segadors" was played toward the start of the inaugural ceremonies, as King Juan Carlos, Queen Sofia, and their two daughters Elena and Cristina took their places in the royal box. As the Catalan hymn played, the King waved and smiled, greeting friends and political leaders seated near the box. But when "Els segadors" ended and the band began to play the "Marcha real", the King assumed the solemn demeanor and respectful posture of one hearing his own national anthem. "Els segadors" had been treated merely as festive music for the entrance of the King, and Catalan reaction ranged from disappointment to undisguised anger (see, for example, Francesc-Marc Àlvaro's column in AVUI, July 28, 1992: 6, and a letter to the editor by Carme Guasch Darné, published in AVUI on 14 August 1992: 9).

Ever since the approval of Barcelona's Olympic candidacy in 1986, there was pressure from citizen groups such as the *Crida a la Solidaritat*, *Òmnium Cultural*, and *Acció Olímpica*, and a political party of increasing importance, *Esquerra Republicana de Catalunya* (ERC), for the IOC to recognize the Catalan Olympic Committee and allow it to select Catalan athletes to compete under the Catalan flag. Joan Antoni Samaranch, president of the IOC and, ironically, himself a Catalan (though one whose rise to prominence in the world of sports is shadowed by his undisguised complicity with the Franco regime) steadfastly refused to countenance such a thing because it would require modification of the Olympic Charter (AVUI, 1 April 1992: 31). However, as Catalans were quick to notice, the IOC permitted, with no modifications to the Charter, the participation of athletes from the countries of the former Soviet Union, wearing the flags of their respective republics, as the "United Team", and made an eleventh-hour decision to reverse an earlier ruling and permit the participation of athletes from Bosnia-Herzegovina as a team under their own flag (AVUI, Olympic supplement, 24 July 1992: 20).

But Catalans did not wait for events to overtake them. On April 23, the day of Catalonia's patron saint St. George (Sant Jordi), a demonstration orchestrated by the youth organization of ERC symbolically re-appropriated the Games for Catalonia by encircling the stadium with a continuous *senyera* (donated by a Catalan cloth manufacturer) more than three kilometers in length, each meter held by a demonstrator. It entered the Guinness Book of Records as the world's longest flag. The arrival of the Olympic flame by boat at the ancient Greek port of Empúries on the northern Catalan coast was met with ceremonies both official and unofficial: members of Acció Olímpica and the Crida a la Solidaritat silently held up large banners reading "Freedom for Catalonia" (in English, for the benefit of the foreign news photographers). The president of the Generalitat, Jordi Pujol, urged Catalans to wave *senyeres* as they watched the Olympic torch pass through the streets of their cities and towns on its way to the stadium. A section in the op-ed pages of AVUI, "Hemeroteca" ('Reading Room'), daily reprinted portions of outraged commentaries on these events in the Spanish press.

The week of the opening of the Games, the Generalitat took out a two-page advertisement in 27 international publications including the *New York Times*, the *International Herald Tribune*, *Time*, *Newsweek*, *Le Monde*, *Stern*, and *Fortune*. It consisted of two maps, the first a blank square showing only Barcelona as a decontextualized point, and below it the question "In Which Country Would You Place This Point?" The second page showed a map of western Europe with no political boundaries except for Catalonia, highlighted in bright red, Barcelona now visible as its capital. The answer to the question —"In Catalonia, Of Course"— was followed by a short text explaining that Catalonia is "a country in Spain with its own culture, language and identity" (see, for example, *Fortune*, July 27, 1992, pp. 213 and 215). An article in the July 30, 1992 edition of AVUI analyzing the response of the Spanish press is titled "Words More Dangerous Than Bombs", a quotation from an article appearing in the news weekly *Cambio 16* of 3 August by José Luís Gutiérrez, comparing Catalan nationalism with the brand of political violence favored by the Basque organization ETA (Basque Homeland and Freedom). *El País*, the liberal Spanish newspaper of record, reported indignantly that the Generalitat had "spent more than 500 million pesetas on its Olympic press campaign" (*El País*, 21 July 1992: 13). *Cambio 16* (27 July 1992, pp. 18–19) retaliated with its own version of the ad, showing a decontextualized Catalonia in red on the first page with the question "In Which Country Would You Place Catalonia?" and on the second page a map of western Europe showing the Spanish state in red, with the answer, "In Spain, Of Course."

5. Cosmopolitan or provincial? The language debate in the context of the 1992 Olympic games

Despite the Barcelona Olympic Organizing Committee's studied unwillingness to take up the issue of the Catalanization of the Olympics, it was criticized in Spain for being *too* Catalan. A little more than a week after the appearance of a column in AVUI (12 April 1992: 14, "Acord olímpic"), in which Pilar Rahola had argued that COOB had opted for the minimum when circumstances would have permitted the maximum, the right-wing Partido Popular weighed in on the subject of language (AVUI, 21 April 1992: 6). Two PP senators representing Guadalajara accused COOB of using Catalan in preference to Castilian in their publications and press communiqués, and suggested that this might be unconstitutional (a favorite strategy of Spanish opponents of legislation passed by the Catalan Parliament). Josep Curto, a deputy representing the PP in the Catalan Parliament, dismissed their remarks as "out of place", and the following day Aleix Vidal-Quadras, the president of the Catalan branch of PP, called them "excessive and alarmist". However, at the same time he took the opportunity to blame not the two senators themselves, but Esquerra Republicana (ERC), the Crida a la Solidaritat, and Acció Olímpica for "provoking" such a reaction (AVUI, 22 April 1992: 9).

As the Olympics approached, there was a more troubling attack on the use of Catalan from within Catalonia. On June 26, 1992, only 29 days before the opening of the Olympics, Xavier Soto, a socialist deputy in the Catalan Parliament, stated in a press release and later confirmed in response to several inquiries that the linguistic normalization policy of the Generalitat "begins to recall the attitude taken toward the Catalan language by the Franco regime", with the terms reversed so that Castilian is now the object of discriminatory policies and practices (AVUI, 27 June 1992: 8). Of immediate concern was the guidebook which the Generalitat was planning to distribute to journalists arriving to cover the Olympics. But Soto went on to say that "this is an affair the Catalan Socialist Party has been aware of for some time, and we no longer believe that it is a matter of involuntary errors, but a deliberate policy".

As the journalist Vicenç Villatoro pointed out the same day in his column (AVUI, 27 June 1992: 12), all parties calling themselves Catalanist had always been united against this accusation of linguistic persecution. Soto's statements to the press broke that consensus, most likely for internal reasons having to do with the troubled relations between Catalan and Spanish socialists in the context of infighting within the Spanish party and its damaging burden of accumulated scandal and corruption charges, some of which threatened the political careers of highly placed Catalan socialists. Nonetheless, it was a significant switching of sides by at least one sector of the Catalan Socialist Party on an issue concerning which it was simply not possible to straddle the fence.

In fact, the use of Catalan during the Olympics in that most important of journalistic media, television, was by no means assured. RTVE (Spanish Radio and Television) had acquired exclusive broadcast rights for the Olympics, and in March 1992, the Catalan Radio and Television Broadcasting Corporation (TVC) was still trying to negotiate with RTVE for the right to broadcast coverage of the Olympic Games in Catalan. Initially, the difficulty seemed to be that the Games could only be broadcast in Europe under the auspices of the European Broadcasters Union (UER), of which RTVE —but not TVC— was a member (AVUI, 11 March 1992: 38). In late April, negotiations were close to the point of breakdown over the price RTVE was asking from TVC for Olympic broadcasting rights (AVUI, 26 April, 1992: 40). On April 29, a majority of the Administrative Council of the Generalitat passed a resolution supporting TVC's efforts to acquire the right to broadcast images of the Games; the socialist representatives on the Council abstained (AVUI, 30 April 1992: 39). By the end of May, TVC still had not been able to arrive at an agreement with RTVE, but was beginning to plan a daily interview program and a nightly news special on the Games (AVUI, 21 May 1992: 47). An agreement was finally signed on 2 July, just 23 days before the opening ceremonies (AVUI, 3 July 1992: 16).

The arrival of a cluster of literary figures in Barcelona just prior to the games added yet another dimension to the debate. Mario Vargas Llosa, the Peruvian writer who ran unsuccessfully against Alberto Fujimori for the presidency of his country, attended a conference of Ibero-American writers in Barcelona in late June 1992. It was a city he had known in the 1970s, when it was still relatively poor. While he was positively impressed by its growth and the wealth embodied in new construction, urban renewal and restoration projects, he also found reason for disappointment. He explained:

> Before, Barcelona represented a great cosmopolitan center in Spain, with its open attitude to culture and its interest in the outside world. ... Now I have the impression, though perhaps I'm wrong, that this attitude has changed. That the greater importance placed on ... defending Catalan peculiarity is what takes precedence, and Catalans are closing themselves off from outside influences as if they were a threat. This would be a tragedy for a city with a great tradition of universalism.
>
> (AVUI, 18 June 1992: 41)

The Catalan novelist and essayist Pere Calders, in his weekly Sunday feature "El davantal" observed,

> I believe, and I too am making use of my right to my own opinion, that Vargas Llosa was referring (in a veiled fashion, in order not to offend) to the Catalans' mania for saving their language. Some people have a very hard time understanding our resistance to sheltering under the protective shadow of the Castilian tongue.... There is something here that we should not ignore: all peoples prefer their maternal language, but Castilian speakers are head over heels in love with theirs.
>
> (AVUI, 28 June 1992)

Vicenç Villatoro, in his column in AVUI (19 June 1992: 12) neatly placed the "provincialism" where it truly belonged, suggesting that perhaps Vargas Llosa's memory of how things really were in the Barcelona of the 1970s had been excessively colored by the passage of time, or that his Barcelona friends were perhaps those who were themselves uncomfortable in an openly Catalan and Catalan-speaking city. In either case, Villatoro argued, Vargas Llosa had committed the entirely human error of treating his own problems as if they were universal.

Other writers were less forgiving. Pilar Rahola, a regular columnist for AVUI and a deputy in the Spanish Cortes for Esquerra Republicana, the only pro-independence Catalan party with parliamentary representation, wrote,

> It seems to me that behind this pretension to universality lies a badly disguised chauvinism. Catalan is perceived as "local" because their Hispanic pride only allows them to perceive it as a second-class language. Catalan "peculiarity" is not quite "culture".
>
> (AVUI, 19 June 1992: 12)

The writer Marta Pessarrodona (AVUI, 1 July 1992: 13), stung into anger and sarcasm by the accusation of "provincialism", declined to name its author:

> My silence recalls that of the author, when he praised the title of one of Maria Aurèlia Capmany's works, *Pedra de toc* ['Touchstone'], only to appropriate it a short time later for a newspaper article without any sort of attribution. After all, why bother to cite a provincial writer?

And as if Vargas Llosa's remarks were insufficiently offensive, the June 11 issue of *The New York Review of Books* —"a publication I love and have subscribed to for the past twenty years," lamented Pessarrodona— carried a review essay by David Gilmour (1992: 6) on Robert Hughes' *Barcelona* and the English translation of Manuel Vázquez Montalbán's *Barcelonas* that ended, rather gratuitously, with the following observation:

> Although Catalonia avoided the political extremism of the Basques, petty provincial extremisms soon asserted themselves. In Barcelona's Picasso Museum, for example, the labels describing the pictures are not printed in English or French or even in Spanish but only in Catalan. Such a gesture antagonizes visitors at the same time that it confirms the city's provincialism.

"A weighty argument, it's true", Pessarrodona continues. "My God, how provincial are the MOMA in New York and London's Tate Gallery (labels in English), and the Louvre in Paris (in French)! ... I want to be as provincial as the whole history of the literature that studies me closely every time I try to make my small contribution to it".

Hughes himself was in Barcelona, having arrived for the formal presentation of the Castilian translation of his book on Barcelona, and made matters worse by delivering himself of the following remark:

> Barcelona ... is a city that has impressed, fascinated, and irritated me. ... What has irritated me the most is a sentiment also found in Australia, a sort of nationalist intellectualism, nostalgic and exaggerated, which is expressed, for example, in the "Freedom for Catalonia" campaign. As if Catalonia weren't already free.
>
> (*El País*, 27 July 1992: 31)

A Catalan reporter quoted Hughes' impatience with "a certain nationalist self-satisfaction that is the result of comfortable living" (AVUI, 25 July 1992: 47). While journalistic assessments of the value of his book were generally positive (there is, after all, no other such serious work on the Catalan capital available in English to the general reader), Catalan observers were also quick to point out its shortcomings; perhaps quicker than they might have been had Hughes not repeated Vargas Llosa's charge of "provincialism". Xavier Moret's article in *El País* (15 July 1992: 23) pointed out that

> In general, Francesc Roca's [Castilian] translation has corrected the abundant errors that might have gone unnoticed by American readers, but would never have been acceptable to readers even slightly acquainted with Barcelona's history.

Francesc Fontbona, a Catalan art historian, observed that the weakest part of the book is the bibliography, and then proceeded to list a few of the many well-known Catalan works on art and architectural history Hughes should have cited (AVUI, 27 August 1992: 11). Again, as Vicenç Villatoro did implicitly and Pilar Rahola explicitly in the case of Vargas Llosa, Fontbona was turning the charge of "provincialism" back at Hughes without using the word itself.

Finally, another Latin American writer, Jorge Edwards, left no doubt that the true source of the foreign visitors' discomfort was language (*La Vanguardia*, 10 July 1992: 6):

> When I came to live in Catalonia at the end of 1973, ... I began to discover, little by little, without any pressure whatsoever, the best of what Catalonia had to offer, from the most humble to the most important; from tomato bread and grilled sardines, let us say, to the spires of the Gothic churches. ... Catalans used to speak with you in Castilian for the sake of courtesy, in the spirit of communication. Now you find with relative frequency —though not always— loquacious professional Catalans trying to impose their language on you by force, while achieving the opposite effect.

The trait that Edwards found so praiseworthy is the very same one that now endangers the process of linguistic normalization from within Catalan society: the peculiar form of diglossia that developed in the repressive atmosphere of the Franco dictatorship, during which, in order to protect themselves, Catalans spoke Castilian automatically with strangers, foreigners or anyone they thought they could identify as a Castilian speaker (see, for example, Prats, Rafanell and Rossich 1994: 95, and Sabater 1992: 23).

6. "Just like Franco, but in reverse": Linguistic normalization and the right-wing Spanish press

Taking note of the accumulation of similar public complaints about the use of Catalan in the context of the Olympic Games by distinguished foreign visitors, Spaniards, and even a few Catalans (see also Balart i Codina 1992), Pilar Rahola wondered in her column if there might be a conspiracy afoot (AVUI 16 July 1992: 10). She concludes that the more likely explanation is a sort of demonstration effect, "a general loss of complexes about certain ideas that were not well regarded in Catalonia —in fact, were the exclusive property of the most marginal variety of Spanish fundamentalism— but remained latent in some sensibilities".

Events during 1993 seem to bear this out. On March 3, Aleix Vidal-Quadras, the president of the Catalan Partido Popular, announced to the press that "I have always been intrigued by the inability of the [Catalan] nationalists to accept that, in private and personal matters, each citizen must be free to choose the language he pleases" (quoted in AVUI, 6 March 1993: 52). "I saw it coming," Joan B. Culla i Clarà wrote in his column in AVUI (8 March 1993: 10).

> In my column of four weeks ago about the ideological face-lift of the Partido Popular, its efforts to project a centrist, moderate image, I warned of the difficulty of coordinating this strategy with Catalan political life, and I predicted a rapid ideological escalation by the ineffable Aleix Vidal-Quadras in his terrain of choice: that of the supposed "linguistic imposition" of Catalan.

In early June 1993, just before the end of the school year, a group of Castilian-speaking parents of children enrolled at a Barcelona public elementary school staged a demonstration to demand "the right of parents to choose the language of instruction for their children", and reject the school's linguistic immersion program for Castilian-speaking children as (according to one parent) "highly negative in pedagogical terms, because it slows down learning, causes children to fail, prevents them from achieving full control of their maternal language and reduces their ability for verbal and abstract reasoning" (quoted in AVUI, 9 June 1993: 20).

"Good heavens!" wrote the Catalan columnist Joan Rendé i Masdeu in mock horror (AVUI, 9 June 1992: 20).

> How dangerous immersion is! If this parent ... is right, then I and everyone else of my generation, who suffered through linguistic immersion in Castilian from our first day at school to our last year at university, ... not just in preschool and elementary school, but for forty years, must be severely and permanently damaged.

But PP wasted little time. On 12 July its executive committee announced the creation of a special commission to look into the question of whether native Castilian speakers in Catalonia, Valencia, the Balearic Islands, Galicia, the Basque Country, and Navarre felt discriminated against by the language policies of these autonomous communities (AVUI, 13 July 1993: 10). "The return of the [Linguistic] 'Manifesto' [of 1981]?" AVUI asked (16 July 1993: 2). Vicenç Villatoro's column in AVUI (14 July 1993: 2) located the origin of this interest in sociolinguistics in the outcome of the 1993 general elections. The Partido Popular had come in second to the Spanish Socialist Workers' Party (PSOE) by the narrowest margin to date. PP had hoped for the support of the Catalan nationalists in the Cortes when the time came to vote for the prime minister, but the deputies representing Convergència i Unió had used their votes to return the socialist Felipe González to office. Outraged, PP was now calling for early elections, certain that it would easily defeat PSOE and punish its Catalan allies the next time.

On Sunday, September 12, 1993, the day after the September 11 Catalan national day, PP rolled out the heavy artillery. A right-wing Spanish newspaper, ABC (which reflects the positions taken by the Partido Popular), ran an enormous front-page picture of the Catalan president, Jordi Pujol, with the following headline (ironic in view of the paper's comfortable acceptance of the Franco regime): "Just Like Franco, But in Reverse: The Persecution of the castilian language in Catalonia". The report inside continued, "The 'Process of Normalization' is not a logical defense of the Catalan language, but an attack on Castilian" (see reproduction of these pages in AVUI, 14 September 1993: 17). The focus of the article was on the place of Catalan in public education, and it was accompanied by large photographs of small groups of parents and their children demonstrating against linguistic immersion programs which, according to the hyperbolic captions, "bring as an immediate consequence the exclusion of Castilian ... in primary education. ... Their children will not know Castilian at all, or will control it so poorly that they will not be able to compete in a world with almost 400 million Spanish speakers". All the parties represented in the Catalan Parliament (even the PP) immediately went on record against these charges, though as Vicenç Villatoro wrote in his column (AVUI, 14 September 1992: 2),

> Talking about this is infinitely exhausting. Personally, what most angers me about the front page of ABC is that it forces us to discuss this piece of foolishness at a time when it would be much more natural to talk about important things, such as the signing of the agreement on Palestinian autonomy. But one has to say something ... so that no one will be able to interpret silence as consent.

Again referring to PP's disappointments in the general elections, he continued, "And this is what I find most disgusting: that for the sake of political games, ... they dig up ghosts, invent falsehoods, and magnify a few isolated hysterical reactions, endangering our greatest source of political capital: peaceful coexistence."

Debate on this affair went on for several months in the press (even the international press), on television, in the Cortes, in the Catalan Parliament, in schools and universities, and in the street. Some of it crystallized around the week-long celebrations in late September in honor of Our Lady of Mercy (La Mercè), the patroness of Barcelona, during which King Juan Carlos and Queen Sofia visited the city to receive its highest honor, the *Medalla d'Or* (Gold Medal), from mayor Pascual Maragall, and to be present for the ceremony dedicating an important street to the memory of the King's father, Juan de Borbón. During Mass in the Basilica of La Mercè, the Archbishop of Barcelona, Ricard Maria Carles, took the opportunity to raise the subject of the attacks on Catalonia in ABC, and to warn that unless political debate became more reasoned and measured, "it could drift into confrontations between persons and peoples". Afterward, during the City Hall ceremony in which the King and Queen received their medal, Mayor Maragall reiterated the need for "respect for the Catalan language and for Catalonia", a statement that was quoted in the newspapers with approval (AVUI, 25 September 1993: 2; *La Vanguardia*, 25 September 1993).

Some days later, however, Pilar Rahola (AVUI, 7 October 1993: 15) observed in her column that while Maragall's words seemed to sound the same note as those of Archbishop Carles, perhaps they were not quite of the same nature. For in the same breath he had hastened to assure the King and Queen that he believed Castilian should also be protected as part of Catalonia's cultural patrimony, a remark he repeated a few days later. In the context of the ABC article and the others that had followed it (for example, AVUI reprinted on 2 October large portions of a particularly aggressive ABC article by Amando de Miguel), this seemed to be an unnecessary offer of aid and comfort to the enemy. Even in the context of the main message of Maragall's speech during the La Mercè festivities — the need for a special city charter for Barcelona— it was unsettling, suggesting that he "administers Catalonia's capital as if it were a city without a nation; aspires to lead a Catalan project, but does not understand it as a *national* project".

Clearly, Rahola had struck an exposed nerve. Her column prompted a harsh critique in highly personal terms from Jaume Sobrequés, a socialist deputy in the Catalan Parliament, describing Maragall's speech as "an immaculate expression of progressive, learned, and European-oriented political Catalanism" and characterizing Rahola as a "pro-independence conservative". Such binary-opposition categories expose, more than anything else, the substantial contradictions from which the Catalan socialists suffer as a party of the left whose Catalanness is constantly being compromised by political subordination to PSOE, whose interests in not only conserving but expanding the power of the Spanish state were embodied in, among other aberrations, an antiterrorist law that violated every generally accepted principle of civil rights, and a secret "dirty war" involving the abduction and murder of individuals suspected of involvement in the Basque organization ETA.

Not content to wait for the PP to announce the results of its inquiries about the persecution of Castilian, Catalan newspapers began to commission their own studies. The results hardly add up to widespread perceptions of a Catalan threat to the continued health of Castilian. *La Vanguardia* discovered that only 26.5 percent of their Spanish respondents believed Castilian to be persecuted in Catalonia; a percentage nearly as great (22.4) had no opinion on the matter, while the remaining 51.1 percent said no. In Catalonia, 84 percent rejected the persecution thesis (*La Vanguardia*, 3 October 1993: 21). Only 30 percent of secondary-school students take most of their courses with Catalan as the medium of instruction (AVUI, 9 October 1993: 16); in primary, secondary, and university education, the use of Catalan as an instructional language hovers around a 60 percent average (AVUI, 24 October 1993: 17); at the University of Barcelona School of Law, less than 40 percent of classes are given in Catalan (AVUI, 9 November 1993: 20).

On 26 September, the Castilian-language Barcelona newspaper *La Vanguardia* published an interview with José María Aznar, the president of the Partido Popular. "Do you believe", he was asked, "that Castilian is now persecuted in Catalonia as Catalan was during the Franco period?" Aznar responded, incredibly, "I don't know what it was like for Catalan during the Franco period. I didn't experience the persecution of Catalan, if in fact it ever happened..." (reprinted in AVUI, 27 September 1993: 12). Asked to explain such breathtaking ignorance on the part of the man who aspired — and was, in fact, later elected—to be the next prime minister of Spain, the newly reelected president of the Catalan PP, Aleix Vidal-Quadras, responded in a manner that was scarcely less surprising:

> Well, let's see. José María Aznar is 40. The period of the repression of Catalan was in the 1940s. Afterwards, things began to loosen up and starting in the 1960s, the truth of the matter is that people spoke Catalan, published in Catalan, there was radio in Catalan. That is to say, there was no more persecution. ... That happened in the 1940s, and Aznar hadn't been born yet. What he means to say is, "I wasn't there".

When the interviewer pressed him for his own view of the matter, Vidal-Quadras said, "No, it's not true that any language is being persecuted in Catalonia" (AVUI, 3 October 1993: 10).

However, Vidal-Quadras also suggested that linguistic immersion programs in schools could be the cause of social conflict (AVUI, 21 October 1993: 13). Perhaps he was thinking of the demonstration shortly after the start of the school year in the coastal resort town of Salou, south of Barcelona, where a group of parents demanded that Castilian be used as the language of instruction (AVUI, 30 September 1993: 22). Somehow, the *New York Times'* European correspondent, Alan Riding, got wind of this. Riding wrote a report undisguisedly sympathetic to the demonstrators, stressing their (groundless) fear of "reprisals", describing the Generalitat's Minister of Education, Joan M. Pujals, as "barely hiding his irritation" as he denied their charges, resurrecting Mario Vargas Llosa's accusation of provincialism, and recalling in shocked tones that the Catalan government "even insisted that Catalan be recognized as an official language ... at the Summer Olympic Games in Barcelona" (*The New York Times*, 23 November 1993). The *International Herald Tribune* reprinted the article on November 24 with an even more inflammatory title than the original, and the following day, AVUI (25 November 1993: 2), in an ironic little note about both reports, suggested that one might have expected a more rigorous standard of accuracy and impartiality in reporting from two such august publications.

Television journalism also made its contribution to the controversy. Several public figures including the Generalitat's Minister of Education, journalists, representatives of the major political parties, and a number of writers and intellectuals, were invited to the studios of the Castilian-language network *Antena 3* for a debate on bilingualism. By the end of the program, all had agreed that Castilian is in no danger from the Generalitat's linguistic normalization policies ... except for the Spanish sociologist Amando de Miguel, whose notoriety had been well established by the Linguistic Manifesto of 1981. He stood firmly behind the argument advanced in that document: the Generalitat was guilty of "linguistic genocide" against Castilian (*La Vanguardia*, 1 October 1993, La Revista: 5). Characteristically, the commentary in Catalan newspapers following the televised debate was ironic rather than angry:

> It is surprising that anyone connected with the media could ask whether in Catalonia it is possible to speak *only* Castilian. ... The reality of Europe is that a large part of its citizens normally use a minimum of three languages. This fact speaks for itself.
>
> (Pere Tió in AVUI, 1 October 1993: 40)

> The great argument [was] that in the modern world there are three or four great languages: English, Arabic, Spanish and Chinese. All the rest are respectable enough, but quite useless in comparison to these. This argument can easily be turned back on itself. What use, for example, is Arabic or Spanish to their millions of speakers in studying economics, unless it is to read material translated from English?
>
> (Emili Teixidor in AVUI, 11 October 1993: 48)

As is often the case, the gentlest but most powerful irony came from the pen of Josep Maria Espinàs (AVUI, 6 October 1993: 48), who took Amando de Miguel to task not for being anti-Catalan, but for being a bad sociologist:

> De Miguel claims that there are "some regions where there are two languages, one which is local, and the other which possesses communicative functions". This is a distinction that should give any student of sociology pause. Is he suggesting that local languages have no communicative functions?

> Another surprising argument is the following: "Castilian is the only language in which Spaniards can communicate with each other". This is false if De Miguel considers Catalans to be Spaniards as well, because it is plain that many Catalans understand each other, and have always done so, speaking Catalan. But it is true if he believes that Catalans are not in fact Spaniards.

It was not the first occasion —nor would it be the last— on which a Catalan took note of the seeming eagerness with which Spanish nationalists demonstrate conclusively the truth of the argument advanced by some Catalan civic groups (most notably the Crida a la Solidaritat) and political parties (especially Esquerra Republicana's youth section, which prints it on T-shirts): "We're not Spaniards, we're Catalans."

7. Epilogue: Interpreting language wars

In late July 1995, José María Aznar, now not only the president of the Partido Popular but also the prime minister of Spain, was in Barcelona on party business. The eminent Catalan historian Josep Benet accepted, though not without reservations, Aznar's invitation to breakfast in one of Barcelona's best and most picturesque restaurants in the hope of opening a dialogue that would remedy the new Spanish political leader's self-confessed ignorance about the post-Civil War repression of Catalonia. Questioned afterwards by reporters, Benet told them the two-hour breakfast had taken place "in an atmosphere of cordiality, sincerity, and mutual respect" (*La Vanguardia*, 21 July 1995: 17). Benet explained to the new prime minister that Spain "must be understood as a plurinational, multicultural, and multilingual entity" and that linguistic normalization was the necessary response to the program of cultural and linguistic genocide attempted against Catalonia by the Franco regime. He also made Aznar a present of his two most recent books, one of which deals with this very subject. In return Aznar offered Benet a copy of his book *Spain: The Second Transition*, and indicated a willingness to continue the dialogue.

At the end of July, a month-long parenthesis opens in the political life of the country as politicians abandon the corridors of power for seaside or mountain holidays (as many of their constituents also do) and prepare at leisure for the opening of the new legislative session in the fall. But on the morning of July 29, Catalans opened their newspapers to read that Aznar had announced that one of his main political objectives would be to "guarantee the constitutional primacy of the Castilian language," a priority second only to the creation of new jobs. In autonomous communities where bilingualism exists, he went on, it is not necessary to undertake any "coercive experiments" promoting the use of local languages (AVUI, 29 July 1995: 11).

This attitude in a Spanish politician of the right was hardly a surprise for Catalans. Josep Benet, questioned by a reporter, said that Aznar is "a typical Spanish nationalist of the Francoist stripe, and the fact that he may occasionally associate with those of us who do not share his views does not mean that he has stopped being one" (AVUI, 30 July 1995: 11). Benet's words sound less harsh in the context of Aznar's own; he characterized Castilian as "Spain's rapid intervention force" (see AVUI's editorial of 30 July 1995: 2). "This is no surprise", Vicenç Villatoro wrote (AVUI, 2 August 1995: 3).

> In the political culture of PP, which is that of the same old Spanish nationalism we have always known, the primacy of Castilian is fundamental. ... But he is cheating, because the Spanish Constitution does not establish any such primacy. ... The primacy of Castilian is part of his party's political project, not a constitutional requirement.

Indeed, as Ignasi Guardans (*La Vanguardia*, 1 November 1995: 19) pointed out, the Generalitat's linguistic normalization law enjoys the blessing of Spain's two highest judicial bodies, the Supreme Court (1994) and the Constitutional Court (1995), as "constitutionally legitimate".

Nor did it astonish anyone, when political life resumed its normal pace in the fall, that Aleix Vidal-Quadras, the president of the Catalan PP and its candidate for president of the Generalitat in the upcoming November autonomous elections, planned to propose that his party's platform should include a position in favor of repealing the Generalitat's 1983 Law of Linguistic Normalization (AVUI, 15 October 1995: 10). However, he was quickly obliged to abandon the proposal in response to public outcry and even some opposition within his own party (AVUI, 18 October 1995: 9; *La Vanguardia*, 19 October 1995: 18). Ostensibly on economic grounds, Vidal-Quadras then proposed the abolition of the Generalitat's *Institució de les Lletres Catalanes*, which promotes Catalan literature and literary scholarship not only in Catalonia but internationally (AVUI, 22 October 1995: 10).

At this writing, debate in the Catalan Parliament on reform of the 1983 Law of Linguistic Normalization is underway. It has occasioned not only the usual protests from the major parties and political figures of both the Spanish right and the Spanish left (and its Catalan allies in PSC; see, for example, an article by Jordi Solé Tura, a former minister of culture in the

Spanish government and currently a socialist deputy in the Catalan Parliament, in *El Periódico*, 26 February 1997: 5), but also conflict between the leaders of the two centrist parties that form the governing nationalist coalition, Convèrgencia i Unió, in the Generalitat. Even a thoughtful journalist whose nationalist credentials have never been in doubt —Vicenç Villatoro, the former editor-in-chief of AVUI— has expressed in print his reservations about a new law of linguistic normalization. Villatoro is concerned that individual citizens' sense of responsibility for the future of their language seems to diminish in direct proportion to the extent that this responsibility is delegated to public administration (AVUI, 12 March 1997: 21). Nor is he alone; a Catalan television producer and journalist who has contributed greatly to the normal use of Catalan in the mass media recently discussed this same concern with me. As in previous phases of the language debate, there are not likely to be winners or losers in any absolute sense. However, the relativities, ambiguities, and contradictions —the raw materials of irony— persist, and shed a certain kind of light on power relations in processes of ideological production and reproduction.

In an article in AVUI (26 August 1993: 11), Pilar Rahola begins by noting that "one of the fundamental principles of journalism —probably one of its most undeniable truths— is that news, by its very nature, is ephemeral". She then proceeds to argue, against this logic of the expiration date, that "the author's importance, ... the seriousness of his argument, and the suspicion that this article was no idle pastime for a summer afternoon ... give me license" to reply in print, some three weeks after the fact, to an article in *El País* (8 August 1993: 9–10) by Mario Vargas Llosa. The latter had used a return visit to Spain as an opportunity to reiterate, in yet stronger terms, the condemnation of Catalan nationalism he articulated on the occasion of the Olympic Games the previous summer. To frame Rahola's argument in Foucauldian terms, her reply is not to a mere news item, but to a "serious speech act" in which she recognizes an underlying "discursive formation", a truth claim taking place "in a context in which truth and falsity have serious social consequences" (see Dreyfus and Rabinow 1982: 48–49).

Vargas Llosa's article is an impassioned defense of the anti-Catalan nationalist thesis advanced by Aleix Vidal-Quadras (1993) in a collection of reprinted op-ed articles to which Vargas Llosa contributed a prologue. The "fundamental question" of the titles of both the book and the article is the intellectual and moral bankruptcy of nationalism, depicted as an appeal to humanity's most atavistic tribal instincts, while civilization, a product of the higher intellectual faculties, moves in the opposite direction toward pluralistic democracy and the emancipation and sovereignty of the individual. Nationalism covers a spectrum ranging from "bloody genocide to the apparently benign 'linguistic normalization'", and although Vargas Llosa concedes that President Pujol is no Radovan Karadzic but a "sensible and tolerant" man, in the last analysis this is of little importance; "however gentle the hand that waves it, the nationalist flag stirs up the basest of human passions".

Rahola's reply draws attention to the odd kinship of ideas that attracts a liberal man of letters to a political project of the right. The contradictory common ground on which they meet is that of Spanish nationalism, the same common ground that united the Catalan socialist mayor of Barcelona, Pascual Maragall, and Joan Antoni Samaranch, the president of the International Olympic Committee and a Catalan who had occupied the quasi-ministerial position of National Sports Delegate in the Franco regime (Balcells 1996: 176), against the Catalan Olympic Committee's request to participate in the Barcelona Games. And the same one that a prominent and much-respected anti-Franco Spanish intellectual resident in Catalonia — the sociologist Amando de Miguel— staked out when he attained a very different kind of prominence as one of the authors of the anti-Catalan "Linguistic Manifesto" of 1981.

The struggle for authoritative entextualization in the language debate — the "fundamental question" posed by Aleix Vidal-Quadras and Mario Vargas Llosa, and addressed by Pilar Rahola— is, I suggest, the struggle between competing definitions of national reality. And I would add that this struggle is not, as Herzfeld (1996: 277) has argued in his analysis of "folk positivism" in the discourse of Greek nationalism, entirely a question of competing essentialisms of a similar order of being. Some essentialisms are more essentialized than others —more naturalized, and thus less "marked" and problematic— and this is the case of Spanish nationalism, because it possesses the state. It is the ironic condition of stateless nations like Catalonia that the "imagined community" (Anderson 1985) is always challenged, by putatively objective scholarship as well as by the state and those who share its interests, as merely imaginary, while the imagined community of state nationalism is treated as objectively real, part of the natural order (DiGiacomo, in press). Catalan journalists and nationalist political leaders persist in speaking of Spanish nationalism precisely because it decenters the taken-for-grantedness of the state and its attributes, exposing their constructedness and suggesting that Spanish identity has no greater claim to truth or reality than does Catalan identity.

I would suggest that the Olympic phase of the linguistic ideological debate, like the debates over maps and the placement and symbolic content of Spanish, Catalan, and Barcelona city flags, generated such extreme tensions, political contradictions, and far-reaching consequences precisely because of the manner in which it called into question the unmarkedness of Spanish state nationalism: not only in the Catalan and Spanish press, but in the international press, in the context of an event of international significance, and at certain important junctures by the deliberate design of both the Catalan government and Catalan civic organizations. To take a single and highly visible example, the Generalitat's cartographic recontextualization in the international press of Barcelona as the capital of Catalonia, "a country in Spain with its own culture, language, and identity", cannot be explained away as an index of Spanish "cultural intimacy", a form of "creative mischief" that "both subverts and sustains the authority of the state" (Herzfeld 1997: 3; 35). The intention was specifically to bracket and refuse complicity in the forms of cultural intimacy upon which the Spanish state and Spanish nationalists tried to insist, to problematize the assumed naturalness and self-evidence of the iconic resemblances on which the nation-state concept is predicated. We can judge the success of the attempt by the outraged responses in even the liberal Spanish press. The news weekly *Cambio 16* (27 July 1992: 18) asked "Where are you, Barcelona? On the eve of the Olympic Games, Jordi Pujol surprises the world with a flourish of ultranationalist vainglory in which Spain is deprived of the Olympics and Barcelona." The article continues, "The long arm of Pujolism reaches everywhere. One day he asks [Catalans] to show respect for the King ... and on the next he urges them to hang only the Catalan flag from their balconies" (20). When the Catalan flag on Barcelona balconies is read in Madrid as a sign of disrespect for the Spanish monarchy, Catalans can be reasonably sure that they are not Spaniards.

Text as an analytic concept has, by now, a long history in cultural anthropology beginning, famously, with Clifford Geertz' conceptualization of culture as an ensemble of social texts —"foreign, faded, full of ellipses, incoherences, suspicious emendations, and tendentious commentaries, but written not in conventionalized graphs of sound but in transient examples of shaped behavior"(Geertz 1973: 10)— and ethnographic interpretation as a "reading" of what is "said" in those "texts." This "text" is a metadiscursive construct, a "way of creating an image of a durable, shared culture immanent in or even undifferentiated from its ensemble of realized or even potential texts" (Silverstein and Urban 1996: 2).

This approach, fruitful as it has been, also reflects an anthropological preference for certain kinds of data over other kinds. Literal (as opposed to metaphorical) texts —literary, journalistic, or scholarly— are seen as secondary rather than primary, products rather than processes. In company with Jaffe (this volume) and Blommaert and Verschueren's recent (1998) analysis of how newspapers contribute to the production of nation-imagining ideologies, what I have tried to do in this chapter is to take such texts seriously as elements in and of ideological practice, following Woolard's (1998: 9) suggestion that conceptions of language are ideological insofar as they are "politically and morally loaded ideas about social experience, social relationships, and group membership."

As in Jaffe's analysis of the translation of French literature into Corsican, writing —in this case, journalism— is a place where Catalans attempt to displace Spanish control. That this contest is not restricted to the Catalan and Spanish press but was played out in the European and North American press as well in the context of the 1992 Olympics is testimony to an ironic feature of language ideology. As Philips (1998: 218) notes in her commentary on Blommaert and Verschueren (1998), the language ideology these authors document assumes that each nation possesses both a culture and a language, but the ideology itself is transnational, shared by mainstream journalism in Germany, Belgium, France, the Netherlands, and Britain, and also by the *International Herald Tribune*, a "western" if not specifically "American" source. This implicit position was the point of departure for all the journalists and commentators who were parties to the Olympic language debate, whether Catalan, Spanish, or foreign, and it made the terms of the debate intelligible to both domestic and international audiences.

The point on which the parties diverged, of course, was that of meaning and value. If ideology, linguistic or otherwise, has been approached as a tool in the contestation of power, it has also been treated as distortion, and the linguistic ideologies of stateless nations perhaps especially so. As Woolard (1998: 8) points out, "even the most doggedly neutral social-scientific uses are tinged with disapprobation," and the highly partisan voices on both sides of the debate I have traced, whether in tones of humor, sarcasm, or outrage, all advance claims about truth and falsity. And this brings me to my own position in the debate. As Jan Blommaert observes in the concluding chapter of this book, I also share with Jaffe and a number of other contributors to this volume a disinclination to hide my own sympathies, which developed in the crucible of the Spanish transition to democracy as it was experienced in Catalonia. One of the first things I learned then is that all interpretations, including scholarly ones, situate the interpreter socially and politically. Assertions of privileged detachment are likely to be read as an implicit defense of hegemonic forces and their dominating power. And my experience with the Olympic language debate, as with others in Catalan political life, leads me to conclude that this reading is accurate.

Notes

1. I read at least one daily Barcelona newspaper, the Catalan-language AVUI, whose editorial views are strongly associated with those of Convergència i Unió, the nationalist coalition that governs the Generalitat (Catalan autonomous government); during election campaigns and other major public events, I read two or three of varying ideological perspectives.
2. Here and elsewhere in the text, translations from Spanish and Catalan are my own.
3. One measure of this is that by October 17, 1986, the day on which the International Olympic Committee announced Barcelona's selection as host of the 1992 Games, some 60,000 individuals had already signed up to work as volunteers, a number that rose to 100,000 in the three weeks following the IOC's announcement (*Diari de Barcelona*, 3 May 1987: 3).

References

Ainaud de Lasarte, Josep M.
1995 *El llibre negre de Catalunya. De Felip V a l'ABC.* Barcelona: Edicions La Campana.

Anderson, Benedict
1985 *Imagined Communities: Reflections on the Origin and Spread of Nationalism.* London: Verso.

Andrews, Colman
1988 *Catalan Cuisine: Europe's Last Great Culinary Secret.* New York: Atheneum.

Argenté, Joan, Jordi Castellanos, Manuel Jorba, Joaquim Molas, Josep Murgades, Josep M. Nadal and Enric Sullà

1979 Una nació sense estat, un poble sense llengua. *Els Marges* 15: 3–13.

AVUI

Concepció Ferrer, "Donar veu a les regions". (9 March 1992: 14).

"TV3 busca l'acord amb TVE per emetre els Jocs". (11 March 1992: 38).

"Samaranch diu que Pujol té raó sobre la catalanitat dels Jocs". (27 March 1992: 44).

"El COE deixa la catalanització dels Jocs a les mans del COI". (1 April 1992: 31).

Josep Espinàs, "Símbols en joc". (1 April 1992: 48).

"La bandera i l'himne de Catalunya seran presents a la ceremònia inaugural dels Jocs". (11 April 1992: 15).

Pilar Rahola, "Acord olímpic". (12 April 1992: 14).

"Satisfacció de Pujol per la presència de la bandera i l'himne catalans als Jocs". (12 April 1992: 17).

"Senadors del PP troben anticonstitucional el progressiu ús del català als Jocs Olímpics". (21 April 1992: 6).

"Vidal-Quadras desautoritza els senadors del PP que van criticar l'ús del català als Jocs". (22 April 1992: 9).

Albert Alay, "Coherència europea i sobirania". (22 April 1992: 13).

"Joan Granados: 'Cada vegada hi ha menys possibilitats que transmetem els Jocs'". (26 April 1992: 40).

"Joan Granados rep suport en la gestió amb RTVE sobre les imatges olímpiques." (30 April 1992: 39).

"Maragall reclama davant Delors un diàleg equilibrat entre ciutats i regions". (9 May 1992: 7).

"Televisió de Catalunya prepara la seva programació d'estiu en funció dels Jocs". (21 May 1992: 47).

"Mario Vargas Llosa diu que 'Europa s'ha convertit ara en el continent jove'". (18 June 1992: 41).

Pilar Rahola, "Provincianisme". (19 June 1992: 12).

Vicenç Villatoro, "Vargas Llosa". (19 June 1992: 12).

"El PSC acusa Pujol de repetir amb el castellà la persecució franquista al català". (27 June 1992: 8).

Vicenç Villatoro, "Ja hi som". (27 June 1992: 12).

Pere Calders, “Llengües i llenguts”. (28 June 1992, Sunday supplement).

Marta Pessarrodona, “Tan provincians”. (1 July 1992: 13).

“Canal Olímpic aplega TVE i TVC en l'empresa que emet els Jocs en català”. (3 July 1992: 16).

Pilar Rahola, “Ofensiva”. (16 July 1992: 10).

“El COI reconeix el Comitè Olímpic de Bòsnia i Hercegovina”. (24 July 1992, Olympic supplement “Barcelona ‘92”: 1 and 20).

“Robert Hughes presenta la versió en castellà del seu polèmic ‘Barcelona’”. (25 July 1992: 47).

Francesc-Marc Àlvaro, “Pacte de Montjuïc”. (28 July 1992: 6).

“Paraules més perilloses que les bombes: determinada premsa de Madrid compara el catalanisme amb ETA”. (30 July 1992: 5).

“‘Els segadors’ i el rei”, letter to the editor by Carme Guasch Darné. (14 August 1992: 9).

Reflexions sobre la Catalunya postolímpica. Interview with Lluis Armet, first lieutenant mayor of Barcelona, by Anna Grau. (19 August 1992: 7).

Francesc Fontbona, “La Barcelona de Robert Hughes”. (27 August 1992: 11).

Ramon Solsona, “Sempre l'han intrigat”. (6 March 1993: 52).

Joan B. Culla i Clarà, “El dependent i el demagog”. (8 March 1993: 10).

Joan Rendé i Masdéu, “Immersió”. (9 June 1993: 20).

“El PP investigarà a les nacionalitats si els castellanoparlants estan sent discriminats”. (13 July 1993: 10).

Vicenç Villatoro, “La discriminació del castellà”. (14 July 1993: 2).

“Torna el ‘Manifiesto’?” (16 July 1993: 2).

Pilar Rahola, “Mario i Alejo”. (26 August 1993: 11).

Viccnç Villatoro, “Això del ‘ABC’”. (14 September 1993: 2).

“L'ABC de la falsedat”. (14 September 1993: 17).

Hemeroteca. Portions of interview with J.M. Aznar reprinted from La Vanguardia, 26 September 1993. (27 September 1993: 12).

“Uns dos-cents pares ocupen una escola de Salou en demanda de classes en castellà”. (30 September 1993: 22).

Pere Tió, “Castellà-català: sumar en comptes de restar”. (1 October 1993: 40).

Interview with Aleix Vidal-Quadras by Lluís Bou. (3 October 1993: 10).

Josep M. Espinàs, "Em comunico amb el lector?" (6 October 1993: 48).

"Unicament el trenta per cent d'alumnes de secundària fan la majoria de classes en català" (9 October 1993: 16).

Emili Teixidor, "Metafísica lingüística". (11 October 1993: 48).

"Vidal-Quadras alerta contra la imposició de la immersió lingüística". (21 October 1993: 13).

"El català no supera el 60% de mitjana a classe". (24 October 1993: 17).

"Menys del 40 per cent de classes de dret de la Universitat de Barcelona es fan en català". (9 November 1993: 20).

"'The New York Times' i la immersió lingüística a Catalunya". (25 November 1993: 2).

"Aznar fixa la primacia del castellà com a gran objectiu del seu govern". (29 July 1995: 11).

"Aznar i l'idioma armat". (30 July 1995: 2 editorial).

"Pujol aconsella a Aznar que canviï l'actitud del PP respecte al català". (30 July 1995: 11).

Vicenç Villatoro, "Primacia". (2 August 1995: 3).

"L'allau de crítiques obliga el PP a frenar l'atac a la llei del català". (15 October 1995: 10).

"Lacalle rebutja la proposta de segregació escolar del PP". (18 October 1995: 9).

"El PP vol suprimir els òrgans de promoció de la cultura catalana a l'exterior". (22 October 1995: 10).

Vicenç Villatoro, "La llei i els costums". (12 March 1997: 21).

Balart i Codina, Pere
1992 *Ser catalán y no ser nacionalista. Penthouse* (Spanish edition) 172: 92–101.

Benet, Josep
1978 *Catalunya sota el règim franquista.* Barcelona: Editorial Blume.

Balcells, Albert
1996 *Catalan Nationalism Past and Present.* London: Macmillan Press.

Blommaert, Jan and Jef Verschueren
1998 The role of language in European nationalist ideologies. In: Schieffelin, Bambi, Kathryn Woolard and Paul Kroskrity (eds.), *Language Ideologies: Practice and Theory.* New York: Oxford University Press, 189–210.

Bou, Enric

1996 La cultura de los prodigios: Catalunya de 1890 a 1990. Paper presented at the symposium "Writing and Cultural Reconstruction in the Basque Country, Catalunya, and Galicia." University of Massachusetts at Amherst and Smith College, October 18–19.

Cambio 16

Juan García and Maria Josep Sangenis, "Dónde estás, Barcelona?" (27 July 1992: 18–21).

José Luís Gutiérrez, "Cataluña y los Juegos Olímpicos". (3 August 1992: 14–15).

Cardona i Martí, Rafael

1995 *El senyal de Catalunya a l'escut i bandera de Barcelona.* Barcelona: Rafael Cardona i Martí.

Congrés de Cultura Catalana

1978 *Congrés de Cultura Catalana, Vol. IV: Manifest i documents.* Barcelona: Curial et al.

Diari de Barcelona

1987 *Un model de llengua pels mitjans de comunicació.* Barcelona: Editorial Empúries.

Diari de Barcelona

"Els voluntaris olímpics seran 'cridats al servei' aquesta tardor". (3 May 1987: 3).

Diario 16

"Por la igualdad de derechos lingüísticos en Cataluña: Manifiesto". (12 March 1981, in the literary supplement *Disidencias).*

"Recuperemos España". (16 March 1981).

DiGiacomo, Susan M.

1985 The Politics of Identity: Nationalism in Catalonia. Ph.D. dissertation, University of Massachusetts at Amherst. Ann Arbor: University Microfilms International.

1986 Images of class and ethnicity in Catalan politics, 1977–1980. In: McDonogh, Gary W. (ed.), *Conflict in Catalonia: Images of an Urban Society.* Gainesville, FL: University Presses of Florida, 72–92.

[In press] "Catalan is everyone's thing": Normalizing a nation. *Meridies.*

Dreyfus, Hubert L. and Paul Rabinow

1982 *Michel Foucault: Beyond Structuralism and Hermeneutics.* Chicago: University of Chicago Press.

The Economist
"A survey of Spain: After the fiesta". (Volume 323, number 7756, 25 April – 1 May 1992).

Ferrer i Gironès, Francesc
1985 *La persecució de la llengua catalana. Història de les mesures preses contra el seu ús des de la Nova Planta fins avui.* Barcelona: Edicions 62.
1986 *Catalunya light...? Els espanyols no són catalans.* Barcelona: El Llamp.

Fuster, Jaume
1978 *El Congrés de Cultura Catalana.* Barcelona: Laia.

Geertz, Clifford
1973 *The Interpretation of Cultures.* New York: Basic Books.

Gilmour, David
1985 *The Transformation of Spain: From Franco to the Constitutional Monarchy.* London: Quartet Books.
1992 Homage to Catalonia. *New York Review of Books*, June 11: 3–6.

Guardiola, Carles-Jordi
1980 *Per la llengua. Llengua i cultura als Països Catalans, 1939–1977.* Barcelona: La Magrana.

Herzfeld, Michael
1996 National spirit or the breath of nature? The expropriation of folk positivism in the discourse of Greek nationalism. In: Silverstein, Michael and Greg Urban (eds), *Natural Histories of Discourse.* Chicago: University of Chicago Press, 277–298.
1997 *Cultural Intimacy: Social Poetics in the Nation-State.* New York: Routledge.

Hughes, Robert
1992 *Barcelona.* New York: Knopf.

International Herald Tribune
Alan Riding, "Catalonians Open A War of Words: In Schools, No More Spanish". (24 November 1993).

Monné, Enric and Lluïsa Selga
1991 *Història de la Crida a la Solidaritat en defensa de la llengua, la cultura, i la nació catalanes.* Barcelona: Edicions La Campana.

The New York Times

"Barcelona, A Four-Time Loser, Wants the '92 Games". (October 17, 1986: A44).

Alan Riding, "Swords Drawn in Spain Over Teaching in Spanish". (23 November 1993)

El País

Xavier Moret, "Las meteduras de pata de un enamorado de Barcelona". (15 July 1992: 23).

"La Generalidad se ha gastado más de 500 millones en su campaña en la prensa internacional". (21 July 1992: 13).

"'Barcelona me ha fascinado e irritado,' dice Robert Hughes". (27 July 1992: 31).

Mario Vargas Llosa, "Cuestión de fondo". (8 August 1993: 9–10).

El Periódico

Jordi Solé Tura, "¿Una nueva ley de la lengua?" (26 February 1997: 5).

Newhouse, John

1997 Europe's rising regionalism. *Foreign Affairs* 76: 67–84.

Philips, Susan U.

1998 Language ideologies in institutions of power: A commentary. In: Schieffelin, Bambi, Kathryn Woolard and Paul Kroskrity (eds.), *Language Ideologies: Practice and Theory*. New York: Oxford University Press, 211–225.

Pi-Sunyer, Oriol

1995 Under four flags: The politics of national identity in the Barcelona Olympics. *PoLAR: Political and Legal Anthropology Review* 18: 35–55.

Prat de la Riba, Enric

1978 *La nacionalitat catalana* [1906]. Barcelona: Edicions 62 i "la Caixa".

Prats, Modest, August Rafanell and Albert Rossich

1994 *El futur de la llengua catalana* (sixth edition, revised and expanded). Barcelona: Empúries.

Recolons i Arquer, Lluís

1979a Els habitants. In: Reixach, Modest (ed.), *Catalunya: Home i territori*. Barcelona: Publicacions de la Fundació Jaume Bofill, 9–77.

1979b El marc demogràfic dels recents moviments migratoris de Catalunya. *Perspectiva Social* 14: 7–34.

Sabater i Siches, Ernest
1992 *Les Paradoxes del català*. Barcelona: Promociones y Publicaciones Universitarias.

Silverstein, Michael and Greg Urban
1996 The natural history of discourse. In: Silverstein, Michael and Greg Urban (eds.), *Natural Histories of Discourse*. Chicago: University of Chicago Press, 1–17.

Solà, Joan
1977 *Del català incorrecte al català correcte. Història dels criteris de correcció lingüística*. Barcelona: Edicions 62.
1980 "El català que ara es parla". *L'Avenç* 27: 47–54.

Strubell i Trueta, Miquel
1978 Immigració i integració lingüística al Principat. *Quaderns d'Alliberament* 2–3: 241–257.
1981 *Llengua i població a Catalunya*. Barcelona: Edicions de la Magrana.

Televisió de Catalunya
1997 *Criteris lingüístics sobre traducció i doblatge*. Barcelona: Edicions 62.

Tubau, Ivan
1990 *El català que ara es parla. Llengua i periodisme a la ràdio i la televisió*. Barcelona: Empúries.

La Vanguardia
Jorge Edwards, "El nacionalismo contra la nación". (10 July 1992: 6).
"El debate del bilingüismo diluye la opinión que ve al castellano perseguido en Cataluña". (1 October 1993, Revista: 5).
"El castellano no está perseguido". (3 October 1993: 21).
"Josep Benet pide a Aznar comprensión y respeto para resolver la cuestión catalana". (21 July 1995: 17).
"El PP propone un vuelco radical en la enseñanza del catalán en primaria". (19 October 1995: 18).
Ignasi Guardans i Cambó, "Jugar con fuego".(1 November 1995: 19).

Vidal-Quadras, Aleix
1993 *Cuestión de fondo (artículos de opinión, 1989–1992)*. Barcelona: Editorial Montesinos.

Woolard, Kathryn A.
1984 A formal measure of language attitudes in Barcelona: a note from work in progress. *International Journal of the Sociology of Language* 47: 63–71.

1985a Catalonia: The dilemma of language rights. In: Wolfson, Nessa and Joan Manes (eds.), *The Language of Inequality*. New York: Mouton, 91–109.

1985b Language variation and cultural hegemony: Toward an integration of sociolinguistic and social theory. *American Ethnologist* 12: 738–748.

1986 The "crisis in the concept of identity" in contemporary Catalonia, 1976–82. In: McDonogh, Gary W. (ed.), *Conflict in Catalonia: Images of an Urban Society*. Gainesville, FL: University Presses of Florida, 54–71.

1989 *Double Talk: Bilingualism and the Politics of Ethnicity in Catalonia*. Stanford: Stanford University Press.

1998 Introduction: Language ideology as a field of inquiry. In: Schieffelin, Bambi, Kathryn Woolard and Paul Kroskrity (eds.), *Language Ideologies: Practice and Theory*. New York: Oxford University Press, 3–47.

Woolard, Kathryn A. and Tae-Joong Gahng
1990 Changing language policies and attitudes in autonomous Catalonia. *Language in Society* 19: 311–330.

Heated language in a cold climate

Monica Heller

1. "Two solitudes"

There is a cliché about Canada which turns up in public discourse again and again, and that is that Canada is composed of "two solitudes", one English-speaking, the other French. The expression comes from the title of a novel by Hugh MacLennan (1945) about life in pre-war Quebec. MacLennan took his title from a poem by Rainer Maria Rilke, in which two solitudes come together, and are united in love. The generalization of the idea to the state of Canada has, however, shifted emphasis away from Rilke's romantic notion, and focuses instead on the seemingly insurmountable obstacles which keep Canada's two major linguistic groups apart. And not just apart; alone, isolated one from the other, unable to share the other's experience, and hence incapable of understanding the other's point of view.

At the same time there is a counterpoint to this image, one symbolized by the opposite pole of Rilke's image and embodied in the vision made popular by former Canadian Prime Minister Pierre Trudeau, of a country in which two groups could live together in harmony and understanding. On the one hand, we can think of Canada as two monolingual societies somehow fated to share the same territory. On the other, there is the reality of having to live together, which has somehow been possible for the last two centuries or so, albeit all the while separate from (even ignorant of) each other, although there is evidence that cohabitation has been paradoxically both harmonious and fraught with strife. Sometimes we talk to each other and achieve what strikes us both as being some kind of understanding. Sometimes we talk to each other but only provoke classic cases of cross-cultural misunderstanding. Sometimes we talk, but our perspectives, informed by different experiences and unequal relations of power, lead to conflict, because our interests are irreconcilably opposed. And sometimes we stop talking to each other altogether.

This is a case where language is important to the image and functioning of nation and state in many different ways. First, as I have suggested, communication between English-speakers and French-speakers (or anglophones and francophones as we like to call them in Canada) is central to any possibility for harmonious cohabitation. Second, for historical reasons, language has become the principal characteristic differentiating groups which clearly think of themselves as distinct. As a result, any inter-group communication is shot through with the political significance of the choice of the language in which to interact.

In this kind of terrain, understanding what people do with language and why they do it is obviously important to the achievement of political goals, that is, to the realization of visions of nation and state on which the possibility for doing other things depends. As a result, it is not surprising that the practice of politics and the practice of various kinds of sociolinguistics in Canada influence each other. It is interesting, although perhaps not surprising, that the nature of that connection is rarely, if ever, discussed or rendered explicit in any way. Clearly, we seem to have something invested in keeping the connection out of the public (or even the private) eye.

My purpose in this paper is to try to break that silence by exploring ways in which ideologies of language, nation and state in Canada have been connected to each other, as well as to the practice of sociolinguistics. In order to do so, I will provide a brief overview of what I consider to be the most relevant dimensions of the historical development of relations between English-speakers and French-speakers in Canada. I will argue that for much of Canadian history since the British conquest in 1759, the relationship between French and English was characterized by an ambivalence over the management of inter-group relations that created the possibility for the maintenance of the social boundary along with the basis for both resistance to the greater power of English-speakers (and hence of English) as well as accommodation to it. In part, these conditions derived from prevailing ideologies of nation and state: for the French, nationalism took a spiritual, ethnic shape, rather than one focused on territory and state. For the English, Canada was understood principally as a component of the British Empire, or later, Commonwealth. Both understood themselves and each other as different "races" or "nations". Under these conditions, there was little basis for direct competition over political, economic or sociocultural resources.

This state of permanent tension was modified in the post-war period, beginning in the early 1960s, with the rise of Quebec territorial state nationalism. Over the last forty years, there has been a new set of permanent tensions in place, derived from new visions of nation and state in Quebec and in the rest of Canada, among French and among English, and which compete with the old visions which have refused to disappear. Québécois nationalism directly challenges the legitimacy of the Canadian state. Perhaps more importantly, its goals have to do with direct competition for the same resources valued by anglophones, and heretofore largely controlled by them.

The conditions of this change have shifted public discourse away from a concern over "race" and "nation", and towards a legitimating ideology of democratic citizenship, without removing at least the concept of "nation" from the core of the legitimating ideologies of state nationalism (no one would dare to talk in terms of "race" any more). But there is a conflict between citizenship and ethnicity as criteria of inclusion, and this has placed language at the centre of post-1960s public discourse on French-English relations.

The major part of this paper will therefore focus on this period, in order to discuss three interlocking processes. The first has to do with the nature of the "new" Quebec nationalism, and the relationship between its ideologies of nation, of state and of language. As in so many other cases, the building of the Québécois state has been accompanied by a focus on linguistic purism, manifested in the valuing of monolingualism (versus bilingualism or multilingualism) in many different ways, and by a concern for language standardization. At the same time, Québécois political mobilization raises certain contradictions. For example, Québécois desires to use political mobilization to gain entry into the modern world necessitate a recognition of the value of English in the global economy. Further, the legitimacy of the state understood as a democratic entity representative of all its citizens necessitates a recognition of the linguistic minorities living in Quebec. And the moral legitimacy of the movement as a strategy for self-determination of a people necessitates recognizing the existence of French-speakers elsewhere in Canada, who, oddly, do not wish to move to Quebec, as well as recognizing the movement's marginalizing impact on speakers of non-standard French.

The second process has to do with the reaction of the federal state, the legitimacy of which (as the representative of all Canadians) is of course directly challenged by Quebec state nationalism. In order to maintain its legitimacy, the Canadian government did two things. First, it entered into the terrain of nation-building first explored by Quebec (hence the flag, the national anthem, and a variety of other trappings of "proper" countries; Breton 1984). Second, it developed an ideology of language and state which valued bilingualism, and which sought to distance itself from ethnocultural definitions of membership (without necessarily finding other ones; hence the endless wringing of hands over Canada's lack of identity). What Canada did, in other words, was to set itself up in competition with Quebec, that is, as an alternative (and somehow better) nation than Quebec, but defined mainly in negative terms; this would be a nation which rejects monolingualism and ethnocultural criteria of belonging.

The third process has to do with the role of linguists and sociolinguists (as well as other students of language issues, such as economists, geographers and demographers) in the management of the first two. This role has been varied; in some cases, academics have actively collaborated in the construction of the Canadian and Quebec states and their legitimating ideologies or else in mobilizing resistance to them, in others they have been constrained by state structures and allocation of resources to work in certain areas, and in still others they have produced critiques of state activity in this area and of their own role in it. Nonetheless it is clear that in some cases their work has been central to the development and implementation of public policy, and in others it has been shaped by it in ways that tend to remain invisible because they are the bureaucratized result of public policy. In all cases, the policies in question, whether federal or provincial, directly derive from the legitimating ideologies of political, social and economic movements. For Canada this means the action and reaction around the rise of Québécois nationalism, and the management of the tensions and contradictions inherent in this state of affairs.

2. 1759 and all that

For many groups, there is an event which takes on the dimensions of an origin myth, an event in the past which is held to have shaped the essence and the destiny of a group, and towards which everyone still orients when thinking about their collective identity. For the British, this is probably the Norman Conquest (hence my sub-title, following a popular satire of British history textbooks, *1066 And All That)*; for the Serbs, it is clearly the Battle of Kosovo in 1389; for the United States, the American Revolution; and so on. The defining moment for the French in Canada, and one that still affects contemporary French-English relations, remains the conquest by the British of New France at the Battle of the Plains of Abraham in 1759. The British interest in New France was partly political and partly economic, as part of the struggle among expansionist imperial powers for world domination; in particular there was a concern for exercising undisputed control over North America and its natural resources, especially, in this instance, of the fur trade (Wolf 1982). But the terrain they conquered had already been settled not just by the native population but also by other Europeans, most of whom were not in any position to go back. Thus began a two centuries long dither about how to deal with the French.

The British had, of course, been fighting with France for years, for centuries, and not just over North America. In many respects, both groups found themselves suddenly having to cope with living with their historical enemy. This became especially dangerous to the British during periods like the American War of Independence, during which the French and the Americans were allied. At the same time, the local French inhabitants had useful knowledge of the land and of the fur trade, which could be usefully exploited; and the French had little choice but to accept the new regime, although of course they did not have to like it.

The legitimizing ideology of imperialism, as has been well-documented, focused (some would say focuses) on the civilizing mission of the imperial powers. This could be, and was at various times and by various people, read in two different ways. At some points, this meant making believers out of the heathen, and bringing the conquered into the fold of the conquering group. At others, it meant maintaining the conquered as a separate, controllable group. In Canada, there were times when the British thought that the best thing to do would be to turn the French into loyal, English-speaking British subjects. There were other times when it was thought best to allow the French to continue to live as French Canadians, as long as they continued to supply the manual labor for the exploitation of primary resources on which Canada's economy was (and in many ways still is) based, and as long as they did not menace the prevailing relations of power.

In the end, the second scenario largely prevailed, although the assimilationist perspective never entirely disappeared. If the British were half-hearted in their occasional assimilation attempts, they nonetheless exerted control in part through their own monolingualism. In order to deal with the structures of political, economic and social power and authority, it was necessary to speak English, or to find someone who did. Thus the British, and later English-speaking Canadians, may rarely have actively campaigned for individual assimilation, but neither were they inclined to accept the existence of institutions beyond their control.

However, the British did permit the persistence of Catholic institutions, which at first were exclusively French (although Irish Catholics came eventually to compete bitterly with the French for control over the Church in Canada). It has been argued that this decision was a strategic one on the part of the British, who sought to exercise control over the French indirectly through their own institutions (Ouellet 1972). For the French this was a compromise which allowed them a certain degree of freedom within structures of British domination.

This institutional separation (for the Church assured education and welfare, and often medical services as well) was accompanied by socio-economic stratification. The French were over-represented among the workers in industries related to primary resource extraction and processing (Canada's economic base; these included forestry and pulp and paper, mining and textiles). There was also a small urban middle class composed of professionals and clerics. On the whole, the French were geographically and socially isolated from the English, although relations between French and English did need to be managed by brokers of some form. There is surprisingly little information about how this happened in Canada's past, although it seems safe to assume that to some extent the boundary was managed by bilingual members of the elite, as well as by those engaged in commerce who either had to deal with both groups as clientele, or else had to articulate relations between English owners and French workers and producers (but see Noël 1990 on the elite's struggle with the British to maintain the use of French). Thus there was space to develop, on the French side, some means of resistance to English domination, or at any rate some means for coping with it. On the English side, this space allowed for the reproduction of relations of power favorable to them, since the French could not compete directly with them for the resources they controlled. At the same time, though, there was the possibility of some kind of collective French threat which the English had to guard against.

Institutional separation also contradicted the imperial rationale for wielding power, that is, that it should lead to the civilizing of the conquered, but in this Canada was not unlike other British colonies where Britain exercised control through local elites rather than through mass assimilation. Still, it was often hard to reconcile the desire to build a dutiful subject nation, member of the British Commonwealth, with the tolerance of such a large group of people within its borders who were unlikely to ever be able to happily think of themselves as British subjects.

The French rationale for accepting the status quo lay in a nationalist ideology which was in fact principally religious. The Church felt that one important way to preserve and propagate the faith among the French was to preserve the language and culture; the motto was "*la foi, la race, la langue*" ('faith, race, language'). Choquette (1987) points out that in Canada we commonly think of the French language as being a privileged path to the Catholic faith; what this belief has produced is, of course, the persistence of the French language itself. The Catholic faith has done as much to preserve French as French has done to preserve Catholicism in Canada. In the following extracts from a text published in 1881 by a journalist named Jules-Paul Tardivel, as cited in Bouthiller and Meynaud (1972: 214–215), we see this link established between language and faith.

> The providential mission of peoples ... Let us take the example of Spain. Isn't it evident that God has wanted Spain to be the mistress of the new continent, that she would control the destinies of America. But Spain has missed her vocation. Instead of working for the spread of the Gospel, she has been concerned only about the accumulation of perishable treasures: she has preferred as her weapon the sword over the Cross. Also, her present influence is inexistent. A handful of impietous republics, caught in civil war, that is the result of her work.
>
> The French Canadian people, small as it might be, undoubtedly has a mission to fulfil in America, a mission analogous to that performed by the French people for a long time in Europe, and which it would have performed for a long time to come if it had not lost itself in the labyrinth of impiety.
>
> The Anglo-Saxon and Germanic races are destined to dominate the continent by virtue of their numbers: this is a fact one has to admit. But the French element also has a role to play.
>
> For centuries, Catholic France has been a source of light, a rich source of generous ideas, a source of inspiration for great works. Only Rome has surpassed it.
>
> Isn't it right to think that the French in Canada have a mission to spread ideas among the other inhabitants of the New World, overly bent on materialism, too attached to earthly goods? Who could doubt that?
>
> But for the Canadian-French people to be able to perform this glorious mission, it has to remain what Providence has wanted it to be: Catholic and French. It has to keep its faith and its tongue in all their purity. If it would keep its tongue and lose its faith, it would become what France has become: a people devoid of its old greatness, a people without influence and prestige. If, on the other hand, it would keep its faith but lose its tongue, it would be blended with its surrounding peoples and would soon be absorbed by them. Individuals would always be able to save themselves, but the mission which Providence seems to have bestowed upon them as a people would be betrayed.
>
> (My translation)

Tardivel's text also points to the way the emphasis on Catholic religious values turned the French away from coveting the material and worldly power and wealth of the English. People today still remember being told in their youth, a few decades ago, that the French in Canada were "*nés pour un petit pain*" ('born for a small loaf'), and that the real rewards would be found in heaven. The effect was to reconcile the French to their lot, and to maintain the power of the Church, on the one hand, and of the English, on the other.

It was the French elite, then, which was largely able to control the definition of what it meant to be French, and to speak French in Canada, through the nineteenth century and into the twentieth. Given the insistence on separateness, and on the importance of the elite, it is not surprising to find a long history in French Canada of linguistic purism (see for example many of the other texts collected in Bouthillier and Meynaud 1972). "*La chasse aux anglicismes*" goes back a long way. The interest in keeping French free of contamination by English was manifested in the way French was taught in schools (anglicisms, for example, were —and are— considered errors), and in columns in newspapers regularly devoted to the subject, as well as to scholarly or amateur publications on the subject. Here is one quote from a 1888 newspaper article by Arthur Buies (cited in Bouthillier and Maynaud 1972: 231, my translation):

> We are infested by anglicism; anglicism overpowers us, drowns us, transforms us and "denatures" us ['nous dénature']. What makes it worse, is that half of the time we are not aware of it, and even worse, that we occasionally refuse to recognize anglicisms when they have been identified to us. We have grown so accustomed to the mixture of the two languages, French and English, that we do not differentiate anymore and that we do not recognize the character, the true nature of each one of them.

Linguistic purism also manifested itself in a concern to purge Canadian French of forms characteristic of the stigmatized working-class. However, there have also long been movements to identify and to preserve what are often called "*canadianismes de bon aloi*", that is, forms invented directly in French (or, occasionally, borrowed from a Native language) to label an object or an activity which did not exist in Europe. Here is a rationale, from a speech given to the Royal Society of Canada by the lawyer and writer Napoléon Legendre in 1884 (cited in Bouthillier and Meynaud 1972: 223, translation mine):

> We, the legitimate representatives of the French language in North America, we have marched with the others and we have put in our share of the work. Why would this work now be put aside, rejected by those who have the mission to study and to judge it? Why would all these expressions that we have been forced to create not be included in the dictionary of the French language, accompanied by a note indicating their place of origin, in the way this has been done for a small number of the terms? That is what I ask; and I firmly believe that we are entitled to it.

These movements can be read as revealing the ambivalent relationship between the French in Canada and the French in France; the latter may act as models, but are often also resented as imperialists almost as oppressive as the English in their contempt for French Canadians. They are also both the source of French Canadian identity, a glorious heritage, and traitors (since the Revolution) to the original cause which brought the French to Canada in the first place. This creates a tension between an acceptance of France as the origin of the value of the French language, and a desire to value what is distinctive about the Canadian variety of the language. The source of the value of French in Canada is both its origins and its distinctiveness. These varied elements of French Canadian linguistic ideology (fear of contamination by English, concern for the "quality" of language, valuing of local forms as long as they are not "jargon", close association with religious values) served to reproduce the relative power of the French elite.

While the social separation of French from English served to reproduce relations of power within the French-speaking community and between the French and the English, at the same time, not only did it create the space for resistance, it created the collective identity on which any kind of collective mobilization might eventually depend (this theme too is present in Tardivel's text, cited above). The French thought of themselves as a French-Canadian nation, as a race, with commonalities wherever they lived across Canada (and even across North America). This collective identity served as the basis for more than one collective uprising against British power (such as that protesting the hanging in the late 19th century of the Métis rebel Louis Riel, or the riots over forced conscription into the British Army in the First World War, or efforts aimed at overturning, or later subverting, Ontario's attempts to prevent schools from using French as a language of instruction). But it was not until the 1950s that this collectivity was able to break through the long-standing inequality which characterized their relations with the British, and indeed bound the two groups inextricably together.

The relationship defined by the Battle of the Plains of Abraham in 1759, and only slightly modified after that, placed the French Canadian clerical and lay elite at the point of articulation between the two groups. They had a vested interest in maintaining their own position of power within French Canadian society, a position which required delicate maneuvering among often contradictory poles. Their power and status were legitimated through an association with the glory of France and of God, and through their ability to keep the British at arm's length without threatening British power. This also required defining French Canada as a distinct nation, in part so as to distance French Canadian society from the secular values of the French Revolution, in part so as to counter-balance British domination of Canada. At the same time, dealing with the British on British terms almost certainly meant speaking more English than perhaps the relatively isolated farmers whose interests they were ostensibly representing (and hence perhaps their own panic with regard to linguistic contamination). The language ideology of the time emphasized distinctiveness and boundedness, the hallmarks of 19th century romantic nationalism. This allowed the French Canadian elite to resist British domination, to link themselves to France while distancing themselves from it, and to claim to legitimately represent the people, whose French was not as good as theirs. But unlike other nationalist movements, this one could not lay claim to territory without directly threatening the British, and this they could not do since their very position of power depended on being the brokers between the British and the French. It was the British who gave their position in French Canadian society meaning and significance.

But this changed after World War II. The religious values, and in particular the religious messianism, which had lain at the heart of French Canadian nationalism fell away. The elite had resources at its disposal which it had not had before, as well as opportunities to use them. By the 1950s, they had begun to re-invent themselves as territorial nationalists, unleashing a change which affects Canadian society to this day.

3. La Révolution tranquille

It is not entirely clear what lay behind the radical shift in relations of power which began to take shape in the 1950s, and which is still unfolding today. While radical, the shift has not been abrupt or violent; hence the appellation "The Quiet Revolution". It has not been violent presumably because it was a revolution from above and not from below. The same lay elite which had been leading French Canadian society for decades, running onto centuries, simply re-invented itself.

There are many theories as to why. One set has to do with the collapse of existing legitimating ideologies, notably that of the Catholic Church (Hobsbawm 1990). Another set has to do with the creation of resources and opportunities for the elite which had previously been non-existent or inaccessible. For example, Clift and Arnopoulos (1979) argue that the financial center of Canada began shifting away from Montreal and towards Toronto after World War II, in part because of the industrial development of southern Ontario (the so-called Golden Horseshoe) as a result of the war, in part because of some astute maneuvering on the part of the Toronto financial elite. This shift caused many members of the English-speaking Montreal financial elite to move west, leaving a vacuum at the management level for the regional market of Quebec. It is also possible that the war created a new industrial base in Quebec (albeit less impressive than that of Ontario), creating a new basis of wealth for the Quebec provincial government, which had always been controlled by the French elite. One might add to this trends towards greater communication, allowing people a better chance to compare themselves to others, attempts to liberalize the Catholic Church across the globe, and other stirrings of liberalization which were to explode in the 1960s as movements for national liberation among colonies and minorities, as feminism, and in the form of many other movements of resistance to old elites and old state structures.

It was a group of intellectuals, among them the future Prime Minister of Canada, Pierre Trudeau, who first began to articulate a new vision of French Canada, in the late 1950s. Their concern was that French Canada was being left by the wayside in the sweep of post-war changes; that French Canada would not be part of the new, modern world, and would not be able to share in its wealth. They also had a commitment to democracy, as the best means for creating equal access to power and wealth in modern society. And yet, French Canadians as a group did not share in power or wealth in Canada. Clearly, the English were mainly to blame for this state of affairs; but so, they argued, were the clergy and the old conservative elite still in power in Quebec City, who had made a fatal compromise with their English-speaking masters. These intellectuals lay the groundwork for a mobilization movement based on common cause between the elite and an emerging middle class, the elite seeking a new power base as leaders of a francophone state and the middle class seeking access to resources previously controlled by the English.

The genius of the new vision was the recognition that in a democratic society where all citizens have a vote, the major source of power French Canadians had collectively was political. At the federal, Canadian, level, this power was diminished by the fact that French Canadians only constituted about one-quarter of the population of the country. However, in Quebec they constituted over four-fifths of the population, and could bring about great changes if they voted as a bloc. The death of the conservative Premier of Quebec in 1959 paved the way for such political changes at the provincial level.

It is the rise to power of the Liberal Party as a result of the elections in 1960 that is commonly held to signal the beginning of the Quiet Revolution. The Liberals took the new vision and made it their own. Their campaign slogan was "*Maîtres chez nous*". They argued that through controlling the apparatus of the Quebec state, they could harness its new wealth to better the lives of French-speaking Québécois, to open avenues to social and economic mobility for francophones, as francophones, in a French-speaking society. French Canadian spiritual nationalism was re-invented as Québécois state nationalism. However, what legitimized it was the subordinate position of francophones as an ethnic group in Canadian society, and the argument that francophones form a distinct nation, which merits its own state. This came to raise a contradiction with which Quebec is still grappling, namely, a contradiction between the ethnic sources of its legitimacy, and the undemocratic nature of the ethnolinguistic ideology of nationalism. A democratic state must represent all its citizens, and in the case of Quebec, not all are ethnic French. But the power of the state of Quebec, as it began to transform itself in this period, lay in its ability to mobilize French-speaking voters as an ethnic bloc.

Over the course of the 1960s, the Liberals systematically worked at the construction of a new, francophone, middle class. They democratized the education system, creating for the first time a broad base of opportunities for young francophones to gain academic credentials, credentials they would need to find jobs in the new economy. They took over provision of services from the Church, and nationalized key industries, notably that involved in the production of hydroelectric power. They thereby assured themselves a continued resource base, and simultaneously provided employment in white-collar civil service jobs for the newly qualified products of the education system. A generation profited from this process, moving from the country to the city, and ascending the ladder of social mobility.

In the 1970s, it became clear that these moves were insufficient. The private sector was still in the hands of the English, and the demographic dominance on which francophone political power depended was being eroded by a plummeting birth rate among francophones and a rising rate of immigration, which tended to contribute to augmenting the English-speaking, not the French-speaking population (there are many reasons for this, going beyond the obvious attraction of English as the language of power in North America and around the world). A series of laws passed by the Quebec government aimed at changing this situation. The first attempts concentrated on the education system, but these failed, since, among other things, education tends to react to values defined elsewhere, not to make them. In 1977 the government took a broader stance, and passed language legislation which is still controversial. However, the most important thing about the new law, from my perspective, is that it focused on making French the language of work. The purpose of this was twofold. The first goal was to facilitate the entry of francophones into the private sector, by allowing them access to jobs without having to learn English, and by privileging a form of linguistic capital which they had, but which most English-speakers did not. The second was to increase the value of French as a form of linguistic capital by harnessing its value to the value of the most important economic resources in Quebec.

Although this language legislation is commonly known as Bill 101, it is important to reflect for a moment on the significance of its real name, "*La Charte de la Langue française*". For a piece of legislation which is actually about economic mobility first and political power second is not phrased at all in those terms. Instead, it is presented as a piece of legislation which is about language. Here is the preface, which sets out the law's underlying philosophy:

> As the distinctive language of a largely francophone people, the French language allows the Québécois people to express its identity.
>
> The National Assembly recognizes the desire of the Québécois to safeguard the quality and the splendor of the French language. It has therefore decided to make French the language of the State and the Law, as well as the normal and habitual language of work, education, communications, commerce and business.
>
> The National Assembly intends to pursue this objective in an atmosphere of justice and openness towards the ethnic minorities, of which it recognizes the precious contributions to the development of Quebec.
>
> The National Assembly acknowledges the right of the Amerindians and the Inuit of Quebec, descendants of the first inhabitants of the country, to maintain and develop their original language and culture.
>
> These principles are in keeping with the universal movement for the revalorization of national cultures, which gives each people the obligation to bring a particular contribution to the international community.
>
> (My translation)

This preface sets out many ways in which a focus on language serves to legitimize economic and political goals, as well as ways in which a particular ideology of language is linked to those goals. The first is to link language and nation in ways that are not clearly ethnic. The Québécois *peuple* is defined as being mainly French-speaking, hence French should be the vehicle of its identity. The text does not, then, limit French to a francophone ethnic group; rather it is to be the distinctive symbol of a nation defined in terms of territory, and more importantly, a particular political structure. The National Assembly makes clear that it must move nationalism away from the ethnic dimension which lay at its source, and towards a form of civic nationalism which is consistent with democratic values. But in order to do so, it must slide quietly from the fact that French is the language of a group of people defined as a people, as a nation, as an ethnocultural group, to setting French up somehow as the property of all citizens of Quebec. What this elides, of course, is the advantage members of the francophone ethnocultural group have as native speakers of French, and as those who control what is to count as French. The contradiction resurfaces elsewhere in the text, which, on the one hand, implicitly recognizes the ethnocultural dimension of making French the language of Quebec by recognizing the rights of "*minorités ethniques*", "*Amérindiens*" and "*Inuit*", and on the other aims at making French everybody's language. Nonetheless, once it is elided in the first paragraph, it is possible to go on and to specify the aims of the law, namely to make French the "normal, habitual" language of Quebec, in keeping with a "universal" movement of national liberation.

What the Quebec government did with this law was to set up an ideology of language and nation which allowed it to avoid confronting the contradiction between the ethnocultural and democratic dimensions of its legitimacy. Anyone can learn a language, and learning one does not have to mean losing another. At the same time, a normal people has the universally recognized right to normal self-determination. And Canada was colonized by the French, as a French nation; their descendants have the right and the duty to uphold that dream (Bouthillier 1994).

The particular vision of language and nation embodied in the Charter is also clearly linked to the political and economic goals of the elite and middle classes at the heart of political mobilization. Quebec should behave publicly as a monolingual zone, and with a language whose quality guarantees the worth of its speakers. Both dimensions are central to the legitimation of Quebec as a French-speaking state, and flow directly from the goals of mobilized Québécois, namely to accede to internationally recognized power and status, as francophones. They set themselves up to compete directly with Canadian anglophones for the same resources, but on new terms. No longer would they compete for access to English; instead they set out to redefine the value of the linguistic capital to which they themselves had privileged access (without, of course, being seen to be doing so).

4. So if they're Québécois, qui sommes-nous?

The rise of Québécois nationalism called into question the legitimacy and identity of two groups: the one million francophones living in parts of Canada other than Quebec, and the federal government. "*Les francophones hors Québec*", as they first came to be called, were obviously directly affected insofar as they had not stopped subscribing to an image of themselves as belonging to a pan-Canadian nation, except that approximately 80% of the members of that nation (those in Quebec) suddenly decided that they were something else instead. This left the remaining 20% or so with an identity crisis (Juteau-Lee 1980). For the federal government, the problem was equally serious, since Quebec directly threatened its legitimacy as the government of all citizens of Canada. The reactions of the two, newly marginalized francophones and the federal government of Canada, are linked, and so I will discuss them together here.

The link lies principally in the attempts on the part of the federal government to redefine its legitimacy on the basis of an ideology of bilingualism. Essentially, the government of Canada had to show that it could represent the interests of anglophones and francophones, and so that therefore it was not in fact necessary to create a monolingual French-speaking independent state in order for francophones to be able to live as francophones, and live well, in North America. It chose to do this by adopting a policy of federal bilingualism, making both French and English official languages of the country, mandating government services in both languages, and financially supporting endeavors to help people learn the second official language of the country (in practice, this almost always meant helping English-speakers learn French, since many French-speakers already spoke English). Needless to say, this was a good thing for minority francophones in the English dominated provinces, who found that the state was suddenly much more sympathetic to their plight than it had ever been before.

The federal government, then, responded to the rise of Quebec nationalism by fostering a new image of Canada. This new Canada had to be seen as everyone's country. This was constructed in two ways. One was to distance the image of Canada away from that of the British Empire, and towards something uniquely Canadian. As Breton (1984) points out, the early 1960s saw the invention of all kinds of new Canadian symbols, the flag and the national anthem being two of the most obvious. The second was to explicitly include francophones as part of the nation by recognizing them as one of Canada's two founding nations, and their language as one of Canada's two official languages. This particular view of Canadian pluralism was quickly extended to include indigenous and immigrant groups, although the relative status of Canada's constituent groups remains a contentious issue. What is perhaps most important to note here is that this view is built on the notion that one can in fact talk about constituent groups as though they were easily identifiable, that is, bounded and homogeneous. Indeed, Canada's favorite image of itself has long been that of a mosaic, in contrast to the American melting pot.

This image of the mosaic has come under fire on two counts. One is that it assumes that all groups are equal, and therefore does not take into account the real relations of power obtaining among them. The second is that the boundaries between groups tend not to be fixed —they tend to overlap— and the groups themselves are usually heterogeneous.

The result is that the federal policy of bilingualism (and multiculturalism) has been viewed with suspicion in several quarters. Francophones tend to fear that it ignores real disparities of power between French and English, putting too much weight on helping English-speakers learn French, thereby helping them to retain their advantage in the marketplace. They also fear that multiculturalism reduces francophones to the status of just another ethnic minority, in ways that also can serve to uphold the power of English as national lingua franca. Immigrants and indigenous groups resent the special status accorded to French, and English-speakers fear the fragmentation of the nation (which one can read as a fear of losing the privileged position that the current arrangement affords them). And within all minority groups there are struggles over who among them gets to define and represent the group, since doing so influences the ways in which the federal government distributes resources designed to advance the federal view and federal interests.

Minority francophones (that is, those in provinces other than Quebec) also find themselves in a position made more complex by their potential for double affiliation to Ottawa (as the capital, "Ottawa" stands in a metonymic relationship to Canada) and to Quebec. On the one hand, it is clear that their improved status is due to pressure emanating from Quebec. In addition, there is strength in numbers, and the more they can make common cause with Quebec, the better their chances of achieving their goals. In fact, a new elite has mobilized in imitation of the Quebec strategy, and lobbied hard over the last fifteen years or so for minority rights. Using the same logic as the Québécois nationalists, they have worked for institutional autonomy (since their demographic dispersion obviates territorial autonomy elsewhere in Canada). The institutional autonomy they have in mind effectively is designed to create the same kind of monolingual francophone social space that Quebec territorial nationalism is designed to create (Heller 1994a). Just as no Québécois would say that one should not learn English, so the official voice of minority francophones values bilingualism. Both hold, however, that as members of a minority, in order to be bilingual, one has to maintain one's first language, and that, in order to do so, monolingual zones are necessary. (Both in Quebec and elsewhere there are dissenting francophone voices who are concerned that such zones may cut off access to the important resource of English; they must seek alternative paths).

On the other hand, the logic of Québécois nationalism precludes the existence of minority francophones, who should, if nationalists are right, disappear, either through assimilation or by moving to Quebec. This is a position which is anathema to many (although by no means all) minority francophones, who have no intention of doing either. As a result, they feel they need Quebec, and should support it, but to support it is to contradict their very existence.

The Québécois vision of unilingualism as the only safe, sane, healthy state for a group of people to live in, profoundly transformed the frame of reference for all inhabitants of Canada. Minority francophones have tried, are still trying, to find a balance between their version of institutional autonomy and the contradictory position they occupy with respect to Quebec's definition of unilingual zones as being fundamentally territorial, that is, linked to political structures. Immigrant and indigenous groups push for a broader and more equitable vision of Canada. The federal government has tried, is still trying, to reinvent Canada as a pluralist, but somehow unified, state, with all the pitfalls of essentialism and naive liberalism that that vision seems to entail.

For all of us, what Quebec did was to push forward language as the terrain on which to carry out our struggles for equitable participation in the resources and power structures of Canadian society. In these struggles, it became useful to legitimize political and economic goals on the grounds of universal truths about language and about the relationship between language and society. Here, of course, "experts" have come to play important roles. In the next section I will explore some of the ways in which research about language has been linked to political ideologies.

5. The politics of the study of language in Canada

The study of language in Canada can be seen as producing legitimating knowledge for political positions. This is the case whether politicians (and others with political goals in mind) justify their positions on the basis of "expert" knowledge about language which was produced in other places under other circumstances, or whether they directly influence knowledge production, influencing research priorities, and putting pressure on researchers (or creating opportunities for them) to gain information which supports their position. In Quebec, as elsewhere in francophone Canada, these processes have tended to produce a focus on the importance of constructing French as a monolingual variety, and of constructing a norm which is somehow both authentic and authoritative. The obverse of this focus has been an equal interest in understanding the obstacles to achieving those goals, whether those obstacles are understood as political, economic, demographic, social, cultural, or linguistic. The federal government and its allies have instead produced a focus on achieving bilingualism, and on its positive cognitive, social, cultural and political effects.

In Quebec, the point of departure is that monolingualism is the "normal" state. One can find thousands of texts which reveal that assumption, whether explicit or implicit, in government documents, in newspaper and magazine articles, in teaching materials, and so on. However, those texts also reveal the work that goes into constructing that assumption, and in nuancing it given the continuing importance of English. That is, it is not possible to take it for granted, nor even necessarily to simply assert, that French monolingualism is the normal state of affairs. For one thing, everyone also wants to learn English; what they do not want is to suffer for not knowing it, or to lose their own language in the process of learning English. For another, not everyone is convinced that you need a monolingual zone in order to accomplish those goals. This has therefore to be justified, usually through the argument that in order to be bilingual one has first to effectively master one's mother tongue, and to be able to use it in a monolingual fashion. Sometimes this argument is simply asserted, but in other instances one does find reference to the psychological literature on language and cognition, and to the sociological literature on multilingualism. Just as one example, here is a short quote from a document produced in 1965 by *l'Office de la langue française*, a Quebec paragovernmental agency whose role is principally to implement government language policy (cited in Bouthillier and Meynaud 1972: 695, my translation):

> Every language is a complex of representations that derives from the grammar as well as from the vocabulary, and by means of which it expresses the mentality of the group of speakers of that language. In its development, a language follows impulses that correspond to the mental demands and the linguistic habits of its speakers.
>
> As soon as, for historical, geographical, economical, psychological or other reasons, these impulses come from without, one can say that the language has entered a critical phase in its development. The linguistic community must then consider itself to be in a state of emergency.

Language contact is here depicted as a threat to the integrity of a language, and hence to the integrity of a nation, a people, as well as to the cognitive and expressive capacities of the members of that nation. The survival of the French nation, depicted as an incontrovertibly important goal, depends on maintaining itself intact, and this depends on maintaining the language, protected from contact with English.

In this perspective, many disciplines have gotten into the act. The survival of French and the survival of the francophone community are seen as two dimensions of the same problem, and therefore one that can be addressed by examining the situation of the French-speaking community and of their use of French and English. The government itself is interested in collecting data on this subject. The census, which as far back as 1871 included a question on ethnicity, now also includes questions on language. A question on mother tongue was added in 1931, and one on language spoken at home in 1971. A question on knowledge of the second official language has also been recently added. Comparisons among these categories of data allow for inferences on patterns of bilingualism, language transfer and assimilation, and have provided endless grist for the mills of sociologists and demographers (cf. Lachapelle and Henripin 1980; Bernard 1988; Castonguay 1996). Essentially what is at stake is showing through census statistics whether or not French is disappearing inside or outside Quebec; whether immigrants and indigenous groups in Quebec learn French or English; and whether English-speakers are learning French. Equally important is associating the patterns discovered with their contexts, notably the relationship between language transfer and exogamy, fertility, socio-economic status, proportion of francophones in the community, or other factors (whether on the basis of census data or other sources of information; see articles in Erfurt 1996, notably those by Vaillancourt on the relationship between linguistic ability and socio-economic status, and Gilbert on the geographical notion of social space and its relation to understanding the reproduction of the francophone community). Each of these issues speaks directly to the concerns of opposing political positions, and serve to support or undermine their arguments and their policies. All assume that it is possible to fairly unequivocally identify some unified thing called a language ("French", "English", and so on), as well as an equally unified thing called an "ethnic group". To do so has however never been easy to do, and has only become more and more difficult as each community has become more and more socially and culturally heterogeneous. Class stratification and social mobility, diversification of economic activities, gender differences, different experiences of schooling, migration and immigration, all contribute to diversifying rather than uniting these groups.

In the search to understand what lies behind these patterns, Canadians have tended to turn towards social psychology (see articles by Landry and Allard as well as by Lepicq and Bourhis in Erfurt 1996). It is assumed that language practices can be understood as functions of individual interest (usually understood as "attitude" or "motivation") and will. The advantage of this conceptualization, both for Ottawa and for Quebec, is that it allows them to maintain the privileging of certain interests while seeming to act in ways that increase access to important resources on a democratic basis. Sociology, anthropology and political science have tended to become engaged in the theorizing of social visions or of relations of power in Canadian society, in which language is not understood as social process, but rather as an essential characteristic, or label.

Thus much of the work on language in Canada, motivated by political interests, takes language as a unified given. Another trend explores language and linguistic processes themselves. Here, interestingly, almost all work has concentrated on the following questions: 1) what do the characteristics of the French language in Canada tell us about its chances of survival and its adequacy as a tool of social development? and 2) how well do people speak French and English, and what contributes to what social psychologists call "additive Bilingualism" (that is, a bilingual repertoire formed of two monolingual-type varieties)? Clearly, the first flows from the interests of francophone nationalists of various kinds, while the second flows from the interests of federalists and to a certain extent of minority francophones.

For the first, linguistics itself becomes important as a diagnostic tool, a way to measure the degree of danger French finds itself in, and to identify important sites and methods of intervention. The same *Office de la langue française* document cited above goes on to analyze the effect of English on French according to the major categories used by descriptive linguistics: phonetics and phonology, morphology, syntax, semantics and the lexicon. It says, further, that "*la morphologie et la syntaxe constituent l'armature de la langue*" ('morphology and syntax are the language's armor'), and that therefore those are the areas where action to uphold the quality of French is most important.

And linguists have indeed become directly engaged in the struggle to make Québécois (or, in some cases, Canadian French, depending on the geographical location and precise political sympathies of the linguist in question) a language to respect, "*une langue de qualité*". This work has been conducted through para-governmental agencies in some cases, notably in the case of linguists (such as Pierre Martel, Jean Corbeil, Denise Daoust, Jacques Maurais and Hélène Cajolet-Laganière) within, or formerly attached to the *Office de la langue française* or its sister agency, the *Conseil de la langue française.* It has taken the form of constructing dictionaries (note the continuity with the desire expressed by Napoléon Legendre in 1884, cited above), inventing technical terminology, writing translation manuals, writing teaching materials, and, generally, debating the importance of developing a Québécois or Canadian norm (cf. Bédard and Maurais 1983; Cajolet-Laganière and Martel 1995). While some, like Cajolet-Laganière and Martel, argue that the construction of a norm is essential to realization of the Québécois dream of national liberation, and to socio-economic power, others like Deshaies (1984) or Maurais (1985) caution that such activities must also be understood as having the potential for creating new relations of inequality (see also Heller 1994a).

In its guise as variationist sociolinguistics, linguistics also became an important tool to demonstrate the legitimacy of the local variety of French as a language. Here the sociolinguistic stance that language is inherently variable, which does not mean it is not rule-governed, served well the interests of a political movement attempting to construct its own linguistic variety as both authentic (only to be found here) and authoritative (as good a language as anyone else's). Here a number of studies have been conducted in Quebec (notably by the team working under Gillian Sankoff and Henrietta Cedergren, and more recently, Gillian Sankoff's student, Pierrette Thibault), in Ontario (notably by Raymond Mougeon) and in the Atlantic provinces (notably by Louise Péronnet, Karin Flikeid and Ruth King; see the article by Mougeon in Erfurt 1996 for an overview of work across all Canada).

Clearly there is something of a tension here, between work focused on legitimating mobilization on the basis of the integrity and authenticity of local linguistic varieties, and work focused on whipping those varieties into shape in order to face the modern world. This tension sometimes takes the form of actual debates, such as that published some years ago in the pages of the Toronto French-language newspaper, *L'Express de Toronto.* Here, a sociologist of communication and a linguist from Laurentian University, Simon Laflamme and Jacques Berger, expressed their view that universities should do extensive work to bring francophone students' linguistic competence up to standard. Two sociolinguists from the Ontario Institute for Studies in Education, Raymond Mougeon and Edouard Beniak, replied that Franco-Ontarian students spoke French that was different, not deficient. Sometimes, however, the tension can be felt within the work of any given sociolinguist or linguist, and in the commentary on it, or work flowing out of it, since both dimensions are real aspects of the reality of francophone life in Canada since the Quiet Revolution (see Heller 1994b for a discussion of how such tensions were played out in the relationship between sociolinguists and the Ontario Ministry of Education officers responsible for curriculum planning in Franco-Ontarian schools). Mougeon (1996: 204 and 206) comments:

> One understands that when they embarked on descriptions of variational phenomena, the sociolinguistic studies of this period attempted to demonstrate that the vernacular usages illustrated the application of rules which differed from those observable in the reference works, but whose logic and social diffusion challenged the idea of the necessity to eliminate them. In doing that, these works tried to have accepted the opposite idea, that the vernacular forms of French in Canada constituted authentic and legitimate linguistic systems and that they were adapted to the communicative needs of their users. ... One must keep in mind that this research has furnished a wide variety of data on spoken French in semi-formal registers, that could hitherto serve as the basis for elaborating norms in the different communities in Canada.
>
> (My translation)

Norms, yes; but norms in the plural, and norms which take into account the sociolinguistic description of authentic francophone vernaculars. This the compromise for which Mougeon argues, and it serves as an example of one way in which sociolinguists can resolve the tension between pressure to promote norms, and the authenticating value of the vernacular.

The federalist perspective places the emphasis on the acquisition of French by English-speakers; in this vein, there is a rich literature dating to the beginning of the Quiet Revolution, although concentrated in the period 1970–1985. Almost all this research lies within the tradition of applied linguistics, with support from social psychology, and most is devoted to the major experiment in second-language teaching to be conducted in Canada, namely French immersion (Heller 1990, 1994a: 85–89; French immersion is a tag for a variety of types of programs which have in common that classes are taught using French as a medium, not simply an object, of instruction).

Most accounts concur that the creation of French immersion programs is linked to the Quiet Revolution and its effects on the value of French in Canadian society. For example, Rebuffot and Lyster document the political mobilization of francophones at that time, and comment:

> In such a climate of revalorization of the language of the majority of the Québécois, the quality of this kind of education becomes a priority, both as a mother tongue in the francophone schools, and as a second language in the anglophone schools.
>
> (Rebuffot and Lyster 1996: 279, my translation)

What we do not learn, however, is how and why the quality of the teaching of French became a priority as a result of the Quiet Revolution. Nor do we learn why the revaluing of French led to a preoccupation among anglophones with how it was taught as a second language at school, whereas (at least in Quebec and parts of Ontario and New Brunswick) access to other ways of learning French through contact with the francophone community was at least theoretically a possibility, both for adults and for children (Heller 1990).

It is clear however that immersion programs across Canada were started as a result of pressure from middle-class anglophone parents, who worked with researchers and the federal government to establish and support these programs at the local level. Neuropsychological, social psychological and psycholinguistic research were bases for arguing for the specific format of immersion:

> Originally, the idea of an initial "language bath" for young children was based on a number of basics. For instance, theories about the flexibility and the maturing of the brain before the age of puberty, about the innate capacity to learn languages, or about the favorable attitude of children towards a different language, have all been influential. Later, emphasis was put on the beneficiary effects of bilingual education from linguistic, cognitive and educational viewpoints, especially when children from majority linguistic groups are concerned.
>
> (Rebuffot and Lyster 1996: 282, my translation)

Parental and governmental concern to establish immersion programs was accompanied by their concern to make sure that the experiment was worthwhile. While a certain amount of attention was paid, at least in the early years, to the effect of immersion on French-English relations, this concern faded rather rapidly from the research agenda, perhaps because the results were less positive than had been hoped (Heller 1990). Instead, research concentrated first mainly on evaluating the extent and nature of learners' proficiency in French, the effect of learning through French in school on English-language proficiency, its sociopsychological effects and its effect on academic achievement (Rebuffot and Lyster 1996: 283). More recently, research has turned to exploring the effect of classroom environment, and in particular of exposure to different kinds of linguistic environments, on proficiency in French. It is evident that the research priority here is measurement and evaluation, and pedagogical intervention, in particular to justify the investment in the teaching and learning of French to which so much time and money has been committed (indeed, it appears that more money at least was invested by the federal government in French-as-a-second-language programs than in programs for minority francophones; Makropoulos 1998). Not surprisingly, research has shown that French immersion is beneficial to English-speaking students, although there is a concern to develop better pedagogical techniques to improve proficiency even more. Little attention has been paid to critiques of French immersion, which argue that since such programs cater to middle-class members of the anglophone majority, all evaluation results must be interpreted in this light (Heller 1990). Even less attention has been paid to the effect of French immersion on the francophone minority; what work there has been has been motivated by the concerns of members of that minority. In the words of one Franco-Ontarian teenager, "*Les anglophones nous ont tout pris, maintenant ils veulent nous prendre notre langue*" ('The anglophones have taken everything from us; now they want to take our language'). This dimension of conflict and competition over linguistic resources is apparent only in the work of francophone minority researchers (see Makropoulos 1998; Bordeleau et al. 1988; Heller 1990).

While both Quebec nationalist and federalist perspectives seem to have impeded the possibility of a critical look at not only the learning of French by anglophones, but more broadly at the social and political dimensions of language contact, precisely such an approach is emerging out of francophone minority contexts. Here, language is treated both as the principal discursive domain in which social and political struggles are waged, but also as a principal means for waging those struggles. There is a concern for examining speakers' representations of language and how these are linked to identity and to relations of power; for understanding the relationship between language practices and the political economy of language; and for understanding the place of language in the construction of community and of social visions, that is, as an element of social movements (see A. Boudreau and Dubois 1993; F. Boudreau and Nielsen 1994; and articles by Heller, Thériault and Cardinal in Erfurt 1996).

Clearly the academic pursuit of knowledge as concerns language in Canada is far from being neutral. It is clearly impregnated with social and political significance from many points of view. The kind of work that gets done is influenced by government policy, which affects what kinds of studies (even what specific studies) the government directly requests or for which it provides funds. Government policy also affects research by creating programs which then generate their own research agenda. Finally, ideologies of language, nation and state stretch far beyond the concrete activity of agents of the state, to influence more broadly the kinds of questions that researchers think are important and interesting, the ways they choose to address those questions, and what, if anything, they choose to do as a result of the knowledge they generate.

6. Borders

Language in Canada is about borders. It is about defining borders, building borders, crossing borders, even ignoring borders, insofar as to deliberately ignore a border you have to accept that there is a border to ignore. The political, social and economic conditions of French-English relations in Canada have shifted over time, even radically since the early 1960s, and yet some dimensions of those conditions and those relations remain the same. The English have always been and remain the most powerful, but need the French in order to sustain that power. The French are able to persist as an identifiable group, and can resist English power, but mainly because the English need them so much. At the same time, because the English are powerful, the French must adapt to them and to their rules. The relationship is one of constant tension, but one which neither group can escape.

In this complex and often contradictory set of relations language plays a greater and greater role. Not only is this the terrain on which borders are constructed, it is also the terrain on which tensions are neutralized, ambiguities constructed, contradictions masked. It is through language that the ideologies of nation and state are produced and reproduced. The Canadian federal government seeks to legitimize itself as the representative of all Canadians by promoting linguistic pluralism, while at the same time it seeks to construct some unifying symbols. To do so requires addressing the real social inequalities that obtain among ethnolinguistic groups, although too often the state opts instead for the discursive construction of a fictive equality. Quebec seeks to legitimize itself as the representative of francophones, and finds itself caught in contradictions between ethnic and civic versions of nationalism. Minority francophones seek to navigate their way between these two competing visions, neither one of which seems to really represent their interests.

In dealing with these tensions, conflict is avoided through the legitimating processes of construction of language ideologies, and through action on the terrain of language, whether that is direct work on what is often called status or corpus language planning (that is, language policy and legislation, or chasing anglicisms, or making dictionaries or teaching French), or more indirectly, doing academic work on language. We have much invested in not examining that action too closely, since one of its primary functions is allowing us to pursue our interests without having to confront contradictions and conflicts. Still, if we don't, then where will we be?

References

Bédard, Edith and Jacques Maurais (eds.)
1983 *La norme linguistique.* Québec: Conseil de la Langue française.

Bernard, Roger
1988 *De Québécois à Ontarois.* Hearst: Le Nordir.

Bordeleau, Gabriel, Pierre Calvé, Lionel Desjarlais and Jean Séguin
1988 *L' Education française à l'heure de l'immersion.* Toronto: Conseil de l'Education franco-ontarienne (Ontario Ministry of Education and Training).

Boudreau, Annette and Lise Dubois
1993 "J'parle pas comme les Français de France, ben c'est du français pareil; j'ai ma *own* p'tite langue." *Cahiers de l'Institut de Linguistique de Louvain* 19: 147–168.

Boudreau, Françoise and Greg Nielsen (eds.)
1994 Les francophonies nord-américaines. *Sociologie et sociétés* 26: 3–196.

Bouthillier, Guy
1994 *À armes égales.* Sillery (Québec): Septentrion.

Bouthillier, Guy and Jean Meynaud
1972 *Le choc des langues au Québec, 1760–1970.* Montreal: Les Presses de l'Université du Québec.

Breton, Raymond
1984 The production and allocation of symbolic resources: an analysis of the linguistic and ethnocultural fields in Canada. *Canadian Review of Sociology and Anthropology* 21: 123–144.

Cajolet-Laganière, Hélène and Pierre Martel
1995 *La qualité de la langue au Québec.* Québec: Institut Québécois de Recherche sur la Culture.

Castonguay, Charles
1996 L'intérêt particulier de la démographie pour le fait français au Canada. In: Erfurt, Jürgen (ed.), *De la polyphonie à la symphonie: Méthodes, théories et faits de la recherche pluridisciplinaire sur le français au Canada.* Leipzig: Leipziger Universitätsverlag, 3–18.

Choquette, Robert
1987 *La foi gardienne de la langue en Ontario, 1900–1950.* Montreal: Bellarmin.

Clift, Dominique and Sheila Arnopoulos
1979 *Le Fait anglais au Québec.* Montreal: Libre Expression.

Deshaies, Denise
1984 Une norme, des normes ou pourquoi pas autre chose? In: Amyot, M. and G. Bibeau (eds.), *Le statut culturel du français au Québec, tome II.* Québec: Éditeur officiel du Québec, 281–290.

Erfurt, Jürgen (ed.)
1996 *De la polyphonie à la symphonie: Méthodes, théories et faits de la recherche pluridisciplinaire sur le français au Canada.* Leipzig: Leipziger Universitätsverlag.

Heller, Monica
1990 French immersion in Canada: a model for Switzerland? *Multilingua* 9: 67–86.
1994a *Crosswords: Language, Ethnicity and Education in French Ontario.* Berlin: Mouton de Gruyter.
1994b La sociolinguistique et l'éducation franco-ontarienne. *Sociologie et sociétés* 26: 155–166.

Hobsbawm, Eric
1990 *Nations and Nationalism Since 1780.* Cambridge: Cambridge University Press.

Juteau-Lee, Danielle
1980 Français d'Amérique, Canadiens, Canadiens-français, Franco-Ontariens, Ontarois: Qui sommes-nous? *Pluriel-Débat* 24: 21–42.

Lachapelle, Réjean and Jacques Henripin
1980 *La situation démolinguistique au Canada.* Montreal: Institute for Research on Public Policy.

MacLennan, Hugh
1945 *Two Solitudes.* Toronto: Collins.

Makropoulos, Josée
1998 *The Status of the French Language and the Development of French Immersion Education.* M.A. thesis, Department of Curriculum, Teaching and Learning, Ontario Institute for Studies in Education, University of Toronto.

Maurais, Jacques
1985 La crise du français au Québec. In: Maurais, Jacques (ed.), *La crise des langues.* Québec: Conseil de la Langue française, 39–84.

Mougeon, Raymond
1996 La recherche sociolinguistique sur le français du Canada. In: Erfurt, Jürgen (ed.), *De la polyphonie à la symphonie: Méthodes, théories et faits de la recherche pluridisciplinaire sur le français au Canada.* Leipzig: Leipziger Universitätsverlag, 183–206.

Noël, Danièle
1990 *Les questions de langue au Québec, 1759–1850.* Québec: Conseil de la langue française.

Ouellet, Fernand
1972 *Éléments d'histoire du Bas-Canada.* Montreal: Hurtubise.

Rebuffot, Jacques and Roy Lyster
1996 L'immersion en français au Canada: contextes, effets et pédagogies. In: Erfurt, Jürgen (ed.), *De la polyphonie à la symphonie: Méthodes, théories et faits de la recherche pluridisciplinaire sur le français au Canada.* Leipzig: Leipziger Universitätsverlag, 277–294.

Wolf, Eric
1982 *Europe and the People Without History.* Berkeley: University of California Press.

The debate on bilingual education in the U.S.: Language ideology as reflected in the practice of bilingual teachers

Sheila M. Shannon

1. Introduction

The Bilingual Education Act of 1968 began a legislative movement in the U.S. to address the education of children in U.S. schools who speak a language other than English. The title suggests that these children are educated through two languages: their native language and English. The amendment to that legislation in 1974 only states that children would be taught in their native language "to the extent necessary to allow a child to progress effectively through the education system." (Schneider 1976 cited in García 1993: 75) The Bilingual Education Act and subsequent legislation address educational equity, not language diversity and use. Schools have been left on their own to determine how languages figure in the equitable treatment of minority language students. The debate on bilingual education has emerged out of this problem. The debate, which has been waged by scholars, educators, politicians, and the general public mainly through the media, is about what form bilingual education should take and the central issue is about the role of the language other than English. This debate has continued over the last thirty years leading to and following from the original Act.

The debate on bilingual education is embedded in the broader debate on the status of English in the U.S. English is the dominant and high status language of the U.S., but there are those (scholars, educators, politicians, and the general public through the media) who have argued that its status should be made official. The history of this question began with the founding of the nation and has continued throughout its building with times, like the present, when it is a major national issue linked to a general nationalist ideology embedded in U.S. history (see Collins, this volume) and re-invigorated during the Reagan years (Billig 1993, 1995). A policy making the status of English official would make the use of other languages problematic. Thus, the debate on bilingual education with its focus on the institutionalization of the use of other languages in the schools draws much of its rhetoric from the official English debate.

The training of teachers for bilingual programs, like teacher training in general, is guided by policies and principles that have emerged from research. For bilingual education, for example, work that identifies effective features and programs that lead to overall academic success for minority language children offers important perspectives for teacher training (e.g., García 1989, 1991, 1992; Ramírez, Yuen, Ramey, and Pasta 1991). Research that has looked beyond the bilingual classroom, however, is beginning to show that the practice of bilingual education is also shaped by language ideologies that prevail at a given time (e.g., Shannon 1995; Wong-Fillmore 1991; Zentella 1990). In the absence of language policy at the federal level and its absence in bilingual education, bilingual teachers rely on language ideology to make sense of their practice.[1]

To understand the debate on bilingual education and its impact on practice, I find a theoretical framework about language hegemony and symbolic domination useful. In this, I draw heavily on the works of Gramsci (1971) and Bourdieu (1991). Language hegemony as used in such a framework can be described as a form of dominance of one language over another. The pattern is quite general; it refers to a macro-social context of languages in competition, and more specifically to the ways in which a society generally ranks the status of the languages spoken within it. Wherever more than one language or language variety exist together, their status in relationship to one another is often asymmetric. One will be perceived as superior, desirable, and necessary, while the other is seen as inferior, undesirable, and extraneous (cf. Shannon 1995: 176).

This article will start from the assumption that the language ideology of English monolingualism is the societal norm in the U.S (following Silverstein 1996). Given the high prominence of Spanish versus English in the American debate on bilingual education, I will focus upon ideologies and practices related to Spanish-English bilingual education. This does not mean, of course, that this is the only debate on bilingual or multilingual education in the U.S. (see e.g. Hymes 1996 for a general argument), nor that the Spanish-English case would be the only *relevant* case in the field of bilingual education in the U.S.[2] Within the framework mentioned above, I sketch how English has achieved its hegemonic status and how Spanish has been relegated to an extraordinarily low status. I then review the main arguments about the role of Spanish in bilingual education. Finally, I present ethnographic evidence of bilingual teachers in practice to illustrate how the hegemonic ideology of English monolingualism emerges in the practice of bilingual education.

2. Language status in the U.S.

The official status of English has been debated since the founding of the nation, although no policy has ever been established at the federal level (Ricento 1996; see Collins, this volume, for a discussion). In her essay "Why no official tongue?", Shirley Brice Heath (1972 [1992]) argues that the new nation's founders associated an official status for English with European monarchy and aristocracy —the things they wanted to get away from— and therefore avoided official recognition of English. Language was thought of in pragmatic terms: building the nation was the work of speakers of several languages, and to designate even the obviously dominant language, English, as singular and official would have alienated important partners in the nation-building process such as the French and German immigrants. Some, however, did argue for an official status for English in some form. In 1780 John Adams, for example, proposed to set up an "American Academy for refining, improving, and ascertaining the English language". (A similar academy never existed in Britain.) His proposal was dismissed by Congress. Adams succeeded, however, in drawing attention to the potential —afterwards amply vindicated (see Phillipson 1992)— that the status of English would have as a world dominant language. He said in his proposal:

> In the last century, Latin was the universal language of Europe . ... In the present century, Latin has been generally laid aside, and French has been substituted in its place, but has not yet become universally established, and, according to present appearances, it is not probable that it will. English is destined to be in the next and succeeding centuries more generally the language of the world than Latin was in the last or French is in the present age.
>
> (Adams 1780 [1992]: 32)

In the late 18th century, however, the vision of a worldwide dominant English was not sufficiently persuasive to convince the Congress to follow Adams' suggestion. Thus English remained an unofficial dominant language, which gradually became so completely hegemonic that the absence of any language legislation in the U.S. surprises observers.

2.1. The status of Spanish

Given the participation of immigrants from all over the world in the construction of the U.S., cultural and linguistic diversity was tolerated if not accepted throughout the early nation-building phases (Higham 1988 [1992]). The bilingual traditions of particularly Germans in the U.S. is evidence of this tolerance and of an historical precedent to bilingualism and bilingual education. It was not until after the first world war that intolerance to immigrant languages began to be witnessed, specifically (and given the context, not surprisingly) aimed at the German language. In contrast to the tolerance towards immigrants' languages, the experiences of Native Americans and Spanish speakers, both residents of the New World, were rather more negative. Colonization and the building of the American nation always involved displacement of Native Americans and aggressive policies aimed at the eradication of their cultures and languages. The Spanish, and later Mexican colonists, were displaced with similar but more covert strategies.

There was scant tolerance for the Native American cultures and languages. The federal government relegated Native American communities to reservations often away from ancestral lands. The government also forced Native American children to leave their families and communities to live in boarding schools. The children were forbidden to speak their own languages or to behave in any way "Indian." The schools had the express purpose of assimilating them thoroughly in the formative "American" culture and the English language (Rheyner 1992). Some mission schools did teach through Native American languages, but never deviating from the goal of getting the children to speak English. The hegemony of English and "Anglo" culture was exercised with impunity by those who believed that this was a benevolent practice, since many shared the assumptions that Native Americans were savages and that civilization was being brought to them through English language and culture.

Westward expansion throughout the 19th century consumed and transformed not only Native American communities, but it also affected Spanish territories and Spanish-speaking communities that had been established over the two previous centuries. Castellanos (1983 [1992]) points out:

> Spaniards held a virtual monopoly over the southern half of this country for one entire century before the arrival of other Europeans ... Spain's domain in the Western Hemisphere between the early sixteenth and nineteenth centuries extended southward to include Mexico, all of Central and South America except Brazil, and most of the Caribbean Islands. It seemed possi-

ble during the sixteenth century that Spanish would become not only the language of the Western Hemisphere, but of the entire world.

(Castellanos 1983 [1992]: 14–15)

Why would a language which at the time shared the status of a world language with German and French have such a low status in the new nation? The reason may be that in the U.S., Spanish was associated with Mexico and not with Spain, and this association facilitated its demotion. Mexico's low status in the U.S. corresponds to the takeover of the northwestern territories of Spain (the U.S. Southwest) in the 19th century and the war with Mexico ending in 1848. Further, the Spanish conquest of what was to become Mexico involved intermarriage with the indigenous population from its earliest times. This practice was not a feature of the Northern European conquest of what is now the U.S. When the Spanish territories broke from Spain, they called the new nation "Mexico", meaning 'mixed people' Thus, the U.S. westward movement overcame the Mexicans with the same racially biased arrogance as the one applied in dealing with the Native American population, and the language of this "mixed" Mexican population was treated along the same inferiorizing lines as its speakers.[3]

Furthermore, the Spanish conquest was both military and religious. Settlements from the 16th century on were typically constructed around a Roman Catholic mission. A religious dimension was characteristically missing from the Northern European conquest and, more importantly, vestiges of anti-Catholic sentiments in the U.S. live on today in presidential voting trends. The U.S. have had only one Catholic (read non-protestant) president elected, and the election of John F. Kennedy was remarkable because he was Catholic. I suspect that this religious factor enhanced (and continues to enhance) views that Mexican-origin people are rightfully awarded low status in the U.S.[4]

Historical accounts of the Mexican experience during the "settling" of the west (e.g. Camarillo 1979; García 1981; Griswold del Castillo 1980) reveal the racist attitudes underlying policy. Schools, for example, were often segregated and the curriculum in those schools was technical rather than academic. García (1981) describes the education of Mexicans in El Paso (Texas) as one in which the students' training was largely confined to personal hygiene and rudimentary technical skills. Whether or not Mexicans spoke English was left up to themselves. Recognizing that speaking English was a way to achieve a higher status, most did so (Barker 1946). Eventually, as Mexican American children attended integrated schools, they were, like the Native Americans, forbidden to speak their home language. They learned English while abandoning their low status language and typically while failing in school.

In his classic study, *Language loyalty in the United States*, Joshua Fishman (1966, in Veltman 1983) reports estimated numbers of speakers of languages other than English, examining changes between 1940 and 1960. Among the largest language groups are German and Spanish. Over the course of two decades the percentage change for German decreased 36.4% while Spanish increased 79.2%.[5] Since 1960,Veltman (1983) reports continued decline for languages other than English, particularly with groups for which immigration is restricted. He also finds that Spanish speakers may retain their language slightly longer, but eventually they too shift to English. On the other hand, the continuous immigration from Mexico and other Spanish-speaking countries (in sociolinguistic terms: a continuous influx of Spanish monolinguals) creates an impression of Spanish speakers being reluctant to learn and speak English.

Spanish speakers live in every state of the Union, but there is a concentration of Mexicans along the border with Mexico, Cubans in southern Florida, and Puerto Ricans in the Northeast. In the last fifty years, the Mexican origin population has become more diffuse. During the 1940s, the federal Bracero Program (a guest worker program) allowed Mexican workers to enter the U.S. legally for seasonal work. When that program was canceled in the 1960s, thousands of Mexicans were well-established in an economy based on migratory working in the U.S. (Bean, Vernez and Keely 1989), while illegal immigration continued to provide an influx of Mexicans in the U.S. Living and working permanently in the U.S. eased the strain of regular illegal border crossings. Eventually entire families reunited permanently north of the border. Some continued in the migratory patterns started in the Bracero Program. Others settled along the migrant stream filling towns and cities from Dallas to Chicago and westward to the state of Washington.

Popular sentiment in the U.S. about illegal immigration from Mexico has always been extremely negative. Recent evidence of the degree of this feeling are the legislative efforts in California to restrict the rights of undocumented residents. The notorious "Proposition 187" was supported by 59% of that state's voters. After the vote, Reynaldo Macías (1995) reported:

> On Tuesday, November 8, 1994, California voters adopted Proposition 187, designed to restrict public schooling, welfare, and non-emergency medical services to persons who are not able to prove their legal immigration or nationality status in the U.S. ... The new law requires public school person-

> nel (including colleges and universities), government workers in welfare offices, and medical personnel to request such documentation before services can be provided. They must also refer and report any such persons or any persons suspected of not being in the country legally, to law enforcement agencies and the Immigration and Naturalization Service of the U.S. Department of Justice. In addition, school personnel are required to report any such persons, or their *parents*.
>
> (Macías 1995: 1)

The strength of this kind of legislation against immigrants has no precedent, and Proposition 187 distinguishes itself for having gone beyond the language question straight to nativism. In California, the state with the largest Latino population within the largest state population in the country, there is no question that the target is Latino.[6] The association of Spanish language with communities of Latinos who are predominantly of (low-status) Mexican origin accounts for the fact that, among minority languages in the U.S., the status of Spanish is one of the lowest.

2.2. The status of English

Although vestiges remain of the early government's reluctance to have an official language policy, the movement to make the status of English official at the federal level in the U.S. began in earnest in the 1980s and coincided with the 1980–1988 Reagan administration. In 1981, a senator and linguist from California, Samuel I. Hayakawa, proposed an English Language Amendment to the U.S. constitution. Although his attempt failed, since then individual states have asked voters for their support making English more or less the official language. Now, more than one third of all states have some constitutional statement about "official" English.

California in particular is a state where language policy is highly relevant. It has a large Mexican and Asian immigrant population, extensive agro-industries with low-skilled workers, and a large school population. Susannah MacKaye's (1987) study of the debate on Proposition 63 —the proposal to make English the official language of that state— provides the typical arguments both for and against such measures. She examined letters to the editor of various major newspapers in California during the debate on Proposition 63. Four key concepts emerged, underlying positions in the debate. Letter writers expressed their beliefs about language as (i) a common bond unifying the nation, (ii) a key to personal and economic success, (iii) a symbol of one's ethnic identity, and (iv) a symbol of nationhood and good citizenship. Those writing in favor of official English in California included Spanish speakers, and voters overwhelmingly supported the proposition.

The following is an excerpt from an editorial that appeared in the *San Francisco Examiner*, October 24, 1986, shortly before voters went to the polls.

> No one should look upon Proposition 63 as an insult to ethnic identity: anyone can retain such identity. This initiative just asserts the obvious —that the citizen who does not become proficient in English is lost in the competition for higher achievement in this state.
>
> Also, it expresses the conviction that the common language is the glue that helps to hold a society together ... The long-term practicalities of national cohesion and the advancement of immigrants in American life, through linguistic assimilation, need to take precedence over temporary emotional responses.
>
> (Crawford 1992: 136–37)

Evaluating the opposition as having "temporary emotional responses" is a standard rhetorical ploy which reduces the weight of the opposition's arguments. The appeal to practicality and unity for society is stated in terms of the benefits for the immigrant. The argument is "this is in everyone's best interests," a classic hegemonic appeal.

MacKaye found that opponents to Proposition 63 argued that unity could be achieved through diversity and that American society benefits from an ideology of multiculturalism and bilingualism. More often, however, she found that opponents were concerned with an underlying racist agenda that such official English measures might have. When similar legislation was proposed in Colorado two years later, an editorial from the *Denver Post* (January 6, 1987 in Crawford 1992) reflects this position.

> More important, the strident rhetoric of the "official language" folks conveys a discouraging air of cultural arrogance that can easily be interpreted as racism by those for whom English is a second language. By inviting thc state to say "shut up" —presumably in a foreign language, so it can be understood— to anyone who walks in the door speaking a foreign language, it offers a phony solution to an exaggerated problem.
>
> (Crawford 1992: 139)

The tone of this argument also dismisses the opposing views with claims of "strident rhetoric," "cultural arrogance," "phony solution" and "exaggerated problem." But the greatest challenge to official English proponents in the editorial is the claim that their agenda is racist.

In writing about the Americanization movement, a general nativist movement of which the official English movement is a part, Joseph Leibowicz (1985 [1992]), a lawyer in New Haven (Connecticut) observes that:

> ... threats to the hegemony of English in the United States may strike at the very heart of our political and cultural institutions. ... But the first important lesson of the Americanization movement must be that attempts to use language for "patriotic ends" must be subjected to the strictest sort of scrutiny, and that elements of jingoism, racism, and xenophobia hiding behind expressed concern for linguistic unity must be identified and rooted out of the debate before proposals to impose English on our official and unofficial life are given any serious consideration.
>
> (Leibowicz 1985 [1992]: 102 and 107)

In the absence of an official language policy and in the debate for such a policy, U.S. society has shifted to an ideology of English monolingualism. But this ideology did not develop independently. It fits within a general nationalistic ideology that became widespread during the Reagan administration. Michael Billig (1993: 70) argues that "[f]ear of communism gave Cold War politicians, such as Reagan and Bush, a moral certainty", as well as a reason to promote an intensely nationalistic ideology. English as a symbol of national identity, pride, unity, support, and devotion became an important feature of this Reaganesque conceptualization of American society.

3. Bilingual education

In his introduction to the 1967 Bilingual Education Act, Texas Democratic Senator Ralph Yarborough (1967 [1992]: 324) argued that schools needed federal assistance for students "whose mother tongue is Spanish." Yarborough was focussed on the persistent educational failure of the children in his state, one with a large and ever increasing Spanish-speaking population. The Bilingual Education Act was passed the following year addressing educational equality for all children whose home language is not English, not just Spanish speakers. The legislation leading to and subsequent to the act has been about the persistent failure of these children in school; it is about children's educational rights.

Lau v. Nichols was the case brought before the Supreme Court in the early 1970s which resulted in what came to be known as the "Lau decision" and "Lau regulations". Although the Bilingual Education Act was in place, the Lau case helped to direct efforts in the education of minority language children. Lau v. Nichols was a class action suit by the non-English-speaking Chinese community against the San Francisco Unified School District. Parents argued that their children were not receiving an equal education because they were being taught in a language they did not understand. Like the Bilingual Education Act, the Lau decision was for something to be done to insure the educational rights of children who arrive at school speaking a language other than English. In formulating the Court's decision, Justice William O. Douglas said (1974 [1992]):

> [T]here is no equality of treatment merely by providing students with the same facilities, textbooks, teachers, and curriculum; for students who do not understand English are effectively foreclosed from any meaningful education. Basic English skills are at the very core of what these public schools teach. Imposition of a requirement that, before a child can effectively participate in the educational program, he must already have acquired those basic skills is to make a mockery of public education. We know that those who do not understand English are certain to find their classroom experiences wholly incomprehensible and in no way meaningful.
>
> (Douglas 1974 [1992]: 253)

Lau and other legislative acts do not specify the form bilingual education should take; they merely state that school districts should make classroom experiences comprehensible to all members of the school population. Legislation has been only about educational rights and not (specifically) about language rights. No one would argue that equal education and the learning of English should not be guaranteed for minority language speakers. It is the role of the minority language in "bilingual" education, which no legislation has dictated explicitly, that is a constant controversy. Thus, it is the one issue that has kept the debate over bilingual education very much alive over the last thirty years. The debate is centered on the role and status of languages other than English in educational institutions —primarily Spanish.

3.1. Opposition to bilingual education

"Hispanics", according to Hawakaya (1985 [1992]), appropriated the Lau decision for themselves (e.g. by hiring Spanish-speaking teachers who could not speak English). Thus, "The only people who have any quarrel with the English language are the Hispanics —at least the Hispanic politicians and "bilingual" teachers and lobbying organizations." (Hayakawa 1985: 99).

Hayakawa, a linguist who became one of the most active campaigners against such regulations, sees bilingual education as a way for Hispanics to make demands and get attention when otherwise they would not have that power to wield. Furthermore, Hayakawa interprets the Lau regulation as internally contradictory in its requirement to teach children English, while teaching them academic subjects in their mother tongue. He apparently takes this regulation to mean that children should be taught English through their home language.

Richard Rodríquez (1985 [1992]), a writer and English scholar whose first language was Spanish, argues that bilingual education is an ideological position taken by middle class Hispanics and foisted on working-class immigrant children. He says that the shift to English and American mainstream culture is one that all children make when they enter school. He does not believe that Spanish belongs in schools. He describes what happened to him as he experienced English at school and Spanish at home:

> I was that child! I faced the stranger's English with pain and guilt and fear. Baptized to English in school, at first I felt myself drowning —the ugly sounds forced down my throat— until slowly, slowly (held in the tender grip of my teachers), suddenly the conviction took: English was my language to use.
>
> (Rodríquez 1985 [1992]: 353)

Similar to Hayakawa's view that Hispanics use bilingual education as a form of resistance, Rodríquez believes that Hispanics seized upon bilingual education as a way to get revenge for their experience of domination in the U.S., what he calls "the injustice of history" (Rodríquez 1985 [1992]: 352).

Linking the public debate on official English with bilingual education became prominent during the Reagan administration. With no policy on the role of the native language in bilingual education, the ideology of English monolingualism became a "default" point of reference. Reagan's Secretary of Education, William Bennett, had the role of minority languages in the education system as his greatest concern, and he opposed any use of a language other than English in bilingual programs. In the following statement, he states his view of the goal of bilingual education (Bennett 1985 [1992]).

> Paradoxically, we have over the last two decades become less clear about the goal [of bilingual education] —English-language literacy— at the same time as we have become more intrusive as to the method. But there ought to be no confusion or embarrassment over our goal. The rise in ethnic consciousness, the resurgence of cultural pride in recent decades, is a healthy thing. The traditions we bring with us, that our forefathers brought with

> them to this land, are too worthwhile to be discarded. But a sense of cultural pride cannot come at the price of proficiency in English, our common language.
>
> (Bennett 1985 [1992]: 362–363)

Bennett's statement reflects the general sentiment that politicians held during the Reagan administration. Ursula Casanova (1991) points out that President Reagan himself spearheaded efforts to discredit bilingual education. The Baker and de Kanter Report, commissioned by Reagan (1981), presented an analysis of bilingual programs and found them to be generally ineffective. Although scholars subsequently regarded the report as unsound, it gained widespread media attention.

Opponents of bilingual education generally target the use of a language other than English in educational programs as problematic and unacceptable. Rosalie Porter, an educator, argues that more English is better (Porter 1990). She believes that time spent in instruction in a language other than English is time wasted. A program whereby children are taught in and spoken to in English only is Porter's view of the most effective approach.

In 1991 a report on the effectiveness of different bilingual program models was issued. Called the Ramírez Report after the principal investigator, David Ramírez, it documented a longitudinal study of immersion English, early exit-transitional, and late-exit transitional programs. Jim Cummins (1994) argues that the study clearly demonstrated that time spent in the native or primary language was time well spent.

> In contrast to students in the immersion and early-exit programs, the late-exit students in the two sites that continued primary language instruction for at least 40 per cent of the time were catching up academically to students in the general population. This is despite the fact that these students received considerably less instruction in English than students in early-exit and immersion programs ...
>
> (Cummins 1994: 174)

Despite these findings, opponents to bilingual education that is not monolingual English have continued their arguments. Keith Baker and Christine Rossell (1996), for example, conducted a review of the effectiveness of bilingual programs. They dismiss as irrelevant findings that document achievement in a language other than English. They argue that the goal of bilingual education must be English oral language proficiency and instruction through English only. To that end, time spent in a language other than English is wasted.

Opposition to the use of a language other than English ranges from views that it is antithetical to the goals of such programs to Reagan's view that it is "absolutely wrong and un-American" (cited in Casanova 1991: 172). There are those, however, who support bilingual education with a restricted use of the native language and with a goal of rapid transition to English monolingualism. Some argue that this position characterizes most bilingual programs. Catherine Snow and Kenji Hakuta, both prominent researchers of bilingual education and bilingualism in the U.S. (1988 [1992]), argue that:

> Bilingual education in its present form may be one of the greatest misnomers of educational programs. What it fosters is monolingualism; bilingual classrooms are efficient revolving doors between home-language monolingualism and English monolingualism.
>
> (Snow and Hakuta 1988 [1992]: 390)

3.2 Proponents of bilingual education

Those who support bilingual education support sustained use of the native language. For a time, scholars such as Hakuta (1986), argued that bilingual education should be based on research clearly showing that bilingualism has been proven to correspond with cognitive and social benefits. Educators and scholars have used those arguments to promote the use of Spanish, for example, in bilingual programs particularly when English-speaking children are enrolled. Hakuta and others, however, have recently put those arguments aside. They now remind us of the paradox of bilingual education programs conceived from an ideology of bilingualism within a society conceived from an ideology of English monolingualism. Snow and Hakuta (1988 [1992]) argue that:

> The crucial characteristic of tension-free bilingual nations is the expectation that it is normal for all citizens to be bilingual. In contrast, in tension-ridden bilingual nations, bilingualism at the individual level is considered abnormal.
>
> (Snow and Hakuta 1988 [1992]: 390)

In this analysis, these authors contend that the U.S. would fit under the tension-ridden nation category. The tension that permeates this society is the conflict of the ideology of monolingualism with that of bilingualism or diversity. It is not "normal" to speak a language other than English nor is it "normal" that, if you do, that you would want to continue to speak after having learned English.

Another prominent scholar, Jim Cummins, has developed theoretical perspectives through which bilingualism and bilingual education can be examined. Like Hakuta and Snow, he has increasingly become critical of bilingual education practice and argues that:

> [M]inority students' school failure is rooted in the ways that schools have reinforced patterns of dominant-subordinated group relations in the wider society by eradicating students' language and culture, suppressing their experience and excluding minority communities from any form of meaningful participation in the life of the school. It follows that if notions like equality of educational opportunity are to be anything more than a rhetorical facade, they must entail a direct challenge to the societal power structure.
>
> (Cummins 1994: 165)

In this statement Cummins reveals bilingual education's struggle with the hegemony of English that earns its strongest support through the ideology of monolingualism. He has become among those who view bilingual education in its larger social context. Lily Wong-Fillmore, another leading scholar who has become disillusioned with the promise of bilingual education, writes about how bilingual programs are regularly sabotaged. She describes what lies behind good and bad programs (Wong-Fillmore 1992):

> In every good program the people who are involved from top to bottom believe in bilingual education and are committed to making it work. There are teachers who know the ethnic language well enough to teach in it and have developed a workable plan for using it in school. English is used in these programs in ways that allow the students to master it eventually, but not in ways that displace the native language.
>
> (Wong-Fillmore 1992: 368)

She argues that there are bad programs because educators do not believe in bilingual education based on an ideology of bilingualism and they harbor resentment that the federal government requires it of them. Above all, she says that it is racism in America that undermines efforts and destroys beliefs.

Bilingual teachers, however, are operating without a guiding policy about the role of the native language. They therefore look to ideologies about language to guide them. The prevailing ideology of English monolingualism is powerfully persuasive. Bilingual teachers may decide that the use of the native language is not in the best interests of the students. The arguments in favor of English only or more English in the education of minority language students are thought to be in their best interests. In light of the nationalistic ideology shifted to and developed in the Reagan years, bilingual education with a diminished role for the language other than English makes some sense.

4. Bilingual teachers in the practice of bilingual education

To illustrate how the absence of a language policy in bilingual education leads teachers to practice it on the basis of a dominant language ideology, I describe how bilingual education is practiced in one school district. The data come from eight years of ethnographic study of bilingualism and bilingual education in a major urban center in the southwestern region of the U.S.[7] The school district is large and serves 66,000 children with over 80 home languages other than English. The vast majority (24,000 or 40%) of those children's home language is Spanish and, of those, most families are Mexican origin. The school district has had some form of bilingual education since the early 1970s.

A major court case brought against the school district in the early 1980s sought school desegregation for African American students. The Latino community followed through on that case arguing that the rights of children whose second language is English were being violated. The judge used a three part precedent from a Texas case, Castañeda v. Pickard, to determine whether the school district was meeting those children's educational needs. The court examined the theoretical underpinnings of the approach the school district used, the actual implementation of the approach, and finally the results. It found that while the district had a sound theory, the implementation and results were problematic and required court ordered remedy. The court "focused in particular on the weak qualifications of the "bilingual" teaching staff, many of whom were monolingual English speakers who, for reasons of seniority, could not be replaced with qualified teachers." (Jiménez 1992: 249)

The remedies that resulted from the court case included requirements for insuring a qualified bilingual teaching staff. Teachers are qualified either by a State endorsement to their teaching certificate (completing a bilingual education program at the university graduate level) or by completing 150 in-service training hours that the district provides.[8] In addition, teachers must pass a Spanish proficiency test. A teacher can be hired for a bilingual position before completing either qualification or passing the test.

Today there are 350 bilingual teachers in this school district. Of those, 25 have the State endorsement. The other 325 teachers are in the district's in-service program.[9] While these steps towards insuring a more qualified teaching staff for the bilingual program are commendable, they have not eliminated the possibility of a teacher being in a bilingual position who does not have adequate proficiency in Spanish to teach through it or one who has and chooses not to. And because teachers can be in the process of completing a qualification, there exists the possibility of a teacher in a position for which they are not fully trained and/or proficient in Spanish. Illustrations of these possibilities follow.

A Mexican immigrant mother whom I will call Sra. Castillo described in a personal narrative her experiences with this school district's bilingual program through which her six children passed. Sra. Castillo had completed two years of a technical school before marrying when she was sixteen. She and her family lived in a large urban area in northern Mexico. With her husband and five children she immigrated to the U.S. when the eldest child was seven years old. They lived in a working-class neighborhood in a two bedroom house they bought with money they saved and that which they received through a workers' compensation claim. Sr. Castillo made some of the considerable and necessary repairs on the house himself.

Sra. Castillo was always actively involved in her children's education. She did not work outside the home and often went to the schools to observe, visit her children's classrooms, be useful and at times to intervene. She was certainly unusual in this respect as few other Mexican immigrant parents got so involved and fewer intervened. It was particularly rare since Sra. Castillo spoke no English (and Sr. Castillo spoke English well). It was around the issue of Spanish at school that Sra. Castillo was most concerned (all translations from Spanish are mine):

> And then, many times the problem is the teacher. It isn't the student nor ourselves, the parents, it is the teacher. I have nothing against the teachers, but many times that is what happens. And like I tell my husband, we have to open our eyes to reality. Many times teachers say they are bilingual and they are not. They are not.

Because Sra. Castillo actually went to the children's classrooms and spoke with teachers she knew just how proficient teachers were in Spanish who claimed to be bilingual. She also could observe how much of the curriculum was being taught through Spanish.

> ... work that they do in the classroom in English and in Spanish and with this teacher one could see that it was all in English, all in English. I couldn't have a conversation with him because he didn't understand me. And then I say it's because of this that my son was more focussed on English because the boy was the whole year in English only. It is not the same the little that we interact here in Spanish at home compared with what he is going to learn at school all day long and every day of the week. Right?

Sra. Castillo believes that a bilingual program has a responsibility for academic Spanish in school. She believes that just the sheer amount of time children spend at school warrants attention to it. Her children's academic performance suffers, she argues, when the teacher cannot teach through both Spanish and English. Sra. Castillo paid close attention to which teachers her children would have, but she never chose to put her children in non-bilingual classrooms even when the teacher was not bilingual. It was usually the case that there were two classrooms at each grade level; one bilingual and the other English-only. In the case of her son that she describes above, she had no option but to keep him in the bilingual classroom. In another instance when her youngest daughter was in first grade with a monolingual English-speaking teacher, Sra. Castillo appealed to the principal to have her daughter tested so that she could pass on to the second grade bilingual classroom (and bilingual teacher). Her daughter successfully met the requirements and was placed in the second grade. It could be that Sra. Castillo's confidence to intervene was enhanced by the time her youngest child entered the school system which allowed her to take a dramatic step. She was well-known at the school and in the school district by this time; having monitored six children's progress through the bilingual program. (See Shannon 1996 for an account and analysis of Sra. Castillo's interaction with the first grade teacher.)

Teachers who were not proficient in Spanish were a problem for Sra. Castillo because she believed that the goal of bilingual education is bilingualism. She saw this as a societal goal and not something that would benefit just her children or just Mexican children.

> And it is very important as much for the family as it is for society —that they learn the two languages. English has as much value as the value that Spanish has. As much value as American culture has, Mexican culture has as much value. And how much I like that my language and my culure be respected and that is why I like respect for the things and the culture both American and English.

She believes mutual respect and a goal of bilingualism can be achieved through bilingual education with the caveat that "*El maestro tiene que ser enteramente bilingüe*" ('The teacher has to be entirely bilingual'). Sra. Castillo maintained these beliefs while encountering bilingual teachers who were not bilingual.

The following examples involve a bilingual teacher in training and the fifth grade bilingual teacher she was placed with. The school is a different one from the one Sra. Castillo's children attended but is in the same school district. This school is also in a working-class neighborhood but predominantly Mexican immigrant families have children in this school. Fewer families own their own houses and more parents are monolingual Spanish speakers. This school also has a bilingual program throughout the six grade levels.

In their fifth grade year, two children (who are subjects of my study of language maintenance and shift) were placed in a fifth grade classroom with a newly hired bilingual teacher. She came from the Midwest and had been interviewed over the telephone by the principal, a month before she was hired. One of the children, Yolanda, is a high achiever, both academically and as a second language learner. Yolanda immigrated from Central Mexico and came to live with her grandmother and aunt. By her fifth grade year and after three years in the bilingual program in this district, Yolanda was a Spanish dominant bilingual. She scored in the 90 percentile on achievement tests in Spanish, and Spanish was the sole language of the home. On informal measures of her English ability, Yolanda could read with comprehension at grade level and scored high on a formal measure of English vocabulary.

The other child, Juan, is not a typical high achiever although he was exceptional in math and computer use. In his fourth grade Spanish literacy class he distinguished himself by becoming expert at the computer skills needed to input, edit, format, and print the students' literary creations. He had been in the bilingual program since first grade and by his fifth grade year, Juan was Spanish dominant and limited in English. Juan is the youngest child of a relatively older couple who are Spanish monolinguals from Mexico. Juan's sister who is five years older than he is bilingual. Juan speaks Spanish only at home and occasionally speaks English with the few peers in his neighborhood who are monolingual English speakers. Juan does not score high in achievement tests in either language. He had not begun to read in English when he entered fifth grade.

At the beginning of the school year, Yolanda reported that her teacher not only did not teach through the medium of Spanish, but that her Spanish was limited, evidenced by the rare occasions when she spoke it. Yolanda was placed in the English curriculum and was not too concerned with her teacher's monolingual behavior. She was comfortable doing her work through English and conducting her social life in the classroom in English. Juan was not forthcoming about his feelings about his teacher's language ability or use. His mother expressed her belief that it was a good thing that the teacher spoke only English because it would improve Juan's English.

In the spring semester a bilingual teacher in training (candidate) was placed in this classroom. Although the university supervisor and school building coordinator were well aware that bilingual education as practiced in this classroom did not coincide with the bilingual ethos the school theoretically promoted, the candidate wanted experience at that grade level.

At the time the candidate was required to prepare and conduct lessons independently of the teacher, she presented a social studies lesson on the topic of pre-Columbian civilization in Mexico. The candidate held a full class lesson standing in front of the students who were all expected to participate. She held a richly illustrated book up before the students and read aloud a paragraph at a time. The book and her reading of it were in English. At the end of a paragraph or two the candidate asked in Spanish if one of the students would like to translate what she had read into Spanish "*en una o dos oraciones.*" ('in one or two sentences') Some students volunteered, Yolanda among them. After the reading, the candidate asked the children what they remembered about the Maya before they proceeded to the Aztecs. She hung a piece of chart paper over the chalkboard and as she went around to each individual student she wrote their response. She told the children they could answer in English or Spanish and repeated the instructions in Spanish. Regardless of which language the child responded in, the candidate wrote the response in English.

A long list emerged by the time the candidate came to Rosa, a student who had been in the U.S. for less than a month and understood no English.[10] The candidate repeated the request in Spanish and Rosa offered "*costumbres*" ('customs'). The candidate added "customs," in English to the list. The candidate spent a few moments discussing Aztec customs, in English. Up until that time Rosa was shriveled up in her desk. Her eyes darted around as it became clear that she would be called on eventually. She heard some children respond in Spanish so when it came time she was able to blurt out in a whisper "*costumbres*". The candidate appropriated the word from her and transformed it into English in the air and on the paper. Rosa shrunk back.

In the coaching session with the University supervisor the candidate expressed her frustration with her teaching. She said she was nervous because of the presence of the supervisor and because she conducted part of the lesson in Spanish. She said she was not properly prepared to do the lesson in both languages since the teacher herself had never modeled that teaching herself. The candidate did not know how to make decisions about using one language or the other or if using both of them was appropriate.

On a subsequent occasion the candidate had the opportunity to take a small group on her own outside of the classroom. The teacher assigned Spanish dominant children to the group. The candidate gave each of the seven children in the group a new copy of a trade book, originally published in Spanish, *Me Llamo María Isabel* ('My Name is María Isabel'). They took turns reading aloud and after each turn, the candidate led a discussion relating what the children were reading to their own experiences. All of the reading and discussion was in Spanish. Seated among the group was Rosa. She participated actively leaning forward into the group and joining in the discussion.

The story in the book is about a Mexican girl who starts school in the U.S. at the fourth grade. In the first chapters the children discover that María Isabel is unhappy at her new school not so much that her teacher does not speak Spanish but that she insists on calling María Isabel, Mary. It leads to embarrassment and a sense of alienation that the girl cannot fathom.

The candidate asked if any of the children had ever had similar experiences. Hands went up, including Rosa's. Rosa said her teacher did not speak Spanish just like the teacher in the book. During the discussion, her teacher came out from the classroom and approached the group. She made schedule arrangements briefly with the candidate and then turned to the children and asked if they liked the book. One boy said he did not because it was about a girl. The teacher laughed and said she would find a book about boys next time and then turned and walked back into the classroom. She had not spoken a word of Spanish. While the teacher was present, Rosa sat back in her chair.

At the coaching session the candidate said that the opportunity to conduct the session in Spanish had been entirely impromptu. The teacher had some extra time and had given the candidate an opportunity to teach an all-Spanish group. The candidate had designed the lesson on the spot. The candidate described the lesson in Spanish as much more effective than the social studies lesson done in two languages. There was no need to translate since all of the children were native Spanish speakers and they were reading from a book written in Spanish.

The candidate discovered that bringing Spanish into the classroom was something she would have to do deliberately. She found that if she ignored it (even entirely as the teacher did) it would not be viewed as problematic. The school district would hire her with limited skills and she could teach with them (or teach in English). To practice bilingual education where Spanish had an important instructional role would take a great deal more effort on her part and she would not necessarily be rewarded for doing so (see Shannon 1996).

5. Discussion

When this school district was taken to court over its bilingual education program, it was found that there were bilingual teachers who spoke no Spanish. The qualification process now in place still produces bilingual teachers who speak no Spanish. The school district's policy on bilingual teacher qualification does not focus on Spanish proficiency with the exception of the test. It is widely known in this school district that teachers prepare for the test to insure a passing score while their actual proficiency in Spanish is limited. It is also not usual for teachers to continue to practice as bilingual teachers with a limited and fossilized form of Spanish. There are cases of teachers who are native speakers of Spanish and who consider the Spanish of the immigrant children and their families to be non-standard and inferior. Some of those teachers refuse to speak Spanish. In fact, bilingual teachers who, for any reason, do not speak Spanish in the classroom will say that the children need English and not Spanish. Many bilingual teachers are not aware of their own language behaviors and would be surprised to see that English dominates and that Spanish and Spanish speakers are negatively affected in a variety of ways as a result (Shannon 1990). All of these attitudes and behaviors can be understood from an ideology of English monolingualism. The school district and the teachers are guided by this ideology, in part, because there is no policy at any level to guide them differently. Even the bilingual teacher hiring policy is based on an ideological position in which Spanish has little or no importance.

Mexican immigrant families are the largest consumers of bilingual education in the U.S. Given the history of attitudes towards these immigrants, their negative experiences about the use of Spanish in bilingual education are not surprising. Sra. Castillo demonstrated an enormous amount of proactivity with her children's education, but she also showed a great deal of tolerance. Most Mexican immigrant mothers behave more like Juan's mother and Yolanda's aunt and grandmother; with a great deal of tolerance and no intervention. Within the prevailing ideology of the hegemony of English, they are the silent and cooperative subordinate group. The symbolic violence (Bourdieu 1991) that occurs when a teacher cannot communicate with a mother, and is supposed to be able to, is part of what Spanish-speakers experience in bilingual education. The children, like Rosa, do likewise. Viewed another way, they receive what is in their best interests. Juan's mother welcomed more English for her son. Yolanda felt proud and successful to get her schooling through English only.

The teacher candidate's experiences provide a window on the socialization process of novice bilingual teachers. The school district, the school, the mentor teacher, and the students themselves were all operating by default in the absence of a policy addressing the role of Spanish in the bilingual education program. English monolingualism was the accepted norm. The candidate could develop as a bilingual teacher based on this language ideology.

6. Conclusion

In her analysis of language ideologies in Canada, Monica Heller (1994) writes:

> The economic and political power of English-speakers has also contributed to the prestige of their language and the high status accorded to their way of doing things. These forms of symbolic capital have been deeply embedded in relations of dominance in Canadian society.
>
> (Heller 1994: 11)

One could replace "Canadian" with "U.S." and accurately describe the language ideologies debate about bilingual education in the U.S. The powerlessness and subordination of Spanish-speakers in the U.S. makes bilingual education that values Spanish problematic. But that is not a complete explanation. The absence of official policy about language in general in U.S. society nor one at the level of bilingual programs means that members of society and participants in bilingual education behave according to language ideologies. Because the debate on official English has been public and pervasive for the last two decades, the rhetoric has been broadcast and heard. The debate on the role of Spanish in bilingual education is another arena for rhetoric to be found. Ultimately, with no policies, practice in bilingual education can be explained further by understanding the ideology of English monolingualism that prevails and helps people make sense of what they do and what is done to them.

The eight years that Reagan was in the White House were a long, intensive period of nationalistic ideology during which time English became a hegemonic language and the ideology of English monolingualism developed. Those ideologies will prevail and strengthen until something causes a shift toward different ones or shifts the language issue away from the nationalism issue. For example, if Spanish became more prestigious it could become cultural capital that English-speakers want. This is illustrated in two-way immersion programs where English-speaking children learn Spanish alongside Spanish-speaking children learning English. However, these programs are operating with a prevailing societal language ideology that favors English. A teacher in one immersion school reported that there is more praise for the English-speaking child learning and speaking Spanish than for the Spanish-speakers' attainment of English (Shannon 1995). Further, program evaluation research of immersion programs detected that, for a variety of possible reasons (such as continued use of English informally among the English-speaking children), their attained fluency in Spanish may be a fossilized or a non-standard variety (Cummins, personal communication, July 1997). A well-articulated policy at the school level as is the case with two-way immersion programs is still affected by society's preference of language ideology. Thus, while a language may gain in status in some domains, power relationships among the speakers of the languages continue to manifest themselves through language.

It is not certain that the new liberalism of the Clinton administration will impact a shift in the dominant language ideology in the U.S. It is clear that well into that political era, the ideology of English monolingualism continues to have the support of American society and its influence on the practice of bilingual education.

Notes

1. I am not arguing that language policy can dictate behavior, but in its absence we cannot point to it as an explanation of behavior.
2. At this point, the 1997 "Ebonics" debate deserves mentioning. I refer to James Collins' paper in this volume for discussion and references.
3. It is popularly believed that the Spanish spoken in Spain is standard Spanish while that which is spoken in Mexico would be non-standard or inferior. The situation can best be compared to that between British English and American English: each variety, in fact, has its own standard and they are basically the same languages.

4. Monica Heller's (1994) analysis of French in Canada contrasts with one of Spanish in the U.S. There, Canadian French is subordinate in status to the French standard from France. In the U.S., the Spanish spoken is no longer associated with Spain, but with Mexico. That association with a nation of less prestige than the U.S. has insured its ever lower status.
5. It is also interesting to note that Italian after Spanish was the largest language group and while they experienced a decline it was only -2.5%.
6. I prefer to use the term Latino (rather than "Hispanic", for example), to refer generally to those in the U.S. with a cultural and linguistic heritage involving the Spanish language as it is my understanding that at the present time they themselves prefer it.
7. I have used pseudonyms in all instances.
8. Teachers who got the endorsement were once also required to take the in-service hours. This is no longer required.
9. These data come from the district office of Testing and Evaluation for the 1997 school year.
10. It is popularly believed that children from Mexico, particularly border cities, come to the U.S. knowing some English. Teachers would be the first to report that this is not often the case. In my experience, it has never been the case.

References

Adams, John
1992 Proposal for an American Language Academy (1780). In: Crawford, James (ed.), *Language Loyalties: A Source Book on the Official English Controversy*. Chicago: The University of Chicago Press, 31–33.

Baker, Keith and Adrienne de Kanter
1981 *Effectiveness of Bilingual Education: A Review of the Literature*. Washington, DC: Office of Planning, Budget, and Evaluation, U.S. Department of Education.

Baker, Keith and Christine Rossell
1996 The effectiveness of transitional bilingual education. *Research in the Teaching of English* 30: 7–74.

Barker, George
1946 *Social Functions of Language in a Mexican-American Community*. (Anthropological Papers of the University of Arizona 22). Tucson: University of Arizona.

Bean, Frank D., George Vernez and Charles B. Keely
1989 *Opening and Closing the Doors: Evaluating Immigration Reform and Control*. Washington, DC: The Urban Institute Press.

Bennett, William J.
1992 The Bilingual Education Act: A failed path. (1985). In: Crawford, James (ed.), *Language Loyalties: A Source Book on the Official English Controversy*. Chicago: The University of Chicago Press, 358–363.

Billig, Michael
1993 Nationalism and Richard Rorty 'The text as a flag for Pax Americana'. *New Left Review* 202: 69–83.
1995 *Banal Nationalism*. London: Sage.

Bourdieu, Pierre
1991 *Language and Symbolic Power*. Cambridge: Polity Press.

Camarillo, Alberto
1979 *Chicanos in a Changing Society: From Mexican Pueblos to American Barrios in Santa Barbara and Southern California. 1848–1930*. Cambridge, MA: Harvard University Press.

Casanova, Ursula
1991 Bilingual education: Politics or pedagogy? In: García, Ofelia (ed.), *Bilingual Education: Focusschrift in Honor of Joshua A. Fishman on the Occasion of his 65th Birthday*. Berlin: Mouton de Gruyter, 167–182.

Castellanos, Diego
1992 A polyglot nation (1983). In: Crawford, James (ed.), *Language Loyalties: A Source Book on the Official English Controversy*. Chicago: The University of Chicago Press, 13–17.

Crawford, James
1992 The debate over official English. In: Crawford, James (ed.), *Language Loyalties: A Source Book on the Official English Controversy*. Chicago: The University of Chicago Press, 87–88.

Cummins, Jim
1994 The discourse of disinformation: The debate on bilingual education and language rights in the United States. In: Skutnabb-Kangas, Tove and Robert Phillipson (eds.), *Linguistic Human Rights: Overcoming Lingusitic Discrimination*. Berlin: Mouton de Gruyter, 159–178.

Douglas, William O.
1992 Lau v. Nichols (1974). In: Crawford, James (ed.), *Language Loyalties: A Source Book on the Official English Controversy*. Chicago: The University of Chicago Press, 251–255.

García, Eugene
1989 Instructional discourse in "effective" Hispanic classrooms. In: Jacobson, R. and C. Faltis (eds.), *Language Distribution Issues in Bilingual Schooling*. Clevedon: Multilingual Matters, 104–120.
1991 *The Education of Linguistically and Culturally Diverse Students: Effective Instructional Practices*. Santa Cruz, CA: Center for Research on Cultural Diversity and Second Language Learning.
1992 Effective instruction for language minority students. *The Teacher* 173: 130–141.
1993 Language, culture, and education. In: Darling-Hammond, Linda (ed.), *Review of Research in Education*. Washington, DC: American Educational Research Association, 51–98.

García, Mario
1981 *Desert Immigrants: The Mexicans of El Paso, 1880–1920*. New Haven, CT: Yale University Press.

Griswold del Castillo, Ricardo
1980 *The Los Angeles Barrio, 1850–1890 A Social History*. Berkeley: University of California Press.

Gramsci, Antonio
1971 *Selections from the Prison Notebooks*. New York: International Publishers.

Hakuta, Kenji
1986 *Mirror of Language: The Debate on Bilingualism*. New York: Basic Books.

Hayakawa, Samuel I.
1992 The case for Official English (1985). In: Crawford, James (ed.), *Language Loyalties: A Source Book on the Official English Controversy*. Chicago: The University of Chicago Press, 94–100.

Heath, Shirley Brice
1992 Why no official tongue? (1972). In: Crawford, James (ed.), *Language Loyalties: A Source Book on the Official English Controversy*. Chicago: The University of Chicago Press, 20–31.

Heller, Monica
1994 *Crosswords: Language, Education and Ethnicity in French Ontario*. Berlin: Mouton de Gruyter.

Higham, John
1992 Crusade for Americanization. (1988). In: Crawford, James (ed.), *Language Loyalties: A Source Book on the Official English Controversy*. Chicago: The University of Chicago Press, 72–84.

Hymes, Dell
1996 *Ethnography, Linguistics, Narrative Inequality: Toward an Understanding of Voice*. London: Taylor and Francis.

Jímenez, Martha
1992 The educational rights of language-minority children (1992). In: Crawford, James (ed.), *Language Loyalties: A Source Book on the Official English Controversy*. Chicago: The University of Chicago Press, 243–251.

Leibowicz, Joseph
1992 Official English: Another americanization campaign? (1985). In: Crawford, James (ed.), *Language Loyalties: A Source Book on the Official English Controversy*. Chicago: The University of Chicago Press, 101–111.

Macías, Reynaldo
1995 California voters support Proposition 187. *Spring Newsletter of Division G, Social Context of Education*, of the American Educational Research Association.

MacKaye, Susannah
1987 *California Proposition 63 and Public Perceptions of Language*. MA dissertation, Stanford University.

Porter, Rosalie Pedalino
1990 *Forked Tongue: The Politics of Bilingual Education*. New York: Basic Books.

Ramírez, J. D., S.D. Yuen, D. R. Ramey and D. J. Pasta
1991 *Final report: Longitudinal study of structure English immersion strategy, early-exit and late-exit transitional bilingual education programs for language-minority children*. San Mateo, CA: Aquirre International.

Rheyner, Jon
1992 Policies toward American Indian Languages (1992). In: Crawford, James (ed.), *Language Loyalties: A Source Book on the Official English Controversy*. Chicago: The University of Chicago Press, 41–47.

Ricento, Thomas
1996 Language policy in the United States. In: Herriman, Michael and Barbara Burnaby (eds.), *Language Policies in English-Dominant Countries: Six Case Studies*. Clevedon: Multilingual Matters, 122–158.

Rickford, John R.
1997 Unequal partnership: Sociolinguistics and the African American speech community. *Language in Society* 26: 161–197.

Rodríquez, Richard
1992 The romantic trap of bilingual education. (1985). In: Crawford, James (ed.), *Language Loyalties: A Source Book on the Official English Controversy*. Chicago: The University of Chicago Press, 351–354.

Shannon, Sheila. M.
1990 An ethnography of a fourth-grade bilingual classroom: Patterns of English and Spanish. In: Bixler-Márquez, D. J., G. K. Green, and J. L. Ornstein-Galicia (eds.), *Mexican-American Spanish in its Societal and Cultural Contexts* (= Rio Grande Series in Language and Linguistics 3). Brownsville: Pan American University, 35–50.

1995 The hegemony of English: A case study of one bilingual classroom as a site of resistance. *Linguistics and Education* 7: 177–202.

1996 The paradox of Latino parental involvement as told through a Mexican Mother's personal experience narrative. *Education and Urban Society* 29: 71–84.

Silverstein, Michael
1996 Monoglot "standard" in America: Standardization and metaphors of linguistic hegemony. In: Brenneis, Donald and Ronald S. Macaulay (eds.), *The Matrix of Language: Contemporary Linguistic Anthropology*. Boulder: Westview, 284–306.

Snow, Catherine E. and Kenji Hakuta
1992 The costs of monolingualism (1988). In: Crawford, James (ed.), *Language Loyalties: A Source Book on the Official English Controversy*. Chicago: The University of Chicago Press, 384–394.

Veltman, Calvin
1983 *Language Shift in the United States*. Berlin: Mouton de Gruyter.

Wong-Fillmore, Lily
1991 When learning a second language means losing the first. *Early Childhood Research Quarterly* 6: 323–346.

1992 Against our best interest: The attempt to sabotage bilingual education. (1992). In: Crawford, James (ed.), *Language Loyalties: A Source Book on the Official English Controversy*. Chicago: The University of Chicago Press, 367–376.

Yarborough, Ralph
1992 Introducing the Bilingual Education Act (1967). In: Crawford, James (ed.), *Language Loyalties: A Source Book on the Official English Controversy*. Chicago: The University of Chicago Press, 322–325.

Zentella, Ana Celia
1990 Returned migration, language, and identity Puerto Rican bilinguals in dos worlds/two mundos. *International Journal of the Sociology of Language* 84: 81–100.

The Ebonics controversy in context: Literacies, subjectivities, and language ideologies in the United States

James Collins

1. Introduction

A short-lived but intense controversy arose when the Oakland, California School Board proposed in December, 1996, that the variety of English spoken by a majority of African-Americans should be recognized and supported in the instruction of the District's more than 52,000 students. The furor of protest and punditry that followed the School Board's proposal is an instructive example of "language ideological debates". The controversy went down in history as the "Ebonics debate", went on during the best part of 1997, and was held at a variety of forums and through a variety of channels, including electronic mail and Internet.

Although the controversy might strike detached observers as a media-generated spectacle of little real substance, there is a deeper significance which emerges when we properly contextualize the Ebonics issue. The Oakland School Board put forth its language policy as part of a strategy to improve the poor educational performance of the district's urban student body. Critics of the proposal were quick to respond that the performance of Oakland students, and of disprivileged minority students more generally, was "not a question of language". On this latter view, linguistic issues are secondary, a distraction from the real causes of people being poorly educated. For some, the real causes were economic —lack of adequate funding, post-school jobs, and so forth; for others, the real causes were moral —lack of effort, motivation, and commitment, on the part of students and their families. Some critics were discursive: Federal Secretary of Education William Riley argued that "Elevating black English to the status of a language is not the way to raise standards of achievement in our schools;" others were sharply derisive: Kweisi Mfume, president of the National Association for the Advancement of Colored People, called the proposal "a cruel joke" (both cited in Leland and Joseph 1997). In what follows I argue that from a historical perspective, all sides to the dispute are partially "right", for questions of language-in-education are inextricable from economic conditions as well as historical projects of remaking moralities.

Given the amount of ink that has flown on the Ebonics debate, I will restrict myself to a sketch of the debate, including the lessons learned from participation in local forums, and then suggest some general features of language ideological debates found in this controversy. These features include the negotiation of text, the equation of language and nation, and struggles to impose symbolic power. In order to develop the theoretical and historical implications of this particular dispute —to understand the way(s) in which a larger historical process as well as a set of existing language ideologies impose upon a momentary and explosive conflict such as the Ebonics debate —I will then present two contextualizing analyses. One critically appropriates Silverstein's (1996) analysis of language ideologies in the United States, asking whether the semiotic processes Silverstein identifies as central to the "culture of standard" are generic to ideologies of language and how the semiotic framework can contribute to a critical, historical understanding. The second contextualizing analysis engages research in the history of education and the history of literacy. Periodizing on the basis of major shifts in the U.S. political economy, this analysis argues for the emergence and transformation of what Cook-Gumperz (1986) has called "schooled literacy"; it identifies the racial exclusion and subordination that were the taken-for-granteds of schooled literacy until the 1960s, and it explores the place of subjectivity in hegemonic and counter-hegemonic struggles over standard language and literacy.

2. The Ebonics debate

I will start by providing a brief chronology of the Ebonics controversy, so that we may follow the temporal unfolding of this particular dispute about language. The issue became public on December 18, 1996 when the Oakland School Board (OSB) passed a resolution stating that "Ebonics" was a language distinct from English that should be recognized, tolerated, and otherwise accounted for in the instruction of the district's predominantly African-American student body (Oakland School Board 1997a). A storm of protest and commentary arose in the next few days, and continued for more than two months, in magazines, television shows, newspapers, on email lists, at public forums, and professional conferences. Within days of the OSB's resolution, William Riley, the federal Secretary of Education, and Pete Wilson, the Governor of the State of California, publically opposed the Oakland proposal, declaring that they would deny funding for any efforts to "teach Ebonics". Radio programs and television news shows devoted air time to the topic, with commentary overwhelmingly against the OSB proposal. Prominent African-American political and cultural figures were consulted. Jesse Jackson opposed the Ebonics resolution as "an unacceptable surrender bordering on disgrace" (quoted in Leland and Joseph 1997). Within a few days, professional email lists, such as that of Division G of the American Education Research Association, were alive with queries, condemnations, and defenses. The Linguistic Society of America discussed the issue at its Winter Meeting in early January, 1997 and voted a resolution in support of the OSB proposal (*Chicago Tribune*, January 7, 1997; see Linguistic Society of America 1997).[1]

Within a month of its initial pronouncement, having faced a barrage of criticism, the School Board modified its original proposal in minor ways, removing a phrase about "genetically based" languages and changing an assertion that Ebonics was "not a dialect of English" to the more defensible claim that aspects of the structure and use of Ebonics derive from African language communities (Oakland School Board 1997b). The OSB did not change the core proposal that Ebonics be recognized as a legitimate medium of instruction and that resources be allocated for preparing teachers and materials to that end. During the months of January and February, forums were held on numerous campuses and at other public locations in cities throughout the country. Experts such as William Labov were interviewed on national radio (Terry Gross, *National Public Radio*, January 31, 1997), and local and national newspapers printed editorial comments on the matter, while the "Letters to the Editor" sections offered a lively exchange of opinions. The controversy continued, though with less prominence, in February, March, and April. The March issue of *On Campus*, a periodical sent to unionized higher education faculty affiliated with the American Federation of Teachers, published "pro" and "con" opinion pieces about the controversy (Asante 1997; Moore 1997). In late April, four months after the controversy began, the African-American Task Force of the OSB, which had prepared the original resolutions, submitted a final report, filled with detailed recommendations for helping to improve the English skills of African-American students, but not mentioning the term Ebonics (*Albany Times Union*, May 6, 1997).

A number of issues were raised and argued over throughout the free-wheeling dispute: Was "Ebonics" a separate language from English, as the original proposal asserted, or merely "slang"? Would recognizing and allowing for minority speech patterns improve students' performance, or would it "ghettoize" the schools? Was the OSB proposal a sincere effort to improve school achievement or an example of race-thinking run amok? And, as noted earlier, was the problem of minority educational performance a question of language, or was language merely a distraction from more important issues such as funding for schools and student motivation?

What is now called Ebonics has long been an object of sociolinguistic research and has over the years been called Negro Nonstandard English, Black English, Black English Vernacular, and most recently African American Vernacular English (AAVE). If we assume modestly that it is learned as the native language variety of 60% of the more than 35 million persons of African American descent in the U.S., then there are probably more than 20 million people for whom this is the "first dialect". Ebonics/AAVE is known to have distinctive features from other varieties of American English. These include phonological processes such as consonant cluster simplification and methathesis in word-final position, so that Ebonics differs from standard English lexical items *cold*, *test*, *desk* as (spelling approximates) *col'*, *tess*, *deks*. These differences result from rule-governed, that is, systematic processes, not from ad-hoc lapses from standard English. As a grammatical system, Ebonics/AAVE contains a complex system of aspectual morphology, in which the so-called *BE* verb, object of much stereotyping, serves as the core of a rich set of distinctions lacking as grammatical categories in standard English (Green 1998). These categories include the "invariant" or "habitual" *BE*, as in *He be workin'* which roughly translates as "he was working in an ongoing or habitual manner, over a number of days." This contrasts with *He workin'*, with the copula deleted, which is the translation equivalent of standard English "He is working."

The aspectual system is also at the heart of the research literature on the creole origins of Ebonics/AAVE. The argument in a nutshell is that Ebonics/AAVE originated in a process of abrupt creolization and subsequent decreolization, involving numerous West African languages and English (Rickford 1998), a sociolinguistic matrix emerging from the plantation-slave system that existed for more than 300 years in continental North America, first in British Colonial America and subsequently in the United States. It is the creolist hypothesis that appears to have informed the highly controversial phrase in the original resolution about "African Language Systems [i.e. Ebonics] [being] genetically based and not a dialect of English" (Oakland School Board 1997a).

In addition to distinct structural features and historical origins, Ebonics/AAVE is known for distinct, controversial, and influential patterns of use. It combines an African legacy of pride in artful language with an American legacy of domination and resistance and the contrapuntal, coded speaking such conditions engender (Scott 1990). Ebonics/AAVE is known for a range of styles of verbal play and challenge such as "Signifyin'", "Markin'", "Playin' the Dozens", and through the vehicle of Rap and Hip Hop music it seems to have captured the attention of the young people of the world (Morgan 1998) while —no surprises here— leaving older folks baffled and indignant at this rude "slang".

Although a fair amount is known about the structure, origin, and use of Ebonics/AAVE, its role in the poor educational performance of African American children remains in dispute. To rephrase the positions mentioned at the beginning of this chapter: Is the poor school performance and educational attainment of African American youth due to a mismatch of home and school language, to a failure of character and motivation, or to unequal and lesser provision of material resources for education? The OSB Task Force on the Education of African American Students looked at these questions and decided that language played a significant role and that language difference (Ebonics versus standard English) provided a rationale for extra resources to change curriculum and teaching practices. In their resolution, the OSB argued that differences between the home language of the students of the African-American majority school district and the English expected in the school played a key role in the poor school performance of the district's African American students (including below average grade levels and disproportionate referrals to Special Education classes and programs: Leland and Joseph 1997; Perry and Delpit 1998) —and that better awareness of Ebonics by teaching staff, along with modifications of curriculum to build bridges between Ebonics and standard English, would enhance overall school performance.

The general point —that taking account of minority children's home language will help their educational performance— is supported by research in the U.S., Canada, and Europe (Cummins 1986), as the original OSB resolution noted, and the resolutions of support by the Linguistic Society of America (1997) and the Committee of Linguists of African Descent (1997) also noted. However, the specific line of argument was inflected to fit the U.S. context. Because financial support for some form of bilingual instruction is legally guaranteed in the contemporary U.S. —admittedly this provision is under assault and shrinking, especially in California— the OSB argued that Ebonics was a separate language from English, that Ebonics-speaking students should be classed as "Limited English Proficient", and hence eligible for special bilingual education monies. The argument that Ebonics is a separate language from English was not tenable, and the OSB changed the claim in a subsequent version of the resolution which argued only that Ebonics is "significantly different" from standard English.[2]

The OSB strategy was understandable in California in the late 1990s, but there were legal precedents for focusing upon dialect (rather than language) difference and educational equity. There had been earlier programs in the U.S. which provided special support for instruction and curriculum that recognized and built upon the linguistic features of Ebonics. In the 1970s there was a widely-publicized court case involving the parents of African American school children and the Ann Arbor (Michigan) School District. In this case it was successfully argued that the reason African American children were disproportionately represented in low-ability reading groups and in the district's special education classrooms was that their language variety was unrecognized or devalued in curriculum, instruction, and assessment. Ruling on the case, Judge Joiner summarized the research consensus that:

> ... there exists a language system which is part of the English language but different in significant respects from the standard English used in the school setting, the commercial world, the worlds of arts and science ... [Black English] is and has been used at some time by 80 percent of the black people of this country and has as its genesis ... a Creole language ... It still flourishes in areas where there are concentrations of black people ... and is used largely by black people in their casual conversation and informal talk.
>
> (cited in Labov 1982: 194)

Joiner ordered the Ann Arbor School District to present a plan to lessen the gap between Black English and the language of "school settings".[3] The Ann Arbor district's plan instituted teacher in-service training, in 20 hours of instruction on the nature and history of Black English, methods for identifying speakers, and ways to distinguish pronunciation differences from reading mistakes (Baugh 1995; Labov 1982).[4]

In its resolution the OSB mentioned "judicial cases in states other than California [that] have recognized the unique language structure of African American pupils" but, as noted, their resolution focused on the bilingual argument and claim. In the broader debate that erupted in response to the OSB proposals there was little expressed recognition that there had been previous efforts to devise Ebonics-sensitive training and materials and that the issue might have a legal basis.[5] Indeed one of the striking features of the Ebonics controversy was how often strong opinion was matched by minimal knowledge of the facts. Whether in casual conversation, local print journalism, or television and radio reportage, few people appeared to have read the OSB resolution or to have a passing knowledge of the research literature on Ebonics, but everyone had an opinion about "teaching Black Dialect in the schools".

In response to the unfolding debate, as well as to apparent confusions we encountered about Ebonics and the OSB resolution, colleagues and I at the State University of New York at Albany organized forums on the issue, initially with students in the Anthropology Department and later for the university at large. In these discussions it quickly emerged that the overall range of facts were complex —they included the OSB resolution and amendments, official responses, the nature of Ebonics, prior arguments in legal cases, and the social science literature about its effects on schooling. At the university forums, most attendees were not speakers of Ebonics, and several positions were voiced. A few simply felt that Ebonics was ignorant speech that should not be used, but the majority were of the opinion that minorities had a right to their own ways of speaking. There was disagreement over whether and how the schools should accommodate to minority speakers, but almost everyone felt that nothing should be done that would impede the learning of standard English, which was often referred to as the "code of power" and the perceived medium of social success. One of the African American students attending the general university forum spoke in defense of the position that language differences, however precious, should not be allowed to hinder success through linguistic assimilation. This position was more acutely expressed in community forums where the majority of the audience were African Americans.

In late January, 1997, as the controversy about the OSB's "Ebonics Resolution" unfolded, I was asked to participate in another forum, this one off-campus. The event was organized by African-American community activists and held in the main Albany Public Library. Most of the more than sixty people in the audience were African-American adults; and how to improve the educational achievement of black youth was a prominent theme of the meeting. There was a sense of urgency to the discussion. Although ethnoracial minorities make up only 25% of the population of Albany, New York, minority children comprise nearly two thirds of the students in the public schools (City School District of Albany 1996).[6] Recently publicized countywide achievement data had shown, once again, that predominantly minority schools, concentrated in the city's poor and working-class neighborhoods, did not score as well on standard achievement tests as the whiter, more affluent city and suburban schools. So the issue of language, schooling, and social equity had local salience as well as being the object of a heated national discussion.

The forum title posed an interesting question "Ebonics: Legitimate Language or Gibberish?" It is the contrast "Legitimate Language" versus "Gibberish" that should attract our attention, for nonstandard varieties of national languages always have a tenuous legitimacy. Although modern linguistics views all languages (and language varieties) as fundamentally equal, many contributions to this book show that the judgment of political states and popular culture is less charitable. In the latter view, there are official languages and standard varieties, legitimate for print, education, and public communication, and there are other languages and nonstandard varieties, which may be appropriate for some groups and purposes, but are seen as inherently restricted, inferior, or flawed. With the term "gibberish", however, we come to a furthest extreme of evaluation and differentiation. For authorities such as *Webster's Seventh New Collegiate Dictionary* (1963), "gibberish" is "unintelligible or meaningless language". It is a striking state of affairs that a major social dialect of American speech —with millions of speakers and an extensive research literature documenting its nature and relationship to other varieties of English— can be thought of as "unintelligible or meaningless language", especially by otherwise politically aware, socially concerned, and culturally affirming African Americans.

This phrasing and contrast probably began with the nationally syndicated columnist Mary McCrory, an Irish American, who in December 1996 accused the Oakland School Board of "legitimating gibberish" (O'Neal 1998: 44). The phrase was picked up by various other print journalists who wrote of "legitimating" dialect, nonstandard or "second-class" languages. In a Letter to the Editor published in the local paper a few weeks before the forum, a local African American minister decried the OSB proposal as "legitimating slang" (Jack 1997). The question posed by the forum, and the prior journalistic equation of Ebonics with "gibberish", should remind us of an older term used by prescriptive grammarians for incorrect language: "barbarisms". We deal in both cases with what is viewed as unschooled, "incorrect" language, and the school has historically played a major role in the creation of internal linguistic differentiation, in the identification and marking of the speech signs of the barbarians within.

None of the panelists speaking that night at the forum accepted the "gibberish" pole of the opposition. But few in the panel or the audience seemed clear about what being a legitimate language might entail. Indeed, I was struck by the sense of contradiction that emerged as the panelists spoke and the audience responded. We all seemed in general agreement that education was a good thing because it improved chances for social mobility. But the sentiment was also frequently expressed that the educational system was rigged by prejudicial curriculum and teaching as well as inadequate financial resources for inner-city schools. This sense of predicament was realistic —an oft-noted expression of African American desire for opportunity and betterment coupled with a historical awareness of inequality and oppression (Mickelson 1990; Ogbu 1979). The sense of quandary over education, however, seemed to exacerbate an ambivalence about Ebonics, identity, and social possibility. Many who spoke at the forum declared that Ebonics was "part of me", a way of speaking associated with the intimacy of family and friends, yet many of those very same people would adamantly declare that Ebonics/AAVE had no place in educational settings. As one high school teacher put it: "[I accept Ebonics] but *I don't want to hear it in my classroom*!" Ebonics was not gibberish, and perhaps it gave voice to cherished memories of self, but its status as legitimate language was far from clear. For many that night it both indexed identity and threatened an idea of betterment that would not tolerate overt black talk.

In the issues raised, as well as the chronology of events, the Ebonics controversy illuminates a number of themes found in other language ideological debates, in particular, themes of textual negotiation, language and nationalism, and language and symbolic power.

First, we may note the explicit modification of positions taken by the OSB as the controversy unfolded. The initial Task Force resolution, in December, argued that African-Americans speak a separate language from English, Ebonics, which genetically derives (in the sense of genetic-historical relationship) from West African and Niger-Congo languages. This position was extensively criticized and, with the exception of Afrocentric scholarship, it has little support in the academic literature. In January, the OSB modified its original resolution, deleting the widely-misunderstood phrase about "genetically-based" languages and shifting to the claim that Ebonics is a variety of English, but one with significant historical influences from West African and Niger-Congo languages. This latter position finds support in research on the "creole" origins of African-American English (Labov 1982; Rickford 1998). Nonetheless, whatever the status of Ebonics, as separate language or dialect of English, the proposal to use it to improve the language skills of black students remained controversial. To select and train teachers for awareness of and sensitivity to this variety of language, to employ it in pedagogical materials, to treat it as an acceptable form of language in classroom settings —all this was wrongheaded and unacceptable to most commentators (Cose 1997; Moore 1997), as we might expect given the prevalent assumption that only standard English is appropriate for instruction in school or for literate expression. As mentioned earlier, the final recommendations of the Task Force, made four months after the controversy erupted, did not mention the term Ebonics. In a sense, by late April the "text" of Ebonics had disappeared, even though the final report maintains the goal of the original proposal —to devote special efforts and resources to improve the "English language skills" of African-American students (*Albany Times Union*, May 6, 1997).

Questions of language and nationalism were raised in manifest form by the controversy. The position that Ebonics is a distinct language from English is associated with the cultural-academic movement known as Afrocentrism, a form of cultural nationalism which emphasizes the consistency, coherence, and unity of African-American traditions, including speech traditions, and their distinctness from the cultural forms and language patterns of the rest of United States (Williams 1975; Asante 1997). Critics of OSB proposals raised various problems with what they saw as a manifest "separatism": citing a "divisive political agenda" of a "Black Nationalist" majority on the Task Force, which undercut class and cross-ethnic solidarities through a focus on language (Farrugio 1997); or asking why African-American speech patterns should be "singl[ed] out ... for a special focus on inter-cultural translation" (Hennessy 1997); or decrying "divisive Ebonics" which would "ghettoiz[e]... our educational system" (Jack 1997) (see also Cose 1997; Leland and Joseph 1997; Moore 1997). At issue in the original proposal and in the critical response is the American ideal of cultural unity and economic mobility through a common language and educational system versus a dissenting and perhaps fragmenting pluralism. Both positions, we should note, assume that print language, disseminated through schools, is essential for the securing or constructing of collective identities, whether the desired outcome is a monocultural or multicultural nation state.

Questions of language and nationalism are also relevant to this case in a specifically legal-institutional sense. As discussed earlier, the original OSB proposal argued that Ebonics was a distinct language from English, that there were special Bilingual Education subsidies for the education of speakers of distinct languages, and that therefore the School District should receive supplementary funds to provide special language services in support of the education of Ebonics-speaking students. As is well known, the United States considers itself an officially monolingual country, despite considerable plurilingualism (see Shannon, this volume). Languages other than English, such as e.g. Spanish or Cantonese, have little or no official or public status, though speakers of other languages have a right, as school children in the public educational system, to have their linguistic difference accounted for, through special bilingual education services. Language rights in the United States are fundamentally individual rights, and they intersect the education system under the "equal opportunity" provisions of the 1965 Civil Rights Act and related litigation (Hernandez-Chavez 1988; Magnin 1990). Speakers of other dialects of English, however, do not have a clear legal claim on special resources, whether their linguistic difference demonstrably affects school performance or not, and notwithstanding the Ann Arbor rulings. The OSB strategy was thus bound up with the specific legal-jural status of *language* difference in the American system of public education.

In addition to the issues of textual negotiation and nationalism, the debate over Ebonics also throws into relief the question of symbolic power. The original OSB proposal was manifestly an effort to claim valued symbolic status for a stigmatized variety of American English, or, in more theory-laden terms, to change the field of value so that Ebonics would have more *cultural-linguistic capital* (Bourdieu 1991). This effort to transform the structure of symbolic value involved several specific proposals: (1) to change the definition of legitimate language so that Ebonics would be acceptable for use in classrooms, by teachers as well as students; (2) to "add value" to Ebonics by providing special training for teachers to learn about the language variety, special credentialing for teachers demonstrating knowledge of the variety and its educational applications, and additional compensation for those so trained or certified; and (3) to devote efforts and money to preparing special curricular materials which draw upon Ebonics, as structural system and as literary heritage. In addition, as discussed earlier, the specific strategy adopted by the OSB, in particular, their initial claim that Ebonics was a separate language from English, must be understood in the context of a specific, legally-defined hierarchy of languages and rights. Standard English is the public, official language; speakers of other languages have individual rights to special educational provision, but speakers of nonstandard varieties of English have no special standing. The effort to transform the value of Ebonics was carried out in the terms laid down by this hierarchy of "school-worthiness": *Standard Language > Other Language > Other Dialect*.

As we have seen, the OSB's effort to legitimate Ebonics *vis-à-vis* standard English was forcefully opposed. Federal officials such as the Secretary of Education and state executives such as the Governor of California condemned the proposal and threatened fiscal retaliation against the Board and the District. Those without direct executive or administrative authority weighed in at the "court of public opinion". As noted earlier, with the exception of a few professional groups, such as the Linguistic Society of America and the Committee of Linguists of African Descent, and a few researchers with substantive knowledge of African-American varieties of language, such as William Labov and John Baugh, most early print commentary was dismissive of the attempt to "[e]levat[e] black English to the status of a language" (Leland and Joseph 1997: 78). Many commentators presented the issue as a natural dichotomy of power: standard English was the language of "empowerment", of success, prosperity, and membership; Ebonics, conversely, was a "disempowering" language of social marginals; it was a divisive, "ghettoizing" language that would perpetuate the exclusion of African-American youth, marking their difference and guaranteeing their subjection (Cose 1997; Lynch 1997; Moore 1997).

3. Standard English and Ebonics as a semiotic system

In the controversy over Ebonics expressed in local forums as well as national media, Ebonics was frequently defined and evaluated in terms of that which it was not: standard English, the sign and vehicle of personal and collective historical improvement. So let us examine ideas about standard English, asking how this language variety came to be viewed as the sole legitimate vehicle of education and the linguistic prerequisite of collective political order and individual mobility. A suggestive beginning to this inquiry is provided by Silverstein (1996) who analyzes contemporary American preoccupations about standard language as emerging from a "culture of standard".

According to Silverstein, the culture of standardization rests on an idealization of linguistic centralization, in which clarity, logic, unity, and market-based social progress depend on appropriation of the monoglot standard. The value-laden apprehension of standard, as a linguistic and social order, involves three semiotic processes: referential displacement, naturalization, and commodification.

In *referential displacement*, standard advocates celebrate clarity and lexical precision against the supposed confusions of dialect, that is, truthful reference becomes the metric of good language, and social differences embedded in language differences become an unfortunate background noise. In this view, speakers of dialects other than the standard dialect "lack vocabulary", rather than having different vocabulary; they "fail to make [or hear] certain sounds", rather than having a different phonology.

That African-American Vernacular English deletes the copula verb form and uses multiple negation is deemed a simplification and source of confusion, rather than a difference complemented by the variety's rich aspectual system.

Central in this analysis is the claim that native speakers assume that reference is primary and that all other uses or consequences of language are peripheral. In this taken-for-granted assumption, which Silverstein has argued is a general if not universal aspect of language use and (mis)apprehension (Silverstein 1976, 1979, 1985), native speakers typically overlook and downplay formal grammatical processes as well as the vast arena of pragmatics.[7] Drawing evidence from a variety of texts — newspaper articles and columns, books prescribing usage, popular texts in fields such economics and biology— Silverstein shows how pervasive is the view of language as a word-based device for signaling referential information and distinctions. It appears to be the folk view of language in journalistic, academic, and everyday culture, prevalent in a variety of textual-institutional sites. In the Ebonics debate, as well as in prior discussions of "dialect", the alleged inability of speakers to be understood — whether because of "sloppy speaking" or "limited vocabulary"— was a typical charge. The view is held, it should be noted, by many educated African Americans, as well as by whites. Tucker Carlson, on *Fox News Network* on December 22, 1996 asserted that Ebonics was not "intelligible English … I mean, this is —this is a language where nobody knows how to conjugate verbs" (cited in O'Neal 1998: 43), while African American columnist William Raspberry claimed that Ebonics "[had] no right or wrong expression, no consistent spellings or pronunciation and no discernible rules" (*Washington Post*, December 26, 1996).[8]

In *naturalization*, the complex, multi-faceted intertwining of language use, social differentiation, social identity, and social purpose are construed as a simple relation between the denotational norm of standard (how things should be said) and the dialectal deviations from this norm. Using standard language as the metric for assessing these speech deviations provides also a fixed perspective on social hierarchy, revealing a seemingly intrinsic link between deviant speech and social place. That is, it essentializes the social category-dialect relation and the standard-dialect relation. Thus Southerners in the U.S., being stereotypically slow-witted, the country bumpkins of the national imaginary, say *tar* for *tire*, *all* for *I'll*, *fixing to* for *about to*; and standard speakers can know Southerners as slow-witted for having said these things. Or, in the controversy over Ebonics, "black slang/English" is known by its "be" verbs and "double negatives", not its systemic structure or contextual complexity of use (Baugh 1983), and speakers are known by their archetypal media images —surly young men, feckless teenage mothers— and not by other, more differentiated images, of say the code-blending power of black preaching traditions (Gumperz 1982, chapter 9; Wills 1994) or African-American aesthetics (Baker 1988; Jordan 1988).

The concept of naturalization is of course not new to the study of ideologies; Roland Barthes analyzed it over forty years ago in his seminal *Mythologies* (1972 [1957]). The central insight is that as historically specific social states and cultural configurations are forgotten as history, they come to be taken-for-granted, and perceived as natural. Critique of the process of social forgetting informs other analyses of language ideology (Fairclough 1989), and the idea of ideology as involving the postulation of essential, natural connections between schematically perceived social types and stereotypic language forms has been discussed as "iconicity" by Gal and Irvine in a comparative study (1997). What Silverstein's analysis suggests is that we see naturalization as part of a cumulative process: referential displacement ignores the pragmatic dimensions of language; and naturalization seizes upon the pragmatic but strips out its multifaceted complexities, organizing a stereotyped ensemble of forms of speech and types of persons (fixed dialects and monodialectal/monolingual speakers) in terms of a particular, modern hierarchy, that of standard versus non-standard(s).

The third process, *commodification*, alerts us to the modern nature of the culture of standard. Commodification involves the objectifying of language, the presentation of standard language as a thing-to-be-had, the possession of which is necessary for market success. Viewed as a universally-available commodity, possession of which enhances economic competitiveness, standard in this formulation comprises a *legitimate hierarchy*. Seen as co-ordinated clusters of positive properties of individual people, standard is "the object of a brisk commerce in goods-and-services" (Silverstein 1996: 291), the true media of equality and access, and the rationale for the known and accepted hierarchy of persons and peoples. This last process, commodification, is of course linked to the capitalist economies, to the homogenizing abstractness of "exchange value" in markets. The term also points to the mystery whereby relations between people —one way of thinking about language and culture— become objectified, rendered a property of things, and given a market value.

It is not a new idea that language can become objectified or thinglike and thus enter into fields of exchange and value. Histories of European and American print, publication, and literature provide many examples (Anderson 1983; Guillory 1993; Warner 1990), and Silverstein and collaborators have analyzed pre-capitalist social formations in Africa (Irvine 1995) and Native America (Silverstein 1984; Moore 1997) in which objectified words, phrases, and discourses are subject to appropriation, inter-generational transmission, and strategic "spending" (ie. consumption-distribution) within a culturally-constituted field of value (see also Hymes 1981; Collins 1998, chapter two). Commodification, however, assumes the ascendency of markets, and it implies as well the primacy of the capitalist system and the commodity form (Lukacs 1971). What gives analytic purchase to this conception in Silverstein's account is his emphasis on hierarchization and individualization and the insight that language may be conceived as *quanta*, as more or less, in a field of evaluation. One of the enduring conundrums of liberal capitalist societies is that class hierarchies must be reconciled with ideals of equality. A familiar way in which such reconciliation is effected is by postulating the individual as the locus of rights and potential for improving her or himself and moving up the social hierarchy (Dumont 1986). Silverstein's argument is that standard is apprehended as gradiently accessible language, a sort of sociolinguistic *mana* that binds individual subjectivities to place in the language-and-social success hierarchy.

Like other commodity ideals, standard is "the object of a brisk trade". The "goods and services" refer to the myriad speech correction and dialect-remediation workshops, consultations, and tutorials that are available, for a fee, in the lower milieux of service-and-corporate America. Such language improvement services batten on the fears of vast lower middle class cohorts that historically faced language prejudice and that internalized "linguistic insecurity" (Labov 1972); such services are advertised in various corporate settings (see Silverstein 1996: 298–299 and note 2); and the clients of such courses, facing the perceived need to "lose the dialect", can be seen testifying in language documentaries such as *American Tongues* and *The Story of English*.

The vision of language as market-tested individual properties is overtly evident in the discourse about Ebonics. Whatever the resonance of this language variety as mother tongue, whatever its success as the medium and marker of peer group loyalties, Ebonics is not "economically feasible", is not "the code of power", not the "language of business", for example, to prominent columnists such as Ellen Goodman ("A 'Language' for a Second-Class Life", *Boston Globe*, December 27 1996) or Brent Staples ("The Trap of Ethnic Identity", *New York Times* January 4, 1997). Standard English is perceived as "the language of business" and as acquirable stuff that allows the possessor to advance in the great chain of being; it has no memory of group, no burden of history. Like a state church, it is open to all, requiring only of the heretofore non-standard speaker that she come alone, with no group and no history.

In Silverstein's account, the brisk commerce in language correction is part of a culture of standard which is most robust in corporate America and not, as we might think, in the public education system. This judgement is, I think, due to the specific period that Silverstein analyzes —the mid and late 1980s. This was a decade when educational alternatives —whether "new math" or "whole language" literacy pedagogy— were part of a general questioning of traditions. Developments during the 1990s, however, suggest that public education remains an important site for struggles over standard. In order to develop this argument, we need to deepen our sense of the historical contexts which inform the Ebonics debate as well as debates about language ideologies in the United States more generally.

4. Historical phases and language/literacy ideologies

When we investigate the history of language ideologies in the United States, we immediately come up against the importance of literacy, print, and schooling in the American project of self-construction. Investigating literacy and schooling, we find that they were part of larger systems of meanings and practices that, following and extending Cook-Gumperz (1986), Graff (1981), and Soltow and Stevens (1981), I will call "economies". These cultural-textual economies correspond, in a rough fashion, to major phases in the political economy of the United States, a political economy in which the question of race has always been of central importance (Davis 1985; Marable 1984). Briefly, we can distinguish three phases, the early-national, mature-national, and late-national phases, and three associated ideological complexes in which ideas about language, political order, and cultural belonging are mixed with ideas about literacy, schooling, and the nature of persons. These complexes foreground the moral, technical, and cultural dimensions of literacy and language, and we may call them the moral economy of literacy, the technical economy of literacy, and the cultural economy of literacy. What this historical sketch will show is how the contradictory dynamics of economic change, democratic aspiration, and racial oppression and resistance pervade the history of language and education, including the recent controversy over Ebonics.

(1) *The early-national phase* spans the 1780s-1880s. It is a period in which colonial conceptions of citizenship and print-based public spheres give way

to Jeffersonian republicanism, with its emphasis on the equality of small producers as the bedrock of literate, civic virtue, which gives way in turn to an industrial economy, increased acceptance of class division and hierarchy, with the promise of equality located in the West-pushing frontier. This phase begins with a close association between what we would now call literacy practices and political subjectivities. As Warner (1990) has argued, in the late colonial period, newspaper publishing, writing, and readership were viewed as essential to the ferment and debate of self-government, to the formation of civic ideals, civic responsibilities, citizen-subjects. This was one strand of a pluralistic culture of literacy of the early 19th century which associated diverse literacy practices with personal and political development (Cook-Gumperz 1986). Its egalitarian and utopian impulses, legacies of Enlightenment thought as well as popular political ferment, were one current in the movement for universal schooling. A second, powerful current in the movement for universal schooling, for "common schools" in the U.S., emphasized the "disciplinary" potential of education, the utility of schooling and literacy, properly organized, for reshaping the character of the working class(es), inculcating virtues of punctuality, sobriety, thrift, and respect for authority, along with reading and writing.

Efforts to fashion a standard American English during this period —most notably Noah Webster's dictionaries and reading programs— expressed the democratic impulses of a common language. Webster particularly hoped to craft in American English a linguistic means that would bypass the known differences of language due to divisions of wealth and region. He ascribed to his spelling reforms both nationalist and democratic aspirations: "Our political harmony is therefore concerned in a uniformity of language"; and "[after spelling reform] [a]ll persons, of every rank, would speak with some degree of precision and uniformity" (cited in Jacoby 1995: 61–62, inserts added).[9]

The Jeffersonian visions of literate, participatory democracy, the common school movement, and the effort to craft a general American English were all based on a fundamental exclusion. African Americans, the bedrock of the southern agrarian economy, were presumed to be unlettered and unschooled as well as unfree. Warner (1990) describes how in the late Colonial Era, blackness, in the figure of the slave, was the contrast that defined white writing: inscription contrasted to speech; knowledge to ignorance; light to dark. With the movement for common schooling, this symbolic hierarchy was potentially threatened; state legislatures throughout the slave-owning South attacked the common school effort and passed specific laws making it a crime to school or otherwise educate an African American, whether free or slave (Nasaw 1979; Zboray 1993). The system of slavery ended with the Civil War of 1861–1865, and the radical reforms of the Reconstruction Period (1865–1876) ushered in a decade of African American political, economic, and educational enfrachisement. But Southern white elites, in concert with the conservative wing of the Republican party, reversed the Reconstruction in the years after 1876, instituting a system of Jim Crow apartheid that lasted until the 1960s (Marable 1984; Zinn 1980).

(2) *The mature-national phase* spans the 1880s-1960s. It is a period initiated by the closing of the Western frontier, a period in which there is a dominant corporatizing of many aspects of American life (workplace, education, mass culture-and-opinion), and connected to that corporatizing, the emergence of technical efficiency, quantification, and elite rationality as dominant values. It is a time of standardization —in language, in markets and taste, and in the scale and organization of schooling. During this phase, schooling comes to be seen as the primary avenue of social mobility, the now-restricted compass of democratic possibility. The school system is professionalized by virtue of public funding, legal support, and consistent curriculum. Early in this period, the social upheavals caused by the change from an agrarian to an industrial economy find expression in the now-familiar idiom of educational crisis: the problems facing the nation are attributed to the lack of "schooled English" or to the inadequate literacy skills of army recruits (Cook-Gumperz 1986; Kaestle et al. 1991; Ohmann 1987; Rose 1989).

During this second phase, as the 19th century ideal of common schooling gives way to the 20th century emphasis on individualized, ability-ranked, curriculum-tracked schooling, there is a corresponding promotion of the idea of individual talent, requiring the separation and ranking of individuals in new ways. This seriation and stratifying is aided by greater technical sophistication in teaching and learning and by the dominance of a testing paradigm that assumes differences on tests are due to differences in individual ability (Cook-Gumperz 1986). As arguments about ability difference and efficient bureaucratic organization justify the 20th century practices of ability grouping and curriculum, literacy shifts from being a moral virtue to being a technical skill. Hence we have a "technical economy of literacy". In this ideological complex, the autonomous "skill" was conceived as a set of socially-neutral aptitudes with standard English, which underpinned the entire project of educability. Standard language literacy was a basic skill, necessary for schooling, and schooling became the primary means of social mobility. As Lasch (1996) has argued, with the closing of the frontier in the late 19th century, an elite discourse of social mobility and meritocracy emerges, in which democratic aspiration shrinks to the notion of an "aristocracy of [schooled] talent", an aristocracy to be sure, but one legitimated by the circulation of an educationally-certified population through its ranks.

This schooled social mobility was increasingly monoglot. In the period from the late 1870s through the 1920s we see the passage of a number of state and federal laws against the de facto multilingualism of the self-described "nation of immigrants". For example, state laws in Wisconsin and Minnesota forbade local school districts from providing bilingual German/English and Norwegian/English instruction. At the federal level, in 1917, the U.S. Congress passed legislation requiring potential immigrants to pass a test of reading and writing in English (Heath 1981).

If it was a period that ushered in an official hierarchy of English versus other languages, it was also the period of an official hierarchy of races. A lynchpin of the Jim Crow system of apartheid was the "separate but equal" doctrine that the U.S. Supreme Court declared constitutional in *Plessy v Ferguson* (1896). This ruling legalized separate treatment in public institutions and throughout civil society as compatible with the Fourteenth Amendment to the Constitution, a provision that supposedly guaranteed "equal treatment under the law" for all U.S. citizens. African Americans were citizens throughout this period but were effectively stripped of most civil rights. Their children attended racially-segregated schools, in the North and West as well as the South, and as is well-established, the black system of education was dramatically underfunded relative to that for whites (Ogbu 1979). Despite the efforts of reformers and radicals, epitomized by Booker T. Washington and W.E.B. DuBois, the steadfast growth of the black press,[10] and the achievements of an urban African American bourgeoisie in the early decades of the 20th century (Baker 1988), the general education and literacy levels of the African American majority always fell significantly below those of whites in national comparisons, whether in the 1880s or 1940s (Kaestle et al. 1991: 125–126).

(3) The *late national phase* spans from the 1960s to the present. Long-term economic crisis has been a dominant feature of this period. As the U.S. political economy has entered an era of heightened globalization and domestic de-industrialization, the lack of fit between the skills and locations of labor and the "needs" of capital have been dramatic (Davis 1985). This late-national period has been characterized by challenges, both political

and intellectual, to the order and assumptions of the mature-national phase. In this uncertain period, questions of language, education, and social order have often been linked.

The 1960s and early 1970s saw the emergence of influential social movements. If the anti-war and student-based counterculture movements can be seen as challenges to the rule by technical elites and experts, the civil rights movement can be seen as challenges to the presumption of equality and assimilation/social mobility for African-Americans, Native Americans, Chicanos and Puerto Ricans (Zinn 1980). An intellectual challenge to explanations of educational failure in terms of individual or cultural deficits led to critical analyses of key features of the technical economy of literacy. In particular, a cottage industry documenting bias in standardized tests called the social neutrality of these tests into question and made manifest their social stratifying function (Hall and Freedle 1975; Marvin 1988). A series of studies investigated nonstandard language use (Labov 1972; Baugh 1983) and socialization to distinct, non-mainstream English languages and cultures, for example, those of African-Americans (Heath 1983) or Native Americans (Philips 1982). In addition, numerous studies of classroom discourse, especially those informed by ethnography of communication commitments (e.g. Hymes et al. 1970; Cook-Gumperz [ed.] 1986) gave lie to the presumed neutrality of classroom communication. One result of the social movements as well as the academic critiques was a growing appreciation of language *and literacy* as more differentiated than previously thought, more connected to social traditions and cultural identities. In brief, this resulted in a concern with "cultural literacies" and with the possibility of education drawing on more than just the official standard language.

However, these critiques of American society and pluralist understandings of language and literacy have in turn been challenged. Since the early 1980s there has been what Apple (1996) calls the "conservative restoration" —an alliance of managerial elites committed to neoliberal market orthodoxy, cultural conservatives committed to "the classics" and "educational standards", and working-class and middle-class authoritarian populists, committed to traditional family, gender, and age relations and traditional and fundamentalist religious values and knowledge. As part of this conservative restoration, there have been successive alarms sounded about social disorder and declining educational standards. Business, political, and conservative intellectual elites have argued forcefully that America was not so much socially divided as educationally deficient (National Commission on Excellence in Education 1983). In this account, job loss is due to working people's lamentable skills, not to capital flight or automation. Not surprisingly, on the national scene a discourse of tougher education standards and a presidential call for a national literacy campaign have been prominent in the 1990s (Educational Researcher 1996). The "Ebonics debate" occurred in the context of this conservative restoration.

5. Conclusion

In the preceding sections, I have argued that social divisions underlie historical as well as contemporary understandings of language, literacy, and schooling. Those divisions originate in the conflicts of class in capitalist society, but we must understand class as a complex project, variously influenced by and influencing racial and gender formations. Attention to the history of literacy also brings out the importance of questions of subjectivity, for in our own cultural tradition, literacy as idea, practice, and negotiation has been about shaping selves, judging character, and measuring minds. A guiding assumption in this tradition has been that literacy leads to social betterment, a strikingly durable element of a now largely-discredited liberalism. The 19th century ideal of social order through rectified language and literacy, caught up in the bureaucratic, stratifying tendencies of American schooling in the 20th century, gives us the "culture of standard": a semiotic ensemble in which referential clarity is next to godliness, social divisions are natural, if not blessed, and a neoliberal scramble for a market-competitive language-and-literacy is humanity's last, best hope for equality.

Silverstein's analysis of the culture of standard addresses present-day American culture, but his account also gives insights into semiotic dimensions of the historical ideologies of literacy just discussed. Referential displacement, the selective emphasis on truthful, referring language over all else, underlies the early-national "moral" connotations of literacy (the first phase) and the mature-national "technical" apprehension of literacy (the second phase). The commodification concept points to the same conjoining of individualization-with-stratification that characterizes the 20th-century technical economy of literacy, and especially the peculiar subjectivity presumed by the modern testing paradigm. In the rise of schooled literacy as the only legitimate literacy, the arbiter of all alternative literacies (Cook-Gumperz 1986), we see a broad process of naturalization, dividing the world into normalized populations of "literates" and "illiterates", with boundaries maintained by commitments to monolingualism and "Standard Only" (Rockhill 1993). But if the first two phases and literacy complexes reveal a dominant pre-occupation with literate selves formed by *langue*-like codes, that is, standard language literacy, how do we understand the late-national "cultural literacy"? Here the pre-occupation is with selves formed through vernacular practices of talk and inscription and through the encounter between vernacular and standard. This latter view of language-and-literacy should be seen, however, not as a transformation or replacement of the earlier emphases but rather as a questioning, criticism, and undermining of those emphases.

A persistent theme of much post-structuralist argument has been that achieving the stability of language, the certainty of representation, entails a struggle of self and social. This is found in Derrida's (1976) criticisms of Saussure and appreciation of Peirce's emphasis on understanding and indexicality, and it is a theme of Kristeva's (1980) charting of desire and language, of subversion of codes by practices, of referential language by the esthetic, of the hard, never-finished business of relating human subjectivity to "the symbolic", the realm of language. This emphasis on the discord of self, social, and language is found also in Bakhtin (1981), criticizing the Saussurean codes, examining the interplay and conflict of dominant and dominated voices in the formation of genres and social discourses, and it is found in Gramsci's (1971) portrayal of national standard language(s) and local dialect(s) as an ongoing historical conflict.

The relevance of all this for our understanding of the recent Ebonics controversy, as well as the emphasis on cultural literacies, is that the post-structuralist and Bakhtinian/Gramscian arguments emphasize the inherent indexing in language of differentiated places, histories, and peoples. Simply put, they argue against a culture of standard. Ethnographic and autobiographical studies of language and literacy have a similar critical message. Against the processes of referential displacement, that is, giving pride of place to the strictly literal dimensions of language, Jordan's (1988) *Ain't Nobody Mean More To Me Than You* argues for the untranslatability of African-American dialect into standard, while Heath's (1983) *Ways With Words* illustrates how class-bound, religious-based philosophies of language may support or subvert an emphasis on literal, referential language. Against the processes of naturalization, Gilyard's (1991) *Voices of the Self* emphasizes a blending of standard and vernacular, a complex switching and mixing, that begins very early in life, marking a Bakhtinian heteroglossia rather than a standard/dialect dichotomy. Similar emphasis on the complex blending of linguistic possibilities is found in Heath's analysis of standard and vernacular, both written and oral, in African-American church services. Against the commodifying of standard and the associated legitimation of hierarchy, we find in Rose's (1989) *Lives on the Boundary* sustained demonstrations that standard English is available to many only through a complex reworking, a struggle, a cultural transformation, a personal disorientation and remaking of self. We find in Gilyard's *Voices* a blunt appraisal of the limits of cultural-linguistic assimilation, and a careful charting of the social costs and risks of "buying into standard".

The post-structuralist and ethnographic deepening of counter-standard literacies provide us with an appropriately sharp perspective on the culture of standard. If, as Silverstein argues, it is centered in a corporate milieux, that is a powerful institutional basis. If, as I have argued, it has been relocated in the public schools in the 1990s, as part of a conservative restoration in education, we must nevertheless remember that hegemonic projects always involve conflict and negotiation. The Ebonics debate was about a proposal to revalue the symbolic status of a nonstandard variety, and the fury of response to that proposal must be seen as having roots in a broader reaction: to the intellectual and aesthetic as well as political challenges to "standards" in the 1960s and 1970s; to the valorization of Ebonics in non-institutional sites through the complex pathways of popular culture; and to the crisis of structural unemployment facing many Americans but especially urban African American populations.

"Market-competitive" language is commodified language, in Silverstein's terms, but I think that language-as-commodity can be more usefully understood from a different theoretical framework, that of *cultural capital*. Gouldner's (1979) study of the "new class" (the professional-managerial class) postulates as an essential condition of that class the possession of cultural capital. In Gouldner's analysis, in order for culture to become capital, there needs to have been a "transformation of culture into *property*, whose incomes could be bequeathed *privately*" (p. 25, emphasis in original). Cultural capital results from transforming culture and language —changing a common inheritance and means of communicating and belonging into things-to-be-had, the possession of which entitles the bearer to claims on income. The symbolic-institutional mechanism for achieving this "private enclosure of the cultural commons" is credentialing, the "certification by someone or some group … in authority … that the individual … possesses certain skills … [and is entitled to] … certain offices, livings, or jobs … (p. 25–26)."

As Bourdieu's writing on the subject reminds us, the school has been a crucial institution in this history of "private enclosure", as language and culture have been seized, shaped, and judged in the unifying techniques of pedagogy, curriculum, and examination (Bourdieu and Passeron 1977; Bourdieu 1991). One result of this schooled history is that some forms of language are deemed worthy commodities, while others are "just trash", or, in the idioms of the Ebonics debate, some languages are "empowering" while others are "ghettoizing slang". The commodification and cultural capital analyses point to common processes: the objectifying and hierarchizing of culture and language; the extension of market logic to hitherto "immaterial" symbolic attributes and capacities. But the cultural capital concept brings out more forcefully the significance of this process, the symbolic violence of cultural expropriation, and the central role played by the school, as generator of society-wide symbolic difference, as arbiter of the cultural-linguistic worth of the possessors and the disposessed.

While discussing symbolic power in the Ebonics affair, we examined specific efforts to change the status of "black English", to improve the linguistic capital of its users. These efforts included having this variety of English accepted for classroom use, special credentials and compensation provided for teachers knowledgeable about Ebonics, and curriculum materials developed in this variety. These efforts occurred in the context of an institutional hierarchy of languages and educational rights that sanctions the opposite state of affairs. Ebonics currently has no legitimacy for classroom use; teachers' competence with African-American English, however pedagogically relevant (Labov 1995), is not given special certification or compensation; and curriculum materials either ignore AAVE or treat is as linguistic error.

With the notion of linguistic difference-as-error, let me return to the view of Ebonics as "gibberish". Earlier I equated this derogatory image of African American Vernacular English with the prescriptive grammarian's view of incorrect (unschooled) usage as "barbarisms". In making this equation, I had in mind Guillory's (1993) historical discussion of the role of the school in regulating access to the means of literacy production and consumption. It is an ancient role, going back to the *scola* of late-imperial Rome, and it involves marking and evaluating an *internal* linguistic differentiation in terms of an *imaginary* community/tradition, to which the schooled literates belong, and to which the unschooled, betrayed by their language, are outsiders, hence "barbarians". Silverstein's analysis of the culture of standard gives us a suggestive account of the assumptions about language that enter into that "imaginary"; the concept of cultural capital reminds us of the violence, symbolic and otherwise, that accompanies the exclusions of the schooled tradition.

But what is at stake is not simply a long history of intricate linguistic prejudice, though there is such a history. Guillory argues (following the work of Bourdieu and others) that the school does not just regulate linguistic difference. The modern school is an elaborate institutional system, and the division between "private" and "public", with the differing resources between the public and private systems and within the public system, contributes to the reproduction of society-wide hierarchies of school-certified symbolic difference. These reflect and reproduce the dynamics of class, race, and language revealed in the controversy over Ebonics. Inequality of economic resources is particularly true of schools in the United States. Ebonics/AAVE is the language of "inner cities", of the urban poor and working class. Its speakers attend schools which are underfunded relative to their suburban and private school counterparts. As students, these youth often have "attitude" or "motivation" problems, as apparently do most linguistic minorities, who are arguably (working-class and peasant) majorities in the world's school systems. As Long (1999) argues in a forceful comparative discussion of the Ebonics issue, these minority/majorities typically experience language difference as a fundamental dimension of their school experience and as a serious obstacle to educational success.

So let me conclude with the question posed at the beginning of this chapter, one which permeated the Ebonics debate: Is poor school performance by African-American youth due to funding, character, or language? The answer must be "all three": Language, economy, and subjectivity. This triad also defines a challenging terrain for ethnographically-oriented approaches to language ideologies.

Acknowledgments

The ideas in this chapter benefitted from discussions in the public forums mentioned in the text, from a lively discussion of the issues at a research seminar of the Centre for Applied Linguistics at Thames Valley University, London, and from critical commentary on earlier drafts by Jan Blommaert, Richard Blot, Michele Foster, and Ben Rampton. Fiona Thompson assisted with editing the final draft. I am indebted to them all.

Notes

1. A good source for the text of original resolutions, revised resolutions, and resolutions of support, as well as documents of declaration is Perry and Delpit (1998).

2. The original claim seems to have emerged from something like the following quandary facing the Board: (1) Given that our students speak a distinct language variety from that of the school and this affects their performance, we need additional resources to build bridges between that variety and the school variety. (2) There are only special monies when the school variety and the home variety are separate languages. (3) Therefore, we hereby declare that Ebonics is a separate language.
3. *Martin Luther King Junior Elementary School Children et al. v. Ann Arbor School District Board.* Federal Supplements: 451 F Supp 1324 (E.D. Mich 1978); 463 F. Supp 1027 (E.D. Mich 1978); 473 F. Supp 1371 (E.D. Mich 1979).
4. See *Africanized English and education*, a special issue of *Linguistics and Education* 7(1–2) (1995), for articles by Baugh on the legal issues and by others on curricular and materials research concerning Ebonics/AAVE.
5. Given the federal system in the U.S. and state and local control of school budgets, court decisions taken in Michigan did not have binding legal force on school policy in other states, such as California, though this does not detract from the basic relevance of the Ann Arbor case to the OSB proposals.
6. This distribution of overall population and school population is basically due to two factors: (1) many of the city's non-minority residents are older or elderly home-owners whose children have finished school (that is, African American households are younger and account for a larger proportion of the city's young people); and (2) many of the non-minority school age children attend parochial or other private schools. This is not an unusual pattern in U.S. cities, though it is often more extreme in areas of relative economic decline, such as the Northeast U.S. Because schooling is financed by local property taxes, there is an annual struggle in Albany, as in many U.S. cities, to convince an older, non-minority population to support tax levees for public education for children who are not their own or those of their friends and who are often seen as racially "other", with all the baggage that carries in the United States. In this context, African American adults who expressed fear or anger that *their* children's education was or might be under-financed were expressing a sensible concern.
7. The idea that a bias or drive for reference is basic to language apprehension and evaluation has been used by a variety of analysts to understand selective apprehension of speech hierarchies (Errington 1985); socialization to Anglo-American law (Mertz 1996); and the oral-to-written translation dynamics of Maya discourse (Haviland 1996). Its universality has been challenged by Hill (1998) in an analysis of Mexicano (Nahuatl) language ideologies, who argues that some speech traditions give salience to pragmatic rather than referential dimensions of language, and both Collins (1996) and Mertz (1996) argue for differential socialization in education to referential or pragmatic aspects of text.
8. A decade earlier, in the documentary *The Story of English: Black on White* (Part 5), the then-superintendent of the Philadelphia School District, Constance Clayton, argued that hypothetical young men who said "I bes ready for comin' here, next week" for "I will come here, next week" would not be understood

by white employers. It is interesting that Clayton, a highly-placed African American official, has constructed an example that does not conform to known rules of Ebonics/AAVE, reminding us that Ebonics is a working class tradition. But what is significant is the claim that the utterance would be unintelligible.

9. We should note Webster's belief that political harmony and relative egalitarianism depend on the "precision and uniformity" of language. A witty example of similar belief, a century later and from a different part of the political spectrum, can be found at the beginning of the film *My Fair Lady.* In a sung speech Professor Henry Higgins, presumably echoing George Bernard Shaw's socialist sympathies, decries Eliza Doolittle's Cockney speech as an reflection of a class-ridden, class-divided society, and praises precise, correct speech.
10. Between 1865 and 1900 over 1200 Black newspapers were established (Marable 1984: 7).

References

Anderson, Benedict
1983 *Imagined Communities*. London: Verso.

Apple, Michael
1996 *Cultural Politics and Education.* New York: Teachers College Press.

Asante, Molefi K.
1997 Should Ebonics be recognized as a language? Yes, Ebonics provides a useful pedagogical strategy. *On Campus*, March 1997: 4.

Baker, Houston
1988 *Afro-American Poetics*. Madison, WI: University of Wisconsin Press.

Bakhtin, Mikhail
1981 *The Dialogic Imagination.* Austin: University of Texas Press.

Barthes, Roland
1972 *Mythologies*. London: Palladin [1957].

Baugh, John
1983 *Black Street Speech.* Austin: University of Texas Press.
1995 The law, linguistics, and education. In: Bloome, D. and J. Lempke (eds.), *Africanized English and Education.* Special issue, *Linguistics and Education* 7: 87–107.

Bourdieu, Pierre
1991 The production and reproduction of legitimate language. In: Bourdieu, Pierre, *Language and Symbolic Power*. Cambridge, MA: Harvard University Press, 43–65.

Bourdieu, Pierre and Jean-Claude Passeron
1977 *Reproduction in Education, Culture and Society*. Newbury Park, CA: Sage Publications.

City School District of Albany
1996 *Comprehensive Assessment Report Summary Data*. Albany, NY: City School District of Albany.

Collins, James
1996 Socialization to text: Structure and contradiction in schooled literacy. In: Silverstein, Michael and Greg Urban (eds.) *Natural Histories of Discourse*. Chicago: University of Chicago Press, 203–228.
1998 *Understanding Tolowa Histories*. New York: Routledge.

Congress of Linguists of African Descent
1997 Resolution in support of the Oakland School Board.

Cook-Gumperz, Jenny
1986 Schooling and literacy. In: *The Social Construction of Literacy*. New York: Cambridge University Press, 16–44.

Cook-Gumperz, Jenny (ed.)
1986 *The Social Construction of Literacy*. New York: Cambridge University Press.

Cose, Ellis
1997 Why Ebonics is irrelevant. *Newsweek*, January 13: 80.

Cummins, Jim
1986 Empowering minority students. *Harvard Education Review* 56: 18–34.

Davis, Mike
1985 *Prisoners of the American Dream*. London: Verso.

Derrida, Jacques
1976 *Of Grammatology*. Baltimore: Johns Hopkins University Press.

Dumont, Luis
1986 *Essays on Individualism*. Chicago: University of Chicago Press.

Educational Researcher
1996 *The relationship between educational research and educational policy*. Special issue, *Educational Researcher* 25(8).

Errington, Joseph
1985 *Language and Social Change in Java*. Athens, OH: Center for International Studies, Ohio University.

Fairclough, Norman
1989 *Language and Power*. London: Longman.

Farrugio, Peter
1997 OUSD Ebonics resolution. Compilation of letters posted on *American Education Research Association Division G Electronic List*, January 7, 1997.

Gal, Susan and Judith Irvine
1997 The boundaries of language and disciplines: How ideologies construct difference. *Social Research* 62: 967–1001.

Gilyard, Keith
1991 *Voices of the Self*. Detroit: Wayne State University Press.

Gouldner, Alvin
1979 *The Future of Intellectuals and the Rise of the New Class*. New York: Continuum.

Gramsci, Antonio
1971 *Selections from the Prison Notebooks*. New York: International Publishers.

Graff, Harvey (ed.)
1981 *Literacy and Social Development in the West*. Cambridge, UK: Cambridge University Press.

Green, Lisa
1998 Aspect and predicate phrases in African-American vernacular English. In: Mufwene, Saliko, John Rickford, Guy Bailey and John Baugh (eds.), *African American English*. New York: Routledge, 37–68.

Guillory, John
1993 *Cultural Capital: The Problem of Literary Canon Formation*. Chicago: University of Chicago Press.

Gumperz, John
1982 *Discourse strategies*. New York: Cambridge University Press.

Hall, William and Roy Freedle
1975 *Culture and Language*. Washington: Hemisphere Press.

Haviland, John
1996 From text to talk in Tzotzil. In: Silverstein, Michael and Greg Urban (eds.), *Natural Histories of Discourse*, University of Chicago Press, 45–78.

Heath, Shirley Brice
1981 English in our language heritage. In: Ferguson, C. and S. Heath (eds.), *Language in the U.S.A*. New York: Cambridge University Press, 6–20.
1983 *Ways With Words*. New York: Cambridge University Press.

Hennessy, A.
1997 Ebonics. Letter posted on *American Education Research Association Division G Electronic List*, January 6, 1997.

Hernandez-Chavez, Eduardo
1988 Language policy and language rights in the United States. In: Skutnabb-Kangas, Tove and Jim Cummins (eds.), *Minority Education*. Philadelphia: Multilingual Matters, 45–56.

Hill, Jane
1998 "Today there is no respect": Nostalgia, "respect", and oppositional discourse in Mexicano (Nahuatl) language ideology. In: Schieffelin, Bambi, Kathryn Woolard and Paul Kroskrity (eds.), *Language ideologies: Practice and Theory*. New York: Oxford University Press, 33–50.

Hymes, Dell
1981 *In Vain I tried to Tell You*. Philadelphia: University of Pennsylvania Press.

Hymes, Dell, Courtney Cazden and Vera John (eds.)
1970 *Functions of Language in the Classroom*. New York: Teachers College.

Irvine, Judith
1995 The family romances of colonial linguistics: Gender and family in nineteenth century representations of African languages. *Pragmatics* 5(2): 139–153.

Jack, Senley
1997 Don't let divisive Ebonics ghettoize our education. Letters to the Editor, *Albany Times Union*, January 11, 1997.

Jacoby, Russell
1995 *Dogmatic Wisdom*. New York: Doubleday.

Jordan, June
1988 Ain't nobody mean more to me than you. *Harvard Education Review* 58: 363–374.

Kaestle, Carl, H. Damon-Moore, L. Stedman, K. Tinsley and W. Trollinger
1991 *Literacy in the United States*. New Haven: Yale University Press.

Kristeva, Julia
1980 *Desire in Language*. New York: Columbia University Press.

Labov, William

1972 *Language in the Inner-City*. Philadelphia: University of Pennsylvania Press.

1982 Objectivity and commitment in linguistic science: the case of the Black English trial in Ann Arbor. *Language in Society* 11: 165–199.

1995 Can reading failure be reversed? In: Gadsden, Vivian and Daniel Wagner (eds.), *Literacy among African-American Youth*. Cresskill, NJ: Hampton Press, 39–68.

Lasch, Christopher

1995 *The Revolt of the Elites and the Betrayal of Democracy*. New York: W.W. Norton.

Leland, J. and N. Joseph

1997 Hooked on Ebonics. *Newsweek*, January 13: 78–79.

Linguistic Society of America

1997 LSA Resolution on the Oakland Ebonics Issue. Posted on *American Education Research Association Division G Electronic List*, January 19, 1997.

Long, Mike

1999 Ebonics, language, and power. In: Blot, Richard (ed.), *Language and Social Identity*. Greenwood, CT: Gordon Breach.

Lukacs, Georg

1971 *History and Class Consciousness*. Boston: MIT Press.

Lynch, Dan

1997 Power and politics of language. *Albany Times Union*, February 27, 1997.

Magnin, Joseph

1990 Language rights as collective rights. In: Adams, Karen and Daniel Brink (eds.), *Perspectives on Official English*. New York: Mouton de Gruyter, 293–300.

Marable, Manning

1984 Prologue: The legacy of the first reconstruction. In: *Race, Reform, and Rebellion*. Jackson: University Press of Mississippi, 1–11.

Marvin, Carolyn

1988 Attributes of authority: Literacy tests and the logic of strategic conduct. *Communication* 11: 63–82.

Mertz, Elizabeth
1996 Recontextualization as socialization. In: Silverstein, Michael and Greg Urban (eds.), *Natural Histories of Discourse*. Chicago: University of Chicago Press, 229–249.

Mickelson, Rosalyn
1990 The attitude-achievement paradox among black adolescent. *Sociology of Education* 63: 44-61.

Moore, Nathan
1997 Should Ebonics be recognized as a language? No, language is not the problem. *On Campus*, March 1997: 4.

Moore, Robert
1997 *"The People are Here Now": The Contemporary Culture of an Ancestral Language*. Doctoral dissertation, University of Chicago.

Morgan, Marcyliena
1998 More than a mood or an attitude. In: Mufwene, Salikoko, John Rickford, Guy Bailey and John Baugh (eds.) *African-American English*. New York: Routledge, 251–281.

Mufwene, Salikoko (ed.)
1993 *Africanisms in Afro-American Language Varieties*. Athens, GA: University of Georgia Press.

Nasaw, David
1979 *Schooled to Order*. Oxford: Oxford University Press.

National Commission on Excellence in Education
1983 *A Nation at Risk*. Washington: U.S. Department of Education.

Oakland School Board
1997a *Resolution of the Board of Education Adopting the Report of the African-American Task Force*. Board of Education, Oakland Unified School District, Document No. 597–0063.

1997b *Amended Resolution of the Board of Education Adopting the Report of the African-American Task Force*. Board of Education, Oakland Unified School District, Document No. 9697–0063.

Ogbu, John
1979 *Minority Education and Caste*. New York: Academic Press.

Ohmann, Richard
1987 *The Politics of Letters*. Middlebury, CN: Wesleyan University Press.

O'Neal, William
1998 If Ebonics isn't a language, then tell me, what is? In: Perry, Theresa and Lisa Delpit (eds.), *The Real Ebonics Debate*. Boston: Beacon, 38–48.

Perry, Theresa and Lisa Delpit (eds.)
1998 *The Real Ebonics Debate*. Boston: Beacon.

Philips, Susan
1982 *The Invisible Culture*. Prospect Heights: Waveland.

Rickford, John
1998 The creole origins of African-American vernacular English. In: Mufwene, Salikoko, John Rickford, Guy Bailey and John Baugh (eds.), *African-American English*. New York: Routledge, 154–200.

Rockhill, Kathleen
1993 Gender, language, and the politics of literacy. In: Street, Brian (ed.), *Cross-cultural Approaches to Literacy*. Cambridge, UK: Cambridge University Press, 156–175.

Rose, Mike
1989 *Lives on the Boundary*. New York: Penguin.

Scott, James
1990 *Domination and the Arts of Resistance*. New Haven, CT: Yale University Press.

Silverstein, Michael
1976 Shifters, linguistic categories and cultural description. In: Basso, Keith and Henry Selby (eds.), *Meaning in Anthropology*. Albuquerque: University of New Mexico Press, 11–55.

1979 Language structure and linguistic ideology. In: Clyne, Paul, William Hanks and Carol Hofbauer (eds.), *The Elements*. Chicago: Chicago Linguistics Society, 193–248.

1984 The "value" of objectual language. Paper delivered at a symposium of the 83rd Annual Meeting of the American Anthropological Association, Denver.

1985 Language and the culture of gender. In: Mertz, Elizabeth and Richard Parmentier (eds.), *Semiotic Mediation*. New York: Academic Press, 219–259.

1996 Monoglot "standard" in America. In: Brenneis, Donald and Ronald Macaulay (eds.), *The Matrix of Language: Contemporary Linguistic Anthropology*. Boulder: Westview, 284–306.

Soltow, Larry and Edward Stevens
1981 *The Rise of Literacy and the Common School in the United States. A Socioeconomic Analysis to 1870*. Chicago: University of Chicago Press.

Warner, Michael
1990 *Letters of the Republic*. Cambridge, MA: Harvard University Press.

Williams, Ronald
1975 *Ebonics*. St. Louis: Institute of Black Studies.

Wills, Gary
1994 Rhetorical leader: Martin Luther King, Jr. In: *Certain trumpets*. New York: Simon and Schuster, 211–224.

Zboray, Ronald
1993 *A Fictive People: Antebellum Economic Development and the American Reading Public*. Oxford: Oxford University Press.

Zinn, Howard
1980 *A People's History of the United States*. New York: Harper Colophon.

Singapore's *Speak Mandarin Campaign*: Language ideological debates and the imagining of the nation

Wendy Bokhorst-Heng

1. Introduction

According to Benedict Anderson, "Communities are to be distinguished, not by their falsity/genuineness, but by the style in which they are imagined" (1991: 6).[1] I take this notion of "imagined communities" as my starting point in this chapter because of the focus it implicitly puts on language. Imagining requires language. But also, around the world, nationalist leaders have used the meanings of language to define this imagining. What is meant by the meanings of language is more than the symbolic use of language, as one might use a national flag or national anthem, in the rallying call of nationalism. Rather, the focus is on how language ideological debates occur within the context of the larger discourses of imagining the nation, how they participate in that process and inform each other.

In this chapter, I will consider the production and reproduction of language meanings within the context of imagining Singapore. If we take into account Kuo and Chen's (1983: 100) observation that "Singapore is known to be a planned society, and its planning framework is, in general, a centralized one," then it is perhaps not surprising that the development of language meanings in Singapore is very much intertwined with the imagining of the nation. Ever since independence, the government in Singapore has imagined a nation that is disciplined, orderly, rugged, efficient, and controlled. Individuality and alternative expressions of national and personal identity are discouraged (Chua 1995). Within this framework, former Prime Minister Lee Kuan Yew has personally developed very particular ideas about language and about how these meanings of language further his view of what is a good society and how that society is to be understood. In particular, while being imagined as multi-ethnic and multilingual, this discourse is more about homogeneity within each ethnic community rather than heterogeneity within the nation.

The production and reproduction of these language ideologies find their nexus in the annual *Speak Mandarin Campaign* (henceforth *SMC*). The

SMC is aimed at the largest ethnic community in Singapore, the Chinese, and its goal is to stimulate the use of one standardized language variety — Mandarin Chinese— rather than the many Chinese dialects spoken by members of that community in Singapore. Thus, the ultimate effect of the *SMC* is one of homogenizing the Chinese community, in itself seen as a necessary building block for building a multicultural, pluralist Singaporean nation.

My discussion falls into three main sections. In section 2, I will provide some general background information about language in Singapore. In section 3, my discussion focuses on language ideology within Singapore's unique structure and within the definition of bilingualism. These two sections provide the historical and ideological context for section 4, in which I discuss language ideological debates in the *Speak Mandarin Campaign*. In so doing, it will be possible to begin to see how and why dominant language ideologies are produced and reproduced. As in the cases discussed by DiGiacomo (Catalonia) and Jaffe (Corsica) elsewhere in this volume, much of the debate has occurred in the mass daily press (see Bokhorst-Heng 1998 for a more detailed discussion of the role of the press in language ideological debates). Section 5 summarizes and concludes the chapter.

2. Singapore: Some background

The Singaporean population comprises three major ethnic groups: 77.5 percent Chinese, 14.2 percent Malays, and 7.1 percent Indians (and 1.2 % "Others"). Of these groups, the Chinese community is the most heterogeneous. In the 1957 census, 11 Chinese dialects were identified as mother-tongues: 39.8 percent claimed Hokkien to be their mother-tongue, 22.6 percent Teowchew, 20 percent Cantonese, 6.8 percent Hainanese, 6.1 percent Hakka, and the remaining 4.7 percent other Chinese and Malaysian dialects. As put by Lee Kuan Yew recently in a book commemorating the 50th anniversary of the British Council in Singapore, "We were a Tower of Babel, trying to find a common tongue" (*ST* 18 April 1997). Since Independence in 1965, the People's Action Party (PAP) government has attempted to reduce this linguistic diversity and to homogenize the Chinese community. Following familiar nationalist rhetoric, the government leaders (and particularly Lee Kuan Yew) have fervently argued that this linguistic diversity is incompatible with the goals of nation-building and have developed policies specifically aimed to solve the problems that such diversity posed for the nation. In part because the Chinese community is particularly divided in its heterogeneity, the government has especially targeted this community. As will be discussed later in this paper, the argument has been that a divided Chinese community would not only be detrimental to the survival of that particular community, but also detrimental to the survival of the nation.

However, it is precisely Singapore's linguistic and cultural diversity that has hindered such arguments from appearing alone. In the first place, the basis of the PAP government's platform at Independence was that the party stood for *all* Singaporeans, in contrast to the government north of the causeway that seemed to promote a Malay Malaysia rather than a Malaysian Malaysia. Thus, "multiracialism" has systematically formed the basis of its political and nationalist agenda. Furthermore, given the fact that Singapore is physically surrounded by Indonesia and Malaysia —two predominantly Malay and Islamic nations— Singapore has had to carefully manage its image. With a predominantly Chinese population, the leaders had to assure their neighbors that Singapore was not an extension of China (and more importantly in the earlier days, of Communism), but was first of all devoted to its position as a Southeast Asian nation.

Thus, for these and other reasons, all efforts to unite the Chinese community have been couched within the larger policies of multiracialism and multilingualism. Revamping the education system was one of the first policy actions of the PAP leaders. Rather than allowing different language-stream schools to continue as had been the practice under British colonialism (Wilson 1978), they introduced bilingualism as a way to unify and nationalize the education system. All students in Malay-, Tamil- and Mandarin-medium schools would learn English as a second language (mostly for Math and Science). All those in English-medium schools would learn the language associated with their ethnicity as a second language (mostly for Civics and History). In effect, this form of bilingualism made English the lingua franca of Singapore, giving the policy the name among local academics "English-knowing bilingualism" (Kachru 1993). Like in most postcolonial African countries, the former colonial language (in this case English) was seen as an ethnically neutral language and thus (among other reasons) introduced for the purposes of national unity and for economic development (see section 2 of Madumulla et al's chapter in this volume). But in contrast to the way in which, for instance, Mozambique has adopted Portuguese (Stroud, this volume), Singapore's leaders have very carefully excluded English from the realm of nationalist discourse and denied it any status as a mother tongue in Singapore. I will return to this at greater length later in this chapter.

Not only did this definition of bilingualism make English the lingua franca, but it also prescribed for each person their "mother-tongue." For all ethnic groups, in a curious twist, "mother-tongue" is defined according to one's father's ethnicity (and which thus may not be the language spoken in the home). If your father is ethnically Chinese, your mother-tongue is Mandarin, if Indian then Tamil, and if Malay then Bahasa Malay. So, even though Mandarin was identified as "mother-tongue" for only 0.1 percent of the Chinese community in the 1957 census, Mandarin was prescribed as such for all ethnic Chinese within the bilingual policy. Within this framework, English cannot be a mother-tongue. The proscriptive definition of bilingualism has thus made bilingualism more a policy about homogenization than heterogeneity, and more about linguistic purism than diversity.

The government's efforts to entrench these three mother-tongues in the various communities were particularly intense in the late 1970s after the bilingual policy received its first official evaluation. In 1978, then Prime Minister (now Senior Minister) Lee Kuan Yew appointed Defence Minister Dr. Goh Keng Swee and the "education team" to evaluate the bilingual policy as it pertained to the Chinese community. In their final report, the committee declared the policy a failure. Less than 40 percent of the students attained the minimum competency level in two languages. The committee saw the continued use of dialects in the home as the main reason for this failure. Because about 85 percent of the students spoke only dialects at home, they were in effect having to learn two languages at school. As well, what they were learning at school was thus not being reinforced at home. On the basis of these findings, and in a rare case of admitting failure, the government concluded that not all children were able to cope with the demands of becoming fully bilingual. However, this is not to say that the policy of bilingualism was to be abandoned. Rather, major changes were made in the education system such that language became the very basis of society. Language-based streaming was introduced, whereby the educational system was stratified according to the different language abilities of the students. The weakest students would receive monolingual education; the best students would receive intensive bilingual training. For all children in Primary school, more than 50 percent of curriculum time would be devoted to language learning. Thus, "effective bilingualism" has become closely aligned with academic, and hence social and economic, success. Since 1987, all schools are now English-medium with "mother-tongue" taught as a second language.

Going by the most recent census conducted in 1990, it appears that the use of "mother-tongue" in the home is taking hold. 29.8 percent of Chinese households use Mandarin as their predominant household language, 50.6 percent one of the dialects, and 19.2 percent English (Tham 1996: 27). While a question of mother-tongue (which appeared only in the 1957 census) cannot be compared on a par with questions on language use, these figures do suggest that there has been a pattern of remarkable language shift away from the use of dialects to Mandarin and English.

While there were real pedagogical and academic concerns motivating the government to make such radical changes in the education system, what the government leaders had to say about language suggests a deeper concern. Furthermore, the fact that these changes coincided with the launching of the first *Speak Mandarin Campaign* also suggests that these policies were entwined in the larger language ideological debates gripping the imagining of the nation. Why Lee Kuan Yew and his government were so concerned about the failure of the bilingual policy has to do with their view of language meanings, with their assumptions of what a "good" society is, and with how they understood the role of language and especially the bilingual policy in the imagining of that society. Most of these views have been engineered by Lee Kuan Yew himself. Between April 1978 and November 1980, he participated in five televised panel discussions in which he presented his view of language and explained the paramount need for the bilingual policy to succeed (Bokhorst-Heng 1998). To these meanings I now turn.

3. English-knowing bilingualism: Crisis management

The bilingual policy has been premised on what Pendley (1983) calls the "functional polarization" of language, or, as Kuo and Jernudd (1994) describe it, the "division of labor between languages." In his 1972 speech at a Singapore Teachers' Union Dinner, Lee Kuan Yew established the parameters of this polarization (*The Mirror*, 20 November 1972):

> When I speak of bilingualism, I do not mean just the facility of speaking two languages. It is more basic than that, first we understand ourselves ... then the facility of the English language gives us access to the science and technology of the West. It also provides a convenient common ground on which ... everybody competes in a neutral medium.
>
> With the language [mother-tongue] go the fables and proverbs. It is the learning of a whole value system, a whole philosophy of life, that can maintain the fabric of our society intact, in spite of exposure to all the current madnesses around the world.

On the one side of this polarization is English, the language needed for instrumental and pragmatic purposes. Professor Jayakumar, then Minister of State (Law and Home Affairs), outlined three pragmatic functions for English (*ST*, 19 August 1982). First, at the national level, "English is the major international language for trade, science and technology and proficiency in the language is essential as Singapore becomes a leading financial and banking centre." This economic consideration is important as economic growth has always been perceived by the PAP government as tantamount to the viability of nationhood. Second, at the individual level, "education in English is the key to the productivity concept. With increasing modernization, skilled workers who know English will be in greater demand ... it is the key to acquisition of skills and training and career advancement." Along the same vein, Lee Kuan Yew saw English as a neutral language linked to meritocracy. English "is our common working language ... It provides a neutral medium, giving no one any advantage in the competition for knowledge and jobs" (*The Mirror* 19 June 1978). Finally, at the community level, when English "is the common language here, it will enable all Singaporeans —regardless of race— to communicate with one another." In this pragmatic view, then, the English language is seen as neutral and culture-less.

Positioned on the other side of this polarization are the three "mother-tongues," Malay, Tamil and Mandarin. As mother-tongues, they are the languages of identity, of ethnicity and of culture. They are the languages of good values, and, in Lee Kuan Yew's words, of a "whole philosophy of life." They are the languages of national cohesion. As put another way by Lee Kuan Yew, while English is for *new knowledge*, to support the development of a modern industrial nation, mother-tongue is for *old knowledge*, to keep the people anchored and focused amidst the changes around them (*ST* 24 November 1979).

What we see in this polarization is a very selective (and often paradoxical) understanding of language. With respect to English, the view is that the language can be separated from culture and technology so that it is possible to adopt the technology accessed through English without necessarily accepting its culture. In contrast, the mother-tongue is seen to somehow inherently embody one's ethnically defined culture. Through mother-tongue education, children would be "inculcated with good eastern values and cultures ... These values will be thus programmed like a computer in the children and form their basic principles in dealing with society and with problems" (Choo Wee Khiang, *Parliamentary Debates*, 17 January 1989, Vol.52, Prt 1, Col.152). Unlike English, it is impossible to separate one's mother-tongue from culture.

While the lines demarcating language meanings within this structure of functional polarization have been presented by Lee Kuan Yew as rational and unproblematic, in practice the model has been very difficult to sustain. Not only is it difficult to separate culture from technology, but it is also difficult to completely divorce culture from language. Yet at the same time, it is difficult to sustain the argument that language inherently embodies culture. However, even this fuzziness in definition has been used by Lee Kuan Yew and other ministers to actually fortify the polar boundaries. This is particularly evident in the maneuvering of the language meanings having to do with English.

During the 1970s, government leaders began to express concern about the increase of individualism, consumerism and liberalism among the people. The late Dr. Tay Eng Soon (Minister of State, Education) noted in a in a speech at the National University of Singapore in 1982, that there was an increase of such undesirable qualities as "hippyism, a libertine pre-occupation with self-gratification, the cult of living for today and for my-self and to hell with others" among the youth (*ST* 13 December 1982). In the context of this discourse, the meanings of English took on added elements. English, the leaders argued, actually posed a threat to the imagining of the nation. The threat of English came in two ways. In the first place, because English is seen as being neutral and mother-tongue to embody one's culture, to learn English at the expense of the mother-tongue would leave a person "deculturalized." In his 1972 speech to the teachers, Lee Kuan Yew explained what he meant by deculturalization in his reference to the Caribbean. It is a "calypso-type society ... speaking pidgin English, mindlessly aping the Americans or British with no basic values or cultures" of their own, and leading a "steel-beating and rum-brewing-and-drinking, happy go lucky life," he said. Frankly, "I do not believe this [kind of society] is worth the building ... worth the preserving" (*The Mirror*, 20 November 1972). What Lee Kuan Yew seems to be suggesting is that to be monolingual in English would invite the danger of having no culture at all. One would be reduced to mindless imitation of the West, not being Asian and not being Western either, with no identity to call one's own.

But there is another (and very contradictory) element to English. Playing on the ambiguous divide within the functional polarization of language, rather than being neutral, English carries cultural meaning as well. Only, the cultural values associated with English are debased and decadent. C. V. Devan Nair (then National Trade Union Congress Secretary General), put it this way: "Through the English language we are enabled to absorb all that modern science and technology can offer us." However, at the same time, most younger Singaporeans also imbibe "the mindless pop culture of the West." This culture and way of life, he says, is one "in which the centres of cognition, perception and feeling are not located in the cerebral cortex, or even in the heart and its cultured emotions. On the contrary, they are located below the waist, and primarily in what may be called the lower vital centres" (*ST* 15 January 1979). English is no longer merely a neutral medium for access to technology, or for inter-racial communication. Rather, it is the gateway to decadence, liberalism, Westernization. Instead of exploring the social changes as associated with concurrent changes in Singapore's economic and political conditions, they were labeled as alien, brought in through the non-mother-tongue. A tension is thus created between the pragmatic needs for English in the imagining of the nation and the potential threat it carries to that imagining.

The answer to this quandary lies in reinforcing the boundaries of the functional polarization of language through what has come to be called the "Asianizing" of Singapore. Because English could potentially lead to deculturalization, Singaporeans needed to be "re-culturalized", they needed to have their Chineseness, Indianness and Malayness restored to them. Because English carried the threat of decadent Westernization, Singaporeans needed a cultural ballast to ground them and protect them. And so, since the late 1970s, through various measures such as moral education programs in the school, the institution of a set of "core" national values, and the creation of different self-help groups for the different communities, the government has sought to re-Asianize the people. Greater emphasis was placed on the prescription of mother-tongues, in the belief that "a race = a culture = a language". Because English cannot be a mother-tongue, its meanings are restricted within the parameters of functional polarization. While the continued dominance of English in Singapore is beyond our discussion here, it is worth noting two things. First of all, by giving greater voice to discussions about the mother-tongue, the social and economic dominance of English is actually retained and strengthened in its disguise (Puru Shotam 1987; Pennycook 1994). Secondly, by reinforcing the boundaries of the functional polarization of language, any claim that might be made for English to be a mother-tongue is denied (Bokhorst-Heng 1998).

Although all three communities are the focus of this Asianizing effort, special attention has been given to the Chinese. In a speech given to the Catholic High School alumni, MP Dr. Ow Chin Hock explained the reasons for this focus: "Unlike the Malay community, Chinese Singaporeans do not have such uniting factors as a common language and religion." In fact, he argued, there is no such thing as *a* Chinese community in Singapore. Rather, "there are three sub-communities: the English educated Chinese, the Chinese educated, and the less educated, dialect-speaking Chinese" (*ST* 16 October 1990). Thus, the newspaper caption read, "Chinese Singaporeans face crisis in values and culture." Because there was nothing within the community to unite them, the re-ethnification of the Chinese community was paramount. It was in this context of crisis intervention that Lee Kuan Yew launched in 1979 what has become an annual *Speak Mandarin Campaign*.

4. The Speak Mandarin Campaign

Three key official arguments have been appealed to by the government in support of the *Speak Mandarin Campaign*. First, there is the *educational* argument: because the continued use of dialects created a burden for children having to learn two languages at school, the use of dialects at home must be restricted and replaced by Mandarin. Second, there is the *cultural* argument: because of the dominance of English, and the threat of deculturalization and Western decadence that came with it, Chinese Singaporeans needed to be re-ethnicized through Mandarin, which would also then provide them with a cultural ballast. And through this re-ethnicization, they would also be united to form *a* Chinese community. Finally, there is the *communicative* argument: Chinese Singaporeans need a lingua franca other than English. The most logical choice was Mandarin, as it was neutral to all dialect groups. While these arguments structure much of the campaign's discourse, the issues are in fact much more complex, and have to do with very specific views of language and how language meanings figure into the imagining of the nation. After first considering the *SMC* as a campaign, I will try to unpack some of these meanings.

4.1. The campaign

Given the fact that imagining the nation in Singapore occurs through very centralized planning, it is perhaps not surprising that the "national campaign" has become the most common genre of government-to-people communication. In his analysis of campaigns in Singapore, Tham Kok Wing (1983) identified sixty-six national campaigns between 1958 and 1982. National campaigns are all planned by the Prime Minister's Office. They have been used to direct and influence public awareness of certain issues, to encourage people to behave in specific desired ways, to control the spread of certain "undesirable" practices or values, as an instrument for policy implementation, to consolidate mass support, and ultimately to psychologically build up the citizenry for the task of nation-building. They have had a wide scope, including Anti-Spitting, Courtesy, and more recently (1996/1997), a Smile campaign. While diverse in their messages, nonetheless the campaigns exhibit a certain stable and generic form, such that they can be seen as a speech genre (Bakhtin1986: 60–102). The general framework is that of crisis management: a crisis is presented, and the government's answer to that crisis is rationalized as being the only answer to that crisis. Thus, when leaders choose the campaign genre to organize their message, they are also organizing how the message will be read and anticipating what assumptions their audience will bring with them.

While the *SMC* has been meant for only the Chinese community, it has been presented in the genre of a national campaign, having its precedence in the pre-Independence national language campaigns. It has been intensely prescriptive in its concerted effort to alter the language behavior of Chinese Singaporeans, to convince them to abandon their use of dialects for the sake of their community and the nation. The *SMC* speeches are almost messianic in their warning of impending crisis should the Chinese fail to unite through the use of Mandarin. In many ways, the *SMC* has been even *larger* than the national campaigns. In terms of duration, it has been by far the longest running campaign. In terms of organization, it has its own secretariat. The campaign involves a completely comprehensive effort, drawing in members of education, mass media, grassroots, the Singapore Chinese Chamber of Commerce and Industry (SCCCI), government leaders, and even the Prime Minister. And its visibility is far greater than any other campaign. As put succinctly by Harrison, "The campaigning for Mandarin has not, as far as can be established, used sky-writing. To find such an omission has been difficult" (1980:177). Banners, posters, and stickers with campaign slogans encouraging the Chinese to speak Mandarin are displayed in public places. T-shirts with the same slogans are worn by students. Advertisements supporting the campaign appear on television, radio and in the cinemas. Numerous activities have been generated in support of the campaign including Mandarin classes (even via telephone and the Internet) and various contests and workshops. No other campaign has seen such a sustained and extensive presence in Singapore.

While on the one hand, the use of a national campaign as the genre within which to organize its message to the Chinese community has allowed for an intensity and scope not possible in other genres, nonetheless, it has also created a number of potentially explosive paradoxes. In the first place, the genre of a *national* campaign for the promotion of Mandarin within the Chinese community has created a blurring of the lines marking what is for ethnic community and what is for nation. And secondly, for the most part national campaigns are concerned with public and social behavior; yet the *SMC* is ultimately about homogenizing the Chinese community by making Mandarin the mother-tongue, the language of the private domain. There has thus been the explosive contradiction between what is public and what is private. As the incongruity between a national, public genre for community-level, private behavior reveals itself particularly in the voices of resistance, I will discuss these conflicts in greater detail in section 4.3. But first, I will turn to the crystallization of language meanings within the campaign, and illustrate this by means of a discussion of one of the campaign's key speeches.

4.2. The crystallization of language meanings: A speech by Goh Chok Tong

As I mentioned, the *SMC* is part of the overall objective of restoring to the Chinese their Chineseness, to *make* Mandarin the mother-tongue of all Chinese Singaporeans. This effort is based on the belief that "a race = a language = a culture", and translated into campaign slogans such as "*hua ren hua yu*" (literally "Chinese people, Chinese language") and, "If you are Chinese, make a statement— in Mandarin." Two key arguments have been presented to support this goal, both couched within the overall framework of a crisis leading to the inevitable conclusion that Mandarin must be the mother-tongue for all Chinese Singaporeans. The first is the *Mandarin versus Dialect* argument, and the second is the *Mandarin versus English* argument. Throughout the campaign, these two debates can be seen weaving in and out of each other, one becoming stronger in one context and the other given greater voice in another. While in many ways, the definitions of language within each contradict each other, they are also dependent on each other in the overall effort of imagining the nation. As will be shown, leaders frequently play these two debates against each other, using their contradiction to both create a tension and then to resolve that tension.

To examine the crystallization of language meanings within these two debates, and their role within the imagining of the nation, I will draw primarily from Goh Chok Tong's speech delivered at the launching ceremony of the 1991 *Speak Mandarin Campaign*. I use his speech because of where it stands historically. While the PAP has held a clear majority of voters' support since Independence, there had been a steady decline throughout the decade of the 1980s: 75.5 percent in 1980, 61.8 percent in 1988, and 61 percent in 1991. The 1991 results were particularly upsetting for the party as the election marked the beginning of Goh Chok Tong's leadership as Prime Minister (Lee Kuan Yew passed on the leadership to Goh on 28 November 1990, and himself became Senior Minister). The declining support caused the PAP leaders to re-examine their ideology and administration. In their post-election analysis, they attributed their losses to the fact that the opposition candidates had used dialects in their campaigning to win the support of the Chinese community (*ST* 14 December 1991). They were forced to acknowledge the voice of resistance in the defining of language meanings. Thus, in some ways, 1991 is a watershed in language meanings, a time when the voice of the people was heard. It is in this context that Goh's 1991 *SMC* speech was given. I will now give the full text of the speech.

> "Mandarin is more than a language"
> Mr Goh Chok Tong
> The Prime Minister
> 30 September 1991
>
> A nation is "a single people traditionally fixed on a well-defined territory, speaking the same language and preferably a language all its own, possessing a distinct culture, and shaped to a common mould by many generations of shared historical experience." [Rupert Emerson in *From Empire to Nation*]. By this definition, Singapore is not yet a nation. We do not speak the same language, and we do not yet possess the many generations of shared historical experience.
>
> Within the same family, it is still very common to find that grandparents, parents and children do not share the same primary language —the language they are most comfortable in. For the grandparents the language they use is very often dialect, for the parents Mandarin; and for the children English. Of course, the three generations do still converse with one another through a combination of dialect, Mandarin and English. But their common vocabulary is unlikely to go beyond 500 words. They will have difficulty discussing any subject in depth. Their conversation will be shallow, limited by each other's command of the other generation's primary language.
>
> I speak Hokkien to my mother. My children speak to me and my wife in English, and Mandarin to their grandmother, my mother. They have dropped dialect. It will take another generation in my family for three generations to share the same one primary language.

Heterogeneous community

In Singapore, communication across families is even more complicated for the older generation. It is not unusual to find two Chinese together who are unable to talk to one another. One may speak Hokkien only while the other Cantonese. How can we ever build a nation if the Chinese community is unable even to speak the same language, be it dialect, Mandarin or English?

You will discover how heterogeneous Singapore is when you go campaigning in an election. No political leader in Singapore can reach out on his own to every Singaporean. No matter how good a linguist he is, he cannot be expected to master the four official languages plus over 20 Chinese and Indian dialects.

It is in our national interest to move into a situation where all Singaporeans can speak to one another in a common language, i.e. English, and to members of his own community in his mother-tongue. For the Chinese, the common mother-tongue should be Mandarin rather than dialect. Unlike Hong Kong, where Cantonese predominates, it will not be politically acceptable if we replace the teaching of Mandarin with any of the major dialects. I do not think we can agree on which dialect to be taught. If we do not succeed in forging Mandarin as the common mother-tongue, the link language for future generations of Chinese Singaporeans will be English only.

Already English is becoming the dominant language among Chinese households. Its use had increased from 10 per cent in 1980 to 21 per cent in 1990.

Language and values

The question is whether with the greater use of English, we may lose some aspects of our identity. These are the traditional values of our forefathers.

Values and language cannot be easily separated. They are intrinsically linked to each other. Values get into our minds and hearts through folklore. For the Chinese these stories and beliefs are preserved in their literature or passed on by word of mouth. Although Chinese literature, idioms and proverbs can be translated into English, their full meaning may be lost in the process.

A Chinese Singaporean who does not know Chinese —either Mandarin or dialect— runs the risk of losing the collective wisdom of the Chinese civilization. This year's campaign slogan is apt. Mandarin is more than a language. Mandarin not only allows the Chinese to communicate with one another but also opens up many chests of treasures —Chinese literature, music, operas, paintings, calligraphy, ceramics and so on. When we can appreciate them, we will feel proud to be part of that rich history which is Chinese.

A sense of history

Having a sense of history is important. It gives us our bearing and makes us understand what we are today. As a country, Singapore's history is short. But if we know Mandarin, we can identify with a 5000 year old civilization.

Last month, the Chinese Chamber of Commerce and Industry organized a congress of Chinese businessmen from all over the world. These were successful men and women. One would expect them to prefer using English, which is the language of trade and business. But I was told that that was not the case. Although the official language of the congress was English, the moment someone spoke in Mandarin, the atmosphere changed. It became more intimate. The use of Mandarin brought out immediately a common understanding among the Chinese businessmen of different nationalities. They felt a common bond. They felt they belonged together.

Making Mandarin popular

Our problem is how to make Mandarin popular with our students. Many parents have voiced the concern that their children may not be able to cope with the learning of Mandarin in schools. I believe we should make learning the language lively and enjoyable. We should put fun and humor to soften the serious task of teaching Chinese.

Last year's "Speak Mandarin Campaign" made some Singaporeans uncomfortable. I fully understand their concerns. Let me assure non-Chinese Singaporeans that the government is not promoting the Chinese language or culture at the expense of the others. In fact, the Ministry of Information and the Arts is working together with the Malay Language Committee to promote standard Malay. The Ministry has also asked the Indian community if it needs help to promote the use of Tamil. We want all the ethnic communities to preserve their language, culture and values. We aim to be a harmonious multi-racial nation.

For the Chinese community, our aim should be a single people, speaking the same primary language, that is Mandarin, possessing a distinct culture and a shared past, and sharing a common destiny for the future.

Such a Chinese community will then be tightly-knit. Provided it is also tolerant and appreciative of the other communities' heritage, able to communicate with them in English, and work with them for a common future, Singapore will grow to become a nation.

If we consider the schema of Goh's text, how his text is organized by authorial intent, we see that his speech follows the argumentation structure common in many of the national campaigns: one which propounds a problem and then provides a solution to that problem. According to one definition, the constitution of a problem involves a "sequential ordering of events, simultaneously employing various devices so as to prepare for the eventual suggested solution as the only rational solution" (Kwok Kian Woon 1983: 71). At the very outset of his speech, Prime Minister Goh establishes the premise of "the problem". He begins his address with the timeless assertion drawn from Rupert Emerson's *From Empire to Nation*: "A nation is 'a single people traditionally fixed on a well-defined territory, speaking the same language and preferably a language all its own, possessing a distinct culture, and shaped to a common mould by many generations of shared historical experience'." Without questioning its applicability to multi-ethnic and multi-linguistic nations such as Singapore, Goh takes this definition as common-sense knowledge, and uses it to measure the degree of nationhood achieved thus far. By this definition, Singapore is not yet a nation. It does not have a *common language* and it does not have a *common history*. This definition thus establishes what Singapore is not, and provides a direction for what Singapore should work towards.

Goh first addresses the challenge of linguistic diversity to Singapore's achievement of nationhood. The problem of linguistic diversity has been a common theme in all of the *SMC* speeches. Already in 1979, Lee Kuan Yew's opening words were, "Chinese Singaporeans face a dilemma," referring to the presence of over 12 dialects within the community and the difficulties that caused for children at school. What is interesting in Goh Chok Tong's speech is that he frames the problem as a *national* problem. Singapore is not yet a nation because it does not have a common language. Yet, in the rest of his speech, he concentrates on the problems of linguistic diversity within just the Chinese community. Thus he uses a *national* framework to address community issues. Providing factual evidence, he problematizes Singapore's linguistic diversity at all levels of society: from the smallest unit, the family,[2] including his own; to the Chinese community, where dialects hinder intra-ethnic communication; and to government, where no political leader "can reach out on his own to every Singaporean." With linguistic diversity permeating family, community and government, "How can we ever build a nation?" Goh asks.

At this point, Goh introduces the inevitable solution: if the main obstacle to the development of full nationhood is the linguistic diversity of dialects, then the obvious solution is linguistic uniformity. "It is in our national interest," he argues, "to move into a situation where all Singaporeans can speak to one another in a common language, i. e., English, and to members of his own community in his mother-tongue." For the Chinese, this common mother-tongue was to be, or become, Mandarin, rather than any dialect.

Goh quickly dismisses dialect as being not even a viable consideration: "I do not think we can agree on which dialect to be taught." He then goes on to imply that if linguistic (dialect) diversity were to continue, Mandarin would not take hold the common mother-tongue. And in that event, English, he predicted, would become the intra-ethnic link language. He then constructs the rest of his argument using the Mandarin versus English dichotomy. But before I turn to this part of his argument, the Mandarin versus Dialects dichotomy needs to be considered a bit more, as it is crucial to understanding the making of a mother-tongue.

4.2.1. Mandarin versus dialects

The 1979 campaign was launched with the call to "*Speak more Mandarin and less dialect*" and "*No dialect, more Mandarin.*" While they agreed with the promotion of Mandarin, many members of the Chinese community took strong offence to this overt call to eliminate the use of dialects. Traditionally, it was dialect-speaking parents and grandparents that played an active role in the transmission of culture and values. And dialects, not Mandarin, were seen as necessary for intimacy, for culture and roots, for family and clan identity, and as the true mother-tongue. And so the campaign slogans were softened to read "*From now on, speak Mandarin, please*" and "*Let's speak Mandarin.*" However, while the slogans were softened, the objective to eliminate the use of dialects remained central to the campaign. This was achieved largely through the dichotic structuring of language meanings. By placing Mandarin and the dialects in contrast with each other, the leaders reinforced both the validity of Mandarin within the imagining of the nation and the inappropriate presence of the dialects. A look at some of the campaign and government speeches shows the centrality of this dichotomy to the formation of language meanings.

– *Dialects are vulgar, polluting, and associated with the uneducated; Mandarin is refined and part of the literary culture.* The vulgarity associated with dialects was noted by Mr. Rabim Ishak, then Senior Minister of State (Foreign Affairs), in a speech at a community center. Although he does not speak Chinese, he said, he has learnt some of the swear words in Cantonese, Hokkien, Teochew and Hainanese. He went on to note that "in Mandarin, the swear words are less common as the language is supposed to be for the refined people" (*ST*, 11 July 1980). And because of the refining effect it would have on the Chinese-speaking community, he supported the *SMC*. In his 1986 campaign speech Goh Chok Tong even called Mandarin a "language of courtesy." He cited a survey conducted by a local polling company which showed that "customers of departmental stores and restaurants who spoke in Mandarin tended to be more polite than those who spoke in dialects."

- *Dialects are divisive, fragmentary, and a major cause of miscommunication and misunderstanding; Mandarin is the language of unity, cohesion, and a bridge between the different members of the Chinese community.* Goh Chok Tong, then Second Defence and Health Minister, pointed out at the opening ceremony of the *SMC* in his constituency that, "The spoken and written form in Mandarin are in unison and do not create problems, unlike dialects where one word can have several meanings depending on the dialect it is spoken in" (*ST*, 9 June 1981). A slide presentation at the opening of the Health Ministry's *SMC* at the School of Nursing also showed the mayhem dialects lead to when misunderstanding occurs in a hospital context. It concluded with the happy ending of patients and nurses communicating in Mandarin (*ST*, 2 October 1985).

– *Dialects are a burden on the young, forcing them to learn two languages when they go to school; Mandarin facilitates academic success.* Lee Kuan Yew believes in a time-management concept of language learning, that there is enough room in the brain for only one language, and that a focus on the one will necessarily exact a cost on the other. "No child, however intelligent, has unlimited data storage capacity," he has argued. "The memory space is finite ... And the more one learns dialect words, the less space there is for Mandarin words" (*ST* 26 October 1981). In this view, dialects are seen to over-burden the young. In one of his televised discussions on language, he argued quite forcefully that, "Dialect will hinder the learning of the child if he uses dialect. I think every parent will be prepared to make a little sacrifice if it is for the future of the child. To speak dialect with your child is to ruin his future" (*ST*, 17 November 1980). Statistics published in the press show that those students who speak Mandarin at home score higher in both languages than those who speak dialect at home, and those effectively bilingual in Mandarin and English score well in all their courses.

– *Dialects have no value, neither culturally nor economically; Mandarin is linked to a 5,000-year old history, rich in culture, and bears immense economic potential with the opening up of China's markets*. In his November 1980 television forum, Lee Kuan Yew stressed that, unlike Mandarin which "has cultural value and will also have economic value twenty years later," dialects "have no economic value in Singapore. Their cultural value is also very low" (*ST* 17 October 1980).

– *Dialects represent the past and are primitive; Mandarin is the future.* A 1980 Singapore Broadcasting Corporation Current Affairs documentary traced Singapore's history. "In the past," the commentator said, the use of dialects by the early immigrants "sufficed for the market place." But, "these conditions have changed ... [As] the future of Singapore lies not as a trading outpost but as a financial, commercial centre, the language competence demand is higher" (*ST* 15 June 1980). In a television forum, Lee Kuan Yew argued, "Mandarin is a developing language; on the other hands, dialect is a stagnant language" (*ST* 10 January 1980).

By contrasting the meanings of dialects with Mandarin, dialects are clearly denied validity in the imagining of the nation and community, and even in the home. Faced with the choice of Mandarin or dialects, the choice, Lee Kuan Yew said in his 1979 Campaign speech, is "obvious." "Indeed," Goh Chok Tong stated, "wise parents will never let their children speak dialect at all" (*ST* 26 October 1981). Thus, although in 1979 Lee Kuan Yew had assured parents that the choice was theirs as to what language they wanted their children to speak in the home, it is clear what that choice should be. In this dichotic structuring of language meanings, then, the government simultaneously created a void by banishing dialects from nation, community, and home, leaving the Chinese community and individual with no mother-tongue, and then filled that void by prescribing Mandarin as their mother-tongue.

4.2.2. Mandarin versus English

In his call for linguistic uniformity, it is significant that Goh does not argue in his speech for linguistic uniformity through English alone, but rather for English plus mother-tongue. In fact, he presents the increasing dominance of English among the Chinese as problematic: "Already English is becoming the dominant language among Chinese households. Its use had increased from 10 per cent in 1980 to 21 percent in 1990." Lee Kuan Yew has argued on more than one occasion that, if dialects were allowed free reign, English might well become the lingua franca of the Chinese community. In his 1979 *SMC* speech, he warned, "Because Singapore is 25 percent non-Chinese, English will be the common language between different ethnic Singaporeans. And if we continue to use dialects, then English will tend to become the common language between Chinese of different dialect groups." The increasing presence of English in the homes of Chinese Singaporeans relates to the second element of nationhood lacking in Singapore: the lack of shared historical experiences and culture. The logic in Goh's argument follows what we have already seen. English is necessary. But English only, without mother-tongue, is undesirable. At the national level, English only would undermine the shared cultural and historical experiences that Emerson said were necessary for nationhood. As Goh put it, "The question is whether with the greater use of English, we may lose some aspects of our identity. These are the traditional values of our forefathers." At the individual level, a person would lose "the collective wisdom of the Chinese civilization" and would lose his/her bearings; he/she would be deculturalized. English cannot become a mother-tongue. As put by Lee Kuan Yew in his 1984 campaign speech, "One abiding reason why we have to persist in bilingualism is that English will not be emotionally acceptable as our mother tongue" (*Campaign speeches* 1989).

This denial of mother-tongue status for English has been challenged in recent years, mostly by those English-educated Chinese who felt threatened when the focus of the campaign turned to them. Their voices appeared in some of the headlines in the *Straits Times*, the main English-language newspaper: "Why Mandarin is not my mother-tongue" (*ST* 23 February 1992), "English a mother-tongue too?" and "English: A Singaporean mother-tongue?" (*ST* 14 June 1994). The answer to these questions has been the continued reiteration of the merits of Mandarin over English with its inherent embodiment of culture and its link to history. At the national level, English-knowing monolingualism would undermine the shared cultural and historical experiences that Emerson said were necessary for nationhood. As Goh put it, "The question is whether with the greater use of English, we may lose some aspects of our identity. These are the traditional values of our forefathers." These are the key to the nation's shared historical experiences. Thus nationhood can only be achieved through bilingualism.

Goh spends the rest of his speech establishing the merits of Mandarin over English in the imagining of the nation. In the first place, he presents the *cultural argument*: Mandarin is "more than just a language ... it also opens up many chests of treasures —Chinese literature, music, operas, paintings, calligraphy, ceramics, and so on." He then offers the *pragmatic argument*, bringing Mandarin out of the context of culture to that of business and commerce in his example of the use of Mandarin at the SCCCI Congress. With the more recent focus of the *SMC* on the English-educated Chinese, the business appeal of Mandarin has grown even stronger. Mandarin has given Singaporeans an edge over its predominantly Malay neighbors in establishing commercial ties with China. However, this pragmatic argument rarely appears alone, and indeed, cannot. For Mandarin to become the established mother-tongue of the Chinese community (especially the

English-medium educated), it must go beyond the neutrality and pragmatism of English. In Goh's account of the SCCCI congress, he uses the device of contrast to take Mandarin there. The moment someone switched from English to Mandarin, "the atmosphere changed." There was intimacy, brotherhood, a common understanding. The assumption built into his account is that, prior to the use of Mandarin, these features were lacking. Thus, not only does Mandarin hold a place in the commercial sector, but it is superior to English. It could unite this group of nationally diverse, but ethnically homogenous, Chinese members, whereas English could not. Thus there is also a third argument, that of *identity*. "Mandarin has more to offer than business" reads a 13 September 1994 *Straits Times* headline. "Don't treat Mandarin as alien language" reads another (8 September 1994). It follows then, that, while the value of English can only be in its neutral role as the language for commerce and for inter-ethnic communication, Mandarin is value-added. And so, while the lines dividing language meanings within the structure of functional polarization are blurred by Mandarin's encroachment in the commercial sector, the divide is rescued by an expansion of the meanings in Mandarin, and ultimately a strengthening of the polarization.

The validity of Mandarin in the nationalist agenda is thus established. Now we come to the climax, the proposed solution. Goh began his speech with a discussion concerning the definition of a nation. The problem is that Singapore is not yet a nation —it does not have a common language and it does not have shared historical experiences. In his speech, he demonstrated how the use of Mandarin can fill both needs. Because of the link between Mandarin and values, and between Mandarin and history, because Mandarin has a place in the commercial sector, and because all Chinese can unite through the use of Mandarin, Chinese Singaporeans must embrace Mandarin. Only then will they become a community, "a single people, speaking the same language, that is Mandarin, possessing a distinct culture and a shared past, and sharing a common destiny for the future". Such a Chinese community, he argues, "will then be tightly-knit;" only then will they be able to contribute to the task of nation building; then "Singapore will grow to become a nation." While Goh does give a disclaimer that this will only be possible if the Chinese community is sensitive to the non-Chinese communities, he does seem to nonetheless suggest that nationhood is contingent on the unity of the Chinese community. There is thus a blurring of the lines between nation and community, in ways reminiscent of the pattern described by Heller (this volume) with regard to the Québécois' insistence of firm mother-tongue monolingualism as a necessary precondition for bilingualism.

4.3. *The voices of resistance*

Earlier in this chapter, I noted how the use of a national campaign for the promotion of Mandarin created two key paradoxes. One has to do with the slippage between nation and community created by the use of a *national* campaign for *community* purposes. The second has to do with the slippage between public and private created by the use of the *public* genre of the national campaign to make Mandarin a mother-tongue, an issue located in the *private* domain of the home. These two paradoxes have translated into areas of resistance, the former mainly voiced by the non-Chinese communities, and the latter by the members of the Chinese community. These are by no means the only voices of resistance; however, they do demonstrate how such resistance has contributed to language ideological debates in Singapore.

4.3.1. Mandarin for nation? For community?

The multiracialist discourse in the "Asianizing of Singapore" paints a picture of Singapore as being a multiethnic nation with three homogenous ethnic communities unproblematically coexisting in equilibrious relation to each other. Singapore has rejected the "melting pot" model in favor of retaining the cultural heritage of the different ethnic communities. The multiracialist discourse also contends that cultural and ethnic identity coexists harmoniously with political loyalty at the national level. Goh Chok Tong captured this harmony in the phrase: "Unity in diversity" (*ST* 14 August 1988). The continuance of ethnic identity has allowed the government to be absolved of many of the responsibilities of cultural maintenance and social welfare, making them the responsibility of the individual communities (Chua Beng Huat 1995).

However, there are a number of problems with this model. In the first place, the sheer disproportionate size of the Chinese community constantly threatens the balance of equilibrium between the different ethnic communities. Chinese-related issues often dominate the agenda, and the non-Chinese communities frequently feel overwhelmed and marginalized (Puru Shotam 1987; Tan Su Hwi 1996). There is often considerable slippage in the government's discourse between nation and community. It is not always clear which is being referenced. A look at the use of pronouns in Goh Chok Tong's 1991 *SMC* speech demonstrates this ambiguity.

In this speech, Goh is clearly attempting to develop a sense of inclusiveness and community, particularly in his frequent use of "we" and "us", together used 18 times. Not only does the choice of pronouns evoke a sense of community, but it also brings everyone into the problem. Together they will work towards solving the problem of nationhood —which is "our problem," "our aim" and in "our national interest." Such inclusive pronouns also evoke a strong sense of Goh's presence in the text, which is made even more visible by his use of "I" (5x) and "me" (2x). In contrast to the use of inclusive pronouns, "they" is used only 8 times —in reference to a family, to his own family, to language and values, and to the Chinese businessmen. Not once was "they" used to refer to an outgroup, or to separate "us" from "them".

It is instructive to note in this context when Goh does *not* use inclusive pronouns. After drawing his audience into the problem with "we" and "us," when it comes to working out the solution in the last paragraph, he retreats. In the last paragraph, he lapses into the traditional community-based rhetoric whereby each community is responsible for its own welfare. In order to remove himself, it seems he needs to extract the human element that had been so present in his text. For the first time, the Chinese community is de-humanized as an "it." If Singapore is to become a nation, it requires not the efforts of "we" or "us," but rather, it requires the efforts of an inanimate Chinese community.

However, while Goh's use of inclusive pronouns create a sense of community and bonding, a closer analysis reveals considerable ambiguity. The use of "we" in some cases clearly refers to Singaporeans (e. g. "We do not yet speak the same language, and we do not yet possess the many generations of shared historical experience"), and in other cases to the Chinese community (e. g. "When we can appreciate them, we will feel proud to be part of that rich history which is Chinese"). But the other references are not so clear. At least the following patterns of reference can be found in the text:

(1) "we" = Singaporeans? Chinese Community? Government?

E.g.: (i) "How can we ever build a nation if the Chinese community is unable even to speak the same language, be it dialect, Mandarin or English?"

(ii) "Unlike Hong Kong, where Cantonese predominates, it will not be politically acceptable if we replace the teaching of Mandarin with any of the major dialects."

(2) "we" = Chinese Singaporeans (presumably)

E.g.: (i) "I do not think we can agree on which dialect to be taught. If we do not succeed in forging mandarin as the common mother-tongue, the link language for future generations of Chinese Singaporeans will be English only."

(ii) "But if we know Mandarin, we can identify with a 5000 year old civilization."

(3) "we"/"us" = Singaporeans? Chinese Community?

E.g.: (i) "The question is whether with the greater use of English, we may lose some aspects of our identity."

(ii) "It gives us our bearing and makes us understand what we are today."

(4) "we" = Chinese Community? Government? Singaporeans? Teachers?

E.g.: (i) "I believe we should make learning the language lively and enjoyable. We should put fun and humor to soften the serious task of teaching Chinese."

(5) "we" = Government? Ministry of Information and the Arts?

E.g.: (i) "We want all the ethnic communities to preserve their language, culture and values. We aim to be a harmonious multi-racial nation."

The ambiguity is compounded by Goh's constant switching between references to nation and community. For example, when Goh details the extent of the problem, he oscillates between Chinese community/family and nation (government). In the beginning of the section on "Heterogeneous community" (and again in the last paragraph), he merges nationhood with community homogeneity. In "A sense of history," he talks about how Singapore's history is short, and so "we" must identify with China's 5000 year-old civilization. As well, the speech (community) was printed in *The Straits Times*, the main "non-ethnic" (national) newspaper.

The ambiguity in Goh's text can be understood at at least two levels. Firstly, the specific reference of the pronouns can be seen as irrelevant to the general aura and effect of the speech. It does not demand intense scrutiny. If anything, and secondly, the ambiguity enhances the overall effect of community. The ambiguity attempts to diffuse any sense of boundary, and to maintain a discourse of multiracialism within the "Asianizing of Singapore."

However, this blurring is precisely what has made the juxtaposition of community and nation within the genre of a national campaign problematic. It is precisely because it is not always clear *who* the campaign speeches are directed at, and who is being drawn into the "we" that the non-Chinese communities have reacted against the campaign. They fear an increase in Chinese chauvinism, and worry that there may be a consequent reduction in the status of their languages and cultures, and that the government might weaken its commitment to multiracialism (*ST* 16 May 1978). The recent focus on Mandarin-versus-English made these questions even more pertinent. English is not confined to just the Chinese community (unlike dialects), and so the lines between community and nation became increasingly vague. The fault-line broke open during the 1990 *SMC*. The theme that year was about speaking Mandarin at work —clearly not a community-specific domain. *The Straits Times* was flooded with letters from both the Chinese and non-Chinese communities condemning the campaign as chauvinistic and exclusionary. As former Senior Minister Rajaratnam noted, people were questioning the government's commitment to multiracialism, and whether the leaders were "doing all this in favor of a Singaporean Singapore" (*ST* 29 October 1990). They were questioning the boundary between nation and (Chinese) ethnic community.

Because of such resistance, the leaders must repeatedly qualify the *SMC's* objectives. First there is the frequent guarantee that the campaign is not about replacing English with Mandarin as the official working language. After the furore of the 1990 campaign, Goh Chok Tong assured Singaporeans that the government's "policy towards the Chinese language has not changed. English will remain the working language in Singapore" (*ST* 27 October 1990). Second, the leaders assert that the promotion of Mandarin is not to diminish the status of the other official ethnic languages. During the 1981 campaign, *SMC* chairman Ho Kah Leong (and Parliamentary Secretary, Education) said, "I want to emphasize here that the government" is not promoting Mandarin "to the exclusion of the other languages. Mandarin WILL NOT replace the other official languages" (*ST* 4 October 1981). Third, the discourse of multi-racialism is frequently brought in to reassure the non-Chinese communities that the campaign is not for them, and not to make Singaporean society more Chinese at the expense of the other communities. The PAP leaders call attention to the government's support for the development of the minority cultures. Brigadier-General Lee Hsien Loong spent considerable time on this theme in his 1988 *SMC* speech:

> *Majlis Pusat* (Central Council of Malay Cultural Organizations) and other Malay cultural organizations organized a Malay Language and Culture Month this year, and Indian cultural organizations organize similar Tamil language activities from time to time. The Government encourages them to do so. Our desire to preserve traditional values is not confined to the Chinese community alone. It is good for the nation that Singaporeans of all races have a clear sense of where they have come from, and why they are here. Each community should take pride in its heritage, retain it and develop upon it.

In his 1991 *SMC* speech, Goh Chok Tong similarly reminded the non-Chinese communities of the government's efforts to promote their languages and cultures. "We want all the ethnic languages to preserve their language, culture and values," he said. "We aim to be a harmonious, multi-racial society." Equilibrium is thus restored through the discourse of the "Asianizing of Singapore" and through the reinstatement of the "a race = a language = a culture" equation.

4.3.2. Public genre for private domain?

Most national campaigns in Singapore are concerned with issues relating to public behavior. On the surface, the *SMC* also appears to be about behavior in the public domain. Lee Kuan Yew stated unequivocally in 1979 that he would not interfere with the home: "I want to be quite clear, we cannot control what is done at home; that we have to leave to the good sense of the parents and the grandparents." He went on to say, "Because administrative action cannot reach the home where dialects, already entrenched, will prevail," the government will focus on "dramatically" altering the pattern of language usage outside the home, in government offices, public transit, hawker stalls and restaurants, shopping centres and so on (*Campaign Speeches* 1989). *Straits Times* Group Editor Peter Lim interpreted Lee Kuan Yew's comments as a policy of non-interference: "While Mr. Lee still seeks to get Singaporeans to stick to two languages and not complicate life for themselves by hanging on to dialects, he concedes that home is where government should not interfere ... he leaves it to the parents to decide. Did I hear a sigh of relief last night?" (*ST*, 24 November 1979). The demarcations between private and public were thus made very explicit.

However, it also is clear that the main objective of the campaign has been to make Mandarin a mother-tongue, the language of the private domain of the home. Quoting again from Lee Kuan Yew, "The ultimate test" of the success of the campaign "is whether Mandarin is spoken at home between parents and their children. That is the meaning of mother tongue" (*ST* 26 October 1981). Shortly after the campaign began, Goh Chok Tong announced that the 1980 census would for the first time include a survey on what languages Singaporeans speak at home. The same question would be asked in the 1990 census "to monitor the success" of the *SMC* (*ST* 19 November 1979).

However, the focus on the home (private), voiced according to the conventions of a national campaign (public) has created an explosive contradiction in the campaign. As with the blurred distinction between nation and community, this contradiction has formed a fault-line along which voices of resistance have emerged. This became particularly problematic in 1980 when, in the view of many, the government's efforts moved too far into the private sphere. In 1980, the Director of Education, Chan Kai Yau, announced that, in a "move to take the *Speak Mandarin* drive one step further" (*ST* 20 November 1980), all students were to be registered in their Hanyu Pinyin names, rather than the dialect names given at birth. His rationale was that pinyinization was necessary to reduce dialect-based identity and to unite the Chinese community. Hanyu Pinyin is a romanized system of transcribing Chinese characters based on Mandarin pronunciation. Most Chinese in Singapore go by the dialect pronunciation of their Chinese names, not Mandarin. The same Chinese character will have different dialect pronunciations, such that, for example, the same name will be Tan in Hokkien, Chan in Cantonese, Sin in Hainanese, and Chen in Mandarin. Thus, by enforcing Hanyu Pinyin, students were required to assume a name different from the one given them by their parents, and different from their father's. Parents were also urged to begin giving their children Mandarin names at birth. Lee Kuan Yew made compliance with this recommendation a measure of one's identification with the Chinese community. In his 1984 *SMC* launch speech, he noted that

> When parents registered their children's names, between August 1982 to July 1984, one-fifth registered only their dialect names, a total rejection. Over one-third registered their dialect names, with full Pinyin in brackets, a concession to their identification with other Chinese of different dialects, a tentative and reluctant acceptance. Nearly one-quarter registered their surnames in dialect and their personal names in Pinyin, a partial acceptance, i.e. they will not give up their total identification with their fathers' and grandfathers' dialect surnames but are prepared to concede an identification with Chinese of other dialects through using Pinyin for their personal names. One-fifth did so in full Pinyin, a full acceptance.
>
> (*Campaign Speeches*, 1989)

By implication, the choice to keep one's name in dialect was an indication that one preferred division and fragmentation over a united Chinese community.

However, names are intensely personal and reflect personal, family, and group identity. A *Straits Times* survey conducted shortly after the policy was announced (21 November 1980) revealed a polarized reaction between the English-educated and the Chinese-educated. Reactions from the English-educated "ranged from mild support to an angry denouncement of it as an 'infringement of the individual's right'." Some letters to the editor expressed the view that the government had "gone overboard," and that the policy was "unconstitutional" (7,9 June 1982). The Chinese-educated considered the move as "logically in step" with the *SMC*, while dialect speakers, who "believe firmly that whatever the government decides is always for their good, said they have no complaint if that is what the government wants" (21 November 1980). Teachers complained that the policy caused confusion, and that it was a futile exercise (*ST* 17 January 1981; 7 June 1982).

But perhaps the strongest voice of resistance was the "silent" one that spoke against registering children's birth names in dialect. After a full decade, it was clear that most Chinese Singaporeans resisted giving their children full pinyin names. According to *The Straits Times* editor, people simply "have not bought" the government's argument for pinyinizing names (23 December 1991). In 1987, Lee Kuan Yew noted that only 12 percent of all Chinese babies born in January to June 1987 were registered with full pinyinized names, compared to 22 percent in 1983. The number of children who had dialect surnames with Hanyu Pinyin personal names increased. The editor saw this pattern as a reflection of "acts of identity": "After all, most parents would want their surnames and their offspring's to be instantly recognizable as one and the same, as an outward mark of their blood bond ... There is also the desire to preserve symbolic links with their dialect groups and the provinces and villages of their forefathers in China" (23 December 1991). Parents clearly drew the line: while complying by giving pinyin personal names, they resisted by keeping their dialect surnames. In the 1991 elections, they also demonstrated their resistance by voting in a member of the Workers Party, Low Thia Khiang in Hougang, who used dialects in his campaigning (*ST*, 14 December 1991). The government responded to the parents' voice of resistance by announcing that students would once again be allowed to register in their dialect names.

5. Conclusion

Before 1991, when it was re-designed and re-issued, each person's identity card included information about one's race and dialect. Since 1991, "dialect" no longer appears. In the prescriptive manner that has characterized the *SMC* all along, it is now assumed that if you are Chinese, your mother-tongue is Mandarin. The linguistic diversity characterizing the Chinese community has thus been homogenized. In this chapter, I have charted some of the key features in this prescription of mother-tongue meanings in the imagining of Singapore. The *Speak Mandarin Campaign* has been the catalyst of this journey, capturing the debates within and over language meanings in the imagining of Singapore. It has been the framework of policy interpretation and implementation, and of resistance to these interpretations and implementations. And it is the framework within which it is possible to go beyond a story of ideology production and re-production by a very domineering government, to one that tells of the tensions, negotiations, paradoxes and resistances by different groups. The story thus becomes one of identifying what has been normalized, how that process has occurred, and of how resistance contributed to the direction and nature of these normalized norms.

The tension between homogenization of communities and the pluralization of the nation, which lies at the heart of the *SMC*, certainly deserves deeper exploration as well as comparison to other cases. In many respects, Lee Kuan Yew's idea of a "multicultural" nation does not seem to differ much from dominant ideas of "monocultural" nations, such as those articulated in many types of modern nationalisms (see e.g. Wilmsen and McAllister (eds.) 1996). In the Singaporean project, as much essentializing of (imagined) community characteristics is going on as in monocultural national projects, and a fair amount of reducing of intra-group differences has also been noted. Only, what is elsewhere perceived as a "nation" (i.e. a "people" with its own language, culture and history) is given the status of "community" in Singapore; the Singaporean nation, by consequence, is a patchwork of internally homogenized communities. Homogenization and essentialization is shifted down one step from "nation" to "community", so as to safeguard the status of "nation" for Singapore and keep it out of reach for the Chinese and other "ethnic" communities. Not surprisingly, and quite similar to many other cases discussed in this volume, an important role is given to language in such homogenizing and essentializing projects. Lee Kuan Yew's statements stand out by the massive amount of theorizing he produces on language in relation to culture, ethnicity, history and society. They prove, among other things, how easily certain linguistic ideologies can be transformed or absorbed into political ideologies, and how easily a rhetoric on language, culture, history and identity can become an instrument of societal streamlining and disciplining.

Notes

1. The author wishes to express her gratitude to Monica Heller and Jan Blommaert for their comments on earlier drafts of this chapter.
2. As was described in a 1993 newspaper article, as a result of the fact that children are learning Mandarin and English in school and because of the *Speak Mandarin Campaign*, a significant number of Chinese households were

shifting away from using dialects towards English and Mandarin. "The result is a communication problem, as dialect-speaking grandparents with English- or Mandarin-speaking grandchildren find themselves at a loss for words. Says Teochew-speaking Madam Tan Yian Hong, 73, whose two grandchildren speak English and Mandarin, "We are like chickens and ducks talking. We carry on in different languages without understanding one another, but hoping somehow that we will." (*ST*, 7 June 1993).

References

Anderson, Benedict
1991 *Imagined Communities: Reflections of the Origins and Spread of Nationalism*. London: Verso.

Bakhtin, M. M.
1981 *The Dialogic Imagination*. Austin: University of Texas Press.
1986 *Speech Genres and Other Late Essays*. Austin: University of Texas Press.

Bokhorst-Heng, Wendy D.
1998 *Language and Imagining the Nation in Singapore*. PhD. dissertation, University of Toronto.

Business Times
[various numbers].

Chua Beng Huat
1995 *Communitarian Ideology and Democracy in Singapore*. London and New York: Routledge.

Chua, S. C.
1962 *State of Singapore: Report on the Census of Population, 1957*. Singapore, Department of Statistics: Government Printing Office.

Harrison, Godfrey
1980 Mandarin and the Mandarins: Language policy and the media in Singapore. *Journal of Multilingual and Multicultural Development* 1: 175–180.

Kachru, Braj B.
1983 *The Other Tongue: English Across Cultures*. Oxford: Pergamon Press.

Kuo, Eddie C. Y. and Björn Jernudd
1994 Balancing macro- and micro-sociolinguistic perspectives in language management: The case of Singapore. In: Gopinathan, S, A. Pakir, Ho Wah Kam and V. Saravanan (eds.), *Language, Society and Education in Singapore: Issues and Trends.* Singapore: Times Academic Press, 25–46.

Kuo, Eddie C. Y. and Peter S. J. Chen
1983 *Communication Policy and Planning in Singapore.* London: Kegan Paul International.

Kwok Kian Woon
1983 Ideology in Singapore: A textual investigation. *Southeast Asian Journal of Social Science* 11: 70–80.

Lee Kuan Yew
1972 Traditional values and national identity. Speech presented at the Singapore Teachers Union's 26th Anniversary Dinner, Shangri-La Hotel, 5 November 1972. *The Mirror*, 20 November 1972, Vol.8, No.47.

1991 Confucianist values should not be lightly abandoned. Excerpts of Interview by Nihon K. Shimbun. 8 January 1988. In: Loy Teck Juan, Seng Han Tong and Pong Cheng Lian (eds.), *Lee Kuan Yew on the Chinese Community in Singapore.* Singapore: Singapore Chinese Chamber of Commerce and Industry and the Singapore Federation of Chinese Clan Associations, 119.

The Mirror
[various numbers].

Pendley, Charles
1983 Language policy and social transformation in contemporary Singapore. *Southeast Asian Journal of Social Science* 11(2), 46–58.

Pennycook, Alastair
1994 *The Cultural Politics of English as an International Language.* London: Longman.

Puru Shotam
1987 *The Social Negotiation of language in the Singaporean Everyday Life World.* PhD dissertation, National University of Singapore.

Singapore Ministry of Communications and Information
1989 *Speak Mandarin Campaign Launching Speeches (1979–1989).* Singapore: Ministry of Communications and Information.

Parliamentary Debates. Republic of Singapore. Official Report
[various years], Singapore.

The Straits Times (*ST*)
[various numbers].

Tan Su Hwi
1996 A critical review of sociolinguistic engineering in Singapore. In: Blommaert, Jan (ed.), *The Politics of Multilingualism and Language Planning*. Antwerp: UIA-GER (Antwerp Papers in Linguistics 87), 107–142.

Tham Kok Wing
1983 National campaigns in Singapore politics. Bachelor of Social Science Honours Academic Exercise, Department of Political Science, National University of Singapore.

Tham Seong Chee
1996 *Multi-lingualism in Singapore: Two Decades of Development*. Census of Population, 1990, Monograph No.6. Singapore: Department of Statistics, Ministry of Trade and Industry.

Wilmsen, Edwin and Patrick McAllister (eds.)
1996 *The Politics of Difference: Ethnic Premises in a World of Power*. Chicago: University of Chicago Press.

Wilson, H. E.
1978 *Social Engineering in Singapore: Educational Policies and Social Change, 1819–1972*. Singapore: Singapore University Press.

Linguistic and political attitudes towards Israeli Hebrew: Ongoing revival versus normalcy

Ron Kuzar

1. Theoretical framework

The language spoken nowadays in Israel is Hebrew, more specifically "modern" or "Israeli" Hebrew. The language has been judged as dead before its modern re-emergence, in light of the straightforward criterion that it lacked native speakers. While the question of the "revival" of Hebrew has often been addressed, the question of the "end of revival", i.e. the normalcy of the language, came up in the 1950s, but has not reached its resolution so far. In fact, it has been kept on a low flame, almost forgotten.

The recognition that scholarly and political circles of discourse have significant mutual relevance has not been taken for granted in the historiography of Hebrew. A rare consideration of this possibility can be observed in Weinberg (1981):

> The "Israel" component of the term [Israeli Hebrew] has no political meaning. Evidently the proclamation of the State of Israel and the consequent catapulting of Hebrew into the position of a national language, the uncontested language of administration, education and the army, meant a tremendous boost to its stature, both psychologically and physically. Yet the bestowing of a name to the new segment of the continuum of Hebrew only coincided with the birth of the state. A fresh name was due because the precipitous development since 1880 had created new linguistic facts and a strain of Hebrew quite apart from other strains. The political event of 1948 [i.e. the establishment of the state, RK] offered an opportunity to take stock, to analyze, to appraise —and since Israel was the center of this new phase of Hebrew, the term "Israeli Hebrew" was quite fitting.
>
> (Weinberg 1981: 62)

While overtly detaching the linguistic issue from any "political meaning", Weinberg correctly recognizes that the establishment of the state "offered an opportunity to take stock." In this paper I intend to show that this opportunity was not coincidental, but rather a meaningful crossroad for the two orbits of discourse: the ideological-political discourse around the policy of *mamlaxtiut* ('statehood') and the scholarly-linguistic debate over the status of Hebrew: is it still in the process of revival or is it a normal language?

Two sources, deriving from different scholarly traditions, inform the conceptual framework within which I wish to tell this controversy: Bruno Latour's view of the historiography of scientific controversies, as laid out in *Science in Action* (Latour 1987), and Antonio Gramsci's view of the role of the intellectual in producing and maintaining hegemonic ideology, as it emerges from his *Prison Notebooks* written between 1916 and 1935 (Forgacs 1988: 189–222, 300–353).

In my reading of Latour, I view the telling of a controversy as a process that involves more than just summarizing main or final opinions of the adversaries. Rather, one has to work one's way up the river, back into the texts documenting the unfolding of the controversy. This process is textual in two ways: first of all, the rhetoric of these texts is very revealing; secondly, by going back to the original texts, we find editor's notes and other bits of format information which add much to our knowledge of the story. These editorial devices of enclosing the texts within an ideological frame, attempt to guide the readers to a limited interpretation, one which they might have overstepped, had the texts been left alone.

But in order to gain a proper understanding of science in the making, one has to go beyond the text, and observe also the different networks —be they economic, academic, or political of sorts— which are recruited to support, or which try to co-opt the adversaries. Latour treated techno-scientific controversies, but his methods are valid *mutatis mutandis* for other kinds of controversy. Latour is not chiefly interested in the theory of social formations, therefore what he calls networks is a relatively flat system of entities expressing and pursuing interests in the world of techno-science. Planting his type of historiography of controversies in a more sensitive social theory will increase explanatory power. Here, the controversy is embedded in the Gramscian model of political structure and ideological hegemony.

Gramsci viewed hegemony as a superstructural mechanism of maintaining the dominance of the ruling class. It is commonplace today to relax the term *ruling class* to mean *dominant political power*, a distinction which on one hand is particularly salient in contexts of nation-building and national conflict, and on the other hand does not commit itself to address the question of nationalism as converging —in the last instance— into class-stratification. In addition to exercising state power directly through legal-official institutions, the holder of power is involved in setting up and participating in voluntary political alliances and cultural networks within civil society, which form a general public consent, organized as a coherent systematic world-view, i.e. as an ideology. This ideology is mediated by the intellectuals who embed it in their disciplinary production. The product with its inlaid ideological strands appears ideologically neutral, and therefore commonsensical and ideologically transparent.[1] The role of intellectuals is the preservation and dissemination of hegemonic (and counter-hegemonic) ideology.

2. Overview of the controversy

By the end of World War I, there was a community of some 85,000 Jews in Palestine, of which over 30,000 were native, often monolingual, Hebrew speakers, using it for all personal and societal functions. At the same time, the newly installed British mandate in Palestine recognized Hebrew as one of its official languages, alongside Arabic and English. The existence of a community of speakers combined with this political recognition of the language could have been viewed as a convenient date for the end of the revival (cf. Nahir 1974: 121–124). However, only in the 1950s this issue came up. It is, therefore, not a trivial question to ask, why it was only in the 1950s that the normalcy of Hebrew was put on the linguistic and cultural agenda, and why it has not been resolved to this day. The question regarding the timing of an act of recognition of a linguistic system is not a new issue in sociolinguistics. It was extensively discussed in Labov's (1982) treatment of the recognition of Black English Vernacular as a dialect of English. In this paper Labov demonstrated how the political, educational, and two versions of linguistic discourses matured and finally converged to produce this recognition.

Figure 1, initially inspired by Latour (1987: 34, Figure 1.2) but going a long way further, underscores some formal aspects of the controversy: the vertical layout represents the first eight years of the decade of the 1950s; the horizontal layout represent the sectors in which the discourse took place, from the leftmost column representing texts in non-Hebrew academic periodicals published overseas, through academic and popularized-academic periodicals in Hebrew in Israel, through the publications of linguists in the daily press (mainly weekend cultural supplements), up to the writing of non-linguist intellectuals (journalists, educators, authors) in the same press media. The rightmost column documents some of the non-textual events, relevant to the discussion. The arrows indicate citations: the head of each arrow points to the work cited. The works represented in the table cover the whole discourse over the question of normalcy versus ongoing revival, save some extremely marginal works which would have added volume to this already very heavy table without affecting the general picture. Each work is represented by a bubble; some works which appeared in sequel-form are represented by connected bubbles.

Some evident facts emerge from this table, before any detailed discussion is undertaken. Rosén's[2] central role in the controversy is observable both from the number of entries in the table and from the number of arrowheads pointing to his works. Some bubbles had to be enlarged to accommodate the large number of arrowheads, thus the fact that it is conspicuous suggests their importance in the debate. We may also note that both Rosén and Blanc[3] were involved in Israeli cultural life, as popularizers of scholarly work. Rosén's radio programs in the *Language Corner* (of which only *Language Processes* is represented in the table) often predated his equivalent written texts. Rosén's main ally, in many respects a partner, was Blanc. Being his junior in age as well as in academic stature, Blanc accompanied Rosén's early struggle in his column *leSon bnei `adam,* ('language of [ordinary] people') in the weekly *masa*. The unity of this bloc of texts is represented in the table by a large curly bracket (needed since some of the citations of Blanc's work were directed to the column in general, not to a particular article).

Two other figures, who will turn out to be major opponents of Rosén (or of the Rosén-Blanc alliance) stand out in the table: one is Ben-Hayyim[4] (Mainly 3.1953 and 27.8.53) and the other is Tsemakh[5] (1954 and 9/16.3.1956).

The controversy flared up in two rounds, which are well represented in the table by the relative vertical depth of the years 1952–1953 and 1955–1956. An external precursor of the normalcy of Hebrew was Weiman (1950), who —unaware of his future role— wrote an innocent report on Modern Hebrew without any revolutionary intentions, simply as an example of a language that would demonstrate a certain question in general linguistics that he was working on. The actual beginning of the first round is Rosén (3.1952), written in French and introducing the new term "*Hébreu israélien*" for the first time. The first round is conducted among linguists only (Rosén, Blanc, Ben-Hayyim, Goshen), and ends with Rabin (9.1954) and Blanc (12.1954a) reporting on it to the world, by way of supporting Rosén's position.

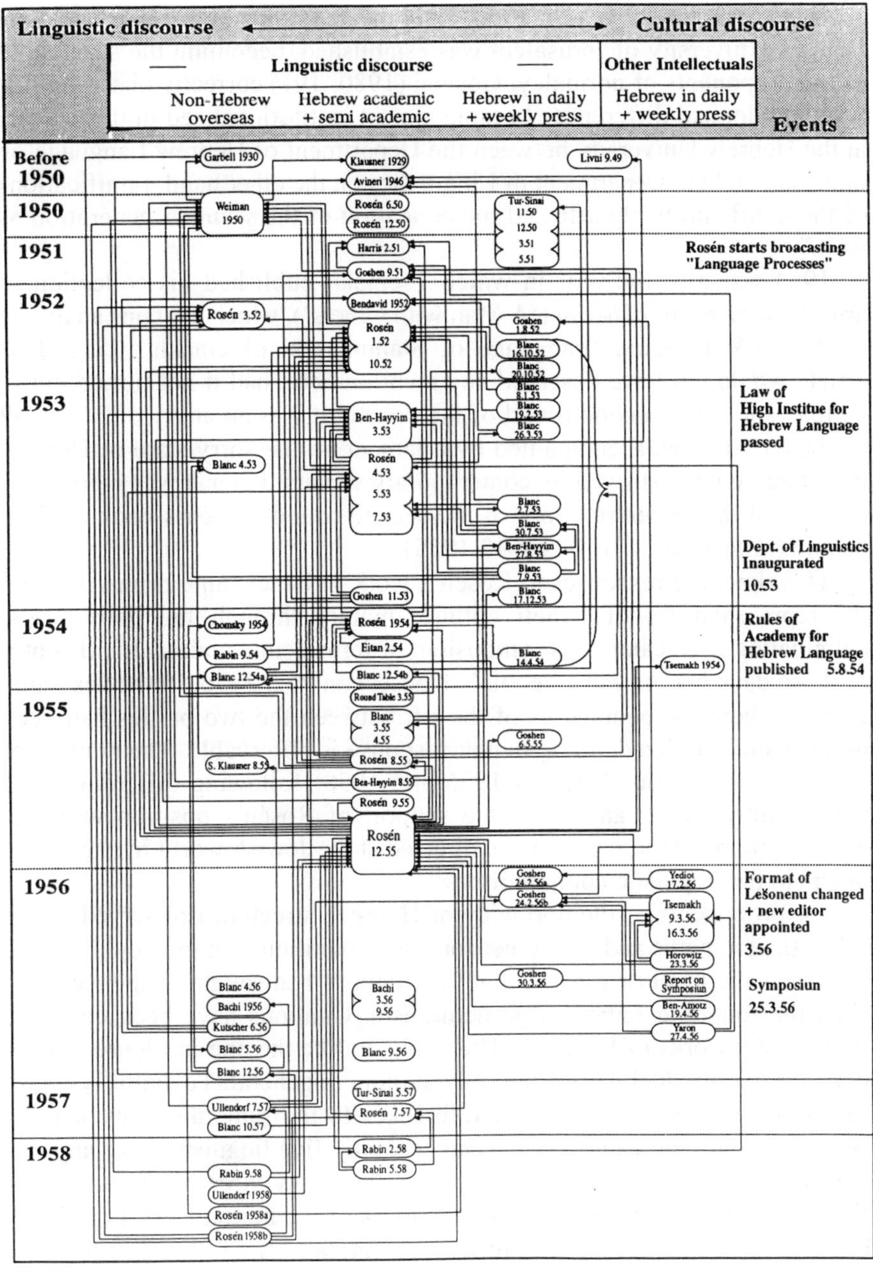
Linguistic discourse
Cultural discourse
Linguistic discourse
Other Intellectuals
Non-Hebrew overseas
Hebrew academic + semi academic
Hebrew in daily + weekly press
Hebrew in daily + weekly press
Events
Before 1950
1950
1951
1952
1953
1954
1955
1956
1957
1958
Garbell 1930
Klausner 1929
Avineri 1946
Livni 9.49
Weiman 1950
Rosén 6.50
Rosén 12.50
Tur-Sinai 11.50 12.50 3.51 5.51
Harris 2.51
Goshen 9.51
Rosén starts broacasting "Language Processes"
Bendavid 1952
Rosén 3.52
Rosén 1.52 10.52
Goshen 1.8.52
Blanc 16.10.52
Blanc 20.10.52
Blanc 8.1.53
Blanc 19.2.53
Blanc 26.3.53
Ben-Hayyim 3.53
Law of High Institue for Hebrew Language passed
Blanc 4.53
Rosén 4.53 5.53 7.53
Blanc 2.7.53
Blanc 30.7.53
Ben-Hayyim 27.8.53
Blanc 7.9.53
Dept. of Linguistics Inaugurated 10.53
Goshen 11.53
Blanc 17.12.53
Chomsky 1954
Rosén 1954
Rules of Academy for Hebrew Language published 5.8.54
Eitan 2.54
Rabin 9.54
Blanc 14.4.54
Tsemakh 1954
Blanc 12.54a
Blanc 12.54b
Round Table 3.55
Blanc 3.55 4.55
Goshen 6.5.55
S. Klausner 8.55
Rosén 8.55
Ben-Hayyim 8.55
Rosén 9.55
Rosén 12.55
Goshen 24.2.56a
Goshen 24.2.56b
Yediot 17.2.56
Tsemakh 9.3.56 16.3.56
Format of Lešonenu changed + new editor appointed 3.56
Horowitz 23.3.56
Goshen 30.3.56
Report on Symposiun
Symposiun 25.3.56
Blanc 4.56
Bachi 3.56 9.56
Bachi 1956
Ben-Amotz 19.4.56
Kutscher 6.56
Yaron 27.4.56
Blanc 5.56
Blanc 9.56
Blanc 12.56
Tur-Sinai 5.57
Ullendorf 7.57
Rosén 7.57
Blanc 10.57
Rabin 2.58
Rabin 5.58
Rabin 9.58
Ullendorf 1958
Rosén 1958a
Rosén 1958b

Figure 1

During the school year of 1953–1954 the department of linguistics at the Hebrew University of Jerusalem was established, becoming the stronghold of the proponents of normalcy. Goshen (1980: 191) correctly observed that "methodological differences became almost institutionalized in those years at the Hebrew University between the Department of Hebrew Language on one hand and the Department of Linguistics on the other hand. ramifications of those rifts probably affected the education of the younger generation as well."

1954 was also the year in which Tsemakh published his collection of articles *`adam `im `akherim* ('A Man with Others'), which contains an article entitled *leSon `ilgim*, 'Language of Stammerers' (Tsemakh 1955). This article would not have deserved any mention here, had it not turned out to be relevant to the second round of the debate. It was an angry didactic call for better Hebrew, accompanied by a lament on the sorry state of Hebrew literature being destroyed by contemporary writers. Later it was marginally mentioned in the central work of the second round, Rosén's book *ha`ivrit Selanu* ('Our Hebrew') (Rosén 12.1955).

This time, the responses to Rosén's work in Israel came primarily from the representatives of Israeli culture, mainly through the daily press, culminating in a scandalous symposium in Jerusalem's main cultural center of those days *beit ha'am* ('People's House') on 25.3.1956. In the academic circles, where the boundaries of the rift between the two parties had been defined and stabilized, no particular response is observable. The number of reports to the world (between 1956 and 1958) following this round was considerably larger, and again the support of Rosén's position was preeminent. Some of the reports were directed at the Jewish world in particular, others to the linguistic community.

For proponents of the normalcy of Hebrew, structuralism served as the theoretical impetus and safety-net for the recognition of normalcy. Figure 2 illustrates the level of support that the linguists had sought in their writing from the founding fathers of structuralism. Citations have been collected from all the works of Figure 1. This table, unlike the one in Figure 1, does not record individual works, but only authors in general. To simplify representation, neither the number of references to the same authority nor the works cited are indicated. As we can see, only five linguists make any reference to the forefathers of structuralism, and only three of them, namely Weiman, Rosén, and Blanc —all supporters of the normalcy of Israeli Hebrew (IH)— extensively mobilized the forefathers of the discipline to support their positions. Goshen, and most significantly Ben-Hayyim, Rosén's main opponent, only cite Bloomfield.

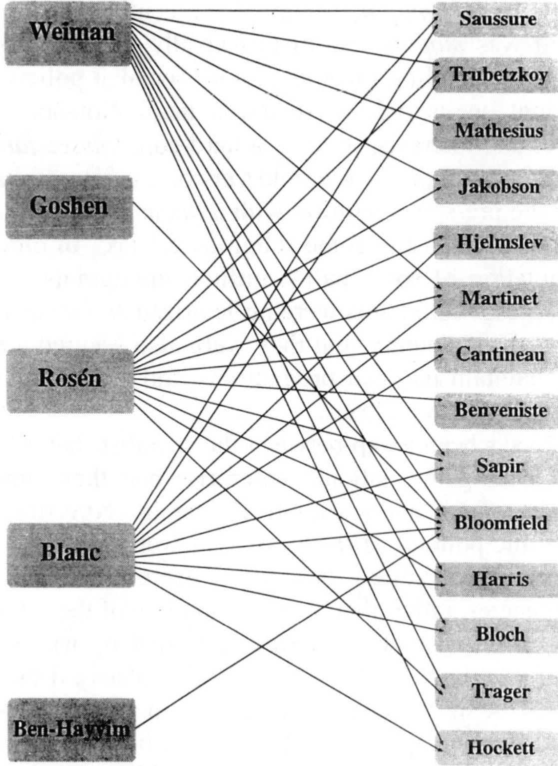

Figure 2

3. Local-political and general-linguistic settings

3.1. Local-political setting: Untying the Zionist package

After the Rhodes cease-fire accords between Israel and its Arab neighbors in 1949, Israel doubled its Jewish population within a few years, primarily through immigration from Arab countries. The absorption of these immigrants was meant to solidify Jewish majority, facilitating the building of a Jewish-Israeli nation-state, which would maximally match all parameters of a prototypical nation-state.

Ben-Gurion's[6] party, *mapai*, occupied the central slot in the political map. On its left was *mapam*, the historical ally of *mapai* as a workers' party, now as always pulling towards a more socialist policy and a Soviet global orientation; on its right were the General Zionists, supporters of bourgeois values and interests, pushing a hard-core *laissez-faire* version of capitalism. Ben-Gurion opted for a mild version of state capitalism, severing for its sake the pre-state coalition with *mapam* and forming an alliance with the General Zionists and some religious parties.[7] In order to quickly absorb the population of some half a million immigrants primarily from Arab countries, these immigrants were proletarized *en masse* and dispersed in frontier areas of the country, but they were also secured a basic subsistence so as to maintain national productivity and a spirit of shared unity against the inimical Arab countries.

There had always been a gap between the socialist rhetoric of socialist-Zionist parties leading the national enterprise and their practice, which supported "productive" ("non-speculative") capital. Nevertheless the government's economic policies of the 1950's, as well as its rejection of neutralism and adoption of Western orientation, were to some extent a break with earlier tendencies, rather than just a little more of the same thing. This break created a discursive rift (and was supported by it), expressing this new ideology of *mamlaxtiyut* ('statehood'): it emphasized the novelty and the advantages of being a state, as opposed to previous class rhetoric; it downgraded voluntarism, epitomized by the socialist *kibbutz* pioneerism of earlier days, replacing it by an exemplary availability for the state's most urgent and demanding tasks; it criticized Stalinism, and on this occasion threw in a rejection of socialism as a workable system.

Ben-Gurion's political mastery led him to appreciate the importance of the intellectual in society. A decade (1949–1961) of his dialogue with three types of intellectuals (scientists, philosophers, and authors) had been lucidly documented —though from an entirely different point of view— in Keren (1983). In 1949 Ben-Gurion summoned to his office thirty five authors (Keren 1983: 118) to discuss "the incorporation of writers and intellectuals into the formulation of national character in the State of Israel." This attempt to mobilize intellectuals to the project of statehood is the *raison d'être* of the whole dialogue. Ben-Gurion both succeeded and failed to form this alliance: to some extent he succeeded in recruiting some court-intellectuals, but many also opposed his political, as well as his scientific, philosophical, and cultural ideas. His main victory, however, was in dictating the cultural thematics, even to many of his opponents. The stronger opposition, around *mapam*, rejected his agenda, and tried to foster a counter-hegemony.

Statehood was not a novelty in Zionist thought. In fact, to become "a nation like all nations" was the utopian dimension of Zionism. Having opted for the maximal model of national normalcy, which totally equates nation and state, Zionism rejected other, less perfect models, such as Switzerland or Belgium. But political independence and territoriality were also important aspects of this model, which had now been materialized. This meant that the Zionist package could now be untied, so that the inventory of elements within Zionism could be checked as either accomplished or unaccomplished. This option opened a new horizon in Zionist-Israeli discourse.

Statehood had to conduct a cultural struggle not only against its forerunner, pre-state volunteerist socialist Zionism. It also found itself fighting the unpremeditated outgrowth of normalcy, modeled after the West: mature modernism which takes the state for granted and promotes individualism. All three orientations —socialist Zionism, capitalist statehood, and *avant-garde* individualistic modernism— were not diametrically opposed ideologies, only shades of the same Zionist nation-building project. They were sensed as distinct enough to kindle and sustain politico-cultural conflicts, but merged enough to maintain cohesive solidarity against the other, any other, be it the Arab countries around Israel, the Arab citizens in Israel, and to some extent the proletarized new immigrants, who were absorbing this ideology, holding off the first powerful outbursts of discontent to later years to come. The partly collaborative parent-offspring relation between these three shades of Zionist ideology, rather than a competitive sibling relation, produced a certain level of benevolent empathy to the opponent: statehood could not totally supplant its beloved forebear, who represented for many people their own personal past, thus serving as their alter-ego, nor could statehood disown its naughty offspring who expressed individuality, loneliness, personal anguish, but never failed the *shibboleth* test of Israeli allegiance: a three-year military service followed by a lifelong service on reserves for a month every year. Statehood was hegemonic in the sense that it was the super-structure that complemented the base of national capitalist political practice. Thus, to the extent that ideological differences had arisen, they were as bitter as a family fight could be: *mapai* was haunted not only by the external conservative counter-hegemonic policies of *mapam*, but also by conservative forces within its own encampment that opposed its transition to statehood. In what follows I will show how the linguistic discourse on Hebrew entered the politico-cultural discourse sketched out above, and how it can be interpreted and mapped within this complex reality.

3.2. General-linguistic settings: Importing structuralism into the study of Hebrew

Without purporting to give a comprehensive nor a balanced account of structuralist theory and practice, I wish to highlight some of its tenets relevant to our discussion:

a) *Every language is worthy of research.* This neogrammarian conception was adopted and expanded by structuralism. Every language, most certainly every spoken language, can be subjected to scientific investigation. There are no superior nor inferior languages; every language that enables the community of its speakers to maintain any communication required by human existence and by the degree of its technological development is a legitimate language. This attitude produced also the recognition that dialects are legitimate objects of knowledge, regardless of their social status. Generally, the linguistic stance is one of scientific description, not of normativist value-judgment.

b) *Behind every language there is a system.* This ensues from the Saussurian *langue/parole* dichotomy, *parole* being the actual manifestation of *langue*: the system. To describe a language is to extract its system out of its manifestations.

c) *"État de langue" is the object of research.* It is the synchronic description that is more salient and innovative in the structuralist project. The point, or the stretch of time, in which the system of a language has been stable, defines an *état de langue*, a 'state of language' of which the system is to be extracted. This is what a structuralist would mean by language in the narrow sense, irrespective of whether it is a dialect or a historical phase of a language in the popular sense. The terms of synchronic description are independent of the diachronic process which actuated it.

IH was ripe for structuralist treatment. It would have deserved descriptive attention, even if it were only one historical phase in a larger sequence of Hebrews, and even if it were only a socially inferior dialect ("children's language", "street language"), merely because it was a stable *état de langue*. Even more so, since in Rosén's view this *état de langue* was the national language of the people and the state of Israel. The view of IH as the latest phase of Hebrew, drawing from its sources but also being a new independent entity, converged with statehood. The Zionist package was untied, Hebrew as an element of Zionism could be evaluated, and if found completed it would re-endorse the project of opening the package and enrich the inventory list of items checked as fulfilled.

4. The two rounds of debate

4.1. The first round of debate

In 1952 Rosén started his article *Remarques descriptives sur le parler hébreu-israélien moderne* saying (3.1952: 4):

> Une nouvelle langue vivante s'est constituée en Israel qui doit faire l'objet d'une description linguistique synchronique. On peut considérer comme forme standard de cette langue celle employée par les bacheliers des lycées et les fonctionnaires officiels. ['A new living language has arisen in Israel, and it should be the object of a synchronic linguistic description. As the standard form of this language, one can take the form used by high school graduates and civil servants.']

Even within the restrictive style of scientific writing, and despite the understated title-category "*remarques*", the novelty of the object of knowledge being declared and the joy of announcing it is tangible. After demonstrating both the continuity (Biblical, Mishnaic Hebrew) and the discontinuity (due to normal and general linguistic processes), as well as the foreign influences (European substratum) as formative features of this language, Rosén felt justified in introducing the new appellation *hébreu israélien* (3.1952: 5):

> C'est pourquoi il faut rejeter l'appelation "hébreu moderne" qui indiquerait seulement une évolution linguistique normale à partir de l'hébreu classique, et employer "hébreu israélien". ['That is why one must reject the name "modern Hebrew", which would merely indicate a normal linguistic evolution from classical Hebrew, and use the name "Israeli Hebrew".']

The break with the past is clear. The introduction of new terminology was not absolutely mandatory. Despite Rosén's reasoning, there are languages that are called modern, even though they have not undergone the relatively smooth history of, say, Greek. But it was a symbolic act, a catchword that linguistically materialized the divide between present and past. By using the attribute Israeli, Rosén associated this object of scientific inquiry with the political entity Israel. In the cultural context of those days his statement harmonized with the call "to formulate national character", aligning his linguistic project with that of statehood.

At this point a word about the role of beliefs and personal intentions is in order. The people discussed here are taken as authors of texts, and only those biographical elements which emerge from the texts (such as Rosén's German mother tongue) are considered relevant. I have not interviewed them or their families about their political opinions, nor have I used any personal letters or journals. This aspect of historical investigation could, possibly, shed more light on the story. Here, only the written evidence of texts is used to construct the semiotic personae which share their name with their real-life counterparts.

In doing so I also assume a measure of distance between intention and role being played by this persona as a split subject.[8] Subjects do not necessarily fall into the rubrics and play the roles that they imagine they do. All the variants of evidence, such as evidence *ex silentio*, coincidence with other texts, co-optation, or even mis-representation by other texts within the cultural discourse —all such evidence should be available as interpretive options. However, I am not using just bare circumstantial evidence; the extraction and interpretation of overt and underlying messages within the passages of the linguistic texts support the politico-cultural interpretation of linguistic positions. Therefore, in our discussion above, whether the real Rosén wished to respond personally to Ben-Gurion's appeal to the intellectuals —this remains to be answered elsewhere; but textually the semiotic persona Rosén did indeed.

It is not accidental that Rosén associated IH with the State of Israel, the outcome of the Zionist project, and not with Zionism itself. In the second round he will modify and refine this statement, but here the emphasis is on the accomplished product, the language of the state. The later interest that Rosén showed in earlier IH, (e.g. Rosén 1992) is not part of the declaration of normalcy. At that point Rosén did not ask: Since when has IH been a normal language? He just stated: now it is.

In a later summary of the controversy Rosén (1977: 40) called the controversy a "*Kulturkampf*-like discussion" and confirmed what might have seemed conjectural:

> Israeli Hebrew was not meant as a geographical designation; I think there was some emotional load in the term when it was finally adopted: the name of Israel symbolized the culmination of the materialization of the aspirations to nationhood in the field of language as well as in the realm of territorial independence. There is no other way to circumscribe what is meant by Israeli Hebrew than to say that it is the national language (*Staatssprache*) of Israel ...
>
> (Rosén 1977: 18–19)

In this retrospective account Rosén put the field of language on a par with the realm of territorial independence as two areas of fulfilled Zionist aspirations. The symbolic act of naming the language after the state, is a forceful intervention in Israeli culture. The incremented number of elements within Zionism already fulfilled re-endorses the opening of the Zionist package and fortifies the rationale of *mapai*'s ideology of statehood. But so far this was only a trial-balloon launched overseas.

In *Language Processes A & B* (1.1952 and 10.1952) Rosén inaugurated IH in Hebrew and in writing (after having done so on the radio). Both in *Remarques* (3.1952) and in *Language Processes A & B,* Rosén used the term IH and presented more or less the same set of facts that demonstrate how IH functioned as a normal language. The rhetoric, however, was very different. *Language Processes A* was introduced as follows:

> In these chapters, which had been previously broadcast in the Language Column of *Kol-Israel* and have been collected to appear now in this booklet, [each issue was a 12x17cm. booklet, RK] my intention was to subject to general linguistics the Hebrew language, as it is accepted in idiomatic live speech untainted by foreignisms. This can be done in light of the growing scientific interest in phenomena of our language, "Israeli" Hebrew.

Here Rosén did not define the language in the sociolinguistic parameters of 3.1952, nor did he perform a speech act of naming. The attribute Israeli appeared in quotation marks, which can only be interpreted as scare-quotes, intended to mitigate the effect of the adjective, and to emphasize its ad-hocery and contingency. After this introductory remark, the language is referred to as "our language", "our living language", "our language today" etc., while "Israeli" Hebrew is mentioned only once more on the last page. In *Language Processes B* (10.1952), "Israeli" Hebrew appears once in the first half, and only towards the end it appears four times as Israeli Hebrew, without quotation marks. Rosén had to prepare the grounds, rather than come out with a straightforward declaration, to introduce the adjective Israeli —collocating with Hebrew— into socially endorsed nomenclature. While in the political milieu Ben-Gurion's statehood was constantly gaining power, on its way to hegemony, Rosén's terminology within the linguistic circles was still subversive. Later, Rosén (4.1953: 3) will admit:

> I shall not deny, that in the two booklets of *Language Processes* that I published I had in mind not only to report the results of my scrutiny into Israeli Hebrew, but also to open a principled discussion, in order to start our introspective self-examination as regards our approach to our spoken language in all its manifestations.

Rosén's initiative was immediately met with objection. Even Part B (Rosén 1.1952) was already prefaced by an editorial note:

> The author, being engaged in investigating and *describing* phenomena of language, purposefully and justifiably excludes from his treatment matters of rectifying and *cultivating* it. Deciding what is correct and incorrect —or in Bloomfield's idiom: what is standard and sub-standard— is not a task of the describing scholar. Ostensibly, one may thus suggest: language *investigation* is one thing; language *cultivation* another. Yet the two professions are con-

> nected: on the one hand, even the investigator notes that certain forms are standard, i.e. not considered erroneous in schools, while others are substandard; on the other hand, clearly a language rectifier must take into account the results of descriptive science, which is the only solid ground for his work. In the following booklets we hope to present also views of other linguists, who see the processes from a different perspective.

The editors, Eli Eitan and Meir Medan, found themselves under extreme pressure after the publication of part A. At that time Ben-Hayyim was the secretary of the Language Committee (forerunner of the Academy of Hebrew Language), the body that published the academic *leSonenu* and the semi-academic *leSonenu la`am*. The fact that he was preparing a response must have been known to the editors. It would not be irrelevant to mention in this context, that Ben-Hayyim devoted the last 37 pages of his response to the cultivation of the living Hebrew language. Other thematic points of contact between the editorial note and Ben-Hayyim's later criticism of Rosén leave little doubt as for his involvement in it.

Ben-Hayyim's intervention was escorted by the massive institutional power that he possessed. An oral response delivered on 3.12.1953 as a lecture commemorating the 30th anniversary of the death of Eliezer Ben-Yehudah, the half-mythologized reviver of Hebrew, was soon expanded into a triple-issue booklet of *leSonenu la`am* (with a record length of 83 pages).

In his response, entitled *Ancient Language in a New Reality*, Ben-Hayyim (3.1953), refrained from any mention of the State of Israel as relevant to the condition of the Hebrew language. In a single reference to Rosén's term "Israeli" Hebrew he asked (3.1953: 58): "is there any other spoken Hebrew that is not Israeli?", thus identifying IH with spoken Hebrew, and flattening the political meaning of Israeli. Throughout the booklet, the term New Hebrew was used, becoming the official designation used in the Department of Hebrew Language at the Hebrew University, as a counter-nomenclature to IH.

After Ben-Hayyim had characterized early Zionist debates on the feasibility of reviving the language as laden with political interests, he (3.1953: 18) stated:

> Thus we are required and are also able to view the process of the renewal of Hebrew, dismissing all political and social factors inappropriately bound together with our problem, while our gaze is lifted to see the truth of reality.

Ben-Hayyim insinuated here that Rosén as a structuralist should not have used political and social factors in his linguistic considerations.

However, the central bone of contention did not involve nomenclature but rather the way that people with different scientific pedigrees grasped reality in different ways. What was at stake here was the form that the substance of language acquired in the views of the researchers as observing subjects. The structuralist pedigree made the contours of the system of language stand out as the main *Gestalt*, marginalizing other phenomena of language as background. Ben-Hayyim's earlier generation, which had neo-grammarian pedigree, was trained to spot the historical sources of words. For him the *Gestalt* was a collection of words, which like a group of undisciplined choir children, jump up and down screaming: "I am from the Bible; I am from the Mishna; I am from Midrash Rabba of Genesis; I am from medieval poetry" etc. (but mainly the first two). Here as well, all other aspects of language got marginalized into pale background.

Ben-Hayyim was not trained and did not practice as a theoretical linguist, which in the 1950's meant being an active structuralist, conversant in the intricacies of the theory. It is not incidental that in these debates Ben-Hayyim makes reference only to Bloomfield's *Language* (see Figure 2), one of a few windows through which outsiders got a glimpse of what structuralism was about. Disregarding, then, the momentary "structuralist" form that Ben-Hayyim's line of argumentation put on, and concentrating on the core of the argument, it boiled down to Ben-Hayyim's (3.1953: 55) following statement:

> Do we not have in our spoken language an internal struggle between a host of elements from variegated and mutually so different "language systems", such as Biblical, Mishnaic, and other layers, which have not yet reached internal equilibrium, have not yet become a uniform system?

Naturally, if Hebrew is a mixture of "struggling elements", then it is not an *état de langue* yet, consequently it cannot be subjected to structuralist synchronic scrutiny. Nothing is the matter with structuralism, reasons Ben-Hayyim; what is wrong is to apply this method to Hebrew at this time. What is, then, the objective of Hebrew scholarship? Extremist normativists —agrees Ben-Hayyim— are wrong in aggravating people with attempts to correct their speaking. Spoken language should be left alone. However, a form of cultural language should be fostered, and it is the task of linguists to participate in this process. This cultural language-in-formation will interact with spoken language, enriching it and being restrained by it. As for the end of this process, says Ben-Hayyim (3.1953: 82):

> In the course of the years —and this is not a matter of a few years— when the systematization of the new Hebrew language is over through the blending of all its present constitutive components, naturally a new grammar of Hebrew will arise. It will come about neither by decree of normative grammarians, nor by advocacy of descriptive grammarians.

Ben-Hayyim's linguistic intervention did not artiulate any political stance. Once Ben-Hayyim stepped forward as the advocate of linguistic conservatism, his position became available to political conservatism, to those forces which opposed statehood, and was potentially insertable in a number of conservative slots. The full-fledged political use of Ben-Hayyim's linguistic positions will emerge in the second round.

Rosén's institutional weakness at this point of the debate was clear: his response *On Standard and Norm, On Processes and Mistakes* (4/5/7.1953), though only twenty pages long, was chopped up into three installments. The following school-year 1953/4 will see the birth of the Department of Linguistics, where Rosén will start to fortify his own institutional stronghold. The department will be headed by the esteemed Egyptologist and structuralist linguist H.J. Polotsky, who rarely participated publicly in these debates (a noteworthy exception being his agreement to chair the symposium on "Our New Language" in 25.3.1956, further discussed below), but clearly took sides by choosing his disciple to build the department with him. In *Standard and Norm* Rosén clarified the difference between standard and norm. He suggested that what the linguist was seeking to describe was the standard of language, some statistical average, while what normativists are looking for is some externally imposed ideal norm. This approach had not eliminated the concept of mistake, it only set clear boundaries around it. A form which deviates from the standard is a mistake and should be eliminated, thus there is room for linguistic education, or cultivation of language, by way of strengthening the standard, not by way of imposing a norm.

Rosén chose to overlook the shortcomings of Ben-Hayyim's "structuralist" argumentation. Instead, he graciously embraced his approval of the structuralist method (4.1953: 6–7):

> ... in his actual contention he accepts the method, and only expresses reservation regarding the truth of my conclusions ... Ben-Hayyim's reservations were said within the method I use —and this satisfies me.

In doing so Rosén used a typical strategy of hegemonic power: he pretended to have a partial alliance with Ben-Hayyim, who was honorably escorted into structuralism. Once there, power relations could not be clearer. This is hegemony's way of enforcing consensus and containing resistance.

As for the definition of IH, Rosén argued that the standard is a statistical average of a certain language stratum (4.1953: 6):

> It is rather hard to determine in each case, what is the social stratum by which the standard is established; in any case, the concept of standard is always tied with the concept "knowers of language". I strove to determine the

> language community by which we should define the standard in Israel —and I arrived at the formula "high-school graduates and state officials when in office" [followed by footnote referring to Rosén 3.1952].

It is clear that at this point Rosén ignored Ben-Hayyim's insinuated criticism of the use of social factors in defining the standard. To be sure, in 1955 Rosén would in fact modify his definition.

The attempt to anchor the standard of a language in a concept such as "knowers of language" does not provide a straightforward explanation to the choice of "the social stratum by which the standard is established." The question remains: who are those *savants*, and how are they nominated? To say that they are selected due to their use of the new system would be entirely circular. The choice —Rosén seems to agree— is purely social. For Rosén they are the elite, the intellectuals, of the national movement, the producers of the oral and written discourse that accompanied it from early Zionism to the mature State of Israel. The vulnerability of this narrow interpretation of such a broad term is evident, for under a different interpretation one could not exclude other sectors from the ranks of "knowers of language."

In Israel of the 1950s high-school education was equivalent to university education in today's culture. The phrase *high-school graduates and state officials* defined precisely the social circle of the Israeli politico-cultural elite. Here again Rosén's linguistic definition of those "knowers of language" coalesced, willy nilly, with the limited applicability of normalcy within statehood, and its elitist political role. The actual boundaries set by Rosén for standard IH as the variant of language used by the elite were not inaccurate. Yet there were at least two other ways of defining the same standard: Rosén's own later modification, which would define as standard that idiom by which a speaker cannot be identified as belonging to any ethnic or social origin, and Rabin's (9.1954: 137) way: "This latter language is a 'standard' in so far as it is being taken over by other speakers." Rosén could not have said this, for methodological reasons: it was a diachronic statement, not to be used in supporting a synchronic definition. At his purely synchronic statement Rosén arrived only later. Of the two contaminated definitions —the social one and the diachronic one— Rosén had environmental support for the former under the aegis of the ideology of statehood.

Blanc, who warmly welcomed Rosén's *Language Processes* and the new scientific spirit they brought with them, in earlier installments of his column *Language of People* in the periodical *masa*, at this point actively joined the debate. He wrote his article *The same Lady* (30.7.1953) invoking in this title the Hebrew expression "the same lady with a different cloak," thus suggesting that Ben-Hayyim is merely another normativist. This article was answered by Ben-Hayyim's *Grammar of People* (27.8.1953), to be answered again by Blanc's *Linguists as People* (7.9.1953). Since Ben-Hayyim's reply does not add new claims to the debates, I will disregard it and treat both of Blanc's installments as one sequence.

Blanc's way into *masa*, one of *mapam*'s cultural vehicles of counter-hegemony, passed through its editor, the poet T. Carmi, a personal friend of his. Both were ideological fellow-travelers, rather than hard-core couriers of its politico-cultural message. Blanc maintained modernist values of respect to individualism as a component of ethical universalism. As Rosén's companion in this struggle he shared with him a devotion to structuralism, but unlike Rosén, his structuralism did not have the overtones of hegemonic statehood, but rather the flavor of individuality, of the distinctions within the state, to be later developed into dialect research of IH. *Masa* turned out to be the convenient niche for voicing his opinions at that time.

At variance with Rosén's forgiving and mobilizing containment strategy towards Ben-Hayyim, Blanc (30.7.1953: 63) drew a clearcut distinction between linguist and philologist and catalogued Ben-Hayyim as the latter. At variance with Rosén's constrained support of linguistic education, Blanc held a radical *laissez-faire* stance (30.7.1953: 66): "the 'cultivation' of language is not a scientific, philological, linguistic, or grammatical matter, but one of aesthetics and art." Another radical position was Blanc's scientistic view that even if the revival of Hebrew was to be seen as a singular event, it could still be treated by regular scientific tools. And to this Blanc (7.9.53) appended the remark:

> Apart from far-fetched speculations, based on superstition such as "You have chosen us from all the nations," I know of no criterion by which it is possible to define New Hebrew as an "unnatural" language.

Blanc here distanced himself from any form of national singularism. Though he often used the term Israeli Hebrew he was not uncomfortable about using the term New Hebrew, since Israeliness was not his main preoccupation. The anti-religious sentiment, here expressed by referring to the liturgical verse in its political usage as superstition, could readily be welcomed by the anti-statehood socialist-Zionist sponsors and readership of *masa*, who had been traditionally anti-religious, and abhorred *mapai*'s pragmatic political alliance with the religious parties in government coalitions, as well as Ben-Gurion's desire to become "a light unto the nations", an exemplary-normal nation. Not only in political, but also in linguistic matters Blanc was at variance with Rosén. But this belongs to the second round of the debate.

While the first round was taking place, the Israeli parliament, the Knesset, passed in 1953 the Law for the Supreme Institute for the Hebrew Language which facilitated the establishment of The Academy of the Hebrew Language. The Academy replaced The Hebrew Language Committee launched and led by Ben-Yehudah in 1890. Ben-Hayyim was appointed editor of *leSonenu*, and its first renewed volume appeared in 3.1956. The Academy decided to maintain continuity: no new series was established; the next volume was to be simply called volume 20. However, the subtitle of *leSonenu* was changed from *A Quarterly for the Amelioration of the Hebrew Language* to *A Journal for the Study of the Hebrew Language and Cognate Subjects*. Thus, a mixed tendency can be observed. On the one hand, another voluntary pre-state organization was taken over by a state organ, being modernized and symbolically normalized. On the other hand, the new institution was not manned with new staff, thereby becoming another stronghold of the conservative forces. Editors were changed, but continuity was preserved in editorial policy. In the years to come a number of monographs and jubilee volumes would be published, among them quite recently Ben-Hayyim's collected papers on Hebrew entitled *The Struggle for a Language* (Ben-Hayyim 1992). No equal time has been granted to the proponents of IH.

4.2. The second round of debate

In 1954 Tsemakh published *The Language of Stammerers*, in which he recapitulated (without explicit reference) Ben-Hayyim's assertion that Hebrew had not yet reached a stable state. Therefore —Tsemakh stretched the argument farther— unlike any normal language, whose main source of vitality is the speaking masses, the speakers of Hebrew are newcomers whose language is broken, thus the source of change must be the esteemed written sources. He said:

> ... once upon a time, in its ancient days, it was a spoken language, one of the extensions of the Semitic idiom. Then it went into reticence, and remained dumb for thousands of years. In our days it broke, with its very own hands, the edict of voicelessness, and returned to the lips of speakers. Let us not forget: Hebrew, unlike other languages of culture in the world, is not a daughter of an ancient language or of some mix of ancient languages. Conversely, to this very day, like Chinese and Arabic, it stayed in its antiquity. This inverted historical evolution inverts any measure of early-and-late in it.
>
> (Tsemakh 1954: 270)

And the conclusion was: since the written sources reflect a fresh young language, a form of fossilized spoken idiom, "he who wishes to rectify his tongue, inevitably ought to dip his quill in these live words, and accept their authority". Stressing that he was not talking solely about words and concepts, but about (1954: 268) "the order of the sentence, its architectural beauty," Tsemakh (1954: 269) admitted to not being capable of "expounding on the formation of the renewed synthetic Hebrew sentence." Where, then, would one seek guidance on how to return to the "Semitic idiom", and what should be done about the synthetic, periodic style used in IH? How would one express oneself in modern ways within Biblical syntax? To these questions Tsemakh had no clear answer other than such advice, as to go back to the mouth of the spring and drink its fresh water, or to let the language come out of bondage and regain its original nature.

In this article not all of Tsemakh's cats had come out of the bag, thus I will put off the more extensive treatment of his positions to his next move in the debate.

Rosén's first move in the second round was a full size book, entitled *Our Hebrew* (12.1955), published by *`am `oved*, the publishing house of the workers union *histadrut* controlled by *mapai.* The editor of *`am `oved*, Shlomo Grodjensky, initiated the publication. Grodjensky was an American Zionist, immersed in Anglo-American culture, who immigrated to Israel and joined the intellectual circles of *mapai.* He supported the individualistic-modernist trends in Israeli culture, and although in the narrow sense Rosén fit into the statehood version of *mapai'*s conceptions, for the more avant-garde modernist that Grodjensky was, Rosén epitomized the individual intellectual, a member of the cultural elite, who single-handedly imported Western thought into the stale category of "Jewish studies", where Hebrew had been traditionally categorized. As such, Rosén seemed worthy of Grodjensky's support.

Our Hebrew is a celebration of victory and an occasion to square accounts with rivals. Against extreme normativists Rosén leveled discordant expressions, such as (12.1955: 113) "falsifying utilitarianism," "lack of principles," (12.1955: 124) "conservative sentiment," "holy lie," (12.1955: 125) "cheap and light-headed opportunism," "mental laziness," etc. A whole chapter was devoted to the "Struggling Elements" in which Rosén further elaborated his view of the way words and linguistic forms of different phases of Hebrew were re-arrayed as a new system. The fifth chapter, containing many "Blanc's notes", is a hundred-page stand-alone phonological analysis of IH.

The first chapter is an assessment of the status of Hebrew among the Semitic languages. Certain critics (e.g. Goshen 24.2.1956) were bewildered by its relevance to the book. However, this surprise should arise only if the book was read as a purely linguistic description detached from the cultural context. When viewed in the context of Rosén's discussion of the periodic style in the fourth chapter (with reference to Tsemakh 1954), and in the context of the last chapter (written by Hannah Rosén, Haiim Rosén's wife), devoted largely to the periodic style in IH —all these discussions together solidify the evidence that supports the claim that not only phonologically and morphologically, but also syntactically and stylistically IH is different yet systematic, hence worthy of its new name.

It is in this work that Rosén responded to the criticism on the social criterion in his definition of IH, adding a definition of standard phenomena to the definition of the speakers of standard language (12.1955: 139): "a phenomenon of habitual language is one, by which its utterer would not be recognized as belonging to a specific ethnic, social, socio-economic, or any other group." Although Rosén was made aware of the infelicitous nature of his social definition, he had not entirely replaced it. He only added the new definition to the old one. In doing so, Rosén conformed to the priorities instated by statehood, i.e. the establishment of a society in which the absorbers would absorb immigration in a way that will reproduce the economic and cultural supremacy of the old-timer Western-oriented privileged classes, and dictate to the absorbees the standards of their new civilization, and their status in it. For them, the standard of IH was externally imposed, so that upwardly social mobility implied the acquisition of standard speech form. Rosén's sociolinguistic definition was a recognition, but as such also a reconfirmation, of the social process.

The issue that ignited the flame of the second round was Rosén's discussion of the period as a syntactic-stylistic feature of IH. The period is characterized by Rosén (12.1955: 129) as having the following features:

> It is of the nature of the period to put a large number of concepts in equal syntactic status ... , to force the hearer's thought to hold its concluding and final evaluation until all the data accumulate, which constitute factors of this evaluation. Further it is of the nature of the period not to let the hearer or reader determine by himself the ways that the mechanism of his thought joins the separate terms, the basic fundamental ideas, which combine into a chained argument when the writer forms the period in his mind.

That IH is periodic is a straightforward clear fact: it breaks away from sequential linearity and forms onion-shaped sentences, adjoined by semantically-explicit subordinative particles and adverbs. This style is sharply opposed to that of Biblical Hebrew, which is non-periodic: more often than not it connects many simple sentences into a linear chain via the connective particle, leaving the logical and semantic value of the parataxis to the interpretive faculty of the reader. It is this style that Tsemakh characterized as Semitic idiom and to which he expressed a wish to return, without specifying the ways to do so. Rosén used two kinds of argumentation in justifying the use of the period. One (12.1955: 128) was based on the need to adjust to modernity. Thanks to the period, speakers of IH are well equipped "to engage in independent linguistic creation in the abstract and developed world of thought of the twentieth century."

However, Rosén went one step farther in his argumentation, claiming (12.1955: 133) that the adoption of the periodic style is a matter of "going in the path of the development of mankind, propelled by the reality of the intellectual progress of the human race," thus reverting to the syntax of Biblical Hebrew, would mean to "reverse by thousands of years the development of the human mind."

Statehood had been persistently accused by its conservative rivals of Westernizing Israel in excess. Rosén's first recommendation, to merely adjust to the modern West, was problematic enough. Rosén augmented its inflammability by evoking a supposedly objective and scientific "development of the human mind." This kind of argument could, perhaps, pass for the convinced elite, but when coming from a native speaker of German, who belonged to this elite, it could also be seen as a sign of cultural patronization. And so it was for Tsemakh: driven by a sense of cultural marginalization, combined with Rosén's (12.1955: 133) explicit and sneering remark about Tsemakh's unwillingness to discuss "the renewed synthetic Hebrew sentence," and further compounded by a sense of loss of all good values of the second *`aliya*[9] ('wave of immigrants') in the new State of Israel, Tsemakh was charged with a triple *casus belli.*

In his article *Hands off!*, Tsemakh (1959 [9/16.3.1956]) recounted the history of Hebrew revival. In this story, only the early phases of the revived language appeared worthy of positive appraisal: the first *`aliya* as a forerunner, the second *`aliya*, Tsemakh's *`aliya,* which translated the dream of revival into a politico-cultural practice, in the Zionist project of nation-building, and the third and fourth *`aliyot* depicted by Tsemakh as a decent continuation and reinforcement of previous achievements. The end of the golden age, according to Tsemakh (1959 [9/16.3.1956]: 166), is marked by the rise of Nazism, and by German immigration, known as the fifth *`aliya.* Being well educated in general knowledge but deficient in Jewish education, this wave of immigrants

> ... at once got absorbed in the community, excelling in talent and knowledge. Its intelligentsia and professionals got high-ranking positions in the university, in teachers' seminars, and in high-schools; those who had been journalists regained their trade; and the engineers and economists became directors of factories and banks.

In other words, the German Jews took command of what Althusser called "ideological state apparatuses", and from that position of power enforced their foreign idiomatics, especially the long periodic complex sentences, upon the defenseless fragile new language. Tsemakh's text is both lamenting and furious and is checkered with vengeful and spiteful *ad hominem* attacks on Rosén and his style. Rosén, though not German but Austrian in origin, embodied Tsemakh's nightmare in all other respects: a German speaking Jew who arrived in Palestine after the rise of Nazism and was holding an influential power position at the university. Rosén was not just doing all that was so evil, but was also supplying the theoretical justification for these deeds (see: 1959 [9/16.3.1956]: 177).

Wherever Tsemakh was using any linguistic argumentation, the influence of Ben-Hayyim's conceptual framework was evident, but always further radicalized. Like Ben-Hayyim, Tsemakh claimed that (1959 [9/16.3.1956]: 163) the revival is still "in a state of mixture and chaos. And no method, even if equipped with the latest and newest tools of research, can impose shape, order, or regime on the arrangement of these yet concealed and obscure matters." While the spoken language cannot be regimented yet, the written language has a clear calling to draw forms and patterns from the ancient sources, and (1959 [9/16.3.1956]: 171) "bestow them with currency in the life that is evolving."

Now, how will the chaos be transformed into a coherent system? This remains to be seen, says Tsemakh, "but we, who possess the Hebrew given to us by the devoted people of the second and third *`aliya* ... as a deposit and heritage —we are responsible and we will determine what will come to pass." In other words, it is the traditional cultural elite, and its knowledgeable representatives, who have the historical task to guide the nation. Here too, Tsemakh takes Ben-Hayyim's principle one step forward, for Ben-Hayyim encouraged all people who by knowledge or by education deal with language to be engaged in the cultivation of language; Tsemakh narrows down the scope of those fitting this criterion to people of the second and third *`aliya*. The deposed shall repossess.

Throughout his article Tsemakh voiced his rejection of the changing agenda, through nostalgia to an unblemished visionary world that had never materialized. The text reads as a confession of the faithful corporal of a revolution who took the rhetoric too seriously for too long. As many men of letters he was prone to be trapped by words and felt cheated by reality, even his very own reality. Though he preserved in his own writing some marginal conservative phenomena of "original" Hebrew, such as preferring the construct form ("language of writing") or the prepositional small-clause ("language that in writing") to the "foreign" noun and adjective ("written language"), his style in Hebrew was highly periodic, as can be seen from the following sentence (1959 [9/16.3.1956]: 163–4):

> And only the immigrants of 1904 (what is called the "second *`aliya*"), and only a few, not all of them, for you have to subtract from their ranks the people of *po`alei-ciyon*, who for reasons of imagined and false popular sentiment adhered to the Chernowitz principles and did not let go of them in our country, and even printed a journal in Yiddish with a very meaningful title "*Der Anfang*" —only the people of 1904 rekindled the torch, and through them Hebrew speech again became more consecrated and widespread within the Jewish community in our country.

At this point, the controversy over Hebrew took on two directions. At the level of popular culture, The Education and Culture Department of the Municipality of Jerusalem organized a symposium on "Our New Language" on the occasion of the publication of *Our Hebrew* (Rosén 12.1955). In a newspaper report on the symposium,[10] the reporter added to the official wording of the occasion of the symposium, i.e. the publication of Our Hebrew, also the phrase "and the sharp criticism of this work by the writer and critic Sh. Tsemakh." The panel of speakers and the names of the discussants from the audience included important representatives of Israeli culture and academia. The reporter mentioned that "it has been a long while since Jerusalem has witnessed such a cultural-linguistic encounter as that which took place on that evening." All these facts, and the polemic that accompanied the events in the press (see Figure 1) indicate how the two discursive orbits got conflated, this time with Goshen (24.2.1956a; 24.2.1956b; 30.3.1956) carried into the discussion and assuming the position of the linguist defending Rosén in the politico-cultural sphere.

The other direction that the controversy took on was the purely linguistic discourse carried out in English in international journals of linguistics and Jewish studies. Most writers gave a balanced account of the controversy, though explicitly or at least tacitly sided with Rosén. The exception this time was Blanc's (12.1956) review of *Our Hebrew* in *Language*. Judging by this review alone, one might fail to identify Blanc as Rosén's supporter and partner. In the introductory and the concluding passages Blanc paid due tribute to Rosén's position as "the first, and ... still the foremost, of a small number of Israeli scholars" (794) in the linguistic discourse over the normalcy and the describability of Israeli Hebrew, and to his actual contributions to the research of Hebrew. Having said this, Blanc launched a mighty attack on Rosén's methodology, and to some extent on his political orientation. The latter can be clearly instantiated in the following passage (Blanc 12.1956: 796):

> He does not, however, completely avoid a certain tendency to ... fight myth with counter myth rather than with science alone. This weakens his case, and his obiter dicta sometimes have unfortunate connotations: the syntactic structure of modern Hebrew, it is said (128), "enables us, and indeed us alone of all the people of Semitic race and speech, to use language creatively and independently in the abstract and advanced universe of 20th-century thought." Antediluvian anthropology (there is no "Semitic race"), dubious ethnolinguistics (the grammar of one's language does not "enable" one to take part in a given culture), and poor Semitics (there is little in Hebrew syntax which cannot easily be matched e.g. by Arabic syntax) do not contribute to the linguistic education of the public.

Rosén's tendency to take pride in the linguistic achievements of IH were understood by Blanc as ideological interference, as myth rather than science. Blanc was not ready to make any concessions to "science alone", and time and again he was showing his disinterest in the milieu of nation-building and the production of national-linguistic haughtiness.

However, it is to a critique of Rosén's methodology, that Blanc devoted most of his review. In a detailed and enumerative examination of Rosén's scientific practice, Blanc contended that Rosén could neither claim that his work followed standard structuralist procedure (12.1956: 796): "on a number of crucial points, his procedure deviates sharply from common practice," nor could he claim that he followed the path of one particular linguist (12.1956: 797): "Surely this is a radical departure from 'basically' Trubetzkoyan phonology."

Blanc's seemingly equivocal attitude to Rosén was not erratic, nor did it exhibit internal development. Blanc was as resolute and scientistic in his linguistics as he was in his social orientation. However, in different circles of discourse he chose to externalize and to suppress different facets of his persuasions. In the Israeli arena, Blanc formed a bloc with Rosén in order to further the interests of structuralism in Israel. In this role, as a proponent of Rosén, Blanc did not criticize Rosén's national particularism. In Israel Blanc let himself be critical of nationalism only when engaged in a debate with Ben-Hayyim (see above his attitude to "You have chosen us from all the nations"), i.e. only of nationalism of the religious brand. In the international arena, where structuralism was dominant, Blanc was exempt from the need to be allied with Rosén, and felt free to pursue his more hard-lined orientation, along two tracks: to cleanse linguistics from national myth by dissociating it from the political agenda of statehood, and to stick to a stringent scientific methodology. This contrasted with Rosén's view of structuralism as a field which is well defined from without, but is an open environment from within, in which a dynamic selection of sources of influence lets one formulate one's own methodological credo. For Blanc, this permissive mode of scholarship was not rigorous enough.

5. Two final remarks

5.1. On the end of the controversy

Having undergone several metamorphoses since the fifties —linguistically, after the advent of generativism and the marginalization of structuralism (see Kuzar 1997), and politically, after the occupation of the territories in 1967— the controversy has not ended yet. Within established academia some institutions have been more liberal and impartial (Both Polotsky and Rosén on one hand and Ben-Hayyim on the other hand received the Israel Prize and were awarded membership in The Israel Academy of Science), while other organizations still support only one party (Ben-Hayyim is a central functionary of the Academy of Hebrew Language; Rosén has never been invited to be a member).

In recent celebrations of the centennial of the inauguration of the Language Committee (1890–1990) a special commemorative volume of *leSonenu la`am* (volume 40–41) was published. It holds 47 articles (337 pages). The volume opens with an article by Ben-Hayyim, bearing the unmistakable title *What is the Historical Unity of Hebrew*. Rosén is not represented, although the volume has a section on "New and Living Hebrew". In Israeli high-schools "History of Hebrew" is taught, without any mention of the issue or the controversy around it. The general tenor of the story in school-books, its spontaneous ideology, is that of ongoing revival and historical unity of Hebrew.

Newspapers and literary magazines occasionally publish articles such as *The Process of Hebrew Language Revival is not over Yet* (B. Ben-Yehuda 1981), *The Struggle over Hebrew as a National Language Goes on* (Atter 1983), and more recently *On the Guard of Hebrew* (Mushon 4.7.1995). The rhetoric is always the same: the identification of the revival of Hebrew with the larger master-project of Zionism, and the contention that both have not yet been materialized.

The historiography of the controversy has been suppressed in circles that lean towards a stronger alliance between state and scholarship, and its materials have been reshuffled. The suppression is evident, for example, in textbooks of The Open University on the history of the Hebrew language (Agmon-Pruchtman and Allon 1994; Schwarzwald [Rodrigue] 1994) in which the controversy is not mentioned. To be sure, the Language Struggle of 1913–1914 is described in the former, and so are other political events. In other words, the textbooks cover not only the history of language in the narrow sense (how one form evolved from another), but also social and organizational aspects of its development.

The reshuffling of the materials of the controversy can be seen in Schwarzwald (Rodrigue) (1994: 14–15). While discussing the names of the language, she mentions Rosén as the source of the name Israeli Hebrew, but leaves out the original political context of the controversy, and plants a new Rosén in the present context:

> Haiim Rosén, who coined the name Israeli Hebrew, treated it as "the Hebrew language used for educational, administrative, commercial, and other needs in the State of Israel." But has this language been alive only since the establishment of the State of Israel? Not at all. Hebrew of this kind was spoken also by the fighters of *palmakh, hagana, `ecel and lexi*[11] alongside other citizens prior to the establishment of the state. The adjective "Israeli" gives it a local dimension, i.e. —the language of *`erec yisra`el*. Thus it creates a partition between the users of Hebrew abroad and those using it in our country, as if only those using it in *`erec yisra`el* have an Israeli Hebrew, while those abroad have a different kind. Though the use of Hebrew abroad is more limited than that in our country, in its features it is similar to the language of our country, therefore the local dimension does not describe the Hebrew of our days.

Note, how Schwarzwald (Rodrigue) identifies Israel (the state) with *`erec yisra`el* (the land), a discursive practice that lines up with the ideology accompanying Greater Israel practices. Furthermore, she construes a community of IH speakers abroad, which in fact does not exist. No community outside Israel speaks modern Hebrew. This fictitious community represents the continued bond between Israel and the Diaspora. The two pairs of terms: Israel/*`erec yisra`el* and Israel/Diaspora symbolize two unfinished Zionist projects in the post-1967 context of occupation, which together form the spontaneous ideological tenets of expansionism, to be read more or less as follows: "The state of Israel is the property of the (Jewish) People of Israel wherever they live, and it expands over the entire land of Israel." Listing all four military organizations as equals is yet another practice of right-wing oriented discourse in Israel.

The reshuffling of terms blurs earlier distinctions, such as Rosén's explicit pronouncement (see above) that the adjective Israeli is not a geographical but a political term, representing territorial independence. This reshuffling contributes to the suppression of the controversy in the collective memory, i.e. as a cultural experience. This suppression, combined with the reshuffling of the terms, fuses the linguistic discourse into the expansionist discourse, exhibiting once again the role of the intellectual in disseminating hegemonic ideology within disciplinary discourse, under the safe shelter of objective and scientific fact. Needless to say, the real author of this text may not view this analysis as representative of her conscious political beliefs, but the persona that emerges from the text does have a clear political profile.

The latter discussion very briefly illustrates that with the political changes and with the shift in hegemonic ideology after 1967, the context of the controversy within Israel changed, nonetheless the axis around which it continued to revolve remained the same: Zionism and its manifestations as a viable factor underlying Israeli political practice and cultural discourse. I think that it is not a prophesy, but a rather solid prediction, to say that as long as the major themes in Israeli politics are defined in terms of the finished/unfinished project of Zionism, its corollary, the status of IH as a finished/unfinished project may, perhaps, undergo further metamorphoses, but cannot be considered settled. But it may also be suggested that recovering such suppressed stories might have a liberating effect both in the narrow fields of linguistic investigation and in the broader cultural domains.

5.2. On the 1950s and the 1990s

The forty years of Hebrew language scholarship between the 1950s and the 1990s have not approached the question from any new angle. Rosén (1977: 15–24) produced a short historiography of his version of the debate, which has never been challenged or discussed. During these decades structuralist work continued to be produced alongside generativist work. The latter has to be divided into two distinct moves. Both are distinct because generativism underwent consecutive phases, and above all because in the first phase (consisting mainly of Standard Theory and Extended Standard Theory) Uzzi Ornan was involved, while the later phases of generativism (Government-Binding and Minimalism) are detached from Ornan's influence, as his theoretical interest shifted to computational linguistics. Ornan, one of the leaders of a political group called Hebrews or Canaanites, cast early Israeli generativism in a peculiar and singular mold, compared to its counterparts worldwide. This part of the story will receive separate attention in a forthcoming publication. Today's generativists are typically graduates of American centers of GB, not students of Ornan. For a generativist of the newer brand the whole question of the existence of Israeli Hebrew is a social question that has nothing to do with linguistics. Linguists strive to describe I-languages (Chomsky 1986: Ch. 2), while E-languages, according to Chomsky (1986: 26) "are not real-world objects but are artificial, somewhat arbitrary, and perhaps not very interesting constructs."

Both structuralist and generativist linguists active today operate under the tacit assumption that Modern Hebrew is a language —in whatever sense— of its own, worthy of scholarly focus. Alongside these schools, a few new directions appeared. Eliezer Rubinstein's generative semantics, which outlived its counterparts in the world, is still practiced by his disciples. Discourse analysis and pragmatics entered the field. Some sociolinguistic work has been carried out, especially as part of a feminist agenda.

These developments clearly testify to a partial victory of Rosén's position, at least in some narrow disciplinary domains (as opposed to state apparatuses such as the Hebrew Language Academy and the educational system), a victory that bears fruits but pays also the prices of its modernist conceptual framework. The lean and skeletal nature of the term *system*, if taken in the serious sense of structuralist theory, resists a critical view of its foundations, and restricts the field of knowledge regarded as interesting and worthy of research. This is why discourse analysis and pragmatics are so often a-theoretical. Once a problematization of the tenets of structuralism is undertaken, and the Saussurean dichotomies are subjected to critical examination, several new paths may open up. The sociolinguistic point of view will have to deal with the mobility of language variation which defies a simplistic view of *la langue*. Blanc, who was a leading dialectologist of Arabic, made some significant contributions to a description of language variation in Israel, which were also acknowledged by Rosén. Not much has been done ever since. In recent decades, a significant shift from ethnolect to sociolect has occurred, from the *mizrakhi* accent of immigrants from Arab countries to a substandard, socially inferior accent, recognized and termed as *frexi* ("*frekhi*") by the educated speakers of IH; it has not merited scholarly attention yet.

Other angles of language variation have barely been discussed (save feminist gender literature). For example, the slow emergence of artistic registers: Hebrew has lacked a way of representing live dialogue in the language of cinema and theater, a deficiency which has only deserved corrective attention in recent years. One may certainly claim that a language that has not developed a full range of registers commensurate with its level of cultural production has not reached a state of full normalcy, even though it has a system.

Another aspect of language refinement is the semantic one. Current Israeli Hebrew certainly has clearer semantic differentiations and a more stable system of collocations than early Israeli Hebrew. Could this lead us to the conclusion that those who claimed that Hebrew had not finished its revival were right? I believe that only a multifaceted approach, which endorses the concept of a system subject to dynamic and dialectical ramification, can start to undertake these questions. Interestingly, the pioneer work in investigating early versus late Israeli Hebrew was carried out by Rosén (1992) (with earlier allusions here and there), followed by some disciples of his. The rejection of structuralism by normativists has not led to a significant contribution to the description and explanation of the phenomena of contemporary Hebrew. The recognition of the imperfections of the structuralist concept of system and its problematization will, surely have a liberating effect, though it obviously owes its root to the structuralists' struggle.

As for the political context, in the 1950s the hegemonic ideology was that of statehood, but it did not yet have a clear, mature hegemonic structure; it was still fighting to establish power. I used the family metaphor to portray the relative solidarity between the forces laying claim to hegemony. Statehood was the sober practically-minded member of the family, running the family-business in the real world; socialist Zionism was the old parent, still sitting at the head of the table, inspiring the family with glorious stories but already retired from business; individualist modernism was the offspring kicking the legs of both parent and grand-parent under the table. Within this setting, the semiotic personae of three linguists: Rosén, Ben-Hayyim, and Blanc became tangential to these family relations. Their texts exemplify the role of the intellectual in a Gramscian model at several levels of congruence with politico-cultural networks: being enlisted, being contained, being co-opted, and being a fellow traveler. Short of an actual statement of allegiance to statehood, Rosén was almost openly and actively enlisted in the ranks of this project. Ben-Hayyim was both contained by Rosén as a structuralist, and co-opted by Tsemakh, whose anti-statehood pro-volunteerism produced a conservative discourse nostalgic for *mapai*'s childhood (second *`aliya*). Blanc's way of recognizing Israeli Hebrew was more individualistic and militant than Rosén's responsible hegemonic conduct, carrying some overtones of anti-statehood, of anti-religious sentiment, and of awareness of dialect and variation, positions which despite their individualism harmonized with the counter-hegemonic melody that *mapam* wished to play. *Mapam*'s attempt to be a counter-hegemony involved by definition the establishment of its own set of alliances, similar to that of a hegemonic structure. Many of the individualists of the modernist trend —by no means all of them— became allied fellow travelers of this counter-hegemonic drive.

The decade of the 1990s, with the peace process that has started in it, resembles the 1950s in that the Zionist package is being reopened again, but this time from a different, post-Zionist angle: it does not take inventory of accomplished/unaccomplished elements, but raises the possibility of the total completion of the project, whereby it suggests also a more potent version of normalcy. Post-Zionism institutes a very threatening challenge to Zionism, because it signals its finality; but at the same time it does not *per se* constitute an anti-Zionist disposition, but merely a historization and periodization of Zionism, which acknowledges its victory, thereby easing the passage of Zionists into it. Even the distinctive mark of Israeliness, the automatic unquestionable availability to military service, is experiencing first cracks.

No political party openly supports this stance, but it seems to have strong infra-structural roots: a growing chunk of the industry and business community has realized that the pre-*Intifada* days of economic gain from the state of occupation are gone for good and all, and that Shimon Peres's vision of a peaceful New Middle-East (even if slowed down by the Netanyahu government) will provide the alternative channels for Israeli capital and commerce. This new economic interest is accompanied by an emergent counter-hegemony, manifest via a loose web of journalists, broadcasters, novelists, poets, playwrights, film-makers, pop-singers, lawyers, and not the least academic scholars. This web is far too complex to attempt any elaborate mapping here. Suffice it to say, that its scholarly academic facet is practiced as a skeptical discourse, which —like its worldwide brethren— feeds on a re-examination of modernist conceptions, and on the tensions between modernist utilitarianism and a relativization of terms that have been stable and serviceable for so long.

It must be clear at this point of my current study, that my own text cannot escape its interpretation as an intervention in the politico-cultural discourse. In my own case, the authorial person and persona are indivisible, therefore a clear statement of intentions seems an honest choice.

In accord with similar developments in the world, there grows in Israel a critical discourse, which —again like its worldwide counterparts— shares with the skeptical discourse the premise of re-appraising the usefulness of modernist frames, but strives to get to its deeper roots by the added preoccupation with the tensions between traditional teleological master-narratives (enlightenment, rationality and reason, social betterment, scientific progress) and their vulnerability to semiotically aware decompositions and deconstructions. This discourse is primarily parasitic, in terms of communication tools and audience, on the carriers and readers of the skeptical discourse, and tolerated by it, perhaps as some sort of a not-always-very-favorable fellow traveler. My study is intended as a contribution to this discourse. As such, it seeks —in its particular domain of knowledge— to renew access to the ideological terms and the historical roots of the controversy over the finality of the revival of IH in Israeli collective memory, and thereby to forestall future "naive" or "objective" treatments of the question, by flagging the option and offering the tools for subjecting them to a similar critique.

Notes

1. In this paper I shall refrain from addressing different readings of Gramsci's conceptions of the state and civil society, abundantly discussed elsewhere.
2. Haiim B. Rosén —Born in Austria: 1922. In Israel since 1938. Ph.D. from Hebrew University: 1948. Was Professor in the Dept. of Linguistics at The Hebrew University and in the Dept. of Hebrew Language at Tel-Aviv University. Today: professor emeritus.
3. Haim Blanc —Born in Rumania: 1926. Grew up in the U.S. In Israel since 1948. Ph.D. from Hebrew University: 1953. Was professor in the Dept. of Arabic at The Hebrew University. Died: 1984.
4. Ze`ev Ben-Hayyim —Born in Poland: 1907. In Israel since 1931. Was professor in the Dept. of Hebrew Language. Today: professor emeritus.
5. Shlomo Tsemakh (Zemach) —Born in Poland: 1886. In Israel since 1904. Educator, writer, and literary critic. Founder and principal of the prestigious Kadourie [kaduri] agricultural high-school, a major breeding-soil of early native Israeli elite (e.g. Dayan and Rabin). Died: 1974.
6. David Ben-Gurion —Leader of the pre-state Jewish community in Palestine and Israel's first prime-minister.
7. The attempt to present a politico-cultural map in terms of political parties is a gross reduction. The individuals active in the field exhibit much more freedom and mobility in and between the more coherent programs and practices of political parties. Nevertheless, we have to bear in mind that in the 1950s, a political party in Israel was not merely an ad hoc association of individuals and interest groups, breaking up and reuniting with every minor change of

political mood, but rather an all-embracing ideological home, which operated massive networks of occupational, recreational, financial, cultural, and social organizations. In this paper, the attribution of characteristics to a certain party (e.g. "*mapai* supported statehood") is merely a reduction that means to say that the population that found its ideological home in *mapai* by and large, and with many variations and internal tensions, could be characterized as such.

8. In the spirit of Althusserian (1971) "interpellation".
9. The waves of immigration (*`aliyot* in plural) relevant to our story are:
   the first *`aliya* (1882–1903),
   the second *`aliya* (1904–14), Tsemakh's *`aliya,*
   the third *`aliya* (1919–1923,
   the fourth *`aliya* (1924–1928),
   the fifth *`aliya* (1929–1939), of the German Jews.
10. The clipping that I obtained is an unauthored report, bearing neither date nor source.
11. The first two were the large combative front units and headquarter and back units of the organized pre-state Jewish population. The *`ecel* (known overseas as the *`irgun*) and *lexi*, known as the *Stern* group or gang, were two right wing oppositional minority military organizations.

References

[This list contains the references for this chapter as well as the primary sources for documenting the debate. Given the importance of chronology in the debate, many of the entries for the latter category carry the day and/or month of publication alongside the year of publication.]

Agmon-Fruchtman, Maya and Immanuel Allon
1994 *prakim betoldot halaSon ha`ivrit:haxativa hamodernit* ('Chapters in the history of the Hebrew language: The modern Division'): *Unit 8.* The Open University.

Althusser, Louis
1971 Ideology and ideological state apparatuses. In: Althusser, Louis, *Lenin and philosophy*. New York: Monthly Review Press, 127–186.

Atter, Moshe
1983 *hama`avak `al ha`ivrit kesafa le`umit nimSax* ('The struggle over Hebrew as a national language goes on'). *ha`uma*, 73.

Avineri, Yitzhak
1946 *kibuSei ha`ivrit bedorenu* ('The conquests of Hebrew in our generation'). Merhavia: Sifriyat Hapoalim.

Bachi, Roberto A.

1956 A statistical analysis of the revival of Hebrew in Israel. *Scripta Hierosolymitana* 3: 179–247.

3.1956 *txiyat halaSon ha`ivrit be`aspaklarya statistit 1* ('Hebrew language revival from a statistical perspective 1'). *leSonenu* 20: 65–82.

9.1956 *txiyat halaSon ha`ivrit be`aspaklarya statistit 2* ('Hebrew Language revival from a statistical perspective 2'). *leSonenu* 21: 41–68.

Ben-Amotz, Dan

13.4.1956 *ma niSma* ('What's up'). *ma`ariv*.

Bendavid, Abba

1952 *leSon hamikra `o leSon xaxamim* ('Biblical language or Rabbinical language'). Tel Aviv: Dvir.

Ben-Hayyim, Ze`ev

3.1953 *laSon `atika bimci`ut xadaSa* ('Ancient Language in New Reality'). = *leSonenu la`am* 35–37. [Reprinted: Ben-Hayyim, Ze`ev 1992: 36–83].

27.8.1953 *dikduk bnei-`adam* ('Grammar of "ordinary" people'). In: Blanc, Haim 1989: 71–78. [Originally in *masa*].

8.1955 *lete`ura Sel ha`ivrit kefi Sehi meduberet* ('On the description of Hebrew as it is spoken'). *tarbic (Tarbitz)* 24: 337–342.

1992 *bemilxamta Sel laSon* ('The struggle for a language'). Jerusalem: Hebrew Language Academy.

Ben-Yehuda, Barukh

1981 *`adayin lo nistayem tahalix haxya`atah Sel halaSon ha`ivrit* ('The process of Hebrew language revival is not over yet'). *`am vasefer*: new series: I.

Blanc, Haim

16.10.1952 *'hiStabSut `o hitpatxut* ('Spoilage or development'). In: Blanc, Haim 1989: 10–13. [Originally in *masa*].

30.10.1952 *`al ta`am vareax* ('On taste and smell'). In: Blanc, Haim 1989: 14–17. [Originally in *masa*].

8.1.1953 *`ivrit `o lo `ivrit* ('Hebrew or not Hebrew'). In: Blanc, Haim 1989: 32–36. [Originally in *masa*].

19.2.1953 *dor holex vedor ba* ('A generation comes; a generation goes'). In: Blanc, Haim 1989: 42–46. [Originally in *masa*].

26.3.1953 *'hilxeta limSixa* ('A law for "the days of" Messiah'). In: Blanc, Haim 1989: 51–54. [Originally in *masa*].

4.1953 Review of Weiman 1950. *Word* 9: 87–90.

2.7.1953 *Sgi`a nora`it `ax lo `ixpatit* ('An awful-ish but couldn't-care-less-ish mistake'). In: Blanc, Haim 1989: 59–62. [Originally in *masa*].

30.7.1953 *`otah hagveret* ('The same lady'). In: Blanc, Haim 1989: 63–70. [Originally in *masa*].

7.9.1953 *habalSanim kivnei `adam* ('The linguists as "ordinary" people'). In: Blanc, Haim 1989: 79–83. [Originally in *masa*].

17.12.1953 *ma hasakana?* ('What is the danger?'). In: Blanc, Haim 1989: 88–94. [Originally in *masa*].

14.4.1954a *ve`ata x.b. rozen...* ('And there came H.B. Rosén...'). In: Blanc, Haim 1989: 104–107. [Originally in *masa*].

12.1954a The growth of Israeli Hebrew. *Middle Eastern Affairs* 5: 385–392.

12.1954b *layesod ha`arvi Sebadibur hayisre`eli* ('On the Arabic element in colloquial Hebrew') Part 1. *leSonenu la`am* 53: 6–14. [All 3 parts reprinted in Blanc, Haim 1989: 135–149].

3.1955 *layesod ha`arvi Sebadibur hayisre`eli* ('On the Arabic element in colloquial Hebrew') Part 2. *leSonenu la`am* 54–55: 27–32.

4.1955 *layesod ha`arvi Sebadibur hayisre`eli'* ('On the Arabic element in colloquial Hebrew') Part 3. *leSonenu la`am* 56: 20–26.

4.1956 A note on Israeli Hebrew "psycho-phonetics". *Word* 12: 106–114.

5.1956 Dialect research in Israel. *Orbis* 5: 185–190.

9.1956 *keta Sel dibur `ivri yisre`eli'* ('A passage of Israeli Hebrew speech'). *leSonenu* 21: 33–39.

12.1956 Review of Rosén 12.1955. *Language* 32: 794–802.

10.1957 Hebrew in Israel: Trends and problems. *Middle East Journal* 11: 397–409.

1989 *leSon bnei-`adam* ('Language of "ordinary" people'). Jerusalem: Bialik Institute.

Chomsky, Noam

1954 Review of Eliezer Riegler (1953) "Modern Hebrew" (New York: Philosophical Library). *Language* 30: 180–181.

1986 *Knowledge of Language.* New York: Praeger.

Eitan, Eli

2.1954 *`al laSon vehistorya* ('On language and history'). [Review of Rosén 1954]. *leSonenu la`am* 45–46: 41–44.

Forgacs, David (ed.)

1988 *A Gramsci Reader*. London: Lawrence and Wishart.

Garbell, Irene
1930 *Fremdsprachliche Einflüsse im Modernen Hebräisch.* PhD. dissertation. Berlin.

Goshen-Gottstein Moshe
9.1951 *halaSon ha`ivrit hameduberet kenose lemexkar* ('Spoken Hebrew language as an object of study'). *leSonenu* 17: 231–240.
1.8.1952 Review of Bendavid 1952. *ha`arec (=Haaretz).*
11.1953 *balSanut mivnit upolitika leSonit* ('Structural linguistics and language politics'). *leSonenu la`am* 43: 17–24.
6.5.1955 *yevu yecu* ('Import export'). *ha`arec (=Haaretz).*
24.2.1956a *barbarismim `alexa*! ('Barbarisms are upon you!'). *ha`arec (=Haaretz).*
24.2.1956b *ha`ivrit Selanu* ('Our Hebrew') [Review of Rosén 12.1955]. *ha`arec (=Haaretz).*
30.3.1956 *`al balSanim, sofrim ve`ahavat yisra`el* ('On linguists, authors, and love of Israel'). *davar.*
1980 *taxbir ha`ivrit haxadaSa: hirhurim `al darxei mexkarah* ('Syntax of New Hebrew: Contemplations on its research methods'). *mexkarim be`ivrit uvilSonot Semiyot: mukdaSim lezixro Sel profesor yexezkel kutSer*: Ramat Gan: Bar-Ilan University Press, 188–201.

Harris, Zelig
2.1951 *hasafa ha`ivrit le`or habalSanut haxadaSa* ('The Hebrew language in light of modern linguistics'). *leSonenu* 17: 128–132.

Horowitz, M. (=M.O.Sh)
23.3.1956 ha`ivrit Selanu — `o lo Selanu ('The Hebrew is ours —or not ours'). *ha`arec* (=Haaretz).

Keren, Michael
1983 *Ben-Gurion and the intellectuals.* DeKalb: Northern Illinois University Press.

Klausner Joseph
1929 *`ivrit `atika ve`ivrit xadaSa* ('Ancient Hebrew and New Hebrew'). *leSonenu* 2: 3–21.

Klausner, Samuel Z.
8.1955 Phonetics, personality and status in Israel. *Word* 11: 209–215.

Kutscher, Ezekiel G.
6.1956 Modern Hebrew and "Israeli" Hebrew. *Conservative Judaism* 10: 28–45.

Kuzar, Ron
1997 Scientificity in linguistic practice: Structuralism. *Semiotica* 113: 223–256.

Labov, William
1982 Objectivity and commitment in linguistic science: The case of the Black English trial in Ann Arbor. *Language in Society* 11: 165–201.

Latour, Bruno
1977 *Science in Action.* Cambridge, MA: Harvard University Press.

Livni, Yitzhak
1949 *hayeS la`ivrit dikduk* ('Does Hebrew have a grammar?'). *molad* 3: 293–302.

Mushon, Levana
4.7.1995 `al miSmar ha`ivrit ('On the guard of Hebrew'). *ha`arec* (=Haaretz).

Nahir, Moshe
1974 *Language Academies, Language Planning, and the Case of the Hebrew Revival.* Ann Arbor: University Microfilms.

Rabin, Chaim
9.1954 Review of Rosén 1954. *Journal of Jewish Studies* 5: 136–137.
9.1958 Language revival: Colloquialism or purism. *Jewish Frontier* 9.1958, section 2: 11–15.
2.1958 *`ivrit beinonit* ('Middle Hebrew'). *leSonenu la`am* 85: 88–92.
5.1958 *lexeker ha`ivrit hasifrutit haxadaSa* ('On the study of new literary Hebrew'). *leSonenu* 22: 246–257.

Rosén, Haiim B.
6.1950 *xiduSei laSon Selo mida`at* ('Unaware neologisms'). *leSonenu la`am.*
12.1950 *draxim behakarat halaSon: b. hadilduk* ('Ways of knowing language: b. Grammar'). *leSonenu la`am.*
1.1952 *Tahalixei LaSon 1* ('Language processes 1'). = *LeSonenu la`am* 25.
3.1952 Remarques descriptives sur le parler hébreu-israélien moderne. *Comptes-rendus du Groupe Linguistique d'Études chamito-sémitiques (GLECS)* 6: 4–7. [Reprinted: Rosén, Haiim 1984, Vol. 2: 26–29].
10.1952 *Tahalixei LaSon 2* ('Language Processes 2'). = *LeSonenu la`am* 32.
4.1953 *`al standard venorma, 'al tahalixim uSgi`ot 1* ('On standard and norm, on processes and mistakes 1'). *leSonenu la`am* 38: 3–8.
5.1953 *`al standard venorma, `al tahalixim uSgi`ot 2* ('On standard and norm, on processes and mistakes 2'). *leSonenu la`am* 39: 3–7.

7.1953 *`al standard venorma, `al tahalixim uSgi`ot 3* ('On standard and norm, on processes and mistakes 3'). *leSonenu la`am* 40: 3–11.

1954 *sixot `al laSon vehistorya* ('Talks on language and history'). Tel Aviv: Joshua Chechik.

8.1955 *dikduk ha`ivrit hayisre`elit* ('Grammar of Israeli Hebrew'). [Review of Weiman 1950]. *tarbic (=Tarbitz)* 24: 234–247.

9.1955 *tahalixei laSon 3* ('Language Processes 3'). = *leSonenu la`am* 62.

12.1955 *ha`ivrit Selanu* ('Our Hebrew'). Tel Aviv: Am Oved.

7.1957 *`ivrit tova* ('Good Hebrew'). Jerusalem: Kiryat-Sepher.

1958a *Sur quelques catégories à expression adnominale en hébreu-israélien. Bulletin de la Société linguistique de Paris* 53: 316–344. [Reprinted: Rosén, Haiim 1984, Vol.2: 41–69].

1958b *L'hébreu-israélien. Revue des Études Juives* 117: 59–90. [Reprinted: Rosén, Haiim 1984, Vol. 2: 70–101.

1977 *Contemporary Hebrew*. The Hague: Mouton.

1984 *East and West: Selected Writings in Linguistics*. Munich: Wilhelm Fink Verlag

1992 *zutot mehitgabSutah Sel ha`ivrit hayisre`elit* ('"Obiterdicta" concerning the crystallization of Israeli Hebrew'). *Societatis Linguisticae Europeae Sodalicium Israelense: Studia V*, 33–39.

Round Table

3.1955 *`al leSon ha"cabarim"'*. ('On the Language of the "Sabre"s'). *leSonenu la`am*, 54–55: 3–17.

Schwarzwald (Rodrigue), Ora

1994 *prakim betoldot halaSon ha`ivrit: haxativa hamodernit* ('Chapters of the history of the Hebrew language: The modern division'): *Unit 9*. The Open University.

Tsemakh (=Zemach), Shlomo

1954 *leSon `ilgim* ('Language of stammerers'). *`adam `im `axerim* ('A man with others'). Tel Aviv: Newman.

9/16.3.1956 *`isfu yedeixem*! ('Hands off!'). *davar*. [Reprinted: Tsemakh, Shlomo 1959: 162–184].

1959 *Sti va`erev*. Tel Aviv: Am-Oved.

Tur-Sinai, N.H.

11.1950 *balSanut uvatlanut 1* ('Linguistics and fiddlesticks 1'). *leSonenu la`am* 14: 4–8.

12.1950 *balSanut uvatlanut 2* ('Linguistics and fiddlesticks 2'). *leSonenu la`am* 15: 3–6.

3.1951 *balSanut uvatlanut 3* ('Linguistics and fiddlesticks 3'). *leSonenu la`am* 17: 3–7.

5.1951 *balSanut uvatlanut 4* ('Linguistics and fiddlesticks 4'). *leSonenu la`am* 18–19: 19–22.

5.1957 *pnei leSonenu bahistorya uvahove.* ('The shape of our language in the history and in the present'). *leSonenu la`am* 80: 193–202.

Ullendorf, Edward

7.1957 Modern Hebrew as a subject of linguistic investigation. *Journal of Semitic Studies* 2: 251–263.

1958 What is a Semitic language? *Orientalia* 27: 66–75.

Weiman, Ralph William

1950 *Native and Foreign Elements in a Language: A Study in General Linguistics Applied to Modern Hebrew*. Philadelphia: Russel Press.

Weinberg, Werner

1981 A concise history of the Hebrew language. In: Nahir, Moshe (ed.), *Hebrew Teaching and Applied Linguistics*. Markham: University Press of America., 19–96.

Yaron, Kalman

27.4.1956 *beSulei hapulmos sviv "ha`ivrit Selanu"* ('Marginalia on the polemic around "our Hebrew"'). *masa.*

Yediot

17.2.1956 *ha`ivrit Se`anu medabrim bah —mahi?'* ('What is the Hebrew that we speak?'). [Review of Rosén 12.1955]. *yedi`ot axronot.*

Politics, ideology and poetic form: The literary debate in Tanzania

Joshua Madumulla, Elena Bertoncini and Jan Blommaert

1. Introduction

In the years between 1968 and 1978, Tanzanian writers and intellectuals found themselves in an intense debate over the nature and meaning of poetry written in the national language, Swahili. The camps were neatly divided: on the one side stood a group of "traditionalists", defending the centuries-old poetic canons of classical Swahili poetry; on the other side stood the "modernists" who demanded the freedom to break away from these established verse forms and who advocated the introduction (and acceptance) of "modern" poetic genres. The debate was fought in letters to the editor, speeches, books, papers and most of all in poems and treatises on literary criticism.

In the debate, a variety of contexts were activated and called into question. First, there was the political context, marked by the introduction of a new socialist political ideology, *Ujamaa*, in Tanzania in 1967. Second, there was the context of Swahili, the old language of the East Coast societies which had been spread over the Tanzanian territory and had acquired the status of national language after independence. Third, there was the context of tradition versus innovation in a revolutionary period, where Africanness had to be expressed through symbols that were not always compatible with the revolutionary ideals of a new socialist culture. And finally, there was the context of emergent classes, status groups, and social and political formations such as the academically trained intellectuals. Together these contexts provided a formidable field of tension in which the debate about literary form soon became inflated with political-ideological meanings and in which crucial questions of identity and culture-political praxis were raised.

The debate thus shows how linguistic *form* —the option of writing "modernist" or "traditional" poetry— can be loaded with ideological and political meaning in a sociolinguistic and political context in which language resources are mobilized for nation-building purposes. The way in which words are being ordered in phrases, in lines, in stanzas, in sequences, is given a political semiotics. Similar insights emerged from Jaffe's exploration of Corsican translator's works: the choice of one communicative action over another was transformed into a political statement, measured on the basis of criteria contained in a nationalist doxa. The specificity of this case must be sought in the particular sociolinguistic context in which the Tanzanian debate develops: a context on the one hand marked by (sometimes extreme) inequality in the distribution of linguistic resources (see further, section 2), and on the other hand marked by the emergence of recognizable "voices" capable of producing adequately politicizable ways of speaking (postcolonial politicians, writers, intellectuals) (Blommaert 1997c). Furthermore, the debate cannot be understood without taking into account the context of decolonization. Actors in the debate make use of the ambiguities in the meaning of cultural and political symbols which may lie at the heart of the semiotics of decolonization and which testify to the emergence of the new traditions and cultural practices described by Ali Mazrui (e.g. 1967a, 1967b, 1978). The debate thus sheds light on the structure of the political processes accompanying a large-scale political, economic and ideological transformation such as that of the introduction of *Ujamaa* in Tanzania.

The debate never came to a real end. Together with the waning of *Ujamaa*, the field of application for some of the theses and principles that had been advanced in the course of the debate gradually vanished. The debate was strongly linked to the fate of *Ujamaa* ideology, and it derived its relevance largely from the potential to align literary discourses to political discourses, dominant ones as well as dissident ones. The literary debate was part of a larger debate on the meaning of *Ujamaa* and on the correct implementation of *Ujamaa*, and as soon as *Ujamaa* lost its grip on the Tanzanian society —in the late 1970s— the literary issues also lost their appeal and their mobilizing potential.

Given the close connection between the literary debate and *Ujamaa* ideology, some introductory background on *Ujamaa* and on the Swahili poetic tradition should be given first. This will be done in section 3. Section 4 will summarize the debate itself and will discuss the main arguments used by protagonists from both camps. Section 5 will conclude this chapter with some reflections on wider historical and sociolinguistic issues. But before that, a brief set of comments must be given on the wider political-linguistic background against which the Tanzanian case can be developed.

2. The politics of language in Africa

Ali Mazrui once remarked that in pre-independence Africa, rhetoric served as a surrogate for real power (1978: 72). Much of what Africans could accomplish in a colonial context, almost by definition marked by extreme power imbalances, depended on their rhetorical skills. Hence, Mazrui argues, the great interest taken by many African leaders in political oratory. But one could extend Mazrui's observation a bit further. Quite a few African leaders were not only interested in the practice of oratory; they were also very much interested in language per se. Language has in many places in postcolonial Africa been a very sensitive political topic and political domain.

The former colonial languages were adopted as official languages in nearly all of the postcolonial states. But this did not mean that things were left as they were. Leaders frequently referred to language in the context of larger political goals and plans. Thus, the introduction of the ex-colonial language was motivated by a desire to build national unity through a "neutral" medium —neutral meaning "not ethnically marked" here— and to use the foreign language in order to establish or maintain the sort of contacts with the western world deemed necessary to attain a desired level of development. Thus also, leaders often tried to "repatriate" French, English or Portuguese and turn them into "African" languages and symbols of Africanness. Stroud (this volume) shows how Portuguese was "repatriated" to suit socialist nation-building goals in Mozambique. In a more complex way, Senegal's Senghor often proclaimed his faith in the universal potential of French, arguing that it had absorbed cultures from all over the world; hence it had been transformed into the medium of *la Civilisation de l'Universel* of which African cultures were now part and parcel. Thus, through the use of French (or English), Africans would give the fullest expression to their modern Africanness (e.g. Senghor 1988: 155–197; see also Meeuwis' discussion of the remarkable Zairian situation: Meeuwis, this volume). Leaders also often intervened in the domain of local languages —often called "ethnic" languages by African leaders and linguists alike. Kamuzu Banda, for instance, decided in 1968 that, "in the interest of national unity", Chinyanja would be adopted as national language of Malawi. But Chinyanja was not typically Malawian, it was also spoken in Zambia, Mozambique and Tanzania, and therefore Banda decided that the language would now be called "Chichewa" (Chauma, Chimimbo and Mtenje 1997: 37–38).

In almost every case, language was brought to stand in relation to issues of national unity, nation-building and identity politics. The colonial legacy of an image of Africa as a nightmarish Tower of Babel had placed sociolinguistic landscaping high on the agenda as a necessary precondition for building a nation out of the multilingual, multiethnic agglomerate grouped in "nations" that were the creation of European diplomats (Mazrui notes: "Africa is landed with the consequences of the consensus of others," 1967a: 7). These attempts at sociolinguistic landscaping often resulted in a pyramidic, hierarchical pattern in which the former colonial language occupied the top, a selection of local languages (usually the most widespread languages) the middle, and the other local languages the bottom of the pyramid. The European language was often the language of higher education, of business, government and the Law; the selected local languages were often "national" languages that could be used during national rituals, and they were often also the languages of primary education and local government; the remaining languages were relegated to the domain of everyday local in-group communication (see e.g. Laitin 1992 for a survey; discussions in Fardon and Furniss (eds.) 1994 and Smieja (ed.) 1997).

Discourses (often also inherited) emerged in which particular languages were associated with politically categorized values and qualities ("English is the language of international contacts"; "Chichewa is the language of freedom") or relegated to particular sociolinguistic domains ("ethnic languages can be used in private life", "Swahili will be used in primary education"). Such discourses had a deeply politicizing effect on almost any form of language use in these societies, and they often led to an acute awareness of the symbolic power of particular forms of language usage among various groups in society. Just like everywhere else, African societies have their linguistic-ideological hierarchies, reflecting and sustaining clear forms of social stratification correlated with the unequal distribution of linguistic resources (especially writing: Blommaert 1998), and containing "marked" language varieties or accents that identify speakers along lines of regional and/or class descent, gender, educational background, and sometimes even political affiliation.

Consequently, problems of voice are extremely salient (and very little understood) in the sociolinguistics of Africa. The outspoken inequality in the distribution of linguistic resources has its effect on who can speak, when and how. Genres such as written discourse in a standard variety of any language (and especially a European language) are the object of extreme inequality, and the capacity or incapacity to use such genres marks the user as either an elite figure or someone from the masses. Written journalism, for instance, is far from a "mass" medium: it is highly elitist, aimed at an audience which is overwhelmingly urban, fully employed, highly literate in more than one language —a very small segment of society in any African country. This is reflected in the figures: in 1980, the largest Tanzanian newspaper in Swahili, *Uhuru*, had an estimated daily readership of 50,000 to 100,000 people, against a population of 17,5 million (Ng'wanakilala 1981: 19). Hence, getting one's opinion printed is not merely an act of expression of "public" —in fact private— "opinion", but it is a very strong form of social and political self-identification and self-disclosure, which categorizes the author as somebody from the upper regions in society.

3. The local context

3.1. Ujamaa *and language*

The United Republic of Tanzania was created through the union of Tanganyika and the islands of Zanzibar and Pemba in 1964. Tanganyika, by far the larger part of the union, had won its independence from Britain in 1961 under the leadership of Julius Nyerere's TANU party (Tanganyika African National Union) and had established a moderate form of African socialism as its state ideology. The protectorate of Zanzibar and Pemba had been independent since 1963, but shortly after independence a bloody revolution ousted the Sultan and replaced the old regime with a radical left-wing government. The union between Tanganyika and the islands caused a shift to the left in TANU (which remained the unitary ruling party after the union), and led to the introduction, in 1967, of a new formalized state ideology for Tanzania, called *Ujamaa* (literally 'familyhood') (cf. Pratt 1976).

Ujamaa had its roots in the older ideology of TANU. This older ideology of African socialism was an unorthodox blend of elements of European socialism and a (largely imagined) anthropological theory of precolonial African societies, which assumed that African rural societies before the advent of the colonizers were characterized by a primitive form of socialism in which property was shared by all, leadership was organized through dialogue and mutual understanding, distinctions between social classes did not exist, and efforts were communal rather than individual (cf. Metz 1982; Mohiddin 1981). As a consequence, some of the crucial elements of socialist orthodoxy (the concept of class and class struggle, historical materialism) were dismissed as irrelevant to African (largely unindustrialized) societies, and a rather minimal socialist strategy was followed in which the equality of all citizens, democracy and the general improvement of living conditions for all through education and health care went hand in hand with a (largely neocolonial) free market economy. This lukewarm form of socialism came under fire from intellectuals (mainly from the University of Dar es Salaam) who advocated a more elaborate and theoretically consistent form of socialism. As said above, the union with Marxist Zanzibar and Pemba strengthened the left wing in the union and legitimized movements towards a more formalized and orthodox form of socialism. At the same time, the union with Zanzibar and Pemba neutralized the threat of a communist government in East Africa. Even though it caused a shift towards a more revolutionary style and rhetoric and a realignment of the international alliances of the union in which the Peoples' Republic of China and the German Democratic Republic became major partners, the radical left wing was effectively minorized inside TANU (Tordoff and Mazrui 1972; Mulei 1972). Exercises in socialist radicalism were largely confined to the intellectuals on University Hill.

In the years following the Arusha Declaration, the University of Dar es Salaam acquired the reputation of being a center of radical political, economic and cultural activities. It became a haven and a meeting place for revolutionaries from other African countries. The South African ANC had a training college in Morogoro, and its cadres participated in debates at the University. The later president of Uganda, Museveni, was a radical left-wing student leader at the University (Othman 1994). Marxist ideology, along with other literatures of that inclination (e.g. Maoism from China and Juche from North Korea) became leading tools of analysis in most subjects, including literature and languages. Many intellectuals of international standing such as Walter Rodney, Ali Mazrui, Samir Amin, Wadada Nabudere, Nathan Shamuyarira, Issa Shivji, Yashar Tandon, George Laming, Alex la Guma, Michael Manley, Giovanni Arrighi and Colin Leys visited the University and gave lectures in ideological or literature classes and public talks. The presence of such radical scholars together with the increase in student exchanges with the German Democratic Republic, North Korea, the Soviet Union and China stimulated the development of a radical socialist tradition.[1]

Ujamaa was a compromise between the moderate and the radical tendencies in the country and in the party. On the one hand, it was a formalized doctrine with a core document, the "Arusha Declaration", and a body of important policy papers which could serve as a basis for exegesis. Also, the first sentence of the Arusha Declaration declared that Tanzania was "a socialist state," a statement so exclusive at that time that it unambiguously aligned Tanzania with other "socialist states" of the Soviet and Chinese kind. One clear consequence of this redefinition of the state was the nationalization of large industries and banks, later followed by attempts at the collectivization of agriculture in *Ujamaa* Villages. On the other hand, the core of the Arusha Declaration and of subsequent key policy papers remained the brand of African socialism as summarized above. The emphasis was still on the development of human capital, class struggle was still absent as a central analytical concept, and in terms of strategy industrialization was replaced by a largely agriculture-based economic self-reliance program. The new doctrine of *Ujamaa* was ambiguous enough to accommodate both moderates and radicals in Tanzania. It was radical enough to deserve the qualification of revolutionary, but it also paid enough lip service to African socialism to appease the anticommunists.

The Arusha declaration marked the beginning of a very intensive nation-building campaign, in which the new revolutionary nation would be built around a new Tanzanian identity based on *Ujamaa*, loyalty to the state, participation in the economic self-reliance programs, and a common language, Swahili. Language was one of the basic "cultural" ingredients of this new Tanzanian identity, and Swahili became the focus of impressive standardization and language planning efforts (Whiteley 1968; Harries 1969; Abdulaziz 1971; Kihore 1976). Swahili had been used by TANU as the language of popular mobilization during the struggle for decolonization, and it had been heavily loaded with symbolic connotations of freedom, equality and Africanness. Shortly after independence, Swahili had been declared the national language of the country, to be used in politics and in the public sphere. Nyerere was a great Swahili orator, and he created a particular political rhetoric in Swahili (cf. Blommaert 1991). Also, creative literature and journalism in Swahili were strongly encouraged, as literacy in Swahili was perceived to be a crucial nation-building and development instrument. English retained the status of official language, and it continued to be the language of post-primary education pending full Swahilization. In the wake of *Ujamaa*, Swahili became even more strongly symbolized as the language of the *Ujamaa* revolution (Blommaert 1994a). The language standardization efforts, started by the British and continued by the Tanzanians after independence, were intensified, and considerable efforts went into the "modernization" and "development" of Swahili (Blommaert 1994b; for a more detailed discussion see Blommaert 1997a).

Yet, the difference between political-ideological fractions was paralleled by a difference between language-ideological fractions. Supporters of a radically socialist interpretation of *Ujamaa* saw the complete Swahilization of the Tanzanian society as a necessary ingredient of cultural decolonization and socialism: it was neither the language of the former colonizer nor that of any particular ethnic group, and so it could become the language of all the independent Tanzanians. To the advocates of full Swahilization, Swahili should become the only language in the country, replacing English as well as local languages. The fact that English remained the language of higher education became a permanent source of annoyance for them. Swahili should become the expression of a new revolutionary-socialist culture in Tanzania, which would replace both the colonial society as well as the pre-revolutionary African ethnic societies (see Mbuguni and Ruhumbika 1974). Against this radical group, a more moderate group (including, from time to time, Nyerere) advocated the continued use of English as a language of higher education, international contact and business, claiming that the exclusion of English from Tanzanian public life would cause the loss of vital political and economic opportunities for the country. With regard to English in education, this group claimed that the Swahilization of the education system would create unaffordable economic as well as pedagogical difficulties. [2]

3.2. The poetic tradition

Swahili is one of the handful of African languages which has a precolonial literary tradition. Poetry is the most popular form in Swahili literature. Written poetry in Swahili has been there for more than five centuries, which is much longer than its other literary counterparts, the novel and the play (see Mulokozi and Sengo 1995; see also Harries 1962; Rollins 1983; Ohly 1985; Mulokozi 1985; Bertoncini 1989; Berwouts 1991 for surveys of Swahili literature). The Arabs are believed to have brought the art of writing to the East African coast during their long and extensive trade and, later, Islamic religious contacts with the coastal people (see Middleton 1992). A series of old poetic genres exists, written in Arabic script and later in Roman script.The best known genre are the long poems in the *utendi* (or *utenzi*) meter. Old poetry also includes short poems in the *shairi* (quatrain) meter. Both *utendi* and *shairi* are quatrains (*tarbia*), whose basic difference lies in the length of the lines and the position of the rhyme. The *utendi* has four hemistitches with end rhymes only; the end rhyme in the fourth hemistitch runs through the entire *utendi*. The *shairi* has four lines with two hemistitches in each line. Each line has a medial and end rhymes. Usually, the medial and end rhyme in the fourth line have, so far, not observed the same running formula. Different poets have come up with their own creativeness of how best to write the fourth line which has most often been taken as the poem's refrain.[3] As time went on, the *shairi* meter gained more popularity than the *utendi*, probably due to its brevity and, hence, ease of composition.

In the 1950s and 1960s, some poets introduced modest innovations into Swahili prosody without making radical departures from the traditional conventions (Mulokozi 1985). The main figure among them, Shaaban Robert, introduced the composition of stanzas of several lines, most of them with mid and end rhymes and a few with end rhymes only. Another innovator, Mathias Mnyampala, introduced the *ngonjera*, a kind of a polemical (and usually *Ujamaa*-inspired) poem in which various characters are engaged in a question-and-answer sort of debate, at the end of which the polemic is resolved and the two contending or conflicting sides are made to concur. This style has been profusely adopted by educational as well as political institutions in their activities.

Although these modest innovations were tolerated by the camp that came to be known as the "traditionalists" (*'wanajadi'*), the general attitude towards Swahili poetry was dogmatic. Amri Abedi's *Sheria za Kutunga Mashairi* ('The Rules of Poetry') (1954) was used in schools and Teacher Training Colleges as a key text in the study of Swahili poetry, and students were requested to write poems in the traditional verse meters. The particular format of traditional verse meters had furthermore been celebrated by European scholars such as Harries (1962) and Knappert (1967, 1979) as one of the great cultural treasures of East Africa and it had contributed to the deeply entrenched view of the Swahili societies in East Africa as extensions of the Orient and of the Swahili language as a blend of Arabic and Bantu languages.

The spoor that had been established by the modest innovators came to be expanded and concretized in the 1970s by those that came to be known as the "modernists" (*'wanamabadiliko'*). During this period, a new generation of talented young poets emerged, led by poets such as Euphrase Kezilahabi, Jared Angira and Ebrahim Hussein. They argued that rigid traditional forms were an obstacle to creative poetic composition; instead, they insisted that content and purpose should be the yardstick to determine the form of a poem. At the same time, in order to show the way, they began writing in free verse. The first publication of this group, Kezilahabi's *Kichomi* ('The Wound') appeared in 1974.

The modernists and their converts were based at the University. As noted earlier, the University of Dar es Salaam had become the site of intense radical political activities in the years following the introduction of *Ujamaa*. In the literature classes as in many other scientific disciplines, Marxist-oriented literature abounded, and a wide variety of Marxist texts were studied and discussed ranging from classics by Marx and Engels, Lenin, and Mao Zedong, over Lu Xun, Kim Il Sung and Frantz Fanon to Tolstoi, Gorki, Lunacharski and several others. One central topic of study and debate raised was the question of conscientization of the Tanzanian masses to create self-awareness. This was sparked off in literature classes in the attempt to define Swahili literature. What were its boundaries and who was its mentor? Where was the abode of the "*Mswahili*" ('the Swahili person') and what was his/her identity? Whose poetry was it?

Despite the presence of a long and exceptional literary tradition in Swahili, and despite the path-breaking new literary works of modern pre-independence writers such as Shaaban Robert, Swahili literature was introduced as an academic discipline at the University of Dar es Salaam as late as 1968. The first anthology of modern literary criticism was edited by Farouk Topan (the literature lecturer and tutor of the young poets at the University) as *Uchambuzi wa Maandishi ya Kiswahili I* ('the analysis of Swahili literary writings I', Topan 1971). Even the name of the corpus, *fasihi*, had not yet taken root by the early 1970s. A couple of coinages were brought forward for consideration including *aadab*, *adabu*, *herufia*, and *lunda*, but the term *fasihi* finally overshadowed the others. The question of appellation is indicative of the whole complex of issues that were brought into the debate, and that all revolve around identity and ownership.

After the introduction of *Ujamaa* in 1967, and as an ingredient of the massive mobilization of human capital that accompanied the nation-building offensive of *Ujamaa*, literary production in Swahili was drawn into the political sphere. In June 1968, Nyerere invited a group of poets to the State House and asked them to

> use their talents in order to promote a better understanding by the people of the land ... of national policies, and particularly of the responsibilities of the citizen resulting from the implementation of the Arusha declaration.
>
> (Harries 1972: 52)

The poets, led by Mathias Mnyampala, formed a literary organization called *UKUTA* (Association for the promotion of Swahili and poetry in Tanzania), with the aim of promoting politically-inspired or politically supportive literary activities. UKUTA became the leading literary organization in *Ujamaa* Tanzania.

4. The long debate

Two general issues of great ideological importance, and one more practical issue dominated the debate. The three issues are, of course, narrowly intertwined, and standpoints on one issue are readily transferred to the others. Still, some distinction can be made:

1. The first issue revolved around the nature of Swahili and its speakers, and touches on questions of legitimate ownership of the language. Whose language is Swahili? And who or what was the historical substrate culture from which standard Swahili originated? The (re)construction of a new (national) history of Swahili is a central preoccupation in this context.

2. The second issue was related to literary works written in Swahili and, more in particular, to questions of inclusion in a category of "Swahili literature": could all works written in Swahili be seen as "Swahili literature"?

3. The third issue was the construction of a stylistic canon for Swahili poetry proper and the transformations in the domain of Swahili poetry that accompanied the debate itself.

On each of the issues, the modernists were opposed to the traditionalists. Poets and intellectuals who defended a "traditional" view of language, culture and poetry were opposed to others who emphasized the radical sociolinguistic, sociocultural and literary break between the past and the present. Both views, and so the totality of the debate, have to be understood in the context of the elaboration of a cultural dimension of *Ujamaa* nation-building: the new socialist nation required a new language, culture, and literature. But which one?

4.1. *Whose language? Swahili and its speakers*

A common problem for many Bantu languages, including Swahili, is that the history of the languages is documented in a series of descriptive/prescriptive works made by (mostly) European scholars during the precolonial and colonial era.[4] Thus, and despite massive investments in local linguistic and sociolinguistic work on Swahili in postcolonial Tanzania, almost all discussions of Swahili drew heavily on the work of scholars such as Meinhof, Werner, Krapf, Hichens, Stigand, Steere, Buettner, Dammann, Johnson, Whiteley, Knappert and others. The opinions voiced in some of these works were not free from traces of colonialism, and especially with regard to the original Swahili culture, emphasis was put on the Arab influence and its "refining" or "civilizing" effects on the African susbtratum cultures. Some authors proposed that the *Waswahili* were a hybrid of Arabs and Bantu people; others contended that the Swahili were a "race" of no particular identity, and so on.

In the context of what came to be known as "cultural decolonization", this view of Swahili language and culture as being products of a far-reaching process of Arabization was strongly contested by Tanzanian scholars. Traditionalists and modernists alike vehemently criticized any hypothesis claiming that Swahili language and its people are either an Afro-Arabic hybrid or belong to no special race. They both opposed these views (albeit with varying degrees of resonance) claiming that the *Waswahili* have been a distinct entity throughout history and still exist today.[5]

This claim is not without problems. On the one hand, the emphasis on a "typically African" identity for the Swahili culture marked the re-appropriation of history by Africans and the beginnings of a tradition of African-nationalist historical revisionism of which Dar es Salaam became a center (Denoon and Kuper 1970). In that sense, it was a logical outcome of a general tendency to Africanize the cultural and intellectual environment, and part and parcel of the emergence of a postcolonial society and culture, completely in line with African socialism and reminiscent of earlier cultural-nationalist African movements such as *négritude*. On the other hand, this battle over the historical identity of the Swahili people created an ethnic group (at least in the traditionalist interpretation, see below), and it associated a language to that group. In that sense, it challenged one of the main ideological arguments with regard to Swahili in Tanzania: the claim that Swahili was not an ethnic language and could therefore become the language of all Tanzanians, without privileged ownership rights for any particular group in society. This was, to some extent, also anti-*Ujamaa*. The egalitarianism (and collectivism) contained in *Ujamaa* was targeted at inter-ethnic differences as much as at social class differences. The re-appropriation of the history of Swahili opened Pandora's box by identifying a set of "original speakers": a group of "*Waswahili*", with a long history stretching into the present, and hence endowed with a status of "original speakers" (including, as we shall see in 3.3, connotations of quality: the "original" speakers are also the "best" speakers).

The most vocal advocate of this view became the late Shihabuddin Chiraghdin (1974). He acknowledged both the expansive quality of Swahili and the fact that Swahili had been absorbed by large numbers of speakers far beyond its original boundaries. Yet, in Chiraghdin's opinion, this should not be an excuse for dispensing with the fact that the language has its rightful owners and place of origin. He emphasized:

> If today the language has spread in a vast area than ever before and is used as a vehicle for national deliberations and hopes, and each individual in the nation is able to employ this vehicle in the implementation of heavier national duties, all this by no means suggests that Swahili language should be disclaimed, and there is no need for doing that, from its original abode.
>
> (Chiraghdin 1974: 36, our translation, here and elsewhere)

Chiraghdin's example was followed by a number of other scholars, and in general, the issue of historical origins was a topic of lively debate.[6] Notwithstanding the overall agreement on the issue, traditionalists and modernists differed on the question of who should be a *Mswahili* and what the boundaries of "Swahili-ness" should be.

One point of view, often voiced, was that any speaker of Swahili can be *Mswahili* as long as s/he becomes a member of a wider community with common cultural ties. This view stresses the historical dynamics of cultural group-formation and refuses to accept an essentialist position which would restrict Swahili-ness to just the community of "original" speakers. Noor Shariff observes:

> Swahili-ness today is not a tribe, but customs of certain people together with their use and observation of a language as the one which nurtured them ... There is no *Mswahili* without a tribe ... One can be a *Mswahili* and at the same time be Indian, or Arab, or Persian or Comorian, etc. Even today there are a few Europeans who are *Waswahili*.
>
> (Shariff 1970: 11)

This view is shared to some extent by Madumulla (1989) and de Vere Allen (1993). Madumulla (a known modernist) focuses attention on the emergence of three distinct groups of Swahili speakers on Mainland Tanzania:

> The first group consists of the immigrants from the coast whose medium of communication and mother-tongue have been Swahili. These are generally found in almost every town centre ... The second and largest group consists of those for whom Swahili is the second or third language. This group does not always claim to be *Waswahili*, although it often operates in Swahili. ... It is by extending the second group that we come to the third group. This is made up of the younger generation who find themselves growing up with Swahili as their first language with an ever decreasing (or non-existent) proficiency in their mother-tongues. A child born to a *Mhaya* father and a *Mngoni* mother, both of whom work and live away from their birthplaces, finds him/herself operating in Swahili at home and, later on, when s/he plays with peers or joins school.
>
> (Madumulla 1989: 20–21)

De Vere Allen, in turn, differentiates between a (genuine) "Swahili" and a Swahilized person, and so arrives at a more or less balanced view. He defines the two groups as follows:

> 1. A Swahili is a person who has (made) his/her home in or around one of the traditional Swahili settlements of the the East African coast or their modern counterparts in the interior; whose lifestyles conforms to that of his/her neighbors; and who has inherited or adopted the Swahili language as his/her preferred tongue;

> 2. A person is Swahilized to the extent that his/her lifestyle conforms to that of one of the groups inhabiting traditional urban settlements on the East African coast or their modern counterparts in the interior, and especially in so far as he/she has adopted the Swahili language as his/her own preferred language.
>
> (De Vere Allen 1993: 15)

This view accepts the expansive nature of Swahili and the extent to which it has not only been declared a national language by some countries, but has also shaped a generation of speakers who have no other language to identify with besides Swahili, although their historical backgrounds and ancestral affiliations have little or no relations with Swahili. Note that this seemingly innocuous sociolinguistics observation presupposes a radically different conception of history than that shared by proponents of a rigid language-ethnic group connection. Accepting the "non-original" speakers as *Waswahili* implies an acceptance of the *political* history of Swahili (as opposed to a *cultural* history) as a language spread over the colonial (later independent) territory by means of language planning, force and coercion. It accepts history *in toto*, not merely as a matter of origins, but as an on-going irreversible process in which origins only play a minor part.

That inclusive outlook to Swahili language and its people was contested by the traditionalists. The most radical reactions pictured this view as an affront whose objective was to deprive the *Waswahili* of their language and bastardize their historical heritage. T.S.Y. Sengo (1987), one of the keen and vociferous proponents of the traditionalist school, identified four "threats to Swahili" contained in the inclusive view:

> (1) The dominance of Swahili scholarship by foreigners;
>
> (2) The corruption of the purity of the language;
>
> (3) The deprivation of the historical speaker of the language;
>
> (4) The conscious attempts to de-Islamize and de-coastalize Swahili.
>
> (T. S. Y. Sengo 1987: 215)

The first point alleges that the original, rightful owners of Swahili have been dispossessed, their place having been taken by "foreigners". By "foreigners", Sengo denotes any person, African or non-African, who is not a native *Mswahili*, and in order to be a native *Mswahili* one's geographical origin must be the East African littoral and its islands. The foreigners, as further alleged, claim to possess superiority, sophistication and highly advanced skills with which they feel "they ought to be the only ones who can write grammars, dictionaries, etc." (1987: 220).

The second point starts from the observation that the standardization efforts made by scholars and experts of Swahili have paid too little attention to Swahili dialects. A number of new Swahili terminologies have been coined from other Bantu languages, without first looking for possibilities in Swahili dialects. This kind of word-coining was regarded by the traditionalists as a form of bastardization. Using this argument, a radical traditionalist group in Mombasa started to develop its own terminologies which appeared from time to time in their journal *Lugha na Utamaduni*. The third point affirms the first one. An additional element here is Sengo's attempt to identify the "*Waswahili* par excellence". To Sengo, the Tanzanians and others who live in the hinterland are said to be "not genuine *Waswahili*" because they only acquired that attribute in the 1970s on political rather than on culture-historical grounds.

The fourth point is an assumption that Swahili-ness is characterized (i) by Islamic culture and (ii) by its coastal origins, and that both essential elements are mirrored in the language. But, Sengo argues, the language developers have set out to cast away the Islamic terminology from Swahili language such as "*Allah*", "*Alhamdulillah*", "*Bisimillah*", etc, in the name of standardization.

Sengo's claims are based on the —now more or less established— observation that there was and is indeed an ethnic group of *Waswahili* (or a cluster of such groups identified as *Waswahili*), and that these *Waswahili* were originally a coastal and Islamic society. It is also a recognized fact that the various Swahili dialects have indeed been overlooked as potential sources of new terminology. At the same time, Sengo clearly advocates a view of Swahili which distinguishes between rightful owners and "co-opted" owners of the language, associates an evaluative-qualitative scale to these distinctions, and stresses a language-culture link which is also dominated by such distinctions: the "original" speakers speak the language best and have the "right" cultural background for the language; others don't, and the differences between the original speakers and the non-original speakers are also differences in quality.

Sengo's claims gave rise to a round of discussions among linguists, folklorists and literary scholars at the University. Madumulla (1989) replied:[7]

> Sengo's arguments on this issue involve two basic assumptions which must be addressed: (1) that the home of a given people can be geographically and culturally determined; and (2) that in the case of the *Waswahili*, the group which Sengo terms the "*Waswahili* per excellence" is still living along the East African littoral. These assumptions raise two questions: first, must a

> people remain pegged within its original geographical boundaries? And second, are people tied down to their "own" culture across the years and centuries? History has proved that the answer to both questions is no. There are numerous examples of people changing their original geographical zones and cultures to the extent of affecting their original linguistic structure. This is an inevitable process in the unstatic nature of life. That the *Waswahili* are presently spread from the Somalian coast to the Mozambican coast by no means implies that there was at some point a spontaneous mushrooming of them all over this area. On the contrary, the process was one of deliberate, gradual immigration, as people crossed over or expanded their former geographical boundaries.
>
> (Madumulla 1989: 19–20)

Sengo and Madumulla both agree on the basic premise that language expresses, and is closely linked to, cultural values; they differ on *which* culture should be contained in Swahili, as well as on *whose* culture it is. Sengo, as an epitome of the traditionalists, advocates an organic view of Swahili, in which the spread of Swahili would mean the spread of the culture of its original speakers. Madumulla on the other hand stresses the discontinuities in the history of the Swahili speakers, and advocates a more open and pluralist (as well as a more socialist) approach to Swahili. Both stances will reflect themselves in the two other issues of the debate.

4.2. Swahili literature or literature in Swahili?

In the years since independence, Swahili has become the language of a booming and fertile literary scene. But in line with the argument on the ownership of the language, not all works written in Swahili are qualified similarly, and two camps can again be distinguished in this field (Bertoncini 1994). The traditionalists restrict the label of "Swahili literature" to the works of authors who are "native *Waswahili*" in the sense outlined earlier; any other literary work written in Swahili is categorized as "literature in Swahili". Against this view, modernists argue that Swahili literature comprises all the works whose authors are inhabitants of countries that declared Swahili to be their national language and in which a majority of the population speaks Swahili.

The matter came up for the first time in writing in 1973 when Sengo and Kiango queried in their book, *Hisi Zetu I* ('Our Wisdom I'), if there was such a thing as Swahili literature, and if so, what it was. The connections to the issue of ownership of the language were immediately made:

> The constraint we face with regard to Swahili is on people to agree being called *Waswahili*. There are lots of notions surrounding the word *Mswahili*. To some, *Mswahili* means anyone who dwells on the coast. To others, it is anybody who put on a robe, a brimless hat, or someone who is a chatter-box, a liar and one who is too charming to the extent of not being taken seriously. To others, *Mswahili* is any Muslim. Still to others, s/he is a half-caste of Afro-Arabic parentage; someone with neither definite tribe nor culture. ... On the basis of that negative view of the word *Mswahili*, many people hesitate being called "*Waswahili*". Tanzania has declared Swahili her national language ... We are convinced that before long the language will be understood and used by everybody in Tanzania and elsewhere ... It is a language which describes our ways of life. But since not all of us in the country agree to be called "*Waswahili*", it becomes difficult for us to be in a position to declare that we indeed have Swahili literature ... If we could come to a consensus that "A *Mswahili* is anybody in a country who has concurred to speak and utilize that language as well as appreciate the culture, habits and customs portrayed and embodied by it", then we could probably say that we have Swahili literature. A *Mswahili* is a Tanzanian if we consider this language to be of Tanzanians.
>
> (Sengo and Kiango 1973: 11)

The field of tension is neatly sketched: if a literature expresses the culture that goes with a language (in the traditionalists' view), then the sudden and politically organized spread of the language (*cum* or *sine* culture, see above) poses a series of complex problems of identity to the observer or the analyst. Are the people who now speak Swahili because it has become the language of the nation all "new" *Waswahili* and hence potential producers of Swahili literature? The traditionalists' answer is negative: these people create a new tradition of writing in Swahili, but one which does not replace the existing, "true" tradition of Swahili literature. "Swahili literature" remains "the literature of the (original) *Waswahili*"; non-*Waswahili* who use Swahili produce "literature in Swahili".

The traditionalists' view was challenged by the modernists, not only on artistic grounds (to be dealt with in the next subsection), but also on socio-political grounds. Modernists claimed that the intricate meter of traditional Swahili poetry creates elitist language, impenetrable and inaccessible for the common man. They felt that rhyme and meter imposed restrictions upon content. Against this, they advocated the use of ordinary speech in poetry, without *mafumbo* (veiled and allusive language) and without rhymes or meter. Content should in no way be restricted by conventions of form. Euphrase Kezilahabi mentioned this as one of his main goals in the programmatic preface to *Kichomi*, adding that from now on the poet would "go down to the people and disseminate [his poetry]" (1974: xiv).

Issues of ownership intersect at this point with issues of the social orientedness of poetry, in other words, with issues of the nature and identity of the audience. Kezilahabi was born in Ukerewe, an island in Lake Victoria, far removed from the original Swahili area. To him and to his supporters, the audience for modern Swahili literature was the totality of the Tanzanian population, and literary style should be adapted to this new audience. Tanzanian writers should write in Swahili, the language of the nation, not in order to reproduce the old coastal culture but in order to reach out to the common man in East Africa, who had become literate through Swahili (cf. Kezilahabi 1980).

The widening of the debate to issues of audience in the 1970s was characteristic of a general questioning among intellectuals and writers in East Africa. Influential authors such as Ngugi wa Thiong'o, Okot p'Bitek, Taaban Lo Liyong, Chris Wanjala and Peter Nazareth (all from Kenya) had arrived at similar questions, mainly focused on the language of writing (English, Swahili or local languages) and on the style of writing and the literary-stylistic canon (see e.g. Okot p'Bitek 1986; Ngugi wa Thiong'o 1981; Wanjala 1978; Nazareth 1978). An undercurrent in all these writings and discussions was the observation that literary production in societies where literacy was a rare and unevenly distributed commodity posed specific problems to authors. Writing always risked to become an elitist act, to be consumed almost exclusively by urban, middle-class elites who could afford to buy books and to read complex, artful realizations of languages other than their mother tongue. One common answer to this problem was to write in Swahili or in local languages; another was to avoid complexities in language and replace them by "ordinary", simple language. The Tanzanian modernists aligned with these views in stressing the exclusivity of *utendi* and other traditional meters. In line with the egalitarianism of *Ujamaa*, such exclusivism could not be tolerated, and Swahili literature should be everybody's literature.

This also applied to the *content* of literature. Literature had to become a vehicle for telling important stories to the people, stories which taught crucial values, historical facts and decisions, along with crucial characteristics of the Tanzanian society and its political system. Ali Mazrui observes that "African literature has, in fact, been a meeting point between African creativity and African political activity at large" (1978: 9). Especially in the field of novel writing, the Tanzanian literature of the 1970s was characterized by a high degree of political awareness, and writers such as Kezilahabi often elaborated on the tension between socialism and antisocial, individualistic forces (Ohly 1981). But also among poets, political topics became popular. The *ngonjera*-genre, developed by the traditionalist Mnyampala, was an explicitly political genre aimed at disseminating the core messages and values of *Ujamaa*. Modernist poets such as Mulokozi often treated political and historical themes in their poetry, feeling that in a sociopolitical environment such as Tanzania, no literature should remain detached from the reality of a society on its road to socialism.

Thus, the issue of ownership of the language was transformed into an issue of the social-communicative nature of literature. The narrow definitions of "Swahili literature" as something that could only be produced and consumed (and, in fact, understood) by the so-called rightful, original owners of the language was felt to be an elitist view. Swahili literature had to be an "open", democratic literature, accessible to all the Tanzanians and written in plain, standardized (and hence, to some, de-Arabized and re-Bantuized) Swahili.

4.3. Poetic rules and practices

The third issue in the debate was that of the poetic canon itself, on the rules of writing poetry. The debate reached its peak in 1975 after the appearance of two publications: Kezilahabi's (1974) collection of poetry *Kichomi* and Kahigi and Mulokozi's (1973) essay *Mashairi ya Kisasa* ('Modern poetry'). The traditionalists launched a protracted offensive against these publications, and they were countered by replies and new publications from the modernist poets (e.g. Mulokozi and Kahigi's *Kunga za Ushairi*, 'The Secrets of Poetry', 1982). The debate continued into the 1980s, and the arguments of the traditionalist school were synthesized in works such as *Mgogoro wa Ushairi* ('The Difficulty of Poetry') by Jumanne M. Mayoka (1984, a follow-up of Amri Abedi's *Sheria za kutunga Ushairi*) and Ibrahim Noor Shariff's *Tungo Zetu* ('Our Creations') (1988).

Apart from the publications mentioned above, the major fora for debating this particular issue also included conferences, seminars and newspapers. Especially the role of the newspapers deserves some comments. The majority of the practicing poets preferred the newspapers as a (rather easily accessible) forum for debate, and especially *Uhuru* —at that time the most important, party-owned national newspaper in Swahili— became a major locus of the literary debate. Poets sent in emotional and sometimes heated poems on poetry and poetic style, written in classical verse-forms. The following poem, a direct attack on the radical modernists Kahigi and Mulokozi, was composed by Saidy de Ghaidy III of Morogoro, a prolific columnist and a strong adversary of the modernists. It appeared in *Uhuru* on July 23, 1975:

Waliposema wahenga, kuwa kipya ni kinyemi
Ilikuwa kuu kinga, kijacho wakakihami
Kwamba kikitia nanga, kiweze na kujihami
Kahigi na Mulokozi, mnapotosha usemi

Mmeipotosha lugha, kufuta yake nidhami
Bayani siyo faragha, na wima hamuinami
Pa gaa kuitwa ghaa, hamchelei wasemi
Kahigi na Mulokozi, mmepotosha usemi

Kipi mlichokitunga, tuelezeni bayani
Si mashairi twapinga, tungo hazijulikani
Au mwasana faranga, kujua tunatamani
Kahigi na Mulokozi, dhana yenu kitu gani?

Mkakitunga kitabu, sura zake kama insha
Semeni: ndiyo adabu, watunzi kutupotosha?
Ole huu ukidhabu, kwetu watudhoofisha
Kahigi na Mulokozi, sana mwatukasirisha

Nawajulisha watunzi, mlio bara na pwani
Kahigi na Mulokozi, waletwe mahakamani
Wahojiwe waziwazi, kipi walichoauni
Kahigi na Mulokozi, watujibu uwanjani

[When our elders declared: a novelty has its charm
Their goal was to protect and defend a new strain;
So that when it reveals itself, it should not be harmed
Kahigi and Mulokozi, you've wronged that saying

You've distorted the language, effacing its laws
Plainness is not secretiveness, upright is not bent
To say "ghaa" instead of "gaa", disregards the speech
Kahigi and Mulokozi, you've wronged the saying

What kind of verse have you composed? you must clearly say
To us it is not poetry, your works are so strange
Or are you looking for money, is it only greed?
Kahigi and Mulokozi: say what is your need?

You've written a book of verse looking like plain prose
Tell us: is it respectful to mislead our youth?
Woe to this distortion, it destroys our strength
Kahigi and Mulokozi, you make us see red

I call upon all poets, both upcountry and coastal
Kahigi and Mulokozi should be summoned to court
Let them be interrogated, what help have they brought
Kahigi and Mulokozi, do confess your fault]

Such poems of stanzas running between 10–20 appeared on an almost daily basis in the newspapers and (less often) in bulletins and journals. Most of the poems attacked the modernists for their impudence of introducing alien and unacceptable elements in Swahili poetry. The modernists, especially Kahigi and Mulokozi (supported by a few other poets) replied. Remarkably, even the radical modernists used classical verse forms in their replies, both to display their knowledgeability in traditional prosodic norms and for the more prosaic reason that, for instance, *Uhuru* refused to print poems that were written in free or blank verse.[8]

The choice of the poetic form as a medium for debating highly sensitive issues is not surprising in view of the politization of the Tanzanian literary field in the 1960s and 1970s. As noted earlier, the production of literature on political topics was enormous during that period, and genres such as the *ngonjera* were deviced specifically for the promotion of *Ujamaa* principles and values (Bulcaen 1994; Blommaert 1997b). Also, letters to the editor in major newspapers such as *Uhuru* often took (and still take) the shape of poems in which political or social themes are raised or discussed. Poetry, written by experts and poets as well as by lay people, is a legitimate genre for sociopolitical debates.

The question of legitimate ownership again emerges as one of the core elements of this aspect of the debate. In particular, poets and critics fought over the cultural origins (and hence, the national and sociopolitical legitimacy) of certain verse forms, and three different claims were articulated by the various protagonists:

(i) modernist poetry reflected European influences and was, hence, non-African;
(ii) modernist poetry reflected Bantu-rhythms and Bantu traditions, and was hence a better reflection of Tanzanian national culture than the coastal and Islamized traditional verse forms;
(iii) traditional poetry, including the importance of rhyme and meter, was deeply influenced by Arabic (hence, non-African) traditions.

The first claim was voiced by the traditionalists, who saw in Kezilahabi's *Kichomi* the expression of a degree of westernization incompatible with the principles of African socialism. The claim was rebutted by arguments stressing that modernization did not equal westernization and that poetic activity and form should be dictated by the topic of the poem rather than by its form. The second and third claim were voiced (often in the same breath) by modernists against traditionalist conceptions of poetic rules and canons (see Bertoncini 1994).

The argument that modernist poetry is deeply "African" in that it articulates and uses "typically Bantu" forms of narrativity and rhythm was developed by Mulokozi and Kahigi (1982). Both authors are linguists with a great interest in Bantu oral tradition, and they claimed that traditional Bantu narratives are unrhymed and have no regular metric pattern. Consequently, unrhymed poetry in Swahili would be fully in line with African traditions, even more so than the rhymed poetry which the *Waswahili* had adopted from the Arabs. The claim is rooted in the modernists' conception of the nature of Swahili and its speakers (see 4.1). To Mulokizi and Kahigi, the national language of Tanzania should express the cultures of inland Tanzania, and not only those of the coastal Swahili societies. Note, in passing, that they do not defend the *Proletkult*-like idea of a unified socialist national culture held by some radical scholars (e.g. Mbuguni and Ruhumbika 1974), but that they see Tanzanian culture as a pluralist blend of Tanzanian ethnic cultures and traditions. Crucial, though, is the restriction of "allowable" influences on modern poetic expressions to *synchronic and local* cultures. Outside influences, European as well as Arabic and regardless of the time-depth of the influencing process, should give way to influences from cultural traditions of groups which occupy the territory of contemporary Tanzania. Allowable are Haya, Sukuma, Nyamwezi influences, but not Arab or European ones, both the Europeans as well as the Arabs having been involved in different forms of colonization and oppression of the Bantu peoples of East Africa.

The most elaborate traditionalist reply to Mulokozi's and Kahigi's arguments was given by Ibrahim Noor Shariff (1988). First, Shariff mentions the fact that the oldest Swahili poem, the *Fumo Liyongo* epic, is rhymed and has a meter.[9] Furthermore, the absence of rhyme and meter in traditional Bantu lore may be caused by inadequate descriptions and analyses by Western scholars. In fact, argues Shariff, oral traditions on the coast and on the island of Pemba are marked by rhyme and meter. Shariff also questions the Arab origins of the Swahili poetic conventions, saying that the direction of borrowing need not have been from Arabs to Africans, but that Arabs might have borrowed rhymes and meters from the *Waswahili* and mentioning the possibility of the independent development of two similar poetic traditions (Arab and Swahili). Instead of being borrowed from Arabic, Shariff claims that the Swahili genres originated from African dance rhythms (the *ngoma* rhythms):

> Anybody claiming that Swahili metrical and rhymed poems have Arab origins should also claim that Swahili *ngoma* dances have Arab origins! Once he has made that claim, let him demonstrate from which part of Arabia these *ngoma* have come.
>
> (Shariff 1988: 201)

And even if some poetic patterns would have been adopted from the Arabs, they would have been "indigenized" by now, after "at least ten centuries" (p. 202) of Arab-African cultural contacts. This stands in contrast to the modern verse forms, which have no roots whatsoever in African traditions but have been introduced instead by intellectuals. Free verse is not rooted in traditions, hence it is not acceptable. For as far as the Arabs go, they

> ... arrived on the Swahili coast several centuries before many of those who call themselves Bantu ... Moreover, the Arabs intermarried with other inhabitants of the East African coast. If a people has its residence somewhere for several centuries, they are as a rule not seen as foreigners, and if there are mutual contacts through marriages, customs and language, then we cannot speak of foreigners at all.
>
> (Shariff 1988: 195)

As a consequence, the Arabs cannot be compared to the Europeans, who came as imperialists and did not leave a profound imprint in the local culture. Hence, there is no reason to celebrate values related to modernization (equated by Shariff to European and Christian, socialist or communist influences) and to denigrate Arab and Islamic influences. The latter have become part of the African cultural heritage whereas the former are but a superficial influence on African cultures.

So far, Shariff's argumentation sticks closely to the lines of argumentation with regard to legitimate ownership of the language sketched in 4.1. Against the modernists' inclusive and pluralist view he poses the view of Swahili as a language inextricably embedded in a particular cultural history, which has stamped it as coastal and influenced by Arab-Islamic traditions. Shariff translates this claim into a standard of qualitative assessment for poetic production. He goes on to argue that modernist poets, who are usually not mother-tongue speakers of Swahili, lack the "feeling" of the language and therefore fail to produce adequate poetic expressions:

> Could it be surprising to see that, even though the modernists' words are in Swahili, the structure of their utterances is inappropriate, especially because many progressists have their own language [mother tongue] and Swahili is a foreign language for many of them?
>
> (Shariff 1988: 205–6)

Shariff here reiterates an earlier critique made by the Zanzibari (i.e. "core-Swahili") writer Said Ahmed Mohamed (made in relation to Swahili novels) that the standardized variety of Swahili which was adopted as the national language of Tanzania is an inadequate medium of literary expression (Mohamed 1981, 1984, cf. also 1995). In Mohamed's opinion, the standard language is "too poor," it lacks some of the most common idiomatic expressions and even a certain amount of words from the general repertoire of Swahili. Many users and even writers lack "flexibility and broadness of choice" in style, so they are "restricted to certain codes and patterns which become repetitive and recurrent in style" (1984: 591), and hence they do not utilize the linguistic means sufficiently. What he appreciates most in a literary work is an elaborated and sophisticated style resulting from a conscious and skillful use of language. To understand and enjoy such sophisticated writings requires a great linguistic competence of the author and the reader, not only at the grammatical level but also at the communicative and cultural levels. On the basis of this criterion he criticizes inland novelists for their lack of communicative and cultural competence in literary Swahili. Comparing the literary style of Kezilahabi's novels to that of the Zanzibari writer Mohamed Suleiman, Mohamed comments:

> Kezilahabi's vocabulary is limited, hence his range of association is narrow —thus his linguistic idiosyncracies fall short of the desired aesthetic effect. This vitiates Kezilahabi's style.
>
> (Mohamed 1981: 73)

As for Suleiman's style, in contrast,

> This kind of verbal display is possible only when the writer has the feeling of his language, thus, this patterning proves even more that Suleiman's command of [the] language is not only his individual talent but a product of [the] social and linguistic environment.
>
> (Mohamed 1981: 153)

The bottom line of Mohamed's argument is that only native speakers reared in an authentic cultural environment, can produce Swahili speech which conforms to criteria of literary aesthetics, subtleness, imagery and so on. Non-native speakers such as Kezilahabi (but also Mulokozi, Kahigi and many other modernists) cannot attain this level of linguistic and cultural competence in Swahili. Hence they do not produce genuine "Swahili literature".[10]

In the debate on poetic form, the question of legitimate ownership is transformed into a debate on degrees of authenticity expressed in differences between "allowable" influences from certain traditions. In line with the overall ideological differences, modernists dissociate themselves from the coastal and Islamic (Arab-influenced) traditions they observe in traditional Swahili verse forms, because the postcolonial national cultural production of Tanzania should reflect a wider range of cultural traditions (those of *all* the Tanzanian peoples) than just the "original" Swahili traditions. The traditionalists, on the other hand, defend the genuinely African background of Swahili poetry, untarnished by alien or undesirable influences associated with colonialism or oppression.

4.4. Summary

To conclude this section, it may be useful to bring the various elements of the debate back together into a coherent pattern. As noted at the outset, the three issues we have isolated for discussion are closely related, and though they represent various dimensions of the debate, they were often voiced together or could only be understood in relation to one another.

The core of the debate is a controversy about what the national language, Swahili, is supposed to signify or symbolize. In a context of strong nationalism and intense nation-building efforts, such as that following the introduction of *Ujamaa*, the sociopolitical nation defined by the Arusha declaration needed to be "filled", completed or complemented with a cultural nation. Given the particular sociolinguistic situation of the country, in which one African language had been widely disseminated in colonial times and strongly ideologized in the struggle for independence, Swahili was a ready target for symbolic nation-building endeavors. It could easily be identified as a marker of Tanzanian identity since it was the language most Tanzanians spoke or understood in various degrees. The controversy arises at the next step, where this language has to be identified with a particular cultural tradition or set of cultural traditions (in other words, where the language needed to be given its classic Herderian complement of culture-historical identity). At this point, Swahili becomes a poly-interpretable concept, and especially the history of the language is called into question. To one camp, the relevant part of the history of Swahili is the precolonial part, in which Swahili could be associated with a centuries-old tradition of Arab-influenced east coast societies. Those societies produced recognizable cultural values and expressions such as Swahili poetry in the classical verse forms. To the other camp, the relevant part of the history is the post-colonial history, in which a new nation emerged, and in which the formerly coastal language became the language of the whole nation. This new nation —a complex of non-coastal cultures— now had the right to leave its mark on Swahili, to influence cultural expressions in Swahili and to express the modernity of the new nation in Swahili. The one camp emphasizes historical continuity, the other historical discontinuity and revolutionary transformations.

It is on the basis of this controversy on the correct or relevant history of Swahili that aesthetic statements can be organized. To the traditionalists, the dissociation between the language and its authentic culture means a loss of "quality" for the language. The language no longer expresses the cultural meanings for which it was made in the first place, it is now made to express meanings which are alien to its "heart and soul". Consequently, the language is no longer as "beautiful" or "rich" as it was in the hands of its authentic users. To the modernists, Swahili is finally re-Bantuized and made into an instrument for the expression of genuinely African meanings, in a poetry which only obeys the rules of adequate expression of thoughts and feelings, not those of rigid and artificial stylistic prescriptions. The poetry, like the language, is now "free", "decolonized", "Africanized" in another sense as that used by the traditionalists. Swahili is no longer the property of any particular group or class: just like all other commodities in the new Tanzanian society, the egalitarianism of *Ujamaa* has made it into everyone's language.

Both argumentative profiles are deeply political. On the one hand, they can only be understood against the historical contingencies of the nation-building offensive which followed the introduction of *Ujamaa* and of wider questions of cultural and intellectual decolonization and re-appropriation and of the sociopolitical relevance of art and literature that dominated the world of artists and intellectuals in east Africa at that time. On the other hand, both views can be (and were) inserted in the political-ideological agendas of particular fractions in the Tanzanian political scene of the time. In particular, they could be seen and read as contributions to the debate on the nature and structure of *Ujamaa* as a strategy of socialist transformation. The traditionalists' arguments could be read as supportive of the "African socialist" tendency, which saw *Ujamaa* as the full implementation of socialist values which were buried in African precolonial traditions. Revitalizing African traditions equaled revitalizing African socialism. The modernists' arguments could in turn be read as supportive of "revolutionary" and Marxist interpretations of *Ujamaa*. To the latter, the introduction of *Ujamaa* created a radical break between the past and the present, and African traditions had either to be abolished and replaced by a new revolutionary Tanzanian culture (in a radical interpretation), or be reordered and blended so as to express the new egalitarianism which marked Ujamaa society (in a more moderate interpretation).

5. Conclusion: The politics of poetry

The multidimensionality of the debate on poetry already demonstrates one of the conditions controlling the political-ideological effect of debates on language: discourses on language have to be able to be inserted into other, more overtly sociopolitical and power-related discourses. They need to be readable *as* indirect political discourses, even though their lexicon and argumentarium is technical or arcane and has nothing to do *stricto sensu* with political relationships or political-ideological positions.

At the same time, this can only work if certain other conditions are met. In Tanzania, one critical condition was the wholesale mobilization of all efforts (economic, political, cultural and intellectual) for the purpose of nation-building. In other words, a debate such as this one, in a domain which would otherwise leave the non-specialist uninterested, could only acquire such a political-ideological significance in a context in which the state had launched a massive attempt at ideological hegemonization of the nation, and in which this ambition was indeed shared by the writers and the intellectuals. The elaborate historical, cultural and literary theories that accompanied the production of different forms of poetry were in themselves a response to Nyerere's appeal to the Tanzanian writers to commit themselves to the aims set forth in the Arusha Declaration, for they proved that Tanzanian writers and intellectuals actively sought to motivate and deepen their practice in terms of social significance, meaning, and political correctness.

Writing poetry in a particular form is thus read (and, indeed, often practiced) metapragmatically as an expression of different forms of political-ideologic alignment, and the literary debate is essentially a hugely inflated metapragmatic debate on the undertones, presuppositions, implicatures and contexts of the poems. The immense symbolization of Swahili in the wake of independence and, even stronger, in the wake of the Arusha Declaration created a rich field of indexicality, in which the sheer act of using the language (as opposed to e.g. English) in a variety of genres (political discourse, literature) could identify the speaker or writer as a member of a politically and socioculturally defined category: as a nationalist, a radical, a moderate, a neocolonialist, a capitalist and so on. This might explain why poetic *form*, rather than content, could become so visible a target of ideological struggle. The actual shape of the language indexed more than it expressed, and the difference between a rhyming stanza and a free-verse stanza could become an act of sociopolitical identification.

A final, but crucial, precondition was the widespread acceptance of a particular linguistic ideology. Swahili can only symbolize or index the complex meanings described above if language is considered to be a vehicle for and a container of cultural identity, if indeed the question as to the cultural "filling" of language is considered to be a relevant one. The controversy on the relevant history of Swahili and on legitimate ownership hinges on the assumption that finding an answer to the question is indeed crucial to an understanding of what the language does in society, what it stands for, and what it can be used for. It is, in other words, crucial in determining the politically correct metapragmatics of Swahili. As such, some linguistic ideologies seem to offer themselves more readily for political-ideological recuperation or incorporation than others. In the case of Tanzania, this particular linguistic ideology became problematic as soon as the idea of a unified nation was launched. If this new nation required a new culture, this culture should have been as unified (and hence, as *singular* — *one* culture) as the nation. And if one language was taken to form and express this unified culture, one particular culture-language package should replace the mosaic of languages and cultural traditions that occupied the territory of Tanzania. This could only be done if Swahili was ethnically unmarked, or to be more precise, if there was no historical association between Swahili and a particular ethnic or cultural group in Tanzania. Scientific evidence had demonstrated the historical and contemporary existence of groups of *Waswahili*, and so this condition was not met. In a debate in which one side defended an "ethnic" Swahili —a politically undesirable stance— and another an "un-ethnic" Swahili —a falsified stance— there was little hope for a compromise, and the project of complementing the politically unified nation with a culturally unified nation (based on the "one nation, one culture, one language" view) was doomed to fail.

Notes

1. In general, Tanzania served as a refuge for freedom fighters and dissidents from all over Eastern and Southern Africa from 1963 onwards. Thus, the Mozambican liberation movement FRELIMO was formed in Tanzania, and dissidents from Rhodesia (Zimbabwe) and South Africa congregated in Dar es Salaam (Pratt 1976: 134–5; Othman 1994).
2. For a summary of the debate on education see Mulokozi (1991) and the papers in Rubagumya (ed. 1990).
3. see for a survey Kaluta Amri Abedi's classic *Sheria za Kutunga Mashairi na Diwani ya Amri Abedi* —'Principles of Kiswahili Prosody and the Anthology of Amri' (1954).

4. Fabian (1986) describes the processes of colonial appropriation of Swahili in the Belgian Congo in great detail. There is a significant degree of continuity between the colonial and the postcolonial linguistic traditions (see Blommaert 1994b).
5. The question as to "who are the *Waswahili*?" has been a popular theme in academic writing (see e.g. Prins 1961; Arens 1975; Eastman 1971). Recent collections of investigations into the anthropology of contemporary Swahili societies are Parkin and Constantin (eds. 1989); Le Guennec-Coppens and Caplan (eds. 1991); Parkin (ed. 1994).
6. In the 1980s and later, some historical and historical-linguistic works appeared which cast new light on the history of the language and its speakers. See e.g. Nurse and Spear (1985), Nurse and Hinnebusch (1993), Middleton (1992), Mazrui and Shariff (1993) and de Vere Allen (1993).
7. The publication dates, and especially the two years separating the papers by Sengo and Madumulla give a false picture of the intensity of the debate. Both papers followed one another rapidly, but the (locally produced) journal in which both papers were published suffered considerable material and financial setbacks during that time. Readers may wish to know that the Madumulla referred to in the text is indeed the first author of this chapter.
8. *Uhuru* thus did not accept the modernists' claim, mentioned in 3.2, that the egalitarianism of *Ujamaa* would be expressed in poetry written in "ordinary" language, and one of the main channels for the mass circulation of poetry (the newspapers) was thus exclusively reserved for "traditional" poetic forms.
9. A very doubtful claim, of course, in view of the essentially oral and performance-bound character of the epic. Fumo Liyongo is believed to have lived around the 9th to 12th centuries, and oral traditions of Liyongo songs still exist today on the east coast.
10. On the other hand, Mohamed himself experiments with traditional metrical forms as well as with free verse. Furthermore, in another article he analyses two free-verse poems (by Kezilahabi and Alamin Mazrui) which, according to him, "exhibit the highest stage of poetic achievement in Swahili, especially in modern Swahili poetry" (1990: 79).

References

Abdulaziz, Mohamed H.

1971 Tanzania's national language policy and the rise of Swahili political culture. In: Whiteley, Wilfred H. (ed.), *Language Use and Social Change*. London: Oxford University Press, 160–178.

Amri Abedi, Kaluta

1954 *Sheria za Kutunga Mashairi na Diwani ya Amri*. Nairobi: East African Literature Bureau.

Arens, W.

1975 The *Waswahili*: the social history of an ethnic group. *Africa* 45: 426–438.

Bertoncini, Elena

1989 *Outline of Swahili Literature. Prose Fiction and Drama.* Leiden: E. J. Brill.

1994 Inland Tanzania: Swahili literature or literature in Swahili? In: Parkin, David (ed.), *Continuity and Autonomy in Swahili Communities.* Wien: Afropub, 205–213.

Berwouts, Kris

1991 *Le Sein de la Mère. Introduction à la Littérature classique et moderne en swahili.* Bruxelles: ASDOC/CEDAF.

Blommaert, Jan

1991 Some problems in the interpretation of Swahili political texts. In: Blommaert, Jan (ed.), *Swahili Studies.* Gent: Academia Press, 109–135.

1994a *Ujamaa* and the creation of the new *Waswahili.* In: Parkin, David (ed.), *Continuity and Autonomy in Swahili Communities.* Wien: Afropub, 65–81.

1994b The metaphors of development and modernization in Tanzanian language policy and research. In: Fardon, Richard and Graham Furniss (eds.), *African Languages, Development and the State.* London: Routledge, 213–226.

1997a *State Ideology and Language: The Politics of Swahili in Tanzania.* Duisburg: Gerhard-Mercator-Universität (LICCAP 3)

1997b The impact of state ideology on language: *Ujamaa* and Swahili literature in Tanzania. In: Tasch, Meike and Birgit Smieja (eds.), *Human Contact Through Language and Linguistics.* Frankfurt: Lang, 253–270.

1997c Intellectuals and ideological leadership in *Ujamaa* Tanzania. *African Languages and Cultures* 10(2): 129–144.

1999 Reconstructing the sociolinguistic image of Africa: Grassroots writing in Shaba (Congo). *Text* 19(2) [in press].

Bulcaen, Chris

1994 Kiswahili literatuur en de Arusha Verklaring. In: Blommaert, Jan (ed.), *Taal, Interaktie en Kontekst in de Afrikastudie.* Antwerp: UIA-GER, 69–101 (Antwerp Papers in Linguistics 77).

Chauma, Moses, Moira Chimombo and Alfred Mtenje
1997 Problems and prospects for the introduction of vernacular languages in primary education: The Malawi experience. In: Smieja, Birgit (ed.), *Proceedings of the LICCA Workshop in Dar es Salaam*. Duisburg: Gerhard-Mercator-Universität, 37–46 (LICCAP 2).

Chiraghdin, Shihabuddin
1974 Kiswahili na Wenyewe. *Mulika* 6.

Denoon, Donald and Adam Kuper
1970 Nationalist historians in search of a nation: The "new historiography" in Dar es Salaam. *African Affairs* 69: 329–349.

de Vere Allen, John
1993 *Swahili Origins. Eastern African Studies*. Columbus: Ohio University Press.

Eastman, Carol
1971 Who are the *Waswahili*? *Africa* 41: 228–236.

Fabian, Johannes
1986 *Language and Colonial Power. The Appropriation of Swahili in the Former Belgian Congo 1880–1938*. Cambridge: Cambridge University Press.

Fardon, Richard and Graham Furniss (eds.)
1994 *African Languages, Development and the State*. London: Routledge

Harries, Lyndon
1962 *Swahili Poetry*. Oxford: Clarendon Press.
1969 Language policy in Tanzania. *Africa* 39: 275–280.
1972 Poetry and politics in Tanzania. *Ba Shiru* 4(3): 52–54.

Kahigi, Kulikoyela K. and Mugyabuso M. Mulokozi
1973 *Mashairi ya Kisasa*. Dar es Salaam: Tanzania Publishing House.

Kezilahabi, Euphrase
1974 *Kichomi*. Nairobi Heinemann.
1980 The Swahili novel and the common man in East Africa. In: Schild, Ulla (ed.), *The East African Experience: Essays on English and Swahili Literature*. Berlin: Reimer, 75–84.

Kihore, Yared
1976 Tanzania's language policy and Kiswahili's historical background. *Kiswahili* 46: 47–69.

Knappert, Jan

1967 *Traditional Swahili Poetry. An Investigation into the Concepts of East African Islam as Reflected in the Utenzi Literature*. Leiden: Brill.

1979 *Four Centuries of Kiswahili Verse*. London: Heinemann.

Laitin, David

1992 *Language Repertoires and State Construction in Africa*. Cambridge: Cambridge University Press.

Le Guennec-Coppens, Françoise and Pat Caplan (eds.)

1991 *Les Swahili entre Afrique et Arabie*. Paris: CREDU-Karthala.

Madumulla, Joshua S.

1989 Another look at Kiswahili scholarship. *Kiswahili* 56: 10–24.

Mayoka, Jumanne M.

1984 *Mgogoro wa Ushairi na Diwani ya Mayoka*. Dar es Salaam: Tanzania Publishing House.

Mazrui, Ali A.

1967a *On Heroes and Uhuru Worship*. London: Longman.

1967b *Towards a Pax Africana: A Study of Ideology and Ambition*. Chicago: University of Chicago Press.

1978 *Political Values and the Educated Class in Africa*. Berkeley: University of California Press.

Mazrui, Ali and Ibrahim Noor Shariff

1993 *The Swahili: Idiom and Identity of an African People*. Trenton: Africa World Press.

Mbuguni, L.A. and Gabriel Ruhumbika

1974 TANU and National Culture. In: Ruhumbika, Gabriel (ed.), *Towards Ujamaa: Twenty Years of TANU Leadership*. Kampala: East African Literature Bureau, 275–287.

Metz, Steven

1982 In lieu of orthodoxy: the socialist theories of Nkrumah and Nyerere. *Journal of Modern African Studies* 20: 377–392.

Middleton, John

1992 *The World of the Swahili: An African Mercantile Civilization*. New Haven: Yale University Press.

Mohamed, Said Ahmed

1981 *The Aesthetic Idiom of Mohamed Suleiman's Writings (Literary Discourse)*. MA thesis, University of Dar es Salaam (mimeo).

1984 Literary Swahili: Its role and contribution to the standard form. *Zeitschrift für Phonetik, Sprachwissenschaft und Kommunikationsforschung* 37(5): 589–598.

1990 Poetry and maturity (the case of Swahili poetry). *Lugha* 4: 78–83.

1995 Towards translatability of the Swahili novel. *Journal of Asian and African Studies* 6: 1–19.

Mohiddin, Ahmed

1981 *African Socialism in Two Countries*. London: Croom Helm.

Mulei, Christopher

1972 The predicament of the left in Tanzania. *East Africa Journal* 9: 29–34.

Mulokozi, Mugyabuso M.

1985 The present state of Swahili literature: A survey. In: Arnold, Stephen (ed.), *African Literature Studies: The Present State*. Washington: Three Continents Press, 171–188.

1991 English versus Kiswahili in Tanzania's secondary education. In: Blommaert, Jan (ed.), *Swahili Studies*. Gent: Academia Press, 7–16.

Mulokozi, Mugyabuso M. and Kulikoyela K. Kahigi

1982 *Kunga za Ushairi na Diwani Yetu*. Dar es Salaam: Tanzania Publishing House.

Mulokozi, Mugyabuso M. and Tibiti S. Y. Sengo

1995 *History of Kiswahili Poetry (AD 1000 – 2000)*. Dar es Salaam: Institute of Kiswahili Research.

Nazareth, Peter

1978 *The Third World Writer. His Social Responsibility*. Nairobi: Kenya Literature Bureau.

Ngugi wa Thiong'o

1981 *Writers in Politics*. London: Heinemann.

Ng'wanakilala, Nkwabi

1981 *Mass Communication and Development of Socialism in Tanzania*. Dar es Salaam: Tanzania Publishing House.

Nurse, Derek and Thomas Hinnebusch

1993 *Swahili and Sabaki: A Linguistic History*. Berkeley: University of California Press.

Nurse, Derek and Thomas Spear

1985 *The Swahili: Reconstructing the History and Language of an African Society, 800–1500*. Philadelphia: University of Pennsylvania Press.

Ohly, Rajmund
1981 *Aggressive Prose. A Case Study in Kiswahili Prose of the Seventies.* Dar es Salaam: Institute of Kiswahili Research.
1985 Literature in Swahili. In: Andrzejewski, B.W., S. Pilasewicz and W. Tyloch (eds.), *Literatures in African Languages.* Cambridge: Cambridge University Press, 460–492.

Okot p'Bitek
1986 *Artist, the Ruler. Essays on Art, Culture and Values.* Nairobi: Heinemann Kenya.

Othman, Haroub
1994 The intellectual and transformation in South Africa. *Dar es Salaam Alumni Newsletter* 1: 9–10.

Parkin, David (ed.)
1994 *Continuity and Autonomy in Swahili Communities: Inland Influences and Strategies of Self-Determination.* Wien: Afropub.

Parkin, David and François Constantin (eds.)
1989 *Social Stratification in Swahili Society.* Special issue of *Africa* 52: 143–220.

Pratt, Cranford
1976 *The Critical Phase in Tanzania 1945–1968: Nyerere and the Emergence of a Socialist Strategy.* Cambridge: Cambridge University Press.

Prins, A. H. J.
1961 *The Swahili Speaking People of Zanzibar and the East African Coast.* London: International African Institute.

Rollins, J. D.
1983 *A History of Swahili Prose.* Leiden: Brill

Rubagumya, Casmir M. (ed.)
1990 *Language in Education in Africa: A Tanzanian Perspective.* Clevedon: Multilingual Matters Ltd.

Senghor, Leopold Sedar
1988 *Ce Que Je Crois.* Paris: Grasset.

Sengo, Tibiti S.Y.
1987 Towards maturity in Kiswahili scholarship. *Kiswahili* 54: 215–224.

Sengo, Tibiti S. and S. D. Kiango
1973 *Hisi Zetu 1.* Dar es Salaam: Institute of Kiswahili Research.

Shariff, Ibrahim Noor

1970 *Kiswahili* 40. Dar es Salaam: Institute of Kiswahili Research.

1988 *Tungo Zetu: Msingi wa Mashairi na Tungo Nyinginezo*. Trenon: Red Sea Press, Inc.

Smieja, Birgit (ed.)

1997 *Proceedings of the LICCA Workshop in Dar es Salaam*. Duisburg: Gerhard-Mercator-Universität (LICCAP 2).

Topan, Farouk

1971 *Uchambuzi wa Maandishi ya Kiswahili. Kitabu cha Kwanza*. Dar es Salaam: Oxford University Press.

Tordoff, William and Ali A. Mazrui

1972 The left and the super-left in Tanzania. *Journal of Modern African Studies* 10: 427–445.

Wanjala, Chris

1978 *The Season of Harvest. A Literary Discussion*. Nairobi: Kenya Literature Bureau.

Whiteley, Wilfred H.

1968 Ideal and reality in national language policy: A case study from Tanzania. In: Fishman, Joshua, Charles Ferguson and Jyoritinda Das Gupta (eds.), *Language Problems of Developing Nations*. New York: John Wiley and Sons, 327–344.

Portuguese as ideology and politics in Mozambique: Semiotic (re)constructions of a postcolony

Christopher Stroud

1. Introduction

A nation-state is far from strictly a politico-economic system; it is also a cultural project (Balibar and Wallerstein 1991), and, perhaps primarily, "a system of cultural signification" (Bhaba 1997: 1), "a powerful regime of order and knowledge that is at once politico-economic, historical, cultural, aesthetic and cosmological" (Malkki 1995: 5).[1] To this can be added that a nation-state is also a discursive project, a system of emblems and indices mediated through images of language. Since Mozambican independence in 1975, language issues have played an important constitutive role in the development of the Mozambican nation-state. The visionary project of the governing socialist party FRELIMO (Frente de Libertação de Moçambique/ Mozambican Liberation Front), the construction of a new Mozambique, was rhetorically mediated through discourses on the Portuguese language.[2] These discourses generated multiple and competing visions of alternative political and social orders.

Mozambican independence was followed by a bloody civil war between FRELIMO and a South African backed guerilla organization, RENAMO (Resistência Nacional de Moçambique/Mozambican National Resistance). Even in the context of this war, issues of language came to constitute a powerful semiotic site where battles between FRELIMO and RENAMO over definitions of Mozambican social and political realities and cultural authenticity were fought.

This chapter will explore the role of language ideological debates, specifically those concerning Portuguese, in the political processes and power dynamics of postcolonial Mozambican nation-state building. It will explore how statements about language were made to stand for, or signify, specific social and political realities (cf. Gal 1992). One focus of the paper will be on discussing the role of multiple, at times contesting, discourses on Portuguese, and on illustrating why certain of these discourses became more prominent and effective at certain times, and not others. In this context, I will note the manifold ways in which different perspectives on language were given an authoritative textualization, that involved personal censorship, intimidation, consensus, persuasion, and violence. In the course of discussing these questions, we will also have occasion to delve into the conceptions or ideologies of Portuguese that were in circulation at the time, and to consider these ideologies with respect to the sociopolitical contexts to which they were a response.[3]

The main point of the chapter is that official Mozambican discourses and meta-commentary on Portuguese have changed and shifted emphases in attempts to tap into, constitute, symbolically represent and naturalize different constituencies of power at different historical periods and under different sociopolitical conditions.

In approaching Mozambican language debates and the manner of their social reproduction and contestation, I take Blommaert's characterization of *debate* in the introductory chapter to this volume as the point of departure, namely more or less historically locatable periods in which "a struggle for authoritative entextualization" takes place. I will therefore explore the patchwork of debates and social processes that have generated and reproduced symbolic meanings of language throughout the development of post-independent Mozambique. Of course, debates need not just be situated events involving actors —or "ideology brokers"— discoursing or contesting legitimate or authoritative representations of language in conference rooms or newspaper columns. An extended use of this term needs to see debates as events that are subject to multiple perspectives, interpretations and reinterpretations, commentary, and action in a plethora of different contexts —a Bahktinian carnivalesque cacophony of voices expressing complicity and opposition.

An account of how images of language are sociohistorically constituted necessarily implies accounts of social and political development, brought about by real historical actors in alliance and conflict (see Blommaert's introductory chapter to this volume). Briggs (1992) has shown that the study of how language ideologies are used to construct and contest social realities requires knowledge of how these ideologies are socially distributed as well as understanding "their location within the processes by which power is produced, naturalized and challenged" (p. 388). In the course of this chapter, different discourses on language will therefore be contextually situated in accounts of Mozambican sociopolitical and developmental realities.

The chapter opens (section 2) with a short historical foray into the events leading up to Mozambican independence, especially treating FRELIMO's revolutionary rhetoric around Portuguese. Section 3 deals with attempts by FRELIMO ideologues to develop a discourse on language that linked an appropriated Mozambican Portuguese to an emerging cultural identity.

This section also treats the question of how the revolutionary myth of Portuguese was inscribed in the institutions of the state so as to symbolize the territory of the new Mozambique in the image of FRELIMO as the mass-party of the Mozambican people. RENAMO's alternative conceptions of Portuguese, *vis-à-vis* national languages particularly, and the way in which language issues were used to articulate resistance to FRELIMO is discussed in section 4. Section 5 details how FRELIMO's representation of Portuguese went through a shift in emphasis in the early 1980s, to highlight more normative concerns of language. It locates this change of tack as contemporaneous with the FRELIMO's failing grip on the power base hitherto sought in mass mobilization. The new discourse on language explicitly subordinated issues of language to the development of a socialist state, and obedience to a vanguard party, thereby shifting the locus of power symbolically inscribed in Portuguese to the FRELIMO elite. In section 6, both FRELIMO's and RENAMO's more recent discourse on language is reviewed, specifically from the perspective of how this discourse is being used to articulate different conceptions of Mozambique's role in global networks. The chapter closes with a concluding section, 6, where the sociohistorical data is discussed from the perspective of how changing discourses on language help construct the transient and ever changing nature of political power.

2. The cultural construction of postcolonial Mozambique

2.1. Becoming independent

Like many newly independent countries, Mozambique (population 15.6 million according to preliminary results from the latest census in 1997, speaking around 20 Bantu languages) has lived through decades of social and cultural transformations which have at times been violent and destructive. After over 500 years of Portuguese colonial subjugation, Mozambique was ushered into independence by FRELIMO, ending almost ten years of "armed" resistance.[4] One month before independence, Samora Machel, the first president of Mozambique, made his legendary journey from Rovuma on the far northern border of the country to Maputo in the south —a major symbolic embodiment of the totality of the new territorial space that now made up independent Mozambique —and thereby set the stage for the beginning of a period of national construction and consolidation.

The task of nation building that confronted FRELIMO was in many ways even more of a challenge in Mozambique than in many other newly liberated ex-colonies. Mozambique was an unstable and fluid colonial construction at the time of her independence, with little sense of national identity. This was due to a number of factors such as the fact that the Portuguese colonialists only managed to gain military control of the country at a comparatively late date (late 19th century), that poor national liquidity had placed the management of the colony in the hands of private and international companies, which had proceeded to divide Mozambique between them, and that, finally, what resistance there had been to Portuguese rule had been local and therefore divisive (Vines 1991). Given the nature of Mozambique at independence, national reconstruction and consolidation had to aim at a radical change of society, involving the creation of new sociocultural and political identities (Abrahamsson and Nilsson 1995: 93). In an important speech, the first president of FRELIMO, Dr. Eduardo Mondlane (1969) characterized the liberation war as

> a process of creating a new reality. While our past was characterized by linguistic, cultural and historical divisions, our future is being established on the basis of unity.

The politics and practice of culture were important instruments in the construction of the new society and the formation of the new citizen. Samora Machel, Mozambique's first president, claimed in 1979 that

> The armed struggle constitutes a cultural liberation; culture constitutes a central and fundamental question of the Revolution

The cultural politics of the revolution also provided the backdrop for how language ideology was debated and how practices of language were understood. A significant moment in the revolutionary discourse on Portuguese was its symbolic appropriation and transformation from a language of colonial oppression to an instrument of the Mozambican peoples' liberation.

2.2. *Fashioning a history for Portuguese*

Elsewhere on the African continent, voices could be heard calling attention to the ways in which metropolitan languages hampered the development of African post-colonial identities. In Mozambique, on the contrary, influential ideologues were instead refashioning Portuguese as an instrument of the new society. Portuguese, the language of oppression during colonial times, was appropriated by the FRELIMO movement. Its ownership was challenged, its alliances reconceived, and its boundaries redrawn —the language was, to all intents and purposes, symbolically taken, along with much else in the way of property that the colonialists left behind them on the eve of their departure, and subsequently transformed into a weapon of the revolution. Samora Machel was cited by the writer and editor Mia

Couto in the magazine *Tempo* (18.01.81) as saying *temos que utilizar a língua do inimigo para derrotar o inimigo. Fazer da língua do nosso inimigo instrumento de combate* ('we have to use the language of the enemy to deter the enemy. Make the language of our enemy into an instrument of combat'). Similar words were pronounced by several of Machel's contemporaries. For example, José Luís Cabaço, then Minister of Information and Propaganda, spoke in the 1970s of "turning Portuguese like the barrel of a gun in the direction from which it came".

One may suspect that the significance of taking over the Portuguese language was enormous. The historian Mbembe (1992a: 18) says that "to a large extent, coloniality was a way of disciplining bodies with the aim of making better use of them —docility and productivity going hand in hand." Portuguese language legislation was part of this effort of coloniality: Colonial language legislation in Mozambique constructed social, residential and occupational space in such a way that employment and access to urban areas and facilities —including housing and education— were the sole prerogative of those who mastered Portuguese. In the majority of cases, this meant white settlers of Portuguese origin and black assimilated Africans, called *assimilados*. To become an *assimilado*, individuals not only had to speak Portuguese, but also show evidence of holding a relevant employment and of living monogamously, i.e. productivity and docility (Marshall 1993).[6] To stake a claim on Portuguese was therefore in itself an act of major significance, full of subversive potential.

Apart from political rhetoric, one way in which the appropriation of Portuguese was mediated was through the literature of the time. The engagement of cultural workers in the liberation struggle had roots back into the 1940s, with authors such as Noémia de Sousa and José Craveirinha. These were later followed by other authors such as Luís Bernardo Honwana and Rui Knopfli (among others), whose work prefigured the collapse of colonialism and exposed injustices and colonial exploitation within a black-nationalist framework.[7]

Luís Bernardo Honwana, particularly, employed a technique in his writings which involved incorporating, without revision or modification, passages of Portuguese speech produced by Mozambican characters replete with errors of simplification and transfer.[8] Honwana's bald literary use of non-standard, and in the eyes of the colonialists, incorrect forms of Portuguese served the oppositional, political, purpose of underscoring the legitimacy of this way of speaking. The force of the strategy depended on the fact that a form of language considered marginal and wrong from the perspective of normative, colonial discourse was, in a specific context, evaluatively transformed to an acceptable form of Portuguese. It is an excellent example of linguistic transgression with clear pointers to Bakhtin's marketplace speech, where the inversion and desecration of official values is typical of carnivalesque activities (see also Mbembe 1992: 1). This literary technique could be interpreted as articulating a politics of identity in transition.

Interesting metaphorical portrayals of this process of adoption and ownership of language can also be found in the combat poetry of the time. Combat poetry by resistance fighters such as Marcelino dos Santos, Fernando Ganhão and Sérgio Vieira, was a way of nurturing and further developing earlier traditions of cultural resistance to colonialism. An important function of this poetry was to mobilize, edify and socialize the liberation forces, with the ultimate aim of providing each individual fighter with revolutionary direction and meaning (Viliya 1996). Marcelino dos Santos, Vice-president of FRELIMO and the First President of the Republican Assembly, commenting on combat poetry said

> Culture is, and constitutes for us, an important factor in the national liberation fight. It carries the essence and the nature of human personal development. We use culture to mobilize the people in the liberation war.

Typical titles such *as Nós somos filhos do povo (*'We are the children of the people'); *Somos combatentes da FRELIMO (*'We are fighters of FRELIMO'); *Forja do homem novo* ('The forging of a new man'), give an idea of the type of topics such poetry touched upon. In this poetry, Portuguese is sometimes portrayed as a weapon. One of the most forceful illustrations of this is in a poem by Sérgio Vieira entitled "Four Parts of a Poem of Education left Incomplete".[9]

> At night in the bases
> deciphering letters
> in the shadow of mango trees
> spelling out words
> under the cry of bombs
> scribbling sentences
>
> word was made bullet
> and the bullet was guided by the word...
>
> from words
> hurricanes were born
> which annihilated the companies
>
> With the sentences they wanted to hide from us
> we lit the great fire
> of the People's war
>
> (cited in Marshall 1993: 109, from Searle 1984: 4, 5)

This poem elegantly depicts how Portuguese is acquired in a very specific second language acquisition context. The act of appropriation is represented as fraught with effort and sacrifice, "taking place at night", "in the shadows; under the cry of bombs" —in itself a testimony to the perceived value of the language. The poem also foregrounds how cultural considerations informed, and were informed by, the war effort; the fight for independence was fueled by knowledge and insight into the meaning of oppression: "word was made bullet and the bullet was guided by the word". Portuguese meant understanding and understanding led to war; "with the sentences they wanted to hide from us, we lit the great fire of the people's war." As with Honwana's texts, the impact of this poem lies in the way it expresses, or relies upon, an act of transgression. Portuguese is used against the colonialists in such a way that both the body and the mind of the colonialists are violated —with bullets and with words.

The modern state establishes relationships between history and territory that involve the state appropriating national histories by "eliminating other national pasts and turning them into variations of its own history" and eradicating the "traditions, histories and memories of dominated nations" (Poulantzas,1980: 113). Part of the first steps towards Mozambican independence was to forge a common national past among the Mozambican people under the umbrella project of the transgressive appropriation of the colonial language. In the spirit of Eduardo Mondlane's cultural politics of unification, the adoption of Portuguese by the liberation movement was part of a rewriting of history.

3. Creating a nation

3.1. Writing Portuguese onto the nation-state

The nation-state is born through processes of homogenization and unification that order and mark out frontiers and national territories (Poulantzas 1980). This demarcation of territorial space and its politization is integral to the exercise of power, and the conquest, regulation, and management of space is therefore a major concern of societies undergoing transition. In Mozambique, FRELIMO achieved control over its political territory by means of control over language —with respect to form, distribution and valorization. The debates and discussions on language issues that took place after independence center on the creation and institutional recognition of a legitimate concept of Mozambican Portuguese that would reflect the cultural, socialist and national identities of the newly independent state. The association of a particular form of Portuguese with the political machinery of FRELIMO contributed to a conception of the new Mozambique in the cast of the party itself.

3.2. *Recreating Portuguese in the image of the future*

Many commentators have characterized FRELIMO's development strategy after independence as an "imaginative project". Portuguese was an integral part of this project of the imagination. Hand in hand with its newly found status as a political inheritance and legacy, Portuguese was being (re)fashioned into the language of the future and as part of the invention of modernity (Urla 1993). In the process, the language itself was constructed as a certain type of entity of the revolutionary imagination.

As the adopted language of the Mozambican future, Portuguese was rhetorically presented as undergoing change and transformation. According to Poulantzas (1980)

> [t]he role of a common language in constituting the modern nation does not refer to a process whereby the State takes over a language, causing it to suffer purely instrumental distortions; it denotes the very *re-creation* of language by the State.
>
> (Poulantzas 1980: 115)

The then Minister of Information and Propaganda, Cabaço, for example, asserted in a speech that Portuguese would become infused with a new status and a new identity. No longer the language of the colonizer but the language of the people, it would be the case that,

> within a few years, a form of Portuguese will be spoken in Mozambique, that is a Mozambican Portuguese that has its own characteristics, ours, that will be a copy of neither Brazilian Portuguese nor any other locality. It will be a Portuguese born out of the participation of our people in the process of national reconstruction.

At this time, the most important characteristics of this new Portuguese were formulated in a discourse of aesthetics; Mozambican Portuguese would be "clear" (*claro*), a Portuguese that was "better" (*melhor*) than European Portuguese because its source was the material, social and spiritual conditions of the revolution. Mozambican Portuguese would further comprise an object of "appreciation" and "emotion". Discourse on language in terms of clarity and simplicity, emotion, and sources of thought can be "deeply enmeshed with conceptions about the nation" (Gal 1992: 448), a point neatly captured in Samora Machel's words, cited by Mia Couto in the magazine *Tempo* (18.01.81)

> we speak here (in Mozambique) a better Portuguese. And why? A clear Portuguese, because we have clear ideas, because we have a clear content and we have clear objectives. ... And we like it very much. Let's cultivate it. It's the national language.

The most fundamental technical process in the imaginative reconstruction of Portuguese was captured in the notion of *enrichment ('enriquecimento')* (Samora Machel 1981*)*. A number of texts from this period give examples of items of new Mozambican Portuguese that were simultaneously said to reflect and structure new human relationships. Such items were commonly words such as e.g. *engajado (*'engaged/commited'), used to refer to those who were ideologically committed to the revolution; *empregado* ('employed'), instead of *doméstico, continuador* ('youth who would continue the revolution') (see Firmino 1995). However, very few authors or language cultivators actually did go on in practice to "enrich" the Portuguese language, that is, to articulate linguistically the spirit of a new revolutionary language and/or taking up and using linguistic variants from emerging contact and second language varieties of Portuguese.[10]

Among those who did, Mia Couto is the enrichment philosophy's most radical exponent. Couto joined the ranks of important cultural and political figures at independence. His work dealt especially with imaginative social experiments, exploring such concepts as *Homem novo* ('the New Man') and articulating and exploring the implications of multiracial societies built on scientific socialist principles.[11]

In his work, Couto incorporates rules and items of usage from Mozambican Portuguese, and, more to the point, actually constructs new items of language through the extrapolation of observed regularities in how Portuguese is used in Mozambique. One such item is the compound lexeme *predispronto*, an amalgamation of *pre* + *dis(posto)* + *pronto*, 'predisposed quickly'. Another is *combustar* instead of *combustão* (see Gonçalves 1995: 23). Couto mixes grammars —Bantu and Portuguese— exploiting the transgressive potential of contact and second language varieties of Portuguese. He plays on linguistic contamination, revealing the ambiguity of the structural forms of Mozambican Portuguese. And he displays a sensitivity towards how admixture of two languages may carry a sense of the ambiguity, flux and coalescence of identities in revolutionary change.

Ba Ka Khosa was another writer who employed yet a different technique of enrichment, namely language mixing. This involved his incorporating loans from Bantu languages into Portuguese texts in an attempt to capture and juxtapose contrasting realities. Most interesting is the way in which Ba Ka Khosa also explicates, or comments on, these juxtaposed realities. He does this in a monologic, Portuguese voice, which subsumes and interprets the Bantu item in another semiotic framework, as in the following text

> *...o odor nauseabundo do sangue que cobriu a aldeia durante aqueles meses fatídicos em que* nkuaia *(ritual anual e sagrado em que os súbditos provenientes de todos os cantos do império à corte se dirigiam).*
>
> (Ba Ka Khosa 1987: 41, quoted in Gonçalves 1995: 22) [my emphasis on Bantu item]

These discourses on language focus on linguistic form, as an object of aesthetics and as a source of linguistic creativity. The political context framing these views on language was one of change and flux, and the creation of new identities in a rhetorical framework of mass mobilization.

3.3. *Institutionalizing appropriated Portuguese*

An important part of the nation-state building process was the inscription of the revolutionary discourse on Portuguese in the machinery of the state. The most significant moment in this political institutionalization of Portuguese was the First National Seminar on the Teaching of Portuguese, convened in 1979 and organized by the Ministry of Education and Culture. This conference retrospectively rationalized the choice of Portuguese as official language, while charging the institutions of the state with cultivating an appropriated, Mozambican form of the language.

The issues discussed at the meeting were numerous, and the participants comprised a broad and representative segment of those actors and interest groups that were concerned with language issues in some way, such as authors, cultural workers, language teachers, curriculum specialists, and politicians. Representatives from other PALOP countries (Países Africanos de Língua Oficial Portuguesa) such as Angola and Cape Verde were also present to share their experiences of language policies and problems. The conference took the form of plenary presentations accompanied by group workshops where set questions were discussed, and solutions proposed and presented. Many of the plenary papers were anonymously authored, a point which further underscores the formal, conference like character of the encounter. From the available documentation of the conference, it is apparent that the interpretation and conceptual treatment of the language issues are conducted within the ordered environment of administration and government protocol.

The political framing of the conference is captured in the opening address by Graça Machel, Minister of Education and Culture (1979: 11), who said,

> It is necessary to normalize and discipline the practice and use of the language we assume as ours. We want one Portuguese in Mozambique, a Portuguese formed by the experiences and realities of the Mozambicans, enriched by linguistic substrates of Bantu origin, tempered by the revolution.
>
> (Machel 1979: 11)

Portuguese had been made mandatory in the People's Assembly and in the FRELIMO Party Campaigns (of Restructuration). It was now the dominant language of the organs of information, the vehicular language of the country and the language of Mozambique's contacts with the outside world. In the opening words of the conference, the ideological position of the government, on Portuguese was reiterated; the status of Portuguese as the official language of Mozambique and as a factor in national unification was reaffirmed. Portuguese was characterized as an instrument with which to access scientific and technical knowledge, and a means with which to understand and participate in the ideology development of the party.

An important facet of the constitution of the modern state is, namely, the *historization* of a language as a symbol of nationalism. One major outcome of this conference was the production of an authoritative, historical narrative on Portuguese. In the most important, and cited, document of the time on the issue of language policy, Fernando Ganhão wrote, or rewrote, what was to become the official history for FRELIMO's choice of Portuguese as Mozambique's official language. Ganhão, a combat poet and fighter, had just taken up an appointment as the first Vice-Chancellor of Eduardo Mondlane University. His point of view was subsequently accorded great weight. Ganhão's paper is a foundational piece for much subsequent debate on language issues in Mozambique, and it is almost obligatorily cited in most work on the topic by language planners and linguists.

As convention would later come to dictate, Ganhão opened his text by referring typically to Portuguese as the language of the oppressor. But he then goes on to point out that since 1962, Portuguese had served to unify FRELIMO members and level out differences between them. Referring to the fact that the majority of FRELIMO's members had spoken hardly any Portuguese at all, and that all of the early daily interactions were in Swahili or English, which were the languages of their political schooling, he said

> It was clear that during the 1st Congress, no resolution was brought up concerning language, but there was a unanimous and tacit acceptance that the documents from the Congress should be edited in Portuguese, because among all the differences this was what was the common denominator for all.

In this quote, Ganhão comes across as portraying Portuguese as a fully-fledged language of consensus, appearing like a phoenix out of the ashes of colonial defeat. One reading that is close at hand is that the party members who used Portuguese did so to express their desire to tone down potentially divisive differences in background, experience and political preference. The act of acquiring the language was also powerfully symbolic, namely an act of solidarity with the party. The implied subtext was that Portuguese was the linguistic emblem of unity.

With such a pedigree, the choice of Portuguese as the official language was a natural next step for revolutionaries bent on forging a united people. The most cited passage by far from Ganhão's speech is when he claims that the choice of Portuguese as the official language was

> a well pondered and carefully examined political decision aimed at achieving one objective, the preservation of national unity and the integrity of the territory.

On the assumption that what works for the party must work for the nation, Portuguese was constituted as the official language of the new order and it was elevated to the major rhetorical means for the creation of a vision of unity and consensus among the Mozambican population. As Portuguese was mythologized as contemporaneous with the birth and consolidation of the nation, so was it bent into the service of symbolizing the new political territory of independent Mozambique. In other words, allegiance to a language was constructed here as tantamount to allegiance to the flag.

Another topic that came to dominate much of the conference was the issue of what *form* of Portuguese would, and should, be spoken in Mozambique. The grand futuristic visions of language and society and the historical reconstructions of the (not-so-glorious) past of Portuguese which were the hall-marks of revolutionary ideologues such as Mia Couto and Vieira were translated into minutes and points for debate and discussion. Pragmatism and the formulation of implementable language policies were the order of the day. In the summing up of the conference, the rhetorical and highly symbolic notion of an appropriated and transformed Mozambican Portuguese was officially dealt with in the following way,[12]

> It was also recommended the preeminent necessity of conducting a study of the basic Portuguese spoken in Mozambique, taking into consideration the principle forms of interference from the mother tongues. This study will permit the discovery of what is happening to the Portuguese language in Mozambique, creating conditions for a later normalization/standardization that would assure a Portuguese language from Rovuma to Maptuo.

The 1st National Conference was not the only forum in which the national role of Portuguese was discussed.[13] Potent instruments in the regulation of public space are mass media, which are particularly important in creating and disseminating nation-state ideologies and in forming notions of citizenship and common purpose (Anderson 1983).[14] It was therefore hardly surprisingly that the question of language use in radio transmissions should surface as one of the issues of major importance in a conference on Radio Mozambique that took place on 26–30 November 1975, hosted by FRELIMO's Department for Information and Propaganda.

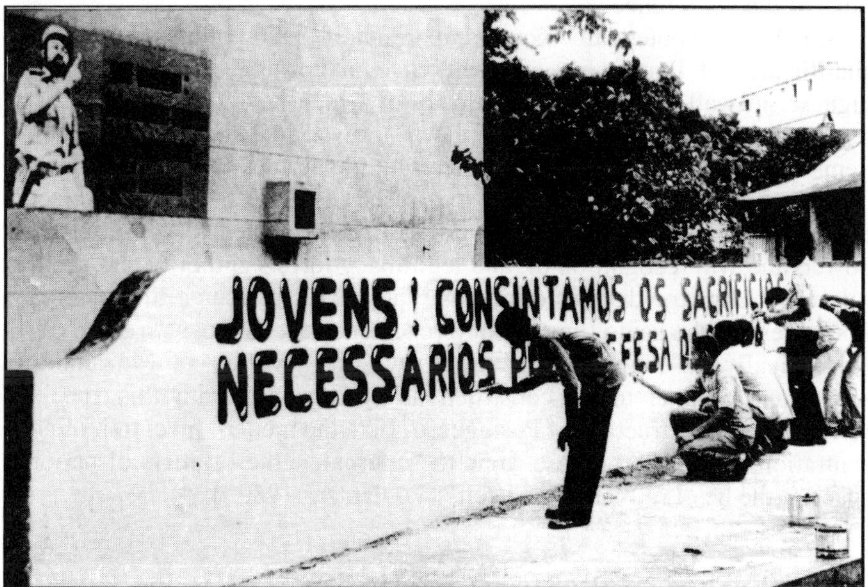

Figure 1. Photo by courtesy of *Noticias*

In the radio debate, as with the other language ideological debates reviewed here, language issues were an integral and formative part of a more comprehensive debate on the revolutionary and moral orientation and development of institutions and individuals. A special paragraph in the reporting from the conference in *Tempo* (1975(271): 60–61) underscored the necessity for radio employees to be true to revolutionary belief and committed and dedicated to the task at hand, namely the reconstruction of Mozambique. Certain departments of the radio were criticized from this perspective, and the "political reliability", or commitment, of their personnel questioned. New policies of recruitment and screening of co-workers were called for. It was also recommended that classical music and music foreign to the beat and pulse of Mozambican rhythms, or that of other sympathetic socialist states, be replaced by more indigenous tones.

This bare-foot approach to cultural expression also came out clearly in the statements made with respect to Portuguese. Of specific interest was the recommendation that because the form of Portuguese hitherto used in radio broadcasts was not the same as that used by the majority of Mozambican speakers, and therefore not easily understood by them, the language of broadcasting should be adapted to better accord with the linguistic realities of Mozambique. Once again, as with the 1st National Conference, a concern with more popular forms of Portuguese dominates the deliberations of the conference.

Another, and potentially more popular, manifestation of the revolutionary significance of Portuguese was reference to Portuguese, or use of Portuguese, in wall paintings, the majority of which have only recently been removed from the city's walls, or been allowed to fade with time. Here, items of Portuguese are embedded in revolutionary depictions of reality.

The perspective on Portuguese expressed in these "discursive projects" can be seen as one expression of how FRELIMO tried to consolidate its power, and win recognition of, and legitimacy for, its authority and right to rule. The language debates during the late 1970s recreated the history of Portuguese at the same time as they redesigned the language, socially and ideologically, in the image of the party. The territory of Mozambique subsequently came to be construed as synonymous with this specific, institutional, construction of Portuguese. Like the modern invention of concentration camps, Portuguese came to "internalize the frontiers of national space at the heart of that space itself" (Poulantzas 1980: 105).

4. Infrapolitics of the powerless or rituals of the weak

4.1. Holes in the net

While FRELIMO was trying to build and consolidate its *nova sociedade*, other forces were doing their best to pull it down. RENAMO, the National Resistance Movement of Mozambique, began to violently undermine fundamental structures of Mozambican civil society in an armed conflict that lasted from the early 1980s until 1992. This conflict, one of the cruelest in the history of Africa, is estimated to have cost 1 million people their lives, left 5 million homeless, traumatized innumerable children, many of whom were forcefully enlisted as soldiers, all but ruined conditions for rural living and destroyed vital infrastructure such as roads, hospitals, schools, and power lines worth a total sum of 18 billion dollars. The governing party FRELIMO seemed unprepared for such an onslaught. Many commentators have suggested that FRELIMO analyzed the nature of the threat to its existence inadequately, interpreting and formulating its national security prerogatives in conventional terms which saw the threat of destabilization as emanating from beyond its borders and not within them. In line with this, an alternative historical revisionist account suggests that the main reason for destabilization was not so much external aggression from hostile neighbors —principally South Africa and Rhodesia— as it was internal dissatisfaction with the FRELIMO government. This was supposed to have been fomented among harassed, primarily rural populations, marginalized by trends in the development of the postindependent society. However, as Abrahamsson and Nilsson (1995) underscore, internal opposition would not have been effective if it had not been for the financial backing, material support and armed interventions of external aggressors such as South Africa and Rhodesia. Marcelino dos Santos, an important member of the FRELIMO politburo, claimed in a newspaper interview that although Mozambique's main problem was external aggression, FRELIMO's "errors provided the holes through which the enemy entered" (Interview in *Domingo*, 10 June 1990, quoted in Hanlon 1991: 5). RENAMO was undoubtedly in an excellent position to tear holes in the fabric of FRELIMO's errors.

The FRELIMO development project was a massive attempt to legitimate the redistribution of power and to establish new forms of authority at all levels of society, locally, regionally and nationally. The Third FRELIMO congress involved a tighter, more exclusive, elite management of power. This meant that FRELIMO destroyed or ignored traditional sources of power, and thereby also lost an "opportunity to link up with the principles of legitimacy which guided the population's 'assessment'..." (Abrahamsson and Nilsson 1995: 86)

FRELIMO's exercise of power had many different repercussions on the rural population of Mozambique. For example, state farms required managers, and the nature and demands of this organization meant that local people could not be accommodated in this role. Generally, as FRELIMO's development policies gained momentum, the peasants and the rural population became more and more marginalized whereas urban groups and people in state apparatus —often Portuguese speaking— became more important (Abrahamsson and Nilsson 1995: 80).

Problems also arose from the locations that FRELIMO had given to the communal villages. Some families had to cover larger distances to get to their fields, and in time, those with distant fields gave up braving RENAMO attacks and instead became day-workers for landholders with plots of land closer to the village. Those families who had the good fortune to have their land located close to the communal villages became influential and active local spokespersons with clear economic interests to protect. In some cases, this implied a radical shift in local patterns of power (Dinerman 1995).

The question of rightful ownership to land was another cause of dissatisfaction. Immediately after independence, peasants in many parts of the country, able to carefully trace ownership back generations, had reclaimed land from Portuguese colonialists. According to FRELIMO however, the land belonged to the state (Abrahamsson and Nilsson 1995), a situation which produced a conflict of interest between the government and the peasants.

Finally, there was also the question of regional imbalance in power that followed in the wake of FRELIMO's strategies. Many of the most influential political leaders at all levels were from the southern part of the country. This opened up the possibility of construing developments during independence in shifting spheres of political and economic power as instantiations of century old antagonisms between North and Central areas of Mozambique, on the one hand, and Southern areas, on the other (Abrahamsson and Nilsson 1995).

There were in other words, any number of reasons for dissatisfaction on behalf of marginalized and dissatisfied segments of the population. These problems were also to provide the leverage for the atrocities of the RENAMO guerilla movement.

4.2. Loud resistance: The semiotics of violence[15]

RENAMO was a classical terrorist, guerilla organization. Its tactics were to burn villages, steal livestock and food, and ambush and kill people. RENAMO cut off ears and breasts, and dismembered their victims. Gang-pressed child recruits were forced to take an active part in the burning of their village and the slaughter of their neighbors and family (cf. Bredin 1994). However grotesque, arbitrary and senseless this violence may appear, nothing, in fact, could be further from the truth. According to Feldman (1991),

> [t]error is a social fact and a cultural construction; techniques and targets of cruelty and destruction are highly symbolically meaningful.
>
> (Feldman 1991: 136)

The significance of RENAMO's terror was very much provided by the ways in which they understood FRELIMO's exercise of power. In a sense, FRELIMO's developmental project was a projection of specific type of order and authority on rural populations. This involved a reorganization of rural space in, for example, the construction of state farms, and the formation of new local centers of power. Spatial organization came to reflect the embodiment and operation of this new power, how it was distributed and where it was located. Important targets for the RENAMO guerilla were subsequently those sites and spatial coordinates that embodied FRELIMO's authority. These were schools, hospitals, and roads linking urban and non-urban areas, i.e. all embodiments of urban conceptions of space and organization.

Figure 2. Photo taken at Maluana, National Highway, no. 1. Courtesy of Sérgio Santimano

Furthermore, because the guerillas needed to enlist the understanding and material support of their constituencies, an important part of their warfare was necessarily semiotic, discursive and interpretive. Guerilla warfare relies upon being able to construct the enemy as a plausible target, in order to rob it of legitimacy. The destruction of state-run farms had such a legitimacy, at least at face value. Because the management of these farms was outside of the control of local people, also imposing structures of interaction and organization of work that was perceived to be alien to traditional Mozambican rural society, RENAMO opposed and tore up land reform whenever it was possible for them to do so.

Not surprisingly, given the importance of Portuguese and the way it was inserted into a politics of control and political development, language issues subsequently became a major target in the ensuing warfare waged by the RENAMO guerilla. After independence, all power, local or otherwise, was mandatorily exercised through Portuguese. There were undoubtedly some practical contingencies that motivated this. As Abrahamsson and Nilsson (1995) point out,

> the war of liberation only reached very limited numbers of the population, and the central leadership's interface with local supporters was small. Consequently, the new administrators came to be recruited mainly from the middle ranks of the liberation army,... Many new administrators came to a district where they lacked political roots, and could not make themselves understood in the local language.[16]
>
> (Abrahamsson and Nilsson 1995: 83)

Portuguese was rhetorically constituted as an urban phenomenon. It was also clearly recognized as an instrument of the state by RENAMO. Portuguese was tangibly part of the division and containment of power, and in the way different groups were constituted as marginal or powerful. Anti-traditionalism, urbanization, co-optation of elites, the pursuit of *o inimigo interno*, 'the enemy within' were all entwined in FRELIMO discourses in and around Portuguese. More to the point, Portuguese and its speakers were semiotized as the constituency. Portuguese was, in a sense, synonymous with the "territory", constituting the political space of FRELIMO.

The enforcement by RENAMO of the use of national languages in the zones they controlled was one tangible demonstration of the semiotics of resistance and violence, and was related to debatable conceptions of language and power propounded by FRELIMO. Bantu languages were also employed within the guerilla movement itself. These practices were partly conditioned by the socioeconomic status and educational level of the guerillas —many did not master Portuguese— but the use of Bantu languages was also emblematic of loyalty to the movement (personal communication, Sr. Lázaro Ernesto, RENAMO's Information Office, Maputo). Finally, speakers of Portuguese were among those most often targeted and killed by RENAMO, especially those with a professional association with the language, such as teachers.

In other words, the conflict between RENAMO and FRELIMO was also one of competing narratives about traditional, contemporary and futuristic ideologies of language and their relationship to power in contests over what was to be recognized as legitimate political authority.

5. In defense of the nation

5.1 "Dreams shattered" (Hanlon 1991: 18)

RENAMO's onslaughts came at a bad time for FRELIMO, as the party already had a troublesome mix of problems to grapple with. After the immediate momentum of independence had worn off, the Mozambican economy started upon a period of heavy stagnation. Production quotas fell drastically, due partly to the mismanagement at all levels of the economy by an enthusiastic and concerned but inexperienced new government and its administration. But Mozambique was also hard hit by the world recession and the deterioration in the terms of trade that followed in its wake. Irrefutably, among the most important factors behind economic and social decline were those related to Mozambique's decision, following U.N. recommendations, to boycott Ian Smith's racist UNT government in Rhodesia. Mozambique was one of the few countries to sincerely do so, and it cost her dearly from economic and military retaliations from South Africa and Rhodesia. During this period, Mozambique along with the rest of sub-Saharan Africa was experiencing the effects of heavy and prolonged drought. The situation was further compounded by the fact that RENAMO proved that FRELIMO was not in a position to protect even the most basic of its populations' interests, namely their right to physical safety. According to Abrahamsson and Nilsson (1995)

> Experiences indicate that opposition to the nation-state project grows when the state cannot deliver essential collective utilities, or guarantee the population's long-term survival... This is essentially a question of how legitimacy develops for a state, or any other form of institutionalized power.
>
> (Abrahamsson and Nilsson 1995: 92)

Besides these problems, there was rising popular opinion and protest against many of FRELIMO's anti-traditionalist stances.

All these developments were rapidly changing an optimistic political climate into one drenched in pessimism (Hanlon 1991: 18). FRELIMO made some serious attempts to respond to this confluence of negative developments, and to counter the populations's dissatisfaction. However, the crisis continued, and led to an increasing loss of control by the state power in many different sectors, threatening the privileges of the coopted, middle-level, Portuguese speaking elites of FRELIMO.[17] FRELIMO's response to these problems was a mix of populism and authoritarianism (Hanlon 1991).

FRELIMO had already undergone a political reorganization. From having been a broad based, popular movement, it had transformed itself into a

Marxist elite party in the Third Party congress in 1977. This strategy aimed to better ensure ideological unity, and to permit FRELIMO to rid itself of the many pre-independence antagonisms that characterized its history (Abrahamsson and Nilsson 1995: 75).[18] Now, in an attempt to meet the crisis, FRELIMO once more opened its doors to debate and decentralized its power.

At the same time, more authoritarian tactics were also in sway. One tangible demonstration of this was the attempt to rejuvenate the dynamics and thrust of the revolution with *Operação Produção* ('Operation Production'), which took place between 1982–1983. Through practices such as mass arrest, curfews and deportations, thousands of citizens with threadbare identity cards were shipped out of the cities, and streets were swept clean of prostitutes, alcoholics, gays and other elements deemed incompatible with FRELIMO's conception of the *Homem novo*. Re-education camps for the political and moral edification of such antisocial elements were introduced in isolated parts of the country.

A complementary mode of response that FRELIMO used to attempt to retain its grip on power was the production of a more authoritarian discourse on language. Despite the earlier popular, political and revolutionary rhetoric of pre-independence (cf. Ganhão, Machel and others mentioned above), and the expression of the same spirit in the concluding note from the 1979 conference, the main discourse on language now was a bolstering and consolidation of a more traditional norm of Portuguese, one closer to the European norm, rather than the celebration of any emergent Portuguese particular to the postcolonial periphery.[19] Malkki (1995), referring to Spencer's (1990) mention of the similarities between nationalist and scholarly constructions of culture in Sri Lanka, argues that the generative order of knowledge is molded in the form of the nation-state. The image of Portuguese officially presented by FRELIMO in the early to mid 1980s bears a structural resemblance to the concerns of the Mozambican state under siege at this time, namely how to contain variation, manage diversity and keep a firm grip on central power.

5.2. Grammatical hegemony

The new discourse on language and its political framing is admirably captured in the most significant document of the 1980s on language policy, the *Contribuição para a definição de uma política linguística na República Popular de Moçambique* ('Contribution to a politics of language in the People's Republic of Mozambique'), written in 1983. In this document, which emanated from the Ministry of Culture and Education, Mozambican language policy is characterized as those policies and practices that contribute to the construction of a socialist state and that furthered the goals of the Mozambican revolution. The text explicitly notes that language politics in other African states are often tied to questions related to the notion of official language, and goes on to say, that in Mozambique, even though African languages are to be valorized, developed and cultivated, and even though their importance for the articulation and development of Mozambican culture is beyond question, Portuguese will nevertheless remain unchallenged as the official language of Mozambique.[20]

The document also addressed the question of the appropriation of Portuguese, and its transformation to a *bona fide* Mozambican variety. In a section entitled *Que Português em Moçambique?* ('What Portuguese in Mozambique?'), the author advises that appropriating Portuguese *não exige, como alguns pretendem, a abolição das regras gramaticais, a liberalização da pronúncia, o descontrole das aquisições lexicais* (p. 15) ('does not imply as some mean abolishing rules of grammar, the liberalization of pronunciation, or loss of control over lexical acquisition'). Claiming that no definitive answer to the problem of choosing a norm of language can be given in a language policy document, the text concludes by noting that it is possible *à identificação e combate daqueles factores linguísticos que podem concorrer para distorcer e prejudicar o desenvolvimento harmonioso da sociedade moçambicana* (p. 18) ('to identify and combat those linguistic features that distort and prejudice the harmonious development of the Mozambican society').

The debate on norm took a further rhetorical step forward with a statement by Samora Machel. Performing an interesting about-turn on the question of norm considering his earlier enthusiasm for a Mozambican Portuguese, the President explicitly advocated a European Portuguese norm. Rosário (1993), referring to a passage from an interview that Machel had given to the Portuguese weekly, *Expresso*, reports him as saying with pride,

> Mozambicans are really forcing themselves to speak a correct Portuguese and are trying to preserve it in a state very close to the norm of Portuguese, because only in that way will it be possible to attain the objectives [planned for] in its adoption in the process of national unity.
>
> (Rosário 1993: 4)

In other words, Machel explicitly connects a specific norm of Portuguese —the European one— to the success of the project of national unification. We witness, to cite Susan Gal, "the happy fusion of a circumscribed and internally homogenous language with a similarly configured nation" (Gal 1992: 449).[21]

Shreds of a more top-down and normative view of Portuguese had, of course, existed previously. When ideologues such as Machel or Couto had spoken about an emergent Mozambican form of Portuguese, enriched by its Mozambican speakers, they seemed to have had in mind a socially *engineered* form of Portuguese that would both reflect and mold the revolutionary consciousness of the new Mozambican citizen —"a better Portuguese" and "a clear Portuguese" (Machel, cited by Couto). Cabaço also had been careful in his speech to distinguish between a Portuguese with a "Mozambican personality" and an error-littered speech that showed non-mastery of the language; speaking of the creativity inherent in adopting Portuguese in this context, he also says that *saber distinguir também isso dos erros com que o Povo possa dominar a língua Portuguesa* ('know how to distinguish these from the errors committed by the people who acquire the Portuguese language'). This wing of discourse on Portuguese, however, became more salient during the early 1980s.

There were other voices at the time, on the periphery of the official scene, which offered alternative views on language, but these had very little headwind in the prevailing political climate. Albino Magaia, for example, wrote on the issue in his weekly chronicle *Ku Lima* in *Tempo* (1980(562): 60–61), noting with consternation that written Portuguese is not the language that is spoken on a day-to-day basis. He lauds the spoken language as a type of language that is, *incomparavelmente mais rica em construções, em significações, muito mais dinâmica* ('incomparably richer in constructions, in meanings and much more dynamic'). He also warned that, *o uso pesado que fazemos do português vem da falta de distinção entre a expressão oficial e a não oficial* ('the heavy use we are making of Portuguese will erase the distinction between the official and non-official expressions').

Likewise, a sociolinguistic project initiated in 1981 under the auspices of UNESCO, comprising both researchers from the University of Eduardo Mondlane (UEM) and the National Institute for Education Development (INDE) had attempted to focus official interest on the legitimacy of the Portuguese spoken by the majority of the members of the Mozambican speech community. The project was, in many respects, a somewhat belated attempt to pick up on the early revolutionary rhetoric around language issues by offering a scientific justification for the political stance on Portuguese as appropriated and transformed. The report from the project cited heavily one of President Machel's speeches to Mozambican students in Cuba, where he was reported to have said, *The língua quando é falada por um povo livre, transforma-se* ('A language when spoken by a free people, transforms itself'). It also referred explicitly to the program for research sketched in the summarizing statement of the 1st National Conference on

Portuguese. In a set of documents prepared for a seminar, the research team argued that second language and contact varieties of Portuguese needed to be given due consideration in educational and social contexts. An incisive paper entitled *O sistema nacional de educação e a situação multilingue do país* ('National system of education and the multilingual situation of the country'), argued for the introduction of bilingual education. A powerful and contrary statement on the role of Portuguese in Mozambican nation-state building was also made in this paper (p.14);

> The mastery of Portuguese should not be seen as a condition "*sine qua non*" for the acquisition of a national consciousness or for the active participation in the revolutionary process. The engagement of the Mozambican people in the National Liberation Struggle is historical proof of this.

Needless to say, at the time, the seminar, planned to be held 16–23 May 1983, was canceled with no motivation given.

5.3. Linguistic terrorism

Blommaert (this volume), inspired by Bourdieu, points out that dominant ideas on language get spread throughout levels of society in *processes of normalization*. These comprise a variety of institutional and semi-institutional practices such as language campaigns, the use of a language in formal education, and the employment of specific languages in the media. All of these processes specify the meaning of language in concrete cases. In the years following, this stance on language was enforced in all public arenas of Mozambique.

Official injunctions and edicts to use Portuguese in public places and official encounters had made it obligatory to use Portuguese in all public sectors of Mozambican society. In fact, a communication from the 5th Congress explicitly condemned the use of local languages in public contexts. A quotidian take on this is well illustrated in the admonishing words from the *Tribunal de Menores* ('The Minors Court'), quoted by Rosário (1993: 1) namely, *É expressamente obrigatório falar a língua oficial* ('It is expressly obligatory to speak the official language').

Briggs, writing of the naturalization of power in Warao discourse, underscores how the "strategic use of linguistic ideologies play an important role in naturalizing social inequality and social power ..." (1992: 397). In this particular case, the close connection between the Portuguese language, the political space of FRELIMO and the legitimacy of the state institutions that owned the language opened up the possibility of ruling out certain uses (or non-uses) of Portuguese as contra-revolutionary. Not to speak Portuguese, or to speak it badly, was available to be used to construct marginal social groupings and to circumscribe a moral space. Expressions of indignation towards those who spoke languages other than Portuguese in public were typical manifestations of this. Letters to the editor at this time printed in publications such as *Tempo* characteristically expressed annoyance and moral indignation about the fact that Bantu languages could be heard in the cities of Mozambique.[22] The first issues of *Tempo* from 1982 contain a number of letters from readers lamenting the public use of Mozambican languages in urban areas. Readers from the north of the country writing under the rubric *Na capital do país só existe uma lingua* ('In the capital of the country, there is only one language') lament the use of Tsonga in Maputo; and Pedro António with his letter *Será que bitonga é a língua nacional* ('Maybe Bitonga is the national language') likewise critizes the use of Bitonga in public situations, depreciatingly referring to it as a *dialecto* ('dialect') —the old Portuguese derogatory term for Mozambican languages. These letters expressed a powerful and censorious citizens' watch of revolutionary spirit, and it is significant that the bulk of them end with the chants,

> Long live FRELIMO! Long live the unity of the Mozambican people! Long live the People's Republic of Mozambique! Eliminate regionalism! Eliminate divisionism! Eliminate tribalism! The fight continues!

Language was also part of the way in which public enemies were characterized. Antisocial, and contra-revolutionary elements were textually and pictorially portrayed as beard-stubbled, hunchbacked, bottle-toting scoundrels whose Portuguese was riddled with ungrammatical elements. A popular such figure of the 1980s was the serial figure *Xiconhoca*. This word is a compound of the Portuguese diminuitive *xico* from *Francisco* and the Changana word for 'snake', *nhoca*. This figure was depicted as the embodiment of evil and depravity.

The character of Xiconhoca is reputably based on a renowned Portuguese warden on one of the Portuguese prison islands off the coast of Maputo. This man was known for his sadistic treatment of prisoners. The grotesque depiction of the figure is an interesting comment on the *inimigo interno* ('internal enemy'). The combination of a historical Portuguese component with an African national component is a telling illustration of how the enemy was perceived.

The fact that the domestic market and state apparatus had required Portuguese speaking manpower meant that Portuguese *per se* came to be strongly associated with important and formal, state controlled, sectors of society. This invariably brought with it an elitization of Portuguese which thereby became an important symbolic capital. Marshall (1993) mentions how ordinary people in low level encounters with petty officialdom could at times be ridiculed and made to feel linguistically insecure if not able to express themselves with a sufficient elegance in Portuguese. This form of linguistic intimidation, where verbal products were relocated into discourses of shame and guilt, contributed to an already existing asymmetrical power relationship between official and client, as well as to a strengthening of the image of Portuguese as an elite language and a language of authority and control. In cases such as this, Portuguese became one of the foremost means in the display of power exercised by government institutions. Because of the grid of associations that Portuguese was embedded within, recognition of the norm and its rightful guardians served to celebrate the institutions that endorsed it. Most importantly, the performance of good Portuguese demonstrated the excellence and legitimacy of the authority's right to talk and to govern.[23]

Figure 3. The text means: *Xiconhoca* is the agent of the enemy. Guide of the invaders, collaborates in the aggression and in the massacres of the people.

Portuguese had historically been adopted as the language of the party, only to subsequently be rhetorically construed as the idiom of the people. In ways similar to the reorganization of FRELIMO in 1977, which removed and encapsulated power to a select few in the higher echelons of leadership, Portuguese was, once more in the history of the nation, turned into a language of the elite. The Portuguese, *ao serviço do Povo* ('in the service of the people') (Cabaço), was replaced —at least "on paper"— by a central and rarified norm of language managed by a cadre of appointed guardians and directorates.

6. Shifting the goalposts: Relocating power, reconsidering language

6.1. Restructuration

During the late 1980s and early 1990s, Mozambique has experienced many fundamental social, economic and political changes. The tragic death of Samora Machel in a plane accident in 1986 and his succession by President Joaquim Chissano coincided with a major restructuring of Mozambique. The collapse of the Eastern European block left a gaping hole in the economic and ideological infrastructures of the country, which ultimately laid the groundwork for a stronger Mozambican orientation towards the old West. The World Bank made it clear that economic and structural reforms were a condition for Mozambique to receive further aid, a point of view that also other donors came to follow. In some cases, this led to significant changes for the worst in the welfare of the population (Hanlon 1991). Concurrently with these developments, pressures were leveled on the democratization of Mozambican society by Western governments, among others.

In 1989, at the 5th Congress, FRELIMO reneged on its status of a vanguard party. By 1990, it had also thrown out the one party state. The civil war ended in the Rome General Peace Accord on the 4th October 1992, and the ensuing period of peace and stability in Mozambique and the region as a whole, finally led to the first multiparty elections taking place on the 27th-28th of October 1994. Perhaps most importantly, the RENAMO movement beame a bona fide democratic, political party. On an international arena, Mozambique also obtained a new geopolitical position as a commonwealth country.

The outcome of all these developments was that Mozambique, economically and structurally, became wedged firmly in the world economy as a peripheral, Third World society. This means among other things that the majority of the population get their income from outside the formal sectors, that education reaches just a minimum of all eligible children, and that state institutions and infrastructures are available to a small segment of the population only. In a global perspective, it also means that Mozambique is heavily dependent on Centre countries for goods, services and knowledge. Mozambican migrant labor to neighboring countries, mainly South Africa and Zimbabwe, is once again a major source of income.

All of these new sociopolitical developments during the late 1980s and early 1990s have found their reflex in language debates. As sites of political power shift and become more elusive in times of transition and change, so do different actors attempt to reformulate what will comprise discourses of power. Particularly interesting in this regard are two new major discursive projects currently under construction by FRELIMO and RENAMO.

6.2. Inward and outward looking

A great deal of contemporary FRELIMO discourse on language is formulated in terms of a reconstructive and reconstitutive rhetoric —a backward-looking sizing up of the past, which simultaneously represents FRELIMO's comment on the present and future sociopolitical and linguistic condition of Mozambique. One prime topic that has led many activists to sharpen their pens is Mozambique's new geopolitical position as a member of the commonwealth. This fact, coupled to the realization that the country is surrounded by Anglophone neighbors, gave rise to persistent rumor in both Mozambican and foreign media during the years 1994–1997 that English might replace Portuguese as the country's official language (cf. Matusse 1994/1997). A flurry of articles in Tempo, Domingo and Savana, by, among others Vieira and Magaia, served this time to buttress Lusophonia from the feared onslaught of English. The linguistic call-to-arms has been accomplished by rallying around the importance of Portuguese for Mozambique. From a historical perspective, Vieira reminds the readership of the weekly Savana of the geopolitical importance of Portuguese in the formation of the Mozambican state in the late 19th century.[24] It is interesting to note that support for Portuguese in this type of discourse is constructed more around the historical merits of the language, and rather less by way of reference to its current political status.[25]

Another theme which has been raised in conjunction with Portuguese in more official circles is its sociopolitical status as a national language. National, African, languages are still associated with authenticity and traditional values, and also increasingly with a more elaborated concept of participatory democracy. However, powerful groups among the Mozambican elite can of late be seen to be elaborating a new understanding of cultural authenticity formulated in terms of the linguistic nativization of Portuguese. Ribeiro (1994), for example, explicitly proposes viewing Portuguese as a national "treasure" on a par with Mozambican national languages.[26] In other words, cultural authenticity and tradition are no longer the sole purveyor of national languages (Stroud and Tuzine ftc.). Furthermore, in oratory and public performance, speakers are increasingly using Portuguese as base language in code switched or interpreted interactions with national languages —an attempt perhaps to slot into the values of tradition codified in national languages but "revamping" them within the cloak of Portuguese.[27]

Furthermore, a notion of citizenship was constructed around the assumption that everybody would have access to Portuguese. The 1990 Constitution, for the first time ever since independence, explicitly mentions language. In article 73, citizens' rights are laid down as follow;

> 1. All citizens have the right to participate in the process of extending and consolidating democracy at all levels of society and government.
>
> 2. All citizens older than eighteen years of age have the right to be elected.
>
> (quoted in Matusse 1995: 7)

In practice, all this means that Portuguese is becoming even more firmly entrenched in Mozambican realities, and a formative factor in the reinvention of tradition; that is, Portuguese is now part of FRELIMO, and more generally, Mozambican history of the revolution and postcolonial development. Discourses on Portuguese are once again refiguring the language in response to FRELIMO's changing perceptions or constructions of where power and authority lay.

RENAMO, on the other hand, in their discourse on language have, if not left the national language platform, at least for the time being retired temporarily, more recently underscoring the desirability of propagating a more center-oriented version of Portuguese. Dhlakama, the President of RENAMO, in an article in Público (1993) complains about the poor support that Lusophone countries, and particularly Portugal, has given to the cultivation of Portuguese in Mozambique, comparing the situation unfavorably with the French input to Francophone countries, or the contributions made by the British Council for the Anglophone. He also mentions that the Portuguese speaking community of the world have a special responsibility to cultivate the language. Dhlakama has also taken upon himself the public role of nurturing contacts with Portugal and especially the Portuguese business community, publicly stating that contacts here are where the future of Mozambique lies. There was also a simultaneous strengthening of Lusophone links, celebrating the commercial and cultural communion that the sharing of a common language allows.

Different discourses on Portuguese among FRELIMO and RENAMO factions encapsulate different orientations to the relationship between national, domestic and global relationships. Whereas FRELIMO is still orientated towards consolidation of national borders and the development of a sense of national identity, RENAMO is opening up toward more global relationships. These different discourses on language clearly reflect each party's perception of where their constituencies and public recognition of legitimacy lie.

7. Conclusion

From independence up until the present moment, discourse and counter-discourse on the status of Portuguese has given voice to different ideologies and realities of power, construed and opposed new social orders, and bolstered and challenged the legitimacy of forms of symbolic authority. In a sense, Mozambican national unity and disunity can also be understood as rhetorically imagined, interpreted and commented upon, and perhaps also partly constituted, (or toppled), through discourse on language.

These sociohistorical data illustrate the claim that the existence of a language is always a discursive project rather than an established fact (cf. Woolard and Schieffelin 1994). In Mozambique during the last twenty years, there have been many different discursive projects on Portuguese. These were frequently contradictory, especially among those in power who participated in these debates. But these discursive projects also illustrate another phenomenon. All of them underscore how language ideologies are a resource in the construction of social and political power, changing as constructions of power change. The different ideologies of language have been used to formulate, and support, different types of reality, different conceptions of power and resistance, and different understandings of social, cultural and personal identity. In this sense, the sociohistorical account also supports Briggs' (1992: 54) suggestion for the Warao that "[i]t may be misleading to speak ... of either 'linguistic ideologies' or 'ideologies of language' in view of the fact that these ideologies will often encompass cultural foci ...". In Mozambique, language issues, specifically those dealing with perspectives on forms of speaking and their political contextualizations have served to entextualize a postcolony's search for a cultural and national identity. FRELIMO's politics of language was in this respect in all essentials a politics of cultural identity.[28]

Notes

1. This paper was written with support from Sarec, grant SWE-95–08. Thanks for constructive criticism to Jan Blommaert (University of Gent), Kenneth Hyltenstam, Don Kulick, and Maria Wingstedt (Stockholm University), Mikael Palme (Uppsala Univiversity), António Tuzine (INDE, Maputo), and Perpétua Gonçalves and Gregório Firmino (Eduardo Mondlane University, Maputo) for comments and suggestions. The responsibility for the ideas and interpretations in the paper is mine alone.
2. For obvious reasons, I cannot deal with the very important issue of language debates on national languages here. For information on the national Mozambican language question, see Stroud (ftc.).
3. It is important to note that the paper deals only with the official discourses on Portuguese, and the purposes to which these have been put under different sociopolitical conditions. Stroud (ftc.) and Stroud and Tuzine (ftc.), on the other hand, explore another set of, no less important, questions in the sociohistory of Mozambican language politics. These are issues such as the concrete historical conditions that led to the choice of Portuguese as the official language and not African languages in the first place, —for example, the linguistic repertoires of the main actors, the lack of a politically autonomous Africanist tradition that was ideologically untainted, the existence of different (politico-) linguistic factions within the dominant discourse, etc. My thanks to Mikael Palme for drawing my attention to this caveat.
4. FRELIMO was formed in 1962 as a group for armed resistance.
5. All translations from Portuguese are my own.
6. Matusse (1995: 3) quotes for example Paixo (1948), the then Secretary of State for Education in Mozambique, who says a nossa missão é de civilização e nacionalização do indígena. A nossa intenção é transformar o indígena num outro português ('Our mission is to civilize and nationalize the native. Our intention is to transform the native into another Portuguese'). In decree 39 666 from 20th May 1954, article 2 contains the definition of an "indigena" ('native') and the conditions for becoming Portuguese. In article 56, one

condition specified is knowledge of Portuguese. The importance of Portuguese is similarly enforced in decree 2 286 from 25th September 1962, where the language is made a basic subject at school, and where failure to attain sufficient grades implied failure of the whole course of study. These decrees were made within the context of a strict political and religious control on behalf of the authorities as to what languages could be used for what functions, the prohibition of written forms of African languages, and the prohibition against using other European languages in public (Matusse 1995).

7. For example, the film-maker Rui Guerra, the painter António Bronze and the author Rui Nogar.
8. Since independence, Honwana has been a prominent figure in language ideological debates, writing extensively on Portuguese and, even more recently on the current ill-fate of Mozambican national languages (Jornal de Letras, artes e ideais, XIV, no. 615: 22–23 1994). Honwana was Secretary of State in the 1980s, in which capacity he was responsible for a 1983 document on the official status of Portuguese, Contributions to a definition of a politics of language in the People's Republic of Mozambique, which contained the first really explicit treatment of a language policy for Mozambique. The importance of this document is apparent from the fact that it is continually referred to in all subsequent work on language policy that has come out of Mozambique since. Honwana was also directly responsible for an authoritative committee text on the status of national languages, also from 1983.
9. Sérgio Vieira later became the chief ideologue of FRELIMO's cultural policy and provided the theoretical rationale for the direction and thrust of political action in the theoretical concept of Homem Novo. He still participates actively in debates on language, and hosts a column in the Sunday weekly, *Domingo*.
10. Matusse (1995: 6) mentions in an amusing aside how the liberation of Portuguese enriched the language by "liberating it from the dictionary". He cites a well-known joke which purports to mirror the type of Portuguese acquired from listening to revolutionary rhetoric: "Woman, tell your husband, mobilize two fish for me, canalize them into the refrigerator, and organize the table strategically, because my adjutant is coming to discuss the maneuvers of the enemy at the railroad".
11. Another contemporary of Couto's was the author Albino Magaia. Both Mia Couto and Albino Magaia were to hold key cultural positions in the early years of postindepence Mozambique as editors of the major periodicals and newspapers, *Notícias* and *Savana* and *Tempo*. These publications were important mainstays for language ideological debates. Couto is the most widely read and most translated Mozambican author. A biologist by trade, currently teaching at Eduardo Mondlande University in Maputo, he is seldom any longer heard in public debates on language. Magaia, a speaker of Ronga, a Bantu language of Maputo, has recently written articles lamenting the decline of national Mozambican languages.

12. Informally, the stance on the norm of Portuguese was different. The then Minister of Education and Culture, (and President Samora Machel's wife), Graça Machel, in response to a question from the floor from a Brazilian representative on the issue of norms, is reported to have explicitly ordained that European Portuguese would be used for purposes of education. She motivated her stand by noting that due to the current dearth of grammarians and dictionary makers, there was as yet no such workable entity as Mozambican Portuguese (cf. Rosário 1993).
13. In general, during the late 70s, there was an enormous public interest in questions of language, specifically dealing with the relationship between Portuguese and national languages. One letter to the editor in *Tempo* (1975(29): 30–31), for example, spends two pages discussing the etymology of the word machimbombo ('bus') under the title "The Secret of the word Machimbombo". More specifically, the point of contention in the text deals with whether this word is an onomatopoeic expression, loaned into Portuguese from the local language Ronga, or whether it is actually a genuine Portuguese item. The author argues quite persuasively, against Magaia's contrary view, that the word was originally coined in Lisbon. He is also concerned that the spelling mirror this. This letter is typical of many that focus on language dealing with questions of historical identity. There were also other contexts where Portuguese was spread. For example, in the early years of the National Literacy Campaign, which reached out into all nooks of the country, all literacy activities were conducted in and through Portuguese. In fact, literacy activities were seen as one way of ensuring the uptake of Portuguese among the broader segments of the Mozambican population. For example, Samora Machel speaking at the Campaign for National Literacy in Maputo (3–7-1978) emphasized the important role of Portuguese in national consolidation.
14. Symptomatic of this importance is that all transmissions on Radio Mozambique open with the vignette "RM, from Rovuma to Maputo", in Portuguese, which giving the geographical coverage of the radio from the most northerly province to the most southern simultaneously functions emblematically as a sort of linguistic marker of the nation. Interestingly, this vignette has never been translated into a national language (cf. Matusse 1993).
15. A fascinating topic for further research would be to investigate what forms of resistance to FRELIMO language policies, if any, occurred among everyday people in hidden, intimate or public contexts. Dinerman (1994) mentions how peasants as a protest against collective farms, built the farms as they were obliged to, but did not live within them. She also mentions the example of how old regulos (Portuguese appointed chiefs), officially divested of their traditional authority by FRELIMO, found new ways to regain/retain their power by proxy through ensuring that close relatives and dependents get elected in their stead. Both of these techniques can succeed in carrying resistance because both build on a show of public complicity with the authority of FRELIMO. (see Scott 1985, for similar examples of economic resistance

among Javanese peasants). Similar forms of resistance for language may also have created pockets of opposition and evasion slap in the middle of public space. But this is a matter for investigation.

16. However, these practical contingencies are surely not the primary reason for the extended, national use of Portuguese. This must be seen as a consequence of the party's ideological stance. For example, in some cases, FRELIMO consciously engineered this type of situation. Teachers for example were transferred to areas where they did not master the local language, ostensibly to ensure their sole use of Portuguese in the classroom Today, as times change, administrators are required —on paper, anyway— to master at least one of the local or regional languages of their districts.
17. At independence, FRELIMO had taken over the apparatus of the Portuguese colonial state, inserting itself into the spaces left by the departing colonialists and the blueprint for much post-independence development had in a sense already been drawn up by the Portuguese when they were masters of the country. FRELIMO adopted much of this, as they did the machinery to make it work. However, as pointed out by many authors (e.g. Firmino 1995, Abrahamsson and Nilsson 1995), this made it necessary to co-opt Portuguese speaking elites to run these state machineries.
18. In the late 1960s, the FRELIMO movement had been plagued by internal disputes between younger, Algerian trained FRELIMO activists and an older generation on a number of issues to do with the management of the so-called liberated areas. These issues touched on the question of FRELIMO's relation to traditional power embodied in the Makonde chiefs, its stand on production policies and control of production, and its views on tribalism/regionalism (Vines 1991: 5–6). Samora Machel on numerous occasions publically characterized tribalism as infiltration (cf Abrahamsson and Nilsson 1995).
19. Other authors read the available documents from this time differently. Firmino (1995) for example, in his excellent and comprehensive review of Mozambican language politics notes how public debates during the 1980s have tended to focus on the valorization of transformed "Mozambican Portuguese" as well as the celebration by e.g. Graça Machel of national languages. However, the documents he cites, some of which I also rely on here, contain passages which permit a different and quite contrary reading. Taking the sociopolitical climate of the time into consideration as well as other material, such as letters to the editor, etc. there is firm justification for exploring and highlighting this contrary reading of the materials.
20. In fact, there is a semblance of a claim in the text that recognizing Portuguese as the nation's official language is almost a prerequisite for the development and cultivation of national languages, the idea being that the expressive potential of African languages would be enhanced through loans and translations from Portuguese.
21. The emphasis on Portuguese even invaded spaces that were a priori intended for African languages. Graça Machel opened the 1st Conference on Mozam-

bican Languages in 1988 with a lengthy speech reiterating the history and national importance of Portuguese.

22. Matusse (1995) mentions in an interesting aside that one of the concerns of the editor of *Tempo* at the time was whether the letters should be corrected linguistically or allowed to stand as they were written —in an appropriated Portuguese.
23. In conjunction with the recent elections, a major televised scandal that gave echoes for weeks after in the daily press was that of a candidate party leader and runner for victory in the first free elections who was judged not to speak Portuguese well enough. This totally discredited him in the eyes of his constituency.
24. A recent contemporary reminder of the turbulent history of frontier making was when factions in the Swazi government laid lay claims to the province of Maputo.
25. The other side of the coin of allegiance to Portuguese can be found in articles by Honwana, and even earlier in the writings of the 1983 language policy document, which wrestle with the political significance and implications of different ways of referring to Mozambique —as a Lusophone country, a member of the countries with Portuguese as official language etc.
26. An invited paper presented to AMOLP (Associação Moçambicana da Língua Portuguesa) at the National Organization of Journalists together with contributions by Magaia and Honwana, among others.
27. National languages are currently enjoying great attention in terms of trial bilingual education programs. The current Minister of Education, A. Nhavoto, has made this issue an important part of his political platform (see Stroud ftc.).
28. For a very relevant and quite similar account of ideology, cultural politics and language debates in another African state, Tanzania, the reader is referred to Madumulla, Bertoncini and Blommaert (this volume).

References

Abrahamsson, H. and A. Nilsson
1995 *Mozambique: The Troubled Transition. From Socialist Construction to Free Market Capitalism.* London: Zed Books.

Anderson, Benedict
1983 *Imagined Communities: Reflections on the Origin and Spread of Nationalism.* London: Verso.

Balibar, Étienne and Immanuel Wallerstein
1991 *Race, Nation, Class: Ambiguous Identities*. New York: Praeger.

Bhaba, Homi (ed.)
1990 *Nation and Narration*. New York: Routledge.

Bredin, Miles
1994 *Blood on the Tracks. A Rail Journey from Angola to Mozambique*. London: Picador.

Briggs, Charles
1992 Linguistic ideologies and the naturalization of power in Warao discourse. In: Kroskrity, Paul, Bambi Schieffelin and Kathryn Woolard (eds.), *Language Ideologies*, 387–400. (Special issue of *Pragmatics* 2, 235–453).

Dinerman, A.
1994 In search of Mozambique. The imaginings of Christian Geffray in 'La Cause des Armes au Mozambique. Anthropologie d'une Guerre Civile'. *Journal of Southern African Studies*, 20: 569–586.

Feldman, Allen
1991 *Formations of Violence. The Narrative of the Body and Political Terror in Northern Ireland.* Chicago: The University of Chicago Press.

Firmino, G.
1995 Revisiting the "language question" in post-colonial Africa: The case of Portuguese and indigenous languages in Mozambique. Unpublublished thesis, Eduardo Mondlane University, Maputo.

Gabinete do Secretário de Estado da Cultura, MEC
1983 *Contribuição para a Definição de uma Política Linguística na República Popular de Moçambique*. Maputo.

Ganhão, F.
1979 O papel da língua Portuguesa em Moçambique. Paper presented at the 1st National Seminar on the Teaching of the Portuguese Language, Maputo.

Gal, Susan
1991 Bartók's Funeral: Representations of Europe in Hungarian political Rhetoric. *American Ethnologist* 18: 440–458.

1992 Multiplicity and contention among ideologies: A commentary. In: Kroskrity, Paul, Bambi. Schieffelin and Kathryn Woolard (eds.), *Language Ideologies*, 445–450. (Special issue of *Pragmatics* 2, 235–453).

1995 Language and the "arts of resistance". *Cultural Anthropology* 10: 407–424.

Gonçalves, P.
1996 *Português de Moçambique: Uma Variedade em Formação*. Maputo: Livraria Universitária e Faculdade de Letras da UEM.

Gross, J.
1993 The politics of unofficial language use. Walloon in Belgium, Tamazight in Morocco. *Critique of Anthropology* 13: 177–208.

Hanlon, J.
1991 *Mozambique. Who Calls the Shots*? London: James Currey.

Hermele, K.
1987 *En ekonomi i spillror. Moçambiques koloniala arv. Moçambique. Kulturhuset Stockholm, 6 Feb-5 Apr 87*. Stockholm: Ljunglöfs.

1988 *Land Struggles and Social Differentiation in Southern Mozambique*. Scandinavian Institue of International Affairs, Uppsala; Research Report 82.

Higonnet, P.
1980 The politics of linguistic terrorism and grammatical hegemony during the French revolution. *Social History* 5: 41–69.

Honwana, L.
1994 *Jornal de Letras, artes e ideais*, XIV(615), 22–23, Lisboa.

Lopes, A. J.
1997 *Política Linguística: Princípios e problemas*. Maputo: Livraria Universitária, UEM.

1997 Language policy in Mozambique: A taboo? In: Herbert, Robert K. (ed.), *African Linguistics at the Crossroads: Papers from Kwaluseni 1994*. Köln: Rudiger Köppe Verlag, 485–500.

Machel, G.
1979 Discurso de abertura. Paper presented at the 1st National Seminar on the Teaching of Portuguese, Maputo.

Malkki, Liisa H.
1995 *Purity and Exile. Violence, Memory and National Cosmology among Hutu Refugees in Tanzania*. Chicago: University of Chicago Press.

Marshall, J.
1993 *Literacy, Power and Democracy in Mozambique. The Governance of Learning from Colonization to the Present*. San Francisco: Westview Press.

Matusse, Renato
1995 *Português: De Língua de Assimilação à Lingua de Unidade Nacional.* Communicação apresentada no II Seminário sobre Transição democratica em Moçambique, Beira, 16 a 20 Outubro.
1997 The future of Portuguese in Mozambique. In: Herbert, Robert K. (ed.), *African Linguistics at the Crossroads:Papers from Kwaluseni 1994.* Köln: Rudiger Köppe Verlag, 541–554.

Mbembe, A.
1992a The banality of power and aesthetics of vulgarity in the postcolony. *Public Culture* 4, 1–30.
1992b Prosaics of servitude and authoritarian civilities. *Public Culture* 5, 123–145.

Mondlane, Eduardo C.
1969 *Lutar por Moçambique.* Lisboa: Livraria Sá da Costa Editora.
1983 *O Sistema Nacional de Educação e a Situação Multilingue do País.* Unpublished paper.

Paixo, B.
1948 *Educação Política e Política Educacional.* Lisboa: Ática SARL.

Poulantzas, Nikos
1980 *State, Power, Socialism.* London:Verso.
1993 Proposta de política cultural de Moçambique, Conferência Nacional sobre cultura, Ministério da Cultura e Juventude, Maputo.

Ribeiro, Fátima
1994 Preserver e divulgar o português, uma das línguas "nacionais" de Moçambique. Special issue of *Português em cordel*, Feb. 1994, 2–6.

Rosário, L.
1982 Língua portuguesa e cultura Moçambicana. De instrumento de consciência e unidade nacional a veículo e expressão de identitade cultural. *Cadernos de Literatura, Coimbra,* 58–66.
1993 *Língua Portuguesa e expressão moçambicana. Discursos: Estudos de língua e literatura Portuguesa, Coimbra* 3: 109–120.

Scott, J. C.
1985 *Weapons of the Weak: Everyday Forms of Peasant Resistance.* New Haven: Yale University Press.
1990 *Domination and the Arts of Resistance: Hidden Transcripts.* New Haven: Yale University Press.

Searle, C.
1984 *Words Unchained. Language and Revolution in Granada*. London: Zed Press.

Siliya, C. J.
1996 *Ensaio Sobre a Cultura em Moçambique*. Maputo: CEGRAF.

Spencer, J.
1990 Writing within: Anthropology, nationalism and culture in Sri Lanka. *Current Anthropology* 31: 283–300.

Stroud, Christopher
The national language question in Mozambique: Towards a concept of linguistic citizenship [forthcoming].

Stroud, Christopher and António Tuzine
Portuguese in the age of Mozambican multiparty politics [forthcoming].

Urla, Jacqueline
1993 Contesting modernities. Language standardization and the production of an ancient/modern Basque culture. *Critique of Anthropology* 13: 101–118.

Vines, A.
1991 *RENAMO. From Terrorism to Democracy in Mozambique*. London: Villiers Publications.

Flemish nationalism in the Belgian Congo versus Zairian anti-imperialism: Continuity and discontinuity in language ideological debates

Michael Meeuwis

1. Three introductory notes

1.1. Historical and geographical situation

This chapter reports on language ideologies and language ideological debates in the Democratic Republic of Congo (formerly Zaire). The cases documented upon are drawn from two epochs in the history of this country, i.e. the epoch of Belgian colonization (±1880–1960) and the epoch of the republic of Zaire (1965–1997).

In 1879, two years after he completed his westward expedition along the Congo river, H.M. Stanley took service under Leopold II, king of the Belgians. At the king's request, during the following five years Stanley founded a number of stations along the river from which to organize further explorations and military conquests. During the same period, this part of Central Africa was also being penetrated by European missionaries. The first missionaries to arrive were Protestants: the Livingstone Inland Mission and the Baptist Missionary Society founded mission stations in the lower Congo area in 1878 and 1879, respectively. The first Catholic mission stations were established by the Priests of the Holy Spirit in the same lower Congo area in 1880 and, in the same year, by the White Fathers on the western shore of Lake Tanganyika. All these Catholic and Protestant congregations soon expanded the number of mission stations in their respective regions and were rapidly followed by other congregations.

By the time of the Berlin conference in 1884–1885, Stanley and his team of administrators, explorers, and settlers had provided Leopold II with a *de facto* dominion over the territory. At this conference, the king succeeded in securing a *de jure* recognition of his possessions. The "Congo Free State", as these possessions were baptized a few months after the conference, remained the king's private property. But free access was granted to entrepeneurs, traders, and missionaries from all Western countries without restrictions or discriminatory privileges as to their nationalities.

On November 15, 1908 Leopold II devolved his powers over the Congo Free State to the Belgian government, marking the start of the history of "the Belgian Congo" properly speaking. The Congo became independent on June 30, 1960, after which it was called the "Republic of the Congo" and later the "Democratic Republic of the Congo". The country's name was changed again in October 1971, when Mobutu, in power since 1965, installed the "Republic of Zaire". Mobutu's reign lasted 32 years. This chapter was in preparation when Laurent-Désiré Kabila completed a 7-month military campaign, eventually leading to the ousting of president Mobutu. On May 17, 1997, Kabila's troops took over the capital Kinshasa, and in a speech delivered the next day Kabila announced the birth of the new "Democratic Republic of Congo".

1.2. The issue

Language ideological debates, or the individual positions that are their building blocks, may be subsequently effective at two levels: (i) the level of debates and ideologies themselves and (ii) the level of language structure and spread. Effectiveness of the first type refers to the maintenance, transformation, and loss of language ideologies through the influence of earlier language ideologies and debates. Effectiveness of the second type pertains to the way in which debates and language ideologies (and their maintenance, transformations, etc.) induce forms of real language change "on the ground". The latter phenomenon is well-documented in the linguistic-anthropological literature (e.g. Mertz 1989; Meeuwis and Brisard 1993; Woolard 1989, 1992; Woolard and Schieffelin 1994).

It must be kept in mind that in both types, effectiveness may but need not always be the mark of language ideological debates. However important ("loud") they may be at the time of their occurrence, some debates may turn out not to be formative at all. Other debates may be formative at only one of the two levels.

In this chapter, I want to reconstruct a debate which has left remarkably few or no traces in terms of language ideologies, but which has been quite consequential at the level of the geographical spread and the structural features of the languages involved. The debate took place among Belgian missionary-linguists working in, and on, the Congo from the 1880s up to independence in 1960. It is well-known that the first linguists (and ethnographers) in most European colonies, especially in Africa, were missionaries (e.g. Welmers 1971; Raison-Jourde 1977; Yates 1980, 1987; Fabian 1984, 1991 [1983], 1986; Samarin 1989c; Hovdhaugen (ed.) 1996). The debate I shall discuss (which was surely not the only linguistic debate among the linguists of the colony) centered around the question as to whether the colonization, "civilization", "education", etc. of the Africans should proceed on the basis of the usage of African lingua francae (such as Lingala and Swahili, among others) or on the basis of the African languages spoken in smaller areas of distribution, i.e. the so-called "vernacular", "local", or "ethnic" languages. The positions taken in this debate have had lasting effects "on the ground": they led to dramatic changes in the geographical spread and in the grammatical structure of the languages that were discussed. The parties agreed that processes of pidginization, including influences from foreign languages, had "corrupted" the lingua francae so much that they were structurally too "poor" and culturally too "detached" from their target populations to be used in their education, Christianization, etc. In order to overcome this "problem", the advocates of the lingua francae soon started coining long lists of lexical items, often accompanied by newly elaborated grammatical norms, which they then transmitted to the Africans through the colonial educational system and through their religious practices. In addition, they introduced the usage of these languages in regions where the Africans had never spoken or heard them before, and where they thus had to learn them as foreign languages. The current geographical areas of expansion of these languages must indeed be traced back to these forms of organized spread in early colonial times (e.g. Meeuwis 1997).

The defenders of the vernacular languages, on the other hand, emphasized the descriptive, non-interventionist task of linguists and warned against the moral turpitude and culturally alienating effects of imposing ethnoculturally exogenous languages, even if these languages were also of African origin. Some protagonists of this view drew on a background of Flemish nationalism which they had developed during their formative years in Belgium (and which they often also continued developing in the colony). Many of them were sympathizers, if not active participants, of the movement which had arisen in Flanders since Belgium's independence in 1830 and which demanded equal linguistic and cultural rights in a society marked by the frenchification of public life. Their "exportations" of Flemish nationalism to the Congo, and the applications to the languages of the colony, will be one of the main foci of attention in this chapter.

At the level of subsequent language ideologies, on the other hand, the colonial debate appears to have "faded out" in postcolonial times. In the postcolonial Congo and in Mobutu's Zaire, the opposition between lingua francae on the one hand and vernacular languages on the other was almost completely absent from the dominant linguistic debates and ideological expressions. In the international context of anti-imperialism and anti-colonialism, it was soon replaced by a discourse in which the main opposition was the one between all the African languages on the one hand (i.e., with no reference to their relative statuses as lingua francae or vernaculars), and French, as the language of the former colonizer, on the other hand.

I will start the documentary part of my argument with a brief description of these language ideologies in Zairian times, which will then allow me to devote the bulk of my contribution to the earlier debate between the colonial linguists and to the impact of Flemish nationalism. It must be mentioned, at this point, that if the postcolonial, "Zairian" debate is said to be discontinuous with regard to this earlier colonial one, this does not mean that it came out of the blue. Nor do I intend to deny that it was partly —in addition to the international context of anti-imperialism— inspired by other colonial ideological antecedents than the ones selected here. The perspective of my argument is historically linear, drawing attention to the fact that language ideological debates clearly identifiable at one moment in history may almost completely disappear from the scene of meta-discourses in subsequent times, however elaborate and explicit they may have been at their own time of occurrence and, most importantly, however lasting their effects may have been at the level of linguistic structure and language spread.

Before proceeding to the documentary part, some methodological remarks with regard to the exportation of Flemish nationalism to the Congo are in order. This exportation has already been suggested by a small number of students of Belgian colonialism, but the research tradition these scholars represent is marked by a methodological gap. This gap presents itself in a fairly essentialist focus on abstract ideological "systems", rather than on identifiable agents of such ideologies and on the historical and geographical contingencies of their biographies.

1.3. Colonialism and historiographic method

In his book on *Colonialism's Culture*, Nicholas Thomas starts off with the remark that "it is becoming increasingly clear that only localized theories and historically specific accounts can provide much insight into the varied articulations of colonizing and counter-colonial representations and practices" (1994: ix). Thomas takes much of the work done in postcolonial critique to task for presenting a depersonalized, homogenizing, and essentialist view of colonial ideology. Drawing on the writings of scholars such as

Bourdieu, he advocates a theory and methodology in which an emphasis on "located subjectivities informs an analytic strategy which situates colonial representations and narratives in terms of agents, locations and periods" (1994: 8). The end result must be a more differentiated view, allowing for the appreciation of "colonialisms" rather than "colonialism" (without, however, losing sight of larger historical and geographical traces which these colonialisms represent and reproduce).

The historiography of language ideologies and linguistic practices (including references to ethnicity and culture) that mediated the Belgians' political and economic colonization of the Congo, and more in particular the link between language ideologies at work in the colony and Flemish nationalism, is in need of exactly this kind of methodological renewal. This link has been previously identified by a number of Africanists (e.g. Yates 1980: 262–263; Young 1965: 248–249, 1976: 193; Verhaegen 1971: 9), but treatment on the topic has so far been characterized by a marked preference for a historiography of "ideas-without-people". In almost all cases, this leads to unfortunate generalizations. In the works mentioned above, observations with regard to Flemish nationalism in the Congo are cursory (an average of one paragraph), as the authors fail to move beyond brief observations of "a similarity" in ideological systems in the Congo and in Flanders. As such, they stop short of providing extensive information on individual biographies and actions. As will be explained below, the introduction and "spread" of Flemish nationalism among certain linguists in the colony was the work of concrete individuals, whose life histories reveal distinctive and highly variable ties to the Flemish nationalist cause in Belgium.

The generalizations resulting from the lack of attention to this kind of individual differentiation are clearest in Barbara Yates's account (1980: 263). She simplifies matters to a view of "the Flemish being against French, in the Congo as in Belgium" in observations such as "many Belgian Catholic missionaries spoke Flemish [and] were reluctant to propagate French because of the perennial linguistic-cultural conflict in Belgium between the Flemings and Walloons" (1980: 263). One type of exportation of Flemish nationalism to the Congo indeed consisted in some Flemish colonials (mostly members of the state or juridical personnel) claiming the right to use Dutch on an equal legal basis as French in their contacts with the colonial administration (see, e.g., the positions taken in the colonial monthly *Band* 1956; also, Van Bilsen 1950; Polomé 1968; Lupukisa 1979). But as will also become clear below, the reluctance of certain Catholic missionaries to use French had very little to do with this type of Flemish nationalism. This exportation of Flemish nationalims did not manifest itself in a dislike of French in particular, but rather in a complex "ideology of the natural", in which the target of criticism was not so much this one language in particular, as any form of linguistic and cultural intervention implying the corruption of the authenticity of ethnic groups.

The equally cursory accounts by scholars such as Crawford Young (1965) and Benoît Verhaegen (1971) do not fall victim to this misconception and understand the role of the ideology of the natural as a theory (and thus as case-independent). Moreover, in contrast to accounts cast in terms of the "anonymous Fleming", Young and Verhaegen provide names, times, and places. Still, they do not establish whether, and to what extent, these "real people" actually drew on individual backgrounds of Flemish activism in Belgium and, if so, whether and how they also applied their Flemish nationalism to the linguistic situations they were confronted with in the colony. The result is yet another type of generalization: the identified individuals are assumed to "carry" an ideology of the natural "because" they were Flemish, and not because of their individually distinctive histories in Flanders. Consider the following paragraph taken from Young (1965), and especially the closing sentence:

> It was the task of four major writers, three missionaries and an administrator, to accredit the thesis of a single Mongo people [one of the ethnic groups of the central Congo basin, see also below, MM]. These four, E. Boelaert, G. Hulstaert, E.P. A. de Rop, and Georges Vanderkerken [sic], became dedicated advocates of Mongohood; Vanderkerken [sic] urged the unification of the Mongo in a single province, Boelaert after independence called for the creation of a Mongo state, and all urged the fusion of Mongo dialects into a single Lomongo, to be used both in education and administration. It is no mere coincidence that all four were Flemish; the parallels are striking between what was advocated for the Mongo and demands then formulated by the growing Flemish nationalist movement for the unification and development of their language and people.
>
> (Young 1965: 248–249)

Was each of these four Flemish men also an actual sympathizer of the "growing Flemish nationalist movement", or did this movement simply grow "alongside" them, as has been the case for so many Flemish people? If they were sympathizers, to what extent? And to what extent did their possible nationalisms actually affect their linguistic views and practices in the colony? Surely, many Flemish missionaries (or other colonials) were not supporters of the Flemish nationalist cause, and many of those who were did not at all find it appropriate to apply this nationalism to the linguistic situation in the colony. The "striking parallels" which Young detects are parallels between abstract ideological systems across different geographical locations and do not refer to continuities within concrete biographies. On the basis of such an approach, contrasting linguistic views advocated by equally ardent nationalists cannot be accounted for; nor can protagonists acting as "sources" for the spread of their Flemish-nationalist language ideologies among non-nationalists be identified. Historiographic data to fill these documentary gaps have, nonetheless, long been available (though mostly exclusively in Dutch) and make such analytic strategies as the one suggested by Nicholas Thomas a feasible enterprise.

2. French versus African languages in the postcolonial debate

The sociolinguistic profile of post-independence Zaire was made up, roughly, of one official language, French, a set of vernacular languages of limited geographical distribution, and four languages of wider distribution, viz. Kikongo, Swahili, Lingala, and Tshiluba. These four languages were privileged in specific social domains, such as education, jurisdiction, the administration, and the media. Despite this *de facto* pattern of diglossia — which was, moreover, marked throughout by many leaks (French or the vernacular languages being used instead when this was judged appropriate for reasons of linguistic competence, etc.)— Kikongo, Swahili, Lingala, and Tshiluba never enjoyed any explicit legal status in Zaire. According to studies conducted by the authors of the *Atlas Linguistique du Zaïre* (Kadima et al. 1983), as well as by Boguo (1988: 55), Matumele (1987: 189), Ngalasso (1986: 16), and Sesep (1988: 3), there was no statement in the Zairian constitution nor in any other Zairian law which explicitly identified these four languages as a specific subclass within the totality of the African languages or which assigned a specific geographical region to each of them. The same, though with certain exceptions, goes for the legislation relative to language use in education. As the series of official decrees and instructions relative to primary and secondary education promulgated since 1960 attests (see CEREDIP 1986), Zairian educational policy makers more than once shifted their position as to whether the medium of instruction was to be French or one of the country's African languages, but this latter category was almost always called upon as one monolithic block, irrespective of a language's status as lingua franca or vernacular. Even if some of the recommendations made by semi-official advisory commissions, such as the 1984 "National Commission of Reform", did mention the four lingua francae as the preferred media of instruction in kindergarten and primary education, their suggestions too, were dominated by an opposition between the ex-colonial and "foreign" language, French, on the one hand, and the totality of the "country's own" languages on the other.

In a considerable portion of the Western sociolinguistic literature on Zaire, it is presupposed that Kikongo, Swahili, Lingala, and Tshiluba were Zaire's four "national languages", which is believed to be an established terminological distinction setting these languages apart from the official language French and from Zaire's many vernacular languages. *Within* Zaire, however, the term "national languages" ('*langues nationales*') was not always used in such a clearly distinctive and unambiguous way (an observation also made by the above-mentioned authors of the *Atlas*, 1983: 13). In the educational legislation referred to above, in the semi-legal recommendations made by the commissions, in the media, in politicians' talk, in academic writings by Zairian linguists, as well as in all informal speech on language issues, the term "national languages" was often a synonym of terms such as "the African languages", "the Zairian languages", "our own languages", "the Bantu languages", "the indigenous languages", and so on. As such, it was an inclusive term, referring to the totality of Zaire's languages of African origin, as opposed to the European language French and without differentiating between lingua francae and vernaculars. In some cases, a Zairian author or speaker would alternate between this inclusive denotation and a more restrictive one, effectively using the term to refer to the set of four languages (Kikongo, Swahili, Lingala, and Tshiluba) in particular. In these cases, however, he or she would mostly be careful to add the number or any other clarification, such as in "the four national languages" (from Nyembwe 1987: 124), "our four national languages" (from Kazadi 1987: 287), "the four 'national' languages (Tshiluba, Swahili, Lingala and Kikongo)" (from Kambaji 1987: 99), etc.[1] These clarifications were necessary because the term "national languages" did not always unambiguously refer to Kikongo, Swahili, Lingala, and Tshiluba. In sum, no thorough conceptual and terminological distinction between these four major languages and the vernaculars was respected, indicative of the low argumentative relevance that was attributed to such a distinction.

Soon after his rise to power in November 1965, Mobutu and his unitary party the *Mouvement Populaire de la Révolution* (MPR), designed the state ideology commonly referred to as *recours à l'authenticité*, *nationalisme zaïrois authentique*, or, simply, *authenticité* (e.g. Gould 1980; Kangafu 1973; Meeuwis 1997; Pauwels 1981; Schatzberg 1988). The basic tenets of *authenticité* reflected a concern with the "mental decolonization" of the Africans. The new state's citizens were said to be strongly alienated from their African roots after decades of colonialism and cultural paternalism. Through *authenticité*, Mobutu wanted the Zairians to regain respect for "their own" cultural identity after decades of looking up to the Western model. The ideology of *authenticité* is best known for its complex set of surface-level symbols (clothing, names, familial jurisdiction, etc.) which served to promote and monitor the loyalty of the population towards the official doctrine. However, given its far-reaching articulation and symbolic elaboration, one of the most striking features of *authenticité* was its lack of a linguistic program (see the contributions to Kazadi and Nyembwe (eds.) 1987; Ngalasso 1986; Nyunda 1986a, 1986b, among many others). After the conception of *authenticité* in the late 1960s and early 1970s, the Zairian authorities hardly ever incorporated the country's African languages into their arguments for the revalorization of traditional African culture, notwithstanding a few ephemeral cases.[2]

From the early 1970s onwards, this lack of a linguistic program in *authenticité* caused fierce reactions on behalf of certain Zairian linguists and other intellectuals concerned with sociocultural issues. The reactions were voiced in an important number of individual publications (Boguo 1988; Bokamba 1976; Kamwangamalu 1997; Kilanga and Bwanga 1988; Mazala and Bwanga 1988; Mbula 1990; Mbulamoko 1991; Muwoko 1991; Nyembwe 1986, 1993; Nyunda 1986a, 1986b; Sesep 1986, 1988), as well as in two national conferences, viz. the "Seminar of Zairian Linguists", held in Lubumbashi on May 22–26, 1974, and the "Conference on the Use of the National Languages in Education and in the Sociocultural Domain", held in Kinshasa on March 11–16, 1985 (Kazadi and Nyembwe (eds.) 1987).[3] The key notion in the linguists' reactions was that of contradiction. These intellectuals found it incomprehensible that a movement such as *authenticité*, which rightly advocated the decolonization of the mind and the return to authentic African values, was devoid of an agenda for fostering the country's African languages. In their vocabulary, language and culture were treated as organic bodies, intricately related to each other. Their claim was that French was a Trojan horse, the linguistic-cultural genius of which led to the cultural alienation of the Zairians. Only the African languages were able to convey the authentic culture and "spirit" of the Zairians. The following quote may serve as an example of this vocabulary.

> Indeed, the French "graft" on the Zairian soul leaves a bitter taste, i.e. an alienated Zairian, who has been turned away from her or his authenticity, from her or his ontological frame of perception, of cognition, of internalization, of reading and of social reality ... In order to enhance the Zairian people's sociocultural, political and socioeconomic integration, it is in our

> ruling body's interest to fight this *francophrénie* and to promote the education of the Zairians from early childhood to adulthood in Zairian languages ... [S]pecial attention should be paid to the education of the Zairian youth in Zairian languages, because this allows them to better perceive, internalize, and resolve the problems their specific environment confronts them with, in the light of the philosophy of *authenticité* conveyed by these languages.
>
> (Kambaji 1987: 98–103)

A number of intellectuals (e.g. Nsuka-zi-Kabuiku 1987) recommended the complete eradication of French from Zairian society, including in the highest official and administrative milieus. French, in their eyes, was nothing but a transitory necessity. Others (e.g. Kambaji 1987) only wanted to reduce the role of French in favor of the African languages, which were to be officially recognized and promoted in education, the media, and other domains. Even if specific suggestions were made as to which particular African language(s) was (were) to be promoted to official and national levels (e.g. Bokamba 1976 and Mataba 1987 for Lingala; Kamwangamalu 1997 for Swahili), authors as a rule attributed only secondary argumentative prominence to this issue, bringing it in as an afterthought to their overall case against French and in favor of the group of African languages as a whole.

It was presupposed that the damaging effects of introducing foreign languages and cultures only applied to European languages, but not to foreign African ones. French was an imposed language and was alien to the age-old cultural heritage and mentality of the Africans, but languages brought in from different areas of the enormous republic were not, because they were "African". Any African language spoken in Zaire was typologically cognate to the other languages, and thus closer to a Zairian's inner being than French in terms of the cultural genius, values, traditions, etc. it communicated. Therefore, the organized dissemination of one or a very limited number of African languages throughout the entire republic, including in regions where they counted as foreign languages, was never considered a relevant issue. Kamwangamalu's publication made this part of the ideology explicit:

> instruction in the national language [which Kamwangamalu suggests should be Swahili, MM] can be a natural substitute for instruction in the mother tongue. Also, compared to French, the mother tongue and the national language are far more related and have much more in common, whether in terms of cultural values or in terms of traditions.
>
> (Kamwangamalu 1997: 77)

In a similar vein, one of the conclusions shared by the scientists participating in the 1985 conference in Kinshasa was that "at the actual stage of Zaire's sociolinguistic situation, there is no apparent conflict between mother tongue and vehicular language" (Kazadi 1987: 286).

Thus, distinctions within the group of African languages, either in terms of status (lingua franca versus vernacular) or in terms of geographical or typological distance, were not prominent in the language ideologies of these Zairian intellectuals. Their debate was dominated by positions in favor of or against French, and thus entailed a homogenizing representation of the African languages. The language ideologies and language ideological debates were, in other words, cast in a binary opposition between French as a symbolic and material attribute of (neo-)colonialism and imperialism on the one hand, and the totality of the African languages as indexes and carriers of authentic culture on the other.

This ideological organization must be linked up with the political wave of anti-colonialism and anti-imperialism that marked the whole of sub-Saharan Africa in the 1960s and 1970s (see, among many others, Mazrui 1967, 1978; Young 1982; see Madumulla et al., this volume for a link with language ideologies). *Authenticité* itself was such an anti-colonialist and anti-imperialist nationalist ideology, and its architects explicitly situated it alongside other trends in the wave of cultural reawakening in Africa. It is important to keep in mind, in this respect, that this wave of reawakening was not a uniform movement across the continent, but displayed fragmentation along political, regional, and even individual lines. The wave opposed Marxists to opportunists, socialists to populists, pan-Africanists to regionalists, etc. With regard to the position of *authenticité*, then, affinities must be sought primarily with those movements that drew substantially on philosophical and humanistic theories (in contrast to those movements in which the political, "down-to-earth" message was foregrounded). As such, the connection of *authenticité* with Senghor's strongly philosophical and humanistic *négritude* was manifest. Mobutu himself declared:

> President Senghor, of whom I've read many publications, has been a model for me. I welcomed his appointment to the *Académie française* as a token of recognition of the rationality and dignity of the Black man. Because the *négritude* which he preached and the *authenticité* which I defend are but one ...
>
> (Mobutu 1989: 36)

Now, if the Zairian linguists mentioned above were in one way or another dissatisfied with the state ideology of *authenticité*, they were only so because of its lack of radicalism. Their objections must, therefore, not be seen as reactionary or moderating with regard to the MPR and its state ideology, but, quite on the contrary, as a form of "ideological hypercorrection" (Meeuwis 1997: 120–126). The "critics" mentioned were part of that body of Zairian intellectuals that counted as the most fervent and loyal followers of Mobutu and the MPR. As the quote from Kambaji shows, their demands for the integration of a linguistic program were not at all aimed at destabilizing, but rather at consolidating the state ideology of *authenticité*. As such, they also wanted to consolidate its role in the transnational mission of African emancipation. They argued that a more radically developed *authenticité* would better serve the struggle of the new African nations against imperialism and neo-colonialism. The urge for a radicalization of *authenticité* on the basis of a state-organized linguistic project, and the ensuing twofold distinction between French on the one hand and the "African" languages as an undifferentiated group on the other, were thus essentially contingent upon the historical situation of Zaire in post-independence Africa.

3. Flemish nationalism and the ideology of the natural in the Congo

3.1. Preliminary remarks: Missionaries and the community of linguists in the colony

As noted in section 1.2 above, missionaries were of primary importance in the first descriptions of the languages found in king Leopold's territory and in the later Belgian colony. On top of this, the first introductions of Flemish nationalist ideology as an ideology of the natural and its application to the territory's linguistic landscape, were also the achievements of missionaries. In what follows, I elaborate on the work of three missionaries in this respect, i.e. A. Vyncke, E. Van Hencxthoven, and G. Hulstaert. Vyncke and Van Hencxthoven, who worked in the Congo between 1880 and the turn of the century, are selected because they represent the oldest cases for which written documents (mostly biographies and editions of their correspondence or diaries) illustrating the introduction of the ideology of the natural exist. Hulstaert arrived in the Congo later on (1925), but he must be included because he was the most influential and most theoretically elaborate proponent of this ideology throughout the entire history of the Belgian Congo. It is a historical fact that in the first years of his linguistic ideologization Hulstaert worked together with a number of other colonials (such as his confrere E. Boelaert and the administrator G. van der Kerken), who had been interested in similar issues since their arrival in the Congo and who were a major source of inspiration to Hulstaert. Nevertheless, of all the linguists who worked in the Congo, it was Hulstaert who most invigorated and theorized the ideology of the natural as based on Flemish nationalism. Through his many scholarly activities and writings, as well as through a massive correspondence, he also disseminated and promoted the ideology among other linguists, and so turned the issue into the object of a public debate.

The group of missionary and other linguists in the colony was not some abstract body without tangible essence or visible only with the benefit of hindsight. Instead, it represented a network of a fairly restricted number of individuals, most of whom knew each other personally or at least professionally, and among whom many immediate exchanges and discussions took place on a regular basis. At least in the years leading up to the end of World War II, the amount of work done by the totality of researchers always remained readily surveyable. Correspondence on linguistic matters and statement-reply discussion papers published in scientific journals were not exceptional, nor were opportunities for meetings such as the Sessions of the Royal Belgian Colonial Institute (*Séances de l'Institut Royal Colonial Belge —Zittingen van het Koninklijk Belgisch Koloniaal Instituut*). In this context, Hulstaert was an important "source" for the spread of nationalist views among other linguists, including those who did not at all sympathize with the Flemish nationalist cause. As I already suggested, through his massive body of publications, as well as through an ongoing correspondence with any colonial administrator, politician, scientist, missionary, or other individual who was in one way or another involved in linguistic policy making or linguistic description, Hulstaert organized what may legitimately be called a wholesale "campaign" for the cause. Hulstaert was a polemic figure, cursed by many, adulated by some, but unavoidable for all.

3.2. Two early missionaries: Amaat Vyncke and Emiel Van Hencxthoven

The missionaries of the order of the White Fathers (*Pères Blancs*, officially *Société des Missionnaires d'Afrique)*, founded in Algiers in 1868 by the French Mgr. Lavigerie, were the first Catholic missionaries to arrive in the eastern parts of what would later become the Congo Free State and the Belgian Congo. Via the caravan routes that started from Zanzibar and Bagamoyo (on the East African coast), the White Fathers first reached the Lake Tanganyika area in 1879 and founded the first mission station of the western lake shore in 1880, namely at Mulweba on the extreme northwestern point of the lake (Delathuy 1992; Heremans 1966; Markowitz 1973). In June 1883, another mission station was founded at Kibanga, a town situated slightly more south on the same western lake shore. The White Fathers of this first period of territorial penetration and initial settlement were all French. The first Flemish missionary to have worked as a White Father on the western shore of Lake Tanganyika was Amaat Vyncke (1850–1888), who arrived in the mission station of Kibanga in January 1884 (*Xaveriana* 1927; Craeynest [1945]).[4]

Amaat Vyncke learned Swahili in Zanzibar, the "waiting room" for all European explorers and missionaries bound for the Great Lakes. On his way west, Swahili was the language he used most often with the leaders, porters, soldiers, and other Arab and African people in the caravan, as well as with the local rulers with whom the caravan had to negotiate. Swahili was also the language used by the White Fathers in the missions already established before Vyncke's arrival, such as in Rumonge and Ujiji on the eastern lake shore and in Mulweba and Kibanga. Thus, during his first years at Kibanga, Vyncke adopted his confreres' and superiors' use of Swahili. Both in the East African region crossed by the caravans and around the Tanganyika lake shores, Vyncke or any other European understood that Swahili was in most cases a lingua franca that did not coincide with the languages the local populations used within more restricted geographical boundaries.

Soon, however, the difference between the two language types attracted Amaat Vyncke's attention. In contrast to his French confreres, Vyncke became acutely aware of this reality and, in particular, of the other missionaries' usage of a lingua franca like Swahili in spite of the presence of vernacular languages. In other words, Vyncke refused to follow the line of least resistance, i.e. to use and adopt Swahili, the language already available and known to Europeans and readily applicable for communication with the Africans. He felt that the children of the mission, and Africans in general, had to be taught and raised in "their own languages", and that future missionaries would have to familiarize themselves with these languages prior to their arrival in the mission. Thus, while his French confreres (some of whom were equally interested in linguistic descriptions and, above all, in the publication of practical learning materials) focused exclusively on the description of Swahili (e.g. the White Father H. Delaunay 1884, 1885; see also Fabian 1984, 1986), Vyncke started to devote his attention to the local languages spoken in his area and was concerned with passing down written knowledge of these languages to later generations of missionaries. Craeynest writes about Vyncke:

> To make things easier for the missionaries to come after him, he would compile a dictionary of the Tanganika languages. "It's a horse's job," he sighed, "Calculate and count: some twelve different local languages, of which only five are (scarcely) known. And then there's the climate, which warns you that half a day of writing is certain to give you the flu. Nonetheless, with God's mercy I hope to labor my way through it and to start printing within a year or so."[5]
>
> (Craeynest [1945]: 152)

Vyncke's perspective on the linguistic realities that surrounded himself and his French confreres was a sequel to his activities in Belgium as an ardent and historically important supporter of the "Flemish Movement" ('*De Vlaamse Beweging*') (see Deleu et al. (eds.) 1973–1975; Wils 1977–1989, 1994; Hermans et al. (eds.) 1992). The Flemish Movement did not emerge in a single social and geographical context. Rather, its sources go back to several, fairly isolated pockets of protests (which may to varying extents have merged by the end of the 19th century). One of these pockets of protests is known as "West-Flemish Particularism" ('*West-Vlaams Particularisme*').[6] It was based in the rural, conservative-Catholic milieus of the Belgian province of West-Flanders, and its main figures included Hugo Verriest, Guido Gezelle, and Albrecht Rodenbach, who were especially active in the West-Flemish towns of Roeselare and Bruges.

Born and raised in this province, Vyncke was a student and personal friend of these three historical figures, and he himself soon became a driving force behind West-Flemish Particularism. In close collaboration with, or at least with the moral support of these figures, Vyncke started such nationalist journals of central importance as *De Vlaamsche Vlagge* ('The Flemish Flag') and *Almanak voor de Leerende Jeugd van Vlaanderen onder de Bescherming der H. Luitgaarde, Patrones van de Vlaamsche Taal en Letterkunde* ('Almanac for the Studying Youth of Flanders under the Protection of Saint Lutgard, Patron Saint of the Flemish Language and Literature').

Typical of West-Flemish Particularism as a branch of the Flemish Movement was the conviction that religion, language, and nationality coalesced into one single unit. Vyncke's nationalism, too, was inextricably connected with his deep Roman Catholic faith. From 1867 to 1869, Vyncke followed the example of many other Flemish young men: he enlisted as a Papal Zouave in the armies of Pope Pius IX, went to Italy, and fought in the Pope's war against Garibaldi and king Victor Emmanuel II (see, e.g. Bittard des Portes 1894; Defives-De Saint Martin 1912; Goddeeris 1978). Upon his return in Flanders, Vyncke founded one of the many "student-zouave corps" of the time. These corps were student organizations recruiting Flemish boys in secondary schools and preparatory seminaries with the intention of hardening them through paramilitary education (physical training, martial techniques, etc.) and to develop among them an unconditional Papal loyalty. More importantly, however, the Zouave leaders of these corps were also concerned with sensitizing the young boys to the Flemish cause, i.e. rendering them aware of "their own identity, culture, and language" and of the treacherous and alienating introduction of French in Flanders. Through these corps, the existing ideological connection between fervent Papal Catholicism and Flemish nationalism was also organized institutionally. Craeynest eloquently formulates what this ideological connection exactly meant to people like Vyncke and other leaders of student-zouave corps:

> To Vyncke, Christian and Flemish were synonyms. His was the strong conviction that the integrity of our own people's soul was not only the Creator's original wish, but that it was also the only reliable guarantee against the destructive forces of myriad imported, perverse ideas, such as latitudinarianism.
>
> (Craeynest [1945]: 211–212)

The "imported, perverse ideas" came, above all, from France: one of the more admonishing creeds of West-Flemish Particularism and the Flemish Movement in general at the time was *Gesta Diaboli per Francos* ('The Devil's Work through French Hands'). Certain Flemish nationalists were convinced that the corruption of the Flemish national character since 1830 was not only the product of the introduction of the French *language*, but also of the introduction of books, methods of education, a frivolous life-style, and latitudinarian views from France. As mentioned, the West-Flemish Particularists also emphasized "original Christianity" as one of the most fundamental features of the Flemish national identity, and to them it was this intrinsically Flemish-Christian soul that was threatened by the frenchification of Flanders. Vyncke himself continuously received harsh criticisms and tokens of incomprehension from his Flemish brothers-in-arms denouncing his membership of a French missionary congregation.

A major theme in the nationalism of the Flemish Movement in the 19th century was the denunciation of the unnatural. The imposition of French in Flanders led to a fundamental distortion of the original national soul of the Flemish people. It made it impossible for the Flemish people to be "its own authentic self" and it led to the adulteration of the purity of the Flemish being, the piety and honesty of a hard-working rural people, their culture, their language, their literary heritage, etc. In this ideology, the Flemishness of the Flemish was an a-historical, natural, of-all-times, God-created reality, while the introduction of French into the schools and in all other forms of public life was a historical accident caused by human intervention, resulting in a situation of unnaturalness, contamination, impurity, deterioration, and captivity. Preservation of the national self and linguistic and cultural freedom therefore constituted the principal war cry in this "ideology of the natural".

The relation between the fervent Catholicism typical of the West-Flemish Particularists and the missionary vocation of many Flemish priests from that Belgian province in the late 19th and early 20th century is evident. To be sure, however, not all of the Belgian missionaries leaving for the Congo were Flemish, and not all Flemish missionaries drew on an active background in, or even some form of sympathy with, the Flemish nationalist cause. Still, certain individuals within what was called "the exportation of Flanders' and God's sons to Central Africa" brought along an exportation of the ideology of the natural, which was accomplished at varying degrees of consciousness and explicit recognition. Like all the other Flemish nationalists, Vyncke, when in Flanders, was never able to accept that "we, Flemish, have been forced to break with our own language and way of living, and to adopt foreign ones" (Craeynest [1945]: 55). Similarly, as soon as he arrived in Africa, Vyncke easily construed the linguistic realities he encountered in Algiers, in Zanzibar, on the road to Lake Tanganyika, and in Kibanga, in terms of an opposition between the one, original language of a people and other, recently imported and imposed languages which corrupted its God-planned authenticity. However far away from home, Vyncke would never renounce his basic concern with the preservation of cultural purity through linguistic protectionism. In one of his letters home he exclaimed: "In Africa always as in Europe, Fleming forever ahead and atop, so I shall continue!" (*Xaveriana* 1927: 19). It is because of this perceptiveness resulting from his Flemish nationalist background that he, in contrast to his fellow missionaries, noticed that the officers on the ship from Algiers to Zanzibar went to school in their native language and not in some European language (Craeynest [1945]: 112), that he noted that the children in Tabora (half-way between the East African coast and Lake Tanganyika) spoke and prayed in their mother tongues ([1945]: 125), and that he encouraged the children in his Kibanga mission to sing in their own local languages ([1945]: 57). It was also the reason why, as explained above, he avoided the exclusive usage of Swahili and developed an urge to learn and describe the local languages.

In the second half of the 1860s, another West-Flemish candidate to join the Zouaves in Rome was the Jesuit Emiel Van Hencxthoven (1852–1906).[7] Due to practical circumstances, however, Van Hencxthoven never actually went to Rome, but his active participation in the student-zouave corps established by Zouave veterans in West-Flanders is amply documented. Van Hencxthoven was born in a militantly Catholic and Flemish family and, as a young man, he attended Hugo Verriest's speeches and manifestations in the early 1870s. His active participation in the student-zouave corps further shaped his Flemish nationalism, streamlining it decisively along the lines of West-Flemish Particularism, including its fundamental Flemish Christianity, and the ideology of the natural.

In 1893, Van Hencxthoven, appointed Superior, and five other Jesuit Fathers arrived in the region immediately south of the actual city of Kinshasa (then Leopoldville, founded by H.M. Stanley in 1881), between the lower Congo and the Kwango river. This is the region where Van Hencxthoven established what would later be called the "Kwango-mission", an area of 400 hectares which at certain moments in history counted more than one hundred Jesuit mission stations. Upon arrival in this region, Van Hencxthoven came into contact with a language he and many other Europeans called "Fiote", a lingua franca arisen out of the contacts between the European state and trade agents, their West African and East African intermediaries, and the local populations (on the history of this language see Hulstaert 1946; Samarin 1984, 1989b, 1990; Bokamba 1993; Mufwene 1988, 1997). Fiote was a language typically tied to vertical modes of communication, the local populations only using it to address state officials and tradesmen and therefore also calling it *Kikongo ya Leta*, 'State Kikongo' (for a list of other names by which this language has been known, see Heine 1970 and Mufwene 1997). Initially, Van Hencxthoven himself also resorted to Fiote in communicating with the orphan children the colonial authorities brought to his mission station in Kisantu (in the first years, these were mostly children liberated by the Belgians during their campaigns against Arab slave traders in the eastern and northeastern Congo). In some of the many other stations of the Jesuit Kwango Mission, however, e.g. in the one in Kimwenza, the language used in the mission school and in all other structures at that time was not Fiote but French. The mission at Kimwenza was run by Father Edward Liagre, who was not a Flemish but a Walloon Jesuit.

Liagre did not theorize on his own linguistic practices, but assumed (as did Vyncke's French confreres) that the medium to be used for the education of Africans was of no intrinsic importance: language selection was to be based on purely practical considerations such as availability, knowledge, spread, etc. Van Hencxthoven's view, which was much more the product of theoretical deliberation, was not as crudely instrumental as Liagre's. To Van Hencxthoven, his confreres' linguistic practices were incomprehensible. Understanding the "depths of the Africans' soul" as well as liberating the Africans from pre-Christian darkness were both unrealizable without knowledge and use of the Africans' own languages. The use of a foreign language was, moreover, an "incorrect policy" in principle, for it involved the introduction of an exogenous vehicle of communication, leading to the denaturalization of the people's original identity.

Schoeters explains how Van Hencxthoven's concern with the cultural isomorphy of the linguistic medium to be used in the Christianization and education of the Africans was contained in the nationalist ideology he developed earlier in Flanders. Referring to a speech delivered by Hugo Verriest in Roeselare in 1872 and attended by the young Van Hencxthoven, Schoeters writes:

> "Flemish, be yourselves Flemish," this was Verriest's pithy conclusion to his glowing speech, by which he set fire to the powder of the Flemish uprising against established French. If, later on in the Congo, Father Van Hencxthoven always respected the Bakongo-negroes' own national character with great zeal and used it as the natural foundation for the construction of Christian civilization, then he acted according to the lessons of this herald of Flanders' resurrection … The success which Father Van Hencxthoven later, in the African jungle, achieved in his Christianization of the Bakongo-negroes was to a great extent due to his concern with reaching the depths of their innermost life through their own language.[8]
>
> (Schoeters [1956]: 15 and 23)

Soon, however, Van Hencxthoven became aware of the fact that Fiote was a language "for the use of the European trade and state agents, which the missionaries too had promoted to the status of general, everyday language" (Schoeters [1956]: 63). Van Hencxthoven was struck by the fact that this language had only recently emerged and was, in fact, itself *not* an original language of the local populations. Its use in the region was expected of the Africans by the progressing Europeans, and its geographical spread was therefore not so much a pre-existing reality which the colonizers first "happened upon" and subsequently "worked by". It was rather an outcome of the unfolding process of colonization itself; in other words, a case of language change and spread on the ground. To Van Hencxthoven, the error made by all Europeans, including the missionaries, in using and imposing this language was as grave as the imposition of French: Fiote was alien to the Africans' original national being and, consequently, had perverse effects. Already by the end of the year of his arrival (1893), he turned away from Fiote, and wrote to his sister in Flanders, "I rejoice that I am already able to stammer a bit of Congolese.[9] That way I'm gradually able to develop more intimate relations with my Black parishioners" (Schoeters [1956]: 65). Schoeters explains how one year later, Van Hencxthoven's early concern with orphan children from the east gradually shifted towards the local children, and that in this context Van Hencxthoven judged his own competence in "Congolese" good enough to substitute it for Fiote. Schoeters' reconstruction, in which the language is called "Kikongo", also nicely conjures up the contrast with Father Liagre's linguistic practices in Kimwenza.

> While French had received a privileged position in Kimwenza (the good Father Liagre would never be able to understand that the opposite was possible, too!), in Kisantu the language of instruction had been the negro-slang of the Lower Congo, "fiote". As long as the little liberated slaves, who spoke almost all the dialects and gibberishes of the Higher Congo, were in the majority, it was hardly possible to consider using another language of communication; however, as soon as the Bakongo-children [the local children, MM] were introduced in the school, the beautiful, melodious Kikongo language, with which Father Superior had familiarized himself in his contacts with the villagers, was evidently given precedence over that argot [Fiote, MM] cherished by civil servants and trade agents.[10]
>
> (Schoeters [1956]: 85)

Like Vyncke's endeavor to replace or complement the usage and knowledge of Swahili with a usage and knowledge of the local languages, Van Hencxthoven consolidated his endeavor to replace Fiote by Kikongo through publications in and descriptions of the language. The language had to be written down for it to be eternalized and to be accepted by all as a "true" language. From 1895 onwards, he started composing prayer books in the language. He was also the driving force behind René Butaye's (one of his lower-ranked confreres in the Kwango Mission and a close follower of his linguistic convictions) scientific publications of the first grammar and the first dictionary of an eastern variant of Kikongo (Butaye 1901a, 1901b, 1909, 1910a, 1910b, 1927).

In 1901, fearing the progress of the Protestant missionaries, Van Hencxthoven extended his Kwango Mission in northeastern direction, founding a mission station at Wombali, near the present-day city of Bandundu. Using Wombali as a stepping stone, Van Hencxthoven and one or two other fellow Jesuits explored the entire region comprised by the Kwilu, Kwa, and Kwango rivers in the course of a few years, and for the first time brought a large part of the local populations into contact with Christianity and Europeans. Van Hencxthoven's linguistic practices in these new territories were characterized both by a furtherance of his ideology of the natural, as well as by a contradiction with this ideology. Schoeters writes about the year 1902:

> In the meantime, Father Van Hencxthoven had attentively studied the many questions and problems posed by the new, completely foreign mission region. One of the first observations he made was a pleasant one: the language of the Bakongo was, if not spoken, then at least quite rapidly understood by the Baboma people of Wombali, and even by the Bayansi, who are situated more to the south. Thus, subsequent missionaries would only have to study one language. Father Cus [one of his fellow-explorers, MM] and himself were convinced that Kikongo should be imposed as the medium of instruction —a conclusion that would prove to have lasting effects.
>
> (Schoeters [1956]: 236)

Van Hencxthoven thus continued his earlier linguistic approach, in that he refused to contribute to the progress of the Europeans' "slang language" Fiote. On the other hand, although he was aware of the fact that the local languages spoken in the newly-explored territories around Wombali were different from the vernacular to which he had devoted all his attention earlier in Kisantu (300 kms to the southwest), he decided to "bring" this vernacular "along" and, thus, to add it as a new language to the range of vernaculars originally spoken there (see also Yates 1980: 269 on this case). Instead of pursuing his policy of the non-imposition of foreign languages, his line of reasoning for the Wombali area was an instrumentalist and linguistically imperialist one. In view of facilitating the linguistic conditions under which the subsequent missionaries were to develop the Wombali mission area, the Kikongo language of the Kisantu area, with which the congregation was already well-acquainted, had to be introduced and imposed upon the Africans in Wombali as the obligatory language of vertical communication.

Van Hencxthoven and his fellow missionaries thus brought the vernacular language of the Kisantu area to regions where it had not been spoken before. Again, this constitutes a case of change in language spread. A language ideological debate, catalyzing individual language ideologies, resulted in the extension of the geographical sphere of Kikongo. Until the present day, the area of expansion of Kikongo still reaches up to the city of Bandundu. We know that this sociolinguistic *fait accompli* must be related to the work of Van Hencxthoven, his confreres, and the Jesuit missionaries who worked in their footsteps. And we also know that it must be related to the exportation of Flemish nationalism to the colony, for even if certain contradictions within the ideological practices may be observed, such as Van Hencxthoven's choice to bring Kikongo to other areas than its original area of expansion, it is still his Flemish nationalism which drove him to stop the spread of Fiote and to turn to the vernacular.

It is also clear that it was not the contingent but rather the theoretical component of this Flemish nationalism which was reproduced in the Congo: at issue was not some aversion to French as the concrete target of Flemish nationalism in Belgium, but rather the more general rejection, within Flemish nationalism as principally based on an ideology of the natural, of *any* form of corruption of cultural and ethnic authenticity. Vyncke's and Van Hencxthoven's rejections of languages other than French (i.e., Swahili and Fiote respectively) are evidence to this point.

3.3. *The debate between G. Hulstaert and E. De Boeck*

In the case of Amaat Vyncke, it is not clear whether his move away from Swahili and towards the local languages was the object of a "debate" in the sense of a direct and explicit confrontation, dialogue, or discussion with his French confreres. It may well have been the case that the matter was never explicitly commented upon by the missionaries in question, but that different individuals simply developed different positions, situated at different levels of awareness and theory formation. In the case of Van Hencxthoven, then, we know that he addressed the issue of linguistic practices to Father Liagre, who stuck to the use of European languages in his mission station. From the biographer's account, we can also conclude that Van Hencxthoven tried to convince other Whites of the evil of Fiote, fellow missionaries as well as state officials, agents, and officers of private factories.

If the case of Van Hencxthoven is already to be situated somewhere halfway along the continuum of explicitness/implicitness, the confrontation between Father Gustaaf Hulstaert (1900–1990) and Mgr. Egide De Boeck (1875–1944) in the northern parts of the colony and about four decades later involved a very public, outspoken, and deliberated exchange of opinions, including an extensive correspondence and other written testimonies available in published form. There is, first of all, a long article containing a discussion between the two missionary-linguists which was published in 1940 (Hulstaert and De Boeck 1940; another, less extensive discussion paper is Tanghe et al. 1940). In addition, the correspondence which Hulstaert and De Boeck exchanged prior to the publication of this article and in which their points of view appear in unpolished form, was edited by Vinck (1994). Secondly, a long list of scientific publications exists through which Gustaaf Hulstaert voiced his grievances and suggestions (e.g. Hulstaert 1939, 1946, 1953, 1981 and another discussion paper known as Bittremieux and Hulstaert 1940), together with the editions of other parts of his correspondence relevant to the matter (e.g. Vinck 1991).[11] In addition to the discussion papers already cited, De Boeck's views also appear in some of his individual publications, especially in the introductions to the many Lingala grammars, dictionaries, and language courses he produced (e.g. De Boeck 1904, 1920, 1942).

E. De Boeck, of the *Congregatio Immaculati Cordis Mariae* (better known as "the Scheutists"), came to the Congo in 1900, and was stationed in Nouvel-Anvers (presently, Mankanza) and later in Lisala, two towns on the right bank of the Congo river in the northwestern equatorial section of the colony. De Boeck immediately picked up Lingala (at that time called "Bangala"), the pidginized lingua franca that had emerged out of the contacts between the first European traders, officials, and missionaries, their non-Congolese, African intermediaries (see above), and the local populations. As was the case with Fiote in the southwest, at the time of De Boeck's arrival the Europeans had been using and imposing Lingala as the medium of vertical communication along the western and northern sections of the Congo river (for both the linguistic and the sociolinguistic history of Lingala, see Tanghe 1930; Hulstaert 1989; Samarin 1989a, 1990; Meeuwis 1997, 1998).[12] By the turn of the century, the use of French as a medium for Christianization (which was applied, as mentioned above, by people like Father Liagre) had already become obsolete throughout almost the entire colony. From the very beginning, De Boeck presented himself as a proponent of the continued organized spread of Lingala throughout the territory's northern and western sections, as well as of the use of this language in the colony's educational system, administration, jurisdiction, etc. His rationale was based on a view generally shared at the time that the colony represented a Tower of Babel (e.g. Tanghe et al. 1940; Fabian 1986, 1991[1983]), i.e. a cluttered plethora of languages, language varieties, and dialects which was in urgent need of simplification from above. In his view, however, it was impossible to accomplish this organized geographical and societal generalization of Lingala without thoroughly intervening in its structures and lexicon. Another opinion, not generalized among all Belgians but certainly appealing to most of the linguists among them, was that Lingala was structurally too "corrupt" and too "poor" a language, and that its grammar and vocabulary were marked by a very low degree of differentiation. From 1901 onwards, De Boeck carried out his massive work of prescriptive interventions in the language: drawing his inspiration mostly from neighboring languages, he designed additional grammatical rules, such as a whole set of morphological differentiations for the tense system (see, e.g. De Boeck's own comments in Tanghe *et al.* 1940: 91), as well as long lists of newly coined words including the name of the language itself. De Boeck enacted all these new norms in a long series of grammars and dictionaries (which started with De Boeck 1903 and 1904) and managed to have them adopted by some of the local populations in the northern areas through the network of schools and parishes which was controlled by his congregation.[13]

Gustaaf Hulstaert, who came to the Congo in September 1925, was a member of the congregation of the Missionaries of the Sacred Heart, operating around the equator in the central basin of the Congo river, where the Mongo people are dominant. Hulstaert immediately developed a linguistic, historical, and ethnological interest in this area and in the Mongo people in particular. Hulstaert and De Boeck soon came into conflict with each other on the issue of Lingala. It is, however, important to note that they actually agreed on a number of pivotal issues. There was, first of all, the shared conviction that the Africans' complete assimilation of the French language was "out of the question": Hulstaert and De Boeck were both products of what became gradually known as the policy of "indigenism" (*indigénisme*), i.e. the Belgian version of indirect rule which stated that at all political, administrative, and educational levels, the "civilization" and "management" of the colonized was to be accomplished preferably on the basis of their own ethnic and cultural structures and institutions. Together, De Boeck and Hulstaert fulminated against certain people in the private sector and the public administration, as well as a considerable number of missionaries, who still swore by the use of French. Secondly, they also agreed that the linguistic landscape of the colony had to be simplified from above. Even if Hulstaert was at times critical of the poor documentation on which many based their representation of the colony as a Tower of Babel (e.g. Hulstaert 1936: 9, 1939: 88), he felt that an organized reduction of the number of languages was a compelling necessity. But this reduction was to be achieved through unification, standardization, and the merging of dialect clusters at the level of large but "existing" ethnolinguistic groups. This was eventually to result in a more limited, but geographically and ethnically representative, number of "languages" (see also Polomé 1968: 305).

What Hulstaert most of all objected to was De Boeck's choice to remedy the colony's linguistic fragmentation by artificially introducing languages into areas where the populations had never used them before. This objection was related to Hulstaert's emphasis on the fundamentally descriptive task of linguistics, which brought him to fiercely criticize De Boeck's prescriptive and interventionist activities.[14] He argued that if Lingala was grammatically and lexically too poor and too devoid of cultural indigenity to serve as a vehicle of education and Christianization, it should be abandoned altogether. The guided, prescriptive correction of Lingala was not only "scientifically incorrect", it could never lead to satisfactory outcomes, as it would still result in the imposition of a foreign and thus culturally alienating language upon the Africans. Hulstaert's objections to Lingala were basically similar to Van Hencxthoven's objections to the imposition of Fiote in the Kwango region. To Hulstaert, the fact that Lingala was a foreign language for many of the Africans confronted with it involved the denaturalization of their cultural and ethnic self. Local populations (and Hulstaert primarily had "his own" Mongo in mind) had to be helped to develop their civilizations on the basis of their own languages, which were not only much richer than "broken" lingua francae such as Lingala, but which also counted as the only isomorphic carriers of the populations' national-cultural genius. In his published discussion paper with De Boeck, he wrote:

> For almost all Blacks, Lingala is not a mother tongue … It remains an artificial and European language, without a negro soul[15] … Who would dare assume the responsibility of replacing a widely spread, rich, harmonious, fluid language, apt to become a perfect cultural language, relying on an admirable oral literature, with a language which is inferior by all standards —with a rudimentary *passe-partout* language … and, by so doing, of causing a civilization to regress in many degrees and of causing the inversion of an incalculable number of years of cultural evolution in a great part of the Congo? For what Mr. E. De Jonghe [an authoritative education specialist and

> linguist in the colony, MM] writes about pidgin, about broken English, about *petit nègre*, etc., is applicable to our case as well: "The populations that are afflicted with these languages are irreparably doomed to intellectual mediocrity."
>
> (Hulstaert and De Boeck 1940: 34–36 and 71–72)

To Hulstaert, hardly any colonial administrator or missionary (De Boeck, for instance) applied the policy of indigenism in a more than superficial fashion. If parts of the colonial body had indeed turned away from the policies of assimilation into French, the majority did not understand that the full implications of indigenism also entailed the refusal to impose foreign cultural elements of *African* origin. In a letter to Father Bühlman, a missionary equally interested in the languages spoken in his mission region, Hulstaert paraphrased his own radical indigenism as follows:

> To me, there is only one *logical* and *coherent* position for an indigenist: the pure position, without compromise: indigenity[16] as it really is and not as we would want it to be; therefore, ancestral language and customs, and not those of another African people. For if the difference between the African and the European is enormous, it is less big yet still very big among the various African peoples themselves.
>
> (Vinck 1991: 43–46, emphasis in original)

Both intellectually and in terms of the level of explicitness governing the debate, Hulstaert's radical indigenism was one of the, if not the, most developed language ideologies of the entire epoch of Belgian colonization. Nevertheless, in terms of content and principles his radical indigenism may be said to represent one more manifestation of the ideology of the natural, of which Vyncke and Van Hencxthoven were two other exponents. To a certain extent, this similarity across Hulstaert's, Vyncke's, and Van Hencxthoven's linguistic preferences may be seen as a product of cross-fertilization. As mentioned above, the linguists of the colony made up a close network of colleagues, acquaintances and friends (or enemies), whose work and opinions were known (or at least knowable) by all those involved. It is certain, to be concrete, that the Jesuits of the Kwango region and the White Fathers of Lake Tanganyika knew each other's work very well (Schoeters [1956]; Thibaut 1911). Van Hencxthoven's views in particular were well known to Mgr. Roelens of the White Fathers. Father Hulstaert, then, was not only well-informed about the linguistic practices applied in missions and schools all over the colony, he was also a personal friend of the important Jesuit linguist succeeding Van Hencxthoven, J. Van Wing (1884–1970).

At least as important as the factor of cross-fertilization was that of *historical concomitance*, i.e. Hulstaert's, Vyncke's, and Van Hencxthoven's shared background in the Flemish nationalist cause. Indeed, Hulstaert's radical indigenism, too, can be traced back to his strong attachment to the Flemish Movement in Belgium. Hulstaert was born in the province of East-Flanders and completed his preparatory seminary and novitiate studies in the province of Brabant (Asse and Louvain). He was, moreover, a member of the generation immediately following the heyday of West-Flemish Particularism. Nevertheless, through personal contacts both in his private life and at school, where he studied with the Flemish novelist Gerard Walschap, he gradually developed a strong Flemish-nationalist conviction that betrayed certain influences from that West-Flemish, religiously inspired branch. Hulstaert more than once stated that his opinion on the linguistic and ethnic situation of the Mongo, as well as on language and ethnicity in the colony in general, was always and very consciously based on nationalist convictions developed in the context of the oppression of the Flemish language in Belgium. By the time Hulstaert came to the Congo, he had already developed an attentiveness towards anything resembling the bastardization, corruption, or erosion of cultural authenticity through foreign influences. The earmarks of his nationalism were an absolute respect for the purity of ethnic groups and national identities, as well as a fundamental belief in the a-historical, God-given, and natural essence of these groups and their identities. Both in Belgium and in the Congo, he worked on the assumption that since these structures were natural and divine and since they had always been there, any form of human intervention possibly leading to a corruption of their naturalness was inadmissible. He more than once reported that his stance was best summarized in the famous verse of the West-Flemish poet and Particularist, Guido Gezelle: "Be Fleming, whom God created Fleming." It is God who created ethnic groups and national identities, and hence, these units should be respected and kept in the original form which God had wanted for them. The fact that he considered the issue of respect for a people's cultural and ethnic identity in the Congo to be perfectly comparable to the situation in Europe also surfaces in a letter he wrote to a Congolese priest in February 1941. In this letter, he attributes the ongoing war in Europe precisely to the lack of such a respect for nations and nationhood among European states.

> I do not accept that education is conducted in a language that is absolutely foreign. That is why I do not accept the option of using Lingala with the Ngombe, Budza, Ngwandi, etc. All this is too dangerous; it is the seed of nationalist revolutions. The history of Europe is full of examples to this effect. ... Changes in a language from generation to generation are natural and without major consequences. They are of all times, including in Europe. But things are completely different when an entire people, an entire tribe has to make the leap in an abrupt way, and above all: when in addition to someone's language, in which their daily, spontaneous life is contained, they have to adopt a second language through which the new civilization (and often religion) are communicated. Whence: a double language, a double and non-unified mentality; whence: spiritual duality, lack of unity of ideas, of emotions, lack of synthesis: the source of all the modern European disruptions, source of all the modern heresies, source of all the modern miseries which are delivering Europe to a barbarity worse than the one in which the first Whites found the Blacks of the Congo ... The anti-natural[17] is a social volcano!
>
> (Vinck 1991: 28–29)

It must be clear that, as was the case for Vyncke and Van Hencxthoven, Hulstaert's reproduction of Flemish nationalism in the Congo was theoretical in nature, involving the application of the ideology of the natural in its general form, rather than through some particular disgust with French. Hulstaert wrote the vast majority of his publications in French (most quotations above are translated from French). In 1937, he started a scientific journal (*Æquatoria)*, the working language of which he and co-founder E. Boelaert decided would be French, and he used French for all formal modes of communication with non-native speakers of Flemish. For people like Hulstaert, the Belgian dispute between Flemish and French was not the main issue in the colony. He stressed that —still a Flemish nationalist— he had no problems whatsoever with using French as an international language of scientific communication. He would clarify that his nationalism (and he often used this qualification himself) had developed from a matter of conjuncture, i.e. the historically contingent injustice suffered by the Flemish in Belgium, to a matter of principle, i.e. an aversion to all forms of corruption of a people's historical, linguistic, ethnic, and cultural naturalness.

4. Concluding remarks

Hulstaert's struggle against Lingala in his region made him produce a massive amount of scientific descriptions of the Lomongo language and, most importantly, guided him towards the unification and codification of this language and its vast cluster of dialects. He worked on one variant (Lonkundo) as the standard variety and produced grammars, dictionaries, and pedagogical materials to consolidate this unification. De Boeck's position in the debate was even more effective at this object-level. He thoroughly "changed" Lingala by inventing not only its new name but also whole sets of grammatical and lexical rules, as well as by using the school and parish networks controlled by his congregation to have local populations adopt this new language and pass it on to following generations. In this context, it is necessary to refer to the historical reconstructions made by Young (1976) and Fabian (1986), among others, showing that the Africans' language use, like their ethnic self-identification, was to a large extent the object of the Europeans' control. In their contacts with Europeans and among themselves, the colonized were often compelled to resort to clearly identified linguistic resources and to behave and present themselves according to very specific patterns of expectation. At times, this monitoring was accomplished through explicit and conscious forms of coercion and punishment. In one of his letters to De Boeck, Hulstaert exclaimed: "every Black man is obliged to speak Lingala because of the State or other Whites, in order to … avoid prison!!" (Vinck 1994: 546). Even in those cases where no such explicit forms of coercion were applied, monitoring and sanctioning were always achieved through implicit processes of hegemony and self-censorship.

Effective as this debate and its individual components may have been at the level of language change and spread, its most important *ideological* ingredient, i.e. the divide between lingua francae and vernacular languages, cannot be said to have been formative of subsequent language ideologies. In the language ideologies dominating the Zairian era, the lingua franca-vernacular divide had become if not a non-issue, at best a marginal one. The most relevant distinction was the one between Zaire's linguistic resources of *African* origin —passable as the media of the nation's cultural heritage— and French as the language introduced by the former, culturally different, oppressor. (The architects of this new ideology thereby overlooked the fact that the geographical spread of these "African" languages, as well as the relations between "standard" and "dialects" and in certain cases their very linguistic structures, were often the result of colonial choices.) Thus, at the level of language ideologies and language ideological debates, the colonial discussion revolving around the choice between lingua francae and vernaculars seems to have vanished as soon as the nation became independent and tried to safeguard its independence and African identity in the face of Western imperialism and neocolonialism. Indeed, even if a weaker variant of indigenism (simply rejecting French without bothering about the non-indigenousness of the lingua francae) was also present in colonial times and may have informed the structure of the debate in the Zairian epoch (with its comparable opposition between French and a unified bloc of African languages), this structure cannot be fully understood without its historical contingency. As argued in section 2, the Zairian intellectuals' preference for such an opposition was to a considerable extent related to the particular historical, international, and political setting in which it was articulated. More precisely, their linguistic debate has to be situated within a more general wave of political and ideological awakening marking the era of decolonization throughout the African continent. The rejection of French in Zairian times must have been more than a simple recycling of an ideology of indigenism developed by colonialists in earlier times, as the proponents of this rejection explicitly linked their demands to various anti-imperialist ideologies emerging in Africa.

Bringing this back to the issue of continuity and discontinuity, some continuity between the colonial debate and the postcolonial one may thus be observed, but this observation in itself cannot account for the historically contingent structure and details of the latter. Such details, to be sure, are crucial for a satisfactory understanding of language ideological developments across time, which includes, in this case, the insight that the history of language ideology is not a linear, mechanical, or organic progress.

The methodological approach implemented here, i.e. the attestation of the historically situated role of "located subjectivities" (Thomas) and the influence of continuities in the biographies of each of them, has allowed me to connect certain positions taken in the colonial epoch with Flemish nationalism and its ideology of the natural. It also allows me, at this point, to stress the individual specificity of the linguistic choices made. There has never been such a thing as a general linguistic policy or practice applied by all missionaries in the colony, not even within the group of Catholic missionaries as opposed to the Protestant ones. As my discussion shows, the clerical segment of the colonial apparatus was actually very much divided in terms of preferred linguistic practices. It is even impossible to link up the different positions with specific congregations; the members of the Missionaries of the Sacred Heart, for instance, did not all embrace Hulstaert's point of view, and certain Scheutists, such as E. De Boeck's own brother and confrere Jules De Boeck (1891–1981), were more in favor of Hulstaert's radical indigenism than of the organized spread of, and normative interventions in, Lingala. It is, in short, inevitable in undertaking the historiographic analysis to attribute the different colonial language ideologies to individuals, and to identify these persons as actual historical figures rather than as representatives of social roles.

This importance of individual specificity also warns us against generalizations within the Flemish camp. On analogy with the situation within the congregations, there has never been a linguistic ideology or practice shared by all Flemish in the colony. Contrary to what analysts such as Yates (1980) and Young (1965) seem to imply due to insufficient degrees of historiographic detail, being a Fleming did not automatically imply being a Flemish nationalist, nor did being a Flemish nationalist automatically imply that one would actually approach the linguistic issues in the colony from the perspective of this nationalism and its ideology of the natural. Many Flemish nationalists among the missionaries and other colonials involved in linguistic decision making simply did not "see" any possible connection between the struggle they vigorously supported in Belgium and the African situation. Hulstaert, as well as some of the individual missionary-linguists he managed to convince, often complained about these Flemish nationalists' incapacity to synthesize and about what he felt to be a glaring contradiction between their rhetoric and practices "back home" and those in the colony. Another Scheutist who shared Hulstaert's ideology of the natural was L. Bittremieux (1880–1946), who worked on the languages in the lower Congo area. In a letter to Hulstaert dated November 4, 1944, Bittremieux qualified the Lingala policy and its entire set of rationalizations as "a sin against the spirit," and highlighted the "contradiction" in the linguistic views of many Flemish nationalists in the Congo as follows:

> So this "sin against the spirit" continues, without provoking any form of protest? And these are the gentlemen who swear by "In Flanders Flemish, in Spanders Spanish"?? —It's really beyond me.[18]
>
> (unedited letter, archives of the *Centre Æquatoria*)

As I hope to have shown, an investigation of the material realities behind ideological systems (i.e. tying these systems down to the histories of tangible agents and to these agents' moves within actual networks) allows us to come up with a more differentiated historiography of colonial practices and ideologies. As long as such a historiography is not provided, such historical processes as the discontinuity in language ideologies from colonial to postcolonial times and the continuity from colonial language ideologies and debates to consolidated cases of language change and spread "on the ground" cannot be apprehended.

Notes

1. All translations from Dutch and French in this chapter are my own.
2. The explicit reasons Mobutu and his regime provided for this absence included references to French as an international language, needed to orient Zaire towards the rest of the world, and as a warranty for operational efficiency in the domains of administration, diplomacy, and technical advancement (see Mobutu 1989: 207–208; also, Meeuwis 1997: chapter 4). Less explicitly declared motives included the fear that the selection and promotion of one or more African languages would be grist to the mill of ethnic and other centrifugal forces. They also —and perhaps more importantly— included Zaire's diplomatic and cultural relationship with France and its *francophonie*. The reluctance of the architects of *authenticité* to promote the African languages to positions where they could be interpreted as competing with French must be related to Zaire's dependence on the enormous financial, diplomatic, and military support it always received from Paris (Kambaji 1987; Meeuwis 1997; Nyunda 1986b).
3. The use of the term "national languages" in the title of the Kinshasa conference is illustrative of the terminological ambiguity which I referred to above. Here, the term is used to refer to all the languages of African origin spoken in Zaire, and not just to Kikongo, Swahili, Lingala, and Tshiluba.
4. *Xaveriana* (1927) is an edition of a selection of the numerous letters Vyncke wrote to his friends and relatives from his departure from Belgium in 1881 onwards. Craeynest ([1945]) is one of Vyncke's biographers. No date of publication is mentioned in Craeynest's biography, but in a footnote on Mgr. Roelens (another White Father), Craeynest mentions that Roelens' episcopal consecration took place in 1896 and that "at present he has been a bishop for 49 years" ([1945]: 205), which allows us to situate the writing of the book in 1945. Whereas *Xaveriana* (1927) is only a selection of Vyncke's correspondence, Craeynest was able to consult the totality of it, and for some information on and quotes from Vyncke I must therefore rely on his reproduction. Other sources on A. Vyncke include Cruysberghs (1951: 157–171), Delathuy (1992: 11), Goddeeris (1978: 316–317), and Monbaliu (1975a). Finally, for

information on this person as well as on many of the other figures to be dealt with below, the reader may also refer to the *Biographie Coloniale Belge – Belgische Koloniale Bibliografie*, which the Royal Belgian Colonial Institute started compiling from 1948 onwards.

5. "The Tanganika languages" is my translation of the original Dutch *de Tanganikatalen*. With regard to this Dutch text as a whole, as well as to a number of other ones to follow, it must be noted that the books from which they come were often written in a particularly archaic and flamboyant style, typical of Flemish writers at the time. My translations are designed to do justice to this original style.
6. The term "particularism" refers to these nationalists' rejection of linking the Flemish culture and language to other "Germanic" regions, such as The Netherlands and Germany. In contrast to some other figures in the Flemish Movement, the Particularists advocated the development of an individual Flemish standard language, preferably based on the western variant, which was said to be the historically most authentic dialect because it was closest to Middle Dutch.
7. Schoeters ([1956]) is one of Van Hencxthoven's biographers. Laveille (1926) is another one, but is less informative from the point of view of Van Hencxthoven's linguistic practices and Flemish nationalism. Schoeters' book does not contain a publication date, but the text on the dust jacket mentions the year 1956 as the 50th anniversary of Van Hencxthoven's death and, probably, as the *raison d'être* of the publication. At certain points in the text, the author also talks about the year 1954 as lying in the very recent past. Other sources of information on Van Hencxthoven and his missionary activities are Delathuy (1986, 1992) and Thibaut (1911).
8. The two tokens of the term "Bakongo-negroes" in this passage are translations of the original Flemish term *de Bakongo-negers*.
9. In the original: *het Kongolees*, the name Van Hencxthoven used for the vernacular language he wanted to promote.
10. It is again necessary to provide the Flemish originals of some of the terms in this passage: "negro-slang" is originally *het neger-bargoens*; "fiote" is also written with lower case in the original text; "gibberishes" is *brabbeltalen*; "argot" is *het taaltje*.
11. A major part of my information on Hulstaert and his linguistic views was also gathered on the occasion of personal meetings with Father Hulstaert in 1988–1989, from an ongoing contact with Father Honoré Vinck, who worked and lived with Hulstaert in Congo up to Hulstaert's death, and from my first consultations (in the form of a pilot research project to be developed in the future) of the archives of the *Centre Æquatoria* (Bamanya, Democratic Republic of Congo), the mission-related research center where Hulstaert worked. Biographical information on Gustaaf Hulstaert is also contained in De Rop (1956: 10–13, 1970, 1980), Vinck (1991, 1987), Lufungula (1986), and Delathuy (1994). Depaepe and Van Rompaey (1995) provide valuable information on Hulstaert's pedagogical views.

12. It is significant that like Fiote, Lingala was in the beginning also called "the language of the State" (*la langue de l'Etat*) by the African language users (Hulstaert 1989: 107). Even if this identification gradually dissappeared as the language acquired native speakers, the initial name remains indicative of the fact that in the first years the language was only used for vertical colonial communication, not for horizontal communication among the Africans themselves.
13. Due to its discrepancy with Lingala as it was originally spoken, this variant has since been designated by the labels "De Boeck's Lingala" (*le lingala de De Boeck*), "school lingala" (*le lingala des écoles*), "literary Lingala" (*le lingala littéraire*) and "written Lingala" (*le lingala écrit*) (as opposed to "spoken Lingala", *le lingala parlé*).
14. As the published correspondence between the two actors now shows (Vinck 1994), both were strongly aware of the differences in their linguistic approaches in this respect. In this correspondence, De Boeck more than once stresses that he is not a trained linguist, interested in scientific-descriptive issues, but that his main concern is with finding practical solutions to the linguistic problems of the colony, whatever changes from above this might entail. Standardization, codification, and norm creation were much higher priorities than the "curiosity" of descriptive scientists. It is important to add that Hulstaert was not a "trained" linguist either (which he often emphasized as well, insisting that this was not necessary to come to a sound and description-based vision). Hulstaert was, however, generally imbued with the status of "scientist", not least due to the international recognition of his monumental linguistic, ethnological, and historical oeuvre (He was, for instance, a *Doctor Honoris Causa* of the Gutenberg University of Mainz, Germany, and of the Université du Zaire-Kinshasa).
15. The original reads *âme nègre*.
16. In the original: *l'indigénat*.
17. The original is: *l'antinaturel*.
18. Bittremieux' coinage of the word "Spanders" (in the Flemish original: *Spaanderen*) instead of "Spain" (*Spanje*) is a pun. The reference to Spain is yet another way to express the ideology of the natural: every nation is entitled to respect for its own language.

References

Band, Tijdschrift voor Vlaams Kultuurleven

1956 *De Taalregeling in Kongo, met Documenten*. Special issue, *Band* 15: 10.

Bittard des Portes, René

1894 *Histoire des Zouaves pontificiaux*. Paris: Emile-Paul.

Bittremieux, Léo and Gustaaf Hulstaert
1943 A propos de la langue unifiée. *Æquatoria* 6(2): 37–41.

Boguo Makeli
1988 Situation des langues zaïroises au Zaïre. *Linguistique et Sciences Humaines* 28: 54–58.

Bokamba, Eyamba G.
1976 Authenticity and the choice of a national language: The case of Zaïre. *Présence Africaine* 99/100: 104–142.
1993 Language variation and change in pervasively multilingual societies: Bantu languages. In: Mufwene, Salikoko and Lioba Moshi (eds.), *Topics in African Linguistics*. Amsterdam: John Benjamins, 207–252.

Butaye, René
1901a *Grammaire congolaise*. Louvain: Ackermans.
1901b *Dictionnaire français-congolais et congolais-français*. Gent: De Witte.
1909 *Dictionnaire kikongo-français, français-kikongo*. Roulers: De Meester.
1910a *Grammaire congolaise*. Roulers: De Meester.
1910b *Dictionnaire kikongo-français et français-kikongo, Suivi d'un Vocabulaire flamand-kikongo et kiswahili-français*. Roulers: De Meester.
1927 *Dictionnaire de Poche kikongo-français, français-kikongo*. Paris: Mission du Kwango.

CEREDIP (Centre de Recherche et de Diffusion de l'Information Pédagogique)
1986 *Recueil des Directives et Instructions officielles*. Kinshasa: Editions du Département de l'Enseignement Primaire et Secondaire.

Craeynest, M.
[1945] *Amaat Vyncke: Vlaanderens Geloofsgezant in Midden-Afrika*. Antwerp: Nieuw-Afrika.

Cruysberghs, K.
1951 *Groten uit ons Volk*. Louvain: Davidsfonds.

De Boeck, Egide
1903 *Buku Moke moa Kotanga Lingala*. Nouvel-Anvers: Mpomba Press.
1904 *Grammaire et Vocabulaire du lingala, ou Langue du Haut-Congo*. Brussels (Polleunis-Ceuterick Printers).
1920 *Cours théorique et pratique de lingala, avec Vocabulaire et Phrases usuelles*. Turnhout (Henri Proost and Cie Printers).
1942 *Cours théorique et pratique de lingala, avec Vocabulaire et Phrases usuelles*. Tongerloo: Saint Norbert (3rd edition).

Defives-De Saint Martin, L.
1912 *Pro Petri Sede: Ou, nos Zouaves belges*. Mechelen.

Delathuy, A. M.
1986 *Jezuïeten in Kongo met Zwaard en Kruis*. Antwerp: EPO.

1992 *Missie en Staat in Oud-Kongo (1880–1914): Witte Paters, Scheutisten, Jezuïeten.* Antwerp: EPO.

1994 *Missie en Staat in Oud-Kongo (1880–1914): Redemptoristen, Trappisten, Norbertijnen, Priesters van het H. Hart, Paters van Mill Hill.* Antwerp: EPO.

Delaunay, Henri
1884 *Grammaire kiswahili.* Tours: Mame.

1885 *Dictionnaire français-kiswahili.* Paris.

Deleu, Jozef, Gaston Durnez, Reginald de Schryver et al. (eds.)
1973–1975 *Encyclopedie van de Vlaamse Beweging.* Tielt: Lannoo.

Depaepe, Marc and Lies Van Rompaey
1995 *In het Teken van de Bevoogding: De Educative Actie in Belgisch-Congo (1908–1960).* Louvain: Garant.

De Rop, Albert
1956 *Bibliografie over de Mongo.* Brussels: Académie Royale des Sciences Coloniales – Koninklijke Academie voor Koloniale Wetenschappen.

1970 A l'occasion du 70è anniversaire de G. Hulstaert. *Africa-Tervuren* 16: 107–112.

1980 G. Hulstaert, missionnaire du Sacré Cœur: Notice biographique. *Annales Æquatoria* 1: 3–11.

Fabian, Johannes
1984 *Language on the Road: Notes on Swahili in Two Nineteenth Century Travelogues.* Hamburg: Helmut Buske.

1986 *Language and Colonial Power: The Appropriation of Swahili in the Former Belgian Congo, 1880–1938.* Cambridge: Cambridge University Press.

1991 Missions and the colonization of African languages. In: Fabian, Johannes, *Time and the Work of Anthropology: Critical Essays 1971–1991.* Chur: Harwood Academic Publishers, 131–153. [First published in 1983, *Canadian Journal of African Studies* 17: 165–187]

Goddeeris, John
1978 *De Pauselijke Zouaven: Met Opgave van de Vrijwilligers uit West-Vlaanderen.* Handzame: Familia et Patria.

Gould, David J.
1980 *Bureaucratic Corruption and Underdevelopment in the Third World: The Case of Zaire*. New York: Pergamon.

Heine, Bernd
1970 *Status and Use of African Lingua Francas*. München: Weltforum Verlag.

Heremans, Roger
1966 *Les Etablissements de l'Association Internatonale Africaine au Lac Tanganika et les Pères Blancs, Mpala et Karéma, 1877–1885*. Tervuren: Musée Royal de l'Afrique Centrale – Koninklijk Museum voor Midden-Afrika.

Hermans, Theo, Louis Vos and Lode Wils (eds.)
1992 *The Flemish Movement: A Documentary History (1780–1990)*. London: Athlone Press.

Hovdhaugen, Even (ed.)
1996 *... and the Word was God: Missionary Linguistics and Missionary Grammar*. Münster: Nodus.

Hulstaert, Gustaaf
1936 Kolonisatie en de inheemsche talen. *Nieuw-Vlaanderen* 2(15): 8; continued in 2(16): 9.
1939 La langue véhiculaire de l'enseignement. *Æquatoria* 2: 85–89.
1946 Les langues indigènes et les Européens au Congo belge. *African Studies* 5: 126–135.
1953 Lingala-invloed op het Lomongo. *Zaïre* 7: 227–244.
1981 Langue et philosophie. *Annales Æquatoria* 2: 1–19.
1989 L'origine du lingala. *Afrikanistische Arbeitspapiere* 17: 81–114.

Hulstaert, Gustaaf and Egide De Boeck
1940 Lingala. *Æquatoria* 3(2): 33–43; continued in 3(3): 65–73 and 3(5): 124–131.

Kadima Kamuleta, Mutombo Huta-Mukana, Bokula Moiso et al.
1983 *Atlas linguistique du Zaïre*. Paris: ACCT and CERDOTOLA.

Kambaji wa Kambaji
1987 Quelques bases sociologiques pour une éducation en langues zaïroises. In: Kazadi N. and N.-T. Nyembwe (eds.), *Utilisation des Langues Nationales: Actes du Colloque sur les Langues Nationales, Kinshasa 11–16 mars 1985*. Special issue, *Linguistique et Sciences Humaines* 27: 96–105.

Kamwangamalu, Nkonko M.
1997 The colonial legacy and language planning in sub-Saharan Africa: The case of Zaire. *Applied Linguistics* 18: 69–85.

Kangafu Kutumbagana
1973 *Discours sur l'Authenticité: Essai sur la Problématique idéologique du "Recours à l'Authenticité"*. Kinshasa: Presses Africaines.

Kazadi Ntole
1987 Rapport général. In: Kazadi and Nyembwe (eds.), *Utilisation des Langues Nationales: Actes du Colloque sur les Langues Nationales, Kinshasa 11–16 mars 1985*. Special issue, *Linguistique et Sciences Humaines* 27: 282–289.

Kazadi Ntole and Nyembwe Ntita-T. (eds.)
1987 *Utilisation des Langues Nationales: Actes du Colloque sur les Langues Nationales, Kinshasa 11–16 mars 1985*. Special issue, *Linguistique et Sciences Humaines* 27.

Kilanga Musinde and Bwanga Zanzi
1988 Quelques remarques sur la situation de la langue française au Zaïre. *Africanistique* 16: 46–56.

Laveille, E.
1926 *L'Evangile au Centre de l'Afrique: Le P. Van Hencxthoven, S. J., Fondateur de la Mission du Kwango (Congo belge) (1852–1906)*. Louvain: Museum Lessianum.

Lufungula Lewono
1986 Vieux souvenirs du R. P. Gustave Hulstaert (interview). *Annales de l'I.S.P./Mbandaka* 5: 1–11.

Lupukisa Wasamba
1979 Problématique du bilinguisme et du plurilinguisme au Zaïre: Héritage colonial et situation actuelle. *African Languages / Langues Africaines* 5: 33–44.

Markowitz, Marvin D.
1973 *Cross and Sword: The Political Role of Christian Missions in the Belgian Congo, 1908–1960.* Stanford: Hoover Institution Press.

Mataba Kamba-Hono
1987 La planification linguistique au Zaïre: Problématique du choix de langues. In: Kazadi N. and N.-T. Nyembwe (eds.), *Utilisation des Langues Nationales: Actes du Colloque sur les Langues Nationales, Kinshasa 11–16 mars 1985*. Special issue, *Linguistique et Sciences Humaines* 27: 127–137.

Matumele Maliya-M.
1987 Langues nationales dans l'administration publique. In: Kazadi N. and N.-T. Nyembwe (eds.), *Utilisation des Langues Nationales: Actes du Colloque sur les Langues Nationales, Kinshasa 11–16 mars 1985.* Special issue, *Linguistique et Sciences Humaines* 27: 186–190.

Mazala M. and Bwanga Zanzi
1988 Bilinguisme et diglossie en milieu scolaire Zaïrois. *Africanistique* 16: 57–73.

Mazrui, Ali A.
1967 *Towards a Pax Africana: A Study of Ideology and Ambition.* Chicago: Chicago University Press.
1978 *Political Values and the Educated Class in Africa.* Berkeley: University of California Press.

Mbula Paluku
1990 Méthodes de travail en terminologie au Zaïre. *Terminologies Nouvelles* 3: 37–41.

Mbulamoko Nzenge Movoambe
1991 Etat des recherches sur le lingala comme groupe linguistique africaine: Contribution aux études sur l'histoire et l'expansion du lingala. *Annales Æquatoria* 12: 377–406.

Meeuwis, Michael
1997 *Constructing Sociolinguistic Consensus: A Linguistic Ethnography of the Zairian Community in Antwerp, Belgium.* Duisburg: LiCCA.
1998 *Lingala.* Newcastle and München: LINCOM Europa.

Meeuwis, Michael and Frank Brisard
1993 *Time and the Diagnosis of Language Change.* Antwerp: UIA-GER (Antwerp Papers in Linguistics 72).

Mertz, Elizabeth
1989 Sociolinguistic creativity: Cape Breton Gaelic's linguistic "tip". In: Dorian, Nancy C. (ed.), *Investigating Obsolescence: Studies in Language Contraction and Death.* Cambridge: Cambridge University Press, 103–116.

Mobutu Sese Seko
1989 *Dignité pour l'Afrique: Entretiens avec Jean-Louis Remilleux.* Paris: Albin Michel.

Monbaliu, Lode
1975a *Ratte Vyncke.* Roeselare.
1975b Brieven van Ratte Vyncke. *Rollariensia* (1975): 1–181.

Mufwene, Salikoko S.

1988 Formal evidence of pidginization/creolization in Kituba. *Journal of African Languages and Linguistics* 10: 33–51.

1997 Kitúba. In: Thomason, Sarah Grey (ed.), *Contact Languages: A Wider Perspective*. Amsterdam: John Benjamins, 173–208.

Muwoko Ndolo Obwong

1991 A propos de l'académie des langues et littératures Zaïroises. *Annales Æquatoria* 12: 497–508.

Ngalasso, Mwatha Musanji

1986 Etat des langues et langues de l'Etat au Zaïre. *Politique Africaine* 23: 7–27.

Nsuka-zi-Kabuiku

1987 Langues nationales et éducation: langues nationales dans l'éducation formelle. In: Kazadi N. and N.-T. Nyembwe (eds.), *Utilisation des Langues Nationales: Actes du Colloque sur les Langues Nationales, Kinshasa 11–16 mars 1985*. Special issue, *Linguistique et Sciences Humaines* 27: 5–17.

Nyembwe Ntita-T.

1986 Fonction véhiculaire et expansion linguistique. *Linguistique et Sciences Humaines* 27(1): 49–67.

1987 Pour une politique linguistique consciente: Eléments de réflexion. In: Kazadi N. and N.-T. Nyembwe (eds.), *Utilisation des Langues Nationales: Actes du Colloque sur les Langues Nationales, Kinshasa 11–16 mars 1985*. Special issue, *Linguistique et Sciences Humaines* 27: 120–126.

1993 Terminologie et développement au Zaïre. *Terminologies Nouvelles* 9: 80–83.

Nyunda ya Rubango

1986a Langue, société et dévéloppement. *Linguistique et Sciences Humaines* 27: 69–88.

1986b Le français au Zaïre: Langue "supérieure" et chances de "survie" dans un pays africain. *Language Problems and Language Planning* 10: 253–271.

Pauwels, J.M.

1981 Twintig jaar Zaïrese wetgeving, 1960–1980. *Rechtskundig Weekblad* 44(35): 2297–2318.

Polomé, Edgard C.
1968 The choice of official languages in the Democratic Republic of the Congo. In: Fishman, J. A., C. A. Ferguson and J. Das Gupta (eds.), *Language Problems of Developing Nations*. New York: Wiley and Sons, 295–312.

Raison-Jourde, Françoise
1977 L'échange inégal de la langue: La pénétration des techniques linguistiques dans une civilisation de l'oral. *Annales: Economies, Sociétés, Civilisations* 32: 639–669.

Samarin, William J.
1984 The linguistic world of field colonialism. *Language in Society* 13: 435–453.
1989a "Official language": The case of Lingala. In: Ammon, Ullrich (ed.), *Status and Function of Languages and Language Varieties*. Berlin: Walter de Gruyter, 386–398.
1989b *The Black Man's Burden: African Colonial Labor on the Congo and Ubangi Rivers, 1880–1900*. Boulder: Westview Press.
1989c Language in the colonization of Central Africa, 1880–1900. *Canadian Journal of African Studies* 23: 232–249.
1990 The origins of Kituba and Lingala. *Journal of African Languages and Linguistics* 12: 47–77.

Schatzberg, Michael G.
1988 *The Dialectics of Oppression in Zaire*. Bloomington: Indiana University Press.

Schoeters, K.
[1956] *Konflikt in Kongo: E.P. Em. Van Hencxthoven S. J. (1852–1906), Stichter van de Kwango-Missie en van de "Kapel-Hoeven"*. Brussels: De Seinhoorn.

Sesep N'Sial
1986 L'expansion du lingala. *Linguistique et Sciences Humaines* 27: 19–48.
1988 Identité nationale, identité ethnique et planification linguistique au Zaïre. *Africanistique* 16: 1–19.

Tanghe, Basil
1930 Le lingala, la langue du fleuve. *Congo* 2: 341–358.

Tanghe, Basil, Egide De Boeck and Gustaaf Hulstaert
1940 Bestaat er wel in de Congoleesche talen een tegenwoordige tijd? *Æquatoria* 3: 90–95.

Thibaut, Emile
1911 *Les Jésuites et les Fermes-Chapelles: A propos d'un Débat récent.* Brussels: Goemaere.

Thomas, Nicholas
1994 *Colonialism's Culture: Anthropology, Travel and Government.* Cambridge: Polity Press.

Van Bilsen, Jef
1950 Au Congo: La question linguistique. *La Revue Nouvelle* 11: 54–61.

Verhaegen, Benoît
1971 *Les Premiers Manifestes politiques à Léopoldville (1950–1956).* Brussels: CEDAF.

Vinck, Honoré
1987 Le Centre Æquatoria de Bamanya: Cinquante ans de recherches africanistes. *Zaïre-Afrique* 27: 79–102.
1991 In memoriam G. Hulstaert (1900–1990). *Annales Æquatoria* 12: 7–76.
1994 Correspondance scientifique Hulstaert-De Boeck, 1940–1941. *Annales Æquatoria* 15: 505–575.

Welmers, William E.
1971 Christian missions and language policies. In: Berry, Jack and Joseph H. Greenberg (eds.), *Linguistics in Sub-Saharan Africa.* The Hague: Mouton, 559–569.

Wils, Lode
1977–1989 *Honderd Jaar Vlaamse Beweging: Geschiedenis van het Davidsfonds.* Louvain: Davidsfonds.
1994 *Vlaanderen, België, Groot-Nederland: Mythe en Geschiedenis.* Louvain: Davidsfonds.

Woolard, Kathryn A.
1989 Language convergence and language death as social processes. In: Dorian, Nancy C. (ed.), *Investigating Obsolescence: Studies in Language Contraction and Death.* Cambridge: Cambridge University Press, 355–367.
1992 Language ideology: Issues and approaches. *Pragmatics* 2: 235–249.

Woolard, Kathryn A. and Bambi B. Schieffelin
1994 Language ideology. *Annual Review of Anthropology* 23: 55–82.

Xaveriana Missie-Uitgaven (Xaveriana Missionary Publishers)
1927 *Missieleven in Afrika: Uit de Brieven van den West-Vlaamschen Missionaris Ameet Vyncke der Witte Paters.* Louvain: Xaveriana.

Yates, Barbara A.

1980 The origins of language policy in Zaïre. *The Journal of Modern African Studies* 18: 257–279.

1987 Knowledge brokers: Books and publishers in early colonial Africa. *History in Africa* 14: 311–340.

Young, Crawford

1965 *Politics in the Congo: Decolonization and Independence*. Princeton: Princeton University Press.

1976 *The Politics of Cultural Pluralism.* Madison: The University of Wisconsin Press.

1982 *Ideology and Development in Africa.* New Haven: Yale University Press.

The debate is closed

Jan Blommaert

Before concluding this book, I wish to comment upon some of the most striking elements that emerged from the various chapters. The overall coherence of the chapters will undoubtedly have struck many readers. I believe that this coherence is not coincidental, and that some of the points of convergence in various chapters may invite new research and new questions to existing data.

In what follows, I will try to systematize some of the main documentary and theoretical findings from the various chapters. I will start by picking up the issue of history and language; next I will return to the hypothetical model of debates sketched in the introductory chapter. After that, I will briefly comment on a number of what I believe to be important contributions and insights adduced by the authors in this book.

1. History and language

A thread running through all the chapters of this book is the view of language as a material thing. Contrary to views widespread in various strands of linguistic and sociolinguistic research, of language as an organic body obeying natural rules and seemingly impervious to human agency, language does not lead a life of its own in this book. The story of the languages discussed here is a story of people who use them, manipulate them, manufacture them, name them.

The patterns in which these interventions occur are discontinuous: there are crucial moments in history during which languages become targets of political, social and cultural intervention, and there are moments in which very little in the way of drama and crisis seems to happen. There are slow movements and rapid movements, periods of intense activity and periods of flow, periods of production, of establishment, of consolidation, of challenge and of decay. In short, the historical patterns in which the emergence and development of ideologically framed concepts of language and language usage occur are broken, fragmented and multilayered, for every moment of intense struggle and debate is intertextual with and develops against the background of previous developments over a longer span of time. This multilayered treatment of time and evolution was perhaps clearest in Collins' treatment of the Ebonics debate, where a highly intensive and fast-moving "*événement*" was set against very slow (and very deep) processes in educational aspects of American nation-building. In the three chapters on Africa, debates were set in the wider context of colonial legacies and nation-building endeavors by postcolonial governments; in most other chapters, debates were framed in wider political-historical developments related to state- and nation-building or regionalism. In each case, "short" time was set against a *durée* background. Time is not a unified concept when it comes to writing the history of languages.

I believe that through this material view of language and this acceptance of fragmented and multilayered time, we have come a long way towards developing a genuinely historical approach to the evolution of language in society. The point of the exercise is summarized by Hymes as follows:

> ... it is an important clarification if we can agree to restrict the term "language" (and the term "dialect") to just this sort of meaning: identification of a historically derived set of resources whose social functioning — organization into used varieties, mutual intelligibility, etc.— is not given by the fact of historical derivation itself, but is problematic, needing to be determined, and calling for other concepts and terms.
>
> (Hymes 1980: 25)

In other words, the story of language must not be an abstract *histoire d'idées* in which developments are narrated as sequences of phases ("first there was this, then there was that"). Rather, it should be a story of different, conflicting, disharmonious practices performed by identifiable actors, in very specific ways, and by means of very specific instruments. Crucial evolutions in the history of languages have to be located in "real" space and time, that is, in socioculturally and politically molded space and time. This, I believe, is the essence of a historical approach *à la* Voloshinov: it is a history of language focused upon the allocation of linguistic resources *as* sociocultural and political resources; of functions of speech seen in terms of metadiscursive power-effects; of difference and inequality in linguistic resources as problematic issues in need of an explanation that goes beyond the linguistic identification of differences.

Perhaps the clearest illustration of this approach can be found in Michael Meeuwis' chapter on languages in the colonial Congo. It also illustrates the potential impact of this approach on existing linguistic and sociolinguistic imagery. The most widespread and authoritative scientific representation of the Bantu linguistic area is that of genetic linguistics. The great Bantuists of the 20th century —Meinhof, Guthrie, Meeussen— are people who produced large-scale comparisons and classifications of the Bantu languages, based upon a monogenetic theory of affiliation (and thus leading, in some work, to sweeping and controversial migration theories, see Vansina 1995). The assumption underlying this representation is an organic one, equating the synchronic distribution of languages to diachronic patterns of language change and movements of people. Meeuwis demonstrates that quite a number of steps have been skipped in this process. First, the sheer acceptance of the existence of languages is based on naming and labeling procedures, and wherever a language name was available there would be a language. Thus, struggles over names for languages were rife, and colonial linguistic archives are littered with discussions about whether or not a certain language "really" existed. I shall return to this point in section 3. Such discussions, as Meeuwis shows, were heavily influenced by normative metapragmatic expectations about what a language *ought to* be, as well as by the practical concerns and personal political-ideological backgrounds of those who engaged in such debates. Second, this practice of colonial intervention in the linguistic and sociolinguistic world of the colony produced and changed languages as well as the conditions under which people used them. Colonialism certainly put an end to the organic evolution of many Bantu languages —assuming that their precolonial evolution was at all organic.

Of course, all of this raises as many questions as it answers. The heterogeneity with which time, history and evolution have been treated by the authors in this book testifies to the uneasy relationship between language as an object of linguistically disciplined thought and language as a sociocultural and political phenomenon. The accomplishment we can claim (and, referring back to the introductory chapter, one promise kept) is that of scratching the surface and laying bare a *potential* for renewed analysis as well as a number of *problems* for renewed analysis.

2. Debates — The model revisited

What most of the chapters in this book have accomplished is to identify contexts under which language becomes an important theme for public debate as well as an important object of politization. These contexts are remarkably similar throughout the different cases discussed in the book. Central is *nation-building*. In almost every paper, language ideological debates occurred in contexts that had to do with the elaboration of a variety of nationalist agendas. Such agendas could be regionalist, and aimed at either the separation of a region from the rest of the state or the increase of sub-state power for a particular region, and usually both this "moderate" and "radical" trend can be distinguished within regionalist movements. This was the case for Corsica, the German-Speaking Swiss, Catalonia, and Quebec, in other words, for those cases that were grouped together as European or European-influenced cases. In each of these cases, linguistic identity is the backbone of claims to cultural uniqueness and hence incompatibility with the existing (multicultural) nation. The Corsicans, German-Swiss, Catalan and Québécois all give pride of place to linguistic difference in their construction of concepts of oppression, marginality and hence liberation.

Underlying this similarity in rhetorical strategies is one and the same theory of language and culture, a theory which holds monolingualism (and by extension monoculturalism) to be the norm or the desired ideal for a society, and which axiomatically projects this monolingualism-monoculturalism onto individuals, each individual being "normally" monolingual and member of one culture. Hymes calls this theory "a "Herderian" conception of the world composed of traditional units of language-and-culture" (1996: 25), and in an attempt to find a name for it, Blommaert and Verschueren (1992) called it "homogeneism".

But the specter of nationalisms was not restricted to regionalisms. The two chapters on the U.S. neatly identified huge breaks in an American self-image —or ideology, see Silverstein (1996)— of monolingualism. Challenges to this ideology, in the shape of Latino immigrants or African Americans claiming linguistic rights on the basis of the very "freedoms" that lay at the heart of the American national imagination, give rise to increased emphases on national unity, homogeneity, and the self-evident nature of the singularity of national characteristics or symbols. And not surprisingly, there too a homogeneistic notion of language is used as a formidable rhetorical weapon in this kind of debate. The same goes for Singapore and Israel, two young states faced with nation-building tasks starting from conditions of multilingualism and multiculturalism. The language suggested in Israel as the medium of expression of and for the new Jewish nation becomes contested as soon as questions about tradition and innovation are being raised. Then, Hebrew becomes essentialized, reified, and inflated with other qualities than purely linguistic ones (viz. ethnic and religious ones). In Singapore, the planning of multilingualism and multiculturalism proceeds along lines that emphasize homogeneity within the building blocs of multilingualism. The Chinese community, previously composed of speakers of different regional varieties of Chinese, is internally homogenized by means of the imposition of standard Mandarin. To those familiar with European discussions on multiculturalism, this pattern sounds familiar. In the context of immigration policies in Europe as well, multiculturalism is often practiced in the form of juxtaposing essentialized and homogenized "cultures", each of them neatly delineated and contained in boundaries of "identity" and "authenticity" (cf. e.g. Blommaert and Verschueren 1998).

Moving somewhat further, the African cases present us with contexts in which nations have to be built *a posteriori*. The struggle for decolonization resulted in the establishment of states; but the states were perceived as in urgent need of nations, and everywhere politicians embarked on massive nation-building campaigns in contexts of extreme multilingualism and multiculturalism. And everywhere, the anticolonial struggle was translated into a struggle for the *Africanization* of the new nations. Remarkably, though, in Tanzania as well as in Mozambique and in Mobutu's Zaire, the theoretical apparatus mobilized for that purpose almost invariably included essentialized and homogenized notions of language and culture, and debates such as the one in Tanzania could only erupt as soon as all the protagonists had agreed on the basic (Herderian) isomorphism of language and culture. The question then became: what particular culture is this language going to express?

The speech of the Singaporean Prime Minister Goh Chok Tong, quoted by Wendy Bokhorst-Heng, was entitled "Mandarin is more than a language." Reading the other chapters in the book we notice that, in the eyes of those waging the debates, this also counts for Corsican, Schwyzertüütsch, Catalan, French, English, Hebrew, Swahili, Portuguese, Lingala, Mongo. Whenever language is drawn into nationalist struggles, it becomes more than "just language". The metadiscourse on language becomes extremely complex and loaded with all kinds of tropic, metaphorical or symbolic associations. The voices articulating this metadiscourse in almost all the cases invoke "expertise" —they are *knowers* of language and therefore also knowledgeable about the associative field surrounding language.

Crucial here is a transposition of one's identity as a linguist, a writer, a translator, into fields of public debate and of political activity, and the linguists, the writers, the translators (and even the missionaries) then produce *political discourse on language*. The role of what I called ideology brokers in the introductory chapter can be summarized as such: they are experts, whose expertise is dragged as a subtext into another type of discourse, not a technical discourse (hence, not "expert" discourse) but a political discourse which is sometimes hard to distinguish from that of "real" politicians. Ron Kuzar repeatedly pointed towards the institutional muscle of Ben-Hayyim, one of the protagonists in the Israeli debate. Samuel Hayakawa, the U.S. Senator and defender of the monoglot standard mentioned by Shannon, can serve as an even better example here. A prominent linguist in his time, he is supposed to "know" in a better, a more documented way as the way we usually suspect politicians to "know" things.

But linguistic work itself, i.e. the core activities of the "knowers" of language, can be politicized and read as political statements. Heller identified the connection between particular preferences in sociolinguistic work and particular political agendas in Canada; the poetic treatises of the Tanzanian young poets were read as Marxist pamphlets by their opponents; the Corsican translators were challenged by their critics for wasting their time on the language-and-culture-perverting activity of translating French books into Corsican. The pattern is again not unfamiliar: state-ideological preferences can be willy-nilly supported and legitimized by expert activities, and states can make sure that experts remain within certain boundaries *qua* choice of research themes and approaches, for instance by means of the allocation of subsidies.

The role of "ideological apparatuses" remains unclear, although in almost every instance discussed in this book, *written* channels played a crucial role. But the cases showed significant differences as to the weight that could be put in the dissemination of particular ideologies of language, as well as to the available resources that could be mobilized for it. The education system evidently remains a crucial channel for linguistic-ideological regimentation, as Shannon, Collins and Watts demonstrated. Modern multimodal mass-media were obvious instruments for ideological reproduction in the cases discussed by DiGiacomo (Catalonia) and Bokhorst-Heng (Singapore), and to some extent also Jaffe (Corsica). The Ebonics battle documented by Collins was fought in a wide variety of media, including the Internet. Newspapers were a forum for the debate in the case of Israel, and though framed in a very different communicative sociology, even in the case of the Tanzanian poets. But in other cases, the debate was almost sectarian and confined to small circles of experts, channeled through letters, reports or in-group publications. The cases discussed by Meeuwis are such small-scale, hardly publicized debates. But it would be mistaken, of course, to reduce debates to one particular medium or channel of production and reproduction. Heller demonstrates the complexity of such processes involving highly exclusive genres such as scientific papers as well as political speeches, whole campaigns, media hypes and so on. In Shannon's case, court rulings are as important speech events as televised scandals. There is rarely a "master text" or an "original text" to the debate; and debates are in themselves characterized by long periods of continuous re-entextualizations, quotations, re-reading of texts, of slow changes in the semantics of key terms, of gradual shifts in the participant structure of the debate, of lows and peaks in the public attention given to the debate. But the end result is usually a doxa, codified or not, implicit or explicit, which is then put into practice in ways that are sometimes orthodox and sometimes not. The refusal of the Tanzanian newspaper to print poetry in free verse is such an implicit doxa, and the way in which bilingual education is put in practice in Shannon's data is a case of a semi-implicit doxa.

So where are we now with the hypothetical model suggested earlier? Quite a bit surely remains to be investigated. But I believe that some parameters have been set for such further research.

3. On labels and names: Language hierarchies

One constant feature of the debates discussed in the chapters is the presence of language hierarchies. In line with what was said before, that language is often more than "just" language, languages and language varieties tend to be *labeled* and *ranked* on the basis of a variety of criteria that have to do with the perceived "quality" of the language or language variety, or, with the degree of "full languageness" of the language or variety. Differences between a "language" and a "dialect", let alone even lower qualifications such as "jargon", "speech" (*parler* in French) or "idiom" are always the product of the politics of representation, and they involve massive projections of power, status, values, norms onto the linguistic phenomenon at hand. Thus, when FRELIMO labeled the Mozambican Bantu languages "dialects", and so aligned itself with colonial discourses on African versus European languages, a whole ideological, metaphorical and associative machinery was set in motion by means of which the language, its speakers, its culture, its social structure, its ideals and aspirations were all branded as inferior to those carried by the "language", Portuguese.

Similarly, when the French Senator threw the question "*Mais où sont vos Rimbaud?*" to the Corsicans, he was imputing far more than a quality assessment about language and linguistic expression to the Corsicans. He was, in fact, ranking French and Corsican on a scale in which language "quality" and language history coincide in such a way that "inferior" languages will always remain inferior, simply because the superior language has a history, a tradition, of superiority. So even if the Corsicans would launch an all-out cultural and literary offensive, producing literature of superlative beauty, still French would remain superior because French had acquired that level of sophistication and literary accomplishment a century ago. This is the double bind activated when cultural activists and language nationalists adopt the hierarchical frame and embark on campaigns for the promotion and the development of their language: by acknowledging the *present* inferiority of their language *vis-à-vis* another language (usually a "model" language, and in that sense Jaffe's choice of *translators* is highly relevant), they acknowledge its *eternal* inferiority. The model language will always have attained the desired level of elaboration or sophistication long before the other language, and quality in the inferior language will always be seen as an emulation or a caricature of that of the model language (cf. Blommaert 1994; Errington 1992).

Ranking can be physical. Sometimes, the mere presence of a language somewhere, the use of a language on a particular occasion, and the sequential order of languages used in multilingual contexts, can be seen as highly relevant and can become a highly sensitive topic of debate. DiGiacomo's description of the Olympic debate in Barcelona is a case in point. Whether or not Catalan would be accepted as a "visible" language during the Olympic Games was the first issue. Then came the sequential order of languages: which one would come first, Castilian or Catalan? Sometimes this competition for public space can result in intricate time-sharing formulas, in which public space is allowed to languages on the basis of complex calculations involving, for instance, the numbers of speakers for each language, or the "national importance" of certain languages (see e.g. Spitulnik 1992).

Concerns with language quality can take on various shapes. But some features prove to be recurrent. Quality and full languageness are, for instance, quite consistently associated with *structure* and *order*. A standardized language is always better than a non-standardized one, and standardization invariably has to do with *writing*, *codification* and *institutionalization*. None of the three criteria is sufficient, but all of them are necessary conditions for quality. None is evident too, and all three of them involve important power effects, forms of disciplining, control and coercion. Second, but not unrelated to the foregoing, quality is associated with *singularity*. Language and language effects need to be singular. People need to be monolingual (either one speaks this language, or one speaks another language), and societies need to be monolingual too. Meanings must be singular, clear and unambiguous —a "language" in the hierarchical sense of the term is always seen as a vehicle of "clear and precise expression" of ideas. The ideology of the "natural" order of things which the Flemish missionaries brought with them to the Congo assumed a direct link between God, the "natural" language of people, and their souls. By praying in their mother tongue, the prayer would come out unfiltered, pure, unobstructed by barriers and obstacles posed by a "foreign" language. Therefore, true Christianity had to be brought to the Africans through their mother tongue.

Third, language quality also involves issues of *ownership*. A "good" language is one that is inherited through generations of speakers. And only when someone is part of the genealogy of the speech community, he or she will be able to speak the language "well", "correctly", or to understand it "completely". This is where tradition comes in. The Swahili poets in Tanzania fought a battle over the rightful ownership of the language. To the modernists Swahili signified the newness of the postcolonial socialist society; consequently they felt free to experiment with the language. The traditionalists situated ownership of Swahili with the traditional coastal Swahili societies, and the age-old verse forms were an expression of respect for this ownership turned into a dogmatic interpretation of "correct language usage". Similarly, Ben-Hayyim and Rosén held very different views on where Hebrew came from. To the former, there was a tradition that needed to be respected lest the language be (unjustifiably) transformed; to the latter, Hebrew was the language of the new state of Israel, and was owned by the people who now spoke it. In Mozambique, Portuguese was snatched away from the colonial oppressor and became the instrument of conscientization, revolutionary propaganda, and national unification. This nation-building purpose involved heavy amounts of disciplining, and language itself became the object of purism, grammatical rigidity, and reification. Issues of ownership invariably involve issues of norms, rules, codes for correct usage of the language. And in discussions of ownership, language is situated in a historical (real or mythical) discourse on the speech community, its evolution and its inheritance from previous generations. Thus, and I add an autobiographical note, in Flanders, the usage of "bad" Dutch in public (e.g. Dutch with clear dialect influences, Gallicisms or other forms of "impurity") can trigger reprimands in which the culprit is reminded of the past generations that fought a hard battle for the preservation and development of Dutch in Belgium.

Fourth, language quality, in practice, requires *expert voices*. Standardization, institutionalization, elaboration and development of languages need to be accompanied by legitimizing and rationalizing discourses of experts.

The power that is excerted through such practices of linguistic landscaping needs to be softened or neutralized by referring to logic, theory, science. The language ideological debates discussed in this book offered a tremendous amount of theorizing, performed by experts from a wide range of backgrounds. It is clear that homogenization, standardization, oligolingualism or the creation of language hierarchies, require more than just brutal power. The acquiescence of the masses, a prerequisite for hegemony in classical theories of ideology, is reached through discourses that generate power through their appeal to the "higher order" of science, logic, rationality, or in one instance, "nature" and God. Hence the reconfirmation of what was said earlier: given the right conditions, linguists and other experts can produce political discourse even when they discuss details of language structure. Even more, given the right conditions they can *only* produce political discourse.

4. Metadiscourse and sociolinguistics

The foregoing remarks underscore the importance of metadiscourse in assessing language situations in countries such as the ones discussed in the book. Apart from "observable" sociolinguistic phenomena ranging from the distribution of languages over forms of language loyalty, language loss, language contact and so on, and apart from phenomena that fall within the scope of "traditional" approaches to language planning such as policy papers, legislative work, the production of standardized language materials and so on, the ways in which language and language situations are being *debated* in societies may offer important sociolinguistic insights.

In such debates, languages and language situations are often changed. The slowly evolving Canadian debate described by Heller transformed the country from an English-hegemonic society into a multilingual society, in which one competing speech community (the Francophones) have won an important place for themselves, and in which the rights and claims of other speech communities now produce a highly complex linguistic-political situation far removed from the apparently relaxed and self-conscious Anglophone hegemony of half a century ago. Similarly, the Speak Mandarin Campaign in Singapore affects the internal structure as well as the external perception of the Chinese communities in Singapore, who are turned from a kaleidoscopic agglomerate into a monolithical sub-society within multilingual and multicultural Singapore. FRELIMO's emphasis on the use of Portuguese has shaped a local —more or less codified— variety of Portuguese, and has at the same time created a sociolinguistic rift between

Portuguese-knowing Mozambicans and Portuguese-ignorant ones. The ideology of German dialect in Switzerland has on the one hand lifted a "dialect" (in the hierarchical sense) to the public and institutional status of a "language" (also in the hierarchical sense), and has on the other hand caused the beginning of a sociolinguistic break between Switzerland and the rest of German-speaking Europe (as well as a widening the intra-Swiss gap between Germanophone and Francophone communities).

So language *is being changed* by debates. Political-linguistic debates intervene in sometimes brutal ways in the history of languages and speech communities, and their effect can overrule "spontaneous" effects of language contact or of language evolution. For one thing, the outcome or the precondition of most of the debates discussed here is a sociolinguistic pattern marked by deep and metadiscursively elaborated inequalities between languages. Never mind Tanzania's 105 languages: what counts in terms of political correctness and social mobility are English and Swahili. Never mind, to bring the argument closer to home, the enormous numbers of Spanish-speaking children in the schools of some American states: what counts is English. It has been long realized that such factors do influence language change. But one might want to look somewhat deeper into the precise mechanisms by means of which political factors intervene in language change, and more in particular, in the discourses *on* language that are applied in the process.

For this is a second important element. Regardless of whether debates "moved" sociolinguistic reality or left it untouched, the structure of the metadiscourse used in the debate is in itself telling. The tropes, associations, symbolizations used in discussing languages, their qualities or disadvantages, and the way in which they ought to be used in society, all reveal a magnificent amount of insights into available ideological sources or traditions, their (lack of) power, their intertextuality with other cases, sources or traditions and so on. This is why inconsequential or marginal debates can be very informative: by showing us the failure of certain bids for power and authority, they might shed light on the historical conditions that made certain forms of power possible and others impossible. The Flemish missionaries' ideology of the natural may have had a respectable pedigree in Flemish nationalism (and may have worked in the context of Belgium). The claim that Africans needed to be given the right to use their own language in order to become Christians and civilized human beings clashed with other deep-rooted colonialist notions of African languages, cultures, civilization, as well as of the purposes of colonization, of images of the desired type of society that would be built in colonial Africa. So what worked in one context failed in another, for reasons that could prove to be a fertile domain of historical-sociolinguistic research.

The purpose of this book consisted partly in demonstrating that the historiography of language needed to be a "real" historiography, that is, a historiography that made use of "real" time, social relations, identifiable actors, power games, and that did away with abstract or reductionist models of linguistic history. Human agency is something which is still looked at with some apprehension in the domain of linguistic history. I believe that the authors in this book have demonstrated that there is a good case for picking up the suggestion and carrying it further.

5. On taking sides

One last feature I want to comment upon is "taking sides". Just like the linguists, educators, philologists, poets, translators, and other "experts" described in this book, the authors of the various chapters are taking sides in what is essentially a political debate. I believe that this is nothing to shy away from; I even believe that it is unavoidable.

Taking sides can take different shapes. There are authors whose sympathies for one or the other "camp" in the debate they describe are barely hidden. Jaffe, DiGiacomo and Shannon can at times be caught expressing sympathies for the minority party in the debate. Jaffe has some sympathy for the translators, DiGiacomo for some Catalans, Shannon for the Latino subjects. Wendy Bokhorst-Heng cannot be said to be enthusiastic about the aims and methods of the Speak Mandarin Campaign. Stroud is critical of FRELIMO's policies, although he does not express great sympathy for RENAMO either. The Madumulla who co-authored the chapter on the Tanzanian poets is himself a well-known "modernist" who participated actively in the debate he and his associates discuss.

But taking sides can also have another dimension. Authors writing on their "home society" probably take a stance which, apart from the function it would have in this book, is also meaningful in the national debate. When Watts describes the Swiss ideology of dialect, he enters into a dialogue with Swiss colleagues, probably on a very different basis than the dialogue he initiates with the wider readership of this book. The same goes for Heller's discussion of scientific work in Canada, for Shannon's and Collins' statements on homogeneism in the U.S., on Kuzar's comments on the status of Hebrew, and on Madumulla's assessment of a debate in which half of his department's colleagues were actively involved. The arguments set forth in the chapters can be "repatriated", they can be re-entextualized out of the context of this book (generically a pristine context) and into the context of a debate that is going on right now, and in which Watts, Heller, Collins, Shannon, Kuzar and Madumulla are actors anyway, since they are *language experts*. Now more than ever, after having written a contribution on their own national debate, this contribution will be seen as an *intervention* in the local debate. Speaking for myself: it will be hard to avoid being questioned about the relevance of this book for the situation in Belgium (where the political history of the 20th century can in fact be told as one big language ideological debate).

It is a circular pattern. Writing the chapters made us discover how deeply political some linguistic opinions can be when they are placed in the context of nationalist debates. At the same time, this discovery in itself placed us right at the heart of the debates some of us were describing. Taking sides is unavoidable: it comes with doing a particular type of questioning of linguistic reality. An attempt at providing a history of language which takes into account social and political factors forces us to voice interpretations of these factors. And in social and political reality, interpretations are partisan, and they almost automatically align the one who formulated the interpretation with one or another political bloc. So be it.

References

Blommaert, Jan

1994 The metaphors of development and modernization in Tanzanian language policy and research. In: Fardon, Richard and Graham Furniss (eds.), *African Languages, Development and the State*. London: Routledge, 213–226.

Blommaert, Jan and Jef Verschueren

1992 The role of language in European nationalist ideologies. In: Kroskrity, Paul, Bambi Schieffelin and Kathryn Woolard (eds.), *Language Ideologies*, 355–375 (Special issue, *Pragmatics* 2(3): 235–453).

1998 *Debating Diversity: Analysing the Discourse of Tolerance*. London: Routledge.

Errington, J. Joseph

1992 On the ideology of Indonesian language development: The state of a language of state. In: Kroskrity, Paul, Bambi Schieffelin and Kathryn Woolard (eds.), *Language Ideologies*, 417–426. (Special issue, *Pragmatics* 2(3): 235–453).

Hymes, Dell

1980 Speech and language: on the origins and foundations of inequality among speakers. In: Hymes, Dell, *Language in Education: Ethnolinguistic Essays*. Washington, DC: Center for Applied Linguistics, 19–61.

1996 *Ethnography, Linguistics, Narrative Inequality: Toward an Understanding of Voice*. London: Taylor and Francis.

Silverstein, Michael

1996 Monoglot "standard" in America: Standardization and metaphors of linguistic hegemony. In: Brenneis, Donald and Ronald Macaulay (eds.), *The Matrix of Language: Contemporary Linguistic Anthropology*. Boulder: Westview, 284–306.

Spitulnik, Debra

1992 Radio time sharing and the negotiation of linguistic pluralism in Zambia. In: Kroskrity, Paul, Bambi Schieffelin and Kathryn Woolard (eds.), *Language Ideologies*, 335–354 (Special issue, *Pragmatics* 2(3): 235–453).

Vansina, Jan

1995 New linguistic evidence and the "Bantu Expansion". *Journal of African History* 36: 173–195.

Name index

Adams, John 173
Arrighi, Jean-Marie 49, 52

Baugh, John 212
Ben-Gurion, David 274ff.
Ben-Hayyim, Ze'ev 270ff., 430, 433
Ben-Yehudah, Eliezer 280
Bennett, William 181
Bittremieux, L. 411
Blanc, Haim 270ff.
Boelaert, E. 386ff.
Braudel, Fernand 3, 6

Casanova, Achille 77
Chiraghdin, Shihabuddin 318
Couto, Mia 347, 351, 355, 373
Cummins, Jim 182

De Boeck, E. 402ff.
de Rop, E.P.A. 386ff.
de Vere Allen, John 319
Dhlakama 370
Dieth, Eugen 83
Douglas, William O. 180

Franchi, Jean-Joseph 39
Franco, Bahamonde, Francisco 107ff.

Ganhão, Fernando 348, 353
Goh Chok Tong 245ff., 429
Goshen-Gottstein, Moshe 270ff.
Gramsci, Antonio 267ff.
Grodjensky, Shlomo 286

Hakuta, Kenji 183ff.
Hayakawa, Samuel I. 177, 180, 430
Honwana, Luís Bernando 347, 373, 376
Hulstaert, G. 386ff., 392
Hymes, Dell 8

Jackson, Jesse 203

Kahigi, Kulikovela K. 325ff.
Kezilahabi, Euphrase 323ff.
Khosa, Ba Ka 352

Labov, William 203, 212
Latour, Bruno 267ff.
Lee Kuan Yew 235–263

Machel, Graça 353, 375
Machel, Samora 345ff.
Madumulla, Joshua 319
McCrory, Mary 208
Mfume, Kweisi 201
Mnyampala, Mathias 316
Mohamed, Said A. 330
Moll, Aina 109
Mondlane, Eduardo 346
Mulokozi, Mugyabuso M. 325ff.

Nichols, Lau v. 179
Nyerere, Julius 311ff.

Ornan, Uzzi 294

Polotsky, H.J. 282ff.

Riley, William 201ff.
Rodríquez, Richard 181
Rosén, Haiim B. 270ff., 433

Schmid, Heinrich 70
Schwarzwald (Rodrigue), Ora 293
Sengo, Tibiti S.Y. 320
Shariff, Ibrahim N. 328
Snow, Catherine 183ff.

Tardivel, Jules-Paul 148
Trudeau, Pierre 143, 153
Tsemakh, Shlomo 270ff.

Van Hencxthoven, E. 392ff.
Vidal-Quadras, Aleix 122ff.
Vieira, Sérgio 348ff., 355, 369, 373
Voloshinov, V.N. 426
Vyncke, A. 392ff.

Weiman, Ralph W. 270ff.
Wilson, Pete 202
Wong-Fillmore, Lily 184

Yarborough, Ralph 179

Subject index

Academy of the Hebrew Language 285
acquisition
second language 349
activism
Flemish 386ff.
additive bilingualism 162
administration *see* Reagan administration
affirmative action 110
African American Vernacular English 204
African socialism 311
African-Americans 201–227
Africanness 307, 309, 313
Afrocentrism 210
Alemannic 71
ambiguity 256
American Education Research Association 203
American Federation of Teachers 203
Amerindians 155
anglicisms 150
anglophones 143–167
Ann Arbor School District 206
anti-colonialism 391
anti-imperialism 381–414
apartheid 219
appropriation 346
Arabization 317ff.
Arusha Declaration 312ff.
assimilation 147, 159, 174, 207, 223, 347, 404
attitudes 6, 31, 41, 74, 92, 161
authenticité 388ff.
authenticity 163, 330, 369, 386, 429
Baker and de Kanter Report 182
Bantu languages 317, 352, 366, 427
'barbarisms' 208
Barcelona 15, 105–134
Belgian Congo 28
Belgium 383ff.
bilingual education 171–194, 205, 365
Bilingual Education Act 19, 171
bilingual programs 182
bilingualism 145, 157–158, 160, 171–194, 237ff., 254
Bill 101, 155
Black English 204, 206
Black English Vernacular 204, 269
see also African American Vernacular
Bracero Program 176
British RP 99
California 176
campaign 243
Canada 16, 143–167
canon 317
capital
cultural 223
linguistic 155, 211, 224
capitalism 30
Castillian 105–134
Catalan 15, 105–134, 432
Catalonia 105–134
Catholicism 148 *see also* Roman Catholic
census 161, 259
Charte de la Langue française 155
Chichewa 309
Chinese 180
Chinyanja 309
choice (language) 109

citizenship 145, 370
civil rights movement 220
civil society 8
codeswitching 91
coercion 409
colonialism 42, 317, 383ff., 427
  see also colonial language
Colorado 178
Committee of Linguists of African Descent 205
commodification 214
community 68
  imaginary 224
  speech 365, 433
Conference on the Use of the National Languages in Education and in the Sociocultural Domain (Zaire) 389
Congo 28, 381–414
Conseil de la langue française 162
consensus 282, 354
contamination
  linguistic 351
Contribuição para a definição de uma política linguística na República Popular de Moçambique 363
conversation analysis 34
correctness
  linguistic 111
  of language 98
Corsican 12, 40–62
  French 430
counter-hegemony 274, 284, 297
  see also hegemony
creolization 204
critical discourse analysis 34
critique
  postcolonial 384
cross-cultural misunderstanding 143
cultural capital 223 *see also* linuistic capital
cultural identity *see* identity
curriculum 205, 209
decolonization 308ff., 388, 429
deculturalization 241ff.
dialect 13–14, 68–100, 206ff., 243ff., 250f., 366, 431, 435
  Alemannic 71
  Savoyan 98
  synecdochic 70
diaspora 293
difference 106, 225
diglossia 41, 53, 62, 387
discourse analysis *see* critical discourse analysis
discursive praxis 32
displacement
  referential 212
diversity 237, 362
  linguistic 249
domination *see* language domination
  symbolic 172
doxa 431
durée 3, 6, 17, 32, 426
Dutch 433

Ebonics 20, 201–227, 426
education 74, 216ff.
  bilingual 171–194, 205, 365
educational performance 205
educational rights 180
educational system 209, 216
elite 151ff., 219, 283
elitization 366
English 19, 23, 71, 171–194, 369, 435
  in Canada 143–167
  in Singapore 235–263
'*enriquecimento*' 351
entextualization 5, 9ff., 105, 131, 431
equality 167
essentialism 61, 131, 159
ethnicity 145

événement 3, 15, 426
'expert' knowledge 159
expertise 18, 24, 159ff., 429, 433

Fiote 398ff.
First National Seminar on the
  Teaching of Portuguese 352
Flanders 383ff., 433
  Flemish activism 386ff.
folklore 83
frame 90
francophones 143–167
francophonie 97
free verse 315
FRELIMO 343ff., 434, 436
French 12, 17, 40–62, 309, 387ff.
  Corsican 430
  in Switzerland 68ff.
  Savoyan dialects of 98
  in Canada 143–167

generativism 292
genetic linguistics 427
genre 310
German 14
  in Switzerland 68ff.
Gestalt 281
'gibberish' 208, 224, 400
habitus 4

Hanyu Pinyin 260
Hebrew 23, 267–299, 428
Hebrew University of Jerusalem 272
hegemony 172, 184, 223, 268ff.,
  282 *see also* counter-hegemony
hegemony 333, 409, 434
heterogeneity 161, 235, 427
heteroglossia 222
hierarchies
  language 431
Hispanics *see* Latino
historical linguistics 4
historicity
  of language 6
historization 353
history *see also* 'natural history'
  national 349
'homogeneism' 428
homogeneity 11, 19, 40, 157, 235
homogenization 350
hypercorrection 72, 91

idealism 7
identity 69, 151, 209, 260, 309,
  316ff.
  cultural 345, 371
  local 69
  national 31, 40, 67
identity card 261
identity politics 309
'ideological state apparatuses' 7, 289
ideology brokers 9, 344, 429
idiom 431
'imagined community' 131, 224, 235
immersion program 122ff., 164ff.,
  193
immigrants 174ff., 219
immigration 154, 176, 287ff., 429
imperialism 30, 147
inclusion *see* inclusive pronouns
indigenism 404, 410
inequality 8
institution
  social 77
institutionalization 11
intellectuals 269ff., 307–335
intention 277
intertextuality 5, 20
Inuit 155
Israel 23, 267–299, 428
Italian
  in Switzerland 68ff.

jargon 431

Kikongo 387ff.
Knesset 285

language
  Bantu 317, 352, 366, 427
  colonial 309
  ethnic 309, 383ff.
  historicity of 6
  local 383ff.
  minority 41, 43, 60, 181
  national 70, 307ff., 360ff., 388
  official 70, 157, 208, 309, 313, 352ff.
  Semitic 287
  standard 202
  vernacular 383ff.
language change 1, 31, 382
language choice 109
language contact 160, 166
language correctness 98, *see also* linguistic correctness
language domination 40–62, *see also* symbolic domination
language hierarchy 431
language legislation 154, 347 *see also* language policy
language mixing 352
language planning 30, 313
language policy 30, 40, 160, 201, 353 *see also* language legislation, identity politics
language revitalization 40
language revival 267–299
language rights 109
language shift 41
language variation 295, 351
Latino 177, 180, 194
Law of Linguistic Normalization 111ff.
legislation (language) 154
legitimacy 144ff.
liberalism 159, 221
Lingala 383ff., 403
lingua francae 158, 237, 243, 383
linguistic capital 155, 211, 224
  see also cultural capital
Linguistic Society of America 203, 205
linguistics 162
  applied 164
  genetic 427
  historical 4, 6
  missionary 383
literacy 95, 202, 216ff., 313, 324
literary form 307–335
literature 347
Lomongo 409
Lusophonia 369ff.

Malawian 309
Malay 237ff.
Mandarin 22, 235–263, 429
mapai 274ff.
Marxism 7, 332
materialism 6, 7
media 15, 92, 105, 355, 430
metadiscourse 434
metapragmatics 333
meter *see utendi and see shairi*
Mexico 175, 194
minority 145, 158, 166, 207
minority language 41, 43, 60, 181
minority rights 158
minority students 201
missionary linguistics 383
misunderstanding
  cross-cultural 143
mixing
  language 352
Mongo 386
monolingualism 19, 145–147, 160, 172, 179ff., 191, 253–254, 428
mother-tongue 238, 242, 253
Mozambique 27, 343–376, 433 *see also* Portuguese

multiculturalism 25, 158, 178, 429
multilingualism 219, 237
multiracialism 237ff.
myth 72ff., 146, 291, 345, 354

nation 235ff.
nation-building 22–26, 31, 236, 268, 275, 291, 307ff., 343ff., 426ff.
nation-state 273, 343, 350ff.
National Association for the Advancement of Colored People 201
nationalism 19, 40, 144ff., 209–210, 268, 381–414
nationhood 249ff.
Native Americans 174
nativization 369
naturalization 213
négritude 318, 391
Negro Nonstandard English 204
network 268, 296
newspaper 105, 133
ngonjera 315ff.
norm 282, 362
normalization 10, 118, 365
Norway 99

Oakland School Board 201ff.
Office de la langue française 160–162

Palestine 269
patois 98
performance 5
pidgin 406
pidginization 383ff.
pluralism 31, 157, 167
plurilingualism 210
poetry 307–335, 348 *see also* UKUTA
Portuguese 27, 343–376, 434
  in Mozambique 343–376, 433
postcolonialism 343–376 *see also* critique
praxis 7
  discursive 32
primary school 89 *see also* education
pronouns
  inclusive 256
Proposition 63, 187 176–177
psychology
  social 161, 164
purism
  linguistic 31, 145, 150, 238

Quebec 17, 143–167
'Quiet Revolution' 152

racism 178, 184
Ramírez Report 182
Reagan administration 177, 179, 181
re-appropriation 346
re-entextualization 436
reference 213, 226 *see also* referential displacement
regionalism 428
'reinvention of tradition' 370
RENAMO 343ff., 436
representation 9, 39, 56
reproduction 5, 10, 15, 89, 95, 105, 130, 148, 235, 344
resistance 77, 246, 282, 255ff., 358–360
resources
  linguistic 310, 426
revisionism 318
revitalization
  of language 40
rights
  educational 180
  language 109
  minority 158

Roman Catholic mission 175
Romansch 68–100
'Romansch Grischun' 70

Savoyan
  as dialect of French 98
school *see also* education
  primary, 89ff
school performance 225
Schriftdeutsch 72, 75, 89–92
Schweizer Fernsehen DRS 94
Schweizer Radio DRS 92
Schwyzertüütsch 14f., 72–74, 89
second-language acquisition 349
second-language teaching 164
self-determination 145, 156
Seminar of Zairian Linguists 389
Semitic languages 287
shairi meter 314
shift
  of language 41
Singapore 22, 235–263, 428, 434
skill 218, 221
slang 203, 208, 400
social institution *see* institution
social psychology 161, 164
socialism
  African 311ff.
socialization 192
sociolinguistics 144–146, 163
Spain 105–134
Spanish 20, 71, 171–194
Speak Mandarin Campaign 235–263, 434, 436
speech 431
speech community 365
spelling 217
standard 208, 282 *see also* substandard
standard language 202
standardization 19, 31, 70, 81, 96, 111, 145, 212, 218, 313, 355, 405, 432
statehood 275ff. *see also* nationhood
structuralism 272ff., 276
students
  minority 201
substandard 295
Swahili 26, 307–335, 383ff., 433, 435
Swiss German 68 *see also* German, *Schwyzertüütsch*
Switzerland 14, 68–100
'symbolic violence' 192
synecdochic dialects *see* dialect

Tamil 237ff.
Tanzania 26, 307–335, 429, 435
teaching *see also* education
  second-language 164
textualization 344
'The Quiet Revolution' 152
time
  social nature of 4
tradition
  reinvention of 370
translation 40–62
tribalism 375
Tshiluba 387ff.
Turkish 71

Ujamaa 307–335 *see also* socialism African
UKUTA 316
United States 19ff., 171–194, 201–227, 428
untranslatability 47, 222
utendi meter 314 *see also shairi* meter

'verbal play' 205
vernacular 164
verse *see* free verse 315
violence 192, 358ff. *see also* symbolic violence
voice 310, 352

Welsh 43
West-Flemish Particularism 395
writing 41

Zaire 28, 381–414
Zionism 273ff.

Language, Power and Social Process

Edited by Monica Heller and Richard J. Watts

Mouton de Gruyter · Berlin · New York

Srikant Sarangi and Celia Roberts
(Editors)

Talk, Work and Institutional Order

Discourse in Medical, Mediation and Management Settings

Cloth. ISBN 3-11-015723-3
Paperback. ISBN 3-11-015722-5
(Language, Power and Social Process 1)

This book takes an interdisciplinary approach to talk and its role in creating workplace practice and relationships. Analytic tools drawn from ethnography, conversation analysis, interactional sociolinguistics and discourse analysis illuminate a range of workplace discourses from medical, mediation and management settings (e.g., hospital rounds, divorce mediation, enterprise bargaining).

The book consists of fourteen specially commissioned contributions to address the thematic focus of how professional knowledge and identities are constituted in discourse vis-à-vis a given institutional order. These discourse practices shed light on what it is to be a member of a profession and how the lives of both clients and professions are affected by institutional processes. In addition to both, clients and professions are affected by institutional processes. In addition to the theoretical insights into workplace discourse and an extended editorial introduction, the final section of the book debates methodological issues and the need to combine disciplinary rigour with diversity.

This book will be a key text for graduate students as well as for lecturers and researchers across a range of disciplines: sociolinguistics, sociology, culture and communication studies, applied linguistics.